Construction Insolvency
Third Edition

AUSTRALIA
Law Book Co.—Sydney

CANADA and **USA**
Carswell—Toronto

HONG KONG
Sweet & Maxwell Asia

NEW ZEALAND
Brookers—Wellington

SINGAPORE and **MALAYSIA**
Sweet & Maxwell Asia
Singapore and Kuala Lumpur

Construction Insolvency: Security, Risk and Renewal in Construction Contracts

Richard Davis, M.A. (Cantab)
Solicitor
Consultant with Pinsent Masons

London
Sweet and Maxwell
2008

Published in 2008 by Sweet & Maxwell of
100 Avenue Road
London NW3 3PF
http://www.sweetandmaxwell.co.uk

Typeset by LBJ Typesetting Ltd of Kingsclere
Printed and bound in Great Britain by MPG Books Ltd, Bodmin, Cornwall

No natural forests were destroyed to make this product; only farmed timber was used and replanted

A CIP catalogue record for this book is available from the British Library

ISBN 978–0–421–96570–6

For James Hillman and friends

Contents

Foreword

The first edition of this work arrived in the midst of the great recession of the twentieth century. The second came in 1999 at the dawn of the new millennium. At this third edition stage, the book is already an established classic in construction insolvency law and an invaluable point of reference.

Although the construction industry was traditionally a high risk area for insolvency, the benign conditions in recent years may have lulled many into a false sense of security. It is precisely in such less troubled times that effort needs to be devoted to putting in place protection from future risks. It is a work like this that enables the reader to safeguard himself, whether as owner, employer, contractor, subcontractor or bondsman from the perils of the future.

Few legal writers have had the time or inclination as this author to consider not only the statutes and case law but also the theoretical and cultural background to their subject. This involves not only some interesting construction insolvencies of the past but also a wide range of cultural references from Greek myths to the poet Rilke.

As one would expect, the author gives detailed treatment to the legal developments since the last edition, for example an analysis of the *Cosslett* case in the House of Lords and its unreported sequel in the High Court. The author not only deals in detail with the decisions themselves but also the practical lessons to be learnt from them within the industry.

There is a very interesting updating of the case law on assignments and their prohibition as well as the use of trusts in this context. Updating of case law is also significant in the ever-increasingly important area of novation, where Ch.15 contains much new interesting material. Even the old chestnut of discharge of guarantors by variation of the principal obligation continues to produce new cases analysed by the author, revealing the pitfalls of inadequate drafting and the dangers of side letters. The danger of security being diluted by the guarantor's subrogation rights as a result of using the wrong form of guarantee is analysed in Ch.19 by reference to the Court of Appeal case of *Liberty Mutual v HSBC Bank* [2002] EWCA 691.

As well as fulfilling its central role of updating and informing, analysing and discussing, this third edition maintains the work's achievement of turning a potentially dry subject into surprisingly interesting reading.

Gabriel Moss Q.C.
3-4 South Square
Gray's Inn
WC1R 5HP

Foreword

Preface

This book was first conceived in the mid-1980s, in the run-up to the reforms brought about by the Insolvency Act 1986. At that time I was asked by Masons (now Pinsent Masons) to review the insolvency-related construction work being handled by the firm. What struck me in particular was the extent to which insolvency was acting as a driver in the development of construction law. I decided to research the relevant case law world wide and look for any recurring patterns there might be. This book is the outcome of that research.

It has been from the outset a practitioner's book: as much a resource for construction professionals and insolvency practitioners as for legal advisers. Initially (1990) it followed the traditional approach of a law book, stating propositions derived from the cases, which were largely relegated to footnotes. In the second edition (1999) I concluded that it would be more true to the subject if there were less abstraction and more analysis of the leading cases, with greater emphasis on the facts than textbooks normally allow. Industry professionals often orient themselves when reading about case law by reference to the standard form used and the location of the project even if such details are not strictly relevant to the decision. Also, by writing for the informed reader rather than the court, it was possible to provide a broader context for the legal discussion.

Thus I would suggest that the law has been "contextualised" in several different ways. First, by applying insolvency principles to a particular industry, they are given "body" and an historical setting. We can relate to stories about particular individuals and companies and the subject comes alive as a result. Second, as similar industry situations present themselves to the courts of all common law jurisdictions, we can appraise the English law approach to this subject against a wider background. We can also compare differing approaches to statutory intervention. Third, by attending to the metaphors inherent in the language of the law, we can develop an "inner eye" for the images at work. Placing the study of law in the context of imaginative traditions is an antidote to the self-importance that sometimes attaches to law as a discipline. It introduces elements of surprise and even subversion, which can be refreshing in the risk-averse legal world. It also contributes to a growing body of work in the universities concerned with images and law. This aspect is developed in the opening and closing chapters. As a general introduction to the hermetic approach, I recommend Patrick Harpur's book *The Philosophers' Secret Fire: A History of the Imagination* (Penguin 2002).

The impetus for including the illustrations came from an exhibition in 2001 at the Fitzwilliam Museum, Cambridge, entitled "Illuminating the Law: Medieval Legal Manuscripts from Cambridge Collections." Some exhibits can be seen online at *http://www.fitzmuseum.cam.ac.uk/gallery/law/*. It was fascinating to discover that legal manuscripts were decorated as well as ecclesiastical ones. The intense colour and beauty of the painting, as well as the inventiveness of the artists, make today's printed law books seem dreary in the extreme. Perhaps these images had a function lost to the modern world: that of acting as windows through which the reader could glimpse something of the divine light of the law. With the arrival of printing, images ceased to appear in legal works. I would suggest that reviving the use of images in this context could have a beneficial effect in deepening our appreciation of law. They can also relieve against the saturnine repression of emotion involved in legal study and repair some of the mutilating effects of over-exposure to Saturn (see Ch.22).

Working between the established legal categories of construction and insolvency has been fruitful in other ways. The law relating to areas such as assignment, novation, and guarantees (chapters 4, 15, and 19) has developed in connection with debts, i.e. one-way obligations. These devices assume great importance in the construction industry where one party becomes insolvent. But difficulties arise in applying the principles arising from debt cases to the complex bilateral obligations of construction contracts. Thus the common law develops through construction insolvency. A similar point can be made in relation to the use of the trust either as the means of payment or as a security device (chapters 9 and 10). The interaction of trust and contract law has been explored in a number of recent construction cases. The Office of Government Commerce has recently indicated that trust accounts will be used on large government contracts from 2008.

A major theme remains the mysterious, animating nature of money: the intangible forms through which it moves (limited companies, bank accounts), the ways in which its flow is regulated (construction contracts, security, the law of debtor and creditor), and the evidence it leaves behind (in this case, buildings, bridges etc). Some psychologists have equated money with imagination, psyche or the life-force.

A combination of economic stability, a fresh approach to employer-contractor relations, high levels of demand for construction work, more intelligent diversification within construction groups, new standard forms, and growth in the public sector through the private finance initiative have increased the industry's understanding of risk. The new sub-title of this book reflects a shift away from studying the effects of insolvency towards an analysis of security as it manifests in the industry, especially in the use of contractual terms functioning as informal security devices (Ch.2). Numerous questions arise: To what extent is it all necessary? Whose interests are being served by it? What effects, social as well as economic, does it have on the industry? The word "renewal" reflects the book's emphasis on the novation process and hints at the creative possibilities latent in the state of insolvency.

Although legal works always cite judicial precedent, they do not usually contain a bibliography of relevant books and articles. I have done so as a resource for those who want to take things further and to bring academic study and legal practice closer together. The bibliography highlights how a subject like construction insolvency is a marketplace where diverse areas of law can meet and mingle: e.g. land law, sale of goods, bailment, banking and finance, arbitration, to name just a few. In similar vein, I have included the final chapter on myth to challenge the perception that, however interesting they may be, such musings ought to be aired elsewhere. First, I am not sure that they would be accepted within the category of jurisprudence as it now exists. (How many books of jurisprudence even mention

Zeus?) Second, I feel that, having emerged as a result of the intensive research and study required for this book, they do actually belong here.

The book has educational origins: many chapters started life as handouts for training seminars at Masons, as papers given at conferences in the UK and South-East Asia, or as lectures at the Centre of Construction Law and Arbitration at King's College, University of London. In these settings, the involvement of professionals from such diverse backgrounds as government, teaching, arbitration, surveying, law, banking, building, design, and engineering ensured a lively interdisciplinary atmosphere in which ideas could be freely entertained without being fixed into a rigid framework. Perhaps the *genius* of the "engineer," in the Roman sense of creative guiding spirit, was at work pointing out the connections between us.

The time-lag since the last edition is so great that little would be gained by summarising the main changes since then. I would just mention that the second edition came out before the decision in *Macob v Morrison Construction* [1999] B.L.R. 93, the first case under the Housing Grants, Construction and Regeneration Act 1996. Since then around 300 cases on this Act have been reported, culminating in *Melville Dundas v George Wimpey* [2007] 1 W.L.R. 1136, a decision of the House of Lords. As well as revising Ch.3 on payment and Ch.5 on set-off to take account of this huge body of case law, I have added a new Ch.12 on the adjudication procedure. Even now, the precise relationship between the Act and major principles of insolvency law is still being worked out.

On the insolvency side, there have been significant developments, notably the Enterprise Act 2002, as a result of which administration and company voluntary arrangement have become the procedures of choice where the company still has value; while administrative receivership has all but disappeared as a secured creditor's remedy. For reasons of space I have omitted chapters on the industry and on security devices in Canada and the US. Although of great interest, it would have been necessary to analyse the statutory regimes of lien and trust, as well as the radically different role of the surety bondsman, which would have made the book too unwieldy. I have however expanded Ch.19 on bonds and guarantees, not least to respond to the perennial problem of unfair calling: see especially *HLC Engenharia v ABN Amro* [2005] EWHC 2074.

In summary this is both a work on construction law focusing on its security and equitable aspects and a work on insolvency law as applied to the complicated contractual relationships of the construction industry. It aims to keep legal principles close to the phenomena which gave rise to them and regards images and metaphors as essential to a depth understanding of the subject. I have referred to cases and materials available as at August 1, 2007.

September 18, 2007

Richard Davis
Pinsent Masons
30 Aylesbury Street
London EC1R OER

Acknowledgements

This new edition could not have been written without my consultancy with Pinsent Masons and I am grateful to the firm for making this possible, especially to Andrew Hibbert, of the UK Construction & Engineering Group, the book's sponsor. I would like to acknowledge the contribution of the firm's information services staff, especially Lynley Barker, Ginny Gilman, Nikki Tees, Janet Heppell, Esther Wheeler and Maggie Chan, not just for helping me find materials but for the good-natured humour with which they greeted my increasingly obscure requests.

I would like to thank the following at Pinsent Masons who have helped with research or read chapters in draft and given useful feedback: Sam Bailey, Fran Button, James Clarke, Peter Clayton, Alison Cull, Alex Darbyshire, Lawrence Davies, Chris Hallam, Duncan Halliwell, Dan Kelmanson, Alastair Lomax, Steve Ovenden, Simon Plunkett, James Pratt, Greg Richards, Katharine Sneddon, Jenna Sutton, Kenny Valentine, Richard Williams, Alan Woolston. John Mackenzie and Shafana Raza unravelled some of the mysteries of Scottish law for me. Minoosh Seifi researched some of the Australian cases.

Thanks also to Gabriel Moss Q.C. for his kind Foreword; to Neil Burton of Burton Marriott Ltd for his case study in Ch.16; to Eleanor Norton of Sweet & Maxwell for her patient nudging as the book took longer and longer to arrive and to Hannah George for taking it through the arduous proof stages; to Linda Jones for kindly allowing me to use the library at the Centre of Construction Law and Management, King's College London; and to Shan Morris for providing me with a copy of her dissertation on Laing Construction. In connection with the chapters on law and myth I have benefited greatly from conversations with James Hillman, Thomas Moore, Joscelyne Samuels, Marie Angelo and Jerry Rothenberg.

The following have kindly agreed to allow the reproduction of copyright material in relation to standard forms: RIBA Publications Limited in respect of JCT forms; The Institution of Civil Engineers, The Association of Consulting Engineers and the Federation of Civil Engineering Contractors in respect of ICE form; The Institution of Chemical Engineers in respect of the I Chem E Guide; the Federation Internationale des Ingenieurs-Conseils in respect of FIDIC; Federation of Civil Engineering Contractors in respect of the ICE Blue Form; HMSO Publications in respect of Crown copyright for GC/Works/1; Building Employers Confederation, Federation of Associations of Specialists and Sub-Contractors and the Committee of Associations of Specialist Engineering Contractors in respect of the Green Form. Extracts from GC/Works/1 are reproduced with the permission of the Controller of Her Majesty's Stationery Office.

I also thank the following for giving permission to quote from their works: David Morrell, *Indictment: Power and Politics in the Construction Industry* (Faber & Faber, 1987); Ann Shearer, *Athene: Image and Energy*

(Penguin Books, 1998); the late Thetis Blacker and The Temenos Academy, "Phoenix Reflections," Temenos Academy Review, 1, Spring 1998, 75-80; James Hillman, *Re-Visioning Psychology* (Harper & Row, 1976), *Kinds of Power: A Guide to its Intelligent Uses*, (Currency Doubleday, 1995), and *Senex & Puer* (Spring Publications, 2005). Other authors are acknowledged separately by full reference to their works in the Bibliography for the relevant chapter.

The Illustrations

The image on the front cover is a detail of Plate 1, which appeared in the *Illustrated London News* on December 22, 1877. It is reproduced from David B. Brownlee, *The Law Courts: The Architecture of George Edmund Street* (1984), by kind permission of The Architectural History Foundation and The Massachusetts Institute of Technology. It seems to have been engraved from a photograph taken from an elevated standpoint. This image is considered in Ch.1.

Plate 2 shows a terracotta plaque in the Museo Nazionale, Taranto, Puglia, Italy, reproduced by permission of The Bridgeman Art Library. It is thought to date from the early fifth century BCE and shows the goddess Aphrodite in her chariot borne by Eros and Psyche. Hermes, with winged feet and helmet, follows behind. Chapter 1 argues that construction insolvency has hermetic depths. This image shows that Hermes and Aphrodite, goddess of love, beauty and sexuality, are close and travel together. She might say that deepening our involvement with law through images is a way of loving.

Plate 3 is a famous photograph of Brunel standing in front of the launching chains of the "Great Eastern," taken in 1857 by Robert Howlett, and is reproduced courtesy of The Bridgeman Art Library. It has been suggested that his somewhat untidy appearance can be attributed to his habit of sleeping in his clothes during the critical period leading to the launching of the ship. The massive chains have something fateful about them as if they are about to engulf him: see the discussion on "binding and loosing" in chapters 1 and 22. Within two years, both Brunel and the photographer were dead.

Plate 5 is a detail of a sculpture by Michelangelo, sometimes called "The Drunkenness of Bacchus" (1496) in the Bargello, Florence, courtesy of The Bridgeman Art Library. Although at first sight the figure of the Roman god Bacchus (the Greek Dionysos) seems to be unbalanced through inebriation, Rafael López-Pedraza has suggested that Michelangelo has created an image of the god as a style of consciousness which does not depend on fixed viewpoints but rather on a fluid response to phenomena. See the discussion on water in Ch.1, and on Dionysos as god of insolvency, in Ch.22.

Plates 4, 6 and 7 are reproduced from Stanislas Klossowski de Rola, *The Golden Game: Alchemical Engravings of the Seventeenth Century* (1998) by kind permission of the publisher, Thames & Hudson. After each engraving the author provides a brief commentary drawing out, but without explaining, its alchemical significance. Intriguingly, he says that images often convey aspects of alchemy which were not recorded in writing. The plates are referred to in Ch.22.

Plate 1. Royal Courts of Justice, London, under construction, 1877

Plate 2. Aphrodite and Hermes, 5th century BCE

Plate 3. Brunel and the launching chains of the Great Eastern, 1857

Plate 4 Saturn in the garden of the philosophers, alchemical engraving, 17th century

Plate 5. Bacchus (detail) by Michelangelo, 1496

Plate 6. "No generation without corruption," alchemical engraving, 17th century

Plate 7. Jupiter (Zeus) begins the alchemical work, 17th century

List of Citations

This book draws on specialist construction and insolvency reports and refers to many overseas cases. The following list of selected citations may be helpful. See also the following:

- *http://www.legalabbrevs.cardiff.ac.uk* provides a comprehensive searchable database of legal citations worldwide.
- *http://www.bailii.org/* gives free access to judgments of UK and overseas courts. The citations placed in italics below are all available at this address online.

A.C.L.R.	Australian Company Law Reports
A.C.S.R.	Australian Corporations and Securities Report
A.C.T.R.	Australian Capital Territories Reports
A.D.R.L.J.	Arbitration and Dispute Resolution Journal
A.L.J.R.	Australian Law Journal Reports
A.L.R.	Australian Law Reports
Alta. L.R.	Alberta Law Reports
A.R.	Alberta Reports (Canada)
B.C.C.	British Company Cases
B.C.L.	Building and Construction Law (Australia)
B.C.L.C.	Butterworths Company Law Cases
Build. L.M.	Building Law Monthly
B.L.R	Building Law Reports
B.P.I.R.	Bankruptcy & Personal Insolvency Reports
Bus. L.R.	Business Law Reports (Canada)
C.B.R.	Canadian Bankruptcy Reports
C.I.L.L.	Construction Industry Law Letter
Con. L.R.	Construction Law Reports
Con. L. Yb.	Construction Law Yearbook
Const. L.J.	Construction Law Journal
C.L.C.	CCH Commercial Law Cases

C.L.D.	Construction Law Digest
C.L.R.	Commonwealth Law Reports
C.L.R.	Construction Law Reports (Canada)
C.L.Y.	Current Law Year Book
D.L.R.	Dominion Law Reports (Canada)
E.G.	Estates Gazette
E.G.D.	Estates Gazette Digest
E.G.L.R.	Estates Gazette Law Reports
EWCA	England and Wales Court of Appeal
EWHC	England and Wales High Court
F.T.L.R.	Financial Times Law Reports
G.L.R.	Gazette Law Reports (New Zealand)
H.K.C	Hong Kong Cases
HKCFI	Hong Kong Court of First Instance
H.K.L.R.	Hong Kong Law Reports
I.C.R.	Industrial Cases Reports
IEHC	High Court of Ireland
I.R.L.R.	Industrial Relations Law Reports
Ll. L. Rep.	Lloyd's List Reports
M.L.J.	Malayan Law Journal
MLJU	Malayan Law Journal Unreporteds
N.B.R.	New Brunswick Reports (Canada)
N.I.L.R.	Northern Ireland Law Reports
N.P.C.	New Property Cases
N.S.R.	Nova Scotia Reports (Canada)
NSWCA	New South Wales Court of Appeal
NSWSC	New South Wales Supreme Court
N.S.W.L.R.	New South Wales Law Reports (Australia)
NTSC	Northern Territories Supreme Court (Australia)
NZCA	New Zealand Court of Appeal
NZSC	New Zealand Supreme Court
N.Z.L.R.	New Zealand Law Reports
O.L.R.	Ontario Law Reports (replaced by O.R.)
O.R.	Ontario Reports (Canada)
P&CR	Property and Compensation Reports

Qd. R.	Queensland Reports
QCA	Queensland Court of Appeal
QSC	Queensland Supreme Court
S.A.	South African Law Reports
S.A.L.R.	South Australian Law Reports
S.A.S.R.	South Australian State Reports
SASC	South Australia Supreme Court
S.C.	Courts of Session Cases (Scottish)
CSOH	Court of Session Outer House (Scottish)
CSIH	Court of Session Inner House (Scottish)
S.C.R.	Supreme Court Reports (Canada)
SGCA	Singapore Court of Appeal
SGHC	Singapore High Court
S.J. (Sol. J.)	Solicitors Journal
S.L.R.	Singapore Law Reports
S.L.T.	Scots Law Times
S.R. (N.S.W.)	State Reports (New South Wales)
S.T.C.	Simons Tax Cases
Tas. S.R.	Tasmanian State Reports
T.L.R.	Times Law Reports
UKHL	United Kingdom House of Lords
VCAT	Victorian Civil and Administrative Tribunal
VICSC	Victoria Supreme Court
V.R.	Victorian Reports (Australia)
VSCA	Victoria Court of Appeal
V.L.R.	Victoria Law Reports (Australia, replacing V.R.)
WASC	Western Australia Supreme Court
WASCA	Western Australia Court of Appeal
W.A.L.R.	West Australia Law Reports (1899–1959)
W.A.R.	Western Australian Reports (1960–current)
W.W.R.	Western Weekly Reports (Canada)

Table of Cases

Table of Statutes

Table of Statutory Instruments

Table of Standard Forms

UK main contracts

UK sub-contracts

Australia

New Zealand

Singapore

Chapter 1

Law in Context

The study of law is often enhanced by placing it in context. Vanessa Finch (2002) for example writes about insolvency against a background of economics and theories of justice. David Milman (2005) provides a backdrop of social and legislative history. In his study of how major projects are put together, Jeffrey Delmon (2005) devotes a lengthy section to the psychology of risk. I drew on these approaches when considering the effect of the Housing Grants, Construction and Regeneration Act 1996 (Davis 1996). The second edition of this book began with a portrait of the construction industry from an economic perspective, with charts showing its structure and its propensity to insolvency compared with other industries. In this new edition, I would like to take a different approach and invite you to enter this subject by spending a few moments contemplating an image (Plate 1). **1–001**

1. The Royal Courts

On the left looms the partly completed Royal Courts of Justice as seen from the Strand. It is an extraordinary sight, veiled in scaffolding, with turrets peeping through, a chimney and other stonework just visible. The hoardings carry advertisements for the Daily Telegraph, Hudson's Household Removals, and "Stolen!" at the Globe Theatre. There is much coming and going in front of Temple Bar, one of the gates to the City of London, which was rebuilt after the Restoration and recently re-erected near St Paul's Cathedral. At one time the upper room was used as a prison; traitors' heads were displayed from the gate until the mid-eighteenth century. Beyond it can be seen the tower of St Dunstan's in the West, dedicated to the patron saint of goldsmiths, a tenth-century scholar and metalworker. **1–002**

Thanks to the researches of David Brownlee, we know that the builder of the Royal Courts, Joseph Bull and Sons, was already insolvent when the image was made and being supported financially by the Office of Works. The lowest of 19 tenderers, Bulls were specialist railway engineering contractors based in Southampton with little experience of large building projects. They over-stretched themselves this time, both financially and geographically. Their problems began with a significant pricing error which meant they had to renegotiate the contract (including the reduction of retention). This was a lump-sum, long-term contract agreed at a time when labour and material costs were rising. Initially, requests for advance payments for equipment and off-site materials were refused but as the contract progressed, the "government had a vested interest in keeping its builder solvent" to avoid "prodigious delays" and made substantial weekly payments, treated as advances, as well as direct payments to stonemasons (Brownlee 1984, 298). The work was completed two years late, and receivers appointed to the contractor a month later.

The irony of the fact that the law courts, where many of the cases discussed in this book were decided, were themselves the product of a construction insolvency is not lost on the judiciary. The example of Joseph Bull and Sons was recently cited in the Court of Appeal. Sedley L.J. observed that s.111 of the Housing Grants, Construction and Regeneration Act 1996 "would have done something to protect the stonecarvers from acting as unpaid bankers to the head contractors" (*Rupert Morgan v Jervis* [2004] B.L.R. 18, at para.17). The image has extended our thinking by introducing an "as if" quality: if the modern statute had applied to the contracts for the construction of the Royal Courts, then roles would have been reversed. The balance of power would have shifted to those lower down the chain of contracts.

What else do we notice in the image? There is a striking contrast between the sheer size of the building in course of erection and the miniature scale of the gate. The artist almost implies that the scaffolding has reached the sky. Another contrast is between the fixing going on in the building work and the flow of life in the street, with all the pushing and pulling, walking and riding in both directions. Much of the scene is in shadow but the sun illuminates a small part of the gate, and the left foreground. The courts are in the fashionable gothic style, the gate harks back to classical times. If we were studying law when this image was made, when the study of Greek and Latin gave access to the myths underlying Western culture, we might well associate this way of thinking with a particular god, known to the Greeks as Hermes (or to the Romans as Mercury). What do I mean by that? As god of imagination, he crosses boundaries, making meaningful connections that light up both sides in an unexpected and fruitful way. This way of being does not work things out but is alive to chance finds made on the road. As well as teaching students to distinguish between cases, a legal education also develops the skill of making connections. This is the hermetic art *par excellence*. Imagination as directed by Hermes is incisive, sophisticated and informed; its cultivation involves meditative work as well as intensive study. The outcome is a particular receptivity to new ideas and images which allows them to feed into a deeper knowledge of the subject. Returning to the image, Hermes might enable us to appreciate where we are standing: in the middle of the road—the Strand, literally the shore or river bank—raised up slightly above the street level. In Plate 2, we can just see the wings on Hermes' feet and helmet that enable him to fly, conveying messages from the gods on Olympus to humans on earth and to the gods below in the underworld.

1–003 The flexible "in between" quality of hermetic thinking is well-suited to the themes of this book. Combining construction and insolvency provides an opportunity for each to learn something about itself through the other's eyes. They concern quite different principles, indeed at first sight they seem to have little in common. This book is a container in which to observe how they react to each other in any number of situations. The book inhabits the hinterland between these categories and is interested in the ebb and flow of money and the involvement of law in the phenomenon of construction insolvency through two of its creations: the contract and the limited company.

As the form of the building takes shape, we know that the builder is falling apart. Is law built by failure? Could there be a secret affinity between them? For a company, insolvency is the equivalent of dying. Again we meet Hermes, this time in classical guise as guide of souls conducting the dead to Hades, the name both of the Greek underworld, which James Hillman (1979), the founder of archetypal psychology, has compared to the imagination, and of the god who rules there. In the context of a book on insolvency, it is worth noting that Hades was known as "Receiver of Many". Going back to the image, we see much hustle and bustle, some at least of which is related to trade and commerce—areas also falling within the pattern of Hermes. It is worth reflecting too that, historically, insolvency principles entered the common law through the law merchant. Hermes is also patron of rhetoric, or word-smithing, and therefore of crucial significance to the art of the advocate. But he does not belong to the civilised world of the law courts. As far as he is concerned, it is as if they had never been built.

Hermes is subversive: he approaches notions of private property and the insistence on strict rights with humour, as in the myth in which he steals Apollo's cattle and then lies about it when Apollo complains to Zeus. He favours exchange without moralising—whether by theft, clever trading, or chance find. Against this rich background of hermetic imagination, we can turn to history for more particulars of our subject. So let us fly with thrice-great Hermes over the Mediterranean Sea to the eastern shores of ancient Sicily and see what we can learn about construction insolvency from our ancestors.

2. Ancestral voices

Dionysius of Syracuse

Dionysius I was born in about 430 BCE and ruled Syracuse, and most of **1–004**
Sicily, from 405 until his death in 367. The most famous story about him is preserved by Cicero, the Roman lawyer and philosopher of the first century BCE. In his *Tusculan Disputations*, he tells how Damocles, "a flatterer", exalted Dionysius for his power and possessions, saying, "never has there been a happier man". "If that is so", replied the tyrant, "would you like a taste of how I live?" Damocles leapt at the chance and was escorted to a gilded couch beautifully decorated with coverings. Dionysius ordered that every luxury be made available to him: gold and silver plate to eat from, exquisitely cooked foods, the rarest incense, and the services of attractive attendants whose only duty was to satisfy his every whim. Damocles was delighted: truly this was the happy life. But directly above Damocles' neck was a sword glinting in the light, suspended from the roof by a horse hair. As he looked up, Damocles felt all his pleasure turn to ashes; a wreath placed on his head slipped down, and he begged to be released back to his former station, saying that he had quite lost his desire to be a happy man.

The tyrant was obsessed by the need for security. Cicero says that Dionysius had a trench dug around his private chamber which could only be crossed by a wooden bridge that he would haul inside when he wanted to be alone and that he never addressed his people in the open, but only from the top of a high tower. A modern history of Sicily records that unlike his predecessors, Dionysius built fortifications rather than temples and theatres, used every possible device to extort money, and moved vast numbers of people from place to place. "All this has a certain intrinsic interest, but it is important too in that it indicates how completely personal the rule of Dionysius was, and was meant to appear. In this respect he created something new in the western world . . ." (Finley et al 1986, 21–22). A man of almost superhuman energy, Dionysius was addicted to power and conquest, and then defending what he'd taken, and yet "his career has something of the poignant futility of a treadmill about it" (at 23). There is something moving too in another story from Cicero concerning two followers of Pythagoras, Damon and Phintias. When one was sentenced to death, the other stood surety for him: very trusting as his life would be forfeited if his friend failed to turn up for his execution. But the condemned man did show up and the surety was released. Dionysius observed: "I would give a lot to be a third person in your friendship."

To our psychologised age, Dionysius displays paranoid characteristics, his inability to trust appears pathological. The "sword of Damocles" is a phrase in common use; the image must articulate something we instinctively recognise in modern life. In terms of this book, it is an archetypal image of the risk of forfeiture: of a contract terminated, or a bond called, or property taken as security, or of a company's life liquidated. Like excessive overheads in business accounts or an overdraft payable on demand, the image of the sword suspended from above is an expression of contingency, that the happy life can be ended with a single blow to the neck.

Nicholas Barbon

1–005 The history of contracting has yet to be written but the name of Nicholas Barbon (1640–1698) will surely feature in it. Son of the Puritan, Praisegod Barbon (or Barebone), Nicholas was a man of many achievements, notably his exploitation of the building boom following the Great Fire of London of 1666, a time when building contracts were becoming increasingly complex (Campbell 2002). Sir John Summerson writes of him:

> "The first we hear of Barbon after his arrival in England is that about 1670 he rebuilt his father's burnt house in Crane Court, Fleet Street, apparently shifting its site to the far end of the Court and giving the new structure a facade of some distinction. Here he lived in a lordly way, directing his mysterious, complex schemes, rarely without great profit and rarely with complete honesty. . . . The houses he built were all very much alike, economically planned to the point of meanness, with coarse ornaments which repeated themselves over and over again. . . . Credit suited him best, for by dint of an odious process of delaying, deceiving, wriggling, and pleading he usually managed to evade the law and ultimately to get away with the business at about half what it would have cost to borrow. . . . When he died, many of his schemes were in utter confusion, and his debts were enormous. It was, also, characteristic of this extremely able, but far from amiable person that, when he died, instructions were found in his will that none of his debts were to be paid" (Summerson 1978, 44–50).

"Credit suited him best"—quite an epitaph. His insolvency at his death seems curiously appropriate. Is Nicholas Barbon an ancestor of the industry's abusive ways or did he just find a congenial home for his dark and tricky nature? As well as property developer, he was also a famous economist, a banker, physician, member of parliament, and innovator in fire insurance. It is nicely ironic to record that one of the leading sets of construction barristers practises in a street built by him in 1682.

It is worth noting that most of London from the late seventeenth century onwards was built by speculators under building leases by which "plots were let at a low ground rent on the understanding that the lessee built at his own expense a house or houses of substantial character, which house or houses, at the end of the lease, became the property of the ground landlord. A building agreement was probably signed in the first instance, to be implemented by the lease when the building was in an advanced state of completion" (Summerson 1978, 39–40). Since the seventeenth century therefore the personal relations between landowners and builders have been inextricably mixed with proprietary rights. The first textbook on building law includes a commentary on the terms usually found in building leases (Emden 1882).

Isambard Kingdom Brunel

Brunel (1806–1859) lived in the heyday of laissez-faire economics when **1–006** freedom of contract was the prevailing legal philosophy. His biographers have concentrated on his achievements as an engineer; they tend not to go into detail about his relationships with contractors. Adrian Vaughan is an exception. He writes: "Throughout his career it was Isambard's technique of management to withhold pay on some pretext and then hold it as hostage against 'good behaviour' for the future" (1991, 21). For the purposes of this book it is interesting to focus on Brunel as paymaster (Plate 3).

Particularly striking is his treatment of Hugh McIntosh, who took over contracts to construct railways to Bath and Bristol after the insolvency of William Ranger led to his exclusion from the works by the Great Western Railway Company. Once contracts were signed, Brunel started to under-certify, withhold payment, order variations but refuse to pay for them or grant an appropriate extension of time. When the contractor protested, Brunel failed to reply to correspondence. He attempted to levy a financial penalty for the contractor's delay but relented, saying that the "fine" would be suspended to ensure his good behaviour.

By 1840, Brunel was withholding £100,000 from McIntosh on another project on the specious ground that he was awaiting an account on an entirely separate contract with Hugh's son, David McIntosh. Brunel continued to argue set-off even after receiving advice from the company's solicitor that it was wrongful. Brunel knew that Hugh McIntosh was solvent, owned his own plant and equipment and employed good engineers. He took credit from the contractor to help the company's cash flow on the project as his own cost estimates had already been exceeded. He also refused to return a bond for £2,000 without cause. The dispute was not resolved until 1865, by which time Brunel and the McIntoshes were dead. The Vice-Chancellor found in favour of the contractor for payment of £100,000 plus 20 years' interest (Vaughan 1991, 139).

Brunel seems to have been what we would today call a workaholic. "Did **1–007** he really need to work so hard?" asks Steven Brindle. "There is no doubt that in Brunel's mind he did, in order to exercise the absolute control over his many projects that he insisted upon" (at 228). A fantasy of domination permeated every aspect of his work: over the design process, the choice of route for the lines, the recruitment of staff, and the drafting and operation of contractual terms. To Brunel, the company's employees were the company's property with no independent life of their own; they were expected to live almost as bonded labourers. Power rested wholly with Brunel. Vaughan gives examples of Brunel's harsh, bullying style; and his jealousy, obsession with status, mistrust of others, inability to delegate, and his "capricious and dictatorial" conduct as certifier of payment (1991, 234). Yet Brunel wrote of himself: "I believe I am naturally idle and all my life is one of slaving and compulsion. I am never my own master and I always have an overwhelming quantity of work which must be done by certain days . . . one's own eye is the only one after all . . . I am obliged to do all myself" (Vaughan 1991: 87, 98, 195). It is interesting to note that Brunel's father, Marc Isambard Brunel, was imprisoned for debt for 10 weeks in 1821 as a result of a downturn in his businesses and the insolvency of his bankers. Marc was also a brilliant engineer but he had no head for business. Vaughan comments that the family lived on the edge of ruin (at 6). He was rescued from the King's Bench Prison in Southwark, where he was living in a small room with his wife, through the intervention of the Duke of Wellington.

Competition between railway companies showed capitalism at its most ruthless. Kostal (1997) has researched the legal and financial background to the growth of the railway industry. Especially interesting is his account of the share market crash of 1845.

> "By late December at least 549 provisionally registered railway companies had 'disappeared', and hundreds more were soon to be wholly abandoned. The fortunes and life-savings of tens of thousands of people had been wiped out. The grim prospect of lawsuits, bankruptcy, and debtors' prison threatened hundreds of noblemen, merchants, barristers, and brokers" (Kostal 1997, 41).

Loss of equity investment came at a time when capital was most needed (at 109). The crash may have had long term effects on the relations between employers and contractors. Firstly, it seems that employers were forced to take credit from the contractors to fund the construction cost (a possible reason for the high percentages of retention at this time). Secondly, the crash had a traumatic effect on all concerned, leading to a desperate desire for as much security as possible, including strict contractual terms functioning as security. Kostal also reveals the roles played by lawyers as company promoters, directors, advisers, and parliamentary agents. The question arises whether this factor has contributed to the legalistic nature of the modern construction industry.

In the nineteenth century "the rate of bankruptcy in the building trade far exceeded that in other trades and occupations" (Lester 1995, 258).

> "Large-scale contracting in the Victorian age was a risky business, and one of the most striking points about it is how many contractors came to grief. Of the ones who feature in Brunel's story, William Ranger and James and Thomas Bedborough became insolvent, and Robert Mudge-Marchant was declared bankrupt. John Scott Russell's business was

> bankrupted by the Great Eastern, and C.J. Mare was bankrupted during the construction of the Saltash Bridge, though they both recovered" (Brindle 2004, 239).

Competitive tendering was the standard means of procurement but the success rate was low, perhaps one in nine tenders.

> "The estimating clerks must have been under continuous pressure to catch enough acceptances to keep the business afloat without inviting disaster by under-pricing—a practice all too common in the lower ranks of the industry as a last gamble under impending bankruptcy" (Summerson 1973, 13).

If Dionysius of Syracuse, Nicholas Barbon, and Isambard Kingdom Brunel are the ancestors of the attitudes and practices of the modern industry, they need to be remembered. Otherwise they will rule us from their graves.

3. Image sense

As well as listening out for ancestral voices we could also pay regard to the **1–008** hints and suggestions latent in the law's use of language, especially its metaphors. This is another way in which the hermetic approach to imagining can enrich our understanding of the law.

The most obvious metaphor is the element of water. To be solvent, a company needs good cash flow as well as a steady flow of work. If the sources of capital dry up, it becomes insolvent and enters liquidation. After the assets are sold, a dividend is paid to creditors and the company is dissolved. We also speak of a company being floated, with money pouring in, a reservoir of capital, a buoyant market, bailing out, going belly-up, a hole in finances, money down the drain, of companies going under, rats deserting the sinking ship, ventures shipwrecked. Here are a few quotations from the cases: "the creditors . . . having offered the company a lifeboat of a CVA": *Souster v Carman Construction Co Ltd* (unreported, December 16, 1999, Peter Smith Q.C.); "rescue that company from the jaws of the liquidation" . . . "pulled the plug": *Official Receiver v Barnes* [2001] B.C.C. 578 (appeal from District Judge Wilby); a company "descended into insolvency" *Vodafone v GNT Holdings (UK) Ltd* [2004] EWCA 1242, para.8, *per* Potter L.J. This association with fluidity feels mysterious. We are a long way away from all the earth-moving of the previous section.

Law is sometimes criticised for not being imaginative and it is true that the legal method strips out everything which is not regarded as relevant to the issue before the court. But this brief look at the language suggests that, however rationalistic and reductive it aspires to be, law is steeped in images which provide subtle understandings. Imagination delights in word play, making connections through the sound as well as the meaning of words. Image is piled on image: the same word evokes multiple meanings that reverberate with each other. "Liquidation" for example refers both to payment (realisation of a debt) and to the consequences of non-payment (winding up). Both debt and debtor can be liquidated: see *Buchler v Talbot* [2004] 2 A.C. 298, para.79 (Lord Millett). While insolvency suggests chaos and confusion, liquidation implies a reduction to order (*liquidare* = melt, clarify, make clear). This water has ambivalent, positive and negative qualities: benevolent in fostering cash flow, malefic in its death-dealing nature. It may hide an aspidochelon. A medieval bestiary describes the creature as follows:

> "There is a monster in the sea which the Greeks call aspidochelon. It was this creature that took up Jonah. This creature raises its back above the waves, and it seems to stay in the same place. The winds blow sea-sand on it and it becomes a level place on which vegetation grows. Sailors believe it is an island, and beach their ships on it. Then they light fires, and when the creature feels the heat of the fire, it dives into the water and drags the ship down with it into the depths" (Barber 1992, 204).

In contrast to the sense of flow, we speak of a bank account being frozen on the issue of a winding up petition, of freezing orders preventing a defendant dealing with an account above a certain limit, of floating charges crystallising into fixed charges, of blocked accounts stopping any movement of funds unless certain conditions are met. The word "insolvency" implies a sudden congealing of the waters.

1–009 A similar idea is expressed through the metaphor of tightening: straitened circumstances, money too tight to mention, capital tied up, tight security, margins squeezed. The process of liquidation is commenced by a winding up petition. The reference is to the winding sheet in which the dead are wrapped for burial. We speak of winding up a debate. There are echoes of the Fates spinning, measuring and cutting the thread of each soul's destiny in Plato's *Republic*. The construction industry uses an instrument known as a surety bond, a medieval form of obligation in which a person binds himself to pay a sum of money. A lien is derived from *ligare* (= to bind), which is also the root of obligation. We speak of legally binding agreements and precedents. The metaphor thus extends to other forms of bond such as the construction contract, or a company's articles of association, even the bundles used in court. Bricklayers arrange courses of bricks in Flemish or English bond. The Latin word *securus* connotes both "free from care" and "firmly fixed".

Loosing is apparent in all forms of release: secured assets are redeemed on performance of the obligation; contracting parties are released from their primary obligations if one accepts the other's repudiation (*repudium* = divorce); the insolvent party is released on a novation. The Latin word *solvere* has the dual meaning of dissolve and untie. A debt with a grace period is still referred to as "*debitum in praesenti solvendum in futuro*," a present debt payable in future. It is possible that "indemnity" too derives from a root that refers to loosing a bond (Onians 1951, 438).

Another dominant metaphor is of balancing and falling. The former is prevalent in company accounts—ledger balances, balance sheets—and also as one of the definitions of insolvency in s.123 of the Insolvency Act 1986 known as the balance sheet test. If a company's liabilities exceed its assets a company is technically insolvent (Ch.8). Debts mount up and become a burden. The image is of a structure becoming unsteady and toppling over. This idea is also behind the knock-on effect whereby the insolvency of one party in the construction chain causes the insolvency of another. We also speak of the domino effect, of a house of cards, and of corporate collapse.

1–010 The court sometimes speaks of money in terms of blood, implicitly likening the company to the human body. For example, Lord Millett has said that "a fixed charge would deprive the company of access to its cash flow which is the life blood of a business": *Agnew v Inland Revenue Commissioner* [2001] 2 A.C. 710, para.7. A company might be starved of cash or need a cash injection. The law also speaks of the body corporate (*corpus* = body). "Company" also has a bodily association, being derived from *cum panis* (= with bread), suggestive of companions setting out on a venture together, like Chaucer's Canterbury pilgrims. In insolvency, there is the general body of creditors, and of course bodies of law. The more we go into this metaphor, playing with the associations of words, the more we enter the world of myth. No more so than with the division of company property by the liquidator and its distribution to the creditors, each receiving the same proportion of his debt. This is a dismemberment, and if we add the blood and the bread we are in religious territory (*religare* = to bind fast). "Turnaround" equates to conversion.

If the revenue realisable by completing a contract is greater than the cost to complete, it is possible that another contractor will agree to novate the contract. Novation is a neglected area of law which is of vital importance in construction insolvency. Derived from Roman law (*renovare* = make new again), *novatio* or *renovatio* is also used in connection with the renewal of institutions such as the medieval Church. When young Francesco Bernadone heard Christ say to him in a vision, "Repair my falling house!" he took it literally and sold some of his father's goods to repair the church of San Damiano. He was promptly disinherited and founded the Franciscan friars whose work brought about a revival of spirituality in the thirteenth century (Attwater 1965, 136). As the friars could not own property, wealthy donors transferred land for the construction of churches to civic authorities to hold "to the use of" the friars, a device which eventually led to the modern trust (Knowles 1948, Vol.1, 133–134). It is interesting to reflect on these connections between property (renovation), law, and spiritual rebirth. *Renovatio* in the Italian Renaissance expressed the spring-like joy of rediscovering the world of the classical gods and goddesses. It was central to the work of the alchemists, one of whose myths concerns the rejuvenation of a drowning king through the mercurial waters, a story with deep resonance with the themes of this book.

Each of these images offers a way of understanding legal process which is not purely conceptual and which places law in a rich cultural setting. Without losing their individuality they can be placed together to form a pattern of correspondences.

- Drying out and dissolving
- Binding-tightening and loosing
- Embodying and dismembering
- Balancing and falling

We can recognise some images which are close together. Fixing for example can be compared with blocking. It is interesting to note that the word "encumbrance" is derived from a French word for blocking a river with a barrage of logs. Stopping a flow is close to the process of freezing. Drying out in the classical Greek world connoted dying, as well as poverty and sickness (Onians 1951, 255). The sensate nature of these expressions enlivens the lawyer's responsiveness to what is happening; the dynamism of natural processes is being mirrored by the law. When we speak of termination, for example, we can imagine a cutting of the bonds. A **1–011** novation is a form of resurrection, and we think of Lazarus. Or the appointment of a liquidator can be viewed as a decapitation of the company's head, as with John the Baptist. Any right of forfeiture evokes the sword of Damocles.

Keeping an ear close to the images that reside in the sound and sense of words is rewarding; it is a useful antidote to the closing-down effect of law's definitions. Law's tendency to abstraction and distance is valuable but can cause dissociation from the world. *Image sense brings substance and body back to legal study.* We might ask: what is the imagination of law like? What is the effect on phenomena of seeing through the legal perspective?

The limited liability company is a legal fiction, a product of the law's imagination which reached maturity as recently as 1855. In itself it is empty or neutral: a company can only operate through rules of attribution which determine whose actions and statements are regarded as those of the company. This lack of definition is very attractive to the imagination, especially to images that are repressed by the legal method, such as those expressing irrationality or instinct. On a formal insolvency the directors, as the mind and will of the company, lose their powers and are displaced by an insolvency practitioner. The company can be said to lose its mind and be possessed by an outsider as the ancients were possessed by gods.

4. Perspectives

1–012 It may be useful to discriminate between construction, insolvency, and law in terms of the perspectives they offer. This is desirable with a law book otherwise everything will appear to be fully under control, in consequence of what we might see as the law's fantasy of mastery. A phenomenologist interested in the fullest possible description and understanding of the matter under inquiry regards an event or thing as having infinite depth; it can never be fully explained or "flattened out" (*planus* = flat), only attended with an open, receptive, mind. The researcher is drawn into, and affected by, the phenomenon.

If we consider "construction" as a way of seeing and knowing the world, independently of its treatment by the law, what would emerge? The question is liberating because the modern industry has become legalistic in the way it sees itself. The root of construction is *struere* (= to pile up, assemble), and implies a perspective that notices the way one thing adds to another, how things fit together. By extension, it could apply to a way of seeing that appreciates how one event relates to another event until a story emerges. The perspective seeks the form in an idea, it is always reaching towards some physical, material manifestation. It seems to depend on the craftsman's unity of hand and eye. Something is being made when we see through this perspective.

By contrast, insolvency brings with it images of destruction, such as death by drowning or dismemberment considered in the previous section. Perhaps we cannot understand the insolvency perspective without first putting to one side our negative associations to these processes. Instead we could value them as much as we value the creative aspects of the construction perspective. This is not easy as insolvency seems to evoke heroic gestures (business rescue, restructuring) which deny its validity or necessity. So what is happening when we see through this perspective? I suggest that it exaggerates something, distorts it to an extreme until it breaks so that something new can appear. The process is disorienting as it involves living without a fixed identity, so that one thing easily turns into another. A literal representation of the Royal Courts under construction evokes the god Hermes, whose archaic attitude to life predates the whole notion of a legal system. Something conscious and familiar is breaking down when we see through this perspective.

Law belongs archetypally to Zeus, who is often imagined as an eagle **1–013**
soaring in the sky: one of the god's names means "He who sees from afar." As father of the gods and ruler on Olympus, Zeus is the ultimate judge and source of power. To see through the legal perspective, perhaps we should ask: what is an eagle like? Swift-thinking and powerful, airy, most high: the associations are with elevation, and the ease with which the bird uses thermal currents. An eagle is also sharp and tenacious, able to cut into material and extract what it's looking for. It is interesting to observe that an eagle is able to rise and fall and rise, connecting above and below. The law also dominates and decides (*de-caedere* = to cut off). There is a connection between judging and healing. According to the Online Etymology Dictionary, the Greek word *krisis* refers to the turning point in a disease and was used as such by Hippocrates and Galen. Its literal meaning is judgment, from *krinein* (= to separate, decide, judge). Something is being decided when we see through this perspective of mastery.

If each element of this book offers a different perspective, law's approach becomes relativised as one among many which can be adopted when attending to the phenomena of construction insolvency. Law always assumes a dominant position and would probably prefer not to have a context. Law naturally speaks in abstractions as if from a mountain peak. The way that textbooks are laid out supports this: with general principles sitting on top of a pile of footnotes. The perspectives of construction and insolvency offer vantage points from which to see what the law is doing. They give us the opportunity of detaching from the legal perspective from time to time to examine our attitudes to the law itself: are they appreciative or exploitative? They allow us to prefer the particular over the general. From the valley floor we can start digging into the common law to see what turns up, looking for the right place to plant new cases. I also wonder about the works that form the subject matter of the cases and where they were carried out and when. Bearing them in mind adds body to legal discussion by impeding the drive to relevance. Who knows, perhaps they have something to say on the matter?

5. Opening questions

What happens if a contractor cannot complete its work because the money **1–014**
coming in is less than the money going out? It sounds like a simple question that invites a practical, systematic answer. Yet it gives access to other questions that touch on complex, unresolved areas of law. In what circumstances should a contract be treated as property capable of being bought and sold? To what extent can a person avoid the *pari passu* rule, the basic tenet of insolvency law that creditors be treated equally? If the contract confers rights not available at common law, do they replace or supplement common law remedies? What allowance ought to be made for

contingent claims owed to or by the contractor? So far as it is possible to give answers to these questions, they seem always to depend on the context. See for example the surprising difficulty in defining a debt in Ch.3.

This chapter has created a portfolio of approaches intended to avoid closing down the phenomena of construction insolvency, including:

- Letting an image tell a story. This slows the busy mind and allows a moment of reverie to happen. In that imaginative space connections appear to make themselves, and we fly to a recently decided case and thence to the possibility of interdisciplinary insights between construction and insolvency. The god Hermes enters an appearance and traces patterns between legal history, the hidden meanings of money, and contrasts between fixing and flowing that will lead us eventually into a greater awareness of images inherent in the legal concepts.
- Remembering to remember the ancestors, real people whose lives were immersed in the patterns of images that shape this book. Their stories are often poignant, bringing a depth of feeling into the law book to stop it drying out. History presses against us, and we are left wondering at the degree to which what happened centuries ago is being re-enacted in the industry today.
- Sensing images allows a parallel process of imagining to emerge which gives life and body to legal work. Perhaps they are "that for the sake of which" the outer work is done. In the background are the waters: life-giving and death-dealing. We've also started to explore the rich imaginal background to novation (Ch.15) and bonds and guarantees (Ch.19), and re-visioned the company as one of the most striking manifestations of the legal imagination.
- Fourthly, the three constituents of this book have been separated out and put back together as perspectives. Although I have written mainly from the legal perspective, it is important to acknowledge that construction and insolvency each offer ways of seeing which are just as valuable. The phenomena under consideration have the capacity to "answer back" and question exactly what is happening when they are reduced to legal categories. The law has not had an especially benign effect on either contractors or debtors.

In sum, this is a book on insolvency as it affects those engaged on construction projects; but it can also be read metaphorically as the very detailed presentation of an image. Researchers often end reports by calling for more research. I have some sympathy with this because questioning tends to open up a field of complexity not apparent at the beginning. One thing always leads to another. The objective of the research may well be to generate questions and learn to love the questions for themselves, as Rilke advises the young poet. In that spirit, here are some of my own:

Can we bring an artist's sensibility to legal work? What might be added to law by this?
Can institutions value the cultural background of law as an essential part of legal education?
Is the "rescue culture" a denial of death?
Is the security demanded in the industry disproportionate to the risks?
Is the cure worse than the disease?

If construction is earth, insolvency is water, and law is air—where is fire?

Is law nothing but the practice of literalism?

What is money that its loss should be so devastating? Why is insolvency feared so much?

Can an awareness of metaphor help a lawyer to "see through" a situation to the just result?

Does the construction industry desire security? Is the instinct for security inseparable from the activity of building?

Do images occur to you as you read? Do you welcome them?

How do you react to the notion of treating a contract or a demand bond as disposable property?

Against this background of history and imagination, the following chapters track the phenomena of construction insolvency, largely through the traditional legal method. In the final chapter I suggest that the knowledge gained can be deepened by seeing it as foreground against the Greek myths, a movement from law into myth.

Chapter 2

Elements of Construction Security

To procure construction work is to wade into a sea of risk. Will it be fit for its purpose? Will it cost more than you can afford? Will delays to completion cause loss to your business? These risks are real enough but they can be managed. Ultimately, they come down to the contractor's ability to remedy the problem, either physically or by paying damages. But what if the contractor becomes insolvent? One answer is to ask the contractor to provide a guarantee from a source that is immune from insolvency or as close to immunity as possible, such as a "first class" bank. In practice however a bank guarantee is just one of a myriad of security devices developed over the last 150 years for use with construction contracts. The aim of this chapter is to separate out the elements which provide security against a contractor's insolvency. Who is demanding what and why? How do the devices impact on each other? Are they all necessary? Is security performing a symbolic rather than a commercial function? These are some of the questions considered. **2–001**

1. Background

"Security" is a legal term of art. If a debtor charges property as security for payment, but defaults on his obligation, the creditor can sell the property and use the proceeds to pay the debt in priority to other creditors; but if the debtor pays the debt he is entitled to have the property released from the charge: *Bristol Airport Plc v Powdrill* [1990] Ch. 744 at 766. "It is this equity of redemption which forms part of the fund held on trust for the company's creditors which arises upon a winding up": *Buchler v Talbot* [2004] 2 A.C. 298, at para.29 *per* Lord Hoffmann. Security is defined by reference to a debtor–creditor relationship. As well as its legal meaning, "security" is often used in a commercial sense. For example in *Shiloh Spinners Ltd v Harding* [1973] A.C. 691 at 723, Lord Wilberforce referred to a forfeiture provision as being added by way of security to secure a stated result. Contractual terms can function as security without creating an equity of redemption (Neate 1990). Sometimes it is not immediately clear whether the court is using security in its legal or its commercial sense. For example in *Technocrats International Inc v Fredic* [2005] 1 B.C.L.C. 467 a payment into court in discharge of a freezing order was held not to grant a security interest in the money to the claimant but merely to act as informal security against the risk of dissipation of assets (para.13). **2–002**

There is also the protection afforded by the common law which applies to the contract unless excluded by agreement, e.g. equitable set-off (Ch.5) or repudiation (Ch.14). The rules of the court can take effect as security, e.g. where an insolvent creditor is not allowed to execute a judgment enforcing an adjudication decision pending the substantive hearing of the dispute, at least without providing security for repayment (Ch.12). Some statutes operate as security, notably s.111 of the Housing Grants, Construction and Regeneration Act 1996 which obliges a debtor to serve a withholding notice as a condition of setting off a cross-claim. In summary, security can be formal if it gives rise to an equity of redemption or informal if it achieves a similar result without giving rise to such an equity. Informal security can be contractual, common law, procedural, or statutory. Broadly, if the security is formal it secures payment; if informal it secures performance. Attitudes towards financial protection depend on who you are: primary or secondary lender, bondholder, investor, project company, end-user, operator, employer, contractor, subcontractor, supplier, guarantor, insurer. The law sees protection in terms of rights and obligations: rights as contractual or proprietary and obligations as primary or secondary. Commercially, protection consists in the cost-effective management of risk. Each approach casts a different light on the subject.

2. Pre-contract security

2–003 This book is primarily concerned with the construction phase of a project and the risks attendant on it, notably the risk of contractor and subcontractor insolvency. As such it does not address procurement and contract strategies (see the guides issued by the Office of Government Commerce), although aspects are mentioned such as the roles played by bonds and guarantees. Nor does it analyse higher level issues of risk management. Instead the book focuses on the interplay between the solvency of contracting parties and the fortunes of the project. The basic question is whether the project makes financial sense. This is likely to involve detailed projections involving many different assumptions. For major projects, the sponsors prepare a financial model which is the key to the "bankability" of the project. Once the model has been agreed, it will form the basis on which lending is structured and be the source of the principles governing the allocation of risk among the various parties.

Pre-qualification is probably the key area for pre-contract financial protection. Pre-qualification comprises at least five elements: the contractor's identity, reputation, expertise, people, and finances. "Identity" refers to group structure, legal domicile, ownership, property and objects. Relevant questions are: is the group involved in capital intensive businesses? are there cross-guarantees? who owns the group's principal assets and where are they? The employer needs to be aware of the company's current workload and be assured that resources promised for the project are not diverted somewhere else. The employer will need to be satisfied on the firm's balance sheet and cash flow positions, current trends, profitability, strength of core areas to withstand downturns in demand, business plans, management accounts and projections, any recent (or planned) major changes with financial consequences, acquisitions, exceptionally large projects, off balance sheet liabilities. Lower down the chain, registration under the construction industry scheme (Ch.21) is some evidence that a subcontractor's tax liabilities are up to date: *Woods (Inspector of Taxes) v Lightpower Ltd* [2005] EWHC 1799, para.13.

After pre-qualification, the next area of pre-contractual protection is the tender process. This enables prospective bidders to be compared against each other to allow the employer to obtain the best value for money (not necessarily the lowest price). As additional protection against wasted costs, tenderers may be required to provide a bid bond (Ch.19). They may also be asked to agree the text of certain documents, e.g. parent company guarantees, before invitations to tender are sent out. The intention is to limit the scope for negotiation after the tender has been accepted. Other legal safeguards at this stage are the use of "subject to contract" on correspondence and draft documents and, where a letter of intent is issued, ensuring that it contains appropriate terms so that the client only becomes liable to pay for work it has asked for, at rates which are reasonable, and subject to a financial cap. Legal capacity and the authority of an agent to enter into a contract are also important. On the facts in *GPN Ltd v O2 (UK) Ltd* [2005] C.I.L.L. 2285 it was held that a quantity surveyor had power to negotiate the terms of a contract but not to bind the employer. After the contractor went into administrative receivership the receivers claimed damages for wrongful omission and/or suspension of work. As no contract had been formed, however, all they could claim was a *quantum meruit* for work that had been done.

3. Security assets in construction

What property is offered as security by contractors? A distinction can be made first between real and personal property. A contractor may own freehold or leasehold land. Personal property can be tangible and intangible. Among the former are: plant, machinery, equipment, tools, building materials, and motor vehicles. Among the latter are: the benefit of contracts (e.g. for building, joint venture, guarantee, hire-purchase or options), shares in group companies or special purpose vehicles, receivables of all kinds (e.g. certified sums, retention, claims), loans made to others, and intellectual property rights. Similarly, the employer offers as security for project finance the benefit of the construction contract and any direct agreements with subcontractors and suppliers, insurance policies, bonds and guarantees, copyright in design documents, etc. (Jones 1992). **2–004**

In the construction industry, debts are probably the most valuable as well as the most vulnerable assets taken as security (Ch.3). A debt is a personal obligation of the debtor as well as a form of property disposable by the creditor. English law has long been content to mix the personal and the proprietary in this way: see *Camdex International Ltd v Bank of Zambia* [1996] 3 All E.R. 431. The common law courts resisted equity's view of a debt as property but lost in the end. A debt is conceptualised as a "thing in action", identifiable by taking proceedings to recover it. The term "receivable" is North American and, though not a term of art, is a useful word to describe any actual or potential money claim, whether inchoate (such as work in progress), conditional (such as retention), or contingent (a claim for damages).

A creditor can make use of a debt or a receivable in several ways: as material for a set-off of a personal obligation he owes the debtor; as a means of payment by way of assignment to a creditor; or as the object of security. In addition, the debtor often has to secure his own obligation by charging other property in favour of the creditor, which may include debts owed to him by others, or, if the creditor is a bank, by the creditor himself: *Re BCCI (No. 8)* [1998] A.C. 214. The debt may be due from another party to the same project. For example, a contractor might make an assignment to the subcontractor of part of a certified sum (*Golden Sand v Easy Success Enterprises* [1999] 2 H.K.C. 356) or transfer to the employer a claim for damages against the subcontractor (compare *Total Liban SA v Vitol Energy SA* [1999] 2 Lloyd's Rep. 700).

A construction contract is obviously more complicated than a debt in that the parties owe obligations to each other, many of them being interdependent, and entrust certain functions to the architect or engineer who owes them both a duty to act impartially. Unless it provides otherwise, a construction contract can be assigned but it is questionable whether certain of the assigned rights remain exercisable only by the assignor, for example those involving the exercise of judgment on his part (Ch.4). Problems of this nature are one reason for the popularity among project lenders of direct agreements (Chs 16, 17). The availability of a debt as a security asset may be restricted by a clause barring the assignment of the contract and difficult questions can arise concerning the effect of a non-assignment provision on security taken over the contract (Ch.4).

4. Formal security

2–005 Under the contract, the employer has the right to performance or to compensation. On the contractor's liquidation, these rights are commuted to the right to a dividend, i.e. a fixed percentage of the employer's claim arrived at by dividing the amount of cash in hand after disposing of the contractor's property by the total amount owed to unsecured non-preferential creditors. The purpose of security is to give the employer a right, in priority to other creditors, to satisfy its claim out of a particular asset of the contractor. If there is a shortfall after having sold the asset, the employer proves for the difference as a dividend. Any surplus is paid to the liquidator for the benefit of other creditors. English law recognises four types of security: charge, mortgage, contractual lien and pledge: *Re Cosslett Contractors* [1998] Ch. 495, Goode 2003, 31–38.

Charge

2–006 A charge has been defined as a present right to have property "made available" for payment of a debt: *National Provincial & Union Bank of England v Charnley* [1924] 1 K.B. 431 at 449. It is "a security interest created without any transfer of title or possession to the beneficiary": *Re BCCI (No. 8)* [1998] A.C. 214 at 226, *per* Lord Hoffmann. The person offering the asset is known as the "chargor" and the person receiving it as the "chargee". The chargor remains the owner but the chargee obtains a security interest. The charge describes the obligation to be secured and identifies the asset (e.g. a specific contract) or class of asset (e.g. "all current contracts") offered as security. A charge may be fixed or floating. It is common for debentures to contain charges of both kinds, identifying the property falling within each.

In theory any kind of property can be made the subject of a fixed charge but as the chargor loses day-to-day control over it, fixed charges are usually granted over assets which are intended to form a permanent part of the business, e.g. interests in land, fixed plant and machinery. An exception is book debts, but a series of cases culminating in *National Westminster Bank Plc v Spectrum Plus* [2005] 2 A.C. 680 have affirmed that to be valid as a fixed charge the bank must both set up an account to receive payment of the debts and restrict the use of that account without its consent. In the event of a default, the chargee can appoint a receiver whose powers over the asset derive from the terms of the charge and from the Law of Property Act 1925. Where the security is taken over land, the charge normally confers wide powers to sell the site, build out or exercise other options. Fixed charge receivers can apply to the court for further powers if those in the charge are insufficient. Goode (2003, para.1–16) identifies five qualities of a fixed security:

- It is a right in an asset rather than against a person.
- The right is given by way of grant or declaration rather than by reservation of rights.
- The right is given to secure an obligation.
- The asset is provided as security not as an out and out transfer.
- The debtor's right to dispose of the asset free of the security is restricted.

"Under a fixed charge the assets charged as security are permanently appropriated to the payment of the sum charged, in such a way as to give the chargee a proprietary interest in the assets" (*National Westminster Bank Plc v Spectrum Plus*, at para.138 *per* Lord Walker).

By contrast, under a floating charge the chargor retains ownership and control and can use assets falling within the categories identified by the charge in the ordinary course of business: ". . . the asset subject to the charge is not finally appropriated to the security until the occurrence of some future event": *National Westminster Bank Plc v Spectrum Plus*, at para.111, *per* Lord Scott. The chargee has a present interest only in the class (or "fund") of assets whose composition changes over time, not in any specific asset. A floating charge is often given over stock in trade and cash at bank and other types of property which the contractor needs to recycle in its business. It could, however, be given over land or any type of property. The charge was formerly enforced by the appointment of an "administrative receiver" having wide powers of managing the company and its business but since the Enterprise Act 2002 the mode of enforcement in the vast majority of cases is the appointment of an administrator (Ch.13). Either event converts the charge from floating to fixed. This process is known as "crystallisation" (Lightman and Moss 2007).

A floating charge may be granted over a building contract, e.g. *MacJordan Construction Ltd v Brookmount Erostin Ltd* [1992] B.C.L.C. 350 at 360. A charge on debts is sometimes coupled with an express assignment: *Durham Bros v Robertson* [1898] 1 Q.B. 765 (equitable assignment by way of charge of receivables securing advance payments). If the charge is floating, the assignment is incomplete until the charge crystallises and notice of that event is given to the debtor: *George Barker (Transport) Ltd v Eynon* [1974] 1 W.L.R. 462 at 467. A judgment creditor can claim specific debts in priority to a debenture holder provided payment is made pursuant to a third party debt order (formerly a garnishee order absolute) before crystallisation. The case law was reviewed in *Wily v St George Partnership Banking Ltd* [1999] B.P.I.R. 1030.

Some jurisdictions provide for the grant of a statutory charge over receivables as security for payment, such as the Queensland Subcontractors' Charges Act 1974, amended in 2002, and the South Australian Workers' Liens Act 1893 (Merity 2002) discussed in the second edition of this book.

Mortgage

2–007 A mortgage involves the transfer of ownership (but not possession) to a mortgagee subject to an equity of redemption. The property is transferred back to the mortgagor on performance of the secured obligation: *Re Bond Worth* [1980] Ch. 228 at 250. In the case of a debt or the benefit of a contract, the transfer is by way of assignment: *Tancred v Delagoa Bay & East Africa Railway* (1889) L.R. 23 Q.B.D. 239 (assignment by way of legal mortgage of a debt); *L/M International Construction v The Circle* (1995) 49 Con. L.R. 12 (assignment by way of legal mortgage of a management contract); *Church v Sage* (1892) 67 L.T. 800 (assignment by way of mortgage of a building contract).

Contractual lien

2–008 Liens and pledges apply only to personal, tangible property. A lien consists in the right to retain an asset for a purpose other than that for which it was originally received (Halsbury, 4th edn, 28, paras 701–781). For example, property originally received for repair can be retained as security for the repairer's charges. Lien is unlike charge or mortgage in that it does not give the lien holder the right to sell the asset, only to detain it pending performance of the secured obligation (chapter 6). If the lien arises under a contract which allows the person in possession to sell it, it is really a pledge. Contractors sometimes claim a "lien on the site" as security for payment but this is conceptually impossible under English law: compare *HG & R Nominees v Caulson* [2000] VSC 126. In other jurisdictions with industry specific legislation, the lien takes effect as a charge on the land or the employer's interest in it (McGuinness 1983; Odams 1996), or over unfixed plant and materials: s.11(3) of the Building and Construction Industry Security of Payment Amendment Act 2002 (New South Wales).

Pledge

2–009 A pledge arises on the delivery of possession of an asset to a creditor by way of security (Halsbury, 4th edn, 36(1), paras 101–140). The creditor ("the pledgee") is entitled to sell the asset in the event of non-payment by the debtor. As with a charge, but unlike a mortgage, ownership remains with the person giving the security ("the pledgor"). In commercial law the pledge is widely used as a security over "documentary intangibles" such as cheques or bills of lading "but it is not possible to pledge ordinary written contracts such as building contracts or hire-purchase agreements, the production of which is not a condition of the obligor's duty of payment or other performance" (Goode 2003, para.1–44). A demand guarantee falls somewhere between these two types of document: it is not a document of title and yet it may be enforceable by simple demand. Such guarantees are regularly assigned although it is not yet clear exactly what rights pass to the assignee: see *HLC Engenharia v ABN Amro* [2005] EWHC 2074, discussed in Ch.19.

Registration

A charge or mortgage granted by a limited company falling within the categories listed in s.396 of the Companies Act 1985 must be registered with the registrar of companies within 21 days of its creation otherwise it will be void against a liquidator, administrator or creditor of the company under s.395. The categories most relevant to the industry are: a charge on land or any interest in land, a charge on book debts, a floating charge, or a charge created or evidenced by an instrument which, if executed by an individual, would require registration as a bill of sale. These sections have been re-enacted in Pt 25 of the Companies Act 2006 which is expected to come into force on October 1, 2008. No material changes have been made. **2–010**

The tendency of the industry to use the construction contract as the source of security makes it vulnerable to arguments that protective devices are invalid on an insolvency as unregistered charges. The court approaches the question whether an arrangement amounts to a charge in two stages: first by considering the language used and asking what rights and obligations the parties intended to create in the asset; second, as a matter of law, by asking whether those rights and obligations were consistent with a fixed or a floating security: *Agnew v Inland Revenue Commissioners* [2001] 2 A.C. 710 at 725. Industry cases include the following:

- A liquidator appointed over an employer argued unsuccessfully that a trust of the contract sum was by way of floating charge and not binding on him for want of registration: *Lovell Construction v Independent Estates* [1994] 1 B.C.L.C. 31 considered in Ch.9.
- An administrative receiver of an employer unsuccessfully argued that, before a retention trust account is set up, a contractor working under a JCT form has a floating charge over the undertaking of the employer securing payment or funding of retention: *MacJordan Construction v Brookmount Erostin* [1992] B.C.L.C. 350 at 360. See Ch.10.
- An administrator of a contractor successfully argued that a power of sale granted to the employer over the contractor's plant and equipment after termination as security for payment of post-termination losses was an unregistered floating charge granted by the contractor: *Smith v Bridgend CBC* [2002] B.L.R. 160. See Ch.6.
- A contractor successfully argued that a retention of title clause, relied on by a supplier in a claim for damages for conversion of its goods by the contractor following the administrative receivership of a sub-contractor, which reserved equitable and beneficial ownership was an unregistered floating charge: *Stroud Architectural Systems Ltd v John*

Laing Construction Ltd (1993) 35 Con. L.R. 135. However the contractor was not a creditor of the insolvent subcontractor within s.395 of the Companies Act 1985 and the charge (or the contractual term which evidenced it) was not invalid as against it. Although the supplier's equitable interest in the goods gave it *locus standi* to claim in conversion, it was not established on the evidence whether the charge had crystallised and become fixed on the specific goods concerned when the conversion took place.

- A subcontractor conceded to the liquidator of a sub-subcontractor that a charge over plant contained in a construction contract was void for non-registration as a bill of sale: *Young v Matthew Hall* [1988] 13 A.C.L.R. 399 (discussed in Ch.6, with other bill of sale cases).
- A liquidator of a contractor failed in a claim for the return of payments made in extinction of the company's overdraft against a bank holding a mortgage of book debts due or to become due under a particular contract. Although the mortgage was unregistered, the loan was fully repaid by the collection of book debts before the commencement of the liquidation: *Re Row Dal Constructions* [1966] V.R. 249. The contractor had not been insolvent when the mortgage was granted.
- A creditor failed in an argument that a pay when paid clause and other rights to withhold payment amounted to an unregistered floating charge or a charge over book debts in *Process Machinery v ACN057 260590* [2002] NSWSC 45. There was no assignment by way of security and a withholding was not equivalent to the grant of a proprietary interest.

5. Proprietary interests

2–011 A creditor may acquire an interest in the debtor's property other than by way of security. On what principles are such claims decided? The question becomes material in the event of the defendant's insolvency. For example, in the recent case of *Re Ballast Plc* [2006] EWHC 3189, a design and build contractor engaged a structural engineer to design aspects of the works. Defects appeared which cost £1 million to put right. The contractor was indemnified under its all risks policy but, after receiving payment from the insurer, went into administration and then liquidation. The insurer was entitled to pursue any cause of action which the contractor had against the engineer by subrogation (see Ch.15). But because it would be claiming in the contractor's name it would lose the right if the contractor were dissolved. For various reasons the liquidators wanted to conclude the winding up and disclaimed the cause of action as onerous property under s.178 of the Insolvency Act 1986. The insurer failed in its application to have the claim vested in it because to be entitled to a vesting order it had to establish a right in the property concerned. Under the law of subrogation, all the insurer had was a personal right to use the contractor's name to recover its loss. If the claim had been pursued to judgment however the insurer would have had a proprietary right to the proceeds but that had not happened here.

Whether a claim is personal or proprietary can be a question of considerable legal subtlety. In the industry, the issue is compounded by the fact that the claim is often embodied in or dependent on the terms of the construction contract rather than some other self-contained document. In this respect cases emerging from the industry sometimes act as engines of legal development. Areas to consider are: the use of the trust as a means of payment and the distinction between a trust and an escrow account in that regard (Chs 9 and 10); the concept of assignment as applied to debts and contracts (Ch.4), and the effect of vesting clauses, land law, and chains of contract on the ownership of plant and materials (Chs 6 and 7).

It may be useful to focus here on the trust. Just as retention is a security for performance, a retention trust is security for payment. Under the trust, the contractor obtains an immediate equitable interest in the trust fund and personal rights against the trustee. The unusual aspect as far as trust law is concerned is the fact that the employer is a self-interested trustee with power to raid the fund to satisfy its own legitimate rights of set-off, which obviously weakens the trust's security function. Retention trusts only provide security for a small percentage of the contract sum. The contractor is occasionally able to negotiate for the whole sum to be held on trust. Such arrangements are intended as the means of payment providing informal security against the employer's insolvency or default. These trusts require very careful drafting to ensure that the express terms of the trust deed match those of the contract or, where the trust is embedded in the contract, that the trustee's rights of recourse and their operation are clearly articulated. Several cases have turned on the contractor's inability to obtain the necessary documents to present to the trustees for payment out of the account. An escrow account is a form of security for payment falling short of a trust. The debtor paying in remains the owner of the benefit of the account but agrees to specific conditions for withdrawal in favour of the creditor. The account is blocked in the sense that only the creditor can call for payment out once the conditions are satisfied but the creditor has no proprietary interest in the account or any rights of tracing. Such arrangements are popular as they are thought to avoid problems over registration of security interests.

6. Common law protection

It is a rule of the common law that anything built on land becomes part of **2–012**
it (Ch.7). The rule will prevail over a retention of title clause of an unpaid supplier provided the landowner had no notice of the clause. The rule gives added support to security taken over land. For example, a bank with a fixed charge over the site as security for payment of a construction loan obtains maximum value under its charge by postponing the appointment of a receiver until practical completion. By so doing, the bank takes the benefit of the contractor's work and materials without having to fund the release of retention. It also obtains the value of uncertified work in progress and work represented by unpaid interim certificates without having to pay for it. Practical completion is often a condition triggering the obligation of tenants to complete their agreements for lease. The common law rule is thus an informal security enhancing a formal security.

Set-off is the primary construction security (Ch.5). A typical industry case is a claim for payment by the contractor which is met by a cross-claim for damages for defects or delay by the employer. The employer is secured for its damages to the extent of the certified sum. Abatement is a defence at common law to a claim for the value of work done and materials supplied. The defence is that the service provided is not to the value contracted for. It has been described as a common law version of equitable set-off. "If the remedy of equitable set-off is available, abatement is not needed. If the circumstances of the case do not warrant equitable set-off, then, in my view, they would not establish an abatement" (*Sim v Rotheram MBC* [1987] Ch. 216 at 259, *per* Scott J.). Abatement is thus a form of security for performance. It disables the builder from recovering more than the value of his work thereby avoiding an unsecured overpayment.

It sometimes comes as a surprise to learn that insolvency, even receivership or liquidation, is not necessarily a breach of contract (Ch.14). Express termination clauses were introduced to allow employers to terminate in the absence of a breach. At common law it is occasionally possible to regard insolvency as an anticipatory breach entitling the employer to terminate the contractor's performance without having to wait until the breach actually happens. Such a power is a back up to the termination clause and comes in useful if the contract is defective in failing to confer adequate post-termination rights.

7. Contractual security

2–013 A contract is not a *tabula rasa*; it is made against the background of the common law which applies unless excluded. Common law rights are frequently restated as terms of the contract, as a reflection in a mirror, but they can be cut down or excluded altogether. Construction contracts tend to qualify the common law rights of the contractor but expand those of the employer. The parties may exclude the common law in its entirety, limiting their rights and obligations to the terms of the contract. The contractor will resist such an attempt since there are some areas which still rely on the implication of a term, e.g. the duty to account for the proceeds of an on demand bond insofar as they exceed the beneficiary's loss: *Cargill v Bangladesh Sugar* [1996] 4 All E.R. 563. Ambiguities may remain in the contract drafting as the consequence of the parties' failure to come to terms. Modern projects can be so complex and involve so many variables that matters can arise which have not been foreseen and dealt with in the express terms. In addition, the need to get on with the work can lead to agreements for variations for example not being properly documented, or even remaining oral, with the inevitable difficulty in getting paid for them. This chapter now turns to the many ways in which construction contracts expand on remedies available at common law. They can be grouped under the following headings: payment, performance, termination.

Payment

Advance payment

2–014 Contractors often request payment in advance to buy materials. On the largest international projects it may be necessary because the cash flow demanded by the contract is beyond the contractor's own resources. The advance is a security for the contractor against the risk of the employer's insolvency or a termination at will at an early stage of the contract. Repayment of the advance is normally secured by a demand guarantee which reduces as the advance is earned by performance (Ch.19). It may sometimes be necessary to ascertain whether a payment was made as an advance (and was therefore repayable by deduction from certificates) or as a loan: *Capital Realty v Chip Thye Enterprises* [2000] 4 S.L.R. 548.

Set-off, abatement and deduction

There are gaps in the common law of set-off which can be filled by appropriate drafting. The major lacuna is where the employer's cross-claim is independent and unliquidated. GC Works/1 is an example of a contract which deals with this problem by allowing each party to set off against the other all cross-claims for damages whether arising under that contract or others between them (Ch.5). Abatement can be extended by agreement to cover contracts for professional services. The contract may confer specific rights of deduction although at times they may be interpreted simply as contractual set-offs. Common examples are liquidated damages and retention. **2–015**

Retention is a percentage of a certified sum withheld by the employer pending completion of the work (Ch.3). It is often considered a form of security for performance by establishing a claim against which the employer can set off a cross-claim for the cost of rectifying defective work: *Calvert v London Dock* (1838) 2 Keen 638. It may be that, on a true construction of the contract, the employer can set off any type of cross-claim against retention, which would then amount to an all-embracing performance security. As well as being defeasible by set-off, the right to payment of retention is conditional on the issue of certificates. As a security device, retention duplicates abatement and equitable set-off. Perhaps the practice of withholding retention ought to have been discontinued after 1841 when the other two devices reached maturity: *Mondel v Steel* (1841) 8 M. & W. 858 (abatement), *Rawson v Samuel* (1841) Cr. & Ph. 161 (equitable set-off), especially since equitable set-off as applied to construction contracts has such a wide scope.

Certification

One of the major protections of the project procurer is the certification process whereby an architect, engineer or project manager decides the level of interim payments (Ch.3). This is intended to ensure the contractor gets a fair payment on account, but the closeness of the certifier to the employer sometimes leads to under-certification. Even so, as the certifier has a duty to act independently of the project procurer, there is a perception among funders that a further buffer is necessary, e.g. the approval of a monitoring agent before a certificate can be issued. Unless the employer has hindered or prevented its issue, a certificate is usually a condition of payment to the contractor. Without a certificate, all the contractor has is a right to have the terms of the contract operated so as to convert work in progress into debt at some future time. This is a major security for performance in the employer. Unless the contractor corrects defective work or brings the works to completion, it will not be entitled to a certificate of payment for the work in question. The certifier has power, by issuing a certificate in a negative sum, to reverse the roles of debtor and creditor. **2–016**

Conditions precedent

2–017 These are useful control mechanisms. Conditions precedent to contract include the execution of bonds and guarantees, collateral warranties, step-in agreements, the provision of opinion letters from foreign lawyers and the execution of formal contract documents. The provision of a bond could alternatively be a condition subsequent: see *Covington Marine Corp v Xiamen Shipbuilding* [2005] EWHC 2912. Conditions precedent to payment include certificates, monitoring agents' approvals, compliance with accounts procedures and "pay to be paid" clauses. It will be a question of construction in each case whether the document is a condition of all payment or of one particular payment. In *Crema v Land Mark Property Developments* [2006] A.C.L.C. 889 the contractor would not agree to a fixed price contract which the funders wanted and a compromise was reached whereby payment above a cap was deferred until after practical completion and, crucially, after repayment of the project loan. In return the contractor was granted a third charge over the site (paras 22–23). The employer became insolvent before completion. A "pay to be paid" clause could make the right to payment contingent on proof of payment of subcontractors from the previous certificate or it might oblige the contractor to pay subcontractors in advance. Some main contracts go further and impose express duties on the contractor to act in a particular way with subcontractors, e.g. to pay them promptly, even making it a condition of the contract that they do so. This can be useful in the event of an insolvency termination where the termination clause has not been properly drafted (Ch.14). The court will not allow the employer to rely on a condition if it has, by its own actions, prevented the contractor from satisfying it: see *Koch Hightex v New Millennium Experience Company* [2000] C.I.L.L. 1595. In that case, the contractor later went into bankruptcy under German law after a bond for £400 million was called by a Saudi employer: *Chiemgauer v NMEC* [2004] B.P.I.R. 42, para.28).

"Pay when paid" clauses

2–018 A "pay when paid" clause in a subcontract is a security for the contractor against the risk of non-payment by the employer under the main contract (Ch.3). Put another way, it is a security for payment. The contractor is secured to the extent that the sum due from the employer represents sums payable to the subcontractors. Where the subcontract falls within the Housing Grants, Construction and Regeneration Act 1996, such clauses are only valid if the non-payment is due to the employer's insolvency, but this is the principal risk managed by a "pay when paid" clause in any event.

Suspension

2–019 A contractor's right to suspend for non-payment is a security against loss of cash flow and a potential security for payment.

Copyright

2–020 If a designer is unpaid, he may be able to use his copyright as a lever to obtain payment. Copyright is a weak security, however, because potential damages for infringement may be much less than the unpaid debt. The designer has to apply pressure on the creditor to settle by issuing proceedings but the court is reluctant to prevent the completion of a building by an injunction restraining the use of the designer's plans (Ch.12). On the other hand the appointment may allow the designer to suspend or revoke the client's licence for non-payment and also bar its assignment without consent. The effectiveness of such terms in this context has not yet been tested in English law.

Performance

Conclusive evidence clauses

Certain terms have a clear security function, e.g. conclusive evidence clauses. These are found in bank guarantees, factoring agreements, construction contracts, finance agreements, and joint venture agreements. In a bank guarantee given to the employer, they reinforce the security by preventing the contractor from challenging the validity of a call, both as regards liability and quantum. For example, the demand may have to be accompanied by a statement that the amount claimed is due and payable under the contract (Ch.19). On an insolvency termination, no specific sum will normally become due until after the final account of the completion contractor has been agreed. A conclusive evidence clause enables the employer to obtain cash on account in the meantime: *Balfour Beatty Civil Engineering v Technical & General Guarantee Co Ltd* (1999) 68 Con. L.R. 180. Such clauses have an effect similar to that of an expert's decision. Lord Denning M.R. once compared them to an interim certificate under a building contract (*Bache v Banque Vernes* [1973] 2 Lloyd's Rep. 437 at 440) before his campaign to treat certificates as immune from set-off and equivalent to cash was halted by the House of Lords: *Gilbert Ash v Modern Engineering* [1974] A.C. 689. Factors use them to prevent the contractor disputing the amount of the debts collected. Contractual set-off clauses sometimes allow the employer to withhold payment by an amount equivalent to a prospective cross-claim. The term is a security because it supports a set-off which would not otherwise be available, effected on the bona fide estimate of the employer's representative. A term that a final certificate is conclusive evidence in proceedings that work was executed to the architect's satisfaction is a security protecting the contractor from suit by the employer or contribution proceedings by the architect: *Oxford University Fixed Assets v Architects Design Partnership* (1999) 64 Con. L.R. 12. Step-in agreements often state that a notice by the funder's agent of an event under a finance or other superior agreement must be accepted as conclusive evidence by the contractor. The funder also attempts to hold the contractor to any estimates of loss submitted before the funder made its decision to step in. In a joint venture agreement, audited accounts are often deemed conclusive evidence as between the parties as to whether the project made a profit or a loss. **2–021**

Limitation clauses

Exclusion clauses also offer security. A clause excluding liability for consequential loss or limiting the contractor's liability to the value of the contract goes some way to meet the risk of an overwhelming contract claim, **2–022** a contributory factor to many construction insolvencies. Similarly, an "entire agreement" clause is security against certain cross-claims, for misrepresentation for example, and preserves the contractor's rights to payment from set-off in respect of them.

Non-assignability clauses

2–023 A non-assignability clause functions as a security for both employer and contractor because it prevents the division of the benefit and burden of the contract (Ch.4). If the employer assigns the right to performance it retains the duty to pay and other obligations. The contractor may be able to suspend for non-payment but there are risks attached. The problem may be under-certification or excessive abatement or set-off where the employer has served the appropriate notices. Allowing the employer to assign also reduces the contractor's rights of set-off. As a result, the contractor's risk increases. If the contractor assigns the right to payment, it will not be devoting the cash flow to its contract with the employer unless perhaps the assignment is part of a factoring arrangement.

Factoring

2–024 Factoring is a method of improving cash flow by assigning debts to a factor in return for earlier payment than would accrue under the contract (Ch.4). It is less common in construction than other industries in view of the non-assignment provisions in the standard forms and the high risk of set-off of unliquidated claims. The contractor has to pay a fee for this service. Under some arrangements, the factor shares some of the risk that the creditor will default in payment.

Indemnities and bonds

2–025 When a bank provides a demand guarantee to the employer at a contractor's request, it usually requires the contractor to provide an indemnity under which the contractor may have to place the bank in funds if the guarantee is called before the bank honours the call (Ch.19). Companies that issue surety bonds also require an indemnity against any sum for which they may be found liable as a result of a breach of the underlying contract. Such indemnities are commonly secured by a cash deposit, a director's personal guarantee or by a charge on land. The indemnities are security, over and above the fees paid at the outset and on renewal of the guarantees, against the risk that the bonds will be enforced.

A demand guarantee is an independent obligation. Some contracts provide that the proceeds of a call must be applied by the employer for the purposes of the contract but usually the contract just obliges the contractor to procure a guarantee in a prescribed form. The court has implied a duty to bring the proceeds into account at the final account stage. Although essential from the contractor's perspective, such a term is only a partial security since the contractor bears the risk of repayment until then and suffers loss of cash flow for which he may not be compensated. It may also have to take proceedings for recovery of the excess over the employer's actual loss.

Solvency requirements

A covenant to observe a solvency ratio is normally contained in bank security documents. With the increasing reliance on public-private financing, solvency warranties are becoming more common in construction contracts as well as parent company guarantees. They might take the form of a covenant to maintain the current net worth of the company as at the date of contract; a duty to satisfy the employer on request of the ability to finance the completion of the contract; or to provide cash flows and updates on other pre-qualification information on request. This ensures that the basic protection given by pre-qualification procedures is continued throughout the contract period. **2–026**

Termination

Express termination clauses

Most contracts allow the employer to terminate the contractor's right to continue work in the event of insolvency. A few make the termination automatic. As a result the contractor is prevented from completing the contract. Termination operates as a security because certain rights to payment only accrue on completion. The employer is able to end the contractor's right to further performance as it is not normally regarded as possessory or proprietary in character. Rumours of insolvency circulate before a receiver is appointed. The contractor's creditors take steps to minimise their own risks by repossessing goods not yet paid for and removing plant and equipment from site. There is a risk of damage if unpaid subcontractors attempt to detach goods previously fixed to the structure. Termination allows the employer to re-enter the site and protect the works. **2–027**

Suspension of payment

The effect of an insolvency termination clause is to empower the employer to build out in its own way and to maximise its claim for compensation against the insolvent contractor. In practice, this is achieved through the legitimised suspension of the contractor's rights to payment to allow the employer time to establish its cross-claim for loss caused by the termination. It is as if the employer is allowed to take as hostage any receivables owed to the contractor and any tangible property on site pending the building out. Suspension of payment is a security for the employer in that it allows it to create a fund against which its own cross-claim for termination losses can be satisfied by set-off: *Melville Dundas v George Wimpey* [2007] 1 W.L.R. 1136, para.13. The draconian nature of suspension of payment is sometimes not fully appreciated. An employer may have refused to pay previously certified sums. The employer's non-payment may have contributed to the contractor's insolvency. Such considerations are swept aside by the termination clause. **2–028**

As well as vertical agreements between parties to the contract chain, termination clauses are highly relevant in horizontal agreements between joint venturers. These follow a similar pattern, in that they exclude the insolvent venturer from further participation in the project and suspend any entitlement to payment of cost or profit share until the project has been completed.

Claims against third parties

2–029 Some of the risk associated with the contractor's insolvency may be shared with the certifier or the employer's advisers. For example, if the builder is overpaid through deliberate over-certification, the architect will be liable to compensate the employer for the excess if it cannot be reovered from the insolvent contractor: *Townsend v Stone Toms* (1984) 27 B.L.R. 26 at 46. Similarly, an architect who recommended an incompetent contractor as reliable but whose work proved to be defective and resulted in a claim in arbitration, was held liable for the costs of the arbitration left unpaid as a result of the contractor's insolvency. The incurring of the costs flowed from the architect's breach of duty and the intervention of insolvency was immaterial to his liability: *Pratt v George Hill* (1987) 38 B.L.R. 25. An architect can also be liable in negligence for failing to check the financial standing of a contractor during the tender process: *Partridge v Morris* [1995] C.I.L.L. 1095. Depending on the context, however, a third party may not be under an obligation to advise the employer on a bidder's solvency: *Football League v Edge Ellison* [2006] EWHC 1462, paras 266–268. Even if there is a duty to advise in relation to a tender, and security in the form of a parent company guarantee is apparently offered by the tenderer but never in fact provided, only nominal damages may be recoverable if the employer would have proceeded without security in any event (para.322) or the parent would have refused to provide it (paras 326–327).

Direct payment

2–030 Privity of contract remains important to the employer as protection against claims by subcontractors, but the employer sometimes needs to intervene in the relationship between contractor and subcontractor to avoid disruption to the work caused by non-payment (Ch.17). Contracts often allow the employer to make payment direct to subcontractors during the contract in cases where the contractor cannot prove payment from previously certified sums or after termination in order to secure the continued performance of the subcontractors and their agreement to work for the completion contractor. To avoid the risk of double payment, the power to make a direct payment is usually coupled with a right to set off the amount of the payment against sums otherwise due to the contractor. A direct payment clause converts a duty to pay the contractor into a power to pay subcontractors and a right to make the set-off. The power to pay direct is a security for performance; the associated right of set-off is a security for payment.

Covenants against removal of plant

2–031 On a termination, the employer wants to keep delays to a minimum. Sometimes, there are problems in sourcing the completion contract. This risk is addressed by covenants not to remove plant and materials from site without the consent of the employer's representative. Such terms reinforce the vesting clauses found in engineering contracts and the employer's powers of detention and use conferred in the termination clause (Ch.6). The employer is thereby secured against the unavailability of important plant and materials.

Contractual estoppel

In order to "feed" its security, the project funder is interested in the employer expeditiously converting its contractual rights into proprietary rights. This can result in contract terms which attempt to pass title to materials as early as possible (Ch.7). Estoppel is a defence preventing a person from denying something he has previously represented to another contract party to be true and on which the other has relied to his detriment. Estoppel can perform a security function where a proprietary right is at stake. DOM/1 contains a form of contractual estoppel in that the sub-contractor agrees not to deny that property in its materials has passed to the employer once the contractor has been paid for them. Similarly, a contractor may agree in a warranty not to rely on the fact of an assignment as a defence that the assignee has suffered no loss. Further, a contract party who countersigns a notice of assignment and returns it to the assignee may be estopped from relying on a non-assignability provision: *Orion Finance v Crown* [1994] 2 B.C.L.C. 607 at 633. **2–032**

8. Bonds and guarantees

There is a vast range of these documents (see Ch.19). They provide two distinct kinds of security: general and specific. In general they are security for performance, protecting against the risk of insolvency or loss of cash flow as well as the risk of assets being switched within a group of companies (e.g. a parent company guarantee). They also address specific risks associated with either payment (e.g. to repay advances) or performance (e.g. maintenance obligations). **2–033**

General purposes

1. Financial long-stop. A guarantee is a reliable source of compensation once liability and quantum have been established. The beneficiary wants certainty rather than speed and takes into account that costs may be involved in enforcing the guarantee. **2–034**
2. Cash flow. The aim here is to provide the beneficiary with both certainty of payment and cash on demand. Although the intention is that the employer will use the proceeds of the bond as cash flow for the project, it has complete discretion over the application of the money. A bond provided on one project might even be called in the event of a dispute on another (Alhajeri 2000, 424). The philosophy is "pay now, argue later". The Australian JCC-D (1994) form provides that payments to a completion contractor as well as direct payments to subcontractors can be recouped from the proceeds of any security provided by the contractor, including an on demand bond: *Ultra Refurbishing v John Goubran* (1997) 13 B.C.L. 330.

3. Group cover. If the contractor is part of a group, it may be difficult to ascertain its financial standing. Even if significant at the start of the contract, the contractor's assets may be switched to another group company later. Obtaining a parent company guarantee gives some comfort but the parent may have no assets except shares in its subsidiaries. Only a composite guarantee jointly and severally from all group companies overcomes group risk but this is usually only given to banks.
4. Allocation of risk. A project risk may be met by a single device such as insurance. If there is no overlapping of remedies, it is possible that a bond may be the only container for a particular risk. An example might be an advance payment bond, where the employer has not required a performance or retention bond.
5. Proof of solvency. It is sometimes said that if a contractor can afford to procure a bond, then it must be strong enough financially to perform the contract: see for example *Greenore Port v Technical & General* [2006] EWHC 3119, para.16.
6. Overcome privity of contract. This is usually the function of a collateral warranty or a direct agreement (e.g. between employer and subcontractor or contractor and funder). Bonds are also used for this purpose, for example, when a funder requires a subcontract bond to be assigned to the employer.
7. Project management. Some bonds allow the bondsman to carry out the works after default by the contractor. Such involvement is usually limited to putting forward a recommendation for the completion contractor. This may help employers who lack the experience or the resources to manage this process themselves such as housing associations or local authorities.
8. "Sword of Damocles". Where the employer and the contractor are in dispute, the employer may make oblique references to the bond or actually threaten to call it unless the contractor accepts the employer's terms. Usually a covert purpose, this has been accepted as the actual function of a performance bond by an Australian court: *Olex Focas v Skodaexport* (1997) 13 B.C.L. 318.
9. Object of security. On a project financing, there can be a tendency to require the creation of an obligation solely as a security asset. This may be a question of habit or the bank may wish to include a value for the obligation in its financial model. This is especially the case with on demand bonds.
10. Unique source of recovery. Contracts frequently exclude or place a limit on certain kinds of liability, e.g. *Shepherd Homes v Encia Remediation* [2007] EWHC 70. As on demand bonds take effect independently of the contract, some employers have used them in an attempt to deprive the contractor of such benefits.
11. "Belt and braces" approach. Project lenders sometimes adopt a "belt and braces" approach to financial protection. The idea behind this seems to be that the integrity of the project is paramount (McGaw 1994). This results in the indiscriminate use of all possible financial

protection measures, regardless of the adequacy of pre-contract procedures or the terms of the contract.

12. Increase the contractor's liability. A contractor who agrees to provide a parent company guarantee or a collateral warranty does so on the basis that it assumes no wider liability than exists under the construction contract. In practice, drafts put forward by intended beneficiaries extend the scope of the contractor's liability, e.g. fitness for purpose obligations in warranties.
13. Compensate for pre-contract errors. Risks are created by the employer failing to ascertain its needs and requirements, rushing the preparation of tender documents or inviting tenders based on incomplete designs. These risks filter through sooner or later to the contractor. The employer may unconsciously project risks of this kind on to a bond. Similarly a bond may be required as part of a variation of the contract. In *Spandeck Engineering v Defence Science & Technology Agency* [2006] SGHC 229 the contractor made pricing errors and tried to persuade the employer to reallocate the original tender breakdown by loading present items with value attached to future work. This would have exposed the employer to additional risk and a bond was requested as a condition of its agreement. On the contractor failing to provide the bond the contract was novated by consent.
14. Personal liability. Where the contractor is a small company, clients sometimes seek personal guarantees from the directors.

Specific purposes

1. Tender. A tender or bid bond is sometimes required as security for the employer's wasted costs should the successful tenderer fail to enter into the contract. **2–035**
2. Advance payment. An advance payment bond is required as security for the earning of advance payment by performance.
3. Performance. A performance bond is required as security for performance generally. Lenders use this term to mean an "on demand" primary obligation; the construction industry uses it to mean a "default" secondary obligation. Each document has to be separately construed to ascertain which of these it is. A performance bond may protect the employer against consequential losses, e.g. for the additional cost of purchasing gas to honour obligations under a gas supply agreement where the contractor was in delay constructing a gas processing plant: *Australian Gasfields v Kvaerner Process Systems* (2002) 18 B.C.L. 116. In Australia, "performance" has also been construed as including a contractor's contingent liability to repay sums awarded in an adjudication: *John Holland v Roads and Traffic Authority of New South Wales* [2007] NSWCA 140.
4. Retention. A retention bond is required as security for repayment of retention released early or never withheld.
5. Efficiency. This bond is used as security for certain obligations after completion, e.g. to satisfy performance and output tests or even

revenue stream: *Roehampton Developments v FAI General Insurance* [2000] WASC 235. It may extend further than this, going some way into the limitation period, in which case it performs a similar function to latent defects insurance.

6. Liquidated damages. A separate bond is sometimes required as additional security for payment of liquidated and ascertained damages.
7. Customs and freight. HM Revenue & Customs may agree to defer payment of VAT and duty if the importer provides a bond as security. Freight bonds are security for payment of duty where equipment originally intended for re-export after completion of a project (and therefore exempt from duty) is left in the country where the works were carried out.
8. Payment. Payment bonds deal with the situation where a contractor has failed to pay others. Advance and down payment bonds cover the risk that the contractor will not earn a prepayment. Stage or repayment bonds are used where the contractor is paid by reference to milestones or dates and cover the risk of overpayment, i.e. if the payment does not reflect the value of the work carried out at that time.
9. Maintenance. This bond secures the contractor's performance during the maintenance period, which might be 12 months after substantial completion. A retention bond is usually available for enforcement from the inception of the contract, whereas a maintenance bond comes into force at the start of the maintenance period. It may be required where the performance bond expires on substantial completion, or the contract concerns a specialist installation which demands a high level of attention after substantial completion, or the contract has an unusually long maintenance period.

Other purposes

2–036 As well as these traditional functions, bonds, guarantees and standby credits are frequently used to plug any risk, real or perceived, that the funder believes is not adequately managed elsewhere. Recent examples in the PFI context have included a bond to secure performance of work deferred until after completion and payment of additional damages over a cap in the contract should the contract sum increase beyond a certain amount. PFI is distorting relationships in the industry. In addition to the practice of assigning the benefit of these securities to the funder at financial close and of requiring direct agreements, the funder may demand bonds direct from subcontractors.

9. Third party agreements

Collateral warranties

2–037 By a collateral warranty a contractor promises a third party (the beneficiary) to carry out the works in accordance with the building contract, i.e. to perform its obligations owed to the employer. Undertaking the same obligation to more than one person opens up the risk of liability for the same damages twice. However as Lord Millett has stated:

> "Since performance of the primary obligation to do the work would have discharged the liability to both parties, so must performance of the secondary obligation to pay damages. Payment of damages to either must pro tanto discharge the liability to both. The problem, in my view, is not one of double recovery, but of ensuring that the damages are paid to the right party" (*Panatown v Alfred McAlpine Construction* [2000] 4 All E.R. 97 at 167, dissenting on other matters).

More recently, in *J Jarvis & Sons v Blue Circle* [2007] EWHC 1262 a contractor gave a collateral warranty to a purchaser and the employer gave a warranty in similar terms to the purchaser in an agreement for the sale of the development. On the purchaser intimating it would bring proceedings for defects, the employer began an arbitration against the contractor for an indemnity against the purchaser's claim. The contractor applied to the court to stay the arbitration on the ground that it could result in payment of damages twice for the same breach—to both employer and purchaser. It was alleged that the employer was a dormant company without assets. Jackson J. rejected the application in part because the employer had offered an undertaking to "pay over" to the purchaser any moneys awarded against the contractor in the arbitration. As a consequence the risk of double payment was so low that the arbitration could not be characterised as oppressive (para.44). A warranty exposes a contractor to liability in damages to purchasers, lenders and tenants of a development under construction. It stands in their eyes as a security for investment, loan or liability to repair. For the developer, a warranty is an essential part of the property offered for sale or letting and in that sense is a security for the whole transaction. If the employer is not the owner of the land, and the contractor provides a warranty to the landowner, the landowner has the prior right to sue for damages for defects or delay: *Panatown v Alfred McAlpine*.

A warranty is like a guarantee in that the contractor's obligation to the beneficiary is co-extensive with its obligations to the employer. It is different in that a surety can rely on all the defences of the principal unless they have been excluded. Under a warranty the contractor's defences are cut down: it could defend by arguing that an alleged defect complied with the specification but not by way of set-off for non-payment. Unlike the position of a guarantor, the contractor under a warranty undertakes a primary obligation. A warranty is inherently riskier than a guarantee. Similar points arise under the Contracts (Rights of Third Parties) Act 1999, which is increasingly used in lieu of collateral warranties.

Depending on its terms a warranty could consist of a unilateral obligation from contractor to beneficiary. On an assignment, in contrast to the position under an assignment of the building contract, there is unlikely to be any equity of the contractor binding the assignee. As a result the beneficiary or its assignee has a valuable security, namely the right to call for performance or payment of damages free of set-off. In this respect a warranty approximates to a debenture which provides for its assignment "free of equities". Collateral warranties often include a copyright licence in favour of the beneficiary in respect of any design elements, together with step-in rights (see below).

A net contribution clause in a warranty gives security to the contractor against the insolvency of others liable to the employer for the same damage. Otherwise the contractor might be liable for the whole loss with only an unsecured right to recover a proportion from others jointly and severally liable. In Australia legislation has been introduced replacing joint and several liability by proportionate liability. This raises the intriguing possibility of an employer with claims against the contractor and a subcontractor (through a warranty) in respect of the same damage being unable to recover its loss in full where the subcontractor is primarily responsible and becomes insolvent (Jones 2007, 87). In such a situation, the "security" constituted by the warranty may both deprive the employer of redress and provide the contractor with informal security against the subcontractor's insolvency!

Direct agreements

2–038 It has become common on PFI projects, or indeed any large contract, for contractors and significant subcontractors to be required to enter into direct agreements (sometimes called "step-in" agreements) with funders (Chs 16, 17). The main purpose of these contracts is to protect the integrity of the project and its anticipated revenues in the event of default in payment to the contractor or to subcontractors such as to give rise to rights of suspension or termination: e.g. *ACA v Sullivan* (2005) 21 B.C.L. 71. The creditor agrees to notify the funder before exercising such rights so as to give the funder the opportunity of substituting a new entity as project company or contractor as the case may be. The funder may agree to be responsible for the accrued debt and the costs arising during the period of "step-in". To that extent, a direct agreement provides security for payment. It is unusual, however, for the funder to commit itself in advance to novate the contract in the event of a default. See *W&J Leigh v CBI Nederland* (Ch.15) for an unusual mandatory novation in this context. The funder may also attempt to restrict its liability through a direct agreement, e.g. by placing a cap on the permissible value of any one variation or capping the aggregate amount of variations under the contract.

Powers of attorney

2–039 A power of attorney reinforces security in a number of contexts. It may be required from a contractor (1) to enable an employer to execute future collateral warranties in the contractor's name as units are sold; (2) to assign the benefit of subcontracts to a completion contractor after termination of the contractor's employment; or (3) to enable an assignee to enforce a demand guarantee by making a demand in the employer's name.

Insurance

2–040 There is an obvious role for insurance in answering a risk that none of the parties is able or willing to meet. In practice, though, it is widely used to support a personal liability of one of the parties, whether to assist the person liable or the beneficiary of the obligation. Areas worthy of specific mention are risks associated with environmental problems on site, latent defects, liquidated damages, loss of profits and bad debts.

10. Statutory security

It is worth noting some statutes that confer security, especially those **2–041** dealing with contract and insolvency law. If a contract is a "construction contract" within the Housing Grants, Construction and Regeneration Act 1996 it must contain certain provisions relating to adjudication and payment. If it fails to do so, the Scheme for Construction Contracts is incorporated by default (Chs 3, 5, and 12). The Scheme consists of terms protecting the creditor and is a form of security for payment. Some aspects of the security afforded to contractors and subcontractors are direct while others are more oblique. The requirement to serve a notice before making a "withholding" against a "sum due" under s.111 protects the contractor from a set-off against the receivable concerned: immunity from set-off is a security for payment. Also in the construction context, the Public Contracts Regulations 2006 provide an indirect form of security for a contractor's costs of tendering and loss of profit. Failure to observe the Regulations confers a civil cause of action on unsuccessful tenderers: *Harmon v House of Commons* (1999) 67 Con. L.R. 1 (on the 1991 Regulations). Other statutes of particular relevance are the Third Parties (Rights against Insurers) Act 1930 and the Contracts (Rights of Third Parties) Act 1999. In *Avraamides v Colwill* [2006] EWCA 1533 an employer had a claim for defects against a contractor (a limited company). The contractor's assets were purchased by the shareholders who undertook to the contractor to complete outstanding orders and "to pay in the normal course of time any liabilities properly incurred by the company" as at the transfer date. As the contractor was left with no assets, the employer claimed against the shareholders pursuant to the transfer agreement invoking the 1999 Act. It was held that these words were insufficient to identify the employer under s.1(3) of the Act so as to allow the employer to enforce the term. "Liabilities" could apply to the company's trade and expense creditors as well as its customers.

The Insolvency Act 1986 provides security for debtors and creditors. If a debtor in financial difficulty begins certain insolvency procedures, its creditors have to obtain permission from the court before bringing or continuing proceedings against it, which is normally refused (Ch.13). The 1986 Act protects creditors against wrongful disposals of the company's property and is thus a form of security for payment (Ch.20). One of the most significant securities afforded by the 1986 Act is the mandatory set-off of all claims where a party becomes bankrupt or enters liquidation. Without it, a liquidator could claim payment in full of sums due to the insolvent company while only paying a dividend on sums claimed against the company (Ch.18). "The effect is to allow the debt which the insolvent company owes to the creditor to be used as security for its debt to him. The creditor is exposed to insolvency risk only for the net balance": *Re BCCI (No. 8)* [1998] A.C. 214, 223, *per* Lord Hoffmann. As a result an application for summary judgment by a liquidator to enforce an adjudicator's decision will normally be refused where the other party asserts a substantial cross-claim. As well as enforcing a set-off, statute also enforces the transfer of property without payment to the original owner where the criteria in s.25 of the Sale of Goods Act 1979 are met (Ch.7). Finally, the regime for the registration of charges laid down by s.395 of the Companies Act 1985 protects creditors dealing with the company by allowing them to assume that, unless property is shown as subject to security by an entry on the register, it is available to meet their unsecured claims. If the charge is registrable but not registered it will not be binding on an administrator, liquidator or creditor of the company.

11. Procedural security

2–042 Technically, legal set-off is a procedural security but it is more convenient to discuss it with equitable set-off (Ch.5). The rules that apply to adjudication, arbitration (Runeland and Blanke 2007) and litigation can enable a creditor to achieve a high level of security in certain situations; it is worth drawing out their security function.

Security against insolvency

2–043 It is not possible to obtain security for a claim for damages in English law: *Lister v Stubbs* (1890) L.R. 45 Ch. D. 1. This is in contrast to the diligence on the dependence available in Scotland and pre-action arrestments common in civil law jurisdictions, although these procedures will not necessarily afford the creditor priority in the defendant's insolvency. Surprisingly perhaps, security for the claim is possible under some international arbitration rules (such as LCIA, WIPO and ICC) and is occasionally ordered: Case No. 1694, Netherlands Arbitration Institute, (1998) XXIII Yearbook Commercial Arbitration 97. Security for costs is a valuable interlocutory remedy in litigation. Under s.726 of the Companies Act 1985 (and CPR Part 25) the court has jurisdiction to order a claimant to provide security for a defendant's costs if there is reason to believe that the plaintiff will be unable to pay them if the defendant is successful. Security may be ordered for the costs of defending a counterclaim, e.g. *Newman v Wenden Properties* [2007] EWHC 336. In that case a counterclaim was brought by an employer which was a shell company with no assets. The development was owned separately by the directors and shareholders of the employer. Security for costs is also available in arbitrations under s.38 of the Arbitration Act 1996 as well as internationally (Gu 2005, especially at 190–191). The court's power to order a non-party to pay the costs is a procedural security. A payment into court is a security giving priority to the claimant in the event of the defendant's insolvency provided the claimant succeeds in its claim: *Sherratt v John Bromley* [1985] 1 Q.B. 1038.

An injunction is sometimes necessary to protect contractual, possessory, proprietary and security rights. In the industry, an injunction forcing the employer to set up a retention trust account under the JCT forms is the means whereby a contractual right to have retention funded is converted into an equitable proprietary right in a trust fund (Ch.10). Until this crucial event occurs, the contractor is an unsecured creditor and the rights of the holder of a floating charge will prevail on the appointment of an administrative receiver or administrator: *MacJordan Construction v Brookmount*

Erostin (1992) 56 B.L.R. 1. Injunctions are also granted where there are mutual allegations of repudiation to deal with disputes over the possession of the site or over entitlement to use plant, equipment and materials in the meantime (Chs 6 and 7). Arbitrators have power to grant injunctive relief under s.48 of the Arbitration Act 1996. Freezing orders are not intended to improve the claimant's position in an insolvency (*Iraqi Ministry of Defence v Arcepey Shipping* [1981] Q.B. 65 at 72), but they can have that effect (*Fourie v Le Roux* [2007] UKHL 1, para.2), e.g. if the assets are preserved for long enough to complete an execution before the start of a formal insolvency procedure. By s.44 of the 1996 Act the court has power to make orders in cases of urgency before an arbitration is on foot to preserve evidence or "assets", which in this context includes contractual rights: *Cetelem v Roust Holdings* [2005] 1 W.L.R. 3555. Finally, the court has an equitable jurisdiction to grant relief against forfeiture of proprietary or possessory rights although this is rarely exercised in construction cases (Ch.14).

Security for cash flow

The adjudication procedure is a procedural security for payment especially **2–044** since (1) adjudicators' decisions are enforced by summary judgment rather than under s.42 of the Arbitration Act 1996 as the Scheme for Construction Contracts envisaged (*Macob v Morrison Construction* [1999] B.L.R. 93); and (2) provided the adjudicator asks himself the right question his decision will be enforced even if it is wrong: *Bouygues v Dahl-Jensen* [2000] B.L.R. 522. If a creditor tries to enforce an adjudication decision against an individual by serving a statutory demand as a prelude to bankruptcy proceedings, and the debtor alleges a cross-claim exceeding the claim, the demand will be set aside even though the cross-claim would not have been a defence to an application for summary judgment: *Parke v Fenton Gretton Partnership* [2001] C.I.L.L. 1712, *Garrow v Society of Lloyd's* [1999] B.P.I.R. 885. There is no equivalent procedure for setting aside a statutory demand served on a company but the court might grant an injunction restraining the issue or advertisement of a winding up petition if satisfied that the company has an arguable set-off (*McDonald's Restaurants v Urbandivide* [1994] 1 B.C.L.C. 306) or, if it has to go to a hearing, dismiss the petition if satisfied that the company had a genuine and serious cross-claim which it had been unable to litigate (*Re Bayoil* [1999] 1 B.C.L.C. 62). If the contractor applies for adjudication on a claim for which there is no defence, the employer may begin a separate adjudication on a different issue in the hope that, if it obtains a favourable decision, the two decisions will be set off by the court when the contractor applies for summary judgment. This tactic failed in *Straume v Bradlor* [2000] B.C.C. 333 because the claim the employer wanted to bring duplicated its defence in the contractor's adjudication. Set-off of sums due under successive adjudications is now unlikely "absent special circumstances": see *Interserve v Cleveland Bridge* [2006] EWHC 741 discussed in para.5–042. To have any chance, it seems that sums ordered under both decisions would have to be due and payable by the hearing of the application for summary judgment. If all else fails, and the court makes an order for summary judgment, it may grant a stay of execution (Ch.12). Depending on the terms of the stay it may amount to a security having the same effect as a set-off. In *Bouygues v Dahl-Jensen* [2000] B.L.R. 522 a stay was granted since the contractor had submitted a proof of debt (for substantial, unliquidated cross-claims in respect of the cost to complete the subcontractor's work after a termination) which the liquidator had not yet considered. If the proof were rejected, the stay was to continue until any appeal against rejection of the proof in the Companies Court had been concluded. It is worth noting that the law report is misleading in that the stay was only granted after a contested application.

In ordinary litigation, the procedures for summary judgment under CPR Part 24 and interim payment under CPR Part 25 remain powerful securities for payment even where the claimant is a company in administration or voluntary liquidation. In *Crimpfil v Barclays Bank* [1995] C.L.C. 385 an interim payment of £1.8 million was ordered on account of the company's claims for damages against the bank for wrongfully terminating its facilities and thereby causing its entry into administration. In *Harmon v House of Commons (No. 2)* (2000) 72 Con. L.R. 21 an interim payment was ordered after it was found that the House of Commons had caused the company's voluntary liquidation by wrongfully failing to award it a contract. An arbitrator also has power to order an interim payment by way of provisional award but only if the parties expressly confer it under s.39 of the Arbitration Act 1996. The powers of dispute review boards are also of significance in this connection. The Panel set up under the Channel Tunnel contract made several important interim orders for payment.

The "fraud exception" is also a form of security. This is the policy of judging applications for injunctions restraining calls under demand guarantees by requiring the applicant to prove the call was fraudulent to the knowledge of the bank. It is so hard to prove fraud that this is effectively a procedural security in aid of the employer's rights under the guarantee (Ch.19). Finally, statutory demands for payment under s.123 of the Insolvency Act 1996 give strong support to an unsecured liquidated claim.

12. Security for payment

2–045 The measures discussed so far provide funders and employers with security for performance, i.e. to ensure the works are constructed to the required quality, time and cost. Contractors seek the same protection, so far as they can, from subcontractors and so on down the contract chain. Looking upwards, contractors seek security for cash flow and payment. There are comparatively few devices available for this purpose.

Pre-contract security

2–046 The contractor needs to ask whether the project makes commercial sense: see generally *Australian Securities and Investments Commission v Edwards* [2005] NSWSC 831 discussed in Ch.20. If it were the employer, would it enter into a transaction of this kind? If the project is speculative, is there a committed end user in terms of a tenant or purchaser? Will the employer make advance payments? Payment problems tend to occur towards the end of a project, which can be the first time the contractor realises the inadequacy of project financing (Mead 2007, 36–37). Perhaps it was always the employer's intention to fund the final stages itself but it has not been able to raise the money. There may be unexpected liability for VAT, extras or loss and expense which were not budgeted for. These risks can be managed to an extent by "pre-qualifying" the employer.

Joint ventures carry the risk that the venturers will fall out (e.g. *Grandine Developments v Le Soleil* [2004] VSC 420) or that a special purpose vehicle will not be financially guaranteed by the shareholders (compare *Ballast v Laurieston Properties* [2005] CSOH 16) or that one venturer will claim that a debt was contracted solely with its co-venturer who is now insolvent (*PJ Davidson v Hanson Quarry Products* [2005] EWHC 298, *JP Mac v Hanson Quarry Products* [2005] EWHC 297). A key question to ask is the extent to which the project will be financed by the employer: compare *Blue Station v Kamyab* (unreported, February 6, 2007, David Donaldson Q.C.). How does it propose to do it? Are there realistic contingency funds? What are the external sources of funding? The Bristol Harbourside Centre, for example, went into a company voluntary arrangement when the Arts Council decided not to fund the project even though it was well into the design stage leaving over a hundred creditors claiming payment (Cavill 1999). The involvement of grant making bodies can cause complications: e.g. *City Link Development Co v Lanarkshire Housing Association* [2005] S.C.L.R. 862. In *Harlow & Milner v Teasdale (No. 3)* [2006] EWHC 1708 the contractor had to suspend its employment for non-payment. There was too great a shortfall between grant money available and the contract sum for the employer to finance the completion of the works; eventually the court made a charging order in favour of the builder and ordered that the property be sold. In an ideal world, the contractor needs access to the financial model, the development appraisal or the finance agreement. The relationship between the finance agreement and the construction contract can become highly material later on, e.g. *Re Jartay Developments* (1983) 22 B.L.R. 134.

Contractual terms

The contractor is given some financial protection by the contract terms, **2–047**
especially the right to suspend or terminate for non-payment. It is comparatively common for limitations to be placed on the nature and amount of the damages recoverable by the employer. Subcontracts enhance the contractor's rights under the common law by allowing specific rights of deduction, e.g. trade and cash discounts. Contingent payment clauses protect the contractor against subcontractor's claims to the extent that they are mirrored in its own claims against the employer. Such "pay when paid" clauses afford a kind of security to the contractor against insolvent employers by passing risk on to subcontractors. The security could be described as the right to treat non-payment to the contractor as payment by it.

Credit insurance

It is possible to insure against non-payment (Wright 1997) but credit **2–048**
insurance is little used because of exceptions to the cover, such as retention, and because premiums are assessed on the contractor's turnover rather than the value of the vulnerable contract in question (Hughes et al 1998,

52). Even if it is available, the policy wording may not reflect industry practice and be unenforceable against the insurer. In *Trade Indemnity v Parkinson* (1995) B.C.L. 39, a subcontractor took out credit insurance. One of the terms of the policy was that subcontracts had to provide a maximum of 45 days for payment after the delivery of goods or provision of services. The insurer was not liable in respect of a bad debt arising through a contractor's insolvency where the subcontract included an entitlement to payment within 14 days after the contractor had been paid subject to actual receipt by the contractor, i.e. a "pay when paid" clause.

Bonds, guarantees etc

2–049 Similarly, bonds in support of payment of the contract sum are rarely used, whether from employers or contractors. There are few precedents in the standard forms. An exception is the payment guarantee to be given by the employer annexed to FIDIC (1999). A third party guarantee is sometimes forthcoming as an inducement to the contractor to return to site after a suspension or termination for the employer's insolvency: *Try Build v Blue Star Garages* (1998) 66 Con. L.R. 90. Interestingly, defaults in payment by employers in China have led to the introduction of payment security bonds of 10 per cent of the contract sum, which have to be filed with the relevant authority as a condition for the grant of a development permit (Chan 2006). In a case in Hong Kong a personal guarantee of a payment schedule given to a subcontractor by a shareholder of the contractor (a joint venture company) was supported by six post-dated cheques signed by the shareholder "for security purposes": *Sun Wah Aluminium Windows v Panyu Fantasy Film City* [2003] HKCFI 774. In *Re Sanpete Builders* [1989] 1 M.L.J. 393 a subcontractor agreed to defer payment for 12 months after the date of payment of each certificate on the contractor's agreement to pay interest and provide promissory notes. Where the employer takes out latent defects insurance under which the insurer waives its rights of subrogation, contractors and those working lower down the contract chain can be protected from future claims. Parent company guarantees are useful but depend on the parent holding the assets of the group. Likewise letters of comfort are useful but are not normally legally binding. Perhaps the weakest security is a personal covenant that the debtor will have access to funds to meet its commitments.

Formal security

2–050 Formal security for payment is rare. It might be obtained for example on a project for a wealthy individual who is based overseas. It tends to arise on unusual projects or in situations where the contractor has the upper hand, e.g. threatening to issue a winding up petition. The employer may offer security as quid pro quo for the contractor's forbearance, e.g. a charge over the site, even if only a second or third charge. A charge on the site has occasionally featured in a standard form, e.g. DECON 1 (1988) issued by the Master Builders Association of New South Wales (Merity 2002, 172). In practice, apart from letters of credit or bank guarantees, the legal device most commonly used to protect payment is the trust. Trusts are used to protect the whole contract sum (Ch.9) or, in the case of JCT forms, retention (Ch.10). In both cases, the trust is usually integrated with the terms of the contract. Although a trust may be set up by way of security, in the industry it is more commonly used as the means of payment.

International comparisons

According to the Cole Report (2003), security for payment practices in the Australian construction industry remain "barbaric and definitely unfair" (vol.8, Ch.14 at 227). The report is probably the most thorough study of a construction industry worldwide. It summarises remedies available in the separate states and annexes a draft federal statute intended to apply across the country. It incorporates various elements of state legislation, including a ban on pay when certified (s.12), a right to apply for payment from the employer once a subcontractor obtains an adjudication decision and permission to enforce it as a judgment (s.43), a trust over retention, cash deposits and bank guarantees when the other contract party "becomes insolvent" (s.57), a trust over goods and materials on site but not paid for in the same event (s.58). These trusts are statutory "deemed trusts" intended to give priority to construction industry creditors in a liquidation. The report might have gone further and extended the trust concept to progress payments but for entrenched opposition in the industry (para.108). Other security devices available in jurisdictions such as Ireland, Scotland, the United States and Canada were considered in the second edition of this book. **2–051**

13. Evaluation of security devices

In 1998, the Reading Construction Forum carried out extensive research on the use of financial protection devices in the industry (Hughes et al 1998). Fig.2.1 indicates the frequency with which some of the devices are used and the percentage by which the contract sum increases annually to pay for them. **2–052**

Protection device	*Frequency (% of contracts on which the device is used)*	*Cost (% annual addition to the contract sum)*
Retention	77 (91 on contracts over £10m)	0.30
Retention bond (default-based	4	0.03
Performance bond (default-based)	45	0.10
Performance bond (demand)	10	0.33
Parent company guarantee	43	Nil
Collateral warranty	55	Uncertain
P.I. Insurance	62	0.40

Source: Hughes et al (1998)

Fig.2.1

The table assumes retention of three per cent which could have earned interest at 10 per cent, half being withheld over a contract period of two years. The performance bonds were assumed to be for 10 per cent of the contract sum. The research found that if all of the devices were used, they could cost an average of 0.34 per cent of the contract sum per annum. The report concluded:

> "In general, the money cost of these various measures is marginal and it is important for industry policy makers to focus more on the costs of loss of liquidity caused by payment problems, whether legitimate or spurious. This is an aspect of protection for payment obligations. Perhaps the industry should be less defensive about performance protection and more proactive about security for payment" (at 59).

Security for payment was given by the employer in only six per cent of the contracts analysed. The selection of protection device appeared to be governed more by a desire to wield bargaining power than an informed assessment of risk. It is tempting to regard the use of contractual security measures as a compensation for inadequate procurement procedures rather than filling a genuine gap in the matrix of risk. Perhaps the starting position ought to be to take adequate pre-contract measures, to draft a fair contract sticking to the common law position as far as possible and to seek the minimum by way of additional security. Apart from tender and maintenance bonds, all other bonds and guarantees in common use are concurrent rather than consecutive (Fig.2.2). In Fig.2.2, the vertical axis sets out the type of document; the horizontal axis the stages of the works.

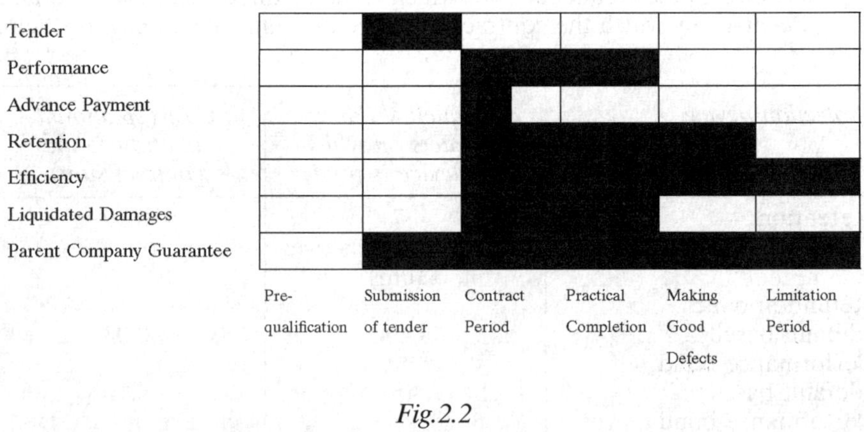

Fig.2.2

It can be seen that the tender bond expires on the entry into the contract by the successful tenderer and the provision of a performance bond. On a major project, where retention is not being withheld, it would not be unusual for there to be concurrent bonds covering performance, retention and advance payment. Although contractors regard retention, and by extension retention bonds, as security for rectification of defects, the employer is often entitled to set off any cross-claim against retention. It follows that, despite its name, retention is really additional performance security. Similarly, although an advance payment bond is security for the advance payment, it also stands as performance security.

It is for the contractor to negotiate specific provisions in the contract and in the bonds that restrict the employer's use of these devices to specific purposes which do not overlap. For example, each bond could say that a claim under one automatically reduces the bonded amounts under the others but this rarely happens in practice. Unless the boundaries between these devices are respected, the position can easily get out of hand. If the contract provides for a 10 per cent performance bond, five per cent cash retention and an advance payment bond for 15 per cent of the contract price, then 30 per cent of the contract sum will be subject to security. It is critical to include appropriate accrual and reduction provisions in bonds dealing with retention and advance payment (Ch.19). It should be noted that, assuming the contractor is paid monthly in arrears and the contract period is, say, two years, the employer has further security in terms of the contractor's uncertified work in progress. This was estimated at four per cent of the contract sum by the Reading survey. If the contractor has undertaken design obligations, the employer should also take the contractor's professional indemnity policy into account.

A performance bond should only be required for good reason. In *Oxus Gold Plc v Templeton Insurance Ltd* [2006] EWHC 864, an employer had difficulty raising finance to build and operate a gold mine in Uzbekistan. To bridge the shortfall between primary finance and the capital required, it attempted to obtain a performance guarantee of the contractor's obligations to stand as security for secondary finance (subordinated debt). It was unsuccessful, although the project was apparently completed under new management (para.200). The guarantee was to be for £12.5 million and support defined levels of cash flow anticipated from the sale of the gold. The case shows the difficulties that can arise where what is essentially a construction document is offered as security for default under a finance agreement. A certain vagueness seems to have affected the negotiations, the parties having different ideas about the nature of the obligation they were seeking: a financial guarantee of payment or a guarantee of performance whether on demand or on proof of default. In the end the proposed surety, Hermes, refused to issue the document given the split between its intended use (to repay the project loan) and actual obligation (secondary guarantee of contractor's performance) (paras 295–296). At para.314, Cooke J. described what happened as an attempt to obtain a performance guarantee "masquerading" as a financial guarantee.

If a bond is thought necessary, financial long-stop and cash flow would be appropriate uses, although a bond protecting cash flow ought to be used only in exceptional circumstances, perhaps where the project is of unusual complexity or very high risk. The transferability of assets within groups makes it reasonable in principle to seek parent company guarantees. If the bond answers a project risk not covered by anything else, then again it would be an appropriate function. Using a bond as evidence of solvency is a mistake, based on a misunderstanding of the way bonds are issued. This is an issue for the pre-qualification and tender stages. Many of the general functions identified above are abuses, as may in context be some of the specific purposes. Perhaps an employer who uses bonds for abusive purposes thinks it is getting an advantage, but its relationship with the contractor will be soured and this cannot be in the interests of the project.

2–051 Given that almost all risks are managed by the contract itself, it would appear that the real reason for requiring all this security is the risk of the contractor's insolvency. Can this be justified? One of the clients interviewed for the Reading report thought it could make money out of a contractor's insolvency. Uncertified work in progress and non-payment could give a six-week buffer. The client may be legally entitled to set off a cross-claim for management time expended in dealing with the problems caused by the insolvency. The focus groups suggested that many clients do so. Last, contractors keen to impress new clients may take on a completion contract at cheaper rates (at 18).

The following questions are worth considering when weighting the protective devices available to employers:

- What percentage of the total project risk can the device bear?
- Does the device consist of cash or is it equivalent to cash?
- How much does it cost to put the device in place? Is the cost passed on to the project procurer?
- Does the device wholly or partly overlap with another device? Is the overlap one of time or obligation?
- Is there security over security, e.g. a charge over a performance bond or a parent company guarantee of a collateral warranty?
- Does the overlap confer any additional benefit on the employer which answers a project risk not otherwise allocated?
- How frequently is the device enforced in practice by the industry (isolating those which are never, or rarely, called upon in practice)?
- Is the function of the protection device recognised as part of the project risk management or is it covert or unofficial, perhaps conferring a benefit over and above that contracted for by the contractor?
- Is the function of the device general and/or specific? If both, can its scope be reduced without disadvantaging the employer?

Many contractual rights function as security. A charge or a mortgage over the benefit of contracts amounts to security over security. There could be a threefold security, for example where a contractor provides a parent company guarantee of a collateral warranty and both are secured by a charge on other property. In the PFI context, there can be even more layers. The question remains whether the risk of the contractor's insolvency is so great as to make all this protection necessary. It is hard to identify the consequences of "over-management" of risk. It is not just a question of increasing the cost of construction. The boundaries between the available devices are not being respected. This blurring is mirrored in the relationships between employers, contractors and subcontractors. An inevitable consequence is conflict and mistrust. The lack of discrimination in the approach to financial protection by employers, perhaps at the insistence of funders, is a contributory factor to the lack of trust in the industry (Latham 1993).

The power imbalance between employers and contractors means that attention is usually focused on financial protection of the paying party rather than security for payment for contractors and subcontractors. Sir Michael Latham tried to redress the balance by recommending that employers set up trust accounts and make a payment monthly in advance into the account as security for the contractor, to "prime the pump" as he put it (Latham 1994). His proposal was universally condemned by clients. Maybe the idea will come back onto the political agenda one day. In the meantime, perhaps there should be a shift away from the emphasis on security and unbalanced contract terms to greater sophistication in pre-contract measures. There is a case for developing financial models that accurately assess insolvency as one of many project risks, allocate the risks among all the project participants, match appropriate protection devices against relevant risks and take proper account of overlaps of time and obligation.

Chapter 3

Debts and Other Receivables

3–001 In the manufacturing industry, an order is completed on delivery of the goods and payment becomes due on receipt of the supplier's invoice. In construction, concepts like completion and entitlement to payment are much more complex. Completion is progressive and has to be defined: phased, practical, making good defects, final. The right to payment depends on a certificate of the employer's representative or on other conditions being met. Interim payments are provisional until final completion and subject to retrospective abatement. Construction contracts are shot through with conditionality. The fact that construction work is carried out using chains of contracts gives rise to the idea that payment is linear. In the industry people speak about payment as if it were a thing, but in law a right to payment is an intangible, enforceable only by bringing proceedings. There is nothing for the contractor to "pass on" (see Ch.17).

1. Qualities of payment

3–002 Payment has temporal, relational and structural qualities. These qualities are apparent from the words used. The language of payment is time. The industry talks of payment as slow, delayed, in arrears or deferred on the one hand and advanced, accelerated or prompt on the other. In relational terms, payment is defined by the identities of payer and payee (not necessarily debtor and creditor). In a simple situation, A agrees to pay B £x. In construction, since the vast majority of work is subcontracted, A agrees to pay B £x of which £y is to be paid to C, £z to D and so on. The industry therefore speaks of payment being made "direct" by A to C or D. Payment is also indirect (by set-off), retained and withheld by A or B. Payment's temporal and relational features are very important, but in construction insolvency its structural qualities are more important still. The industry speaks of "payment structures" when distinguishing between, say, payment by value over time (interim certificates) and payment of a percentage of the contract sum by work stage (milestones). The "structure" of a payment is also apt to describe inherent limitations in the chose in action. For example, retention is a conditional debt defeasible by set-off. The failure to bring the works to completion means the condition will never be satisfied, providing the employer with a complete defence to proceedings. The debt is also defeasible if the employer has a right of recourse under the contract.

A construction contract is very unusual in that the consideration is continually being negotiated. A agrees to pay B £x to be valued by C and certified by D, where C is the employer's quantity surveyor and D is the architect. Inherent in any construction receivable is the exercise of judgment by A (in respect of abatement, deduction and set-off), C (in exercise of its duties of valuation) and D (in exercise of its duties of checking C's valuation and certification). A further structural consideration is whether the payment is secured, guaranteed, or contingent (in the sense of a pay when paid clause). The consequences of non-payment are not as immediate as those of ceasing work. Non-payment of one or two certified sums is unlikely to be a repudiation whereas ceasing work could well be an abandonment of the contract. For all these reasons construction receivables are regarded as "flawed" and "vulnerable" compared with those of other industries. This chapter examines various of the structural qualities of payment. Set-off is dealt with in Chs 5 and 18 while direct payment is considered in Ch.17.

2. Construction receivables

Definition

3–003 It is hard to say exactly what a receivable is. Its elusiveness reflects the mercurial nature of money. At its broadest, a receivable embraces any actual or potential right to payment. It can include a present debt which may never confer the right to sue the creditor to judgment and an inchoate entitlement which may never become a debt. It is not much easier to tell when a receivable is a debt because, instead of enunciating clear principles in this area, the court has tended to resolve the issue before it by applying a subtly different definition of a debt. A debt is like a chameleon adapting itself to its environment. For example, set-off, assignability, statutory demands, winding up petitions, attachment of debts, retention, and charges over book debts adopt slightly different criteria. "Indebtedness" is not a term of art; it can include payment obligations which are present, future, contingent, conditional, defeasible, maturing, accruing due, due, and payable: *Banner Lane Realisations v Berisford Plc* [1997] 1 B.C.L.C. 380. For the purposes of obtaining a judgment against a debtor, the receivable must be payable. Hence the standard definition of a debt as a liquidated sum of money which is due and payable and enforceable by action: *Ogdens v Weinberg* (1896) 95 L.T. 567. However, this does not mean that a receivable falling in the other categories listed above would not be regarded as a debt for other purposes.

This section attempts to set out some general principles and then to apply them to receivables arising under a construction contract. It is worth noting that any definition of a debt will not apply in all situations since the parties to a contract can choose whatever criteria they like for when and how a debt will arise. The accrual of a right to payment, and its correlative duty to pay, may entitle the creditor to issue proceedings but not to obtain judgment. Judgment can only be obtained where all the contractual conditions for recovery of the debt have been satisfied. The most common is the expiry of a grace period. The court has often treated "due" and "payable" as synonymous: *Re Fastnedge, ex parte Kemp* (1874) L.R. 9 Ch. App. 383 (bankruptcy); *Re Elgar Heights* (1985) 9 A.C.L.R. 846 (company insolvency). But an assignment of sums "due" can include sums "owing" rather than those immediately "payable": see e.g. *Southern Cross Interiors v Deputy Commissioner of Taxation* [2001] NSWSC 621, at para.27. In that case (a preference claim) it was argued that, as creditors had not pressed for payment after the grace period of 30 days had expired, their debts were due but not payable and therefore non-payment could not satisfy the test of insolvency under the Australian Corporations Act 2001 (which required failure to pay debts that were due and payable). The argument was rejected: in the absence of express or implied agreement to extend the time for payment, a course of dealing giving rise to an estoppel, or well-established industry practice, a debt is due and payable at the time prescribed by the contract (para.54). Where a contract allows time for payment, it is common to refer to a debt becoming "due" at the beginning of the period and "payable" at the end. If there is no grace period, a debt will become due and payable at the same time. Although it sounds paradoxical, it depends on the construction of the contract whether a receivable can become a debt before it becomes due for payment. For example, under a sale of goods payable by instalments, the contract may be construed as creating a debt for the whole price on delivery of the goods which accrues due as each instalment date is reached. It is uncertain exactly how far this concept of a debt "accruing due" goes. Some would extend it to situations where a seller has provided the consideration but a condition of a purely administrative nature has not been satisfied or even where the condition is structural so that the debt itself is conditional.

The position under a construction contract is complicated because the contractor's right to payment is usually dependent on the issue of a certificate by a third party. However, it is possible for a receivable to become a debt due for immediate payment without a certificate. This can arise where the contract provides for payment monthly in advance on receipt of the contractor's invoice. Alternatively, the contract may provide for stage payments, e.g. on the achievement of second stage brickwork or the building being watertight. In *Avonwood Homes v Jaffer* [2003] VCAT 443, a builder went into liquidation before reaching fixing stage and the liquidator could not recover payment for that stage. Specific sums may be payable on agreed dates under a cash flow schedule regardless of the amount of work actually done: *Henry Boot v Alstom* [2005] B.L.R. 437, para.60. In either case, the debt will become payable as each stage or date is reached.

The Housing Grants, Construction and Regeneration Act 1996 now **3–004**
provides that every contract falling within its ambit must have an adequate mechanism for ascertaining when a sum becomes due and the "final date for payment", which simply seems to mean the date it becomes payable. The Act does not define a debt for the purposes of a construction contract and appears to say nothing about the structural issues which can arise. In *Community Development v Engwirda Construction* (1969) 120 C.L.R. 455 at 459, it was said that, on entering into a lump sum contract for building work, the employer becomes liable to pay the lump sum as a debt. However, the debt is conditional on the contractor providing the consideration: *Attorney General v McMillan & Lockwood* [1991] N.Z.L.R. 53. The debt will not become enforceable until all contract terms for payment have been satisfied. It is not clear, however, whether, after having provided the consideration by doing the work, but before the work has been certified for payment, the contractor has a debt accruing due or simply an inchoate right to have the contract terms of certification operated.

The question was recently considered in relation to ICE (6th edn) in *Henry Boot v Alstom* [2005] B.L.R. 437. It was treated purely as a question of construction of the contract. Both parties raised disputes in connection with the final certificate which were referred to a judge arbitrator. The employer successfully argued that the contractor's claims were statute barred because the relevant causes of action had arisen when the work was done, i.e. more than six years before the arbitration commenced, and was not dependent on the issue of certificates. The Court of Appeal allowed the contractor's appeal holding that: (1) the right to payment arises when a certificate is not paid or not issued when it should have been, and (2) the contractor had a continuing right to have the sum certified in later certificates, including the final certificate. It is interesting to note that Dyson L.J. did not employ the language of debtor and creditor but spoke of the right to payment. He focused on the certificate as condition precedent to payment rather than to debt; perhaps he saw no distinction; in the context of a limitation argument it is natural to concentrate on the moment when a debt becomes enforceable by court proceedings. The decision has been criticised (MacLaughlin 2006). The idea that the contractor's right to payment accrues brick by brick or day by day is the mirror image of the actual position in law from the employer's point of view. Assuming the employer owns the land, it acquires the value of the builder's work and materials immediately they are added to the land (Ch.7). However, as the employer might say, the builder agreed to build a house not just to lay bricks, and even the right to interim payment is a concession. The contractor's submission seems to be based on equity or the sense of justice; if the employer repudiates the contract there is no doubt that the contractor is entitled to damages representing the value of work in progress at that moment irrespective of certification. Such a claim could also be relied on as an equitable set-off before damages are assessed by the court. The persistence of the accrual theory may derive from a primitive, almost magical relationship to the land as both giver of the materials and receiver of the building made from them. The passing of money may be an acknowledgment of the builder's role in this mystery.

The court has also considered the issue in the context of arrestment in Scottish law and in the attachment of debts. A third party debt order may be obtained in respect of debts "due or accruing due" to the contractor under RSC Order 49. Under English law, the creditor can only attach a certified sum although it is immaterial whether the sum is payable at the date of attachment: *Dunlop & Ranken v Hendall Steel* [1957] 3 All E.R. 344. It appears that retention cannot be attached until certified for release: *Grant Plant Hire v Trickey* (1961) 105 S.J. 255, *Drew v Josolyne* (1887) L.R. 18 Q.B.D. 590, *Earle v Hemsworth Rural DC* (1928) 140 L.T. 69. This view limits "accruing due" to the situation where the debt is in existence and will become payable by effluxion of time. Such a construction is apt for the attachment procedure, otherwise the court could become involved in questions of interpretation of the standard forms which are unsuited for consideration at the enforcement stage, but is inconsistent with the law's general approach to debts: *O'Driscoll v Manchester Insurance Committee* [1915] 3 K.B. 499, *Tapp v Jones* (1875) L.R. 10 Q.B. 591, Prentice (1983). It appears to confuse the distinction between a condition precedent to a debt coming into existence and its recoverability by action. Compare this approach with the Canadian case of *Sandy v Yukon Construction* (1961) 33 W.W.R. 490 in which a judgment creditor of a subcontractor obtained a garnishee order against the contractor. The subcontract provided that amounts should not become payable to the subcontractor until 14 days after the contractor received the appropriate architect's certificate and payment from the employer. No sums were payable when the order was served but money was later paid into court. It was held that the order attached money accruing due to the subcontractor even though it did not become payable until a later date. It was unnecessary for the contractor's debt to be enforceable by the subcontractor at the date of the garnishee order. This case can be compared with *Lim Boon Kwee v Impexital* [1998] 2 S.L.R. 953, in which a garnishee order obtained against a contractor by a sub-subcontractor did not attach to the first half of retention even though it had been certified and paid to the contractor because the contractor had a valid right of set-off against it. The second half of retention was not due as it had not been certified at the date of the order but, in any event, the subcontract contained a valid pay when paid clause under which any sum owed to the subcontractor was a contingent debt until receipt of payment by the contractor.

Classification

A receivable is not a term of art but is a useful word to describe all actual **3–005**
or potential rights to payment. A contractor's receivables are quite complex and, to an extent, vary depending on the type of contract chosen by the parties. They could be classified under four headings: the contract sum, damages, a claim for quantum meruit and others (fig.3.1).

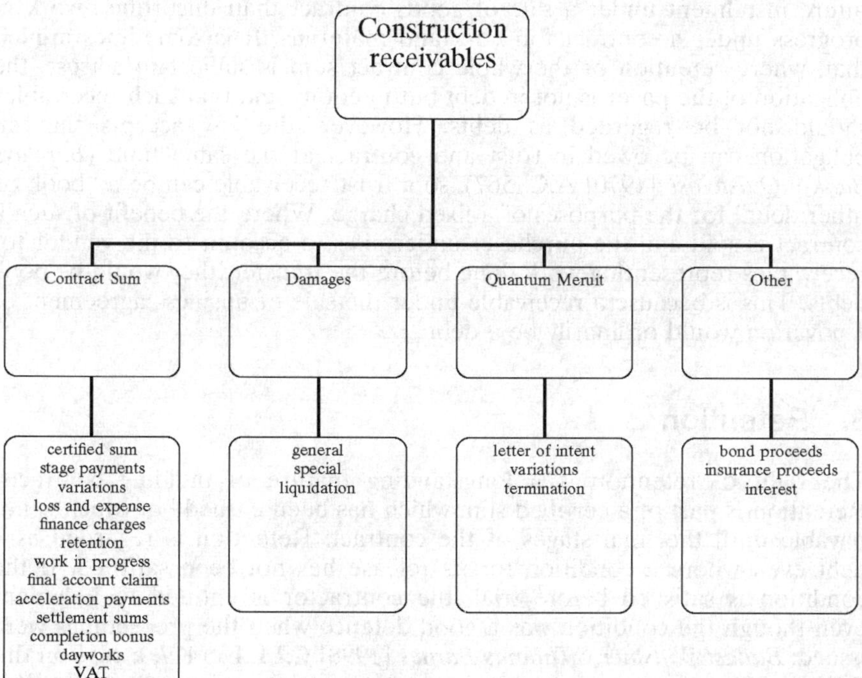

Fig. 3.1

A receivable needs to be a debt in the strict sense, i.e. recoverable by action, before it can be the subject of a statutory demand under s.123 of the Insolvency Act 1986. There is a need for certainty in that context since non-payment of a valid demand deems the debtor to be insolvent. It is possible that the criteria for a book debt are wider and embrace not only certified sums but also retention and claims made under the contract which are normally recorded in the contractor's books (see below). Any receivable can be assigned, however inchoate, even under a future contract: *Tailby v Official Receiver* (1888) L.R. 13 App. Cas. 523. To be eligible for legal set-off, a cross-claim must be for a debt in the strict sense, whereas contractual set-off and set-off in bankruptcy and liquidation apply even to inchoate uncertified amounts, ascertainment being a matter either for the contract or the insolvency procedure. A cross-claim for equitable set-off need not be ascertained.

Fixed charges are taken over book debts and other debts now and from time to time due or owing to the company. If a receivable falls within this description, the charge holder will gain priority over preferential creditors. The description of charged assets may be wider than this, e.g. "all receivables, debts . . . now or at any time hereafter belonging to the mortgagor" (*Re Armagh Shoes* [1984] B.C.L.C. 405). The expression "other debts" can include an obligation by a purchaser of a business to pay the price by instalments: *M O'Donnell & Sons v Midland Bank* [2001] EWCA 2108.

Retention is a special case. Although it is not recoverable by action until certified for release, it is quantified by each interim certificate and is thus regarded as a conditional debt (see below). Retention is closer perhaps to a future instalment under a sale of goods contract than uncertified work in progress under a contract for work and materials. It is sometimes argued that, where retention or the whole contract sum is subject to a trust, the obligation of the payer is not in debt but in equity and that such receivables should not be regarded as debts. However, the law accepts that an obligation can be owed in trust and contract at the same time (*Barclays Bank v Quistclose* [1970] A.C. 567), so a trust receivable can be a "book or other debt" for the purposes of a fixed charge. Where the benefit of such a contract is sold and the purchaser undertakes to account to the vendor for receivables representing work done before the transfer, they would be book debts. This is because a receivable under the sale of business agreement or a novation would ordinarily be a debt.

3. Retention

3–006 The right of retention is a longstanding feature of building contracts. Retention is part of a certified sum which has been earned but which is not payable until the final stages of the contract. Retention is regarded as a debt even where a condition for its release has not been satisfied. If the condition is satisfied before trial, the contractor is entitled to judgment even though the condition was a good defence when the proceedings were issued: *Ballast Wiltshier v Thomas Barnes* [1998] C.I.L.L. 1417, a case on the DOM/1 form of subcontract. Until retention falls for release, however, it is not regarded as a "debt due or accruing due" which can be attached by a judgment creditor: *Grant Plant Hire v Trickey* (1961) 105 S.J. 255. In order to avoid bringing retention into account on a repudiation by the contractor, very clear words would be necessary: *Tony Cox Ltd v Jim 5* (1996) 14 Build. L.M. 6. In *Birse v Eastern Telegraph* [2004] EWHC 2512 a final account dispute under JCT 80 was settled on the basis that money be withheld by the employer pending the completion of snagging items and a timetable laid down for the staged release of retention following defects certificates. Two years later the architect issued an instruction not to make good any defects until further notice and the contractor left site. The employer issued proceedings claiming £1.5 million damages for defects. It was held that the employer could retain £13,000 (all that remained by then of the money withheld) as there were still outstanding snagging items but had to release over £400,000 held as retention, since the architect's instruction rendered it impossible to operate the terms of the settlement agreement, subject only to any valid cross-claim there may be. The retention clause in the settlement agreement was not a forfeiture provision (paras 34–35). See also *Melville Dundas v Hotel Corporation of Edinburgh* 2007 S.C. 12 discussed in Ch.16.

The term "retention" is used in the UK, Australia and New Zealand (see Loftus 2002 for international comparisons). Confusingly, "retention fund" and "retention moneys" are also used, whether or not the employer has segregated retention from its own property by paying an equivalent amount into an account: *G&M Aldridge v Walsh* (unreported, June 2000, CA (Vic)), paras 9–11. Such imprecise language has caused confusion in the context of the retention trust which is considered in more detail in chapter 10. American contracts use "retainage" but this appears to have the same function as retention (Sweet and Schreier 2004). Canadian statutes and standard forms use "holdback". Although this is a percentage of the contract sum retained by the employer, it fulfils a different function from retention and is not directly comparable (Goldsmith and Heintzman 1988).

Commercial function

Retention is usually a fixed percentage of the contract sum. In the **3–007**
nineteenth century as much as 25 per cent was withheld: *Tooth v Hallett* (1869) L.R. 4 Ch. App. 242. Nowadays, the norm is three per cent or five per cent but higher percentages are still encountered, e.g. 10 per cent in Eastern Europe (Champion 2005, 415). In some jurisdictions the maximum percentage is fixed by statute. The timing of its release depends on the terms of the contract. Usually, half is paid to the contractor on practical completion (or substantial completion or taking over), and the balance after the end of the defects liability period (also known as the maintenance period), but this is not necessarily so. For a matrix of retention provisions in the standard forms and major contractors' terms and conditions see the House of Commons report (2002, annex A). In an Australian case, the taking over provisions in a standard form were deleted and the following words substituted: "the retention amount shall be payable in six months after the Certificate of Acceptance is granted, which shall not be withheld unduly, providing all works are wind and weathertight": *Watkins v Cairns Meat* [1963] Qd. R. 21. The court referred to deleted words from which it was inferred that the parties had intended something different from a taking over certificate. The clause meant that retention was to be released

only six months after defects had been completed, even though the employer had gone into occupation of the building. In the context of PFI projects see section 23.3, Standardisation of PFI Contracts (SoPC), Version 4 (March 2007).

The timing of payment of retention is the clue to its principal function, which is said to be "to encourage the contractor to fulfil his obligations during and after the completion of the works and to provide some form of insurance to the client should he fail to do so" (Banwell 1964, para.9.1). According to this definition, retention has a dual purpose: an incentive to the contractor and protection of the employer: *Calvert v London Dock* (1838) 2 Keen 393. Retention is protection against failure to rectify defects, at least as far as the second half is concerned, since a certificate of making good is a condition of its recoverability. On the other hand it was recently described as "security for default in any respect": *Birse v Eastern Telegraph*, *per* Judge Humphrey LLoyd Q.C., at para.34. Retention has been described as a forced loan providing free financing to the employer (McGuinness 1983). It is also seen as a safeguard against over valuation: it does have the quality of provisional abatement about it. It is a simple claim against which the employer can set off a cross-claim in the event of the contractor's default. The JCT forms also anticipate deductions from retention in respect of liquidated damages for delay, insurance premiums, the cost of completion of part of the work by an alternative contractor, or direct payment made to subcontractors or suppliers. Retention is defeasible in respect of these other risks. These two aspects, conditionality and defeasiblity, make retention a flawed asset in the contractor's balance sheet (Hayton 1994a). As retention accumulates gradually during the contract period, it is only towards the end of a contract that it gives worthwhile protection. It is at this time that the employer may need it most as, apart from any final account balance due to the contractor, there will be no further sums against which the employer can set off a cross-claim: *Morgan v Allen* [1971] Tas. S.R. 285. There are many objections to retention. It is said to be a disproportionate remedy applied across the board whereas only a small proportion of contractors fail to honour defects obligations. The sums withheld would frequently not be sufficient to cover the cost of rectifying defective work. No claims were made by clients against retention insurance schemes set up by lift and steelwork contractors. Here is some of the evidence submitted to the House of Commons Trade and Industry Committee:

> "I then asked him if the steel structure that we have erected had any faults or problems to which he replied no. I was then also informed that there was a problem with the tarmac in the car park as it had weeds growing through it. This was another reason why the retention was being held back. I explained to Mr Smith that we were being punished for other people's alleged mistakes and quite matter of fact he agreed. Ev 60
>
> Our latest monthly management figures show retention to the value of £257,000 on outstanding cash of £2,859,000, i.e. 9 per cent. Without this retention money outstanding, we could finance extra business to the value of £1,500,000 based on turning our money over six times per year. Ev 62.
>
> [Contractors] very often use this as a way to blackmail subcontractors into doing additional work that was not in the original contract. Ev 63.
>
> How many extra men, computers, vehicles and other assets to increase our business could we have acquired if we did not have to invest this

money in the construction industry? In practice everything is done to frustrate the receipt of retention moneys. Ev 64

The abuse of retention can act as a restriction to the growth and development of [SMEs] . . . Ev 65

Our retention account is usually between £80,000 and £100,000 per year, and this equates to far in excess of the amount of profit that the company makes. Ev 65

Eliminating retention helps to build teams. It's all about the subcontractors and by eliminating retentions you can show them that you're not going to hold them back. Ev 67

By the time retention is payable, often staff have moved on, the file has been archived and the costs on both sides to clear the matter inefficiently accumulate. Ev 94

. . . unless the subcontractor maintains a constant vigilance, it will not know when it has become entitled to be paid. This leads to the situation where some subcontractors employ a staff member purely to chase retentions. Ev 94

It is ironic therefore that results from the Housing Forum Demonstration Projects report in February 2002 shows that defects are fewer on projects without retention. Ev 95

It is never on time. It is like living with a parasite that will never go away." Ev 105.

Significance of retention

It is useful to summarise the reasons why retention is important. Margins in 3–008 the construction industry are low when compared to other sectors. Even if the retention is only three per cent, its non-recovery may deprive the contractor of its profit on the contract or even push it into loss (BSRIA 2002). In theory the cost of retention to a contractor is loss of interest but, if it could not have borrowed the amount of the retention, its cost may be better expressed as the loss of opportunity.

> "This might be a profit on a development or it might be the ability to pay off an existing loan or to finance the business and avoid insolvency. The focus group interviews revealed that the true cost of retention was . . . the problem of the final payment never being released at all" (Hughes 1998, 22).

Provided the employer remains solvent, however, retention is relatively neutral to contractors as they obtain back-to-back retentions from subcontractors. It is the subcontractors and those beneath them in the contract chain (SMEs—small or medium sized enterprises) who bear the cash flow disadvantages of the retention system (Hopper 1996). It is worth noting that JCT subcontract form (2004) provides for retention to be released on practical completion of the subcontract works rather then being held up until completion of the main contract. This approach is becoming more common.

The retention percentage can be increased by agreement if other security such as a performance bond cannot be obtained. This may arise because the contractor has exhausted its bonding capacity at its bank or for other reasons. Although retention counts as an asset in the contractor's balance sheet it is vulnerable. Apart from the additional credit and working capital which it represents to the employer during the execution of the works, the employer has free use of half of the retention during the maintenance period which could be 12 months or more. As the retention is usually unsecured, and the contractor may have less contact with the employer during the maintenance period, it becomes progressively less recoverable as time goes by. The Cork Committee received extensive representations on retention when reviewing the law and practice relating to insolvency but concluded that it fell outside its terms of reference (Cork 1982, paras 1057–1075). On the contractor's insolvency, the employer, the contractor's general creditors and its lender all look towards the retention to satisfy their claims. Priority disputes over retention are considered in Ch.10.

The "presumption against payment"

3–009 One of the peculiarities of the construction industry is that, on the formal insolvency of a contractor, there is almost a presumption against payment of genuine debts to the insolvency practitioner. This even applies where the contractor has fully performed so that the second half of retention is due and payable. The employer sometimes argues that it has suffered a loss in such a case because, if a defect were to arise during the limitation period, it would not be remedied. This has been described as loss of "expectancy" or "the chance of a remedy" (Bingham 1993). The employer therefore withholds the retention until the limitation period has expired. The issue was addressed in SPI Technical Bulletin 13 which advised insolvency practitioners to "take a robust line" with employers in this situation. In law, an employer would not have any right to withhold payment unless perhaps the contractor had covenanted not to become insolvent before the expiry of the limitation period or the contract contained a right of set-off in respect of a prospective breach.

Alternatives to retention

3–010 Some standard forms provide for other forms of security in lieu of retention. For example the Australian form AS 4000-1997 defines security as:

> "cash, retention moneys, bonds or inscribed stock or their equivalent issued by a national, state or territory government, interest bearing deposit in a bank . . ., an approved unconditional undertaking . . . or an approved performance undertaking given by an approved financial institution or insurance company or other form approved by the party having the benefit of the security."

In the UK, it is more common for retention to be replaced (or released early) by a retention bond or a maintenance bond but there are significant problems with this approach (see Ch.19). Philip Wood has considered other alternatives, such as charge back or trust back arrangements whereby the contractor charges or declares itself trustee of amounts representing a given percentage of the contract value (Wood 1989, 227). The Banwell Committee suggested an experiment under which contractors would tender on the alternative bases that retention was and was not withheld. It considered that retention in excess of three per cent was unjustified where the contractor had both pre-qualified and been chosen through selective tendering (1964, para.9.11). In two recent reports of the House of Commons Trade and Industry Committee (2002, 2003) retention was viewed as an outdated concept which should be discontinued although legislation was not thought appropriate. Some see the growth of partnering and framework arrangements as sufficient protection: if the contractor fails to rectify defects it gets no repeat business. The DTI maintains that the need for retention will fall away if contractors do work which is "defect-free". Better definitions of practical completion may also help (Champion 2005, 412). Some standard contracts such as the JCT major projects form (2003) now omit retention without providing an alternative, an indication that the concept is regarded as disproportionate at least for the more sophisticated client.

4. *Quantum meruit*

A receivable frequently encountered in the construction industry is the **3–011** claim for a *quantum meruit*. This is a right to be paid a reasonable sum in certain situations, e.g. for work done at the employer's request without a contract or where variations are ordered outside the scope of the contract. It has been held in Australia that a *quantum meruit* for work in progress remaining uncertified at the date of termination could not be a debt because it was not ascertained or readily ascertainable by the court: *Geraldton Building v Woodmore* (1993) 8 A.C.S.R. 585. The court applied *Ogdens v Weinberg* (1896) 95 L.T. 567 which defined a debt as a sum recoverable by an action for debt which had to be ascertained or capable of being ascertained by the court. There is however contrary Australian authority which holds that a claim under a *quantum meruit* is a claim in debt because formerly it was one in respect of which an *indebitatus* or common count would lie: *Alexander v Ajax Insurance* [1956] V.L.R. 436 at 445. See also *The Aldora* [1975] Q.B. 748 at 751. In *Amantilla v Telefusion* [1987] C.I.L.L. 316, when considering a *quantum meruit* for variations included in a final account claim brought by a receiver and manager appointed over a contractor, Judge John Davies Q.C. followed the second approach.

> "A quantum meruit claim for a reasonable sum lay in debt because it was for money due under a contract; it was a liquidated pecuniary claim because a 'reasonable sum' was a sufficiently certain contractual description for its amount to be ascertainable. Such a claim was for a specific sum and was no less specific for being described in words rather than in figures. The nature of a claim for unliquidated damages was wholly different; the function of the court was not one of interpreting the contract, but of deciding, in accordance with legal principles, what compensation, if any, should be paid to redress any harm done by its breach. A claim for unliquidated damages could not be a liquidated pecuniary claim, even if claimed at a definite figure" (at 316).

A claim for a *quantum meruit* could be regarded as a debt for the purposes of legal set-off: *Lagos v Grunwaldt* [1910] 1 K.B. 41 at 48, *Aectra v Exmar* [1994] 1 W.L.R. 1634 at 1647. The classification may also depend on the basis of calculation of the reasonable sum.

5. Funding cash flow

3–012 Contractors are usually paid monthly in arrears. At the outset, dates are agreed for monthly valuations of the contractor's work. Under standard forms of building contract, the contractor provides the quantity surveyor appointed by the employer with sufficient information for him to value the work seven days before each of the agreed dates. The quantity surveyor then submits his valuation to the architect appointed under the contract who issues an interim certificate by which the employer has to pay the net sum due to the contractor within 14 days or such other period as is stated in the contract. The contractor will, as far as possible, so arrange its affairs that it does not have to meet outgoings until payment has been received under an interim certificate. This is achieved in the case of subcontractors by appropriate contract terms. In many cases, a significant amount of labour on-site is engaged by labour-only subcontractors who will not be paid until the contractor is paid. Builders' merchants give credit to approved contractors which also assists cash flow. Nevertheless it is necessary for a contractor to meet some site outgoings and it has to meet its head office overheads in the meantime. The delay between payments and receipts gives rise to the requirement for working capital.

Working capital consists of current assets including cash, debtors and stock. Stock in the case of a construction company largely consists of materials and work in progress. Unless an advance payment has been made, there is at least a month's delay before a project starts to generate cash and so the contractor must look to other sources of finance to fund its working capital. These sources consist of debt and equity. With most small to medium contractors, debt is provided by means of a bank overdraft, trade credit or unsecured loans from the directors. Motor vehicles, plant and equipment are commonly financed by hire purchase or leasing. Factoring is not as common as in other sectors as construction contracts tend to be long term and there is a serious risk that the factor's claim would be defeated by set-off (Salinger 2000). Funding debt by means of an overdraft and trade credit is a cause of instability because both sources of finance are short term. Once these have been exhausted, the contractor may have no other source from which to pay its creditors (Kenley 2003).

Medium to large contractors are better placed since they can fund debt by means of term loans, bond issues and other methods. Equity means shareholders' funds. These consist of the capital contributed by the company's shareholders, retained profits from previous years' trading, reserves established by revaluation of properties and the share premium account representing the premiums received from the issue of shares at a price above their nominal value. An equity investment depends on the financial success of the company. Its reward consists in dividends declared by the company but the investor takes a high risk which is not secured against the company's assets. A debt investment is not so dependent on the company's financial success. Its reward is interest payable at agreed rates and the investor's risk is lower as the debt is normally secured against the company's assets (Ch.2). The relationship which debt bears to equity ("gearing") is one of the major financial ratios by which a contractor's financial health can be assessed. Gearing indicates a company's ability to borrow in order to meet short-term commitments.

It is also important to know the extent to which a company can pay interest on its borrowing out of its operating profits ("profit before interest and tax"). The proportion which interest bears to profit ("interest strain") is the other major solvency ratio. The level of gearing is important but the ultimate cause of insolvency is lack of liquidity. Creditor pressure may be such that the contractor has no time to dispose of assets or organise a rights issue to raise cash. There are two guides to liquidity: the current ratio, which is the proportion which current assets bear to current liabilities, and the acid test ratio, which is the proportion which current assets less stock bear to current liabilities. A contractor's margin is the proportion which profit (before interest and tax) bears to sales. Profitability can be assessed by return on capital employed. This is the proportion which profit, before interest and tax, bears to the capital employed in the business. Capital employed is the total of fixed assets and working capital. Once a contract has been under way for some months, it should start to generate positive cash flow. This is enhanced by the practice adopted by many contractors of weighting items occurring early in the contract known as "front-end loading". In July 2007 the Office of Government Commerce published a *Guide to Best 'Fair Payment' Practices* (OGC 2007) which will be introduced for use on public sector work as from January 1, 2008. Improved payment processes are expected to produce savings of 2.5 per cent on construction costs. The guide includes a model Fair Payment Charter which, although not legally binding, will be signed by the client at the outset, and by the contractor and subcontractors before they are appointed (para.10). A major element is a commitment to pay subcontractors and sub-subcontractors within 30 days of the main contract valuation. If a project bank account is used (see Ch.9), this could be reduced to 21 days (para.18).

6. Housing Grants, Construction and Regeneration Act 1996

Payment under a contract entered into after May 1, 1998 may be governed **3–013** by the Housing Grants, Construction and Regeneration Act 1996. This Act applies to all construction contracts entered into in the UK except those with residential occupiers and in certain specialist sectors, such as oil and gas, mining, nuclear, and manufacture of building components. It is intended to provide "a framework for fairer contracts and better working relationships within the construction industry" (DOE 1995). It requires the parties to agree a procedure for payment which complies with the 1996 Act. Failure to do so will result in the implication of the Scheme for Construction Contracts (England and Wales) Regulations 1998 (SI 1998/649) by default in order to supplement or replace the non-compliant contractual term.

When and how does a debt arise?

This section focuses on the creation of the debt; issues on abatement and **3–014** set-off against the sum due are considered in Ch.5. Before the 1996 Act, the standard form of domestic subcontract, DOM/1, provided for monthly payments to the subcontractor, the first being due one month after the subcontractor started work on site. Payment was within 17 days of the date it became due. So if the subcontractor started on July 1, its first payment would be due on August 1, and payable on August 18. The next payment would be due on September 1 and so on. There was no requirement for domestic subcontractors to submit applications for payment, although they usually did. Their works were valued by the employer's quantity surveyor when he valued the whole of the main contract works for certification. Then it was for the main contractor to allocate an amount to each domestic subcontractor's work and make the payments. In practice, this contractual mechanism was often not operated (Price 1994). Instead, subcontractors were paid within a certain period after the date of a certificate issued under the main contract or after the contractor had been paid. This left the subcontractor in a difficult position as DOM/1 did not reflect what actually happened.

By s.109 of the 1996 Act a subcontractor, as well as the contractor, has the right to be paid by instalments, stage payments or other periodic payments unless either the contract period is less than 45 days or the parties estimate that the work will take less than that. The parties are "free to agree" the intervals of payments or the circumstances in which they become due. If not set out in the contract, the Scheme provides that payment intervals will be monthly in arrears. The 1996 Act does not require an instalment to represent the value of the work done since the previous instalment. Under a deferred payment contract, for example, there might be 10 instalments, nine for nominal amounts and the tenth for £10 million. Section 110(1) is intended to provide greater clarity in this area. It requires that every construction contract should provide an "adequate mechanism" for deciding what is due, when it becomes due and when it becomes payable. The parties are "free to agree" all these things but, in the absence of agreement, the Scheme provides that the amount due will be the value of the work less previous payments. It will become payable within 17 days after it becomes due (or 45 days in the case of a final payment). Obviously, there is scope for discussion as to what is an "adequate mechanism". Section 110(2) requires the contractor, no later than five days after a payment has become due, to serve a payment notice stating the amount if any of the payment made or proposed to be made and the basis on which that amount was calculated. If the Scheme applies, the payment notice must be served within five days after receipt of the subcontractor's application for payment. Any withholding notice must be served at least seven days before the final date for payment.

Both building and engineering forms have been amended following the 1996 Act. Under JCT forms, payment becomes due on the issue of an architect's certificate. The employer issues a payment notice no later than five days after that. The final date for payment as defined in the 1996 Act is 14 days from the certificate. If the employer wishes to make a set-off against the payment, it must serve a withholding notice not later than five days before the final date for payment. ICE (7th edn) takes a different approach. The engineer's certificate takes effect as the payment notice. Payment is due on the certificate which must be issued within 25 days of delivery of the contractor's monthly statement. The final date for payment is 28 days after delivery of the monthly statement, i.e. three days after the certificate. The withholding notice must be given at least one day before the final date for payment.

Case study

The 1996 Act and the Scheme provide a framework which is to apply across **3–015** a large part of the industry: a top-down, "one size fits all" approach. But it can be difficult to apply the statute to the diverse ways that payment is organised. In addition, there have been problems interpreting the statutory wording and in understanding the interrelationship between the document or event marking the creation of the debt and the requirement for payment and withholding notices. As a way in to this subject it is proposed to examine one case in detail and then to outline the current areas of controversy.

In *Alstom Signalling v Jarvis Facilities* [2004] EWHC 1285 Alstom was engaged by Railtrack to design and install plant on a railway extension. Alstom subcontracted the signalling and telecoms work to Jarvis under an amended I Chem E form with a target cost and pain/gain sharing mechanism (explained in other litigation between the parties: [2004] EWHC 1232). There were monthly payment intervals tied in to Railtrack's reporting cycle. Jarvis submitted a request for payment every 28 days with details of actual and anticipated cost for the month. Within the same week Alstom had to raise any queries on the information provided. Failing a satisfactory response, it could exclude the disputed items and issue a certificate within 14 days of the request for payment showing the sum due. The final date for payment was seven days after Railtrack's certificate for the same period under the main contract. After substantial completion, Jarvis made two further interim applications but Alstom considered nothing was due owing to the contractual operation of the pain-share mechanism. References to adjudication were made by both parties under which Jarvis was successful but Judge Humphrey LLoyd Q.C. refused to enforce them. He also granted declarations on the construction of the contract and the Scheme. The adjudicator based his decision on his perception of the purpose of the 1996 Act: "that the withholding notice must reflect the difference between application and certificate—not between certificate and payment to be made" (para.5). He interpreted Jarvis's request for payment as establishing the sum due subject only to *ex post facto* adjustment following Alstom's queries. He also found that the definition of the final date for payment by reference to a certificate from the employer was too uncertain to comply with the 1996 Act and that the Scheme applied in default.

The court held that the subcontract complied with s.110. There was no reason why an "adequate mechanism" dealing with payment under the subcontract could not rely on periods, certificates or events laid down by the main contract.

> "Provided that the event is readily recognizable and will produce a date by reference to which the final date can be set, there is no reason why it cannot be used. Payment of a subcontractor by reference to the date of a main contract certificate accords with industry practice . . ." (para.22).

The presence or absence of a withholding certificate was irrelevant to the creation of the debt whether the Scheme applied or not (para.35). The subcontract allowed the contractor to make deductions from the amount requested before issuing a certificate. In this case, the certificate performed the role of the payment notice and showed a nil value.

Areas of controversy

3–016 The first area concerns public policy. In giving effect to the Act the court is concerned to do three things: to interpret the actual words of the statute, to enable the Act to fulfil its purpose, and to do justice. The Act was not imposed by an interventionist government; it was lobbied for by the industry as a way out of its own seemingly intractable problems. In the end it was the product of compromises which continued to be made right up to the end of the parliamentary process. As such it is not an easy statute to give effect to. Care is needed when adopting a purposive approach. In *Alstom v Jarvis*, it led the adjudicator to disregard the actual words of the statute. In other cases it has led to arguably unjust results, e.g. where the claimant in an adjudication is entitled to enforce a decision free of set-off even though it repudiated the contract after the final date for payment of the claim. What is justice and purpose in this context? It is often stated that in adjudication the industry accepted a disputes procedure that was bound to involve "rough justice". The truth may be rather that certain outcomes of the Act were not predicted or at least not fully appreciated by the industry groups, e.g. the court's decision not to review the merits when enforcing adjudication decisions; the prohibition of set-off against adjudicator's decisions; or the inability to set off liquidated damages, even though an entitlement logically follows from an adjudication decision, for want of a notice under s.111: compare *Balfour Beatty v Serco* [2004] EWHC 3336, *RJ Knapman Ltd v Richards* [2006] EWHC 2518. Is the primary goal of the Act to provide certainty of expectation to creditors, especially to subcontractors, so that they know how and when their debts accrue and in what amounts? Or is it to alter the balance of power in the industry by prohibiting certain practices and procedures on grounds of fairness, even though they pass the certainty test? It seems that the decisions of the Technology and Construction Court disclose a difference of opinion among the judges although recently a more interventionist trend has become apparent.

The second area of controversy concerns the question of the adequacy of the payment mechanism. As *Alstom v Jarvis* shows, there is a distinction between reducing an application in order to arrive at the sum due and abating a sum due. The former is part of the valuation process, the latter a defence to payment. Under a design and build contract the contractor serves an application and the employer has a short time to challenge it. If items are disputed only the balance becomes due. If the employer fails to respond the whole application becomes due: see *Watkin Jones v Lidl* (2002) 86 Con. L.R. 155. But in both cases the employer can reduce the sum due on grounds of abatement provided it serves a notice which complies with s.111 within the period before the final date for payment.

The requirement for a payment notice is the seed of confusion in practice since it can satisfy both s.110 and s.111. It can mark the creation of the debt and allow the payer to reduce the debt to the amount payable. The government is proposing to remove this requirement (DTI 2006, 18). The DTI has recently concluded that many contracts still lack an adequate mechanism of payment or at least a means of communicating it to creditors and proposes to amend s.110(1) so that all contracts provide for the issue of a certificate either by the payer, the payee (by means of an application), or a third party named in the contract. It intends to make "pay what certified" clauses unenforceable. A certificate by a third party under another contract would not be sufficient and the Scheme would apply in such a case (DTI 2006, 18).

The third area worth noting is the need for a clear final date for payment. Perhaps the most interesting aspect of *Alstom v Jarvis* was the court's approach to the Railtrack certificate. In applying the certainty principle Judge LLoyd Q.C. considered he was giving effect to the purpose of the Act and responding to the commercial needs of the industry. But to the DTI the idea of pay when certified offends the principle of fairness which the Act was brought in to promote. It is therefore considering prohibiting such arrangements. "However the current use of pay-when-certified clauses suggests that a significant regulatory intervention of this kind may require separate primary legislation" (DTI 2006, 19). This aspect is taken further in the next section on contingent payment.

7. Pay when paid

On a construction project, the contractor bears the risk of the employer's **3–017** insolvency, unless the subcontract clearly provides otherwise. "Where one has a chain of contractual rights and liabilities, the party in the middle is normally exposed to the risk of insolvency on the part of the other parties. If the [JCT] scheme set out to avoid that consequence, I would expect it to do so by clear and express provision": *Birse Construction Ltd v Co-Operative Wholesale Society Ltd* (1997) 84 B.L.R. 58 at 75, *per* Phillips L.J. Pay when paid clauses in construction contracts are now regulated by s.113(1) of the Housing Grants, Construction and Regeneration Act 1996. Before looking at the 1996 Act it is useful to bear in mind the background to these clauses (Yendall 1997, Murphy 1989). Problems tend to arise in connection with the termination and completion of the main contract, disputes between employer and contractor, and the employer's insolvency.

The general background

Outside insolvency, although not directly in issue, the efficacy of pay when **3–018** paid clauses was impliedly accepted by the House of Lords in *Gilbert Ash v Modern Engineering* [1974] A.C. 689 where the subcontract stated:

> "14. Payments (both interim and final) as stated overleaf will be made to the subcontractor as and when the value of such works under the terms of the principal contract is included in a certificate to the contractor and the contractor receives the monies due thereunder."

Viscount Dilhorne commented: "Under the subcontract [the contractor] became only liable to pay when he received the money from the employer" (at 711). English cases have focused on the effectiveness of a pay when paid clause on completion or termination of the main contract.

In *Rushpass v G Percy Trentham* (unreported, May 10, 1991), a main contract under JCT 81 was determined. The termination was disputed and referred to arbitration. The subcontractor was entitled to payment "within 7 days of receipt by [the main contractor] of payment of the said work pursuant to the said main contract". The subcontract provided that where the main contract was determined, the subcontract would automatically determine and the subcontractor's rights would be the same as those of the main contractor in that situation under JCT 81. The subcontractor obtained summary judgment on the ground that JCT 81 did not provide for contingent payment.

> "If a pay when paid clause is to survive the determination of a contract, then it must be clearly drafted in order to achieve that effect. In the present case not only is it not so clearly drafted but for the reasons set out above, the drafting of [the termination clause] clearly precludes such a construction."

If the reason for non-payment is due to the contractor's default, e.g. in bringing about the termination of the main contract, it cannot rely on the pay when paid clause: *Durabella Ltd v J Jarvis & Sons Ltd* (2001) 83 Con. L.R. 145, para.17. In *Churchfield Construction v Waymans* (unreported, July 25, 1996), a contractor was in dispute with an employer over a claim for loss and expense. Practical completion of the main contract had been achieved. The contractor had agreed a final account with a domestic subcontractor and there was no dispute as to defects or otherwise between them. The subcontract provided for payment within 28 days after any interim certificate which included the value of work done by that subcontractor provided that the contractor had received payment in respect of it. It appears that the amount claimed by the subcontractor had not been certified or paid to the contractor. Garland J. awarded summary judgment to the subcontractor:

> "I read these provisions as being abundantly clear that the pay when paid provision bites only on interim certificates and not once the works have reached the stage of practical completion, still less of course, final certificate . . . [The subcontractors] were only dependent on pay when paid so far as interim certificates were concerned . . . I averred in passing that these pay when paid clauses can cause great difficulties, and are not to be encouraged at every stage".

These cases imply that a pay when paid clause would have been effective before practical completion or termination and even on those events if the subcontract terms had been clear enough. The validity of a clause making payment contingent on the employer's solvency is recognised by s.113: *Durabella Ltd v J Jarvis & Sons Ltd* (2001) 83 Con. L.R. 145, paras 20–21. Before the 1996 Act, there was some doubt over the effectiveness of a pay when paid clause on the employer's insolvency, mainly because clauses in regular use referred to payment but not the cause of non-payment. For example, under the FCEC form of subcontract, a contractor had to pay the subcontractor "within 7 days of his receiving from the employer on account of the main work any payment which includes a sum in respect of the subcontract works". The Green Form had a similar provision.

The use of pay when paid clauses is associated with the introduction of management contracting as a means of procurement in the 1960s. Until 1987, when the JCT issued a standard form, contractors used their own forms of subcontract or had special conditions for use with the standard forms of subcontract: *A Davies & Co v William Old* (1969) 113 S.J. 262, compare *Maidenhead Electrical Services v Johnson* (1997) 15 C.L.D. 10-03.

There is a significant body of case law in the US, Canada, New Zealand, Singapore and Malaysia on the ability of a pay when paid clause to withstand the employer's insolvency (Subramaniam 2006). Broadly speaking, in the US there are two opposing lines of authority for and against the validity of pay when paid clauses (Hill and Evans 1998). The courts of Canada have tended to validate them as conditions precedent to payment unless non-payment has been caused by a default of the contractor: *Timbro Developments v Grimsby Diesel* (1988) 32 C.L.R. 32. The courts of New Zealand have tended to invalidate pay when paid clauses. The main issue is whether the restriction imposed by the clause is intended to be temporal (pay when paid) or structural (pay if paid): e.g. *Smith and Smith Glass v Winstone* [1992] 2 N.Z.L.R. 473 which concerned a claim by a sub-subcontractor after the contractor had gone into receivership. The sub-subcontract was in similar terms to the FCEC subcontract. It was held that to be effective against the contractor's insolvency, the pay when paid clause would have to be a condition precedent rather than an ordinary term of payment but the words used were not strong enough to support such a construction. The courts of Singapore and Malaysia have preferred to take a literal approach and generally enforced pay when paid clauses. For example, in *Interpro Engineering v Sin Heng Construction* [1998] 1 S.L.R. 694, the High Court of Singapore considered a clause in a sub-subcontract which provided: "[The Plaintiff's] entitlement to payment of the net sum each time shall arise progressively as and when a progress payment . . . is received from [the contractor]". The court considered the clause to be "reasonably straightforward and unambiguous" (at 698). Because the contractor had not been paid the amount in question, the claim by the sub-subcontractor had to fail. The court observed:

> "While the courts will readily wrap a caring arm around the weak and the meek, they cannot do so in every instance. Everyone negotiates his own contract. He is at liberty to give and take as much as he can mutually agree with the other side. The sub-contractor *per se* is not a special species which requires special principles of law to give him a generous dose of legal protection" (at 698).

This case is perhaps the high water mark of decisions upholding pay when paid clauses. See also *Pernas Otis Elevator v Syarikat Pembinaan* [2003] 394 MLJU 1.

Meaning of "payment"

What is payment for this purpose? The main area of contention is whether **3–019** the subcontractor can argue that the contractor has been paid if the employer has set off a cross-claim greater than the amount owed to the contractor. "Payment is a consensual act and thus requires the accord of both creditor and debtor": *Canmer International Inc v UK Mutual Steamship* [2005] 2 Lloyd's Rep. 479, *per* Gloster J., at para.53. Thus payment can be made by a contractual set-off but not by legal or equitable set-off (see also Wood 1989, 725–727; Goode 1988, 147–148; Goode 1983). In a recent dispute over a tax statute, a set-off has been held to amount to payment: *Burton v Mellham* [2006] 1 W.L.R. 2820. Contrast *Ribblesdale v Forbes*

(1916) 140 L.T. 483 in which the Court of Appeal characterised equitable set-off as relief against the liability to pay. In *Durabella Ltd v J Jarvis & Sons* (2001) 83 Con. L.R. 145, the contractor was working under a letter of intent with the employer but entered into a subcontract under DOM/1 which incorporated its own pay when paid clause. The employer terminated the letter of intent before completion of the works, but after the subcontract works had been completed. The contractor settled its claims against the employer and relied on a term in the settlement agreement that no part of the sum due from the employer was attributable to the subcontractor's work. Judge Humphrey LLoyd Q.C. rejected this contention in the light of evidence that the term had been imposed by the contractor and had no evidential value. It had been inserted with intent to mislead the court. In the absence of any contemporary breakdown of the settlement figure, the contractor had failed to prove it had not been paid and could not rely on the pay when paid clause.

Other contingencies

3–020 Payment may depend on contingencies other than receipt of payment from a party up the line. Consider the following examples:

- a PFI arrangement under which the project company is intended to act only as a conduit for payment between government and contractor so that payment is contingent on authorisation under the concession agreement;
- a contract funded by lottery money under which rights to payment may be subject to compliance with requirements of external bodies before funding can be released;
- a secured payment contract where payment is deferred until a particular stage or until completion;
- conditions of payment to subcontractors such as a certificate from the main contractor or a certificate from the employer under the main contract which the contractor makes a condition precedent under the subcontract;
- strict contractual deadlines for submission of applications or requirements for specific levels of detail, in default of which payment is deferred until the following period.

These conditions are sometimes characterised as "pay when certified" or "pay when entitled". A right to payment may depend on an application being made under a superior contract: *Bovis Construction v Ergon* (unreported, March 30, 1994, CA). This case arose out of the insolvency of the Olympia & York Group, the employer on the Canary Wharf project. Ergon achieved practical completion of its work and signed an agreement in full and final settlement of its final account before the employer went into administration. The issue was who was to bear the loss: Bovis as management contractor or Ergon as works contractor. Ergon obtained summary judgment but lost on appeal. On its true construction, the works contract entitled Ergon to payment within 21 days after Bovis submitted an application to the employer. Bovis had not done this when the employer went into administration and there was no allegation of breach in having failed to do so.

The effect of s.113

Section 113(1) provides that pay when paid clauses will now be effective only on insolvency. It states: 3–021

> "A provision making payment under a construction contract conditional on the payer receiving payment from a third person is ineffective, unless that third person, or any other person payment by whom is under the contract (directly or indirectly) a condition of payment by that third person, is insolvent."

The section represents a compromise between various interest groups in the industry. It was included as a surrogate for the trust of the main contract sum proposed by Sir Michael Latham (Davis 2000, at 165).

The definition of insolvency for companies in s.113(2) is limited to formal insolvency events, e.g. an administration order, the appointment of a receiver and a resolution or an order for winding up. It does not include informal insolvency or voluntary arrangements or compositions with creditors. This omission can lead to an anomaly. If the employer enters administration, the contractor can rely on a pay when paid clause as a complete defence to proceedings brought by subcontractors. One of the purposes of the administration might be to facilitate a voluntary arrangement. If that purpose is successful, could the contractor lose the protection of the pay when paid clause? If so, the contractor may well vote against the arrangement. Perhaps this situation could arise where only the contractor's employment has been terminated and the subcontracts remain in being. Even if the operation of s.113 is "once and for all", it may encourage a contractor to seek the employer's formal insolvency when previously it may not have done so.

Contractors will have to take a policy decision whether or not to include a pay when paid clause in their subcontracts. If they wish to do so, it is essential that they draft their own clause and make sure it is properly incorporated: *Aqua Design v Kier* [2003] B.L.R. 111. This is because there is no pay when paid clause in the Scheme. However, if the contract contains a valid pay when paid clause it will not be invalidated simply because another payment term is held to contravene the 1996 Act so as to bring the Scheme into play. This is because the Scheme applies by default only to the non-compliant term: *Hills Electrical & Mechanical v Dawn Construction* [2004] S.L.T. 477. In that case it appears that the employer had gone into administration and a subcontractor was attempting to prevent the contractor from relying on a pay when paid clause by arguing that another payment term was invalid (see para.4), although this is not expressly stated. The 1996 Act does not resolve other difficulties with pay when paid clauses created by ambiguous or confusing drafting. Reference will still have to be made to the principles to be derived from the cases (McCosker 1995).

Contracts entered into under the Private Finance Initiative are expressly 3–022
excluded from the 1996 Act: s.106(1)(b), SI 1998/648. In this context, there is a chain of contracts between government, project company (or concessionaire), and contractor. The 1996 Act can apply to a contract as between

the project company and the contractor. There are indications that the court is adopting a wide interpretation of s.113 which may invalidate conditions precedent to payment such as those canvassed in the previous section: *Midland Expressway v Carillion Construction* (2005) 106 Con.L.R. 154. In that case, the Secretary of State for Transport entered into a concession agreement with Midland Expressway to design, construct and operate a toll road. Midland Expressway as project company entered into a design and construct contract with a consortium of four contractors. Variations were ordered by the Secretary of State under the concession agreement and the work was carried out. The contractor claimed £11.5 million as the cost of the variations but received only £1.5 million from the employer. The contractor served a notice of referral to adjudication. The employer applied for an injunction restraining the adjudication, arguing that the contractor had to wait until the employer's application for payment in respect of the varied work had been dealt with under the concession agreement. (Compare the discussion on name-borrowing and subcontract benefits in Ch.9.) This contention was rejected as it conflicted with s.108 of the 1996 Act. The Secretary of State had refused to join in a tripartite adjudication. The employer then relied on two other provisions in the design and construct contract: (1) that the contractor's rights to payment for the variation should not exceed the amount (if any) to which the employer was entitled under the concession agreement; and (2) that the contractor would only be entitled to payment for the variation once it was clear that the employer would obtain "equivalent project relief" and had received the funds to pay the contractor or confirmed that it had funds available to it. The risk was of the project company incurring a liability to the contractor which it could not pass on to the Secretary of State. Jackson J. held that both clauses infringed s.113 and were not available as defences to the contractor's claim.

The decision has been criticised on the ground that the first provision does not make payment contingent on prior payment but on prior certification (Sheridan 2006). In the language of this chapter, the argument would be that the provision concerns the structure of the debt rather than the time of payment. In other words, it is an inherent restriction or flaw in the formation of the receivable justified by the basic concept of PFI of which the contractor had notice. Contingent entitlement to payment (variously called pay when certified or pay when entitled) is regarded as the raison d'être of the special purpose vehicle in the PFI chain (Buisson 2004). The distinction between factors constituting a debt and conditions for its realisation can be very subtle and is made more often in commercial and insolvency disputes than construction cases. In *Midland Expressway v Carillion*, Jackson J. stated: "Contracting parties cannot escape the operation of s.113 by the use of circumlocution" (para.71). The question also arises whether the approach of Lord Hoffmann in the recent decision in *Melville Dundas v George Wimpey* [2007] 1 W.L.R. 1136 to the construction of s.109(2) of the 1996 Act might cast doubt on the decision of Jackson J. in *Midland Expressway v Carillion*. Section 109(2) reads as follows: "The parties are free to agree the amounts of the payments and the intervals at which, or circumstances in which, they become due." In Lord Hoffmann's opinion, "The reference to 'circumstances' shows that Parliament did not require that stage payments should become inexorably due at fixed intervals but that liability to pay them could be subject to contingency" (para.9). He even went so far as to say that an agreement might conceivably deny the contractor a right to be paid by instalments and still comply with the 1996 Act (para.11). Could he have had equivalent project relief in mind?

The decision in *Midland Expressway v Carillion* has made it necessary to consider ways of financing payment to the contractor in the interim, e.g. unsecured loans to the employer from the contractor or its parent or an agreement to defer the final date for payment to the contractor until the employer has been paid or a longstop date. Buisson (2004) sees the case as a clash between two public policies: the need to protect contractors and subcontractors from payment abuse and the further promotion of PFI as a means of procuring public works; and advocates the exclusion of the first tier of subcontracts beneath a contractor working on a PFI project from the 1996 Act altogether.

The building and engineering forms take different approaches to s.113. DOM/1 was initially amended to include an insolvency pay when paid clause (Amendment 10), but a subsequent re-issue of the form published in 1998 omitted this clause. The intention is therefore that the contractor bears the risk of the employer's insolvency. This is also the approach under the 2005 Standard Building Sub-Contract Conditions. By contrast, the Blue Forms of engineering sub-contract published by FCEC and CECA for use with ICE (6th edn) contain a pay when paid clause which conforms with s.113.

8. Book debts

It was seen in Ch.2 that certain charges granted by a company have to be registered under s.395 of the Companies Act 1985 in order to be enforceable against a liquidator or administrator appointed to the company. One of these is a charge on book debts. "The question of what is a book debt has regrettably remained one of those mysteries of company law" (Oditah 1991, 23). Whether a debt is a book debt is a mixed question of law and accounting practice. A book debt has been defined as a debt arising in the course of a business which is normally entered in the books of a business of that description whether actually entered or not: *Shipley v Marshall* (1863) 14 C.B. N.S. 566. Classification depends on the accounting treatment given to the industry concerned and the activity undertaken in that industry. The definition of a book debt is capable of changing from time to time. **3–023**

In the case of contingency contracts such as insurance policies or surety bonds, receivables will not be book debts in view of uncertainty whether they will arise or not: *Paul & Frank v Discount Bank* [1967] Ch. 348. If the insured event has occurred, however, the insurance claim can amount to a debt but may well not be entered as such in a company's accounts and therefore not be a book debt: *Coakley v Argent Credit* (June 4, 1998, Rimer J.). It is worth distinguishing two issues:

- Is the arrangement a fixed charge over a book debt which, if not properly registered under s.395, is unenforceable against a liquidator, administrator or creditor of the company?
- Is the arrangement a fixed charge on an "other" debt, i.e. a debt which is not a book debt, so as to confer priority on the charge holder over other creditors?

In the first, the court has to decide whether the instrument falls within accepted definitions of fixed charge and book debt so as to require registration. In the second, the enquiry is limited to whether the arrangement constitutes a fixed charge and whether the receivable can properly be said to be a debt at all. If the contract is not contingent, such as a building contract, a debt could be a book debt even though the right to payment does not arise until some time in the future: *Independent Automatic Sales Ltd v Knowles & Foster* [1962] 3 All E.R. 27. In that case, the court defined a book debt as "a debt arising in the course of the business and due or growing due to the proprietor of that business". It was seen earlier that "growing due" has been construed in several different ways, e.g. in a different context, the Court of Appeal construed the phrase as "something that in the course of the trade or business will ripen into a debt, although not a debt, and only in an inchoate state at the commencement of the bankruptcy": *Blakey v Trustees of Property of Pendlebury* [1931] 2 Ch. 255 at 264, *per* Lord Hanworth M.R.

Cases in the construction industry have not yielded a clear or comprehensive test. Under a classification proposed by Trevor Frid (2001), work which has been measured but not yet certified for payment is a future book debt. He would also extend the concept of a future book debt to unmeasured work which has been completed by the start of a formal insolvency procedure. With an ordinary lump sum building contract, however, this may not be feasible until practical or sectional completion; in such a case it seems more likely that unmeasured work would constitute work in progress falling within the ambit of a floating charge. Even if the receivable is a book debt, it may have been the subject of an outright assignment rather than a charge. In one case, a contractor resolved that one of its shareholders should complete outstanding contracts and receive 50 per cent of any resulting profits. It was held that the arrangement was an equitable assignment of the profits: *Re Lawson Constructions* [1942] S.A.S.R. 201. In another case, it was held that debts arising under road construction contracts undertaken by a person whose normal business was that of a storekeeper were not book debts because they did not arise out of that person's normal business: *Robertson v Grigg* (1932) 47 C.L.R. 257. The authorities were reviewed in *Contemporary Cottages v Margin Traders* [1981] 2 N.Z.L.R. 114. A contractor carried on the business of selling and erecting prefabricated cottages. Having obtained a contract to build a cottage, it manufactured units for assembly and subcontracted the construction of the units on site. The benefit of each contract was assigned to a finance company as security for loans and notice of assignment was given to each employer. Assignments were generally made before commencement of construction and in all cases before completion. Under some of the contracts the price was payable by way of a small deposit, the balance of the purchase price save a small retention within 14 days of notice that the package was ready for delivery, and the balance within seven days after completion. It was held that all categories were book debts. A receivable is still a book debt under a present contract even if it only comes into existence when work is completed (see Gough 1996, 680).

What of contractors' claims? In *Re National Westminster Finance* [1991] 1 Qd. R. 130, the court considered a construction company whose main business "was the construction of home units and commercial buildings for sale". The case concerned the status of money held in the company's solicitor's account in respect of damages recovered from defaulting purchasers who had agreed to buy building units.

It was held that:

> "When received by the present solicitors, the relevant amounts of damages took on the character of debts due to the company, because, subject to clause 3 of the agreement they were the company's money and held by the present solicitors on the company's behalf . . . The evidence shows that these amounts were due to the company on account of or in connection with its construction business, so that they should be regarded as 'book debts' of the company falling within the scope of the above statutory definition" (at 136, *per* de Jersey J.).

It has also been held that money received where a claim is compromised constitutes a book debt since the original obligation was transformed by the compromise into an obligation to pay a lesser sum: *Perrins v State Bank of Victoria* [1991] 1 V.R. 749 at 756. It is possible that a book debt will arise under a nominated subcontract as soon as an award is issued under a main contract arbitration which identifies sums in respect of measured work and loss and expense claimed by the subcontractor: *Birse Construction v Co-Operative Wholesale Society* (1997) 84 B.L.R. 58.

Before a claim has been settled or converted into a judgment or an award, its status is less clear. An argument could be made that "loss and expense" and "finance charges" under a JCT form or "costs" under an ICE form are debts in the sense that they are earned by performance under the express terms of the contract. The contractor might routinely enter amounts for such items in a "claims ledger" before they have been ascertained. It is possible that they are all debts "growing due" to the contractor and, in view of their accounting treatment in the contractor's records, are properly regarded as book debts, but this would depend on the court taking a relaxed view on the question of ascertainability.

In summary, it seems likely that construction book debts will not be limited to sums certified for payment. Sums to be invoiced by the contractor under contracts with different payment structures are future book debts, becoming recoverable once the payment event giving rise to the invoice occurs. Its conditionality and defeasibility gives retention a different quality but it is arguable that it is a book debt even before being certified for release. Conditionality is not the same as contingency: *Re Brush Aggregates* [1983] B.C.L.C. 320. Retention is sufficiently certain to be a debt: only its recoverability is uncertain until after completion. An agreed final account could be a book debt even though the contract makes a certificate a condition of payment.

Chapter 4

Assignment

This chapter concerns problems which arise on the assignment of a construction contract. Various questions arise: Is there a contractual restriction on assignment? If so, is it an absolute bar or subject to conditions? What is the nature of the assigned property? Is the right assigned subject to the independent judgment of the architect or the engineer? Is it subject to a contingency? Assignment forces us to think about the nature of a construction contract. **4–001**

1. Functions of assignment

Assignment is a versatile device which is widely used in the construction industry, especially by way of security. Commonly, an employer assigns agreements relating to a development to the lender as security for a loan to acquire the site and meet the construction cost. In *Re Warren* [1938] Ch. 725 a builder financed the development of four houses on a bank overdraft guaranteed by the vendor of the land who also made a small cash advance in consideration of the builder's agreement to pay the proceeds of sale to the vendor's solicitors to be applied first in repayment of the overdraft. The last payment to the vendor was made on the day the builder went bankrupt. It was held that the contract was an equitable assignment of the anticipated proceeds of sale from the development and the trustee in bankruptcy was not entitled to the sum paid to the vendor. Trade credit is sometimes given to contractors and subcontractors by assignment of receivables. In the early case of *Lett v Morris* (1831) 4 Sim. 607 a builder agreed to demolish and rebuild a tavern for £2,360 payable by instalments. A timber merchant agreed to give credit of up to £700 on security of payment of £80 from each of the first three instalments and £460 from the balance. The arrangement was held to be a valid assignment to the timber merchant. Such arrangements are no longer common because contractors undertake to lending banks not to offer their receivables as security to another creditor ("negative pledge" clauses). **4–002**

Even where assignments of debts are permitted, they may not be accepted by factoring companies in view of the involvement of third party certifiers in the creation of the debt and the comparative ease with which debtors in the industry can make a set-off (Salinger 2000). Some institutions however have a policy of allowing the assignment of receivables by contractors to finance trade credit: *Fairfax Gerrard Contracts v London Fire and Emergency* [2004] All E.R. (D) 152, at para.34, discussed in Ch.15.

In *Yeandle v Wynn Realisations Ltd* (1995) 47 Con. L.R. 1, a contractor in administration had a contract with a local authority under ICE (5th edn). A subcontractor under the FCEC Blue Form claimed extra remuneration for unforeseen ground conditions but the engineer rejected the claim. The subcontractor then assigned its debts, including receivables under the subcontract, to a factor at a discount. The factoring agreement was guaranteed by the managing director. The subcontractor went into liquidation and the factor enforced the director's guarantee. The factor's claim was settled and the debts re-assigned to the subcontractor who then assigned to the director all moneys payable by the contractor pursuant to the subcontract. The director failed in his claim as assignee against the contractor as the assignment did not pass the right to challenge the engineer's original decision.

Assignment is also used as a means of facilitating the sale of a business (*Powergen Retail v British Sugar* [2006] EWHC 316) and the settlement of disputes (*South East Thames RHA v YJ Lovell* (1985) 32 B.L.R. 127). An example is *Total Liban v Vitol Energy* [1999] 2 Lloyd's Rep. 700, in which Vitol agreed to sell gasoline to a buyer who agreed to sell it on to Total. The gasoline was defective and Total sued the buyer who sued Vitol in turn. The buyer lacked the resources either to pursue the claim against Vitol or to meet any award an arbitrator might make in favour of Total. The buyer therefore assigned to Total all its rights as against Vitol, the buyer claiming an indemnity in respect of Total's claim against Vitol. This is the reverse of a name-borrowing arbitration (see Ch.9) in that it amounts to a claim by way of assignment by the employer against the subcontractor, the contractor stepping out of the picture. The question arises as to whether the power to invoke the name-borrowing provision is assignable, for example by a subcontractor to a sub-subcontractor.

Assignment is used in leasing agreements in respect of plant and equipment and is often used in the transfer of assets between companies in a group. Assignment is also important in the transfer of collateral warranties (Cartwright 1990, 1993). A debtor may assign property in part payment in response to pressure from its creditors. In *Jones v Farrell* (1857) 1 De G&J 208 a timber merchant had already given substantial credit to two partners trading as a contractor in relation to a factory under construction. Partly as payment and partly as security for a further advance, the contractor assigned £1,000 which was to become due from the employer. One of the partners became insolvent and the other absconded before the supplier had been paid and the employer refused to pay him without an indemnity. It was held that the employer was obliged to pay the supplier as the arrangement was a valid equitable assignment. By contrast in *Yongnam Engineering v Yeo* [2006] SGHC 62 on the insolvency of the main contractor, the employer transferred to a nominated subcontractor the 23rd floor of the office block under construction for an agreed price, payable by way of set-off against the sums owing by the contractor under the subcontract. The arrangement unravelled when it emerged that the mortgagee of the development refused to release its security over that part of the property.

2. Benefit and burden

4–003 If the property concerned is a chattel or land an assignee acquires the right to possession; but an assignment of a chose in action such as a debt, goodwill, intellectual property or the benefit of a contract can only be enforced by taking proceedings. A contract is a chose made up of four distinct elements: the benefit and burden respectively of both the seller and the buyer. Only the benefit is assignable. The buyer can assign the right to the goods but not the duty to pay for them, and the seller can assign the right to payment but not the duty to deliver them: *Nokes v Doncaster Amalgamated Collieries* [1940] A.C. 1014. With a construction contract things are rather more complicated. From an employer's point of view, the benefit and burden of a construction contract extend much further than the right to the building on completion and the duty to pay the contract price (fig.4.1).

Benefit	*Burden*
to issue variation orders	to pay
to terminate in certain events	to appoint the professional team
to levy liquidated damages	to give possession of the site
to claim general damages	to co-operate, or not to hinder or prevent
to possession of the building on completion or in sections	to procure the performance of the professional team: the proper issue of instructions, certificates and valuation of the work
to be jointly named in an insurance policy taken out by the contractor	not to interfere with the independent functions of the certifier
	to insure against certain risks

Fig.4.1

So where an employer assigned the benefit of a contract in JCT 80 form to a funder after practical completion, it was held not to have passed the burden of having to fund retention on request from the contractor: *Finnegan v Ford Sellar Morris (No. 2)* (1991) 27 Con. L.R. 41. Similarly, if a builder is paid monthly in advance and assigns its right to payment, the employer cannot claim against the assignee for repayment of sums not earned by performance: *Pan Ocean Shipping Co Ltd v Creditcorp Ltd* [1994] 1 All E.R. 470. The duty to earn the advance is part of the burden which remains with the builder.

It is sometimes assumed that an assignee of an employer's rights can exercise all of the rights making up the benefit of a contract, but there are dicta to the contrary: "A contract that A will build a house for B, and follow his instructions on such variations as the contract may allow, cannot be converted by assignment into an obligation to follow the instructions of C": *Linden Gardens Trust Ltd v Lenesta Sludge Disposal Ltd* (1992) 30 Con. L.R. 1 at 13, *per* Staughton L.J. Although the judgment of the Court of Appeal from which this quotation is taken was overturned on appeal, this particular point was not questioned in the House of Lords. Staughton L.J. repeated it later in *L/M International Construction v The Circle Limited Partnership* (1995) 49 Con. L.R. 12 at 22:

> "When the benefit of a contract is assigned, the character of the obligation is not changed. Before the assignment the [construction]

> managers were, in some respects, obliged to act on the instructions or directions of the [employer]. The assignment could not change that and render them subject to the orders of [the assignee banks]. A new agreement would be needed to achieve that."

This view has attracted support:

> "The better view appears to be that the employer who has wide powers of variations and of expending Prime Cost sums cannot assign the contract benefit while the building is uncompleted. The contractor expects that employer to be the one exercising the benefits as well as remaining subject to the burdens" (Megens and Ang 1994, 324–325).

This may be putting things too high, although in assessing whether an assignment of the benefit of a construction contract was to the prejudice of the contractor, the court has stated that the employer could not "extend the job at will by calling for extras": *Charlotte Thirty and Bison v Croker* (1990) 24 Con. L.R. 46 at 55, *per* Judge Malcolm Potter. Tolhurst (1999) puts the position slightly differently:

> "It is suggested that the obligor is not placed in any worse position (in law) by reason of the assignment as long as the assignee exercises only those powers inherent in the assigned right and the obligor's duty is not varied (at 562) . . . Assignment . . . is governed by principles of equity. Rights which are the subject of an agreement can only be enforced (or denied) to the extent that it is conscionable to do so . . . [which] depends on the nature of the right assigned and the legitimate expectations of parties in respect of that right" (at 557).

See for example *HLC Engenharia v ABN Amro* [2005] EWHC 2074, discussed in Ch.19, in which the court granted an injunction restraining payment of a call under an on demand bond made by an assignee.

The reported cases tend to concern the assignment of money obligations such as liquidated damages or general damages awarded as a surrogate for performance. Under the general law however assignees are entitled to specific performance or injunctions in respect of non-money obligations if such relief would have been available to the assignor (Jones and Goodhart 1996). From the employer's point of view, the benefit of a construction contract includes the right to call for further performance from the contractor as well as a right to damages. In the absence of clear words to the contrary, an assignment of the benefit of the contract transfers both kinds of right.

In *Linden Gardens v Lenesta Sludge* [1994] 1 A.C. 85 the House of Lords spoke of the right to performance mainly in terms of the right to possession of the building on completion free from defects. There was no discussion of other rights which form part of the benefit but which are exercised through the architect, such as the right to issue instructions or variation orders. It is the unique position of the certifier that makes it hard to fit construction contracts into the law of assignment, which has historically developed in cases concerning the transfer of debts. Perhaps this is the crucial point: it is not so much that certain aspects of the employer's benefit are by nature personal but that the benefit of the power to vary the works is subject to the burden of doing so through a third party who owes independent obligations to the contractor. Could this be an example of the "pure principle of benefit and burden" (see below)? Perhaps Lightman J. had this kind of situation in mind in when he said that: "If the contract requires any judgment to be exercised whether by the obligor or the obligee, an assignment cannot alter who is to exercise it or how that judgment is to be exercised or vest the right to make that judgment in the court": *Don King v Warren* [2000] Ch. 291 at 321.

3. Freedom to assign

Unless the contract provides otherwise a creditor can assign a debt without **4–004**
the debtor's consent because it is in the interests of society as a whole that property should be freely transferable. It has long been accepted that it is immaterial to a debtor who it pays provided it gets a good discharge.

> "The special right of ignoring altogether the consent of the person upon whom the obligation lies to the substitution of one person for another as the recipient of the benefit would seem in principle and in common justice to be confined to those cases where it can make no difference to the person on whom the obligation lies to which of two persons he is to discharge it . . ." (*Tolhurst v Associated Portland Cement Ltd* [1902] 2 K.B. 660 at 668, *per* Collins M.R.).

Exceptions

The freedom to assign is subject to a few exceptions. The following cannot **4–005**
be assigned: the burden of the contract; a contract which is personal to the parties (to paint a portrait); a bare cause of action, unless the assignment concerns the transfer of a property right or the assignee has a genuine commercial interest in the action (*Trendtex Trading Corp v Credit Suisse* [1982] A.C. 679); and in some insolvency situations, e.g. a liquidator cannot assign a claim for wrongful trading (*Re Oasis Merchandising* [1997] B.C.C. 282).

The court is prepared to assume that it is of no importance to the contractor who is to take the benefit of its work, or to the employer as to whom it pays. On the other hand it is of concern to the contractor that the employer in whom it placed confidence by entering into contract retains the liability to pay, and to the employer that the contractor entrusted with the works actually carries them out.

Disadvantages to the contractor

This assumption that there is no detriment to either party in allowing the **4–006**
benefit and burden of a contract to be split is not well founded in practice. For example, a project funder may require the employer to assign the benefit of the contract, i.e. the right to call for performance. If this occurs, the contractor owes a duty to the funder to continue working but can only

look to the employer for payment (fig.4.2). As the works proceed, their value may be under-certified or the employer may make wrongful set-offs against certified sums. Either matter can seriously damage the contractor's cash flow but may not in the circumstances be sufficient to justify the contractor in suspending work or leaving site.

	Benefit	*Burden*
Employer	None	Duty to pay
Contractor	Right to payment	Duty to carry out and complete building
Lender (assignee of benefit)	Right to the building on completion	None

Fig.4.2

In such situations, the contractor cannot protest that continued under-certification will delay completion as the duty to complete will be owed to the funder. Indeed, the funder will probably be pressing the contractor to maintain programme. If the employer becomes insolvent, but no event occurs entitling the contractor to terminate its employment, the contractor could be obliged to continue even in the knowledge of an increasing risk of under-payment. Had the benefit and burden not been split, it would have been easier for the contractor to "go slow" and await a repudiation by the employer, as only then could the contractor safely suspend the works or leave site. Unfortunately for the contractor this process could take several months.

If it decided to abandon the site during that period, the contractor could find itself in repudiation and the funder would be entitled to claim as damages the increased cost of having the works completed by a new contractor together with consequential losses. Commercially, if the contractor dealt only with the employer, it might be able to leave site much earlier. Depending on the circumstances, it may be that "the assignee cannot insist on the continued performance of the contract unless either his assignor is able and willing to satisfy the obligation to pay, or the assignee himself is willing to do it for him" (*Cooper v Micklefield Coal* (1912) 107 L.T. 457 at 458, *per* Hamilton J.). This position is only partly alleviated by the new statutory power of suspension conferred by s.112 of the Housing Grants, Construction and Regeneration Act 1996.

Case illustration

4–007 This point is well illustrated by *Brice v Bannister* (1878) L.R. 3 Q.B.D. 569 which concerned a shipbuilding contract under which the builder was to receive £1,375 in stage payments. The builder experienced financial difficulty and persuaded the owner to make advance payments ahead of the agreed stages. The builder owed a solicitor a substantial amount and assigned £100 "out of money due or to become due" to him under the contract. Notice of the assignment was immediately given to the owner. At the date of the assignment, the builder had received £1,015 leaving a balance of only £360 of the contract price unpaid. The amount the builder had received was more than the value of the work done and it would require considerably more than £360 to finish the ship. The builder became unable to continue without further payments from the owner who was concerned at the extra cost of terminating the contract and engaging another builder. The report is unclear but this appears to be the reason why the owner continued to pay the builder rather than the assignee.

Although the court sympathised with the owner, he was found liable to pay the £100 to the solicitor. As the cost to complete exceeded the balance of the contract price, the owner had no choice but to fund the builder to completion. Having allowed the builder to split the benefit and the burden, the owner had to pay twice. In fact, the owner may have been fortunate that only £100 of the balance of £360 had been assigned. It might still have been cheaper for the owner to have risked additional liability to the assignee than the greater cost of the completion contractor although this was presumably outweighed by the legal costs involved. The report is silent on the value of the work at the date of receipt of the notice of assignment.

Other disadvantages to debtors

Assignment can have other adverse consequences to a debtor. First, there is **4–008** the inconvenience of having to pay someone other than the creditor. In the nineteenth century, it was recognised it would be tiresome for a gentleman to have to pay the assignees of his tailor and other tradesmen. To avoid problems his only recourse was to pay the assignee without delay and produce the receipt to his creditor or to interplead and allow the various claimants to the debt to fight it out amongst themselves: *Jones v Farrell* (1857) 1 De G&J 208. It would certainly be very inconvenient if all the subcontractors employed on a project were to assign sums due to them from the contractor. Assignment adds to a contractor's risk because there is always the possibility that it will be overlooked and the assignor paid by mistake: *Malayawata Steel v Government of Malaysia* [1980] 2 M.L.J. 103 (P.C.).

These concerns are minor compared with the fact that after receipt of notice of assignment, the debtor can build up no new rights of set-off. In the absence of assignment, a debtor could (unless prohibited by the contract) set off a cross-claim under an entirely different contract provided it represented a debt which was payable when the claim was brought: *Stooke v Taylor* (1880) L.R. 5 Q.B.D. 569. If the creditor assigns its claim, the debtor is denied this right of set-off unless its debt had already accrued due, e.g. *Marathon Electrical Manufacturing Corp v Mashreqbank* [1997] 2 B.C.L.C. 460. Thus, by allowing a creditor to assign its claim, a debtor can lose a right of set-off it would otherwise have had. The injustice of this is obvious when one considers that assignment is supposed to be a special right exercisable only where the identity of the payee is not a significant factor for the debtor. In *Pan Ocean v Creditcorp* [1994] 1 All E.R. 470, the House of Lords had to decide between the relative importance of two principles of assignment: (1) that a debtor should not be placed in a worse position by reason of an assignment; and (2) that an assignee is not liable for the burden of the contract. It seems that the second carried more weight.

The same situation arises when an administrative receiver is appointed because the appointment crystallises a floating charge and operates as an equitable assignment of all the charged assets to the floating charge holder: *Biggerstaff v Rowatt's Wharf* [1896] 2 Ch. 93. The right of a receiver to resist cross-claims arising after the debtor receives notice of assignment is loosely known as "receivership set-off". Although strictly the subject belongs to the law of assignment, it will for convenience be dealt with in Ch.18.

"Subject to equities"

4–009 An assignment is subject to equities, such as any right of set-off in existence at the date of receipt of notice of assignment (see generally Ch.18). In the industry an equity binding an assignee may also be created by a compromise under the contract. In *Bowden v John Laing* (unreported, May 12, 2000, CA), a brickwork subcontractor obtained working capital from an equipment manufacturer and an entrepreneur and made an assignment to the former of all sums payable under its subcontract with Laing. The subcontract was terminated by Laing on grounds of delay. The director of the subcontractor compromised its final account claim at nil in view of Laing's cross-claim. A claim by the assignee was rejected on the ground that the director had the authority to do what he did notwithstanding the assignment. An argument that the director had given the assignee an irrevocable authority to conduct the affairs of the subcontractor as his agent was rejected. Similarly a consensual termination of a contract will release a debtor's liability to an assignee if the assigned debt only becomes due if the contract is fully performed: *Babson v Village of Ulysses* 52 NW Rep (2d) 320 (1952). In *Ruggieri v Magnox Electric Plc* (unreported, April 14, 2000, CA) a director as assignee of a contractor which had gone into compulsory liquidation obtained legal aid to recover a debt from the employer pursuant to a settlement agreement. The claim was rejected by the Court of Appeal on the ground that the agreement only entitled the contractor to claim from the employer in respect of sums paid to a subcontractor but on the evidence it had failed to do so before it went into liquidation.

The rationale is that a debtor should be in no worse position by reason of an assignment. It follows that an assignee is not entitled to higher damages than the assignor could have recovered. In a number of construction cases, defendants have unsuccessfully relied on this principle in an attempt to avoid liability to an assignee altogether. The most recent is *Technotrade Ltd v Larkstore Ltd* [2006] B.L.R. 345. During construction work a landslide occurred causing damage to adjoining properties. The owners sued the employer (Larkstore) who was unable to pass on the liability to its design and build contractor since the contractor was insolvent. Instead the employer brought Part 20 proceedings against an expert soil inspection company (Technotrade) as assignee of Technotrade's contract with the original owner of the site. It was assumed that the landslip could be attributed to negligent advice contained in a report prepared by Technotrade on which Larkstore had relied. Technotrade submitted that, as the original owner had sold the site to Larkstore before the landslip occurred, it had suffered no loss. And as the appointment was not assigned until after that event, Larkstore had no cause of action. Logically it followed that the assignee could recover nothing. Its claim fell into a legal "black hole": the party with the cause of action had suffered no loss; the party who suffered the loss had no cause of action.

The Court of Appeal re-examined the basis of the law of assignment. The rule which limited the assignee's damages to those suffered by the assignor was to protect the debtor; it was not intended to give it an escape route from liability. The true analysis was that the cause of action was complete at the time of the defective report: loss often follows some time after the breach. If the original owner had developed the site itself it would have been entitled to substantial damages. As assignee Larkstore acquired the cause of action "which always brought with it potential or inchoate liability for all the losses which would ultimately, subject to matters of causation and remoteness, flow from it" (at para.85, *per* Rix L.J.). There was no restriction on assignment in the appointment itself.

Notice of assignment

A debtor may be asked to confirm receipt of the notice of assignment. In **4–010** some cases, the notice will set out a new term not contained in the contract, e.g. a duty to pay without set-off or counterclaim. Care is needed lest, by counter-signing the notice of assignment, the debtor undertake a wider obligation to the assignee than it originally had to its creditor: *Alstom Transport v Elequip Projects* [2004] EWHC 2897.

Conditional benefit

There are two possible exceptions to the rule that only the benefit can be **4–011** assigned: the "conditional benefit" rule and "the pure principle of benefit and burden". Where a contract confers only conditional or qualified rights, an assignee takes them subject to the condition or qualification. "Such restrictions or qualifications are an intrinsic part of the right: you take the right as it stands, and you cannot pick out the good and reject the bad": *Tito v Waddell (No.2)* [1977] Ch. 106 at 290, *per* Megarry V.C. A conditional right under a construction contract would include a right subject to a condition precedent. For example, the contract may make the execution of a collateral warranty or the provision of a bond a condition precedent to the continuing right to payment. An assignee of the right to payment would have to satisfy the condition before being able to enforce the right. In this sense, the benefit is inextricably bound to the burden and cannot be separated. The pure principle of benefit and burden is a more elusive concept. The principle is that a person who takes the benefit must bear the burden. How can this principle be reconciled with the rule that only the benefit can be assigned? In *Tito v Waddell* Megarry V.C. stated:

> "It may be founded on acceptance, so that he who accepts the benefit is taken also to have accepted the burden, or it may be a rule of law, so that he who accepts the benefit is bound by the burden, irrespective of any acceptance of it. In the conditional benefit type of case it may perhaps be easier to rest the doctrine on acceptance than in cases of the pure principle of benefit and burden: if you accept the benefit you cannot escape the consequence that you have accepted what forms part of the

benefit, or is annexed to it, whereas under the pure principle, the burden may be the price the law compels you to pay for taking the benefit" (at 308–309).

It was held that the pure principle of benefit and burden applied. There, the benefit was a right to mine phosphate and the burden was an obligation to restore the land to its former owners and replant it with trees when the phosphate had been extracted. The replanting was not a condition of the right to mine. The assignment was the culmination of a complex series of changes of control from a company to special commissioners who were replaced from time to time. It is difficult to see how the pure principle can apply to a construction contract. Some guidance may be found in the judge's view that the principle would apply where a person takes an assignment of the whole contract from a company on the point of going into liquidation and undertakes to discharge the burden and to indemnify the company (at 287). This is close to the facts in *Chatsworth Investments v Cussins* [1969] 1 All E.R. 143 and might be a better explanation for the decision in that case than implied novation. The pure principle has been criticised in later cases: in *Carbofuels v Dampskibs* (unreported, July 11, 1996) Morison J. even questioned its existence:

"In any event, I can see no policy reason for it. The time when it would be most needed, namely when a company was being stripped of its assets leaving the creditors in the air, would be the time when it would not apply, because it would be unlikely that when carrying out that task the assignee and the assignor shared a common intention to transfer liabilities. If they had such an intention it is unlikely that, if asked, the covenantee would have refused consent; and, if he consented, then the law of novation is sufficient to cover the position." (transcript, p.33)

4. Non-assignment clauses

Standard clauses

4–012 Construction contracts often contain a clause preventing either party from assigning the benefit without the other's consent, e.g. clause 7.1 of JCT 05, clause 1.7 of FIDIC (1999), clause 3 of ICE (7th edn). Assignment in breach of such a clause will be invalid as between the assignee and the other contract parties: *Linden Gardens v Lenesta Sludge* [1994] 1 A.C. 85. In that case Lord Browne-Wilkinson stated that: "A party to a building contract . . . can have a genuine commercial interest in seeking to ensure that he is in contractual relations only with a person whom he has selected as the other party to the contract" (at 107). There are many reasons for this. He gave as an example the fact that some employers are more reasonable than others in dealing with disputes: see also *Explora Group Plc v Hesco Bastion* [2005] EWCA 646, para.96. A contractor suing the employer for payment might be met by the defence of abatement even though a cross-claim in respect of defects had been assigned. The contractor might have to join the assignee in the proceedings to avoid being penalised twice for the same breach (at 105). In *Modern Weighbridge v ANR*

(1996) 12 B.C.L. 224 an assignee failed to recover the balance of the contract price from the employer due to a non-assignability clause in the contract. The assignee could not establish an estoppel against the employer because although the assignee acted to its detriment in completing the contract for the assignor, to the knowledge of the employer, the employer had made it clear throughout that it did not consent to the assignment.

Linden Gardens concerned clause 17 of JCT 63 which provides: "The Employer shall not without written consent of the Contractor assign this Contract". The court construed "assign this contract" as "assign the benefit of this contract". The standard forms vary in their treatment of non-assignability. Clause 3 of ICE (4th edn) provides: "The Contractor shall not assign the Contract or any part thereof or any benefit or interest therein or thereunder without the written consent of the Employer". This was an effective restriction on the assignment of the whole benefit: *Helstan Securities Ltd v Hertfordshire CC* [1978] 3 All E.R. 262. A contract can restrict the assignment of part of the benefit leaving the remainder freely assignable but it would have to be clearly drafted: *Flood v Shand Construction Ltd* (1996) 81 B.L.R. 31.

Unreasonably withholding consent

If a contract bars assignment without prior written consent, and adds a **4–013** proviso that such consent shall not be unreasonably withheld, e.g. clause 3 of ICE (7th edn), the question arises as to the relevance and interpretation of the proviso in the context of a construction contract. In *Hendry v Chartsearch, The Times*, September 16, 1998, the Court of Appeal considered a claim under a facilities management agreement which contained such a clause. One of the parties passed a special resolution assigning various causes of action under the agreement to one of its directors without seeking the other party's consent. Two of the judges in the Court of Appeal held that this was fatal to the director's claim. The assignment was not a breach of contract but was without legal effect so far as the other party to the contract was concerned. "Consent is not withheld if it is not asked for; and if it is not withheld it cannot be said to be unreasonably withheld" (*per* Millett L.J.). The question whether, had consent been sought in advance, it could have been reasonably withheld, was irrelevant. Evans L.J. disagreed, considering that such enquiry was needed.

On the facts, the assigning company was insolvent and had been struck off the Companies Register. The other party complained that legal aid would be available to the director although not to the company, and security for costs could have been ordered against the company but not against the director. Evans L.J. thought that the availability of legal aid would not have been a reasonable ground to withhold consent but that the loss of the right to apply for security for costs would have been. It remained open to the director to volunteer security for costs and thereby validate the assignment but he had chosen not to do so. The director sued as equitable assignee as the resolution took effect as an agreement to assign. He claimed that the other party had set out to destroy the business by starving his company of cash and taking over its products and staff without paying for them. Among other things, the director argued that the other party had received notice of the assignment and made no objection, but the court held that any such inaction could not make the assignment effective in law. A non-assignability clause can survive the repudiation of the contract: it was reasonable to withhold consent to assignment in this case as the relationship between the parties had broken down and was likely to result in litigation.

By contrast, in *ANC v Clark Goldring and Page* [2001] B.C.C. 479 a clause prevented assignments by franchisees of a parcel collection and delivery service without the prior written consent of the franchisor which was not to be unreasonably withheld provided (a) the franchisee was not in breach at the time; and (b) the proposed assignee agreed to pay the assignor's costs of the assignment, be bound by the agreement, and sign a specific undertaking to comply with the restrictive covenants. The court heard two claims together, by assignees of insolvent franchisees. In one, the franchisee had entered a company voluntary arrangement; and in the other, a creditors' voluntary liquidation. In both cases, the assignment was on the basis that a percentage of the proceeds of a successful claim would be paid to the company. The court held both assignments valid because, on its true construction, the intent of the agreement was to give a franchisee freedom to assign, provided the franchisor was protected against unfair competition, as well as incompetence on the part of the assignee, by new enforceable undertakings being put in place. Once the agreement had come to an end, such a prohibition on assignment could serve no useful purpose.

In *Orion Finance v Crown Financial Management* [1994] 2 B.C.L.C. 607, a computer lease contained a clause preventing assignment without the consent of the end user. The dealer assigned the right to rental under the agreement without consent to Orion as security for payment under a hire purchase agreement. Orion gave notice of the assignment to the end user who counter-signed the notice. The court held that the end user was estopped from relying on the non-assignability clause. Objectively, the assignment was one to which no reasonable objection could have been made. Subjectively, the end user always knew the dealer intended to assign the lease and was aware that Orion did not know about the non-assignability clause. By countersigning the notice, the end user had represented to Orion that there was no assignability point to be taken. Similarly, in *British Gas v Eastern Electricity, The Times*, November 29, 1996, the court held that the withholding of consent for a collateral purpose was not reasonable (see Ch.15). Nor would it be reasonable to withhold consent at trial, having been informed of the assignment before it was made and having made no objection: *Midland Land v Warren Energy* [1997] C.I.L.L. 1222. A clause in a contract for the construction, operation and management of a waste facility which provided that the contract was personal to the contractor who was not entitled to assign it without the employer's consent, barred the assignment of the contract by a liquidator appointed to the contractor: *Quadmost v Reprotech* [2001] B.P.I.R. 349. Imposing a requirement for consent can work both ways: such a clause can be used by a contractor as a lever to extract payment from an employer: *Lemina v Phillips Construction* (1988) B.C.L. 56. On the other hand, a contractor in financial difficulties whose lender asks for an assignment of the benefit of contracts as security might be forced to reveal its financial position to the employer as a condition of obtaining its consent. As a result, the employer might start delaying payment or preparing claims against the contractor.

Inter-group transfers

4–014 In the course of litigation, it sometimes comes to light that the plaintiff has transferred its cause of action to another company within the same group as part of a reorganisation. In *John Young & Co v The Rugby Group* (unreported, December 19, 2000, Judge Richard Seymour Q.C.), this fact emerged from a witness statement filed in support of an application for summary judgment by the contractor for £1.1 million for work done. The employer, relying on the non-assignment clause in MF/1 (rev 3), argued that it constituted a complete defence to a claim. This plea was rejected because the assignment in the inter-company agreement was subject to the assignee obtaining any necessary consents from other contract parties. Following completion the assignor acted as undisclosed agent for the assignee in carrying on its business. If such consent was not forthcoming, the assignor would hold the benefit of the contract on trust for the assignee. On the facts in this case, the assignment had no legal effect and to the extent that the assignor was in breach of contract in purporting to assign it, it had no effect on the contractor's rights to enforce the contract.

It is worth comparing this decision with two Scottish cases. In *WJ Harte Construction v Scottish Homes* (1992) S.C. 99, following a group reorganisation, the works were carried out by an associated company of the contractor who executed the JCT 80 form. The change was disclosed to the employer who agreed to it. The court held that the arrangement fell short of a novation and that the work had been carried out on behalf of the original contractor as its agent (see further on this case in Ch.15). Similarly in *Laurence McIntosh v Balfour Beatty* [2006] CSOH 197 a partnership trading as Laurence McIntosh & Sons entered into a standard form works contract with Balfour Beatty as management contractor for work at the National Library of Scotland. During the contract, the partnership was incorporated as Laurence McIntosh Ltd and its business and assets transferred to the company. A letter was sent to Balfour Beatty's accounts department informing them of a change to their bank account details which gave the name of the company, but there was no actual notice of an assignment. The works contract contained a term requiring the contractor's consent to assign. The company later issued proceedings against Balfour Beatty claiming an extension of time of 67 weeks and over £630,000 as loss and expense. Lord Drummond Young dismissed the claim on the ground that the company was not a valid assignee when it was brought, having acted in law merely as the ad hoc agent of the partnership. The letter was not addressed to anyone at Balfour Beatty with contract-making authority.

In summary the reasons why parties opt for non-assignability clauses in their contracts vary from case to case:

- they remove the risk of double payment by overlooking an assignment;
- they relieve the debtor of the inconvenience of having to deal with a potentially large number of assignees;
- they avoid the problem which arose in *Brice v Bannister* where the employer was exposed because of advance payments it had made;
- they recognise the fact that some creditors are faster than others in enforcing their rights; and
- they can cut down the debtor's rights to legal and liquidation set-off.

5. Qualified assignment

4–015 A contract may permit assignment subject to certain conditions. Only the employer may be allowed to assign or only some rights may be assignable. This occurs in assignments of sale of business agreements where the original purchaser excludes from the assignment the benefit of warranties and indemnities given by the original vendor. A construction example is the FCEC form of subcontract which only permits the assignment of "sums which are or may become due and payable". This means that other rights would in this context be unassignable: e.g. to claim general damages (*Flood v Shand Construction* (1996) 81 B.L.R. 31), to bring an arbitration (*Herkules Piling v Tilbury Construction* [1992] C.I.L.L. 770), or to apply to set aside an engineer's rejection of a claim for additional remuneration due to adverse ground conditions (*Yeandle v Wynn Realisations Ltd* (1995) 47 Con. L.R. 1). It is also possible to limit the number of assignments that can be made. This occurs in collateral warranties where only one or two assignments may be allowed. An assignment may place restrictions on further assignment, e.g. that any further dealing in the debt has to be authorised in writing by the original assignor: *Bowden v John Laing* (unreported, May 12, 2000, CA). The benefit may become assignable at a particular stage of the contract, e.g. clause 19.1.2 of JCT 80 which allows assignment only after practical completion where the employer has also transferred its interest in or granted a lease of the whole of the property concerned. The contract gives the parties the option of incorporating this qualification on assignability or making assignability dependent on consent. Finally the contract may be assignable only to a named person or class, e.g. to a named banker or to "any lender to the project" or "any group company". In such a case, it will be a question of construction of the clause as to whether the assignee will be subject to the same restriction: *Dumford Trading v Oao Atlantrybflot* [2005] EWCA 24, *Essar Steel v The Argo Fund* [2006] 2 Lloyd's Rep. 134; compare *British Energy v Credit Suisse* [2007] EWHC 1428. See also *Esso Australia v Southern Pacific Petroleum* [2005] VSCA 228 which concerned a joint venture agreement which allowed assignment to a "related corporation" provided the assignor guaranteed its performance. Simplifying the facts a little, one party, Southern, became insolvent and wished to enter an arrangement with creditors under which it would sell its interest in the joint venture to a new special purpose vehicle. Southern as assignor would give a guarantee to the other joint venturer and then go into liquidation. The court considered that the arrangement was not in breach of the joint venture agreement and refused to grant an injunction restraining the assignment.

6. Effect of restrictions on assignment

4–016 It was held in *Linden Gardens* that:

> "a prohibition on assignment normally only invalidates the assignment as against the other party to the contract so as to prevent a transfer of the chose in action: in the absence of the clearest words it cannot operate to invalidate the contract as between the assignor and the assignee and even

then it may be ineffective on the grounds of public policy" ([1994] 1 A.C. 85 at 108, *per* Lord Browne-Wilkinson).

This is illustrated by *Attwood and Reid v Stephens* [1932] N.Z.L.R. 1332 which concerned road contracts for a public works department which denied the contractor the right to "assign all or any of the moneys payable or to become payable under the contract or all or any part of any other benefit whatsoever arising or which may arise under the contract, without the previous consent in writing of the engineer-in-chief" and provided that any money assigned in breach of the contract was to be forfeited to the employer. The case concerned a priority dispute between the contractor's assignee and one of its creditors who had obtained a garnishee order. It was held that assignments which had been made were valid and took priority over the garnishee. Where the contract has a non-assignment clause and the debtor pays the assignor, it will not be obliged to pay again to the assignee but the assignor will hold the money on trust for the assignee or its successor in title. If a creditor in financial difficulty assigns the same debt to more than one person, the first to give notice of assignment to the debtor will take priority provided the assignee was unaware of any prior assignment: *Dearle v Hall* (1828) 3 Russ. 1.

7. Assignment by way of trust

A declaration of trust can avoid the effect of a non-assignment clause **4–017** (Allcock 1983, 343). In *Don King v Warren* [2000] Ch. 291, affirmed [2000] Ch. 327, management and promotion agreements between Frank Warren and professional boxers were unassignable by nature as personal contracts or through non-assignability clauses. Warren entered into partnership with King and agreed to hold the agreements "for the benefit of the partnership absolutely". This was held to be a valid declaration of trust of the benefit of the agreements. The trust extended to all rights under the agreements and was not limited to the fruits, i.e. money derived from them. Lightman J. considered that non-assignability was "still undeveloped" as a field of law (at 318). As a consequence, Warren had to bring the benefit of these agreements into account as part of the winding up of the partnership: see *Re Turcan* (1889) L.R. 40 Ch. D. 5, at 11. The decision has been criticised on the basis that if assignment—"the most outright of dispositions"—is barred, it would be anomalous to allow lower degrees of transfer such as trust or charge (Turner 2004).

To what extent could a beneficiary in this situation make a claim directly against the other contract party? There is authority to the effect that if a trustee of a contract refuses to enforce the rights held on trust, the beneficiary can sue in its own name joining the trustee as defendant: *Vandepitte v Preferred Accident Insurance* [1933] A.C. 70. However the court will in each case examine the reason why the trust was declared. In the commercial context the "procedural short cut" of allowing the beneficiary to sue in its own name may not be permitted. In *Don King v Warren* (at 321) Lightman J. stated that ". . . in a case where the subject matter of the trust is a non-assignable contract and there are outstanding obligations to be performed by the trustee, the beneficiary under the contract cannot interfere". In view of the reciprocal nature of the obligations brought into play by a construction contract it seems to follow that a trust is likely to be restricted for practical purposes to the fruits of the contract once they have been obtained by the trustee. In *Barbados Trust Co v Bank of Zambia* [2006] 1 Lloyd's Rep. 723, for example, Langley J. refused to allow the beneficiary to sue the other contract party direct to recover an advance made in respect of a letter of credit facility where the trustee had declined to take proceedings itself. On appeal it was not necessary to decide whether the *Vandepitte* procedure was available as it was held that the assignment to the trustee itself had not been valid: [2007] EWCA 148.

It has been suggested by McKnight (2003) that, on the facts in *Don King v Warren*, the court would have come to the opposite conclusion had it properly applied the principles of contractual interpretation laid down in *Investors Compensation Scheme v West Bromwich Building Society* [1998] 1 W.L.R. 896. It is true that every construction of a document will depend on the surrounding circumstances but it seems probable that clear words will still be required to support a construction that common law rights such as assignment or set-off have been excluded: *Liberty Mutual Insurance Co (UK) Ltd v HSBC Bank* [2002] EWCA 691, paras 49–58 (subrogation rights). In addition, most cases on non-assignability arising in the construction industry concern standard forms rather than the ad hoc agreement prepared in *Don King v Warren*. There remains the possibility that a non-assignability clause may be overcome where one group company enters into a contract as undisclosed principal for another: consider *Karl Construction v Palisade Properties* [2002] S.C. 270.

8. Security assignments

4–018 Perhaps the most common assignment in the industry is of the benefit of a building contract by way of security. In *Durham Brothers v Robertson* [1898] 1 Q.B. 765 the Court of Appeal had to construe the following wording:

> "In consideration of money advanced from time to time we hereby charge the sum of 1,080 [pounds] which will become due to us from [the employer] on the completion of the above buildings, as security for the advances, and we hereby assign our interest in the above-mentioned sum until the money with added interest be repaid to you."

The lender gave notice of assignment but failed in an action against the employer on the ground that the document created an equitable assignment by way of charge which did not entitle the lender to sue in its own name.

If an assignment is by way of charge, the assignor retains the right to sue for any loss suffered through breach by the debtor. If there is an outright assignment coupled with an entitlement to re-assignment once the secured obligation has been performed, it takes effect as an assignment by way of legal mortgage: *Tancred v Delagoa Bay Railway* (1889) L.R. 23 Q.B.D. 239. By this arrangement, the mortgagor remains the beneficial owner of the property subject to the mortgagee's security interest. It follows that, despite the assignment, the assignor-mortgagor retains the right to sue for its own losses during the period of the assignment. If the assignee issued proceedings, it could only recover the loss actually suffered by the assignor and would then hold the proceeds on trust for the assignor as mortgagee. After reassignment, the original assignor sues on its own account and not as successor in title to the assignee: *L/M International v The Circle Limited Partnership* (1995) 49 Con. L.R. 12.

In the Australian case of *Re Turner Corporation* (1995) 17 A.C.S.R. 761 it was conceded that the presence of a non-assignment clause in a contract meant that a charge could not attach to the non-assignable contractual rights, but was the concession properly made? After all a chargor remains the owner of the charged asset. Could the prohibition have restricted the mode of enforcement rather than the grant of a valid charge, so that a debenture holder could direct the company to recover the debts on its behalf by allowing the receiver to collect them in the name of the company in the usual way? The only English authority appears to be *Foamcrete v Thrust Engineering* [2002] B.C.C. 221. In that case a supplier granted a fixed charge over book debts and a floating charge over its undertaking to a bank and later entered into a contract to supply goods to Thrust which contained a restriction on assignment. On the supplier's liquidation, which caused the floating charge to become fixed, the bank transferred the debenture to Foamcrete who sued to recover a debt owed by Thrust which fell due after the liquidation. Thrust relied on the non-assignment clause. Mummery L.J. pointed out that the debenture was granted before the contract was entered into. He then stated that by virtue of the floating charge the bank acquired a beneficial interest in all future debts from Thrust. The charge had to take priority over the prohibition on assignment otherwise the supplier could remove assets from its scope by including a non-assignment clause in its contracts, which would defeat the purpose of the charge (para.32). Mummery L.J. implied that *Linden Gardens v Lenesta Sludge* [1994] 1 A.C. 85 applied only to cases in which a person entered into a contract containing a non-assignment clause and then broke it by assigning that contract whereas *Foamcrete* was not such a case (para.27).

This approach has been criticised as a misunderstanding of *Linden Gardens* (Tettenborn 2001). It also ignores the argument that the crystallisation of the charge was an equitable assignment which post-dated the contract: compare *Starelec v Kumagai Gumi* [2002] QSC 137. It also seems to take no account of the supplier's right to trade in the ordinary course of business, which included the right to enter into contracts containing non-assignment clauses. Such terms are found in all of the construction standard forms. By analogy, in *MacJordan Construction v Brookmount Erostin* (1992) 56 B.L.R. 1 it was accepted by the Court of Appeal that setting up a trust fund to protect retention under a JCT form would be an act in the ordinary course of business of the employer (see Ch.10).

To avoid this kind of problem, tender documents frequently make it a condition of the building contract that the contractor will consent to the assignment of the benefit by the employer to a lender. A charge may be created over a purportedly non-assignable right if there has been an effective waiver of the prohibition on assignment or an estoppel precludes reliance on it: *Orion Finance v Crown Financial Management* [1994] 2 B.C.L.C. 607. Otherwise, the charge may be effective only as between chargor and chargee, e.g. by conferring a proprietary interest in the proceeds of any charged property recovered by the charger: Lightman and Moss 2007, para.25–018. Compare *Bawejem v MC Fabrications* [1999] B.C.C. 157.

9. Acknowledgement

4–019 Acknowledgement arises where A holds a fund on behalf of B, B directs A to pay C from the fund, A accepts the direction, and A promises to pay C direct. In that event C can seek restitution from A by an action for money had and received (Chitty 2004, para.29–194). It has been suggested that this principle might apply where a contractor asks an employer to make a direct payment to a subcontractor and, in response to the contractor's request, the employer promises the subcontractor to pay it direct (Prentice 1983). If this situation falls within the principle of acknowledgement, the subcontractor may have an action for money had and received against the employer enforceable on the contractor's liquidation. The problem with this argument is that the employer does not normally hold a fund for the contractor. The nearest equivalent would be some kind of construction trust. The difficulty then would be that the employer could not accept the direction because it could lead to personal liability for breach of trust. There is authority that the employer need not hold a fund and that acknowledgement can be effective where the employer merely owes a debt to the contractor (*Shamia v Joory* [1958] 1 Q.B. 448) but this decision has been criticised as "plainly erroneous" (Goode 2004, 62).

10. Flawed assignments

4–020 It was seen earlier how the assignment of the benefit of a construction contract may only pass the right to payment rather than the right to order a variation. By the same reasoning, it is possible that the assignment of an on demand bond may transfer the right to the proceeds of a call but not the power to sign the demand: consider *HLC Engenharia v ABN Amro* [2005] EWHC 2074 discussed in chapter 19. If a default guarantee is assigned, but there is no assignment of the underlying contract or obligation, the assignee cannot enforce the guarantee: *Hutchens v Deaville Investments* (1986) 68 A.L.R. 367. The rationale is that a creditor cannot convert one obligation into two: the original contract duties owed to itself and the guarantor's duties owed to the assignee. This reflects the secondary nature of a guarantor's obligation (Ch.19). To make a contract truly non-assignable it appears from the foregoing that it needs to be explicit and prohibit all means of transfer: assignment, trust, mortgage, acknowledgement, or any disposition or dealing whether absolutely or by way of security without consent.

11. Formalities

4–021 Assignment is an informal process. "All that is necessary is that the debtor should be given to understand that the debt has been made over by the creditor to some third person" (*William Brandt's Sons & Co v Dunlop Rubber Company* [1905] A.C. 454 at 462, *per* Lord Macnaghten). There are two overriding practical considerations: When can the assignee sue the debtor? Who does the debtor have to pay in order to get a good discharge? The answer depends on whether the assignment is legal or equitable (Fig.4.3).

Legal	*Equitable*
Formalities required—must be in writing signed by the assignor	No formalities required—could be oral provided there is adequate evidence
Written notice must be given to the debtor	No requirement for notice (although notice would preserve priority over later assignees and ensure that debtor can only obtain a good discharge by paying assignee)
Debtor can only obtain a good discharge by paying assignee	Debtor can obtain good discharge by paying assignor (unless notice of assignment has been served)
Assignee can sue in its own name	Assignee needs to add assignor as co-plaintiff or, if it refuses, as co-defendant
No consideration required	Probably no consideration required
Must be absolute, i.e. whole debt or interest must be transferred.	Need not be absolute, assignor could retain some interest
Must not be by way of charge only	Can be by way of charge only

Fig.4.3

Legal and equitable assignment

4–022 An assignee can only take proceedings in its own name to enforce the chose without having to join the assignor where the assignment is legal. A legal assignment is one which complies with s.136 of the Law of Property Act 1925:

> "(1) Any absolute assignment by writing under the hand of the assignor (not purporting to be by way of charge only) of any debt or other legal thing in action, of which express notice in writing has been given to the debtor, trustee or other person from whom the assignor would have been entitled to claim such debt or thing in action, is effectual in law (subject to equities having priority over the right of the assignee) to pass and transfer from the date of such notice (a) the legal right to such debt or thing in action; (b) all legal and other remedies for the same; and (c) the power to give a good discharge for the same without the concurrence of the assignor."

The following can only take effect as an equitable assignment: oral assignments, assignments by way of charge, assignments of part of a chose, assignments where notice is not given to the debtor, and agreements to assign: *Phelps v Spon-Smith & Co* [2001] B.P.I.R. 326. An equitable assignee can sue in its own name but has to join the assignor. After an assignment, the assignor cannot sue in its own name without joining the assignee: *Three Rivers DC v Bank of England* [1996] Q.B. 292. Section 136 only excludes security assignments by way of charge; an assignment by way of mortgage will fall within the section if the other conditions are met: *Tancred v Delagoa Bay Railway Co* (1889) L.R. 23 Q.B.D. 239. Giving notice of assignment has at least four advantages:

- until it receives notice, the debtor can obtain a good discharge by paying the assignor;
- giving notice ensures priority to the assignee over successive dealings with the chose;
- the notice may bring the assignment within s.136 and allow the assignee to sue in its own name; and
- after receipt of the notice, the debtor cannot raise any fresh and independent equities in defence to an action brought by the assignee.

The reason why a particular assignment of a debt is equitable rather than legal may also affect the ownership of its proceeds. If the only reason is lack of notice, the proceeds are received by the assignor on trust for the assignee but if it is because the assignment is by way of security the position is more complicated. If the assignment is by way of specific equitable charge, the proceeds remain in the assignor's ownership but cannot be used without the assignee's consent. If the proceeds fall within a floating charge, the assignor can deal with them in the ordinary course of business (Ch.2). Before enforcement, the assignee only has a security interest in the proceeds. Once either charge has been enforced, for example by the appointment of a receiver, property in the proceeds passes to the assignee. The effect of a fixed charge is similar to an escrow arrangement in that the debt will belong absolutely to the assignor but be subject to contractual restrictions that only the assignee can fulfil.

(b) Construction examples

4–023 A term in a nominated subcontract that the contractor holds the subcontractor's proportion of retention on trust has been held to be an equitable assignment to the subcontractor of the appropriate proportion of the contractor's interest in the retention: *Re Tout and Finch* [1954] 1 W.L.R. 178. In an insolvency situation, time is often of the essence. Whether acting for a creditor pressing for payment or an insolvency practitioner wishing to conclude an agreement, equitable assignment may be the most expeditious means of transfer. For example, in *Golden Sand v Easy Success Enterprises* (1999) 2 H.K.C. 356 a contractor in financial difficulty was unable to prove payment of nominated subcontractors who approached the employer for direct payment under the equivalent of clause 27(c) of JCT 63. Instead, it was agreed between the employer, the contractor and nominated subcontractors that all future payments to nominated subcontractors would be made direct by the employer. The works were completed, the defects liability period expired and the final account was agreed. Approximately $380,000 was due to one of the nominated subcontractors which included retention of $175,000. Before this was paid by the employer, the contractor went into liquidation. It was held by the High Court of Hong Kong that the direct payment agreement divested the contractor of its rights in respect of money due to nominated subcontractors (the element representing retention being subject to a trust in any case). The court ordered payment to the nominated subcontractor of money the employer had paid into court. The basis of the decision seems to have been that the agreement amounted to an equitable assignment to the subcontractors of the proportions of certified sums ascertainable from the architect's certificates. In both cases, it seems that the assignment was equitable because it was only part of a chose, namely the debt owed by the employer.

12. Priorities

A contractor may pacify its most aggressive creditors, particularly those **4–024** threatening to issue a winding up petition, by assigning sums due or to become due from employers. In the event of the contractor's formal insolvency, such assignments can give rise to competing claims between the assignee, the employer, an insolvency practitioner appointed over the contractor, a secured creditor, an execution creditor, a guarantor, and the subcontractors or suppliers on the project concerned. The question of priorities will be looked at first where money assigned has already been earned by the date of notice of assignment and then where it has not been earned. The distinction is also relevant in ascertaining what assets are retained by receivers or administrators under a sale of business agreement: e.g. *Explora Group v Hesco Bastion* [2005] EWCA 646. In that case an analogy was drawn between earned and unearned agency commission and existing and future fruits of a contract in the context of non-assignability clauses (para.101).

Money already earned

An assignment for value of a sum already earned before liquidation will be **4–025** valid against a liquidator even if payment does not become due until after the start of the liquidation. So where six-sevenths of the work had been performed and two-sevenths remained to be paid for, an assignment of less than one-seventh of the contract sum before the contractor's bankruptcy was valid against the trustee even though it did not become due for payment until after the trustee had completed the work: *Re Toward Ex p. Moss* (1884) L.R. 14 Q.B.D. 310; *G&T Earle v Hemsworth RDC* (1929) 140 L.T. 69. There is no distinction between an assignment of the value of work payable on completion of an agreed stage and an assignment of retention: *Drew v Josolyne* (1887) L.R. 18 Q.B.D. 590. See also *Aicken & Son v Bradley* [1916] N.Z.L.R. 659.

What is the position where a contractor has a claim for a quantum meruit? As the test is whether the sum assigned has been earned by the date of assignment not whether it is due or payable, it appears that an assignment of sums due or to become due on a quantum meruit ought to be valid against a contractor's liquidator, although there appears to be no authority. The same appears to be the case where the contract provides for payment against interim certificates. On the same argument, an assignment of sums due or to become due would include the value of uncertified work in progress executed before liquidation because the value had been earned and merely required ascertainment. It is therefore important for an insolvency practitioner to value the work completed before the commencement of the insolvency procedure before deciding whether to complete a contract.

An employer does not want to pay twice for the same work. An assignee will be anxious to obtain payment of the whole amount assigned. An administrator wants to ensure that the company recovers the amount budgeted against the cost to complete in order to recover the projected profit. A bank or other holder of a valid fixed charge over book debts will take priority against an assignee of sums due or to become due insofar as they are represented by certified sums or retention at the date of liquidation: *Re Jason Construction* (1972) 16 C.B.R. 297. It is thought that this principle would apply also to an assignment of an entitlement under an arbitration award: *Bank of New South Wales v The King* [1918] N.Z.L.R. 945.

Money not yet earned

4–026 In the example referred to above, if the fractions had been reversed and two-sevenths of the work was still to be done but only one-seventh of its value remained to be paid for, an assignee would not take priority against the contractor's trustee in bankruptcy or liquidator if the latter completed the contract because there was nothing due at the date of the assignment: *Tooth v Hallett* (1869) L.R. 4 Ch. App. 242. Compare the Canadian case of *Creditel v Terrace Corporation* (1983) 50 C.B.R. 87 where no money became payable to the assignee as the trustee elected not to continue the contract. The same applies to an assignment of profits where it can be shown that they would only be earned at the end of a contract: *Hewitt v Official Assignee of Barnes and Keble* [1930] N.Z.L.R. 416, *Re Jones Ex p. Nichols* (1883) L.R. 22 Ch. D. 782. It is important to examine the terms of the assignment. If the assignee is entitled to be paid out of specific progress payments (e.g. from the first and second certificates), it will not take priority over a liquidator if those particular payments are insufficient to pay the assignee in full: *Gardner and Yeoman v Watson* (1937) G.L.R. 141.

The assignee may also lose priority if, after deduction of liquidated damages payable prior to receipt of the notice of assignment, there is no net sum payable to the assignor: *White v Ensor* (1882) 11 N.Z.L.R. 207. Compare *Fulton v Dornwell* (1885) 4 N.Z.L.R. 207 where an assigned debt was extinguished by the cost to complete and the employer was held to have acted reasonably and mitigated its loss. See also *Re Yeadon Waterworks v Wright* (1895) 72 L.T. 538.

Chapter 5

Set–off, Abatement and Deduction

As an informal security for payment, set-off plays a crucial role in construction insolvency. The concept has generated a large body of industry-related case law. This chapter gives a concise overview of set-off and abatement at common law by reference to construction cases; explores how the standard forms expand, restate or reduce the rights of the parties at common law; describes the type of industry claims that can be set off and the problems that arise in practice; notes how certain litigation procedures achieve an outcome equivalent to set-off; and summarises limitations on the common law imposed by statute; ending with an examination of the relevant terms of the Housing Grants, Construction and Regeneration Act 1996 and a discussion of their relation to the general law. The effect on set-off where one of the parties is insolvent is considered in Ch.18. Set-off is the primary construction security. Any alteration to rights of set-off will adjust the allocation of insolvency risk. **5–001**

1. General principles

If A is claiming money from B and B has a money claim against A, set-off is the process by which the two claims are set against each other producing a balance. If A brings a claim, B will have a cross-claim. Set-off is a progressive defence to payment to the extent that the cross-claim approaches the amount of the claim. Once it equals or exceeds the claim, the cross-claim amounts to a complete defence (Wood 1989, 1995; Derham 2003). Set-off differs from abatement, counterclaim and valuation (fig.5.1). **5–002**

Abatement is a defence that a claim should be reduced by the value of goods or services not in accordance with the contract. Counterclaim is not a defence but a separate cause of action which the rules of the court allow a defendant to assert in proceedings brought by a claimant. Valuation is neither a defence nor a claim but a procedure for bringing a claim into existence by converting work in progress into debt. All three aspects are considered later.

Set-off cannot arise if either claim or cross-claim is for property other than money. A cross-claim for delivery up of a chattel or for possession of land cannot be set off against a money claim. Nor can set-off apply unless both claims are owed between the same persons in the same capacity. A cannot set off against B a cross-claim which it brings as trustee for C. This is because B's claim is against A whereas the cross-claim against B is really made by C. Thus it is not possible to set off against a claim for rent due

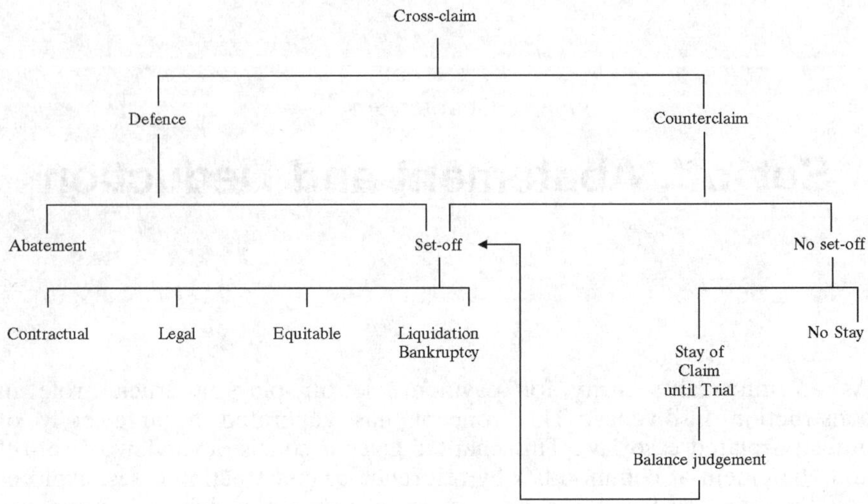

Fig.5.1

from a corporate tenant a cross-claim for building work carried out by shareholders of the tenant: *Hamilton Ice Arena v Speirs* [2001] NZCA 308. Set-off performs various functions. Where both parties are solvent, set-off exists for commercial convenience: why insist on two payments, when one will do? If a dispute arises, set-off avoids unnecessary proceedings: why have two actions if a claim for the balance will do?

2. Equitable set-off

5–003 This is also known as "transaction set-off" (Wood 1989). Equitable set-off arises where the two claims are so closely connected that it would be unjust to allow one to proceed without setting off the other: *Federal Commerce & Navigation Co Ltd v Molena* [1978] Q.B. 927 at 974. It does not matter whether they are liquidated or unliquidated: a cross-claim for damages can be set off against a claim in debt and vice versa. Unliquidated claims can also be set off against each other: *Bim Kemi AB v Blackburn Chemicals* [2001] 2 Lloyd's Rep. 93. In that case the Court of Appeal adopted a two-stage test:

- Is the cross-claim "flowing out of and inseparably connected with the dealings and transactions which also give rise to the claim" even though it may arise under a separate contract? (*Bank of Boston v European Grain* [1989] 1 A.C. 106 at 112, *per* Lord Brandon)
- Would it be manifestly unjust to allow the claimant to succeed on its claim without bringing the cross-claim into account? (*Federal Commerce v Molena*)

There are thus two elements: the degree of connection and the question of justice. A positive answer to the first question will usually result in a negative answer to the second. An exception is a claim for freight which the court has long enforced free of set-off (*Bim Kemi* at para.38), and presumably industry claims based on a valid adjudicator's decision (Ch.12). For a stark example of a refusal of equitable set-off in respect of claims arising under the same contract see *Sankey and Yeomans v Helping Hands Group* [2000] C.P. Rep. 11.

Equitable set-off is not simply a matter of discretion for the judge. It involves a careful and thorough examination of the facts and the application of equitable principles. It is as if the cross-claim were woven into the fabric of the claim. The creditor must have defaulted on the very obligation for which he seeks payment (Wood 1989, para.1–20). Originally equity intervened to provide relief where a debtor had an equity (a cross-claim) which "impeached the title to the legal demand" (the claim): *Rawson v Samuel* (1841) Cr.& Ph.161. It was a question of conscience. The court asks: Does the cross-claim ethically undermine the claim? Does it subvert the whole legitimacy and foundation of the claim? Has either party acted manipulatively? See *Eller v Grovecrest Investments* [1995] 2 W.L.R. 278, *Esso Petroleum v Milton* [1997] 2 All E.R. 593, *Star Rider v Inntrepreneur* [1998] 16 E.G. 140, *NextCall Telecom v BT* [2000] All E.R. (D) 2371.

Set-off allowed

The cases referred to above can be compared with *Hanak v Green* [1958] 2 Q.B. 9 (discussed below) and *Government of Newfoundland v Newfoundland Railway Co* (1888) L.R. 13 App. Cas. 199, analysed in Ch.18. Set-off was allowed in both cases. Consider also *Railtrack Telecom Services v Marconi* [2002] EWHC 1546 in which a cross-claim for damages for misrepresentation in connection with one contract (to identify sites adjacent to railway lines on which to erect masts for mobile phones) was held eligible for set-off against a claim for an ascertained sum due following the exercise of a put option to purchase shares in a telecoms joint venture company under another. The two agreements were intertwined, "part of one larger joint venture which embraces them both" (at para.27, *per* Morison J.). The cross-claim was weak, however, and the court ordered the defendant to pay £20 million, the amount of the put option, into court as a condition of being allowed to defend the proceedings. Similarly in a Malaysian case a purchaser agreed to buy land from a builder who in turn agreed to construct a "shophouse" on the land within 18 months. It was completed five months late, by which time the purchaser still owed the final instalment of the purchase price. The purchaser successfully claimed the amount by which liquidated damages for the builder's delay exceeded the unpaid balance of the price. She was not in breach of contract in withholding the final instalment since she was entitled to an equitable set-off which extinguished the builder's claim: *SEA Housing v Lee Poh Choo* [1982] 2 M.L.J. 33. More recently in *Safeway Stores v Interserve* (2005) 105 Con. L.R. 60, defects in a supermarket car park emerged after practical completion. The owner engaged independent contractors to rectify them and attempted to recover the cost from the contractor under a collateral warranty. The contractor had been engaged under JCT 80 by an employer with a separate contract with the owner, Safeway. The employer was also a party to the warranty but had gone into liquidation owing the contractor £1.2 million on its final account. Clause 3.3 of the warranty provided: "The Contractor shall 5–004 owe no duty or have any liability under this deed which are greater or of longer duration than that which it owes to the Developer under the Building Contract." Ramsey J. held that the contractor's unsatisfied claim against the employer operated as a complete defence by way of equitable set-off against the owner's claim. The purpose of clause 3.3 was "to restrict [the contractor's] liability to Safeway to its equivalent liability to [the employer] under the building contract" (para.51). The court also considered that Safeway would have been bound by any settlement in respect of the defects reached between employer and contractor (para.53).

Set-off denied

5–005 In *Aboussafy v Abacus Cities* [1981] 4 W.W.R. 660 there were three separate contracts between employer and contractor. In 1974 the contractor sold the site to the employer, in 1975 the contractor agreed to build on the site for the employer, and in 1977 the contractor agreed to manage the building for the employer. The contractor went into receivership and the receiver sued for recovery of sums due under the management agreement. The employer unsuccessfully claimed a set-off in relation to cross-claims it had under the sale and construction contracts. The cross-claims were unliquidated so legal set-off was not available; and the three contracts were not sufficiently connected to qualify for equitable set-off. In another Canadian case, *Dominion Lumber v A&S Builders* (1999) 45 C.L.R. (2d) 303, equitable set-off was denied as between a claim by a supplier for the price of materials delivered to subcontractors on site A as agent for the contractor and a cross-claim by the contractor for damages for delayed delivery to site B. The two sites were unconnected and there was no link between the claims, e.g. it was not suggested that late delivery on site B was caused by non-payment on site A. Although the contractor and the supplier had a running account which was settled every month, invoices being issued for each delivery, on the evidence they had agreed to treat each contract separately.

3. Abatement

5–006 Abatement is a defence that a claim for the price should be reduced by the value of goods or services which are not in accordance with the contract: *Mondel v Steel* (1841) 8 M. & W. 858. A payment obligation can be "discharged" by abatement: *Gilbert Ash v Modern Engineering* [1974] A.C. 689 at 722. A valuation of the goods or services supplied is made and then deducted from the value which they would have had if they had conformed. It may be possible to do this by referring to the contractor's tender or invoice, but if he has charged a lump sum a fair assessment has to be made, supported if necessary by an expert's report. In some cases diminution in value can be determined by reference to the cost of repair although "the cost of remedial works does not become the measure of abatement. It is merely a factor which may be used either in isolation or in conjunction with other factors for determining diminution in value" (*Multiplex v Cleveland Bridge* [2006] EWHC 1341 at para.652, *per* Jackson J. distinguishing *Duquemin v Slater* (1993) 35 Con. L.R. 147). Cost of repair was adopted as the method of ascertaining abatement in *Multiplex* as the partially completed steelwork had no market value in a conventional sense; it only had value to the contractor who was under an obligation to complete the structure (para.654). The defence goes to the quality of the product or service rather than the performance of some other obligation. A contractor's claim for payment cannot therefore be reduced by the loss suffered by the employer through the supplier's delay: *Mellowes Archital v Bell Projects* (1997) 87 B.L.R. 26. Abatement is by reference to the value of the service as a whole rather than specific parts. If a contractor agrees to construct a reinforced concrete beam but omits the steel, it appears the employer can abate the whole price rather than just the value of the missing reinforcement: *Hodgson v Miller Construction* (unreported, 1995, noted in Jones 1999).

Abatement applies to the supply of work and labour but probably not to contracts for professional services such as an architect's appointment: *Hutchinson v Harris* (1978) 10 B.L.R. 19. This distinction is not always easy to make. Relevant factors are the nature of the personnel involved, the scope of work and the question whether the obligations assumed are those ordinarily undertaken by professionals: *Foster Wheeler v Chevron* (unreported, February 29, 1996, Judge Humphrey LLoyd Q.C.). Abatement is a common law doctrine but it is now contained in s.53 of the Sale of Goods Act 1979 as far as contracts for the sale of goods are concerned.

The same facts can give rise to abatement and equitable set-off as alternatives: *Barnett v Peter Cox* (1995) 45 Con. L.R. 131. It is possible that the cost of rectifying defective work could be the same as the difference between the value of the work done and the value it would have had if it been carried out in accordance with the contract: consider *Barrett Steel v Amec* (1997) 15 C.L.D. 10–07. This might be the case if the replacement builder is not called upon to take down defective work and make good or perhaps where the cost of labour or materials falls after the original work is done. In most cases, however, the amount of an equitable set-off will be higher than an abatement in order to take account of preparatory work, increased costs and the possibility that the original builder may have underestimated for the work in its tender. The right to abate is implicit in the words "work properly executed" in clause 30 of JCT 1998: consider *Barrett Steel v Amec*; *Multiplex v Cleveland Bridge*, para.662. In *Ellis Tylin v Co-operative Retail Services* [1999] B.L.R. 205 at 221, the employer reserved an express right of abatement under a maintenance contract, with an additional right to deduct a 10 per cent retention from future payments if the work represented by the abatement was not done.

It was recently said of abatement, set-off and counterclaim that "such niceties and their discussion is and has for some time been distinctly passé": *Birse v Eastern Telegraph* [2004] EWHC 2512, at para.35, *per* Judge Humphrey LLoyd Q.C. Even so, there may still be the need to distinguish between them in the context of exclusion or limitation clauses. It is a question of construction whether the contract excludes abatement or equitable set-off or both: *Acsim v Danish Contracting* (1989) 47 B.L.R. 55. Abatement is not subject to the law of limitation in view of its character as a defence at common law. Neither is equitable set-off as it amounts to an equitable defence on the merits: *Filross Securities v Midgeley* [1998] 3 E.G.L.R. 43. If the cross-claim is in reality a counterclaim, it cannot be set off in equity if it has a shorter limitation period than the claim and the claimant waits until after the cross-claim has expired before issuing proceedings: *Aries Tanker v Total Transport* [1971] 1 W.L.R. 185. Similarly a legal set-off cannot be made if the debt the subject of the cross-claim is statute-barred. In *Multiplex v Cleveland Bridge*, at para.97, the contractor advanced a claim for remedial work by way of abatement rather than set-off of damages in order to evade a cap on the subcontractor's liability for damages contained in the contract but the court did not consider this issue.

4. Legal set-off

5–007 Legal set-off is also known as "independent" or "statutory" set-off. Its origins lie in an eighteenth-century statute which was passed to remedy the mischief of a debtor being sent to prison for non-payment when he had a cross-claim which could not be taken into account because it was not connected with the claim. The statute has been repealed but legal set-off is preserved in the rules of the court (CPR Part 16.6) because it prevents circuity of action: *Fuller v Happy Shopper Markets* [2001] 1 W.L.R. 1681, para.21.

Liquidated/ascertainable	*Unquantified*
Sums due	Work in progress
Invoiced sum	*Quantum meruit*
Book debts	Future debts
Rent/mesne profits	General damages
Freight	Interest as special damages
Taxed costs	Untaxed costs
Judgment debt	Order for damages to be assessed
Liquidated damages	Restitutionary claims
Contractual interest	Damages in tort

Fig.5.2

The main requirement is that the claims on both sides have to be liquidated debts or money demands which can be ascertained with certainty at the time of pleading: *Hanak v Green* [1958] 2 Q.B. 9. If not already liquidated by the time the defence is served, the quantum of the claims must be easily ascertainable without estimation or valuation: *Aectra Refinery v Exmar* [1994] 1 W.L.R. 1634, at 1649–1651. See fig.5.2. Legal set-off is available only in judicial proceedings; it is not available where the cross-claim has been referred to arbitration or, it appears, adjudication (see below). There is a distinction between the time a right to set-off arises and the time it takes effect. The cross-claim only operates as a defence if judgment is entered: *Stein v Blake* [1996] 1 A.C. 243 at 251. Legal set-off:

> "is not a substantive defence to the claim but a procedure for taking an account of the balance due between the parties . . . It entitles the defendant to require that the merits of an unrelated cross-claim be tried in the same action and converts the plaintiff's original cause of action into the right to a balance due on the taking of the account" (*Aectra Refinery v Exmar* [1994] 1 W.L.R. 1634 at 1648, *per* Hoffmann L.J.).

Legal set-off is a defensive right: it can be used as a shield, not as a sword. The court encourages the claimant to give credit for the debtor's cross-claim where legal set-off is available, so much so that if credit is not given, the claimant may be penalised in costs: *Stooke v Taylor* (1880) L.R. 5 Q.B.D. 569.

Set-off allowed

The classic example of legal set-off in the industry is a claim for liquidated **5–008** damages by the employer under one contract which is answered by a cross-claim for a certified sum by the contractor under another. There is authority that liquidated damages constitute a debt for the purpose of this kind of set-off: *Fletcher v Dyche* (1787) 2 Term Rep. 32, *Hargreaves v Action 2000* [1993] B.C.L.C. 1111 at 1113. This right is normally restated in the contract and may be cut down by a condition that the architect issues a certificate of delay before the employer can set off or deduct liquidated damages. Another possible application is where a contractor is carrying out more than one contract for an employer. The employer may have a liquidated cross-claim if the contractor fails to comply with an architect's instruction and the employer engages an alternative contractor for that purpose. Clause 4.1 of JCT 98 provides that the cost is recoverable from the defaulting contractor either by deduction from sums due or as a debt. Legal set-off is more likely to occur between suppliers where mutual trading is on the basis of invoices, as in the manufacturing and retailing industries.

Set-off denied

A cross-claim for an over-payment which relies for quantification on a **5–009** surveyor's report prepared for one of the parties will be treated as unliquidated: *Hargreaves v Action 2000* (1992) 36 Con. L.R. 74. The case concerned nine subcontracts all signed on the same day which concerned nine petrol stations which the contractor was building for an employer. The subcontractor went into receivership and there was a sum due from the contractor on one of the subcontracts. On the receiver issuing proceedings, the contractor defended by way of set off of cross-claims for overpayment arising under two of the others. The cross-claims could not be set off in equity as they were unconnected or at law because they were unquantifiable without the intervention of an agreed third party or the court and the receiver succeeded in his claim. Contrast the court's treatment of claims for quantum meruit considered in Ch.3. See also *OCWS Logistics v Soon Men Construction* (1999) 2 S.L.R. 376.

Alternative pleas

In *Fuller v Happy Shopper Markets* [2001] 1 W.L.R. 1681 it was argued that **5–010** the defence of equitable set-off is only available in cases where legal set-off has been denied (para.26). This submission was rejected but Lightman J. went on to hold that the correct approach is to consider equitable set-off first. Only if the defendant fails on that ground is it necessary to consider legal set-off. Similarly, where the facts give rise to claims for abatement and equitable set-off, the court should look at the equitable set-off claim first, citing *Sim v Rotherham Council MBC* [1987] Ch. 216 at 258.

5. Contractual set-off

5–011 In its purest form, contractual set-off creates a set-off where none existed before, but it is also a way of describing terms which expand, restate, exclude, or cut down common law remedies.

Expanding the common law

5–012 There is a gap in the common law: set-off is not available where the cross-claim is both unrelated to the claim and unquantifiable without reference to a third party: *Axel Johnson v MG Mineral* [1992] 1 W.L.R. 270. A contract can fill this gap and expand on the common law in several ways: (1) by allowing set-off of unliquidated cross-claims arising from unrelated contracts or unconnected claims; (2) by conferring express rights of deduction; and (3) by allowing either or both parties to exercise group set-off. Provisions of this kind give rise to a contractual set-off.

Set-off across contracts

5–013 The contract in *Gilbert Ash v Modern Engineering* [1974] A.C. 689 allowed set-off ". . . in connection with this or any other contract". See also *Pillar v Croudace* (unreported, December 19, 1984, Judge Sir William Stabb Q.C.) referred to later. Clause 24 of GC/Works/4 (1998) allows set-off by the government against any sums due to the contractor of claims arising "under or in respect of the Contract or under or in respect of any other contract between the Contractor and the Crown". The new form of subcontract for use on government contracts steps down to subcontract level the right to set off against contracts contained in the main contract. Outside insolvency, in one case the government of Hong Kong failed in an attempt to set off across contracts in respect of cross-claims against a contractor (LLoyd 1992).

Deduction

5–014 As well as expanding common law set-off, contracts also confer rights of deduction which are not available under the common law. In the industry, these include retention of a percentage of the value of work done until completion and cash discount of a percentage of the difference between the value of the work done and the retention: *Team Services v Kier* (1993) 63 B.L.R. 76.

Group set-off

5–015 There is little case law dealing with group set-off clauses in ordinary commercial contracts: see for example *Sinochem International v Mobil Sales* [1999] 2 Lloyd's Rep. 769 (set-off claim failed), *Pillar v Croudace* (unreported, December 19, 1984, Judge Sir William Stabb Q.C.). In *Gallemos v*

Barratt Falkirk [1990] S.L.T. 98, Gallemos purchased the business and assets of a contractor which had gone into receivership. The business concerned the supply of timber framed housing kits to developers. It then entered into a contract with Barratt Falkirk for this purpose. It was a condition of the contract that Gallemos sourced components from another company in the Barratt group, Barratt Construction. Unfortunately, Construction had previously dealt with the insolvent contractor from whom Gallemos purchased the business and required security for payment. This took the form of a clause which would be included in all acknowledgement forms sent in response to orders placed by Gallemos:

> "We Barratt Construction Limited reserve the right to contra any monies overdue by you from the following Barratt Companies and if payment is not made within 60 days we will effect contra as necessary from these companies named below assuming they are a debtor of yours."

The clause set out the names of seven companies of which Barratt Falkirk was one. When Gallemos went into receivership, it was owed £33,500 by Falkirk and owed £32,000 to Construction. Falkirk tendered the balance of £1,500 to the receivers who rejected it and sued for the whole debt. The dispute was narrowed when it was found that it was only possible to match acknowledgments to orders totalling £19,000. It was agreed that the clause formed part of the contract in respect of those orders. The court treated the issue as one of assignment by way of security rather than set-off. This was apparently because of lack of mutuality as the other Barratt companies were not parties to the contract. (It was not argued that Construction entered into each contract with Gallemos for itself and as agent for each company in the Barratt group.) The assignment argument assumed that on Construction's confirmation of each order, Gallemos would make a security assignment of such sums as may from time to time be owing from any of the named Barratt companies. On default of payment by Gallemos within 60 days, Construction could enforce the security and call for payment as assignee from whichever of the Barratt companies happened to be indebted to Gallemos at the time (or more than one if necessary to discharge the debt). In deciding in favour of the receivers, the court held that the clause fell short of the requirements for an assignment, not least because there was insufficient evidence of intention to assign by Gallemos.

It is worth noting clause 51 in GC/Works/1 (1998) which allows set-off not only across all contracts between the parties but across any contract there may be between companies forming part of the contractor's group and government departments who together comprise the Crown. It is especially unusual in giving the contractor group companies reciprocal rights of set-off against the government departments. Although this clause would be effective from the Crown's point of view in allowing any government cross-claim to be set off, it may not be enforceable by an associate of the contractor for reasons similar to those applied in *Gallemos v Barratt*. Where a prospective employer is a member of a group of companies, the contractor may, without acquiring any rights against them, be asked to invoice one or more other companies in the group. This can result in confusion over the identity of the contracting party, e.g. *Planned Storage Systems v DPN Design Consultants* [2002] EWHC 2670. It is possible for a group set-off arrangement to arise informally if one group company acts as agent for another but the necessary constituents of an agency relationship would have to be made out, e.g. *Wates Building Group v Jones* (1996) 59 Con. L.R. 97.

Restating the common law

5–016 It is common for construction contracts to restate the common law without intending to affect either party's rights. The only problem with this approach is that, where a clause only sets out some of the rights available at common law, it opens up the possibility that the parties intended to exclude the common law except for those rights: *Perar v General Surety* (1994) 66 B.L.R. 72. In *Dawnays Ltd v Minter Ltd* [1971] 1 W.L.R. 1205 Lord Denning M.R. treated a clause of this type as the peg on which to hang the proposition that claims for payment under a certificate were exempt from set-off unless and until cross-claims were upheld in a court order or arbitrator's award. This became known as the "rule" in *Dawnays*' case. The court had before it a claim by a subcontractor for payment under a certificate which was met by a contractor's cross-claim for damages for delay. The contract provided that:

> "The contractor shall notwithstanding anything in this subcontract be entitled to deduct from or set off against any money due from him to the subcontractor (including any retention money) any sum or sums which the subcontractor is liable to pay to the contractor under this subcontract."

Set-off was refused as the court construed this clause (in particular the word "liable") as restricting the contractor's right of set-off to liquidated and ascertained sums established by a judgment or an arbitration award or otherwise admitted due. It is not stated in the judgment whether submissions were made on the question whether the general law had been excluded. Damages were estimated initially at £47,000 and later revised to £61,000 and exceeded the subcontractor's claim. The court seems to have considered that the revision to the calculation indicated a lack of credibility in the cross-claim as a whole and rejected it as shadowy; although from the report it does appear that the delays were on the critical path of the works. It also seems that the architect had not issued a certificate of delay which may have been a condition precedent to the set-off of any cross-claim for delay-related costs. The decision could perhaps be justified on either of these grounds but the court went on to elaborate a general principle that interim certificates created a special class of debt against which set-off was not possible apart from cases of fraud.

> "Every businessman knows the reason why interim certificates are issued and why they have to be honoured. It is so that the subcontractor can have the money in hand to get on with his work and the further work he has to do . . . An interim certificate is to be regarded virtually as cash, like a bill of exchange. It must be honoured. Payment must not be withheld on account of cross-claims, whether good or bad-except so far as the contract specifically provides. Otherwise any main contractor could always get out of payment by making all sorts of unfounded cross-claims.

All the more so in a case like the present, where the main contractors have actually received the money" (at 1209, *per* Lord Denning M.R.).

Lord Denning thus departed from the mainstream of existing law by attempting to restrict equitable set-off to sums which have been adjudged or admitted. This case was followed in a series of later decisions of the Court of Appeal before they were all overruled by the House of Lords in *Gilbert Ash v Modern Engineering* [1974] A.C. 689. The general law is therefore that a certified sum is not insulated from set-off like freight or a bill of exchange unless the contract clearly provides otherwise.

Modifying the general law

The majority of industry disputes over set-off concern the contractual exclusion or restriction of common law rights. The precise effect of the contractual term on the general law is a question of construction in each case. **5–017**

Express exclusion

In the leading case of *Gilbert Ash v Modern Engineering* [1974] A.C. 689 it was decided that the parties to a building contract had not excluded the common law. The case concerned a subcontract which included the following term: **5–018**

> "If the subcontractor fails to comply with any of the conditions of this subcontract, the contractor reserves the right to suspend or withhold payment of any monies due or becoming due to the subcontractor. . . . The contractor also reserves the right to deduct from any payments certified as due to the subcontractor and/or otherwise to recover the amount of any bona fide contra accounts and/or other claims which he, the contractor, may have against the subcontractor in connection with this or any other contract."

It was held that the first paragraph was unenforceable as a penalty since it would permit the contractor to withhold an indeterminate amount for a trivial breach. Lord Reid thought that the second paragraph was "intended to supersede and be substituted for the common law right of set off" (at 698), but the majority were of the view that it did not go far enough to exclude the contractor's rights under the general law.

> "So when one is concerned with a building contract one starts with the presumption that each party is to be entitled to all those remedies for its breach as would arise by operation of law, including the remedy of setting up a breach of warranty in diminution or extinction of the price of material supplied or work executed under the contract. To rebut that presumption one must be able to find in the contract clear unequivocal words in which the parties have expressed their agreement that this remedy shall not be available in respect of breaches of that particular contract" (at 718, *per* Lord Diplock).

The absence of "clear unequivocal words" excluding the law of abatement and equitable set-off meant that the set-off clause was treated as restating the common law and the contractor was entitled to set off its cross-claims for defects and delay against the subcontractor's claim for payment. The Court of Appeal has confirmed that it is equally open to the parties to exclude legal set-off: *BICC v Burndy* [1985] 1 Ch. 232 at 248. By contrast, a term in a guarantee that payment would be made "in full, without any set-off or counterclaim by the Guarantor, free and clear of and without any deduction or withholding" was sufficient to exclude the common law: *Try Build v Blue Star Garages* (1998) 66 Con. L.R. 90, discussed in Ch.16. Project finance contracts intend the contractor to pay liquidated damages in cash rather than by way of set-off against the final payment due to it. Hence set-off is usually excluded in principle (Vinter and Price 2005). The parties may vary the contract to exclude set-off against specific receivables. In *Henry Walker Etlin Contracting v Mostia Constructions* [2001] QSC 89 for example a subcontractor argued that an acceleration agreement reached with the contractor included a term that variations would be paid for without set-off in return for an increased retention.

Exclusion by implication

5–019 The common law of abatement and set-off may also be excluded by implication: *Gilbert Ash v Modern Engineering* [1974] A.C. 689 at 723, *per* Lord Salmon; see also *Melville Dundas v Hotel Corporation of Edinburgh* [2007] S.C. 12, discussed in Ch. 16. In a series of decisions, the Australian courts have construed construction contracts as excluding the common law of set-off by implication, taking into account the fact that the parties agree to continue the works even though a disputes procedure has been invoked and the presence of many express rights of deduction: *Algons Engineering v Abigroup Contractors* (1998) 14 B.C.L. 215. See also *Hempseed v Durham Developments* [1998] 3 N.Z.L.R. 265 and *Pembenaan v Dr Leela's Medical Centre* [1995] 2 M.L.J. 57, *John Sisk & Sons v Lawter Products* (unreported, High Court of Ireland, November 13, 1976). Such arguments are not likely to be persuasive in the UK (Derham 2003, paras 5.104–5.109). An argument based on the implied exclusion of set-off was rejected in *BOC Group v Centeon* (1999) 63 Con. L.R. 104. A contract may provide that its terms are exhaustive of the parties' rights and remedies against each other: *Strachan & Henshaw v Stein Industrie* (1997) 87 B.L.R. 52.

Excluding abatement

5–020 In *Mottram Consultants v Bernard Sunley* [1975] 2 Lloyd's Rep. 197 there were no "clear unequivocal words" excluding abatement and set-off but there had been clear words conferring such rights which were deleted by the parties. The House of Lords took the deleted words into account when construing the contract and held that the common law had been excluded. It appears that abatement was excluded by the parties' deletion of the word "deduct" as the right of "deduction" had been specifically referred to in *Mondel v Steel*. The term "deduction" is not a legal term of art. If a clause merely prohibits deduction, it may in context not be clear enough to exclude common law set-off: *Connaught Restaurants v Indoor Leisure* [1994] 1 W.L.R. 501, *Valeo Materiaux v VTL Automotive* [2005] EWHC 1855, para.57. In context a term excluding the right to withhold payment of "sums properly due" may not be sufficient to exclude set-off: consider *Esso Petroleum v Milton* [1997] 2 All E.R. 593.

Excluding set-off but not abatement

On its true construction, a contract may exclude set-off but not abatement: *Acsim v Danish Contracting* (1989) 47 B.L.R. 55. The case concerned a set-off provision in the Blue Form of non-nominated subcontract as amended by the parties: "The rights of the parties to this subcontract in respect of set-off are fully set out in these conditions and no other rights whatsoever shall be implied as terms of this subcontract relating to set-off." The court construed this clause as excluding rights of set-off under the general law but not the principle of abatement and the contractor was allowed to abate the claim. **5–021**

Agreements for lease

There have been several cases arising out of agreements for lease in which the parties agree that the tenant will take up a lease on practical completion. It would be open to the tenant to set off against the landlord's claim for rent a cross-claim for damages for defects in the building: *British Anzani v International Marine* [1980] Q.B. 137. If the land is sold, the tenant can still set off a cross-claim for defects against the assignee's claim for rent falling due before he bought the land: *Muscat v Smith* [2003] 1 W.L.R. 853. But equitable set-off would not be available against rent falling due after the assignment: *Mortgage Corporation v Ubah* (1997) 73 P. & C.R. 500. As a matter of policy, as opposed to legal principle, it is difficult to see why a distinction should be drawn between set-off against rent accruing before and after an assignment: *Edlington Properties v JH Fenner* [2005] N.P.C. 119 (at para.28). **5–022**

Exclusion by receivers

A commercial reason for excluding set-off is to protect the creditor in case it gets into financial difficulty or the charge holder where receivers are appointed: *John Dee v WMH Ltd* [1997] B.C.C. 518 at 522, affirmed [1998] B.C.C. 972 at 976. On their appointment, receivers often write to customers asking them to agree to place further orders on terms that payment is made free of set-off. The receivers' letter may also attempt to exclude set-off in respect of existing contractual obligations: see *Alstom Transport v Elequip Projects* [2004] EWHC 2897 discussed in chapter 18, and *Melville Dundas v Hotel Corporation of Edinburgh* [2007] S.C. 12, discussed in Ch.16. **5–023**

6. Arbitration and adjudication

As a consequence of its historical origins, legal set-off is not available where either claim is subject to arbitration: *Aectra Refinery v Exmar* [1994] 1 W.L.R. 1634. This restricts the availability of legal set-off in the industry. In that case there was a claim for a sum due pursuant to a settlement agreement which was met by a cross-claim for a liquidated sum arising under a separate dispute which had been stayed to arbitration. The cross- **5–024** claim could not be set off since it was not being pursued by a court action. By contrast, in *Glencore Grain v Agros Trading* [1999] 2 Lloyd's Rep. 410, legal set-off was allowed even though both claim and cross-claim were brought to enforce arbitration awards as the claims had by the date of the action both become debts enforceable in court.

This restriction does not apply to equitable set-off which is available even where the cross-claim has been stayed to arbitration: *Aectra Refinery v Exmar* [1994] 1 W.L.R. 1634 at 1649. So for example in *Bim Kemi AB v Blackburn Chemicals* [2001] 2 Lloyd's Rep. 93 set-off was allowed of a cross-claim which had been stayed to ICC arbitration in Stockholm "on the grounds of the potential injustice, delay and extra cost which would arise from a requirement to conduct a separate arbitration" (at para.15, *per* Potter L.J.). The claim was for damages for repudiation of an oral agreement which had no provision for arbitration.

In an arbitration, the position seems to be that a cross-claim may be set off where it amounts to an abatement or an equitable set-off but not where the respondent claims legal set-off or makes a counterclaim which is not also an equitable set-off: Aeberli (1992), Berger (1999). This is on the basis that abatement and equitable set-off are in the nature of substantive defences and may, depending on its terms, fall within the scope of the arbitration agreement: *Ronly Holdings v JSC Zestafoni* [2004] B.L.R. 323, *Metal Distributors v ZCCM Investment Holdings* [2005] EWHC 156. For example set-off was refused in *Econet Satellite Systems v Vee Networks* [2006] 2 Lloyd's Rep. 423 because on their true construction the UNCITRAL arbitration rules restricted set-off to cross-claims arising under the same contract as the claim. There is no authority on the question whether legal set-off can be argued in an adjudication but by analogy with arbitration it would appear that such a defence would fall outside the adjudicator's jurisdiction. This is a further benefit of adjudication to claimants.

7. Industry claims and cross-claims

5–025 Claims by contractors are usually for payment of liquidated sums under certificates or some other payment mechanism or unliquidated claims for damages or loss and expense, finance charges, or *quantum meruit*. Claims by employers are either liquidated (liquidated damages and other sums which the contract deems to be recoverable as a debt) or unliquidated, e.g. damages claims for delay or defects or to recover an overpayment. See generally Ch.3.

Delay and disruption

Equitable set-off

5–026 A contractor's claim for payment for work done and materials supplied may be defeated by equitable set-off of a cross-claim for delay. In *Young v Kitchen* (1878) L.R. 3 Ex. D. 127 a contractor agreed to construct two buildings for an employer. On completion, over £6,000 became due and payable which the contractor assigned to Young. Young gave notice of assignment to the employer. On the employer's failure to pay, Young as assignee sued for the balance of the contract sum but was met by a cross-claim of £2,400 for delay and £800 for defects. Both buildings were completed late and the employer was unable to let them for commercial purposes. It was held that the employer was entitled to set off its cross-claim for damages against the assignee's claim. Although it was unliquidated, the cross-claim flowed out of the same transaction and the criteria for equitable set-off were satisfied. In *Ellis Mechanical Services v Wates Construction* (1976) 2 B.L.R. 57 a subcontractor claimed release of retention after the main contract had been terminated. The contractor's cross-claim included an element of delay-related costs incurred on a different contract between the parties that had not been terminated. It appears that set-off was refused because the two contracts were not sufficiently connected. The Court of Appeal later considered a claim by a subcontractor for an interim payment which was met by a cross-claim from the contractor for general damages based on a nine-week delay overtopping the claim: *NEI Thompson v Wimpey* (1987) 39 B.L.R. 65. Applying *Gilbert Ash v Modern Engineering*, it was decided that the contractor could "rely on their cross-claim by way of set-off under the rule in Mondel v Steel" (at 73, *per* Lloyd L.J.). This is not strictly correct because that case concerned abatement and delay costs could not abate the claim. The real basis of this decision appears to have been equitable set-off along the lines of *Young v Kitchen*.

Contractual set-off

In *Gilbert Ash v Modern Engineering*, part of the contractor's cross-claim **5–027** against the subcontractor related to delay. The House of Lords allowed equitable set-off of the delay costs although the decision may also be justified on the basis that the delay costs could be set off under an express term. In practice, set-off for delay requires substantiation otherwise a cross-claim is at risk of being rejected, as in the Australian case of *Melbourne Glass v Coby Constructions* (1998) 14 B.C.L. 409, and *Sable Contractors v Bluett Shipping* [1979] 2 Lloyd's Rep. 33 in which a cross-claim for rent under a prospective lease failed as being too speculative. In *MJ Gleeson v Taylor Woodrow* (1989) 49 B.L.R. 95, a management contractor's cross-claim for delay against a subcontractor's claim was refused on the ground that liquidated damages had already been deducted under the contract: to allow set-off would permit double recovery. The management contractor was responsible for certifying interim payments and deducted both liquidated and general damages for delay before ascertaining the certified sum.

> "The only thing that was wrong about [the management contractor's] statement of account was that it treated the deductions which I have mentioned as a certifiable matter capable of reducing the sum certified . . . That would be tantamount to saying that a cross-claim unrelated to the value of work done and materials supplied diminishes their value which would, of course, be nonsense" (at 106, *per* Judge John Davies Q.C.).

Such deductions could only give rise to a set-off (*Mellowes Archital v Bell Projects* (1997) 87 B.L.R. 26) but that had already been made by deducting liquidated damages. Even if the contractor complied with the set-off procedure, it might still be refused set-off in the absence of the necessary certificate of delay, e.g. if the architect's certificate under clause 12 of NSC/4 had not been issued before the date on which the payments became due. See also *John Mowlem v Carlton Gate* (1990) 21 Con. L.R. 113; *RM Douglas v Bass Leisure* (1990) 53 B.L.R. 119.

Disruption

5–028 If the issue turns on a short point of law or on the construction of the contract, the court will decide it on an application for summary judgment. The Court of Appeal has refused a contractor's claim for set-off based on disruption on the ground that, properly construed, clause 23 of NSC/4a required compliance with the set-off machinery in respect of disruption as well as delay: see *Pillar v DJ Higgins* (1986) 10 Con. L.R. 46. The cases do not often deal separately with set-off for disruption: see *Chatbrown v Alfred McAlpine* (1986) 11 Con. L.R. 1 which concerned clause 15(2) of the Blue Form (1971 edition, July 1978 Revision), and *Pitchmastic v Birse Construction* (unreported, May 19, 2000, Dyson J.), on an amended DOM/2 form.

Defective work

5–029 Cross-claims in respect of defective work give rise to equitable set-off of the cost of rectification or an abatement of the claim by the value of the defective work: *Lowe v Holme* (1883) L.R. 10 Q.B.D. 286. The claim may depend on the conduct of the employer. If it refuses to allow the contractor access to rectify defects appearing during the defects liability period the employer's set-off may be restricted to the cost to the contractor of rectifying them: *Pearce & High v Baxter* (1999) 66 Con. L.R. 110. *Hanak v Green* [1958] 2 Q.B. 9 has been described as "the foundation stone of the modern law" of equitable set-off: *Raytheon v Space Cargo* (unreported, July 27, 2000, *per* Judge Raymond Jack Q.C.). In *Hanak v Green* the employer claimed the cost of rectifying defects. The contractor had cross-claims for variations on a *quantum meruit*, expenses incurred through a denial of access to the site and damages for trespass to goods (the employer had disposed of some of his workmen's tools). The Court of Appeal allowed set-off in respect of all of three cross-claims. Those for *quantum meruit* and damages in tort did not strictly arise out of the contract but were nevertheless held to be so closely associated with the claim as to satisfy the criteria for equitable set-off. This shows the liberal attitude adopted by the English courts to equitable set-off where claim and cross-claim arise out of the same project. It is difficult to understand how a claim for damages for trespass to goods could "impeach" a defects claim unless perhaps they were needed to rectify the defective work. This aspect was not necessary for the decision and only Sellers L.J. actually dealt with it. The allowance of set-off of the claim for a *quantum meruit* has also been criticised (Spry 1969, Meagher, Gummow and Lehane 2002, Derham 2003). This case was however later approved in *Gilbert Ash v Modern Engineering*. In the Australian case of *Leighton Contractors v East Gippsland Catchment Management Authority* (2001) 17 B.C.L. 35, a construction manager was refused summary judgment on a claim for payment of his fee on the ground that the employer had an equitable set-off in respect of defective work carried out by trade contractors. The fee was based on time spent and expenses incurred. It appears that the cross-claim was eligible for set-off as damages for breach of the manager's duties of supervision and approving the trade contractors' invoices for payment. The court left undecided whether the employer also had a defence of abatement against the construction manager's fee. Compare with *L/M International v The Circle Limited Partnership* (1992) 37 Con. L.R. 72 at 153.

Over-valuation

In *Acsim v Danish Contracting* (1989) 47 B.L.R. 55 a subcontractor's claim for payment was reduced on the basis that it did not represent "the total value of the subcontract works properly executed and of the materials and goods properly on site." The contractor had the right "to show that the subcontractor had not in fact earned all of the sum claimed, or . . . to defend the action by showing that by reason of breach of contract the work was worth less than the sum claimed" (at 70, *per* Ralph Gibson L.J.). The court concluded that the contractor had a defence in respect of work omitted from the contract, unauthorised variations deemed to have been included in the contract sum, over-valuation of authorised variations, over-valuation of incomplete work, and work not properly executed. There can also be room for argument about the correctness of a method of measurement, the true interpretation of a bill item, the effect of an instruction etc. Some of these arguments formed the basis of the contractor's unsuccessful argument in *Ellis Mechanical Services v Wates Construction* (1976) 2 B.L.R. 57, in which Lord Denning M.R. stated: **5–030**

> "That is all very well; but, as all of us with experience of building and construction cases are aware, there is inevitably something due. In most cases it can be said with certainty that £x is due. In such a case the court gives judgment for the £x and gives leave to defend as to the balance. Otherwise it would mean that the builders and contractors could be kept out of a great portion of their money indefinitely by the employer simply saying 'I want to investigate the accounts'" (at 62).

In that case set-off was refused on the basis that:

> "The ordinary practice is that there must be some real basis, not a shadowy basis, for showing that there is an issue worthy of investigation by the courts. The defendants' answer amounts to no more than 'We dispute the claim'. That is not enough" (at 64, *per* Lawton L.J.).

Valuation arguments of this kind are particularly well suited to adjudication by an industry professional. See also *NEI Thompson v Wimpey* (1987) 39 B.L.R. 65.

Quantum meruit

One of the peculiarities of the industry is that the parties sometimes fail to form a contract at all, even where substantial works are involved. In *Pillar v Croudace* (unreported, December 19, 1984, Judge Sir William Stabb Q.C.) **5–031** a subcontractor's claim for an interim payment under the Green Form was met by a counterclaim from the contractor in respect of charges and services rendered, defective work and damages for delay and disruption. The subcontract provided that: "Notwithstanding anything contained in this subcontract, Croudace Limited or any associated companies will be entitled to deduct from this subcontract, any monies due, whether under this subcontract or otherwise." On the evidence, the court concluded that no contract had been formed and dismissed the subcontractor's application for summary judgment but granted leave to the subcontractor to amend its pleading to claim payment on a *quantum meruit*. Exactly how the contractor ensures that its cross-claims are taken into account in the process of valuing the subcontractor's work on that basis is not entirely clear.

Prospective claims

5–032 The court requires clear words to show the parties' intention that a bona fide estimate of future loss would be sufficient to justify a set-off. The introduction of construction management as a new form of procurement led to many one-off contract forms which included clauses of this kind. In *Rosehaugh v Redpath Dorman Long* (1990) 50 B.L.R. 69 two claims were made by the employer for £5.2 million and £3.1 million respectively, representing bona fide estimates of the construction manager. Summary judgment was refused by the Court of Appeal: the trade contractor had arguable cross-claims for variations, loss and expense or damages, and its set-off rights had not been excluded by the contract. The text of a similar prospective set-off clause is given in *Mowlem v Eagle Star* (1992) 33 Con. L.R. 131 at 135. See also *Birse v Eastern Telegraph* [2004] EWHC 2512, at para.22. As part of the final accounting process following an insolvency termination under the NEC3 form, the project manager has power to deduct an amount representing a forecast of the anticipated additional cost to complete.

8. Counterclaims and summary procedures

Counterclaims

5–033 A counterclaim is a cross-claim which the rules of the court allow to be asserted in proceedings brought by the creditor: *Stooke v Taylor* (1880) L.R. 5 Q.B.D. 569. A counterclaim differs from set-off and abatement in three ways. It can be used to claim any form of relief and is not restricted to a claim for money. Set-off admits a claim and then asserts a cross-claim up to the value of the claim whereas a counterclaim does not use a claim but is asserted independently of it. A counterclaim is offensive in character and puts forward an autonomous cause of action, whereas set-off and abatement are essentially defensive. There are some cross-claims which can only take effect as a counterclaim: (1) a cross-claim which is unliquidated and independent of the claim; (2) where set-off is excluded by the contract or where a condition precedent to set-off has not been complied with; and (3) if the cross-claim exceeds the claim, the excess can only be advanced as a counterclaim. If a counterclaim falls within any of the recognised categories of set-off discussed earlier, it will be allowed as a set-off in the proceedings. In contrast a claim in respect of defective work advanced by an employer in response to a contractor's claim for a quantum meruit cannot be properly characterised as a counterclaim: *ERDC Group v Brunel University* [2006] B.L.R. 205, para.123. Whether a counterclaim can be set off is highly material when considering an application for security for costs against a defendant. In *L/M International v The Circle Limited Partnership* (1992) 37 Con. L.R. 72, the court ordered an employer to provide security for a counterclaim of £15 million against a construction manager suing for an unpaid balance of prime cost. The report includes a discussion on the nature of equitable set-off under a construction management agreement.

Summary procedures

Where a claimant can show that the defendant has no reasonable prospect **5–034** of successfully defending its claim, it may obtain an order for summary judgment under CPR Part 24. This procedure is restricted to cases where there is no real dispute on the facts and, if there is a point of law involved, that it can be easily and crisply dealt with by the court. If it is possible but improbable that a defence to the claim will succeed, the court has discretion to make a conditional order requiring a payment into court to be made or particular steps taken. The court also has power under CPR Part 25 to order a defendant to make an interim payment of such amount as it thinks just where liability is admitted or the court is satisfied that if the action proceeded to trial, the plaintiff would obtain judgment for a substantial sum. A substantial interim payment was awarded in *Harmon v House of Commons (No. 2)* (2000) 72 Con. L.R. 21 to a contractor which entered voluntary liquidation after its tender for a substantial public works contract was wrongfully rejected. The court held that, had it been awarded the contract, it would not have gone into liquidation. The company was awarded its tender costs, loss of profit and other sums. In such applications the court takes into account any set-off or counterclaim on which the defendant might be entitled to rely. The court estimates the prospects of success on the counterclaim and only considers an interim payment as a proportion of a balance judgment after having deducted the counterclaim from the claim: *Shanning v Wimpey* [1985] 3 All E.R. 475, *Imodco v Wimpey* (1987) 40 B.L.R. 1, *Crown House v Amec* (1990) 6 Const. L.J. 141. The security function of the counterclaim is therefore preserved in its entirety. If the court stays execution of the creditor's judgment pending the hearing of the counterclaim, the result is the same as if set-off had been ordered. Special difficulties arise in the context of adjudication (see chapter 12). In a case where an administrator of a steel erection subcontractor applied for an interim payment, it was held that, taking counterclaims into account, the court could not make the order (*Smallman Construction v Redpath Dorman Long* (1988) 47 B.L.R. 15), but when the case was remitted to the Official Referee, he was prepared to order summary judgment of part of the claim as the counterclaims could not be set off.

9. Statutory and other limitations

Legal set-off, liquidation set-off and bankruptcy set-off are all derived from **5–035** statute. As well as creating rights of set-off, however, statute restricts them in certain situations. The most significant are contractual terms deemed to be unfair, or to contravene the policy of insolvency law or fail to comply with construction industry legislation.

Unfair Contract Terms Act 1977

5–036 Where a set-off exclusion clause is contained in standard terms of business, it may fall within the ambit of the Unfair Contract Terms Act 1977 and be unenforceable as unreasonable. The issue for the court is whether a relevant term, when construed as a whole, is reasonable, rather than the particular part relied upon as excluding set-off rights: *Esso Petroleum v Milton* [1997] 2 All E.R. 593 at 602. A clause in a contract for the provision of mechanical plant was held unreasonable on the ground that it prevented the withholding of payment by reason of any "payment, credit, set-off, counterclaim, allegation of incorrect or defective goods or for any other reason whatsoever which the customer may allege excludes him for performing his obligations hereunder": *Stewart Gill v Horatio Meyer* [1992] 2 All E.R. 257. In contrast, a term was held to be reasonable where it excluded set-off against payment "in cash or as otherwise agreed [of] all sums immediately when due". The term was contained in standard conditions adopted by the freight forwarding industry after extensive negotiations between representative bodies and was in widespread use: *Schenkers v Overland Shoes* [1998] 1 Lloyd's Rep. 498. The 1977 Act also applies to attempts to exclude set-off for cross-claims for misrepresentation: *Skipskredittforeningen v Emperor Navigation* [1998] 1 Lloyd's Rep. 66. The aim is to strike down clauses limiting liability rather than setting out a procedure for dealing with claims. There is no policy bar against a clause excluding set-off of cross-claims for fraud. It is clauses excluding liability for fraud which are at risk.

Insolvency Act 1986

5–037 Contracts attempting to exclude liquidation or bankruptcy set-off will not be upheld by the courts: *National Westminster Bank v Halesowen* [1972] 1 All E.R. 641, *British Eagle v Air France* [1975] 2 All E.R. 390. This is because they contravene the *pari passu* rule that unsecured creditors receive the same proportion of their debt by way of dividend: s.107 of the Insolvency Act 1986.

Housing Grants, Construction and Regeneration Act 1996

5–038 This Act is considered below. It prohibits any "withholding" against a sum due unless prior notice has been given. There are two scenarios: set-off against a payment falling due under the contract, and set-off against an amount ordered to be paid by an adjudicator. The Act applies to contractual set-off as well as set-off and abatement at common law.

Common law restrictions

5–039 Apart from statute, there are some common law restrictions on set-off. The first is that a claim brought on a dishonoured cheque is immune from set-off unless the cross-claim is based in fraud, duress, invalidity or a total failure of consideration: *Nova (Jersey) Knit v Kammgarn* [1977] 2 All E.R. 463. The second is that set-off is not available where the claim is brought in respect of a cancelled direct debit arrangement, subject to the same exceptions: *Esso Petroleum v Milton* [1997] 2 All E.R. 593.

10. Housing Grants, Construction and Regeneration Act 1996

The background to the 1996 Act is given in chapter 3, which discussed ss.109, 110(1), and 113. Set-off and abatement in connection with contracts falling within the Act are regulated by ss.110(2) and 111 (see TeCSA 2004 for case summaries). **5–040**

> "110(2). Every construction contract shall provide for the giving of notice by a party not later than five days after the date on which a payment becomes due from him under the contract, or would have become due if (a) the other party had carried out his obligations under the contract, and (b) no set-off or abatement was permitted by reference to any sum claimed to be due under one or more other contracts, specifying the amount (if any) of the payment made or proposed to be made, and the basis on which that amount was calculated.
>
> 111(1). A party to a construction contract may not withhold payment after the final date for payment of a sum due under the contract unless he has given an effective notice of intention to withhold payment. The notice mentioned in section 110(2) may suffice as a notice of intention to withhold payment if it complies with the requirements of the section. (2) To be effective such a notice must specify (a) the amount proposed to be withheld and the ground for withholding payment, or (b) if there is more than one ground, each ground and the amount attributable to it, and must be given not later than the prescribed period before the final date for payment."

Withholding under the contract

"Withholding" is not a term of art, it can have a wide meaning: *Marubeni Corp v Sea Containers* (unreported, May 17, 1995, Waller J.). Employers often abate certified sums on the ground that they are only liable to pay sums "properly due". This gave rise to an argument that abatement adjusted the receivable by reducing the sum due against which withholding was made (Barrett 1998). In *Rupert Morgan Building v Jervis* [2004] B.L.R. 18 the Court of Appeal gave "withholding" a wide construction so as to include both set-off and abatement on the ground that both cause damage to a contractor's cash flow. "Withholding" does not however refer to valuation and it remains open to the paying party to control the constitution of the receivable through the valuation process. Section 111 implies that set-off has to be considered in stages: **5–041**

- First, is the notice "effective", i.e. does it comply with the formal requirements of the section?
- Second, is the ground relied upon eligible for abatement or set-off at common law or permitted under the contract?

- Third, is the amount proposed to be withheld properly "attributable" to the ground?

The case law has focused on the first stage since if the notice is not formally effective there is no need to go further. But it is possible to satisfy the first test but fail the others. These aspects have not come before the court since equitable set-off will apply in the vast majority of cases and, in any event, they are for the adjudicator to decide. The court has described s.111 as laying down a "comprehensive code" dealing with set-off where the 1996 Act applies: *VHE Construction v RBSTB Trust Co* [2000] B.L.R. 187, para.66; *Ale Heavylift v MSD (Darlington) Ltd* [2006] EWHC 2080, at para.67. It sometimes appears as if the withholding notice has displaced the common law of set-off and abatement as the legal mechanism for dealing with cash flow disputes, but the 1996 Act has not abolished the common law categories; in the absence of an effective notice they are merely suspended until the next payment period. This is apparent from the terms of s.110(2)(b) and the reference to the "ground for withholding" in s.111(2)(a). It seems that this refers to two matters: the nature of the payer's cross-claim and the category of set-off or abatement relied upon. It does not follow from a finding that the notice is formally effective that the withholding is valid. After all, if the payer did not have to substantiate the ground it could evade payment by a series of notices based on spurious cross-claims. In other words, although the notice is necessary, it is not sufficient. This conclusion highlights a risk to the unpaid contractor invoking the statutory right to suspend under s.112 (see Ch.14). The 1996 Act operates as a statutory gloss on the common law. If a contract provides for notice before set-off, it is acknowledging the application of common law to the contract, even though it places a restriction on its operation. The Act forces disclosure in advance and to that extent requires paying parties to be efficient in their contract administration. An area of potential injustice is where the cross-claim is based on a repudiation by the receiving party which occurs after the final date for payment.

Because adjudicators' decisions are usually enforced, even if manifestly wrong, it follows that, in cases where the 1996 Act applies, the common law of set-off and abatement has in effect been excluded from the ambit of the court. Many disputes referred to adjudication do not proceed further. In those that do, the need for the set-off may have disappeared by the time the substantive hearing takes place. The court's opinion on the underlying dispute, in particular on any point of law involved, would be obiter. There is unlikely to be the same degree of legal argument before the court as was formerly the case. This appears to be the price paid for a quick and comparatively cheap procedure. Hiving off disputes to adjudicators may mean that set-off as part of construction law will stop developing. Approaches may develop among adjudicators which are inconsistent with legal principle but which cannot be challenged. On the other hand the scope of equitable set-off in the industry is so wide that a cross-claim is more likely than not to qualify for set-off. Many aspects of common law set-off are restated in the express terms so that it may not matter in practice if the adjudicator misunderstands the law. The one area of difficulty could be legal set-off (see above).

Withholding against an adjudication decision

This fundamental issue is not directly addressed in the 1996 Act or the Scheme. Section 108(3) states: "The contract shall provide that the decision of the adjudicator is binding until the dispute is finally determined by legal proceedings, by arbitration . . . or by agreement." The Scheme is in similar terms, with the additional obligation to "comply with it" in the interim (para.23(2)). In this area, more than any other, the court has suffered the conflict between the literal words of the statute, the policy they are thought to implement, and its overriding duty to do justice. **5–042**

After a series of decisions, some of which are conflicting (Carey 2004), the weight of authority has come down in favour of the proposition that a withholding notice must normally be served in order to set off against an adjudicator's decision. In *Interserve v Cleveland Bridge* [2006] EWHC 741, a subcontractor applied to enforce an adjudicator's decision for payment of £1.3 million. During the court hearing, the same adjudicator in a subsequent dispute ordered payment of £1.4 million by the subcontractor to the contractor. Jackson J. refused to set off the amount ordered by the second decision and granted summary judgment to the subcontractor. The sum due under the first decision had been unpaid for 10 weeks. The sum due under the second would not become payable for another 10 days and the subcontractor was not yet in breach in respect of that obligation. The court held that summary judgment was in accord with the policy of the 1996 Act, its true interpretation, and previous authority.

One of the purposes of the 1996 Act was "to ensure that payments passed promptly down the line to contractors, subcontractors and suppliers, without the hold-ups which had become endemic in the construction industry by the 1990s" (para.33). Where there are successive adjudications, "absent special circumstances, the losing party must comply with the adjudicator's decision. He cannot withhold payment on the ground of anticipated recovery in a future adjudication based upon different issues" (para.43). Otherwise, "The result might be that no adjudicator's decision is implemented; each award simply takes its place in the running balance between the parties. Such an outcome is plainly contrary to the policy of the 1996 Act" (para.46).

The decision was based on ss.108(3) and 111(1) together with the CIC Model Adjudication Procedure by which the parties agreed to implement any decision without delay whether or not the dispute was taken further. The cases relied on were *VHE Construction v RBSTB Trust Co* [2000] B.L.R. 187; *Ferson Contractors v Levolux* [2003] B.L.R. 118; *MJ Gleeson v Devonshire Green* (unreported, March 19, 2004, Judge Gilliland Q.C.); *David McLean Contractors v The Albany Building* (unreported, November 10, 2005, Judge Gilliland Q.C.). Subsequent cases have followed the reasoning in *Interserve*. In *William Verry v Camden LBC* [2006] All E.R.(D) 292 the parties agreed to comply with a decision without prejudice to their other rights under the contract. Ramsey J. did not construe the reservation of common law rights as allowing the employer to withhold payment of the decision on the ground that a subsequent certificate had been issued showing a balance in its favour. All the reservation did was to preserve the employer's rights to pursue its claim for overpayment by separate action after having honoured the decision. In a different context Lord Hoffmann appeared to take a different view of the effect of a reservation of rights on the 1996 Act and this aspect of the decision may need to be reconsidered: see *Melville Dundas v George Wimpey* [2007] 1 W.L.R. 1136. In *Hillview v Botes Building* [2006] EWHC 1365 an employer sought to enforce an adjudication decision in respect of liquidated damages to which the contractor admitted it had no defence. The contract was JCT 98 with contractor's design incorporating the CIC adjudication procedure. Shortly before the decision was issued the contractor submitted its final account and applied for summary judgment on it. It argued as follows: that the two applications should be heard together, or that the enforcement application ought to be disposed of at trial rather than by way of summary hearing, or that judgment should be entered against it only for the difference between the two claims, or that a stay of execution be granted. There was no allegation of insolvency against the employer. Judge Toulmin Q.C. enforced the decision. However he observed that as the contractor's application for summary judgment was fixed for hearing within two weeks:

> "If there had been a serious risk in those circumstances that money paid over on a provisional basis would not be recovered promptly in the event that Botes succeeded in obtaining summary judgment . . . I should have given sympathetic consideration to granting a stay for the short time until that date or making other orders to secure the sum which had not been paid" (para.33).

Perhaps this is an example of the "special circumstances" referred to by Jackson J. above.

Other cases have reasoned that the seven-day period for compliance with an adjudication decision referred to in s.111(4) re-sets the final date for payment and allows the other party to serve a withholding notice in respect of a new cross-claim not raised in the adjudication: *Conor Engineering v Les Constructions Industrielles* [2004] B.L.R. 212, compare *Solland International v Daraydan Holdings* (2002) 83 Con. L.R. 109. Following *Interserve*, it appears that this argument is untenable. The period is only part of the adjudication machinery; it is not intended to set a new final date for payment as that term is used in s.111.

The status of an adjudication decision has become clearer. According to the conservative view the terms of the 1996 Act and the Scheme that a decision was binding and had to be complied with equated the decision with an ordinary contract term. Set-off against it could be seen as compliance since it recognised the validity of the claim. Under the more radical view which has prevailed a decision has an inherent immunity from set-off. Both views gave a purposive effect to the 1996 Act. The conservative approach gave effect to the 1996 Act against the background of the common law. The 1996 Act required that certain terms be embodied in construction contracts. As contractual terms, many believed that they were not sufficiently clear to rebut the presumption in *Gilbert Ash v Modern Engineering* that underlying common law rights were not excluded as against the decision. The claimant would still be protected against spurious set-offs by the court's ability on the application for summary judgment (a) to limit cross-claims available for set-off against a decision to those arising after the final date for payment of the claim; and (b) to reject the cross-claim as shadowy or as ineligible for set-off within the recognised categories. In practice the vast majority of decisions would be honoured.

Construction contracts involve a constant interplay of mutual, interdependent rights and obligations. It remains to be seen whether the radical view goes too far in separating claim from cross-claim, undermining the juridical basis of equitable set-off in the cause of cash flow.

Withholding across contracts

This is possible in cases where the claim and cross-claim are so closely related as to make it unjust to allow one without taking the other into account (equitable set-off) or are both debts or easily ascertainable with certainty without the need for valuation (legal set-off) or the contract expressly allows it. In its analysis of responses to a recent consultation document the DTI stated: "It seems reasonable to consider that perhaps 20% of contracts contain cross contract set-off clauses" (DTI 2006, 49). Two-thirds of respondents thought that equitable set-off was flexible enough to meet the industry's needs and that the use of contractual clauses permitting set-off across contracts should be allowed only in the context of framework agreements (at 48). The DTI's conclusion was that legislative intervention to invalidate such clauses was not justified: **5–043**

> ". . . a prohibition of cross-contract set-off clauses would need to include a statutory definition of closely related contracts as a general exception to the prohibition. As well as including framework agreements this would be needed to provide sufficient certainty over when the practice is possible via principles of equity. However well defined, we believe it is inevitable that litigation would arise over how the statutory definition applied and when it is possible to set off between contracts. A further perverse impact could be that contracting parties seek to exploit this exception in more contracts than currently include cross-contract set-off clauses. A further point to note is that this is an area which insolvency law generally leaves to parties to agree in their contracts" (at 24).

It is noticeable that legal set-off, where the claim and cross-claim do not have to be related, is not mentioned. All a contractual term normally does is to supplement the common law by filling the lacuna between legal and equitable set-off (see above, para.5–012). Equitable set-off was introduced to do justice between the parties, legal set-off on practical grounds. A contractual set-off clause is appropriate where the parties wish to treat all their dealings on the same footing rather than contract by contract. As such it seems unexceptionable. But if it is invalidated, is it necessary to make any exceptions? The common law will continue to provide some protection. It does not seem relevant to bring in insolvency law, other perhaps than as an argument in favour of contractual set-off clauses. On bankruptcy or liquidation, a set-off is applied across contracts by statute whatever the contracts may say (see Ch.18). A contractual term would merely anticipate what applies in that event.

Finally it is worth mentioning s.110(2). This section deals with service of a payment notice within five days after a payment becomes due "or would have become due if (a) the other party had carried out his obligations under the contract, and (b) no set-off or abatement was permitted by reference to any sum claimed to be due under one or more other contracts". The 1996 Act thus "equates what is due with what would be payable if the contractor . . . had carried out its obligations and there was no set-off or abatement under some other contract": *Alstom Signalling v Jarvis Facilities* [2004] EWHC 1285, para.26, *per* Judge Humphrey LLoyd Q.C. Section 110(2) and the second sentence of s.111(1) were introduced at a very late stage in the legislative process, only a few weeks before the Bill gained Royal Assent at the end of July 1996. Section 110(2) is oddly drafted. As a defence to a money claim, set-off does not normally prevent a sum becoming due, except for equitable set-off where claim and cross-claim are mutually interdependent. Similarly, abatement of a claim can only arise from defective performance of the contract under which the claim arose. The section is, however, clear enough in providing that the payment notice must state the gross amount before any withholdings are made.

International comparisons

5–044 The reforms made by the Housing Grants, Construction and Regeneration Act 1996 have inspired construction-specific legislation in other jurisdictions such as Australia and New Zealand (Dawson 2003), and Singapore (Chan 2005). A number of interesting comparisons can be made. The first concerns the purpose of the legislation. Under the Building and Construction Industry Security of Payment Act 1999 of New South Wales a failure to serve a payment schedule in response to a payment claim resulted in a "debt due" for payment, but in proceedings to recover the debt it was not clear whether the debtor could defend by setting off a cross-claim. In other words it was not clear from the statutory language whether its aim was to promote clarity as to when a construction receivable arose or to make the resulting debt immune from set-off. The 1999 Act was amended by the Building and Construction Industry Security of Payment Act Amendment Act 2002 to make it clear that immunity from set-off was indeed to be accorded to a debt arising by virtue of the Act: ss.15(4) and 16(4). The English and Australian statutes are not directly comparable, but broadly speaking it seems that what required an amending statute in New South Wales has been dealt with by judicial intervention in the UK.

The second aspect worth noting is that the New South Wales legislation has extended the definition of pay when paid to any provision which "makes the liability to pay money owing or the due date for payment of money owing, contingent or dependent on the operation of another contract": s.12(2)(c) of the 2002 Act. This section appears to invalidate "pay when certified" and stands as a precedent should the DTI ever take that aspect further. Thirdly if an adjudication decision under the New South Wales legislation is not paid the claimant can request an adjudication certificate from the authority to whom the application was made. Such a certificate entitles the claimant to suspend work and, on being filed as a judgment at court, to a debt certificate under the Contractors' Debts Act 1997. Service of the debt certificate on the employer operates as a statutory assignment under that Act to the subcontractor of any receivable then owing to the contractor up to the amount of the debt. Reference should also be made to the Cole Report (2003), the most recent study of payment practices in the Australian construction industry, which includes a draft federal statute which draws on the New South Wales legislation in particular.

Summary

Set-off is best seen as a series of layers (common law, contract, statute, insolvency) which require an archaeological approach. This reflects the hoarding instincts of the law, e.g. the right to legal set-off was not lost when the original need for it disappeared. The relation between the 1996 Act and the common law appears to be as follows: **5–045**

1. To exclude the common law of set-off requires clear unequivocal words or implication: *Gilbert Ash v Modern Engineering* [1974] A.C. 689.
2. Simply including an adjudication procedure in a contract not governed by the Act will not exclude the common law: *Parsons Plastics v Purac* [2003] B.L.R. 334.
3. The Act is procedural in effect and is not intended to exclude the parties' underlying rights of set-off and abatement, although a failure to follow the notice procedure under ss.110(2) or 111 may lead to the postponement of the right of set-off or abatement to the next sum falling due for payment.
4. To that extent the terms imported by the Act or the Scheme rebut the presumption that common law rights have not been restricted or limited in some way.
5. The same applies to a contract not governed by the Act which includes similar terms as far as set-off and abatement are concerned: *Lovell Projects v Legg and Carver* [2003] B.L.R. 452.

Chapter 6

Plant and Equipment

Since the nineteenth century, terms have been included in construction contracts in respect of plant and equipment which attempt to place the employer in the position of a secured creditor in the event of the contractor's insolvency. Such terms rarely use the explicit language of a banking document. As a consequence, a large body of case law has developed which turns on the precise words used (Wallace 1995). The context of the dispute has led the court to construe similar wording in different, sometimes opposite, ways. This chapter explores the issues which arise when the terms of the contract confer property or security interests in the contractor's plant. **6–001**

1. Historical background

The nineteenth-century cases cast a long shadow and it is hard to understand them without some awareness of the historical background. When domestic work was carried out under building lease agreements, employers bought materials themselves or made advance payments to builders for that purpose (Emden 1882, Summerson 1978). These agreements provided that the materials would become the employer's property on being brought to site. In *Blake v Izard* (1867) 16 W.R. 108 counsel for the employer submitted that: **6–002**

> "the lessors now very often sell the materials to the builders, and advance so largely on the works as they progress that builders without any capital accept large contracts, and become virtually merely the foremen of the lessors. In this case, the materials were originally nearly all the property of the lessors, and the lessors would, without such an agreement as this, have no security for the value of their materials until they were used on the land, and so became part and parcel of the freehold. The builder having no capital to purchase them with, is, by giving this security to the landlord, enabled to get everything that he wants, either directly from the landlord, or by the otherwise unsecured pecuniary advances of the landlord from tradesmen who are paid with the landlord's money."

From quite early on, plant and equipment was included within the scope of these clauses. It is not clear whether this derived from building leases or arose out of the need for heavy plant for the construction of the railways, e.g. *Banbury v Daniel* (1884) 54 L.J. Ch. 265, a railway contract under which the contractor was paid 75 per cent of the value of the plant in advance.

Whatever their original function, vesting clauses gradually disappeared from building contracts and contractors simply agreed not to remove materials from site without the architect's consent. This change may have occurred through the emergence and increasing financial strength of main contractors, the growing use of subcontractors or the replacement of building lease agreements by other forms of contract. Possibly, statutory intervention such as the Sale of Goods Act 1893 had an effect (see Ch.7). At any rate, Alfred Hudson did not include vesting clauses in the precedents in his book on building contracts published in 1891. Plant vesting clauses are still used in contracts for engineering work (clause 70.2 of NEC3 extends the concept to materials) but their function is not clearly articulated. In what follows, it is therefore worth bearing in mind the following questions:

- What commercial function does the vesting clause have? Is it just another device to manage insolvency risk?
- How does the clause respond to the diversity of plant and equipment and their various different uses on the project?
- How does the vesting clause relate to other terms, e.g. as to payment or termination?

2. Definitions

6–003 Plant and equipment are not terms of art; their meaning shifts from contract to contract (Lonergan 2005). Some contracts do not distinguish between them. The main issue is whether the chattel is to form part of the permanent works or to act as the means of construction. Thus "plant" may refer to a structure fixed to the land as part of the permanent works e.g. a chemical plant. "Equipment" has two senses: (a) items intended to be fixed but as temporary works, e.g. a tower crane; and (b) a range of items from hand tools at one end of the spectrum to a tunnel boring machine at the other. Some equipment may be left in the ground even though not originally intended as part of the permanent works, e.g. sheet piling for a cofferdam. Valuable items constitute potential security assets for the employer. Part 2 of FIDIC (4th edn) gives the example of a dredger for reclamation work whose capital value might exceed the contract sum.

The main commercial risk attaching to plant and equipment is lack of availability to meet the programme. This might be caused by periods of high activity in the industry when suppliers cannot meet the demand for specific plant, problems in the design or manufacture of the plant leading to delays in replacement, the contractor diverting the plant to other contracts, the contractor defaulting in payment to leasing companies leading to repossession, as well as claims by the contractor's creditors. Availability risk affects both temporary and permanent works. Further questions arise:

- What is the connection between availability risk and the interests in plant and equipment granted to the employer?
- Removal of plant from site can be an early warning sign of a contractor's insolvency. Does the court view availability risk merely as a sub-set of insolvency risk?

- If the item in question is not intended for the permanent works (in the same way as goods and materials are) why should the employer stipulate for a right of property rather than a security interest?

3. Rights against plant and equipment

It is useful to consider the employer's rights against the contractor's plant and equipment under three headings: contract, property and security (Barber 1998). **6–004**

Contractual rights

A distinction needs to be drawn between the position before and after a termination. Before termination, the employer's main concern is that the contractor brings plant and equipment needed for the project onto site at the appropriate time and dedicates it to the works. Contracts therefore provide that the contractor shall not remove plant and equipment from site without the engineer's consent. This is intended to meet availability risk. While the contract is ongoing, removal without consent will be a breach but is not usually a termination event. Even if the breach is repudiatory, the employer may not want to accept the repudiation. It may prefer the contractor to return the plant. The utility of a prohibition against removal depends on the court's willingness to order specific performance. The court regards such a term as a personal right against the contractor; it appears not to give rise to a contractual lien (see the discussion later on the *Cosslett* case). In the context of goods and materials a right of detention before termination has been held to transfer a property interest even in the absence of a vesting clause: see *P4 Ltd v Unite Integrated Solutions* [2006] EWHC 2640, para.120, discussed in Ch.7. If correct, such an analysis could apply to plant which is intended to become part of the land. A right to damages for breach of the prohibition against removal will not be valuable if the contractor is insolvent. Thus, contractual rights alone are not sufficient to manage availability risk. **6–005**

The reported cases focus on the position after termination. In that event the standard forms allow the employer to seize and use the contractor's plant. Issues arise as to the enforceability of such terms on insolvency, e.g. as infringements of the *pari passu* rule or as unregistered charges. These aspects are considered later. Such rights do not necessarily affect the ownership of the plant. These may be some of the reasons why the employer has tried to improve its position by obtaining property interests in the contractor's plant.

The most famous dispute over contractors' plant is probably the "Battle of Mickleton Tunnel". In 1846, Robert Mudge-Marchant took over a contract to build the Mickleton Tunnel purchasing wagons, timber and machinery from the previous contractor. Brunel was the certifying engineer on the project (see Ch.1). By 1851, over £34,000 had been withheld by the employer and the contractor suspended work. The employer instructed Brunel to evict the contractor and seize his plant worth £10,000 as compensation for £6,300 allegedly owing by him. The contractor refused to leave and ordered his men to stand guard over the plant. Brunel assembled an army of 3000 navvies and the contractor "surrendered" in the hope of a settlement (Vaughan 1991, 187).

Property rights

6–006 The employer has various options. Does it want to own the contractor's plant outright or to obtain some lesser right? Is the proprietary interest intended to be permanent or for a specific period or subject to a condition? At what stage is the right vested? Unfortunately, language used in contracts is often highly ambiguous. The courts have had to consider the meaning of vesting clauses for different purposes: for example, whether building lease agreements were registrable as bills of sale, whether plant fell within with the "reputed ownership" of a bankrupt (a concept abolished by s.235 of the Insolvency Act 1985), or whether the employer had a property interest sufficient to take priority over the contractor's judgment creditors.

Outright transfers

6–007 If the contract says that title passes to the employer on delivery, the employer acquires unlimited ownership rights. In *Goodman v Napier Harbour Board* [1939] N.Z.L.R. 97 the employer determined the contract on grounds not associated with insolvency and seized and sold the contractor's plant. The contract contained a vesting clause:

> "All plant and material delivered or brought on to the works for the purpose of being used or employed in or about the same shall be the absolute property of the Board in like manner as though they had been legally vested in the Board by absolute assignment . . ."

The clause restricted the removal of plant during the contract and prevented any assignment or other dealing without the engineer's consent. The termination clause provided that the plant should become the absolute property of the employer without payment. The court was impressed by the clarity of the vesting clause and rejected the contractor's claim for damages in conversion. The termination clause did not detract from the vesting clause; it merely allowed the employer to keep its own property. *Bennett and White v Municipal District of Sugar City* [1951] A.C. 786 is a similar case. The contractor was assessed for tax on plant and equipment used on a government contract. The contract provided:

> "15. All machinery, tools, plant, materials, equipment, articles and things whatsoever, provided by the contractor . . . shall from the time of their being so provided become, and, until the final completion of the said work, shall be the property of His Majesty . . ."

Tax was payable only on items owned by the contractor or in its legal possession. Lord Reid construed these words literally so as to pass ownership to the employer on delivery to site. There was then "a notional or actual bailment or redelivery of possession to the builders for the purpose of carrying out the building contract" (at 815), so the contractor remained in legal possession. Both employer and contractor had legal interests in the plant, the former derived from an absolute title, the latter from possession (Goode 2004, at 35). It was submitted that, as the contractor did not have exclusive control over the plant, in view of the engineer's powers, it could not have legal possession. This argument was rejected as it "would seem to confuse control of operations with control of the physical instruments by which the operations are to be carried out. These may well be in different persons" (at 815). This aspect assumed some importance in the *Cosslett* case discussed below. Alternatively, perhaps it could have been held that the plant was in the shared possession of contractor and employer (Goode 2004, at 43). In the end, the contractor avoided liability on other grounds.

Deemed transfer

If the contract "deems" the employer to be the owner or says the employer **6–008**
is to "be considered" as the owner for the purposes of the contract, the court regards the contract as ambiguous and enquires further: *Smith v Bridgend CBC* [2002] B.L.R. 160. It might be construed as transferring an equitable interest. This occurred in *Brown v Bateman* (1867) L.R. 2 C.P. 272, which concerned materials which were deemed by the terms of a building lease to be attached to the land on delivery. Lord Reid's reference to bailment in *Bennett and White* suggests the employer in that case had the general property in the plant and the contractor the special property. Jonathan Parker J., reasoning on similar lines at first instance in *Cosslett* where the wording was different, thought the employer had the special property: *Cosslett (Contractors) Ltd v Mid-Glamorgan CC* (1995) 78 B.L.R. 104, at 127. In doubtful cases the court may choose not to give effect to the provision, leaving it to the employer to rely on any protection afforded by a termination clause: *Re Keen & Keen Ex p. Collins* [1902] 1 K.B. 555.

Transfer and retransfer

Vesting clauses sometimes provide for plant and equipment vested in the **6–009**
employer on delivery to site to be transferred back to the contractor on completion. Although consistent with a chattel mortgage, such clauses may in context have purely contractual effect. In *Hart v Porthgain* [1903] 1 Ch. 690 a contractor agreed to erect a temporary dam to keep out the sea during excavations for the construction of a harbour. The contract provided that:

> "All such plant and materials shall be considered the property of the Company until the engineers shall have certified the completion of the contract, and no plant or materials shall be removed or taken away without the consent or order in writing of the engineers."

The contractor went bankrupt after building the temporary works. Farwell J. held that the clause:

> "vests the property in the materials in the company at law subject to a condition that, when the engineer shall have certified the completion of the contract, the contractor shall be at liberty to remove them. . . . In my opinion these clauses are put in for the purpose, not merely of enabling

the contract to be performed, but also as a due security for its performance" (at 694–6).

Despite the reference to "security", it seems that there was an absolute transfer of property: *Cosslett (Contractors) Ltd v Mid-Glamorgan CC* (1995) 78 B.L.R. 104 at 119.

In *Re Keen & Keen Ex p. Collins* [1902] 1 K.B. 555 (a reputed ownership case), the contract was in essentially the same terms as in *Hart v Porthgain* but the court reached the opposite conclusion that the words were not sufficient to pass ownership. The court placed reliance on the restriction on removal of plant from site during the contract as evidence that the parties did not intend to transfer ownership. In *Cosslett (Contractors) Ltd v Mid-Glamorgan CC* (1997) 85 B.L.R. 1 at 16, Millett L.J. seemed to prefer the reasoning of *Keen & Keen*.

Security interests

6–010 There can be a fine line between an equitable interest (property) and an equitable charge (security). English law recognises four forms of security: mortgage, charge, contractual lien and pledge (see Ch.2). In the context of plant and equipment the case law has focused on fixed and floating charges granted by the construction contract.

4. Fixed charges

6–011 It is rare for the court to construe a construction contract as creating a fixed charge. In *Brown v Bateman* (1867) L.R. 2 C.P. 272 the court left open whether the employer with the benefit of a vesting clause obtained an equitable interest or an equitable charge. If the latter it would appear to have been a fixed charge. At first instance in *Cosslett (Contractors) Ltd v Mid-Glamorgan CC* (1995) 78 B.L.R. 104, Jonathan Parker J. held that clauses 53 and 63 of ICE (5th edn) amounted to a fixed equitable charge over plant but his analysis was rejected on appeal in favour of a floating charge.

The contract in *Young v Matthew Hall Mechanical & Electrical Engineers* [1988] 13 A.C.L.R. 399 was more explicit. The case concerned the effect of an express charge in a termination clause in an engineering sub-subcontract which had been terminated by the subcontractor (Matthew Hall). A few weeks later a liquidator was appointed to the sub-subcontractor (Nordtech) who claimed delivery up of plant and equipment in the possession of the subcontractor on the ground that the sub-subcontract constituted an unregistered charge under the Western Australian equivalent of s.395 of the Companies Act 1985. There was no vesting provision but the contract had an extended termination clause:

> "19.5 . . . On the completion of such work all tools and equipment and the surplus of the materials so taken possession of shall be handed over to Nordtech but without payment or allowance for the fair wear and tear they may have sustained in the meantime, provided that, if there be a deficiency as referred to in this article, and if Nordtech fails to make

good such deficiency [they] may be sold and a sufficient part of the moneys received retained by Matthew Hall and applied in payment of such deficiency.

19.6 (a) If default is made by Nordtech and not remedied and Matthew Hall exercises all or any of the powers provided by art 19.3 then (to the full extent permitted by law and by Nordtech's existing contractual obligations to others): (i) Matthew Hall shall have and Nordtech hereby grants to Matthew Hall a charge over all construction equipment owned by Nordtech and the right to register bills of sale over such construction equipment; and (ii) Matthew Hall shall have the right to retain possession of all construction equipment owned by Nordtech and then situated on the work site for the purposes of ensuring the completion of the works pursuant to the powers granted to Matthew Hall in this art 19; (b) Nordtech acknowledges and agrees that construction equipment brought onto the work site for the purpose of the works is deemed to be in the possession of Matthew Hall for so long as it remains on the work site; and (c) Matthew Hall's rights pursuant to para (a) of this art 19.6 shall be extinguished with respect to any item of construction equipment if Matthew Hall gives written approval to Nordtech pursuant to art 6.6 of the subcontract for any such item to be removed from the work site and in that event Matthew Hall will at the request and expense of Nordtech supply to Nordtech a Memorandum of Satisfaction of any bill of sale which Matthew Hall has registered over such item of construction equipment."

Matthew Hall conceded that the charge and the power of sale were void against the liquidator for want of registration as bills of sale but the court held that the rights of possession and user remained enforceable as terms of the contract. They were not enough to confer a security interest; if anything, they amounted to a lien which would be lost if the employer lost possession. Since the charge only came into effect on a termination, it was not registrable until that event happened. The terms of the sub-subcontract in this case are radically different from the English cases. By the time the charge came into effect, the only liability it could secure would be any net deficiency.

5. Floating charges

The law in this area is governed by the decision of the House of Lords in *Smith v Bridgend CBC* [2002] B.L.R. 160 which arose out of the administration of a contractor, Cosslett (Contractors) Ltd. In that case the contractor agreed with a local authority to provide and operate two coal washing plants designed to separate coal from shale. The employer made an advance payment of £1.8 million to the contractor to buy the plant, repayable by deduction from operating charges over the next four years. The local authority intended to sell the coal and use the shale in land reclamation. Presumably it was intended that the plants would then be removed by the contractor at the end of that period as they remained in its ownership throughout. Two years into the contract, the contractor went into administration and left site following disputes with the employer. Administration was not a termination event under the contract. The **6–012** engineer certified that the contractor had abandoned the site and it was expelled under clause 63. The employer took possession of the plant and later transferred it to another contractor as part of an agreement to complete the washing operations. Thus the plant never became part of the land, nor was it the means of constructing the works. It was a temporary structure to enable a process to be carried out on site by the contractor. There are two strands to the subsequent litigation which are relevant to the industry: first, a claim for delivery up of the plant which failed because the employer retained an interim right to possession; second, a claim for damages for conversion which succeeded as the employer failed to return the plant when it ought to have done. The first strand will be considered here, the conversion claim later.

The claim for delivery up

6–013 Before the works were completed, the administrator sought an order for delivery up of the plant under s.234 of the Insolvency Act 1986 or payment for its use. He failed at first instance and in the Court of Appeal but on different grounds.

The employer's rights before termination are set out in clause 53:

> "53(1) For the purpose of this clause: (a) the expression 'Plant' shall mean any constructional plant coal washing plant temporary works . . . (2) All plant, goods and materials owned by the Contractor or by any company in which the Contractor has a controlling interest shall when on site be deemed to be the property of the Employer. The washing plant must be owned by the Contractor or by a company in which the Contractor has a controlling interest . . . (6) No Plant (except hired Plant) goods or materials or any part thereof shall be removed from the Site without the written consent of the Engineer which consent shall not be unreasonably withheld where the same are no longer immediately required for the purposes of the completion of the Works but the Employer will permit the Contractor the exclusive use of all such Plant goods and materials in and for the completion of the Works until the occurrence of any event which gives the Employer the right to exclude the Contractor from the Site and proceed with the completion of the Works."

On termination, the employer becomes entitled to:

> "63(1) . . . complete the Works and the Employer or such other contractor may use for such completion so much of the Constructional Plant Temporary Works goods and materials which have been deemed to become the property of the Employer . . . [and] may at any time sell any of the said Constructional Plant Temporary Works and unused goods and materials and apply the proceeds of sale in or towards the satisfaction of any sums due or which may become due to him from the Contractor under the contract . . ."

Both the trial judge and the Court of Appeal agreed that clause 53 was not clear enough to give the employer a property right in the plant. The issue was whether the employer had obtained a contractual right or a security interest, and, if the latter, whether the security was enforceable against the contractor in administration.

Jonathan Parker J. concluded that the contractor had granted the employer a fixed equitable charge over the plant: fixed, in the light of the restriction against removal in clause 53; equitable, in that the vesting provisions showed an intention to confer an interest short of ownership; and a charge, in view of the power of sale in clause 63 and the right to set off the proceeds against sums due or to become due to the contractor: *Cosslett (Contractors) Ltd v Mid-Glamorgan CC* (1995) 78 B.L.R. 104. The claim for delivery up failed.

The Court of Appeal also dismissed the claim but for different reasons. It concluded that clause 53 was purely contractual whereas clause 63 conferred a floating charge over the plant securing the contractor's contingent liability for any final account deficiency. Before termination there was no liability which a charge could secure since there was no debt owing by the contractor. After termination, the charge could only secure a payment obligation as the contractor's duty to perform had been commuted to a potential liability to account. Although the floating charge had not been registered and was therefore unenforceable against the administrator, it did not taint the employer's other rights under clause 63 to take possession and use the plant for the purposes of a completion contract: *Cosslett (Contractors) Ltd v Mid-Glamorgan CC* (1997) 85 B.L.R. 1. The House of Lords agreed with this approach. The case was followed recently in *Greenore Port v Technical & General* [2006] EWHC 3119, para.41.

Commentary on the *Cosslett* case

It was a key part of the ratio that it was the engineer and not the employer **6–014** who had the discretion to refuse to allow plant to be removed from site. The engineer acted independently on operational grounds (compare the *Bennett & White* case above). It follows that he could not take into account the wishes of the employer as charge holder, e.g. to keep plant on site as a potential fund in case the contractor became insolvent. The essential ingredient of a fixed charge, that control over the assets lay with the chargee, was not made out. In this respect, the case is analogous to *National Westminster Bank v Spectrum Plus* [2005] 2 A.C. 680 which concerned a fixed charge over debts. But here the case turned on the unique position of the engineer as both agent of the employer and independent certifier. Several questions arise: Would the result have been different if the power to retain the plant on site lay with the employer not the engineer (as in *Young v Matthew Hall*)? Should the ICE form be amended to that effect? Could the engineer be justified in withholding his consent to removal if there were, at the time the contractor made its request, circumstances making it likely that a termination event would occur? Planning for an imminent post-termination completion contract using the contractor's plant could be an operational matter. In such a case, the interests of the employer as procurer of the works and as charge-holder would coincide: compare the contractor's "Armageddon plan" in *Multiplex v Cleveland Bridge* [2006] EWHC 1341, para.605. But are such interests ever separable?

The court separated out the rights of user and sale. One was contractual, the other a security. The employer argued in the House of Lords that the power of sale was simply a right to enable it to clear the site and feed a contractual set-off. This reflected an assumption in the industry that the standard form was not intended to create a charge. The employer's submission is consistent with the approach in *Reeves v Barlow* (1884) L.R. 12 Q.B.D. 436 considered below in which the Court of Appeal rejected a claim that a vesting clause was registrable as a bill of sale. In that case the court appeared to lean in principle against interpreting terms protective of employers under building contracts as registrable securities. The finding that the security was a floating charge may have turned on the particular type of plant concerned in this case and the way it was defined in the contract. If the washing plants had not been included in the definition of plant in clause 53 or regarded as constructional plant in clause 63 the position may have been different. Lord Scott stated that the categorisation of the right was a question of law not dependent on the intentions of the parties (para.53). The charge was a future security which did not come into existence until the employer served its seven day notice of default under clause 63. However it could still be registered as a floating charge as from the execution of the contract (para.63). The grant of the charge would be in the ordinary course of business of an engineering contractor, rather like the obligation to fund retention under a JCT contract (Ch.10). Will lenders to the employer require amendments to contracts of this kind by stipulating for a fixed charge? In ICE (7th edn) the deeming provision has been dropped but the power of sale of plant on a termination has been replicated in clause 65(2) almost unchanged.

Ironically, after an administration lasting nearly 10 years, the claims of the ordinary unsecured creditors were all statute barred with the exception of the employer whose contract had been under seal. As a result, the assets of the company, including the damages paid to it by the employer, would be shared by way of dividend between the employer and the preferential creditors in the subsequent liquidation. From the ordinary creditor's point of view, the litigation had been successful but no money had been recovered: *Cosslett (Contractors) Ltd v Mid-Glamorgan CC* [2004] EWHC 658. Had the company been placed in liquidation some years previously, its claims could have been continued by a liquidator and the creditors' rights to prove their debts would have been preserved. The employer's decision to execute the contract under seal gave it a procedural security in circumstances which could hardly have been foreseen; a security which not only preserved its rights over a longer period of time, but gave it priority over all the other unsecured creditors, as if they had agreed at the outset that their own claims should be subordinated in the event of liquidation.

6. Lien

6–015 In the *Cosslett* litigation, counsel for the employer argued that clauses 53 and 63 when taken together amounted to a possessory lien coupled with a power of sale, relying on *Great Eastern Railway v Lord's Trustee* [1909] A.C. 109. This was rejected on the ground that the employer's rights were not derived from the voluntary delivery of possession. It only obtained possession through an express right arising on the contractor's default. Such an approach was more in keeping with an equitable charge than a lien: *Cosslett (Contractors) Ltd v Mid-Glamorgan CC* (1997) 85 B.L.R. 1 at 14, 18. Distinguishing between these two types of security can be a subtle matter: see *Re Hamlet International* [1998] 2 B.C.L.C. 164, discussed in Pickin (1998).

There are comparatively few modern cases involving the lien in the UK construction industry. In *Crowfoot v London Dock Company* (1834) 2 C&M 637 a contractor went bankrupt before completing the contract. Retention was 25 per cent of the contract sum payable within one month after full completion. He was to be paid under engineer's certificates issued every two months. This was not enough to finance the work and the employer agreed to make advances to the contractor in consideration of his agreement that all the plant, equipment and materials on site and to be brought to site should be a security for the advances. On the contractor's bankruptcy, the employer marked the plant with its initials and used it to complete the works. It emerged that the contractor had been overpaid by £13,000. The plant was worth £5,000 and the contractor's assignee sued the employer for its value. The assignee's claim failed since the effect of the contractor's agreement was to give the company a lien over the plant as security for its outstanding debt. See also *Hawthorn v Newcastle upon Tyne Railway* (1840) 3 Q.B. 734, *Re Waugh Ex p. Dickin* (1876) L.R. 4 Ch. D. 524, *Byford v Russell* [1907] 2 K.B. 522, *Forestry Commission v Stefanetto* (1975) 133 C.L.R. 507, *Egan v State Transport* (1982) 31 S.A.S.R. 481, *Phontos v New South Wales Land & Housing Corporation* (1988) B.C.L. 45.

7. Pledge

It has been argued that if the ICE form confers a formal security it is as **6–016** likely to be a pledge as anything else (Palmer 1996, 1997). Against this is the fact that the contractor has possession of the plant until the event arises which activates the employer's power of sale. The possessory element of the pledge could be supplied by construing the employer's position before termination as that of a bailee with special property in the plant, even though under clause 63 the employer's right to possession is expressly made contingent on a termination. The only clear delivery of possession is involuntary through the operation of the termination clause. Professor Palmer counters this by arguing that a pledge can arise where possession of a chattel has been given for some other purpose: *Barrett v Livesey* (unreported, November 6, 1980, CA).

In the only other relevant case in this area, *Kerr v Dundee Gas Light Company* (1861) Ct. of Sess. 343, the contract conferred an express pledge on the employer in respect of plant and materials brought to site "for the due performance of the contract". After the original contractor went bankrupt, the works were completed and the employer had to return the plant. It could not sell it and set off the proceeds of sale against sums due from the bankrupt because on its true construction the liability secured by the pledge was completion of the works rather than payment of any deficiency. The pledge secured completion risk by ensuring the continued availability of the plant *as a pledged asset*. A pledge can secure any form of obligation, not just liability to pay money (Paterson 1993). The power of sale in the ICE form could be consistent with a pledge or a charge. If one accepts that the intention of the parties was primarily to secure performance, then a pledge is a more appropriate form of security. It is a pity that pledge was not considered in *Smith v Bridgend CBC* [2002] B.L.R. 160. On the performance aspect of plant as a security asset, see also *Forestry Commission v Stefanetto* (1975) 133 C.L.R. 507.

8. Challenges to vesting clauses

6–017 Vesting clauses have been challenged in the following situations: on a disputed termination, as a penalty, as contravening the *pari passu* rule, in claims for conversion, and as an unregistered bill of sale. See also Ch.7 for analogous situations concerning goods and materials.

Disputed termination

6–018 Where a termination is disputed and the contractor has left site, what is to happen to its plant and equipment? There are various possibilities.

The contractor's interests can be protected either by being allowed to collect its property or by the employer undertaking to the court to pay damages should it later appear that it terminated without just cause: *Mohan and Holmes v Dundalk Railway* (1880) L.R. Ir. 477; *Callaghan v City of Glasgow* 1988 S.L.T. 227 (obligation to return plant or pay its value); *Wood v Rural Sanitary Authority of Tendring* (1886) 3 T.L.R. 272 (plant returned); *Corporation of Cork v Rooney* (1881) 7 L.R. Ir. 191 (undertaking in damages); *Roberts v Maurbeth Investments* [1974] 1 N.S.W.L.R. 93 (contractor allowed to collect plant); *Re Winter Ex p. Bolland* (1878) L.R. 8 Ch. D. 228. A contractor was allowed to repossess its plant in *Attorney-General v Ko Hon Mau* (1988) 44 B.L.R. 144. The case concerned the Hong Kong Public Works Highways Maintenance Contract (1972 edn) which had a vesting clause providing for re-vesting on completion or termination for non-payment or if the employer obstructed the issue of a certificate. The contractor terminated but the employer cross-claimed for an entitlement to terminate for failure to proceed with due diligence. The court was asked to rule on the fate of the plant pending an arbitration.

> "The contractor puts its value at HK$1.8 million. This he says he wishes to realise to satisfy the pressing demands of his creditors. Government wishes to retain the apparent 'security' the plant affords (in addition to that provided by the HK$0.45 million performance bond provided under the contract); to use the plant on site; and if necessary to sell it to its advantage. Underneath the rival claims to possession lie the competing claims of creditors between whom hereafter different considerations may apply" (at 150, *per* Hunter J.A.).

On balance, the court allowed the contractor to repossess its plant. The employer therefore lost its security but the court may have been influenced by the fact that the contractor had also provided a bond. The court may decide the issue of whether the termination was valid. In *Dalkia Utilities v Celtech* [2006] 1 Lloyd's Rep. 599, the contractor agreed to build and operate a combined heat and power plant for 15 years. The contract provided that the facility was to remain in the contractor's ownership throughout to enable it to claim capital allowances but on a termination by either party the employer should be entitled to keep it. The contractor was granted a lease of the site. There were mutual allegations of termination. Christopher Clarke J. held that the contractor validly terminated the contract. The plant was a tenant's fixture which the contractor would be entitled to remove if the employer failed to pay the termination sum (para.154).

In deciding whether, on a balance of convenience, the employer should be allowed to use the contractor's plant for the purpose of completing the works pending determination of the validity of its actions, the court takes all the circumstances into account. In *Groutco v Prince Constructions* (1987) B.C.L. 372 a contractor was allowed to retain a subcontractor's plant until their dispute on the validity of the termination of the subcontract had been concluded, otherwise the court felt the contractor would have lost any proprietary rights it may have had. See also *Re Yeadon Waterworks* (1895) 72 L.T. 538 (CA) (sell or free use of the contractor's property); *Forestry Commission v Stefanetto* [1975] 133 C.L.R. 507; *TMC Constructions v Collins Radio Constructors* [1992] NTSC 20. If the contract gives the employer the right on the contractor's default either to cancel the contract or take over the works and use the contractor's plant, the employer cannot use the plant if it decides to cancel the contract: *Phontos v New South Wales Land & Housing Corporation* (1988) B.C.L. 45. That case concerned a disputed termination but the court assumed for the purpose of the contractor's application for delivery up that the employer had validly cancelled the contract. The contract gave the employer a lien over the plant until the contractor had paid the net deficiency arising once the contract had been completed. Since the lien only arose where the works had been taken over, however, it was held that the contractor was entitled to the immediate return of its plant. The contract also contained a restriction on removal of the plant but this was only effective while the contractor was carrying out the work. Once the contract was cancelled, the restriction was removed.

The court also has power to order the sale of plant and equipment under CPR Part 25: *Bank of Scotland v Neath Port Talbot CBC* [2006] EWHC 2276. In that case the plant consisted of a waste recycling facility designed to operate for 25 years as part of a PFI contract. Problems were experienced with output levels and the local authority terminated the contract. The authority claimed that the termination clause vested the plant in itself free of legal charges granted by the contractor to its bank. This was disputed by the bank which was asserting its rights as charge holder. There was some urgency as a delay in resolving the fate of the plant could mean loss of access to EU structural funds to finance a replacement contract. David Richards J. ordered a sale by an independent agent who would invite bids from the market, including both the authority and the bank.

Penalty arguments

Although penalty arguments are usually encountered in construction law in **6–019**
connection with payment of money, e.g. liquidated damages for delay, they can be made in relation to any provision whereby property is retained or

forfeited, including it appears rights reserved in termination clauses which apply on an event of default which is not a breach but which is regarded as within the domain of the party causing or permitting the event to arise: *Integral Home Loans v Interstar Wholesale Finance* [2007] NSWSC 406. In a case concerning a road making contract, it was held that forfeiture of plant on termination of the contract was a penalty: *Bysouth v Shire of Blackburn and Mitcham* [1928] V.L.R. 562. There was a vesting clause but it only concerned materials. The court may have been influenced by the fact that the employer was entitled to terminate for trivial breaches, e.g. execution of work on a Sunday. The court also found that the notice given under the contract was invalid. A right of seizure in a termination clause was also held to constitute a penalty in *Egan v State Transport Authority* (1979) 24 S.A.S.R. 5. In *Forestry Commission v Stefanetto* (1975) 133 C.L.R. 507 the employer was entitled to seize and use the contractor's plant and equipment on a termination. The contract provided:

> "The Contractor shall have no right to any compensation or allowance for any action taken by the Principal pursuant to this subclause, other than a right to require the Principal to maintain in good working order the Constructional Plant referred to in the preceding paragraph. On completion of the work all Constructional Plant and the surplus of the materials and other things so taken possession of will be handed over to the Contractor, but without payment or allowance for the fair wear and tear they may have sustained in the meantime provided however, that if there is a deficiency as referred to in sub-clause 43.4 and if the Contractor fails to make good that deficiency, the Principal may retain in his possession the said Constructional Plant, materials and other things until the deficiency is made good pursuant to the provisions of sub-clause 43.4."

It was held that this provision was not a penalty.

> "It must be observed that the appellant is not primarily interested in obtaining damages for breach of the contract. It is primarily concerned with the completion of the work within a stipulated time. Both the provisions as to liquidated damages and as to the provision of security are means to that end, coupled with an ease of recovery of damages in the event of breach. But the possession and use of the machinery and plant are, to my mind, a direct means of achieving the purpose of the contract, namely, the completion of the work. They are not a means of providing the appellant with any form of compensation in respect of the breach of the agreement. . . . It seems that the provision allowing the appellant to complete the work with the aid of the respondent's plant is both reasonable and in the interest of both the parties, i.e. the interest of both parties to effect early completion. True it is that the respondent is denied the immediate use of the machinery and plant: but he is in default" (at 515–516, *per* Barwick C.J.).

The *pari passu* rule

6–20 Where the contract has no vesting clause but allows the employer to seize and sell the contractor's plant on the contractor's bankruptcy or liquidation, it will be struck down as infringing the *pari passu* rule now contained in s.107 of the Insolvency Act 1986. In *Re Harrison Ex p. Jay* (1880) L.R. 14 Ch. D. 19 the contract provided that on the contractor's bankruptcy: "all improvements, materials, implements, plant, chattels, and effects [on site] . . . shall be and become absolutely forfeited" to the employer who could:

> "re-enter and take possession of [the site], chattels, and effects, without any formal proceeding, and . . . relet or sell the same to any person, or otherwise use and enjoy the same as fully as if this agreement had never been entered into."

The contractor went bankrupt and the Court of Appeal had to decide between competing claims to wood, bricks, tiles, scaffolding and other building materials by the employer and the contractor's trustee. The court had no hesitation in deciding that they belonged to the trustee. James L.J. stated that:

> "a simple stipulation that, upon a man becoming bankrupt, that which was his property up to the date of the bankruptcy should go over to someone else and be taken away from his creditors, is void as being a violation of the policy of the bankrupt law . . . everything that [the contractor] was bound to do under the agreement had been performed by him up to the date of the bankruptcy, and therefore no right was vested in the lessor except by virtue of the bankruptcy" (at 25).

A power to forfeit plant may, however, be upheld where the right is exercised on another ground in the absence of insolvency: *Davies v Mayor of Swansea* (1853) 22 L.J. Ex. 297. A right to forfeit must have arisen before the start of the bankruptcy. For example, in *Roach v Great Western Railway Company* [1841] 1 Q.B. 51, two partners acted together as contractor. The contract provided that on their default, their tools and materials on site should "be in all respects considered as the absolute property" of the employer. They did not vest in the employer on delivery to site. The contractors were in delay and the engineer (Brunel) served a seven-day notice prior to termination. Before the period expired, both partners went bankrupt. It was held that the contractors would only have been in default after the notice had expired. As bankruptcy had intervened, title had passed to the contractors' trustees. In *Cosslett (Contractors) Ltd v Mid-Glamorgan CC* [2002] B.L.R. 160 it was held that the power of sale over plant in clause 63 of ICE (5th edn) was not a forfeiture provision and the employer was under a duty to take reasonable care to obtain the best price (paras 56–57), on which see *Ashtenne (AIF) Ltd v O'Neill* [2006] EWHC 2884.

Conversion

Where a contract allowed the employer to use the contractor's plant and **6–021**
materials "without making any payment for the same, or being answerable for any loss, damages or deterioration which might happen thereto (save from unlawful neglect or default of [the employer])," it was held that the employer was entitled to use the plant and materials without being liable in conversion to the contractor: *Mohan and Holmes v Dundalk* (1880) L.R. Ir. 477. But in the absence of a valid user clause, the employer can be liable in tort for converting the contractor's goods.

A substantial interim payment on account of damages for conversion was ordered by Judge Toulmin Q.C. in the course of the *Cosslett* litigation (see section 4 above). After the Court of Appeal refused the administrator's application for delivery up of coal washing plants on the ground that the contract allowed the employer to retain them until the works were completed, it emerged that the council had agreed to transfer the plant to the completion contractor. The employer argued that, although the power of sale was void as against the administrator, it remained enforceable against the company. This argument was rejected by the House of Lords who reinstated the award of damages at first instance: *Smith v Bridgend CBC* [2002] B.L.R. 160. Lord Scott thought that the employer's disposal of the plants was repudiatory in character and that, had it occurred before the initial application before Jonathan Parker J. it might well have entitled the contractor to an order for delivery up (para.73). The employer's cross-claim of £2.2 million consisting of the additional cost to complete together with unearned advance payments were unsecured debts in the subsequent liquidation.

In *Egan v State Transport Authority* (1982) 31 S.A.S.R. 481 the contract provided that on termination the employer could seize the contractor's plant and materials which would then become the employer's property. The employer wrongfully terminated but relied on these express rights against the plant and materials. Fifteen years later, after extensive litigation, the court declared the termination wrongful and awarded damages in conversion or detinue at the contractor's election. Exemplary damages in detinue were also awarded against the employer.

> "The immediate effects of the termination were traumatic. Men were stranded in remote areas without pay. Recent large deliveries and materials were not paid for. Creditors contacted the police and Egan was threatened with arrest and possible imprisonment. In the longer term he was a man left without an occupation; his credit worthiness and general business reputation were in ruins; he was foreclosed by clause 35 from claiming damages for breach of contract; he was harried by hostile creditors, the number and extent of whose claims had just been revealed to the railways. These disastrous consequences arose out of the initial unlawful detention of plant and further detention in the early stages more than out of the subsequent conversions of plant in later months and years" (at 532, *per* White J.).

The court had declared the seizure clause to be a penalty at an earlier trial: *Egan v State Transport Authority* (1979) 24 S.A.S.R. 5. Detinue was abolished as a tort in English law by the Torts (Interference with Goods) Act 1977, but the remedy of delivery up was retained under s.3 of that Act.

Unregistered bills of sale

6–022 An insolvency practitioner encountering a vesting clause for the first time might well conclude it was void as against the company as an unregistered bill of sale. In the cases, however, such clauses have always fallen outside the relevant legislation. Why is this? The issue is still a live one, e.g. the question whether clause 63 of ICE (5th edn) was a registrable bill of sale was raised but not decided in *Smith v Bridgend CBC* [2002] B.L.R. 160, at para.64.

Under the Bills of Sale Act 1878 a bill of sale is a document executed by an individual which is falls into one of three categories:

1. An assignment, a transfer or other assurance of goods or chattels, or
2. A licence to possession of chattels as security for a debt, or
3. An agreement by which an equitable right to or a charge or a security on personal chattels is conferred.

If the bill is given as security for payment of money, it is a "security bill", otherwise it is called an "absolute bill": Halsbury, 4th edn, 2002 reissue, para.602. Both types must be witnessed, show consideration and be registered in the Central Office of the Royal Courts of Justice within seven days in order to be valid against a trustee in bankruptcy or an execution creditor: Halsbury, paras 735, 825.

Under s.396 of the Companies Act 1985 "a charge created or evidenced by an instrument which, if executed by an individual, would require registration as a bill of sale" is void against a liquidator, administrator or creditor of the company under s.395 unless details are delivered to the Registrar of Companies within 21 days of its creation. We are therefore in the same territory as the unregistered floating charge considered in the Cosslett litigation (see also Ch.2).

In *Brown v Bateman* (1867) L.R. 2 C.P. 272, the contract provided that **6–023** all materials brought onto site for the purposes of the works "should be considered as immediately attached to and belonging to the premises." The court rejected an execution creditor's claim that the clause was a bill of sale. It expressed no view whether the words used were clear enough to transfer the materials to the employer outright but considered they were sufficient to create "a clear equitable right" or "an equitable charge". However, at the time the case was decided, neither was capable of being a bill of sale. In *Blake v Izard* (1867) 16 W.R. 108, the contract provided that all materials brought on to site "should become the property of" the employer. The court again rejected a claim by an execution creditor:

> "This Court has in the case of Brown v Bateman decided to respect the evident intention of the parties under these agreements. It was intended to preserve the rights of landlords [under building leases], and I consider it was a most wholesome decision. It has been contended that it is a bill of sale, or that it comes within the scope of the Bills of Sale Act, but I apprehend that that question is set at rest by Brown v Bateman, which shews that stipulations of the nature of building agreements are not within the scope of the Bills of Sale Act" (*per* Willes J.).

Here the court reveals a policy basis for the earlier decision, to protect the interests of landowners. This may explain why *Brown v Bateman* was not distinguished: the equitable interest arose as the materials were considered part of the land. In *Blake v Izard*, they became the property of the employer and there was no deemed incorporation. These cases were decided under the Bills of Sale Act 1854 which concerned the first and second categories of bill.

In *Re Garrud Ex p. Newitt* (1881) L.R. 16 Ch. D. 522, the contract had no vesting clause but gave the employer a right to re-enter and forfeit any materials on site "as and for liquidated and settled damages". On the contractor's bankruptcy, the trustee argued that the clause was void as an unregistered bill. In the absence of a vesting clause, the first and third categories of bill could not apply. The second category was also rejected on the ground that the clause was given as security for damages rather than debt. (This is questionable as liquidated damages are regarded as a debt for some purposes: see Ch.5.) Alternatively, the materials were taken not as security for the debt but in discharge of it. This case was relied on by Lord Scott in *Smith v Bridgend CBC* [2002] B.L.R. 160, at para.54.

The Bills of Sale Act 1878 added the third category of bill, namely agreements transferring an equitable interest or conferring a charge or security over chattels. Emden (1st edn, 1882 at 154) concluded that, as a result: "the difficulties arising in those decisions [*Brown v Bateman; Re Garrud, Ex p. Newitt]* upon this point have been removed by the Bills of Sale Act 1878, and that agreements of this description would be within the words of Section 4". Emden's opinion was not, however, accepted in the next case to come before the court: *Reeves v Barlow* (1884) L.R. 12 Q.B.D. 436. The contract provided that: "all building and other materials brought by the intended lessee upon the land shall, whether affixed to the freehold or not, become the property of the intended lessor." Once again the court rejected the claim of an execution creditor that the clause was an unregistered bill of sale. The Court of Appeal considered that the two earlier decisions were "unshaken decisions of a court of great weight" which "we are not prepared to review." The third category of bill was not relevant because, as soon as the materials were delivered to site:

> "property in them passed in law, and nothing was left upon which any equity as distinct from law could attach . . . The builder's agreement accordingly was at no time an equitable assignment of anything, but a mere legal contract that, upon the happening of a particular event, the property in law should pass in certain chattels which that event itself would identify without the necessity of any further act on the part of anybody, and which could not be identified before" (at 442, *per* Bowen L.J.).

In the construction context, even if the vesting clause were an unregistered bill of sale, the court seems to be saying that the bringing of materials to site or their fixing to the structure, depending on the terms of the contract, would render the bill spent: Halsbury, paras 615, 624, 630. See also *Welsh Development Agency v Export Finance* [1990] B.C.C. 393 at 411. *Reeves v Barlow* is firmly established and has been followed many times (e.g. *Tapper v Bodley* (1884) 3 N.Z.L.R. 4; *Bennett and White v Municipal District of Sugar City* [1951] A.C. 786), but it does not say that a vesting clause in a construction contract can never be registrable as a bill of sale. Each contract has to be construed separately.

It may be useful to consider a case where an assignment by a contractor was a bill of sale. In *Church v Sage* (1893) 67 L.T. 800 a builder assigned the benefit of a building contract together with all plant and materials on site or to be brought on site during the contract as security for a loan. In a priority dispute between an assignee and an execution creditor it was held that the latter should prevail as the assignment was an unregistered bill of sale.

> ". . . this was a legal assignment of the existing plant and materials, with a power to take possession, and as regards the future plant and materials, either an equitable assignment . . . or an agreement whereby a right in equity to the chattels, or a charge or security upon them was created" (at 801, *per* Wright J.).

The following points may be of relevance when considering the question posed at the beginning of this section. If plant is designed specifically for the contract, it will be identifiable before being brought to site. Delivery to site is not necessarily a transfer of possession to the employer. Some financial obligations owed by contractors are debts. It may remain arguable that a vesting clause requires registration where the employer is not the owner of the land: *Church v Sage* (1893) 67 L.T. 800. The policy basis of *Blake v Izard* could be reviewed in the light of changes in social conditions. It is clear, however, that a simple provision for payment under interim certificates cannot be a bill of sale: *Davidson and Davidson v Claffey Constructions* (1985) W.A.L.R. 29.

9. Third party interests

The discussion so far has assumed that the contractor owns the plant. In **6–024** practice plant may be brought onto site by subcontractors, be hired or leased by the contractor or subcontractor, or be supplied by a subsidiary of the contractor.

Subcontractors

Where a vesting clause in the main contract is not mirrored in the **6–025** subcontract, the court will not infer it merely because the subcontractor agrees to carry out work in accordance with the terms of the main contract: *Dawber Williamson v Humberside CC* (1979) 14 B.L.R. 70. In *Triangle v John Burroughs* [1958] (3) S.A. 810, the main contract contained a clause vesting plant and machinery in the employer together with rights of enforcement similar to ICE (5th edn). Some of the work was to be done by a nominated subcontractor but the subcontract did not contain a clause vesting the subcontractor's plant and equipment in either contractor or employer. The court considered that the vesting clause in the main contract, having been inserted for the benefit of the building owner, should be construed against it. As it only referred to plant brought to site by the contractor, it could not include plant delivered by subcontractors. It would be unjust to construe the clause in any other way as it could lead to the subcontractor's plant being forfeited if the main contract were terminated through no fault of the subcontractor. In any event, there was no privity of contract permitting the employer to enforce direct against the subcontractor.

To overcome this difficulty, clause 11 of the CECA Blue Form (1998) designed for use with ICE (6th edn) provides for ownership in the subcontractor's plant to pass to the contractor immediately before it is due to vest in the employer and then revert to the subcontractor immediately after it has re-vested in the contractor. The standard forms also require contractors to ensure that subcontracts include back-to-back vesting provisions, e.g. clause 54.7 of FIDIC (4th edn). Where there is no incorporation of terms and the subcontract does not contain a vesting clause neither employer nor contractor is entitled to retain the subcontractor's plant: *Perbadanan v Teo Kai Huat* [1982] M.L.J. 165.

Where the plant is hired or leased

6–026 An order will not normally be made in respect of plant which has been hired or leased by the contractor: *Forestry Commission v Stefanetto* (1975) 133 C.L.R. 507. Standard forms such as ICE, FIDIC and the Singapore SIA form contain elaborate provisions enabling the engineer to identify plant not in the ownership of the contractor so that arrangements can be made for the employer to take over the contractor's hire or lease agreements after termination. If a contract is terminated by consent it may be possible to agree a novation of the contractor's arrangement with the plant's owner in favour of the employer: see *Crouch Mining v The Scottish Coal Co* [2003] CSOH 217 discussed in chapter 15.

In *TR Nominees v Multiplex* (1996) 12 B.C.L. 219, the hirer failed in a claim for delivery up of two tower cranes and a hoist hired to a subcontractor which had repudiated its subcontract. The evidence was that the equipment would be needed for a further nine months. The application failed for two reasons: first, there was a common director between the hirer and the subcontractor and it was not at all clear whether the hirer had an immediate right to possession for non-payment under the hire agreement. In any case, the balance of convenience lay with the contractor for various reasons: the hirer had no present use for the plant; its true claim was for damages in conversion; the inconvenience of dismantling the cranes and the hoist would be considerable; the hirer's financial position meant that an undertaking in damages would be of little value; and the order sought was in the nature of final relief. No condition was imposed that the contractor should pay a reasonable hiring charge as it would represent payment of damages before trial (inappropriate in the absence of facts which could support a freezing order), the payments would be irrecoverable if the contractor ultimately succeeded and, if the subcontractor went into liquidation, the contractor would be exposed to the risk of double payment.

Subsidiaries

6–027 Clause 53 of ICE (5th edn) attempts to vest in the employer all plant brought to site owned by the contractor "or by any company in which the contractor has a controlling interest". It is questionable whether this is enforceable against a subsidiary of the contractor in the absence of privity of contract or authorisation to the parent to act as its agent for this purpose. However, Millett L.J. has suggested that the court will grant specific performance of the obligation "by requiring the [contractor] to exercise its powers of control over the subsidiary and thus procure compliance with its own obligations" (*Cosslett (Contractors) Ltd v Mid-Glamorgan CC* (1997) 85 B.L.R. 1 at 17). In attempting to bind the whole group, clause 53 resembles a group set-off clause or cross-guarantee.

Chapter 7

Goods and Materials

1. General principles

This chapter concerns the interplay between two principles of common law. The first is from land law: *quicquid plantatur solo, solo cedit* (Holdsworth 1956)—anything which is fixed (literally "planted") in the earth becomes part of it. The second is from commercial law: *nemo dat quod non habet* (Goode 2004)—no person can give what he does not have. In other words, only an owner can confer ownership. Sellers invoke the second of these principles by using retention (or reservation) of title clauses by which ownership will not pass to the purchaser until the goods have been paid for (McCormack 1995, Goode 1989). But in the context of construction work, the first principle prevails so that a retention of title clause will be defeated if goods are fixed to the land: *Re Yorkshire Joinery* (1967) 111 S.J. 71; *Aircool Installations v British Telecommunications* (unreported, April 26, 1995, Judge Quentin Edwards Q.C.), *G James Safety Glass v Joffe Group* (2003) 19 B.C.L. 304. Where the employer is not the owner of the land, the supplier has no cause of action against the landowner for the price: *Gough v Wood* [1894] 1 Q.B. 713; *Crossley v Lee* [1908] 1 K.B. 86. There is thus a tension between employers who do not want to pay for goods until they have title and suppliers who do not want to pass title until they have been paid. **7–001**

The greater the number of intermediate parties between the supplier and the landowner the more complex the position becomes. The *quicquid plantatur* rule transfers risk to the contractor just as a pay when paid clause transfers risk to subcontractors. A retention of title clause might be seen as the supplier's answer to the pay when paid clause: money going down the chain is held up by a pay when paid clause; title going up the chain is held back by a retention of title clause. Standard forms of main and subcontract attempt to resolve this tension. The intention behind the JCT scheme, for example, is that title to unfixed materials delivered to site should pass to the employer as soon as the employer pays the contractor for them even if the supplier or subcontractor has not been paid.

The general rule is that title to materials supplied under a building contract will pass to the landowner on incorporation into the works: *Sims v London Necropolis Co* (1885) 1 T.L.R. 584; *Tripp v Armitage* (1839) 4 M. & W. 687 at 698. Where the contract provides for payment under interim certificates, there is authority that title to unfixed materials will pass to the employer on the issue of the relevant certificate: *Banbury Railway v Daniel* (1884) 54 L.J. Ch. 265. But there is more recent authority that title to unfixed materials will only pass to the employer on events such as certification or payment if the main contract clearly says so: *Egan v State Transport Authority* (1982) 31 S.A.S.R. 481, 537, 542; compare *Allco Steel Corporation v Australian Capital Development Corporation* (November 14, 1996, CA (NSW) noted in (1997) 14(4) Build. L.M. 1). This is the assumption behind the interlocking provisions of the standard forms of main and subcontract under which title passes to the employer on payment of the contractor (e.g. JCT 98, clause 16.1) and the subcontractor agrees not to deny that the employer has become the owner of its materials in that event even if the subcontractor has not been paid for them (e.g. DOM/1, clause 21.4.5): *P4 Ltd v Unite Integrated Solutions* [2006] EWHC 2640, para.144.

In practice, the same questions keep recurring: Have the goods or materials been delivered to site? Have they been fixed so as to become part of the land? Are they governed by a contract of sale or a contract for the supply of goods and services? What remedies are available to the unpaid supplier? What defences or other rights are available to the person in possession of the goods? This chapter considers these issues.

2. Fixed materials

7–002 The *quicquid plantatur* rule derives from Roman law, as far back as the Twelve Tables of the fifth century BCE (Buckland 1963). The policy behind it was to prevent the needless demolition of buildings. The Roman concept of *accessio* applied where ownership of a thing was acquired by incorporation into another thing. This could be a movable to another movable (a jewel set in a ring), immovable to immovable (silt attaching to a river bank) and a movable to an immovable (building on land). The last situation was known as *inaedificatio*. The principles of Roman law were adopted by medieval lawyers and the *quicquid plantatur* rule gradually emerged as part of the common law. It concerned three categories: heirs and executors, tenants for life and remaindermen, and landlords and tenants.

The strict rule was relaxed in the case of the last category because it was recognised that a tenant would need to fix things to the land for business purposes. The law was restated in *Elwes v Maw* (1802) 3 East 38 which concerned a tenant farmer who had erected buildings for the better running of the farm. Before the end of the term, he demolished the buildings and removed the materials but was held liable in conversion to the freeholder. The exception given to trading tenants did not apply as farming was not regarded as a trade. It was held (to quote one of the authorities cited in the case) that after the end of the term the buildings "became a gift in law to him in reversion and were not removable" (at 52, *per* Lord Ellenborough C.J.).

There appears to be only one exception: where a builder works on another's land by mistake and the owner stands back and accepts the benefit without alerting the builder to his mistake, the owner can be held liable to compensate the builder: *Ramsden v Dyson* (1866) L.R. 1 H.L. 129. As a consequence of these common law rules, a contractor or subcontractor working on a modern construction project confers a gratuitous benefit on the landowner as title to its materials vanishes on their being transformed into land. In the absence of agreement, e.g. for an equitable lien, the builder acquires no proprietary interest in the land by virtue of its work capable of registration against the title: *HG & R Nominees v Caulson* [2000] VSC 126. Credit opens up the risk of non-payment and the owner of the land benefits at the expense of those carrying out the work. The potential injustice of this situation has long been recognised and recommendations have been made to change the law but without success (Crowther 1971, Latham 1994). Nevertheless, the law of restitution continues to develop and may assist the unpaid contractor in appropriate circumstances: *W Cook Builders v Lumber* [2007] SASC 20 discussed in Ch.13.

The *quicquid plantatur* rule "is an absolute rule of law, not depending on intention" (*Elwes v Brigg Gas Co* (1886) L.R. 33 Ch. D. 562 at 567, *per* Chitty J.) The criteria are set out in *Holland v Hodgson* (1872) L.R. 7 C.P. 328:

> "There is no doubt that the general maxim of law is that what is annexed to the land becomes part of the land, but it is very difficult, if not impossible, to say with precision what constitutes an annexation sufficient for this purpose. It is a question which must depend on the circumstances of each case, and mainly on two circumstances as indicating the intention, viz., the degree of annexation and the object of the annexation. . . . Perhaps the true rule is that articles not otherwise attached to the land than by their own weight are not to be considered as part of the land unless the circumstances are such as to show that they were intended to be part of the land, the onus of showing that they are so intended lying on those who assert that they have ceased to be chattels; and that, on the contrary, an article which is affixed to the land, even slightly, is to be considered as part of the land, unless the circumstances are such as to show that it was intended all along to continue a chattel, the onus lying on those who contend that it is a chattel" (at 334–335, *per* Blackburn J.).

A minimal degree of annexation thus shifts the burden of proof that a chattel is a fixture away from the landowner: *Reynolds v Ashby* [1904] A.C. 466; *Scottish Discount v Blin* [1985] S.L.T. 123; *Lockwood Buildings v Trust Bank* [1995] 1 N.Z.L.R. 22; *Gebrueder Buehler v Peter Chi* [1988] 2 M.L.J. 69; and the Australian case of *Re Starline Furniture* [1982] 6 A.C.L.R. 312 in which a liquidator who detached and sold fixtures was made to account for the proceeds to the mortgagor of the land. Each case depends on its own facts and the intention of the parties is relevant only insofar as it can be derived from the degree and purpose of annexation: *Hobson v Gorringe* [1897] 1 Ch. 181 at 193; *Mellhuish v BMI* [1995] 4 All E.R. 453 at 461. The court will not admit extraneous evidence of the subjective intentions of the parties but the amount of damage which would be caused to the building or the chattel by its removal is a relevant factor: *Holland v Hodgson* (1872) L.R. 7 C.P. 328; *Chelsea Yacht and Boat Co v Pope* [2001] 2 All E.R. 409, para.24. The court takes account of changing times: *Leigh v Taylor* [1902] A.C. 157 at 162.

In *Elitestone v Morris* [1997] 2 All E.R. 513, the House of Lords **7–003** considered materials from three perspectives: as chattels, as fixtures and as part of the land. In that case a chalet resting on a concrete base had become part of the land since it could not be taken down and re-erected elsewhere like a portakabin but only enjoyed *in situ*. Thus, building components which are fixed to a built structure will be fixtures and may or may not be part of the land depending on the degree and purpose of annexation. In the Australian case of *Belgrave Nominees v Barlin-Scott* [1984] V.R. 947 the court granted a mandatory injunction ordering a subcontractor to return air-conditioning plant it had removed from a building on the basis that it had become a fixture. See also *People's Park v Schindler Lifts* (1993) 1 S.L.R. 591 (lifts and escalators were fixtures); *Aircool Installations v British Telecommunications* (unreported, April 26, 1995, Judge Quentin Edwards Q.C.) (air conditioning units were fixtures); *G James Safety Glass v Joffe Group* (2003) 19 B.C.L. 304 (glass panels were fixtures); *Dalkia Utilities v Celtech International* [2006] 1 Lloyd's Rep. 599, para.31 (heating plant was a fixture).

Modern building techniques and new technology, especially computers, are likely to challenge the criteria of a fixture as time goes by. In the Canadian case of *Credit Valley Cable v Peel* (1980) 27 O.R. (2d) 433, for example, it was held that television cable installed in conduits within an apartment building was not a fixture because it was not for the permanent enjoyment of the building but was merely a service to the residents. Compare *Hulme v Brigham* [1943] 1 K.B. 204 (printing machines remained chattels); *Blower v Alta* (1983) 50 A.R. 66, affirmed 68 A.R. 156 (two-ton crane sitting on track bolted to floor remained a chattel); *Canadian Imperial Bank of Commerce v Alberta Assessment Appeal Board* (1990) 75 Alta. L.R. (2d) 362 (bank cash dispensing machines remained chattels).

The status of a chattel may determine whether a contract falls within the Housing Grants, Construction and Regeneration Act 1996. In *Gibson Lea v Makro* [2001] B.L.R. 407, a shop fitter failed in an argument that a contract to supply and install wall equipment was for "the carrying out of construction operations" within s.104(1) of the 1996 Act. By s.105 "construction operations" are defined as works "forming, or to form, part of the land." Judge Richard Seymour Q.C. held that the common law test applied. Although the equipment was screwed to timber fixing plates that were bolted to the structure, it was intended to be easily moveable to respond to the employer's business needs and not to form part of the land.

3. Unfixed materials

7–004 A supplier's right to repossess unfixed materials will depend on the terms of the contract and in particular whether it is for the sale of goods or the supply of goods and services. The House of Lords has acknowledged that the expression "contract for work and materials" is "one of considerable imprecision" and that many work and materials contracts closely resemble contracts of sale: *Young & Marten v McManus Childs* [1969] 1 A.C. 454 at 476, *per* Lord Wilberforce. For example, in *Pritchett & Gold v Currie* [1916] 2 Ch. 515 a subcontractor agreed to supply and erect a battery. The contractor went into liquidation before the battery was installed and the subcontractor sued the contractor and the employer who paid the balance of the contract sum into court. It was held that there were two contracts: one for the sale of the battery and another for its installation. The consequence was that title to the battery passed on delivery so that the money in court belonged to the liquidator. If the contract had been for work and materials title would have passed to the employer on installation. Similarly a contract to supply and hang wallpaper has been held to be two contracts, one of sale and the other for services: *Wyett v Smith and Smith*

[1908] 28 N.Z.L.R. 79. But a contract to supply and lay a carpet was held to be a contract for the sale of goods in *Philip Head v Showfronts* [1970] 1 Lloyd's Rep. 140. The higher the work content, the more likely the contract will be for work and materials: *Brooks Robinson v Rothfield* [1951] V.L.R. 405; *Collins Trading v Maher* [1969] V.R. 20; *Otis v Girvan* (1990) 2 ACLB 70. If the agreement provides for progress payments on account of the contract price it is more likely to be a contract for work and materials governed by the Supply of Goods and Services Act 1982.

Contracts for sale of goods

Under s.25 of the Sale of Goods Act 1979: 7–005

> "where a person having bought or agreed to buy goods obtains, with the consent of the seller, possession of the goods . . . the delivery or transfer by that person [the purchaser] . . . of the goods . . . under any sale, pledge, or other disposition thereof, to any person [the sub-purchaser] receiving the same in good faith and without notice of any lien or other right of the original seller in respect of the goods . . ." transfers title to the sub-purchaser.

This is an exception to the *nemo dat* rule referred to at the beginning of this chapter and is a valuable security for performance in the industry.

In *Archivent v Strathclyde General Council* (1984) 27 B.L.R. 98 Archivent was a direct supplier to a contractor. Its terms included a simple retention of title clause. The main contract was in the JCT 63 form. Archivent had not traded with this contractor before and its normal policy was to ask for cash before delivery. By an oversight it delivered ventilators to site without obtaining payment in advance. By the time the contractor went into receivership some of the goods had been fixed. Although the contractor had been paid for them it had not paid the supplier. The supplier claimed delivery up of the ventilators or payment of their value. It was held that s.25 applied: title to the unfixed goods passed to the employer as soon as it paid the contractor for them. It was crucial that (a) the goods were delivered to site under a contract of sale, and (b) the employer could prove it had paid the contractor in good faith and without notice of the retention of title clause.

The decision is also of interest because of the implicit finding that the transfer to the employer under JCT 63 satisfied the requirement of a "sale, pledge or other disposition" in s.25. As JCT 63 is a contract for work and materials, the transfer could not have been a sale, and even if there had been a constructive delivery to the employer it was not by way of pledge. The only basis for the decision was that the transfer was a "disposition" (see Goode 2004 at 46, 429). This view is supported by *P4 Ltd v Unite Integrated Solutions* [2006] EWHC 2640. In that case, a mechanical and electrical subcontractor entered a voluntary arrangement and then liquidation before having paid a specialist lighting supplier. The supplier applied for summary judgment against the contractor for damages in conversion relying on a retention of title clause in its terms and conditions. Apart from a minor element, the claim failed because the retention of title clause was not incorporated into the supply contract, and even if it had been, the contractor would have had a good defence under s.25.

One of the issues was whether the subcontractor had been paid. It was not possible to identify the supplier's goods in subcontract valuations or to match them against interim payments under the main contract. The subcontractor had however compromised a dispute with the contractor on terms that it received £190,000. On analysis, Ramsey J. found that this sum included all of the goods falling within the supply contract whether actually delivered to site or not (para.171). The settlement agreement altered the mode, but not the effect, of payment under the subcontract (para.176). The payment of £190,000 was sufficient to transfer title to the contractor under clause 21.4.5.3 of DOM/2 (to the extent it had not been transferred to the employer under clause 21.4.5.2 on payment of the contractor under JCT 98), including items delivered between the date of the payment and the subcontractor's subsequent insolvency. Although it was not necessary for his decision on the facts, Ramsey J. also held that a disposition under s.25 does not require full transfer of title. A transfer of an interest, legal or equitable, in the goods is sufficient, relying on *Worcester Finance v Cooden Engineering* [1972] 1 Q.B. 210. By clause 21.4.5.1 of DOM/2 the subcontractor cannot remove goods delivered to site other than for use in the works without the contractor's consent. Such restriction is sufficient to transfer an interest in the goods to the contractor (para.119). (Alternatively, perhaps the clause is not intended to have proprietary effect but to operate as the tangible equivalent of a blocked bank account.)

These cases can be contrasted with *Hanson v Rapid Civil Engineering* (1987) 38 B.L.R. 106 in which the requirements of s.25 were not satisfied. The supplier had traded with the contractor for some years on a running account basis. The supplier's terms included a retention of title clause. The contractor went into receivership without paying the supplier for timber products delivered to various sites. On two projects, the main contracts provided for monthly progress payments including the value of unfixed materials, but property in the materials was not to pass to the employer until it had paid for them. (There was no provision for certificates.) In the absence of payment there could be no "disposition". Unless the contract otherwise provides, an interim payment is on account of the contract sum and does not pass ownership of materials even if their value has been certified: *Egan v State Transport* (1982) 31 S.A.S.R. 481 at 542.

Contracts for work and materials

7–006 The parties to a construction contract are free to agree that property in materials shall pass other than on incorporation: e.g. on "appropriation" off site, on delivery to site, when their value is included in a valuation or a certificate, when the contractor or subcontractor is paid or on some other event: *Bateman v Eric Reed* [1960] 4 S.A. 151; *Grills v Dellios* [1988] V.R. 136. In *Dawber Williamson v Humberside CC* (1979) 14 B.L.R. 70, a domestic subcontractor agreed to supply and fix roofing slates. Sixteen tons of Welsh slates were delivered to site but had not been fixed by the time the contractor went into liquidation. At that time, the contractor had been paid for them but had not paid the subcontractor. The subcontractor fixed the slates by separate agreement with the employer without prejudice to its claim for the value of the goods. The starting point for Mais J. was that title to building materials passed on incorporation which had not occurred at the commencement of the liquidation: *Seath v Moore* (1886) L.R. 11 App. Cas. 350 at 381. So the question was, had that common law position been altered by statute or contract?

The employer initially argued that title had passed under s.25 of the Sale of Goods Act 1893 (equivalent to s.25 of the 1979 Act) but this defence failed as the slates were supplied under a contract for work and materials. The subcontract appears to have been in the Blue Form and provided for title to unfixed materials to pass on payment by the contractor but in this case the subcontractor had not been paid. Thus the contractor had no title to pass to the employer. The employer relied on the fact that the subcontractor was deemed to have notice of the terms of the main contract (JCT 63), including clause 14 by which title to unfixed materials delivered to site passes to the employer on payment to the contractor. But the court considered such notice to be insufficient to overcome the absence of privity as between employer and subcontractor. The payment terms in main and subcontract were not sufficiently back to back, and therefore clause 14 could only work where the contractor had title himself. The subcontractor obtained judgment for the value of the slates and damages for conversion. Compare *Jack Frost v Minister of Public Works* [1980] 3 S.A. 20, in which the main contract was not incorporated and an unpaid subcontractor repossessed its materials on the contractor's liquidation even though the employer had paid the contractor for them.

A similar argument based on incorporation of terms succeeded in *Sauter Automation v Goodman* (1986) 34 B.L.R. 81. A supplier agreed with a contractor to supply and commission a boiler control panel which was to be installed by others. The contractor went into liquidation after the panel had been delivered to site but before paying the supplier. The employer wanted to use the equipment. The supplier claimed the goods or their value relying on a retention of title clause in its terms and conditions but failed. First, the contractor's acceptance of the supplier's tender amounted to a counter-offer which had been accepted by the supplier's conduct in delivering the goods: compare *P4 Ltd v Unite Integrated Solutions* [2006] EWHC 2640. Thus the contract between them did not incorporate a retention of title clause and property in the goods passed on delivery. Even if there had been a valid clause imposing a trust on the proceeds of sale, Mervyn Davies J. (at 91) would have refused to make any order until after the accounting process had been concluded under the termination clause of the main contract and it was known whether any sum would become payable to the liquidator which could be attributed with certainty to the supplier's goods. Second, the contract incorporated the terms of the main contract (GC/Works/1), substituting "supplier" for "contractor", and the supplier was bound, among other terms, by clause 3 which vested its goods in the contractor on delivery to site. The main contract termination clause would have allowed the employer to pay the supplier direct but the employer was evidently not prepared to do so. Although GC/Works/1 is a contract for work and materials, it seems that the supplier genuinely had a contract for the sale of goods as the commissioning element made up a small proportion of the contract sum. Section 25 could have applied but did not because the employer had not paid the contractor.

In response to the decision in this case, clause 19.4 of JCT 80 was amended to oblige contractors to include in subcontracts a term that title to materials should pass to the employer as soon as the contractor was paid, and that the subcontractor should not deny that that had happened. This may also reflect the industry's experiences during the recession of the early 1980s (Williams 1987). A similar provision is contained in clause 3.9 of JCT 2005. Contractors sometimes offer "certificates of indemnity" against loss sustained should it later appear that the contractor had no title as an inducement for the architect to certify payment for off-site materials but these are unsecured promises which depend on the contractor's continuing solvency. Architects are nervous about certifying for off-site materials without proof of ownership in view of the potential risk of a negligence claim by the employer.

4. Remedies

7–007 So far this chapter has examined how s.25 and the standard forms operate as exceptions to the *nemo dat* rule. An unpaid supplier with a retention of title clause has various remedies: repossession or "self help" action, a declaration of ownership, an order for delivery up, an injunction restraining dealings with its goods or their proceeds of sale, or damages in conversion. If the supplier can establish that it still owns the goods and that damages would not be an adequate remedy, the prospect of an injunction depends on showing that the balance of convenience is in the supplier's favour. This section looks in more detail at the remedies available.

Repossession

7–008 "Self-help" by subcontractors removing goods from site is not uncommon, e.g. in *Dalinga v Antina* [1979] 2 S.A. 56 a lift installation subcontractor disabled a lift by removing a vital mechanism to force payment. In the Canadian case of *McNeill v Ja Ron Construction* (1979) 35 N.S.R. 2d 150, a subcontractor who suspected he might not be paid laid a septic tank in the ground but took care not to connect it to the house. On the contractor absconding, the subcontractor simply turned up with a lorry and removed the tank and other items. It was held that the subcontractor had not committed any trespass as the employer had never revoked the contractor's licence to the site which the subcontractor also enjoyed. The employer was liable in conversion to the subcontractor for refusing to hand over other items taken before the subcontractor could come back and collect them. Applying *Tripp v Armitage* (1839) 4 M. & W. 687, in the absence of any express provision regarding passing of title, a subcontractor's materials would only pass to the landowner on incorporation, which had not occurred. The subcontractor caused no damage to the owner's property in removing the septic tank which had since been installed on another site. This situation could happen in England where the contractor is informally insolvent but no termination event has yet occurred allowing the employer to terminate its employment.

Where the materials are fixed to the land but are "tenant's fixtures" so that as between landlord and tenant they are removable before the end of the term, it has been held that a retention of title supplier could require the tenant (with whom he was in contract) to detach the materials or to exercise the tenant's right of removal: *Re Galway Concrete* [1983] I.L.R.M. 402. The court expressed the view that the supplier would have a right of re-entry to detach its materials even without an express term to that effect but this aspect is questionable. See also *Taymech v Rush & Tompkins* (1990) S.L.T. 681 (removal of an inhibition after receivers appointed).

Where the supplier is in contract with the owner of the land and reserves a right of re-entry in the event of non-payment for the purpose of detaching its goods the supplier obtains an equitable interest in the land: *Re Samuel Allen* [1907] 1 Ch. 575; *Re Morrison, Jones & Taylor* [1914] 1 Ch. 50. If the right of re-entry is exercised and the materials are detached, they regain their former identity as chattels. The supplier's equitable interest takes priority over a later equitable interest, e.g. where a receiver is appointed under a floating charge over land, but will be defeated by anyone taking a later legal interest in good faith for value without notice of the supplier's interest: *Kay's Leasing Corporation v CSR Provident* [1962] V.R. 429.

In *Whenuapai Joinery v Trust Bank* [1994] 1 N.Z.L.R. 406 a secured creditor took priority over a supplier's equitable interest. The bank provided a loan to finance the work against a mortgage over the property. A joinery supplier made substantial deliveries to site and was owed nearly $180,000. His terms included a retention of title clause with a right of re-entry to detach joinery which had been fixed to the building. Following the collapse of the New Zealand property market, the developer was unable to complete the project. The supplier re-entered and removed its joinery and the bank entered into possession and sold the property. (The joinery was in fact used to complete the works without prejudice to all parties' claims.) The bank succeeded in its claim against the supplier on the ground that the joinery had become a fixture. The mortgage, which took effect as a fixed equitable charge, prohibited the removal, dismantling or structural alteration of buildings or improvements by the developer without the written consent of the bank which had not been given. Although the supplier had an equitable interest in the joinery which had been fixed the bank took priority as it had gone into possession before the supplier had re-entered without notice of the supplier's rights. On appeal, the court held the bank's priority did not stem from the act of possession but from the prohibition against removal.

A retention of title clause may well not be sufficient protection for suppliers on construction projects. Notice needs to be given to the employer and the landowner. A right of re-entry and repossession can only be effective where a supplier is in contract with the landowner and registers his interest in the land if registration is appropriate.

Delivery up

The objective of the unpaid supplier or subcontractor is not usually the **7–009** return of its materials but payment. Where payment can be adequately protected, the court is unlikely to grant an injunction for delivery up, even if the paying party is insolvent. In *Lipe v Leyland DAF* [1993] B.C.C. 385 a supplier claimed about £100,000 in respect of vehicle parts. A major part of Leyland's business consisted in the sale of spare parts. If the supplier's claim succeeded, it would be followed by hundreds of others which would wreck the receivers' chances of selling the business as a going concern. The receivers offered the supplier a personal undertaking in their own names that should its claim be accepted, the receivers would either return the goods or if they had been sold pay the suppliers their invoice values. The supplier rejected the undertaking since it would have had to take on trust the receivers' ability to pay. Hoffmann L.J. considered that those dealing with receivers can rely on the fact that as agents of the company they are entitled to an indemnity from the company's assets and that as professionals receivers would not risk bankruptcy by incurring personal liability unless they were satisfied that the company could meet its liabilities. In the circumstances, to grant an injunction would be to yield to unfair commercial pressure from the supplier. Although undoubtedly a fair result, the reasoning came as a surprise to the construction industry. The frequency of enquiries as to the level of receivers' professional indemnity insurance suggests that creditors do place some reliance on their personal assets. In *Mayflower Foods v Barnard* (unreported, August 9, 1996, noted in (1997) 14(1) Build. L.M. 1, (1998) 15(2) Build. L.M. 7) Judge Hegarty Q.C. discharged an injunction obtained ex parte preventing administrative receivers from disposing of equipment fixed to business premises as part of the sale of the business as a going concern in circumstances where the receivers had given an undertaking along the lines of that offered in *Lipe v Leyland DAF*. The undertaking extended to consequential losses that might be suffered by the claimant, who was the equipment lessor, and any liability the receivers might have for inducing or procuring a breach of the lease, damages being limited to the value of the goods. See also *Bank of Scotland v Neath Port Talbot BC* [2006] EWHC 2276 considered in Ch.6.

An injunction for delivery up was refused in *Alucraft v Costain Australia* (1991) 7 B.C.L. 179. Costain as main contractor delivered materials to Alucraft as subcontractor for processing and fabrication into cladding. Alucraft issued proceedings alleging that Costain had repudiated the subcontract, claiming damages. Costain contended that it had properly terminated, counter-claiming for a mandatory injunction for the return of materials. The injunction was refused on the ground that damages were an adequate remedy and that the balance of convenience lay with Alucraft. The particular facts were important. Alucraft accepted that Costain could collect fabricated panels which had been paid for. There were sufficient quantities of completed panels on site to ensure that the progress of the works would not be impeded by refusing an injunction. Alucraft undertook to return glass and aluminium which had not yet been used in the fabrication process but Alucraft had a lien on partially or fully fabricated panels which had not been paid for, which extended to the added value of the materials accrued from the fabrication process. Alucraft was entitled to retain raw steel, reinforcement, fixings, rubber sections, silicone and insulation which had not been used but for which it had not been paid. The position in this case can be compared with the practice of the employer providing free issue materials to the contractor: *Rossco Civil Engineering v Dwr Cymru* (unreported, July 15, 2004, Recorder Dermod O'Brien Q.C.), paras 11, 43–50.

Where the obligations of the contractor are carried out informally by one of its subsidiaries, the court may imply a contract between them having terms which are back to back with those of the main contract, including the termination clause. Thus, an administrator appointed to a subsidiary in this scenario may have no right to materials or their value brought into being for the benefit of the employer: compare *SCI Games v Argonaut Games* [2005] EWHC 1403. The subsidiary may also be liable to the employer in tort for interfering in the performance by the contractor of its obligations by preventing it from delivering up the materials in breach of the terms of the main contract of which it was aware and impliedly agreed to observe.

Restraining orders

In *UCA France v Fisher Foods* [2003] B.P.I.R. 299, Jackson J. granted an injunction restraining administrative receivers from parting with the proceeds of sale of goods sold before or after their appointment. Damages would not be an adequate remedy because the contract was governed by French law and the supplier had brought an action in France to determine the validity of the retention of title clause which would be heard within three months. No hardship would be caused to either party by granting an injunction in the interim. A receiver's powers to withhold monopoly supplies were restricted in *Land Rover v UPF* [2003] 2 B.C.L.C. 222 (specific performance in the form of a mandatory injunction ordered against a company in receivership). 7–010

Injunctions are also granted in relation to the goods themselves. In *Modern Structural (Scotland) Plastics v Tayloroof* (unreported, December 3, 1990, Sh Ct) a supplier of goods under retention of title to a subcontractor obtained an interim interdict (injunction) against a contractor restraining it from intromitting (converting) its goods or removing them from site, and an order that they be delivered up, following the subcontractor's entry into liquidation. The orders were overturned on appeal, on the contractor giving evidence that it had paid the subcontractor for the goods in question before the commencement of the winding-up, and had an arguable defence under s.25. The contractor stated that its inability to use the supplier's goods would cause eight weeks' delay to the project. Liquidated damages of £10,000 per week would be due under the main contract and the contractor might also be liable for disruption to other trades. Two-thirds of the goods claimed were fixed before the subcontractor went into liquidation. The balance of convenience lay with the contractor and the interdict was recalled (discharged). In *Thomas Graham v Glenrothes* [1967] S.C. 284 the Court of Session held it was arguable that s.25 was satisfied where goods were supplied direct to a contractor and their value included in a certificate of which 80 per cent had been paid to the contractor before it went into liquidation. The employer then sold the goods to the completion contractor. Presumably it was possible to appropriate the payment to specific goods. In the absence of payment the simple appropriation of materials by the employer after terminating the contractor's employment is unlikely to be a disposition within the meaning of the section: *Forsythe International v Silver Shipping* [1994] 1 W.L.R. 1334. In *Remm Construction v Allco* (1990) 53 S.A.S.R. 471 a subcontract for the supply and erection of structural steel was "forfeited" by the contractor on the ground of delay. The contractor had paid the subcontractor for raw steel and steel in course of fabrication off site at sub-subcontractors' premises. Other payments in respect of the steel had not been made because the contractor claimed a set-off and relied on a right to suspend payment conferred by the forfeiture clause. The subcontractor warned the sub-subcontractors not to co-operate with the contractor, who obtained an injunction against the subcontractor preventing it from interfering. The balance of convenience lay in favour of minimising delay to the project rather than conferring a security for payment on the subcontractor for claims it was pursuing in arbitration. The subcontractor argued that, although it had been paid, property in the steel had not passed to the contractor because it had not been appropriated to the contract. This was rejected, as "appropriation" was a sale of goods concept of no application to the subcontract in this case. The court seems to have assumed that the contractor owned the steel: as between contractor and subcontractor, the court would stop the subcontractor interfering in the contractor's attempts to negotiate with the sub-subcontractors; but as between the contractor and the sub-subcontractors, the latter may have retained ownership under the terms of their sub-subcontracts. Interestingly, the court held that the right to pay sub-subcontractors direct conferred by the contract operated independently of the forfeiture clause. The fact that the forfeiture clause conferred an express right to use "on site" materials but was silent about "off-site" materials was not relevant.

Conversion

7–011 After the contract has been terminated, the court may grant an injunction restraining removal of goods and materials and in appropriate cases award damages to the employer in conversion: *Marsden v Sambell* (1880) 43 L.T. 120. The conversion can consist in selling the goods, fixing them to the land or simply refusing to return them. The claimant must be the owner or the person entitled to immediate possession of the goods. This can in context include an assignor: *P4 Ltd v Unite Integrated Solutions* [2006] EWHC 2640, para.108, *Mayflower Foods v Barnard* (unreported, August 9, 1996, noted in (1997) 14(1) Build. L.M. 1).

If both main and subcontracts reserve title to unfixed materials until payment, the employer will become the owner of the materials when the subcontractor is paid for them even if that occurs after the employer pays the contractor: *Allco Steel v Australian Capital Development Corporation* (November 14, 1996, CA (NSW), noted in (1997) 14(4) Build. L.M. 1). The case concerned a subcontract for the supply and erection of structural steel. At the time the main contract was terminated by the employer, the steel had not been delivered to site. The contractor had been paid for it but had not paid the subcontractor. At that time title therefore remained with the subcontractor. There was then a deed of release under the subcontract under which the contractor made a payment to the subcontractor who was allowed to keep the steel. On the subcontractor selling the materials, the employer successfully claimed damages in conversion. The Court of Appeal of New South Wales held that it did not matter in what order payment for the steel had been made. Section 25 could not have applied since the contractor was not a buyer in possession and the subcontract was probably a contract for work and materials. The subcontractor may also have authorised the contractor to pass title to the employer in the ordinary course of business.

In *Stroud Architectural Systems v John Laing* (1993) 35 Con. L.R. 135 a supplier to a subcontractor claimed damages in conversion against a contractor in respect of glazing units which had been delivered to site but not paid for before the subcontractor went into administrative receivership. The claim relied on a retention of title clause reserving "equitable and beneficial ownership" to the goods. The court rejected the claim on the ground that the clause created an unregistered floating charge by the subcontractor in favour of the supplier, following *Re Bond Worth* [1980] 1 Ch. 228. Since title had passed to the subcontractor, the supplier had no interest in the goods and therefore no right to conversion damages.

5. Insolvency practitioners

As well as the legal and commercial issues arising out of the ownership of goods and materials on a construction insolvency, insolvency practitioners have the practical challenge of finding out exactly what has happened, which materials have been paid for, and where title might have passed to the employer through the interlocking terms of main and subcontracts or under s.25 of the Sale of Goods Act 1979. As a contractor has relatively few tangible assets, materials quickly become the focus of disputes. These may be more emotional than rational, the materials symbolising salvage from the wreck even if they have minimal economic value. If the value of the materials at stake is relatively low, it is worth noting that the court may penalise a party in costs for failing to agree to mediate its claim: *P4 Ltd v Unite Integrated Solutions* [2006] EWHC 2924. **7–012**

Administrative receivers can find themselves in difficult situations where ownership of materials is disputed. Unpaid suppliers will turn to the remedies reviewed in the previous section and may issue proceedings against the receivers as well as the company. The receivers' aim may be to maintain the status quo by keeping loose materials on site while novations are negotiated. Offering the supplier a personal undertaking to return the goods or pay their invoice value may be the only way to achieve short term respite from creditor pressure.

The position of an administrator is significantly better. First, he has a statutory power to dispose of property, with the permission of the court, in which a third party has a security interest: para.71, Sch.B1 of the Insolvency Act 1986. A security interest for this purpose includes a "retention of title agreement" which is defined as:

> "an agreement for the sale of goods to a company, being an agreement (a) which does not constitute a charge on the goods, but (b) under which, if the seller is not paid and the company is wound up, the seller will have priority over all other creditors of the company as respects the goods or any property representing the goods" (s.251 of the Insolvency Act 1986).

To the extent that building materials are supplied under a contract of sale therefore, they can bc disposed of by the company in administration free of the supplier's retention of title claim. The company has to account to the supplier for the net proceeds of the disposal and, if they are below the market value of the goods, must make up the difference. Disposal in the context of a construction contract also means fixing to the land. Although the administrator is allowed to "dispose" of the materials, s.251 uses the word "sale" rather than disposal. It seems to follow from this that an administrator's power under para.71 does not extend to materials supplied under contracts for goods and services, i.e. most subcontracts: compare the way in which these terms were construed by the court in *P4 Ltd v Unite Integrated Solutions* [2006] EWHC 2640.

Second, the supplier cannot issue proceedings against the company without the administrator's permission or that of the court: para.43, Sch.B1 of the Insolvency Act 1986. In practice an application for permission may be coupled with an application for relief, e.g. an injunction. The criteria are set out in detail in *Re Atlantic Computer Systems* [1992] Ch. 505. Permission will normally be given if it is unlikely to impede the achievement of the purpose of the administration. Otherwise, a balancing exercise is carried out: will substantially greater harm be caused to the company in allowing the creditor to repossess its goods than to the creditor in allowing the administrator to dispose of them and account for their value? If a contractor is in administration, and the goods are being disposed of to the employer, it may be relevant to inquire whether there are likely to be any risks of non-payment under the main contract. Under standard forms of building contract, a certificate can be issued in a negative amount, reflecting a downwards revaluation of the works. If the contractor relies on a future payment from the employer to fund payment to the owner of the goods, and the architect issues a negative certificate or the employer exercises a right of set-off, the supplier will have been prejudiced by not being allowed to repossess its materials. Similarly, if a subcontractor is in administration, and the subcontract makes payment conditional on receipt of money from the employer (pay when paid) or on an event or document under the main contract (pay when certified), the supplier may be placed at risk of non-payment by being refused possession of its goods.

Chapter 8

Informal Insolvency

What is insolvency, as understood from the legal perspective? In chapter 1 it was suggested that law literalises and fixes phenomena. It does this primarily through defining them in its own terms. This chapter therefore begins with the statutory definitions of insolvency and how they have been applied to the industry. The literal approach of law is concerned with cause and effect. The chapter continues with an investigation of the causes and indicators of insolvency as manifested by contractors, with reference to some of the large companies which have been affected in recent years. It concludes with a discussion of the main options available outside formal insolvency. 8–001

1. Meaning of "insolvency"

"Insolvency" covers the financial failure of individuals and companies and their position before and after the start of a formal insolvency procedure. The Insolvency Act l986 provides two alternative tests. 8–002

The going concern test

Under the going concern test, also known as the "cash flow test", "commercial insolvency" or "practical insolvency", a company is insolvent if it is "unable to pay its debts as they fall due": s.123(1) of the Insolvency Act 1986. It is important at the outset to distinguish inability to pay, deferment of payment and refusal to pay. Inability to pay is the consequence of inadequate cash flow and shortage of working capital which can have many different causes. Non-payment may be the result of a deliberate policy of postponing payment of debts until the last possible moment, e.g. service of a winding up petition. This is a dangerous line to take because of the serious effect of a petition on a company's credit rating and the confidence of its lender. Refusal to pay may result from defective performance by the subcontractor. Even where the contractor is unable to pay, it will not be insolvent under the going concern test if it has a defence to the subcontractor's claim. Hence the need to understand the different ways in which receivables arise in the industry (Ch.3). A temporary inability to pay may not amount to insolvency if the creditors do not press for payment and the company will soon receive funds to pay them, perhaps by collecting a substantial debt or borrowing additional working capital. 8–003

It can be difficult to prove inability to pay. The best evidence is a written admission, which may be forthcoming if the contractor is driven to relying on the creditors' goodwill in a last ditch attempt to avoid formal insolvency. In the absence of other evidence, insolvency can be proved by the service of a statutory demand under s.123(1)(a) of the Insolvency Act 1986. This is a simple form which is served at the registered office of the company requiring it to pay a due debt exceeding £750 within 21 days. If payment is not made within that period, and the company has no justifiable reason for non-payment, it is deemed to be insolvent and no further proof of insolvency will be required at the hearing of a winding up petition. There is no requirement that the creditor must serve a statutory demand. In *Re Taylor's Industrial Flooring* [1990] B.C.C. 44 the court stated that the vast majority of creditors seeking a winding up order do not serve statutory demands as the 21–day period merely gives the company time in which to dissipate its assets. Where "a debt is due and an invoice sent and the debt is not disputed then the failure of the debtor company to pay the debt is itself evidence of inability to pay" (at 50, *per* Dillon L.J.). In that case, a plant hire company invoiced a contractor for its charges. The contractor raised an argument that its credit period had not expired but this was rejected by the court on a finding of fact. A winding up order will not usually be made if the debt can be disputed on *bona fide* and substantial grounds or the debtor has a genuine and serious cross-claim which it has been unable to litigate (see Ch.11).

The balance sheet test

8–004 Also called "absolute" insolvency (Scotland), this test assesses a company's solvency by reference to its assets and liabilities rather than its cash flow. Under the balance sheet test a company is insolvent "if it is proved to the satisfaction of the court that the value of the company's assets is less than the amount of its liabilities, taking into account its contingent and prospective liabilities": s.123(2) of the Insolvency Act 1986. It is more difficult to apply than the going concern test. Although the 1986 Act contemplates that a snapshot will be taken as at a particular date, rather like a balance sheet, the criteria for inclusion and valuation of an asset are not necessarily the same as those which apply to a statutory audit. In the industry a housebuilder may fail the balance sheet test if its land bank is revalued downwards but remain able to meet its debts as they fall due. To an external unsecured creditor the company appears solvent; to a secured lender with the right to enforce its security if certain financial ratios are not maintained it may be insolvent. In practice, provided the going concern test is satisfied, the company has time to trade out of its difficulties.

How the tests are applied

8–005 Which test is relevant depends on the context. In general both apply on applications to restrain petitions for winding up or their advertisement as well as on the hearing of petitions for winding up or administration orders (Ch.11). The going concern test is particularly relevant to applications to stay execution of a judgment (Ch.12) or to complete an execution by a charging order or a third party debt order or to set up a retention trust or to justify an arrestment (Scotland). The balance sheet test applies in actions for wrongful trading, transaction at an undervalue and preference (Ch.20) and the disqualification of directors (Ch.21). It is also relevant to applications for security for costs. Either test may be used where a construction contract allows one party to suspend or terminate on the "insolvency" of the other (Ch.14). The same may apply to other rights, e.g. to call a demand guarantee or enforce a charge or mortgage or declare a dividend. Expert accounting evidence is admissible. There may be issues arising out of the construction of statements of standard accounting practice and financial reporting standards: *Re Colt Telecom* [2002] EWHC 2815 (creditor's petition for an administration order). To a large extent such issues are not industry specific. Similar techniques for inflating the value of assets and concealing the extent of liabilities are used across industries. Are there any particular themes emerging from industry related cases? The following aspects are worth noting.

On the asset side, the court takes into account present rather than contingent assets: *Byblos Bank v Al-Khudhairy* (1986) 2 B.C.C. 99,549. Controversial areas include the approach taken to the recognition and recoverability of revenue and profit on long term contracts under SSAP 9. In *Jarvis v PricewaterhouseCoopers* (unreported, July 13, 2000) a contractor wanted to include income of £15 million in respect of two claims. The auditor did not think they were sufficiently certain of recovery to constitute income without proof of payment or an acknowledgment from the debtor that the sum was due. The auditor subsequently resigned and filed a statement under s.394 of the Companies Act 1985 that it had done so because it had had to expand the scope of its audit to appraise the subjective approach of the management and had not been paid for this work. The contractor issued proceedings for an order that the statement not be sent out but later discontinued them. Lightman J. commented that, in delivering its statement of reasons for resignation, the auditor's role was analogous to that of a trustee (para.16). A change in accounting treatment can have a dramatic effect on a contractor's balance sheet. In 2002, for example, Amey adopted a policy of writing off bidding costs on PFI projects rather than capitalising them, and of recognising the level of risk at the early stages of projects when deciding how much profit to include. As a result, the 2001 accounts which recorded a profit of £55 million actually showed a loss of £18 million (Harrison 2002). A change from a conservative method that includes profit only on completion may signal manipulation of the accounts: see *Tong Tien See Construction v Tong Tien See* [2002] 3 S.L.R. 76, at para.65. Debtors can be maintained at artificially high levels by failing to make a provision against bad debts. Similarly maintaining the value of assets such as plant and equipment at cost rather than allowing for depreciation can falsify the position: *Taylor Projects v Brick* [2005] NSWSC 571. There may be evidence that the employer on a major project on which the subcontractor's claim against the contractor arose is in liquidation: *Re Sanpete Builders* [1989] 1 M.L.J. 393 at 400. The directors may dishonestly include uncertified sums as contingent assets when they have been paid and already included as cash at bank or include receivables which have in fact been assigned to someone else: *Chip Thye Enterprises v Phay* [2004] S.L.R. 434. Retention was not treated as an asset for accounting purposes on a security for costs application where liability was disputed by the paying party: *Europa Holdings v Circle Industries* (1992) 33 Con. L.R. 34 at 40.

Assets shown as a loan account or retained profits may in fact be paid out to directors before a contractor goes into liquidation: e.g. *Hart Investments v Larchpark* [2007] EWHC 291 at para.26. In *White Constructions v White* [2005] NSWCA 173 a contractor's assets consisted mainly in money borrowed from related companies. There was evidence of a group policy that payment of an inter-company loan would not be required unless the debtor was able to make it. The court accepted that the loans in question were not payable on demand but upon a contingency which had not yet occurred as the contractor could not afford to pay them (para.148).

Where the contractor is involved in property development, problems may arise on the treatment of interest on land acquisition and construction costs and on the valuation of the land and buildings in course of construction. Valuations of flats for example need to be tested against advertised prices: *Barry D Trentham v Lawfield Investments* [2002] S.C. 401. Projected profit has to be based on realistic cost assumptions. In *Ace Contractors v Westgarth Developments* (June 1, 1999, Fed Ct (Aus)) an employer had to replace a contractor who (it appears) had defaulted. In the meantime it entered into a direct contract with Ace, a former subcontractor on the project. Ace petitioned to wind up the employer for non-payment. One of the reasons that Weinberg J. was not satisfied that the employer had established its solvency was that it had based the cost to complete the project on the balance of the available funding, an assumption described by the contractor's accounting expert as "heroic."

In a large construction group assets and contracts may be switched around for legitimate reasons. In *Lewis v Doran* [2005] NSWCA 243 (see Ch.20) this was to separate the construction from the property side so that the property company would find it easier to obtain finance. On the other hand, a loss making contract may be transferred to a subsidiary with no assets with the aim of avoiding liability to the employer in the event of a default. The original contract party may rely on all kinds of legal argument to justify this *ex post facto* especially novation and agency. "Front" companies are not unusual. In jurisdictions with compulsory builders' registration the group company with the licence will tender and obtain the contract but the work may be carried out by another group company: *Tong Tien See Construction v Tong Tien See* [2002] 3 S.L.R. 76. With a family company group, the tender may be made in the name of a company bearing the founder's name but the contract entered into by a company operated by one of his sons. A director may not disclose full details of loans made by him or the extent of the company's liability for interest: *Barry D Trentham v Lawfield Investments* [2002] S.C. 401. A contractor may argue that liability to certain subcontractors ought not to be taken into account as it is subject to payment from the employer. Allegations are sometimes made of oral pay when paid clauses in order to avoid subcontractors' claims. Liabilities financed off balance sheet and not required to be shown in audited accounts may have to be taken into account in the balance sheet test. There may be an under-funded final salary pension scheme. It is the treatment of contingent and prospective liabilities which gives rise to most difficulty.

Valuation of contingent liabilities

8–006 Resolving a claim for defective work may require a lengthy trial and be the subject of considerable disagreement between experts. The court may conclude that the contractor is not liable at all because the defects were wholly attributable to the architect's design. Even if the contractor is found liable, the court may conclude that damages should be restricted to the cost of repair rather than replacement. Thus, depending upon the circumstances, it is possible to say that a defects claim could be worth everything or nothing. In these circumstances, how should the court apply the balance sheet test? One approach is to take the whole value of the claim into account but this could be unfair to the contractor. The creditor may be using its claim oppressively in order to stifle the contractor's genuine cross-claim. Both parties' views may be tenable at the date of the test but the employer's claim may be sufficient to convert a fully solvent contractor into a grossly insolvent one. In the event of difficulty, the court could adjourn the application to allow the contingent claim to be valued. This may be done by litigation or arbitration or by the procedure for appealing against rejection of proof. These methods would promote certainty but be a slow and expensive means of valuation. Adjudication is another possibility.

Totty and Moss propose taking a range of potential liability (at A1.08). They suggest that the lowest figure in the range should be deducted from the highest figure in order to ascertain the area of uncertainty. The figure representing the area of uncertainty is then multiplied by the percentage probability that the claim will succeed, and the result is then added to the lowest figure in the range to arrive at a valuation. UK GAAP disapproves of a method of valuation which relies upon the multiplication of a claim by a probability factor. The addition of the minimum value of the claim in the calculation proposed by Totty and Moss adds credibility to their approach but it presupposes that it is possible to arrive at realistic figures to establish the range in the first place. Where the claim depends upon the existence of a contract, and this is in dispute, the range may be between 0 and 100 per cent.

What are the alternatives? Valuation of contingent claims is necessary in the following contexts: the statutory audit of companies, security for costs applications, and breach of warranty claims. Auditors are concerned with questions of accrual and disclosure in accounts so as to show a "true and fair view". Where a contingency is reasonably certain to occur (95 to 100 per cent likelihood) it will be included. Where it is probable (50 to 95 per cent likelihood) an amount is accrued if it can be estimated with reasonable accuracy, otherwise it is disclosed in a note to the accounts. Where an outcome is possible (five to 50 per cent likelihood) no amount is accrued but the potential liability is disclosed. Where liability is unlikely (less than five per cent) disclosure is not required although good practice may recommend it. As with Totty and Moss's approach, the application of auditing techniques presupposes that liability and a range of quantum can be established. The auditor's approach is therefore of limited value to the balance sheet test. Where there is evidence that a plaintiff will be unable to pay a defendant's costs if the defendant succeeds in its defence, the court may order the plaintiff to provide security for costs under s.726 of the Companies Act 1985. The judges of the Technology and Construction Court have found it difficult to assess the probability of success in defects claims. If they experience difficulty given their experience of the industry and familiarity with the issues, courts with insolvency jurisdiction may find themselves in an even more difficult position. Attempts to value contingent liabilities in the context of agreements for the sale of shares or assets in the company have not enjoyed greater success: *Trollope and Colls v Gresham* (1984) 2 C.L.D. 7.16. Claims in the construction industry, whether made by employer, contractor or subcontractor, are often inflated. They suffer from "exaggerations which in all good faith everybody is inclined to make in estimating the expenses which they can recoup from someone else" (*Chandless v Whitton*, unreported, December 10, 1986, Browne-Wilkinson V.C.). The acceptance of the full value of the contingent claim for the purpose of the balance sheet test fails to take this important factor into account.

The *pari passu* rule

8–007 A creditor with a security interest or proprietary right in the debtor's property is much more likely to be paid in the event of the debtor's insolvency. An ordinary unsecured creditor often receives little or nothing. Hence the scramble for assets which precedes many insolvencies. The position for ordinary unsecured creditors changes with the start of a liquidation or a bankruptcy when a creditor's debt is converted into the right to claim in the proceeds of sale of the assets after they have been realised by the insolvency practitioner. The claim is known as a "proof of debt" which, if admitted, entitles the creditor to a dividend, each creditor receiving the same percentage of its debt: s.107 of the Insolvency Act 1986, r.4.181 of the Insolvency Rules 1986. This principle of fair treatment is known as the *pari passu* rule ("with the same step"): see *Re Redman (Builders) Ltd* [1964] 1 W.L.R. 541. This rule forms the background to much of insolvency law (Ch.13). It is the basis of the liquidator's power to claw back property transferred by the company before the start of the procedure by avoiding transactions which have unjustly enriched one person at the expense of the general body of creditors. This applies to transactions with directors, shadow directors, connected persons, associates, creditors, sureties, participators in fraud and others (Ch.20). The idea is that the transactions have, by diminishing the company's assets, conferred an unfair or improper advantage on the other party. It is the fact that the company participated in these transactions which justifies their avoidance.

2. Causes of insolvency

8–008 Contractors are renowned for having low profit margins, low fixed assets and low capital but high cash flow and high return on capital employed. Financing is generated internally from positive cash flow and retained profits and externally from short term finance, usually an overdraft repayable on demand. Short term finance can support working capital, stock and work in progress; but for growth, long term external finance is needed in the form of equity investment and long term loans.

Structural aspects

8–009 Hillebrandt and Cannon (1989) point out that, as a consequence of positive cash flow and the lack of an asset base, the industry has particular characteristics which make it vulnerable to insolvency. Firstly, contractors need to diversify in order to use the cash earned from contracting to generate higher profits, create assets as security for loans and seek financial stability by venturing into businesses counter-cyclical to construction. Diversification was a major cause of insolvency between 1989 and 1995. Whether the move was into property as with Rush & Tompkins and Lilley or into subcontracting and materials supply as with Conder, failed acquisitions poisoning the financial health of the group have been a feature. Secondly, there are no financial barriers to entry into the industry. Ease of entry has a number of consequences: a proliferation of small firms with little management expertise, a tendency to over-capacity even at the height of a market, and an industry where market forces are at their most ruthless. Yet calls for a licensing system have not found favour in the UK. During the recession of 1989–1993 there is evidence that even formal insolvency was not sufficient to balance supply and demand. One analysis found that the combined turnover of the 10 largest contractors who became formally insolvent in the previous three years was £2.1 billion whereas the loss of capacity suffered by the industry over the same period was only half that amount (*Contract Journal*, May 5, 1994). Thirdly the predominance of family firms also contributes to the level of financial failure. This is because ingrained attitudes lead to financial complacency and an inability to adapt to a changing market. Fourthly, conglomerates seeking positive cash flow are attracted to contractors. One thinks of Lonrho which bought Sunley. Sunley in turn purchased Turriff on its insolvency, only for Sunley Turriff to purchase part of Lilley on its receivership. Sunley itself went into administration in 2003. Fifthly, management buy-outs are more feasible than in other industries. Buy-outs have been a common exit from receivership: examples are Graham Wood, Conder Structures and Henry Barrett. However, there have been cases where a management buy-out has been followed by receivership due in part to the level of debt required to finance it. An example is Elliott Northern, where the business was acquired through a buy-out from the receiver of JA Elliott, which went into receivership in 1993 and was then dispersed through novations. With the Dew Group in 1992 it was possible to plan the receivership by appointing receivers to the parent company, allowing the target company to continue trading while a buy-out was negotiated. From time to time, contractors experience a sharp decline in demand leading to reduced turnover and lost cash flow. In the 1990s recession, excessive competition forced many to tender at below cost. Tenders for long term contracts were based on prices for subcontractors and materials which later increased sharply. These features cannot be sustained by the unstable sources of finance used by contractors. Cash reserves built up in previous years are lost and contractors have to turn to their bankers and shareholders for support. Haig (2000) demonstrates with brief case studies how significant upwards rent reviews, and the adoption of a more restrictive planning policy by a local authority, as well as the effect of family problems, can also affect a contractor's solvency.

(b) Fluctuating demand

Demand for the industry's products is cyclical and fluctuates in accordance **8–010**
with Government policy and the general economic climate. In *Re UDL Civil Contractors* [2000] HKCFI 519, schemes of arrangement were sanctioned in

respect of a large construction group in Hong Kong. The group's insolvency resulted from the recession in South-east Asia in the late 1990s, specifically from "the unexpected calling of loans from major financial creditors of the Subsidiaries which triggered off a chain reaction leading to the refusal of credit arrangements by trade creditors and default in payment by the Subsidiaries" (*per* Le Pichon J., at p.10 of transcript). Loss of market may occur suddenly in specialist areas, e.g. the crisis in the fit-out sector in 2004. Insolvency is more likely to occur in the construction industry than most others. It has been suggested however that the way the figures are compiled and presented gives a misleading picture of the relation between construction and other industries (Hillebrandt 1984). "There is a greater chance of a construction firm failing than other firms but it is less than twice as much, not five times as much as some statements imply" (Hillebrandt 1977). The industry appears so prominent because it is the largest industrial category which is not subdivided in the statistics and is bound to have a larger number of failures because of its unusual fragmentation.

It has been said that "the construction industry, more than almost any other, faces continuous and at times violent changes in work load, in work mix and in the method of managing the process. It is almost by definition changing its product all the time" (Hillebrandt and Cannon 1989, xix). Management of change means adapting strategy to the processes of growth, recession, recovery and so on (Lansley 1987, 5, 141). Failure to adapt has historically been a prime cause of insolvency in this sector. Sustained economic growth over the last 10 years, coupled with improvements to payment procedures, and cultural shifts towards longer term relationship building with employers, have combined to mitigate this feature. In hindsight perhaps the recession of the 1990s had a cleansing effect by clearing out a layer of medium-sized firms and by changing the claims culture which was afflicting the industry. For some, the trend towards partnering and framework agreements is beneficial in providing a stable work load; but it can lead to loss of market for those who are left out.

Poor financial control

8–011 Successful contractors are expert at cash control and management. They have evolved highly sophisticated techniques of cash flow forecasting and monitoring. A well managed contractor maintains detailed financial, cost and management accounts which allocate cost in as much detail as possible to specific contracts and to individual elements within them but, unfortunately, many fall short of this standard. Many contractors fail to collect debts, particularly retentions, allowing them to accumulate until their age makes them difficult to collect. The adage of cash flow is to "collect early and pay late". Late payment is, however, a two-edged sword. It is a serious problem in the industry and a contributory factor to the large number of insolvencies.

The Banwell report concluded:

> "Prompt payment for work done is of such importance and all concerned are so sensitive to delay that the industry generally must be

willing to make use of procedures which will ensure that contractual obligations are met promptly and that there is no impediment to the proper flow of money" (1964, para.9.6).

Delay in payment affects all parties involved in the contractual chain. It is hard to say what difference the Late Payment of Commercial Debts (Interest) Act 1998 as amended has made (see Barber 2007). Last in line is the builders' merchant, colloquially known as the "industry's banker".

Generating working capital from operations is a hallmark of the industry. "The funds generated from operations are potentially far greater than the value of the organisation managing them. This, properly managed, gives the contracting organisation significant opportunities, but leads also to significant risk for the system" (Kenley 2003, 256). The practices and techniques involved have been called "cash farming". The term was apparently coined by Gyles in his (1992) report on productivity in the construction industry in New South Wales. The Gyles Report refers to two studies of failed contractors, Girvan and KB Hutcherson Group, in which cash flow was generated by managing the timing of payments. Cash flow was diverted to another part of the business when it was needed for the construction side; or it was relied on too heavily instead of equity and debt finance. In both cases a sudden dip in cash flow resulted in insolvency (Kenley 2003, 232).

Most capital is usually needed at the inception of a contract. If a contractor is over-reliant on "cash farming", it is vulnerable when it begins to take on a number of contracts running concurrently. This may happen to a small company that suddenly "takes off", and wins more work than it can reasonably handle. The real danger seems to stem from the fact that a contractor may be blinded by good cash flow and believe that the money is his to spend, rather than the consequence of trade credit which will have to be repaid. Instead of preserving the funds or investing on the money markets with provision for immediate or short term availability, the contractor may spend it on fixed assets or luxury goods. As a consequence, there is no "safety buffer" to fall back on if demand falls and it becomes necessary for a time to tender at lower rates. This is a potential disadvantage of front end loading, the practice of weighting a tender so that the prices of items of work early in the programme are artificially raised and items towards the end of the job lowered. Kenley (2003, 248) gives an example of how this can go wrong. A contract was front end loaded but the information was withheld from the contract administrator. Early subcontracts which should have generated a margin of 25 per cent were let at five per cent, the target margin for the project. A significant part of the work was done at this percentage. The error was only discovered when the project was two-thirds completed. Ironically, the employer realised that the rates for finishing trades were low and ordered additional work based on them.

The "knock-on effect"

The vast majority of contractors are small firms with few employees. Small **8–012**
firms often fail because of the financial failure of another company higher in the contractual chain. A significant number of insolvencies occur as a

direct result of the insolvency of another party. This phenomenon is known as the "domino" or "knock-on" effect. It has three aspects. First, the knock-on effect is felt up or down the chain. The insolvency of a contractor may bring down a series of subcontractors and suppliers; but it may also cause the failure of an employer set up for a project which becomes unviable after the contractor's failure. Secondly, the effect can be felt across different companies in the same group. Thirdly, the knock-on effect is experienced across industrial sectors. The property industry is cyclical and experiences boom and bust periods. A sharp decline in the property market reduces the demand for construction work which causes insolvency among contractors. The fall in orders is felt by subcontractors, suppliers and manufacturers of plant, equipment and transport. A slump in house-building inevitably leads to a contraction in demand for home furnishings, household appliances and DIY services. The failure of a parent company may lead to the collapse of the entire group. This may arise where each company has guaranteed the liabilities of the others. Similarly, the failure of one partner may cause the insolvency of the joint venture company if the other partner is unable or unwilling to assume responsibility for its debts. The failure of one partner may also lead to the insolvency of the other. A common reaction to a substantial bad debt is the purchase of work at low or negative margins in order to maintain turnover e.g. *Kenna & Brown v Kenna* [1999] NSWSC 533. Suddenly winning more work may give the appearance of doing well; but suicidal bidding of this kind only makes the problem worse, increasing the risk of further insolvencies. The knock-on effect occurs in other situations, e.g. the insolvency of Independent Insurance in 2001, leaving contractors to bear their own claims as well as losing premiums. In the eighteenth and nineteenth centuries banking insolvency was a significant cause of insolvency among contractors.

How can the knock-on effect be avoided? Protection against insolvency can be obtained by a combination of measures, especially by avoiding excessive concentration on a particular client, industrial sector, region or even country. A pattern of growth commonly seen is where a small contractor forms a relationship with one particular client. If that client becomes insolvent or decides to place its work elsewhere, the contractor cannot support its overheads and debt and is forced into insolvency. In *Re Harris Simons* [1989] 1 W.L.R. 368 a contractor went into administration after increasing its turnover from £830,000 in 1985 to £17 million in 1987 and £27 million in 1988. Almost all of the increase was attributable to one client. The contractor became unable to pay its debts after substantial sums were withheld as a result of a dispute. This is a potential risk in "partnering". The same point applies to companies concentrating in one sector. During the 1980s, many contractors expanded into house-building and commercial property and were badly affected when both markets collapsed in 1989. Diversification during a recession is extremely difficult because the influx of competition drives down margins forcing newcomers to buy in work with the attendant risks referred to earlier. Geographical spread ought to give some protection against insolvency since demand fluctuates across the country. Finding work overseas is not necessarily the answer: the property ventures in the US undertaken by Rush & Tompkins were a significant cause of its receivership and liquidation in 1990.

Overwhelming contract claims

If a construction contract goes wrong, it can go badly wrong. An exceptional claim against the contractor under one contract can be enough to cause insolvency. One example is liability for liquidated damages following a failure to complete the works on time. The greatest danger is that management is forced to concentrate on one problem contract and the effort to extricate the company draws in resources from the rest of the company or group. There have been some striking examples in recent years, notably the contract for the construction of the Kariba Dam in Zambia undertaken by Mitchell Construction in the early 1970s. In his account of the contract and the subsequent receivership of the company, David Morrell, Mitchell's former chairman, argues that problems on the Kariba contract arose out of chronic under-certification and the refusal by the employer to allow compensation for unforeseen ground conditions: **8–013**

> "The most crucial fact we faced was that between October 1971 and April 1972 we had suffered an adverse cash flow at Kariba of £1 million and, at a time when we should really have been in our stride, work was almost at a standstill. In the previous October we had raised £1 million through the issue of debenture stock, because it was considered prudent to augment the company's working capital; but in those few months the whole of that sum had disappeared down a large hole in Central Africa. Not only that, but the drain was continuing and would go on unless and until the engineer acknowledged that the rock was treacherous and gave us some financial relief. Our reaction in April 1972, when the storm clouds had unmistakably gathered, was twofold. We stopped tendering for new projects. At the same time we turned our attention to trying to collect some of the huge sums which were owing to us. We also made some internal reorganisation in order to limit the disruption to the rest of our business. In cutting back on tendering we were, of course, taking the opposite action to a contractor who is seriously unstable. He is likely to seek his solution in a vastly inflated order book, with a great deal of 'front-end loading', in the hope of gaining liquidity relief while putting his house in order. Our position was different. We had many assets to protect, and our biggest fear was that they would all be absorbed by this one disastrous contract" (Morrell 1987, 165).

By January 1973, when the receiver was appointed, Mr Morrell estimates that Mitchell had been under certified by £4.1 million. Under-certification is an area of risk in contracting which the contractor is not well placed to resist. Another example of an overwhelming contract claim bringing down a substantial contractor is that of Davy Corporation. Davy was founded in 1830 but was forced to dispose of its main businesses in 1991 following a disastrous contract for the conversion of an oil rig in the North Sea. The contract sum was in excess of £120 million and agreed as a fixed price, no allowance being made for progress payments. Davy's problems started with the withdrawal of a joint venture partner and were compounded by increased safety requirements, industrial relations problems and difficulties experienced in the course of construction. Liquidated damages eventually exceeded the contract sum.

Significant losses on major projects caused John Laing plc to sell its construction business to O'Rourke Holdings for a nominal sum in 2001. John Laing re-focused its core business on investment and PFI projects, returning to profitability in 2003. In a detailed case study, Morris (2005) analyses several contracts on which Laing Construction agreed to a target price (with pain/gain share mechanism) but subject to a guaranteed maximum price. The company then experienced serious cost overruns which it could not claim from the employer. She also questions whether other features such as the company's family ownership and control and the relative autonomy given to subsidiaries could have contributed to its financial difficulties. It was the fact that the group had diversified and acquired valuable assets in property and homes which it could sell that enabled it to successfully reorganise itself. But diversification can sometimes work against the solvency of construction groups.

Imprudent diversification

8–014 Contractors look to other sectors in search of higher profits than are to be made from contracting. Successful contractors need outlets to invest positive cash flow. During the 1980s, many contractors were tempted into property development for these reasons, but have since withdrawn from the sector or have become insolvent. The largest insolvency was the Rush & Tompkins Group which went into receivership in April 1990 with liabilities thought to exceed £300 million. The company was formed in 1930 and was floated on the Stock Exchange in 1971. Its core business of contracting and minor civil engineering was reasonably successful. The company experienced a liquidity problem in 1986 but was able to reduce borrowing by a rights issue. New management was introduced which decided to close the civil engineering side and diversify into property development. The company would enter into a joint venture with a partner who provided the land and obtained planning permission. Projects were financed through a jointly owned company whose assets would be charged to the lender. Rush & Tompkins assumed all the risk, however, because it guaranteed the liabilities of the joint venture company and acted as contractor to it. A further rights issue was planned in 1989 but was not proceeded with. Cash flow problems emerged towards the end of 1989 and a programme of property disposals was launched, but by February 1990 additional financing was sought from the company's bank which was refused. After additional security was provided in March 1990, the bank lent a small amount of new money, but, after negotiations for further equity from existing shareholders failed, the company's shares were suspended in early April 1990 and, two weeks later, the company ceased trading. Receivers were appointed by the bank on 48 hours' notice. Unusually, for such a large company, there had been no prior investigating accountant's report. Diversification can also be achieved by moving from one method of procurement to another. An example from the early 1990s is Harry Neal, a long established contractor, which decided to move from lump sum to management contracting but could not adjust to the different culture. Insolvency could also result from an acquisition which turns out to be a financial liability. Similarly while some companies have experienced problems after moving from management contracting or construction management to design and build and PFI projects, others such have successfully moved out of contracting into PFI. On a smaller scale, it was reported that one of the reasons why a roofing contractor became insolvent was its expansion into "total envelope solutions", i.e. also providing cladding and guttering. Although contract values increased as a result, so did the level of technical expertise and the company's exposure to fluctuations in materials prices, the volatility in metals being much greater than in asphalt (Leftly 2006). Substantial sums can be incurred in supporting a new subsidiary, even by means of an orderly wind down of its activities, and in litigation to recover losses from the vendor. For some, the urge to build an empire is just too strong: many insolvencies have resulted from corporate aggrandisement.

"Phoenix" companies

In its recent survey of the construction industry in Australia, the Cole Commission concluded that the industry "has particular characteristics which make it vulnerable to phoenix company activity" (Cole 2003, Vol.8, ch.12, para.93). Phoenix trading occurred "most commonly in building sub-industries which have large workforces of semi or unskilled labour, and where labour costs are a significant part of the running costs of the business" (para.6), especially formworking, scaffolding, concreting, bricklaying, plastering, gyprock fixing and steel-fixing. A major feature is non-payment of the equivalent of PAYE and National Insurance Contributions. Three scenarios were identified. Under the first, a contractor trades for a short time (six months to two years) and builds up large debts, then goes into liquidation. A new company is formed which takes over the old company's assets and business for nothing while leaving the liabilities with the insolvent company. The second scenario involves the formation of a management company to hold the assets of the business which are hired at exorbitant rates to a phoenix company which employs all the staff and supplies labour to contractors but does not account for tax. The phoenix company is allowed to go into liquidation and is replaced by another company. In the third situation, the group consists of three companies dealing with management (i.e. owning plant and equipment etc), sales (i.e. contracting) and supply of labour. "Sales" receives all group income, while "Management" owns all group assets. "Sales" may pay hire charges or rent to "Management" at inflated rates. But "Sales" only pays "Labour" enough for wages net of tax. "Labour" as the phoenix company is allowed to go into liquidation, leaving "Sales" and "Management" to carry on trading with a new labour supply company. "Sales" may be successful in tendering for new work as it does not budget for tax liabilities. The Cole Report includes a detailed case study of one formwork group, Emerson Industries, which illustrates these features. Non-payment of tax may not be planned at the inception of trading; it may arise because a contractor cannot raise sufficient capital and is tendering at below cost to survive (Ch.21). In the UK s.216 of the Insolvency Act 1986 aims to prevent the use of phoenix companies by imposing personal liability on a director of a company bearing the same or similar name to a previous company which has become insolvent of which he was a director (Ch.20). 8–015

Other causes

8–016 Many companies rely on the continued support of a parent to remain viable. For example, withdrawal of parent company support led to the administration of Ballast in 2003 (Leftly 2003). See also *Wallace-Smith v Thiess Intraco* (2005) 218 A.L.R. 1 in which an Australian company became insolvent after withdrawal of support by its UK parent.

3. Indicators of insolvency

8–017 Most indicators of insolvency are matters of common sense but sometimes the same action can be interpreted either as prudent management or a distress signal. An early indicator of insolvency could be a missed payment deadline or a request for an extended payment period. A request for accelerated payment or reduced retention is frequently a sign of a cash flow problem: *Re DKG Contractors* [1990] B.C.C. 903 at 911. In the medium term, increasing creditor pressure results in the service of writs and notices of arbitration. Damaging rumours may start to circulate on site. A contractor in difficulty tries to reschedule payments by raising disputes, making unjustified contra charges or set-offs and by refusing to make payments on account when only a small element is in dispute. A cash crisis causes rapid management turnover on and off site. It has been argued that the return on scarce managers who are difficult to replace should be considered as a criterion of financial performance rather than return on capital employed, management expertise being the principal scarce resource limiting the expansion of a construction business (Hillebrandt and Cannon 1989, at 71). Reduction in site supervisory staff leads to defective workmanship which aggravates the company's difficulties in getting paid. A company may become known for under-bidding to win work and take on excessive numbers of surveyors to launch claims against employers.

An auditor's report qualified on a going concern basis is an indicator that the company is on the road to formal insolvency in the short to medium term as also is the late filing of accounts. Accounts do not, however, necessarily tell the whole story (see above). Access to internal accounts is difficult to obtain for all but secured lenders and these may be inaccurate. Credit references are one source of information but mistakes can be made. In *Loughton Contracts v Dun & Bradstreet* [2006] EWHC 1224 an agency wrongfully published a negative financial report on the claimant and was liable in damages for libel. If a company is quoted on the Stock Exchange, its share price is one indication of its financial worth but this can be illusory if information available to analysts fails to disclose the true picture. Research by Abidali (1990) referred to in Morris (2005) analysing financial ratios taken from the accounts of construction companies, eleven of which had failed, found that predictive techniques such as Z-score and A-score had to be adjusted for use when pre-qualifying contractors. The financial press publishes details of transactions by directors in shares of their own companies, but this is not necessarily a distress signal: it may simply record a particular director's need for cash rather than any problem with the company.

By the time a creditor becomes aware of a problem, it may be too late. A company may be forced to admit to its client that it cannot continue trading without *ex gratia* payments. The client may feel that it is in its own best interest to make such payments rather than suffer the consequential costs of engaging a completion contractor, as happened with Joseph Bull and Sons building the Royal Courts of Justice (Ch.1). At the terminal stage, the contractor may be refused trade credit. Before a company goes into administration or liquidation, there is a twilight period when it is known to be financially vulnerable. During this period, creditors stalk the company's assets hungry for payment or security to improve their position in the impending insolvency. The law of the jungle prevails and the most powerful (or the best advised) succeed in getting paid in priority to others.

4. Informal insolvency procedures

When asked for money, investors turn to a company's balance sheet. **8–018**
What assets does it have? Unlike property companies, contracting firms have relatively few tangible assets which can be carved up and redistributed among the creditors or offered as security to lenders (see Ch.2). A company which has never diversified out of contracting will have debtors, retention, claims and work in progress: all of them assets derived from construction contracts which are regarded by banks as a flawed form of security. Small contractors may also own a lease, stock and vehicles but these are unlikely to be of much value to a lender.

Independent business review

In reviewing its options a contractor has to consider the interests of **8–019**
lenders (including banks, venture capitalists and holders of debt instruments), trade creditors such as subcontractors and suppliers, bondsmen, employers, preferential creditors, shareholders, landlords, asset lessors, public utilities and employees. If a contractor approaches a bank with a request to increase the overdraft facility, the bank may require the contractor to commission a viability report or independent business review from an accountant (ICAEW 1992). This may be either the result of a full investigation which may take weeks or a quick review lasting a day or two, known as a "quick and dirty". Such a review may conclude that the business cannot be saved and that the bank should take immediate action. The overdraft limit is likely to be cut causing an immediate cash flow crisis resulting in the voluntary liquidation of the company unless the directors can find another source of short term finance. The reduction may be followed by a requirement that the overdraft limit is further reduced by the amounts of additional sums paid into it. Timing is important and the bank may act immediately after a large payment is received from an employer before the contractor can pay trade creditors. This is more likely where a contractor has failed to keep the bank fully informed or where there is no market for its services. Surveys by the Association of Business Recovery Professionals record loss of market as the most common reason for company failure (R3 2004, 25). If a more detailed investigation is commissioned, what factors will influence the lending decision? The key question is whether the business

is viable. Viability is in the eye of the beholder (Adamson 1991). An objective assessment can only be made by an outsider. This is usually an independent insolvency accountant (rather than the company's auditor). Some firms publish special briefings on the industry for the benefit of lenders (Grant Thornton 1999). An initial review is taken of the company's cash flow since uninterrupted cash flow enables a company to continue trading while the options are sorted out. The best approach is to look for positive aspects of the business while recognising the negative ones. The accountant will also appraise the quality of the management. The report is then presented to the bank and a lending decision made. This can result in the company entering "intensive care" and conditions of further lending being imposed.

"Intensive care"

8–020 There is a wide range of possibilities to consider, either alone or in conjunction with each other.

1. Operational measures. These include cutting overheads and "non-productive" staff (White 2000), managing working capital by improving collections and obtaining more generous credit, alternative finance such as factoring, asset refinancing or venture capital.
2. Reorganisation. This involves an alteration to the group's structure by winding down loss-making businesses, merging separate businesses or divisions to reduce cost and create "synergy" or separating businesses to take advantage of new markets. Where businesses are discontinued, careful timing is required to take advantage of tax losses and allowances. Tax is a major concern in the swaps of businesses and shares between group members, sale and lease backs, hive down and sale arrangements, the creation of new subsidiaries and asset refinancing.
3. Merger or takeover.

   > "For example, in 1996, Wimpey swapped their quarrying and contracting activities for Tarmac's house-building division. In December 1998, Bovis and WS Atkins proposed a merger. Tarmac created an offshoot Carillion in 1999 but was itself bought over by Anglo American in 2000. Anglo American then sold a substantial part of Tarmac on to Hanson. Tilbury-Douglas changed its name to Interserve Project Services Ltd to reflect its move from being a construction contractor to a support services company" (Morris 2005, 29).

4. Secondment. Secondment of managers from one part of the group to another may be sufficient. Alternatively, the appointment to the board of a "company doctor", "turnaround specialist" or an insolvency practitioner is worth considering.
5. Rescheduling. Rescheduling is the postponement of payment of the principal or interest on a debt: see *Try Build v Blue Star Garages* (1998) 66 Con. L.R. 90. For example, a trustee of an 8 per cent loan

note maturing in 2009 might agree to reschedule repayment of the principal to 2012 provided that interest is paid at 10 per cent after 2009. Rescheduling can include the reduction of interest rates, waiver of debt and other possibilities.

6. Moratorium. A moratorium is a consensual freeze on the enforcement of rights contingent on an agreed date or event. For example, where a company has comparatively few creditors, they might be prepared to suspend their rights pending the completion of a major contract and an orderly wind down of the company's affairs: *Re Barrington and Associates* [1989] V.R. 940. In practice, a moratorium is implemented in conjunction with one or more of the other options.
7. Composition. A composition is a contract between the company and its creditors to pay less than the face value of its debts. For example, the creditors might agree to accept 60 pence in the pound in full and final satisfaction of their debts to enable the company to continue trading.
8. Subordination. Major shareholders, suppliers, as well as other group companies who have lent money may agree to subordinate their claims in order to induce a company's bankers not to enforce their security in the hope of enabling the company to trade out of what may often be temporary liquidity problems.
9. Arrangement. The word "arrangement" is wide enough to embrace most informal processes, as well as voluntary arrangements under the Insolvency Act 1986 considered in Ch.13, and schemes of arrangement under the Companies Act 1985 (Goode 2005, para.1–25).
10. Rationalisation. Similar to reorganisation but involving the disposal of assets or businesses. The decision to sell depends on whether the proceeds of sale will exceed the loss of cash flow generated by those assets or businesses. An example is Jarvis's decision to sell a stake in its PFI investment on London Underground in 2004. Morris (2005, 54) states that: "John Laing plc had transformed from a company averaging £1.4 billion turnover with losses of £30 million in 2002 to a reduced £480 million turnover in 2003 with profits of £20 million when the disposal program had been completed."
11. Restructuring. Restructuring is the alteration of a company's balance sheet by agreement between the company and its lenders, e.g. Eurotunnel. It may include elements of all of the above together with an alteration to the company's share capital. This is now considered in more detail.

Large-scale restructuring

A restructuring can be an expensive process involving heavy professional fees of merchant banks, accountants and lawyers in addition to the costs of redundancies and asset disposals. Restructuring may preserve the financial viability of other businesses in the region who are clients of the lenders, preserve a significant customer for future lending, and enable the customer to continue to pay interest and leave open the possibility of the **8–021** bank's recovering the principal after the business has recovered sufficiently to be sold or floated. Restructuring is more likely to take place where the contractor has acquired tangible assets in the form of property and subsidiary companies with viable businesses. The aim is to persuade the company's lenders that they have more to gain by co-operating with each other than by enforcing their securities. The company will involve subsidiaries and shareholders where it is contemplated that a rights issue, a debt-equity conversion or a guarantee will be required. Trade creditors will not usually be involved but continue to be paid in the ordinary course of business in order to prevent a winding up petition being issued. Under the London Approach developed by the Bank of England, lenders act in unison and agree to allow the company to continue to draw on facilities which have not been exhausted (Kent 1997). Lenders also agree to postpone enforcement of their securities and in appropriate cases to provide further working capital in proportion to their existing commitments on the basis that further advances will be given priority. There are three stages: standstill, refinancing and workout.

The aim of a standstill is to arrive at a short term interim agreement between the banks in order to stabilise the position. The lawyers acting for the banks will need the following information: a group structure chart, full details of joint ventures and other off balance sheet activities, existing facilities and security, an inventory of the company's property, copies of all negative pledges etc (White 1998). The standstill agreement will deal with waiver of default, a moratorium and the basis on which new money is to be provided. It may also lay down further conditions precedent to drawdown. A standstill enables the banks to work out what their respective positions would be on a notional liquidation of the borrower. This will influence their respective negotiating positions when dealing with the refinancing agreement. A steering committee is chaired by a co-ordinating bank which is often the clearing bank with the largest debt. The committee represents a number of diverse interests including banks, leasing companies, bondholders etc. Their loans may be secured or unsecured, long or short term, from a parent or subsidiary, guaranteed, subordinated etc. The company will take advice from its lawyers, auditors and merchant bank who may be appointed especially to advise on the restructuring.

The refinancing agreement will determine the basis on which the company's existing and future borrowing is to be dealt with. This will vary in each case. The agreement should authorise the steering committee to approve the terms of all asset disposals and lay down the priority in which the proceeds of sale are to be paid to the banks. It will also provide the machinery for the conversion of debt into equity (as occurred for example with Costain and YJ Lovell), the subordination of existing borrowing to enable lenders of new money to take prior security and a moratorium on the enforcement of existing securities. The agreement will provide a termination date for completion of the rescue or the wind down as the case may be and the refinancing period will end by expiry, default or repayment. Detailed monitoring arrangements are needed. Default under the refinancing agreement may include the presentation of a winding up petition which is not withdrawn within, say, 10 business days. Changes in the termination date or interest rates would probably require the unanimous approval of the banks, whereas other matters might require the approval only of the steering committee or of a group of banks.

After the refinancing agreement has been executed, the workout has to be closely monitored. Banks do not want a permanent stake in construction companies and will take an active interest in the means whereby their shareholding can be realised. If problems emerge during the workout which were not previously known, the company may be forced into administration or liquidation. The restructuring of Lilley failed through the discovery of large "black holes" in the balance sheet of joint venture companies which had environmental problems which might have cost £14 million to put right.

Small to medium enterprises

For the smaller company or group, the elaborate procedure outlined in the previous section will not be appropriate. In recent years, especially since the Enterprise Act 2002, it has become common for "turnaround professionals" to be appointed to the boards of companies in financial difficulty. As well as the range of possibilities canvassed under the heading "intensive care" above, other options have become popular such as invoice discounting, the disposal of loans on the secondary debt market, and the facilitation of an "early exit" whereby the business or assets of a company are disposed of before its cash flow dries up. Asset-based lenders and private equity funds are playing a more prominent role. For example, Alchemy Partners invested in Sunley Turriff for several years before the contractor entered administration in 2003. Endless LLP describe on their website how they provided investment support for a management buyout of DavyMarkham Ltd, a heavy engineering company which supplied the boring machine used on the Channel Tunnel project, as part of a broader turnaround strategy. A case study by the Society of Turnaround Professionals (*www.stp.org.uk*) in respect of Multi-national Niche Engineering Group, which supplies the oil and gas sector, focused on operational changes and the settlement of litigation against the company.

Lending criteria

What are the factors that influence a lender when deciding whether to accept one of these options rather than appointing an administrator? The bank's perspective is governed by a number of factors. The first is stability. If the borrower's position is unstable, lenders may prefer to enforce their security than risk its erosion by creditors enforcing judgments against the company's assets. One of the factors preventing the restructuring of Lilley was the extent of creditor pressure: over 300 writs had been issued against the company by the time receivers were appointed. The second factor is security. If lenders are fully secured, or nearly so, they are more likely to appoint administrators than agree a restructuring. Conder was not supported because the banks were almost fully secured. Costain was supported because a receivership would not have resulted in a good recovery for the banks who were forced to take risks to get their money back. With Lilley, a restructuring would still have left the banks 50 per cent secured and a receivership was thought to be **8–022** the better option. Where possible, the bank will improve its security before taking steps to enforce it, as happened with Rush & Tompkins. The third factor is the prospect of recovery. Banks will appraise the quality of the management and the underlying viability of the business. Banks place comparatively little weight on the value of contractors' claims and discount the chances of contractors squeezing margins from sub-contractors and suppliers especially as a market begins to rise. Evidence of previous tendering on negative margins is also likely to deter lenders. Another relevant factor is the question of new money. Banks regard the conversion of debt into equity and the provision of new money as options of last resort. If new money is required, they are happier for shareholders to raise it through a rights issue or a new placing of shares or for a venture capitalist to provide it on the basis of new security taking priority over existing security. If debts are so great that interest would not be recovered for many years, banks might prefer to convert the interest rather than the principal into secured loan stock or preference shares. Retention of debt with the option of conversion into shares later is a more attractive proposition than conversion into equity at the start of a restructuring. If a contractor has a weak balance sheet, it will be excluded from tender lists, be unattractive as a joint venture partner and fall prey to aggressive creditors who might not otherwise have woken up to the existence of a financial problem until after a rights issue had been underwritten. The lender may wish to avoid unduly negative publicity. It may also feel under an obligation arising out of a long business relationship with its customer although this aspect is much less important than it once was. Some banks prefer to form a view at the earliest possible stage as to whether they should continue to support the customer or terminate the relationship.

Impediments to informal procedures

8–023 Inevitably the process of trading through insolvency involves many areas of law. A major restructuring, for example, requires expertise in company law, security law, tax, insolvency, pensions, employment, finance and commercial law. As the intention would be to continue paying trade creditors, the restructuring may pay little attention to the terms of the company's ongoing contracts. The use of on demand bonds causes considerable problems. It was reported that the restructuring of Costain involved a special facility of £65 million for these bonds. On demand bonds are increasingly used on UK projects and can result in bank facilities being needlessly committed to the detriment of the contractor's working capital position. A bondsman can also exert considerable pressure over banks involved in a rescue.

> "Once the bond provider has paid it becomes an actual, rather than a contingent, creditor and is in a position to pull the group down unless it is bound by the terms of the rescue not to do so. Accordingly the lead bank has to make the difficult decision, at the outset, whether to bring the bond providers within the rescue party knowing that many of them will not be familiar with the rescue culture, or whether to take the gamble that the company will perform all its contracts properly so that

a bond will never be called. However, if the lead bank's judgment is wrong, and the bond is called then the bond provider who has paid is in a singularly strong position to force the rest of the creditor group to put the company in funds to reimburse the bond provider lest it destroy the whole rescue" (White 1998).

Another area of concern is the power of an unsecured creditor to present a winding up petition based on a contingent or prospective debt, e.g. where a contract has been completed but a final account not yet agreed. If the creditor can show an entitlement to a minimum sum and that the company is insolvent, it will be able to present a petition which the company's lenders may be forced to settle. There is also a concern by directors that they could become liable to contribute to the assets of the company for wrongful trading. Although this risk is probably small in many cases, it is always present in any restructuring (see Ch.20).

Chapter 9

Construction Trusts

1. General principles

If a trustee becomes insolvent, the trust property does not form part of his estate for distribution to creditors: s.283 of the Insolvency Act 1986. The trust is therefore useful protection against insolvency. It was developed by the courts of equity in the family context and has since been extended to commercial areas such as debt instruments (Hayton 2003, 36–48). In these areas the trust is declared by a formal deed. If used in the construction industry, the trust is more likely to be evidenced by a clause in the building contract or a side letter. Construction trusts often give rise to a conflict, or an apparent conflict, between contractual and equitable principles. As security against insolvency, trust arrangements are sometimes challenged by liquidators or administrators on the ground that they amount to a charge registrable under s.395 of the Companies Act 1985. **9–001**

Creation of a trust

There are three essential requirements for a trust: the settlor must intend to create a trust over property belonging to him; the property transferred to the trustee and held on trust must be ascertained and identified; and the trustee must know the identity of the beneficiary of the trust to whom he is accountable. **9–002**

It is not essential that the word "trust" is used provided the settlor's intention is clear: *Re Kayford* [1975] 1 W.L.R. 279. Setting money aside into a separate account is helpful but not conclusive evidence of a trust. In *Re Multi Guarantee* [1987] B.C.L.C. 257, money was paid into a joint account in the names of the parties' solicitors pending resolution of a dispute. One of the parties intended the account to be held on trust for its customers but the other envisaged its being used for general purposes after the dispute had been resolved. There were no agreed terms on how money could be withdrawn from the account. It was held that the money had been paid to the solicitors for a purpose which had never been finalised and it reverted by resulting trust to the person who had paid it in.

This case can be contrasted with *Glen Eight v Home Building* [2005] NSWSC 309. In that case a design and build contractor agreed to pay subcontractors before it could become entitled to progress payments from the employer. In the event of non-payment the superintendent could direct that an account be opened in the joint names of employer and contractor.

All moneys in the account "would be held in trust for the Principal for the purpose of paying suppliers and subcontractors to the works". On the contractor's default in payment of subcontractors, the parties agreed a variation to the payment procedure whereby an account was set up and the contractor notified the employer each month of the amounts due to subcontractors. After both employer and contractor signed cheques drawn on the account, the employer would pay in the appropriate amounts to cover the cheques which were then sent to the subcontractors. When the contractor entered voluntary administration there was $1.8 million in the account. McDougall J. continued an injunction restraining the administrators from dealing with the fund on the ground that there was a serious question to be tried as to whether a trust had been constituted in favour of the subcontractors, with a resulting trust for the employer in the event that the primary trust failed. The main difficulty concerned the requisite intention. The contract term could not be relied upon as it was not invoked by the superintendent but the fact that the only payments in and out of the account were for defined subcontractors pointed towards an intention to create a trust.

An intention to create a trust can be negatived by express provision. In *Anaconda Operations v Fluor Daniel* [1999] VSCA 214 a contract to design and construct a cobalt and nickel extraction plant included the following clause: "The Owner does not hold any Approved Security or the proceeds of any Approved Security on trust for the Contractor". As a result, the court discharged an injunction which had been granted restraining the employer from dealing with $45 million representing the proceeds of two retention bonds, and ordered an inquiry as to damages.

It must be possible to ascertain the subject matter of the trust. If A declares a trust in favour of B of "£5,000 of the £10,000 standing in my account" no trust is created unless and until A transfers £5,000 into a new account: *Re Goldcorp Exchange* [1994] 2 All E.R. 806. Similarly, a trust of retention under a JCT form will not come into existence until the employer sets money aside because "retention" is a conditional debt owed to the contractor; it is not the employer's property (see Ch.10). A trust of the benefit of a contract will apply to all present and future choses in action in respect of it. Thus, the trust would extend to any debt arising out of the contract, any cheque representing that debt, and any cash or credit to a bank account representing that cheque.

There must also be a beneficiary to whom the trustee can be accountable. This is illustrated by *OT Computers v First National Tricity Finance* [2003] EWHC 1010. A week before it went into administration, a company set up two trust accounts at a bank, one in respect of customer deposits and the other to pay "urgent suppliers". The sums paid into these accounts came from the company's general funds. This was not a *Quistclose* trust (see para.9–014 below). There was no doubt that the directors had the necessary intention to create a trust or that both accounts represented trust property. In the case of the customers, it was possible to ascertain the identity of the beneficiaries as at the date the account was opened and a valid trust was created. But Pumfrey J. held the same could not be said for the suppliers because it was open to question which of them could be described as "urgent". The purpose of the trust was to vest an immediate interest in the suppliers in question. The trust in this case was fixed rather than discretionary and it was necessary to identify each member of the class. The word "urgent" was too vague to have this effect.

A trustee can hold property on trust for itself and another as beneficiaries. The terms of the trust may entitle the trustee to specific rights against the trust property without naming the trustee as co-beneficiary. As an active self-interested trustee, A would hold the property subject to its express rights on trust for B as beneficiary. This is a defining characteristic of construction trusts (Hayton 1994a). The question arises as to how such a trustee exercises its rights against the fund. **9–003**

In *ESPL v Radio & General Engineering* [2005] 2 M.L.J. 422, a mechanical and electrical subcontract provided: "Sub-Contractor will receive the payments made by Contractor and will hold the right to receive such payments as a trust fund to be applied first to the payment of labourers, suppliers, Sub-Sub-Contractors and others responsible for the Work justifying such payments. . ." The subcontractor (Radio) entered into a sub-subcontract with ESPL which incorporated the terms of the subcontract by reference and provided for the opening of a joint account in the names of Radio and ESPL. Radio agreed that all moneys received in relation to the sub-subcontract works would be deposited into the account and disbursed "in the mutually agreed manner set out in the attached appendix". However, the appendix merely recorded that the account would be jointly operated by signatories nominated by both parties. The account was set up and operated, the contractor being authorised to make payments representing the sub-subcontract works directly into the account.

Disputes arose during the works over alleged defects. Radio invoked a default clause and had the defects remedied at its own expense, setting off the cost against sums due to ESPL, arguing that its duty to pay sums received from the contractor into the fund was reduced, or extinguished, by its right of set-off. The Malaysian Court of Appeal disagreed. It was held that the arrangement constituted a valid trust and a mandatory injunction was ordered that payment in full should be made into the account.

The court seems to have accepted that the contractor would be entitled to payment out of the account (or to withhold future payments in) once it had obtained an arbitration award establishing its claims in relation to the quality of the work. It appears that the subcontract made an award a condition of set-off following the invocation of the default clause although the report is not clear (see paras 5 and 25 of the judgment). In this respect the decision is consistent with cases on the retention trust such as *Henry Boot v The Croydon Hotel* (1985) 36 B.L.R. 41 (see Ch.10).

Proprietary claims

One of the major differences between a trust and an escrow account is that in the case of a trust, the beneficiary has well-established procedures available to trace trust property which has been misapplied. In *Foskett v McKeown* [2001] 1 A.C. 102, Lord Millett distinguished between tracing and following as ways of ascertaining what has happened to the trust property. **9–004**

> "Following is the process of following the same asset as it moves from hand to hand. Tracing is the process of identifying a new asset as the substitute for the old. Where one asset is exchanged for another, a claimant can elect whether to follow the original asset into the hands of

> the new owner or to trace its value into the new asset in the hands of the same owner. . . The transmission of a claimant's property rights from one asset to its traceable proceeds is part of our law of property, not of the law of unjust enrichment. . . . Property rights are determined by fixed rules and settled principles. They are not discretionary. They do not depend upon ideas of what is 'fair, just and reasonable'. . . . Tracing is thus neither a claim nor a remedy. It is merely the process by which a claimant demonstrates what has happened to his property, identifies its proceeds and the persons who have handled or received them, and justifies his claim that the proceeds can properly be regarded as representing his property" (at 127–128).

Trust assets can be traced into all kinds of property. There are detailed rules dealing with bank accounts. An account is a debt owed by the bank to its customer. There will normally be many payments in and out of the account. When making a withdrawal, the customer is deemed to be taking out the earliest payment in: *Clayton's case* (1817) 1 Mer. 572. If a customer pays trust money into his personal account, he is deemed to make withdrawals of his own money first as the law assumes he would not intend to commit a breach of trust. Where trust money, or the proceeds of sale of trust property, are mixed with the trustee's own money, the beneficiary is entitled to a charge over the account as security for the trust property. If trust money is used to buy an asset, the beneficiary can either claim the asset or a lien over it: *Re Hallett's Estate* (1880) L.R. 13 Ch. D. 696. Where an asset is purchased from a mixed fund containing trust money and the trustee's own funds, it is subject to a charge securing payment of the misappropriated assets: *Re Oatway* [1903] 2 Ch. 356. If the asset increases in value, the beneficiary becomes entitled to a proportionate share of the increase: *Re Tilley's Will Trusts* [1967] 1 Ch. 1179. If at any time a mixed account goes into overdraft, the beneficiary loses all tracing rights: *Roscoe v Winder* [1915] 1 Ch. 62.

Personal claims

9–005 If a person receives property in breach of trust and parts with it without accounting to the beneficiary, he may be personally liable as constructive trustee. He will be liable for "knowing receipt" where he has actual knowledge, or turns a blind eye to the obvious, or deliberately fails to make enquiries which an honest person would make: *Trustor v Smallbone* (No. 2) [2001] 1 W.L.R. 1177. It was appropriate in that case to pierce the corporate veil and recognise receipt by a company as that of the individuals in control of it because the company had been used as a device or façade to conceal the true facts. A person can be accountable as an accessory to a breach of trust even if he has not personally handled trust property. A person can be liable for "knowing assistance" if he is dishonest even if the original breach of trust was committed honestly and in good faith: *Royal Brunei Airlines v Tan* [1995] 3 All E.R. 97. It is, however, essential to prove the dishonesty of the person assisting the breach of trust. These aspects are considered further in para.9–027 below.

2. Construction trusts

9–006 When a trust is used in connection with a construction contract it is usually intended as the means of payment. The trust account may be the source of payment for the whole contract sum, or part such as retention, or an element in dispute. The trust can be evidenced by a clause in the contract, or a collateral agreement, or a separate trust deed. It may benefit the contractor or the subcontractors or both. Whatever method is used, the trust will consist of a mixture of contractual and trust obligations. In essence, the terms of the trust will be the terms of the contract.

Trusts of the contract sum

There are many ways in which a trust can be used to protect the contract sum. The most useful from the contractor's point of view is the "*Lovell* trust" since the employer makes a payment into the account one month in advance of the work being carried out: *Lovell Construction v Independent Estates* [1994] 1 B.C.L.C. 31. A similar arrangement is used on international contracts where the employer's lack of access to foreign currency to pay the contractor can be overcome by a sophisticated form of barter: *Rafidain Bank v Saipem* [1994] C.L.C. 253. **9–007**

Some subcontracting organisations advocate the "cascade" "systems", whereby sums received on account of the contract sum are held on trust by the contractor to pay itself, its subcontractors and suppliers. The subcontractors receive payment for themselves and their sub-subcontractors and so on down the chain until the last supplier to the project has been paid. Under this system, which is operated in parts of the US and Canada, the trust is not expressly written into the contract but arises by statutory implication. It is not the means of payment but a source of proprietary and personal remedies (Glaholt 1999; Reynolds 1996).

In *Constructing the Team* (Latham 1994), Sir Michael Latham put forward a composite scheme protecting the contractor and the first line of subcontractors and suppliers. The employer sets aside a fund on trust for itself and the contractor to pay the contractor in accordance with the building contract. If the contractor becomes insolvent before completion, the primary trust fails and a secondary trust arises in respect of any balance in the account in favour of the first line of subcontractors who share rateably in the fund. This ingenious solution resolves the problem created by *British Eagle v Air France* [1975] 1 W.L.R. 758, since a statutory trust would not offend the *pari passu* rule (Ch.8). It was accepted as a viable solution by the contractors but rejected by employers' organisations.

Two UK standard forms have included a trust of the contract sum. Under SEACC (1993), the employer opens a special account from which the contractor and specialist subcontractors are paid. The principal feature of the trust is that the employer loses all rights of set-off against the fund even in respect of liquidated damages. Contrary to Latham's recommendation that the trust should be included as a core clause, there is also a trust in optional clause V of The Engineering and Construction Contract (2nd edn, 1995). The trust option has been omitted in the third edition (NEC 2005). For a comparison between the *Lovell* trust, SEACC and NEC see Davis (1996). Payment trusts have apparently been used on large projects in Australia by the Commonwealth Department of Defence (Cole 2003, Vol.8, Ch.14, para.102) and on a contract for the Defence Estates Organisation in Andover, UK (Klein 2006).

In a significant move, the Office of Government Commerce is now advocating the use of what it calls "project bank accounts" on suitable public sector projects (OGC 2007, para.18). Benefits are stated to include: "transparent management of cash flow, a reduction of financing charges across the supply chain, less opportunity for payment abuse and reduced impact of insolvency of a supply chain member" (para.21). The mechanism to achieve this is a trust deed to which client, contractor and subcontractors are made parties. The OGC has provided a precedent (OGC 2007, App. A) from which it appears that the trust will, as with *Lovell Construction v Independent Estates* considered in para.9–016 below, be used as the means of payment rather than as security for payment. Unlike the *Lovell* trust, however, moneys will only be deposited after the work has been carried out and certified for payment. The illustrative trust deed is silent on questions of abatement and set-off. Presumably such matters will be dealt with before the ascertainment of sums due to the participants in the construction process since once payment is made into the account, sums are automatically disbursed through the CHAPS banking system direct to the bank accounts of the contractor and scheduled subcontractors.

The intention is that as from January 1, 2008 "public sector clients should progressively specify use of Project Bank Accounts where practicable and cost effective" (para.18). This is clarified later to mean larger one-off projects (para.87). Although called "a trust for the whole supply chain" (para.79) it will not apply to the "smaller chain members" (para.90) such as labour-only subcontractors (para.104). It will be crucial to dovetail the provisions of the trust deed with the terms of the main and subcontracts, especially those dealing with valuation, disputes, termination and set-off. It is worth comparing the OGC trust deed with other formal arrangements such as the *Lovell* trust, SEACC and the NEC trust option (see Davis 1996).

Retention trusts

9–008 Trusts of retention are only found in the JCT standard forms, i.e. the Standard Form of Building Contract (JCT 63, 80, 98, 05), the Standard Form With Contractor's Design (JCT 81, 98), the Intermediate Form (IFC 84, 98), the Fixed Fee Form (JCT 67), and the Management Contract (JCT 87, 98). The trust is stepped down into the conditions of nominated subcontract (NSC/C) and works contract (WC/2) but not to named subcontracts (NAM/C) or domestic subcontracts (DOM/1 and DOM/2). This subject is considered in detail in Ch.10.

Stakeholder accounts

9–009 Some JCT forms of subcontract provided for payment to a trustee-stakeholder to hold on trust for the contractor and the subcontractor until otherwise directed by an arbitrator or the parties, e.g. cl.22 of NAM/SC. Interest was added to the fund and the stakeholder was entitled to deduct its expenses from the fund. In *Drake & Scull Engineering v McLaughlin & Harvey* (1992) 60 B.L.R. 102 the court granted an injunction to enforce an order of an adjudicator that the contractor pay to a trustee-stakeholder the amount found due to a subcontractor as security pending a re-hearing of the dispute in arbitration. This form of relief was expressly provided for in

DOM/1. The advantage is that the claim is secured in the interim; the disadvantage is that the claimant suffers a loss of cash flow.

The policy of the Housing Grants, Construction and Regeneration Act 1996 is to facilitate cash flow in the industry. As a result, statutory adjudicators have no power to order payment to a stakeholder. However, a practice has developed of including contractual terms permitting or even compelling adjudicators to make such orders, especially where there is evidence that the claimant is or about to become insolvent. The Department of Trade & Industry proposes to amend the Act to prohibit the use of such terms as they suspend the effect of an adjudicator's decision until final determination (DTI 2006, 30). Respondents to the DTI's consultation exercise felt that only the court should have this power in the form of its jurisdiction to order a payment into court or a stay of execution (DTI 2006, 26–27), even though the power to stay execution has only been exercised so far where the claimant is in formal insolvency (Ch.12).

Escrow accounts

Occasionally an employer agrees to provide security for payment. The simplest method is a payment guarantee from a bank but for reasons of its own the employer may prefer simply to deposit part or all of the contract sum in a bank account, e.g. the Australian standard form described in Merity (2002, 173). The employer may then execute a charge over the account as security for its payment obligations or declare itself trustee of the fund to pay the contractor from it in accordance with interim certificates. **9–010**

Deposit charges

In *ASRS Establishment Ltd* [2000] 2 B.C.L.C. 631 an escrow account was set up as security for performance by a purchaser (ASRS) under a share sale agreement. The vendor later executed in favour of the claimant what was called a fixed charge over "all book debts, bank account credit balances and other debts and claims . . . due or owing to the company". The account was not expressly mentioned and probably unknown to the charge holder at the time. It was held by the Court of Appeal that the vendor had created a floating charge as it retained the ability to deal with property falling within that description in the ordinary course of business. Robert Walker L.J. stated that there seemed to be no reported case concerning a credit balance in an escrow account similar to that created in this case. He held that the escrow moneys came within the residual class of "other debts and claims" (para.40). This case can be contrasted with *Obaray v Gateway (London) Ltd* [2004] 1 B.C.L.C. 555 which concerned a deed of deposit securing payment of rent or other sums falling due under a lease. The deed provided that a sum representing a half-year's rental was to be paid to the landlord who would hold it in a separate account, repayable at the end of the lease after payment from the account of all sums owing as a result of the tenant's default. The deed also charged the account to secure the tenant's obligations under the lease. On the tenant's liquidation, it was held that the landlord was entitled to deduct sums owing before accounting to the liquidator for the balance of the deposit even though the express charge **9–011** had not been registered. Although Judge Hazel Williamson Q.C. construed the landlord's right of deduction as a charge, she held it was not registrable under s.396 Companies Act 1985 (paras 71–72). The arrangement could also be viewed as creating a trust over the deposit in favour of the tenant on the terms of the deed (para.58). As the landlord was only ever obliged to repay the deposit net of any deduction, liquidation set-off under r.4.90 of the Insolvency Rules 1986 could not arise.

Escrow as means of payment

9–012 In *Bouygues v Shanghai Links* [1998] 2 H.K.L.R.D. 479, affirmed [1998] 4 HKC 206, the contract was FIDIC (4th edn) and concerned a substantial development with a contract sum of US$ 33.25 million. The employer was a special purpose vehicle company formed under Chinese law and had no assets apart from the development. Its parent was incorporated in the British West Indies and its sole asset was the right to use the land to which the development related for 70 years. It was a condition of the contract that the contractor's duty to start work depended on its receiving satisfactory arrangements for payment. The contractor was satisfied by a letter in the following terms from the employer's parent:

> "We advise that under an agreement entered into by the [defendant], all of the funds required to pay the US$33,250,000 Contract Price will be deposited in a segregated US$ account of the [defendant] at Standard Chartered Bank in Hong Kong. Payment of the Contract Price under the Contract will be made from this account and funds can be paid out of this account by the signature of Barry Hansen and one other director of the [defendant]."

The contractor accepted the escrow account in lieu of a payment guarantee. Before the contract was completed, there were mutual allegations of termination. The contractor claimed $3 million in respect of an unpaid certified sum and a further $11 million for post-termination losses. Both the contractor's claims and the employer's cross-claims were referred to arbitration.

The contractor claimed a declaration that the parent held the account on trust to pay whatever was found due to the contractor in the arbitration and an injunction preventing any withdrawals from the account pending the arbitrator's award. If the trust claim failed, the contractor argued that the parent had agreed that the account would only be used to pay sums due from the employer under the construction contract and that the injunction should be granted to prevent a breach of the parent's agreement. The court rejected both the contractor's trust argument and the parent's defence that all it had provided was a non-binding "letter of comfort". The court held the letter to be an actionable promise by the parent that the matters referred to would be carried out.

The account was a security in the sense that it could not have been the parties' intention that the parent could make withdrawals before the contract price had been paid in full. However, the court found that "contract price" in this context was a term of art and meant "the totality of the sums payable to the plaintiffs for the performance of their obligations under the construction contract" (at 496 *per* Brian Keith J.); but it did not extend to sums falling due to the contractor after a termination. In that event, the account was intended to finance a completion contract, otherwise "in the absence of other sources of funding the construction of the development would grind to a halt" (at 497).

Investors had written to the contractor in similar terms to the parent's letter but with an additional clause: "We agree that payment of the Contract Price will be made to you according to terms and conditions of the construction contract . . ." The court construed these words as referring to the timing of payments rather than to any sums which might become due in connection with the contract. The provisions dealing with payment of the contract price as defined in FIDIC were replaced by a separate payment regime on termination so that even the $3 million were not payable from the escrow account. The contractor had only raised the question of security for payment at a late stage so as not to put the employer off. Had it pressed for clearer wording, or a properly constituted trust, there was a risk it would not have obtained the contract.

Escrow as security for damages

In *Re Namco* [2003] 2 B.C.L.C. 78 the court considered the validity of an **9–013** escrow agreement. It was in the context of applications for provisional liquidators to be appointed and for permission under s.130 of the Insolvency Act 1986 to continue a claim against the company: the issues in the case did not need to be decided. The agreement provided that an amount was to be deposited as security for payment of any damages for breach of a charterparty for which Namco may be found liable. The agreement named a firm of solicitors to act as escrow agent. Namco ceased trading and breached the terms of the charterparty. In order to withdraw the money, the other party (Seatruck) had to produce either an arbitration award or a consent signed by both parties. But Namco refused to agree to the release and Seatruck applied to the Commercial Court for specific performance of the escrow agreement, obliging Namco to sign a joint notice that could be served on the escrow agent. Seatruck applied for summary judgment.

A few days before that hearing, Namco applied for the appointment of provisional liquidators, primarily to allow them to challenge the escrow agreement as an unregistered registrable charge. Blackburne J. considered that s.395 would not avoid such a charge as against provisional liquidators; if that was wrong, it would not be a proper exercise of the court's jurisdiction to assist the company to put itself into a better position as against one of its creditors, given that it was the company's duty to register the charge in the first place. Had he appointed provisional liquidators, the judge would have granted Seatruck permission under s.130 to continue the existing proceedings. The outcome of the application to the Commercial Court is not known.

Escrow and litigation

Compare this use of security with that in *Technocrats International v Fredic* **9–014** [2005] 1 B.C.L.C. 467. In that case, £700,000 was paid to one of the parties' solicitors to hold until further order as security for the applicant's claims. On compliance, a freezing order was discharged. When the defendant company went into administration, the applicant argued that it had an enforceable security interest in the money. It was held that security in this context meant protection against the risk of dissipation of assets rather than security against the defendant's insolvency (para.17). Interestingly, the court thought that the position might have been different if the defendant had procured a bank guarantee instead of making the payment (para.15): see *Polly Peck International v Asil Nadir* [1992] 2 Lloyd's Rep. 238 at 249. A freezing order does not impose an obligation on the defendant to satisfy any judgment debt out of moneys paid into an account and there could be no equitable charge over the fund within the principle in *Palmer v Carey* [1926] A.C. 703 at 706–707.

"Quistclose" trusts

9–015 Money advanced to enable a debtor to pay its creditors but which has not been paid to them by the time the debtor goes into liquidation is held on a resulting trust in favour of the person who advanced the money: *Barclays Bank v Quistclose Investments* [1970] A.C. 567. This case has recently been reconsidered in *Twinsecra v Yardley* [2002] 2 A.C. 164 in which Lord Millett stated: "Arrangements of this kind are not intended to provide security for repayment of the loan, but to prevent the money from being applied otherwise than in accordance with the lender's wishes" (para.72). Lord Millett regarded the *Quistclose* trust as "a simple commercial arrangement akin . . . to a retention of title clause" (para.81), which enabled the debtor to avoid formal insolvency by paying off its existing creditors, or allowed it to continue trading by providing it with working capital with which to incur fresh liabilities.

This concept was applied to the construction industry in *Re McKeown* [1974] N.I.L.R. 226. A contractor borrowed money to pay an arbitrator's fees before taking up the award. The loan was on condition that it be used to pay the arbitrator's fees only and that it was to be repaid out of the proceeds of the award. The contractor went bankrupt after taking up the award but before receiving payment. It was held that the loan had been advanced for a specific purpose and did not form part of the bankrupt's estate, which could only receive the proceeds of the arbitration award subject to the obligation to repay the loan from it first.

More recently, in *Re Niagara Mechanical Services* [2000] 2 B.C.L.C. 425, a contractor went into administration and agreed improved payment terms with the employer to enable the works to continue. The employer then learned of a subcontractor claiming to be owed £60,000 who had not been included in the cash flow agreement. He was due to commission the air conditioning and the employer agreed to pay the administrators this sum to ensure the subcontractor returned to site. The administrators accepted the money on account of sums due and failed to pay the subcontractor. It was held that they received the money for a specific purpose. Having failed to apply it for that purpose, they were under an equitable obligation to return it to the employer.

The *Quistclose* trust has also been applied in the context of direct payment to a sub-subcontractor on the impending insolvency of the subcontractor (*Analogy v Bell Basic Industries* (1996) 12 B.C.L. 291, discussed in Ch.20); payment of retention by the employer (*Re Old Inns* (1994) 13 A.C.S.R. 141); an agreement entered into by a funder before the liquidation of the contractor, to pay subcontractors and suppliers direct to complete a specific project (*Re Barrington and Associates* [1989] V.R. 940); and payment to solicitors by an investor in a property development (*Templeton Insurance v Penningtons* [2006] EWHC 685. The concept has also been applied to money deposited as security for payment under a finance lease of construction equipment. On the lessor executing a release the account was held by the insolvent bank on resulting trust for the contractor: *Thiess Watkins White v Equitycorp* [1991] 1 Qd. R. 82.

3. Trust or charge?

The main contract

The main English authority on the question whether a trust of the main contract sum can be a registrable charge is *Lovell Construction v Independent Estates* [1994] 1 B.C.L.C. 31. The facts of this case are worth careful study. **9–016**

The facts in Lovell v Independent

Independent was incorporated in 1989 at the height of a property boom. The company purchased a property in London NW1 for £14 million with funding from Gota Bank against a mortgage on the property and all present and future contracts relating to it. In the middle of 1991, Lovell agreed to redevelop the property for a contract sum of £16 million, on condition that interim payments were channelled through an escrow account. The contract was in the JCT 80 form, amended to allow Lovell to terminate its employment if payments were not made in advance into the escrow account, and also to require the architect to send copies of his certificates to the parties' solicitors. **9–017**

The escrow agreement stated that its purpose was to facilitate payment under the building contract through an account that was to be opened at Barclays in the names of the parties' solicitors. The account was to continue until the final certificate, except in the event of insolvency, in which case the architect was to value the works in accordance with the termination clause in the contract and, if appropriate, certify further payment to Lovell. On receipt of the architect's certificate, the trustees were to pay Lovell by telegraphic transfer and the trust would terminate at which point any surplus in the account was to be repaid to Independent.

The escrow agreement stated that any money paid into the account was "deemed to be impressed with a trust in favour of Lovell", although interest was to be for Independent's sole benefit. Payments into the account were to be made in accordance with an agreed schedule. Any certificate by the architect after an insolvency termination could only have been issued under the escrow agreement, as the termination clause in JCT 80 was silent on the point.

The parties instructed their solicitors to open an account and to transfer sums to Lovell immediately on receipt of interim certificates provided there were sufficient funds in the account. The only exception was where the architect had certified Lovell to be in delay, in which case the solicitors were to abate payment by the amount of any liquidated damages levied by Independent.

By early 1992, the property market had collapsed and the project was no longer viable. Lovell requested additional security and Independent procured from Gota Bank a standby letter of credit for £1 million payable on demand on receipt of Lovell's certificate that an interim certificate had not been honoured "by reason of there being no sum standing to the credit of the escrow account." The letter of credit was to expire at the end of June 1992. In early March, the bank served Lovell with notice of assignment of the benefit of the building contract and the escrow agreement which had been effected by the mortgage executed by Independent several years previously. At the end of March, the bank appointed receivers in respect of the site and the agreements.

Lovell mistakenly believed that fixed charge receivership entitled them to terminate their employment and they served notice purporting to do so. The same day Independent convened a meeting of creditors under s.98 of the Insolvency Act 1986. Liquidators were appointed at a creditors' meeting held towards the end of April. At this point, the architect issued a certificate in favour of Lovell under the escrow agreement for final payment out of the account. However, the certificate was ineffective since the architect's power to issue it only arose on a valid termination of the building contract. It had also become clear that the sums due to Lovell would exceed the amount in the account and they would have to make a call on the standby letter of credit. The difficulty was that the architect had issued an invalid certificate and was concerned at its position and the fact that it might not be paid in view of Independent's insolvency. By this time, there were only two weeks left before the letter of credit was to expire.

Rival claims to the account

9–018 At this point, the liquidator claimed the balance standing in the account by challenging the status of the escrow agreement. He argued that the agreement amounted to a floating charge in favour of Lovell of the credit balance standing in the account from time to time, securing Independent's payment obligations under the building contract. As the charge had not been registered under s.395 of the Companies Act 1985, it could not be binding on him. Gota Bank had a valid security over the escrow agreement and so it seems that the liquidator's efforts could only have benefited the bank. The bank was also exposed under the letter of credit.

Lovell served a fresh notice of termination under the contract, relying this time on the fact that Independent had gone into creditors' voluntary liquidation. It also issued proceedings before the Official Referee which were primarily intended to procure the architect's certificate under the escrow agreement, non-payment of which was a condition precedent to a valid call under the letter of credit. Lovell applied for leave to amend its proceedings to claim a declaration that the escrow account was not a registrable charge under s.395 of the Companies Act 1985.

In the end, this was the only issue which had to be decided by the court. Lovell's application was against the company in liquidation, the bank and the receivers. The liquidator was joined so as to ensure compliance with any direction to the architect to issue a certificate under the escrow agreement and to enable the court to hear his submissions on the security issue. The receivers were joined as claimants to the money in the escrow account and as parties interested in the architect's power to certify under the agreement. Neither they nor the bank played an active role.

The liquidator argued that Independent's right to any surplus in the account after Lovell had been paid was an equity of redemption. He argued that Independent's right to have liquidated damages deducted from payments out of the account was inconsistent with a trust. On its true construction, the whole arrangement was a security because Independent never lost its right to pay Lovell under the building contract. If it chose to do so, it would be entitled to redeem the money standing in the account to the extent of the interim certificate it had paid. If the arrangement did amount to a trust, it was a trust by way of security, similar to that in *Compaq Computer v Abercorn* [1993] B.C.L.C. 602. Lovell argued in reply that, taken together, the amended JCT 80 form and the escrow agreement were simply the means of payment and that, even if the trust were a security, it was not registrable under s.395.

The court's findings

After hearing detailed argument, the court held in favour of Lovell: **9–019**

> "It was the intention of the parties that the joint account should be a conduit by which moneys due from Independent to Lovell pursuant to certificates issued by [the architect] should be channelled to Lovell. This was not in substitution of any rights Lovell had under the JCT contract. These were additional rights and in one sense can be described as a form of security, but it appears reasonable to infer that it was the intention of the parties that Lovell would look to the joint account rather than to their rights under [the building contract] for the honouring of certificates. . . I have reached the conclusion that the machinery established by the escrow agreement was for effecting payment and was not for establishing security. Since on the happening of certain events moneys in the account might be paid out either to Lovell or Independent, both had a beneficial interest in the moneys. I find that the escrow agreement established a trust and not by way of charge under which the legal interest was in the trustees and the beneficial interests were in Lovell and Independent" (at 36–37, *per* Judge James Fox-Andrews Q.C.).

There was no need for the court to consider the question of registrability. In the end the architect certified again under the escrow agreement, and the balance in the account was paid out to Lovell who were able to claim under the letter of credit before it expired.

Commentary

The decision is in line with previous authorities such as *Carreras Rothmans v Freeman Matthews Treasure* [1985] 1 All E.R. 155, as well as the Australian case of *Associated Alloys v ACN* (2000) 202 C.L.R. 588, considered at para.9–023 below. The argument that the trust amounted to a charge over a book debt appears to be misconceived. To fall within s.396 of the Companies Act 1985, a charge has to be in respect of debts owed to the chargor, i.e. Independent. In this case, the account was a debt owed by the bank to the trustees, who were primarily accountable to Lovell. It is true that Independent was entitled to any surplus in the account after the contract sum had been paid but even this is unlikely to be accepted as a **9–020** book debt: *Re Brightlife* [1987] Ch. 200. It is only ascertainable after the "secured" obligation has been fully discharged, when the solicitors have become bare trustees in favour of Independent, dropping out of the picture as between Independent and Barclays.

In this connection, a trust over collections pursuant to a subordination agreement was held not to be a charge in *Re SSSL Realisations* [2005] 1 B.C.L.C. 1, on the ground that the trust property could not extend further than the amount of the indemnity to which the bondsman was entitled. Even if it were, it could not be registrable as a book debt because it only applied to the proceeds once collected not to the pre-existing debt.

Lovell's position would have been made easier if fixed charge receivership had been an insolvency termination event under JCT 80 (JCT 05 has not amended the termination clause in this respect). Gota Bank had a floating charge over the undertaking of Independent, but chose to appoint receivers under their fixed charges.

Although the escrow agreement was tied in to the payment clause of JCT 80, it was not fully integrated with the termination clause, in that quantification of the amount due to the contractor on termination for the employer's insolvency was not dealt with. The architect was not made a party to the escrow agreement and was concerned about his jurisdiction to issue the certificate.

In *Zauner Construction v No. 2 Pitt Street* [2001] VSC 154 the parties entered into an arrangement similar to the *Lovell* trust, established pursuant to a trust deed entered into simultaneously with the main contract. A schedule detailed the amounts to be paid into the account at monthly intervals. On the employer's failure to pay the third instalment into the account, the contractor suspended the works pursuant to a right granted by the deed. This entitled the contractor to common law damages; however, a parallel right of suspension under the main contract entitled it to delay and disruption costs. During the period of suspension, the contractor made claims for prolongation costs which were certified for payment. The court ordered summary judgment on the basis that the certificates had to be honoured even if they had to be adjusted later to reflect whatever was the true construction of the parties' agreement.

Subcontract trusts

9–021 An escrow or trust account may be set up at the subcontractor level by opening a joint account: see *ESPL v Radio & General Engineering* [2005] 2 M.L.J. 422, and *Glen Eight v Home Building* [2005] NSWSC 309 considered above. In *Celtic Contractors v Infinite Environmental Services* [2003] B.L.R. 340, a bank account was opened in the joint names of the contractor and a subcontractor. A payment would be made into the account by the project funder on receipt of a certificate from the employer's representative showing the amount due to the subcontractor. The precise machinery for payment out is not given in the report. The subcontractor considered that the arrangement amounted to a charge over the account securing payment under the subcontract.

The contractor wanted to engage another subcontractor, Celtic. However, Celtic had previously dealt with another company controlled by the directors of the contractor and wanted security for payment. Instead of setting up a new joint account it was agreed by all three parties that Celtic would be paid from the existing account, with the employer's representative certifying the amount due to the two subcontractors. Payment was to be made from the account in the following order of priority: the existing subcontractor, Celtic, and then the contractor.

The arrangement was evidenced by a letter from the subcontractor acting as "honest broker" between the parties. It was intended to be formalised in a legal agreement but this was not done. Celtic subsequently fell out with the contractor over valuation and sought an injunction freezing any dealings with the account below a minimum sum. The injunction was granted *ex parte* but was later discharged on the ground that the tripartite arrangement was not sufficiently clear to vest an equitable interest in the account in Celtic. No other evidence was submitted to support the making of a freezing order and the injunction therefore had to be discharged.

It is not clear whether the subcontractor actually had a charge over the account (which would have taken effect as an equitable charge not requiring registration), or whether the terms of its subcontract, together with the bank mandate setting up the account, were sufficient to bind the contractor to pay sums due to it in priority to the contractor to the extent of moneys in the account. It is possible that none of the parties understood the legal effect of the arrangement they had entered into.

Retention trusts

The question whether the retention trust operates as a charge has not so far **9–022**
been raised in the case law. In the Australian case of *Re Old Inns* (1994) 13 A.C.S.R. 141, it was assumed that a joint account in the names of employer and contractor, which was opened in lieu of a bank guarantee for the contractor's obligations during the defects liability period, was a charge. However, the court held that it was not a book debt and remained binding on the liquidator of the employer even though it had not been registered under the New South Wales Company Code. The court followed *Re Brightlife* [1987] Ch. 200. The account was set up pursuant to cl.10.21 of the Australian JCC-B 1985 form, which specifically provided that the account or the guarantee were to stand as "security" for the contractor's defects period obligations: compare *Obaray v Gateway (London) Ltd* [2004] 1 B.C.L.C. 555 considered earlier.

The fact that a charge over retention might cause practical difficulties in the industry is not necessarily a reason against it: *Re Welsh Irish Ferries Ltd* [1985] W.L.R. 610. An argument for its existence might run as follows:

(1) By paying money into a separate account, the employer has appropriated property for the discharge of a debt and charged the account as security for payment of retention.

(2) The equity of redemption would be the right to withdraw the money in the account by satisfying the retention from another source.

(3) The arrangement has certain characteristics of a charge: the contractor is given a right in the fund; the contractor's interest has been conferred by the employer rather than reserved by it; the arrangement restricts the employer's rights of disposition of the money in the account; interest on the fund is payable to the employer.

This view is supported by a retention of title case which held that a clause constituting the buyer as trustee of hire charges arising from use of the goods until the seller had been paid was a registrable charge: *Tatung v Galex* (1989) 5 B.C.C. 325.

Against this, it can be argued by analogy with *Lovell v Independent* that the parties intended to create a trust as the means of payment of the retention. The trust device is the most appropriate vehicle for this purpose as it identifies the retention, recognises the claims of contractor and employer, and protects the money in the event of the employer's liquidation. As the retention accrues, the employer's contractual duties in respect of it are discharged by payment into the account and the contractor's rights to payment from the account arise by operation of the trust provisions: *Swiss Bank v Lloyd's Bank* [1980] 2 All E.R. 419, 426.

If this is correct, the contractor's remedy in the event that the employer fails to release retention when it becomes due, is not to sue the employer in debt but to seek a declaration that it has performed the contract, and obtain an order that the fund be paid out: see *Associated Alloys v ACN* (2000) 202 C.L.R. 588 below. In another retention of title case, the House of Lords tested whether a seller had a security interest by asking whether it retained the ultimate right to the goods: *Armour v Thyssen* [1990] 3 All E.R. 481. In this context the contractor has the ultimate right to the fund, subject to the employer's rights of deduction. The employer only has a right to the fund on the contractor's default. This is the reverse of the position which would have applied had the trust operated as a charge. The fact that the employer cannot mix its own money with the retention fund also points towards a trust: *Re ILG Travel* [1995] 2 B.C.L.C. 128, 156. In *Re Old Inns* (1994) 13 A.C.S.R. 141, the court agreed that the security had been given by the contractor not the employer. A trust is more consistent with the intention of the parties as expressed in the JCT forms.

If the retention trust is a charge, is it registrable? It is not registrable as a book debt: see the earlier discussion on the *Lovell* trust. A retention trust clause can be compared to a floating charge. Just as the charge is an incomplete assignment until a receiver is appointed, so the trust clause is a purely contractual right to have moneys set aside. However, there the resemblance ends because the charge holder has a present interest in the fund of assets caught by the charge and control over the receiver's appointment, whereas the contractor is dependent on the employer's co-operation, or the court's assistance, to constitute a trust. In the interim, the borrower is entitled to dispose of assets falling within the floating charge provided it does so in the ordinary course of business, whereas if the employer makes no attempt to segregate retention and simply uses it as working capital, it does so in ordinary breach of contract. It appears therefore that a security over retention would not be registrable (Hayton 1994a).

Proceeds of sub-sale

9–023 It is also worth mentioning *Associated Alloys v ACN* (2000) 202 C.L.R. 588, in which the High Court of Australia upheld as a trust rather than a charge a retention of title clause in a steel supplier's invoice.

The relevant part of the clause:

> "In the event that the [buyer] uses the goods/product in some manufacturing or construction process of its own or some third party, then the [buyer] shall hold such part of the proceeds of such manufacturing or construction process as relates to the goods/product in trust for the [seller]. Such part shall be deemed to equal in dollar terms the amount owing by the [buyer] to the [seller] at the time of the receipt of such proceeds."

The steel was fabricated into pressure vessels, heat exchangers and columns, and was intended for a Korean sub-buyer. The seller went into administration and then liquidation. The court construed the clause as an agreement to constitute a trust of future-acquired property, namely the moneys received by the buyer (para.48). Receipt of the proceeds by the buyer would discharge the debt created by the supplier's invoices. The constitution of the trust would thus discharge the debt by performance (para.45). However the supplier failed on the facts as it could not demonstrate that payments from the sub-buyer were related to the steel supplied under any particular invoice (para.53). The buyer had also not set aside the payments into a separate account. The decision may be hard to reconcile with *Tatung v Galex* (1989) 5 B.C.C. 325, referred to above.

4. Subcontract benefits

There are several other ways in which a subcontractor might claim priority in the insolvency of the contractor: "name-borrowing" and the procurement of the benefit of the main contract. Under the standard forms these are restricted to nominated subcontractors and works contractors but the principles are sometimes used more widely when drafting one-off contracts. **9–024**

Standard form clauses

Name-borrowing is the right to bring an arbitration in the contractor's name against the employer where the subcontractor is dissatisfied with an architect's instruction, an extension of time, or the amount of a certified sum. In all three cases: **9–025**

> "Subject to the Sub-Contractor giving the Contractor such indemnity and security as the Contractor may reasonably require the Contractor shall allow the Sub-Contractor to use the Contractor's name and if necessary will join with the Sub-Contractor in arbitration proceedings at the instigation of the Sub-Contractor to decide the matter as aforesaid" (cll.2.7, 3.11 and 4.20 of NSC/C).

The second avenue open to a nominated subcontractor is cl.1.13 of NSC/C which provides:

> "The Contractor will so far as he lawfully can at the request of the Sub-Contractor obtain for him any rights or benefits of the provisions of the

Main Contract so far as the same are applicable to the Sub-contract Works and not inconsistent with the express terms of the Sub-contract but not further or otherwise."

"Benefit" in this context extends to bringing an arbitration, but if the employer becomes insolvent before meeting the award the contractor remains liable to pay the subcontractor. It cannot argue that the "benefit" was the right to payment rather than payment itself: *Birse Construction v Co-Operative Wholesale Society* (1997) 58 B.L.R. 58 at 77. A clause 1.13 claim applies to the whole of the main contract. An arbitration under it would be between the main contractor and the employer and controlled by the contractor.

A name-borrowing arbitration is limited to three specific heads of claim and takes effect as an arbitration by the subcontractor in the name of the contractor but under the control of the subcontractor: *Gordon Durham v Haden Young* (1990) 52 B.L.R. 61. In that case, a name-borrowing arbitration was completed and the arbitrator granted the subcontractor an extension of time and loss and expense. The employer was ordered to pay the subcontractor directly "as effective claimants herein" within 14 days in full and final satisfaction of its claim. The award was issued by consent between the employer and the subcontractor. No insolvency was involved.

These two forms of relief are also available in management contracting. Clause 4.27 of WC/2 allows the works contractor to borrow the contractor's name and arbitrate against the employer if it disputes the amount certified in its favour. Clause 1.11 is in similar terms to cl.1.13 of the nominated subcontract. In *Belgravia Property Co v S&R (London) Ltd* [2001] B.L.R. 424 a works contractor attempted to bring a name-borrowing arbitration in its own name without having provided an indemnity or security to the contractor. The employer applied to the court under s.32 of the Arbitration Act 1996 for a declaration on whether the arbitrator had jurisdiction. Judge Humphrey LLoyd Q.C. stayed the arbitration as the contractor was entitled to withhold its consent until proper indemnity and security had been provided. However, if the works contractor did so, the proceedings would be regularised with retrospective effect. The judgment contains an analysis of previous case law.

It is worth comparing these cases with *FPM Constructions v Australian Recreation Systems* [2004] NSWCA 318, which concerned a contract to design, build and operate a leisure centre between a local authority and a joint venture company formed by an architect, a contractor and a leisure company. After completion of the construction work, the architect and the contractor transferred their shares in the company to the operator. At that time the company was pursuing an arbitration against the local authority by which it was in effect passing on claims made by the architect and the builder under their subcontracts with the company. The parties to the joint venture agreed that any fruits of the arbitration would be paid to the person whose claim they represented and that if in the reasonable the opinion of the company's solicitor there was no further advantage in continuing the arbitration, it had power to terminate it. When the company terminated it in the light of uncertainty as to the company's ability to recover its costs, it was held to have done in breach of contract.

Where the contractor is insolvent

If the contractor is insolvent, and the subcontractor succeeds against the employer, or the contractor obtains a benefit for the subcontractor under cl.1.13, can the contractor's insolvency practitioner claim the benefit from the subcontractor? The answer turns on the construction of NSC/C. Take first the name-borrowing procedure. A claim is usually brought in the name of another by an insurer exercising a right of subrogation in the name of the insured, an equitable assignee suing in the name of the assignor, or a beneficiary of a trust claiming in the name of the trustee. In each case the nominal claimant would receive any damages subject to the other's proprietary interest: an equitable lien or charge in the case of subrogation (*Napier and Ettrick v Hunter* [1993] 1 All E.R. 385); a trust in the other two cases. Such an interest would protect the subcontractor against the contractor's insolvency. The right to use the other's name is a consequence of an existing proprietary right. But if the right to sue in another's name is conferred by contract and is not the consequence of a proprietary interest, the beneficiary only has a personal claim for the damages. The name-borrowing provision could be seen as consistent with privity of contract, its purpose being to enable an arbitrator "to decide the matter" referred to him. **9–026**

Outside the name-borrowing context, the courts have consistently rejected the notion that the contractor receives money from the employer representing subcontractors' work as trustee for the subcontractors. The question arose in *George E Taylor v G Percy Trentham* (1980) 16 B.L.R. 15 where a contractor claimed a sum which had been withheld by the employer under a certificate. The sum represented a claim which the employer had against a subcontractor under a direct warranty under which the subcontractor was liable to the employer for delay. The employer had no right of set-off under the main contract in respect of this sum but it argued that the contractor had no beneficial interest in the money since it would have been bound to pass it on to the subcontractor. This argument was rejected by Judge Sir William Stabb Q.C., although he went on to speculate that the employer might have been able to set off the cross-claim against the subcontractor had the subcontractor made a claim for direct payment under the warranty.

Defences to trust arguments

An argument that a name-borrowing clause took effect as a trust of the claim might be met by two defences: **9–027**

(1) if the parties had intended a trust, they would have used clear language as in the retention trust clause;

(2) there is a strong presumption against importing trust obligations into commercial contracts unless the context is clear.

On any view, the approach taken in NSC/C is not clear. A contractor receives a nominated subcontractor's proportion of certified sums in its own right unless they concern retention. The same applies to any loss and expense certified by the architect. It would seem strange that a nominated subcontractor could alter this situation by invoking the name-borrowing procedure. Such a result would adversely affect the contractor's rights of set-off in respect of cross-claims against the subcontractor. The clause provides the subcontractor with one of the rights of a trust beneficiary but does not constitute a trust. In *Lorne Stewart v William Sindall* (1986) 35 B.L.R. 109, Judge Lewis Hawser Q.C. rejected an argument that the arrangement was an assignment (at 128). The language falls short of either assignment or trust and it seems more probable that the court would hold the name-borrowing provision to be an elaborate contractual device which is not intended to disrupt the normal payment chain. It is not an express equivalent of the implied term that led to the equitable lien in *Napier's* case, i.e. that the insured would pay to the insurer any damages received from a third person attributable to the insurance proceeds it had received (at 409). The subcontractor faces similar difficulties with a clause 1.13 claim: see *Schott-Kem v G Percy Trentham* (unreported, 15 May 1985, CA) discussed in Ch.17.

Alternatively the subcontractor might argue that the contractor entered into the main contract for its benefit. In such a case, the contractor would hold the benefit on trust for the subcontractor: *Lloyd's v Harper* (1880) 16 Ch. D. 290. Construing the subcontract as a whole it does not seem to fall in this category. The question is whether it could fall within the principle in *Lloyd's v Harper* to the limited extent of cl.1.13. It is hard to resist the conclusion that all cl.1.13 does is to prevent the contractor sitting on its rights under the main contract: to the extent that they overlap and are consistent with a nominated subcontract, it is reasonable that they should be exercised against the employer. But to the extent that the claim is successful against the employer, the contractor accounts to the subcontractor in its own right for the proceeds and not as trustee or assignor. Clause 1.11 expressly excludes privity of contract as between the employer and the subcontractor.

"Passing on" money

9–028 The same principles apply to cl.10(2) of the FCEC form of subcontract which provides:

> ". . . the Contractor shall take all reasonable steps to secure from the Employer such contractual benefits, if any, as may be claimable in accordance with the Main Contract on account of any adverse physical conditions . . . On receiving any such contractual benefits from the Employer . . . the Contractor shall in turn pass on to the Sub-Contractor such proportion if any thereof as may in all the circumstances be fair and reasonable."

It has been stated that the duty to "pass on" a proportion of the benefit "imposes a legal obligation on the main contractors": *Mooney v Henry Boot* (1996) 80 B.L.R. 66 at 78, *per* Staughton L.J. A legal obligation can co-exist with an equitable obligation in the same transaction: *Barclays Bank v Quistclose* [1970] A.C. 567 at 581. The way that the words apparently reify the proportion could lead to an argument that it must be held on trust for the subcontractor. But the language is commercial and is more likely to reflect the industry's linear idea of payment discussed in Ch.3. In other words, although the contractor's claim may be calculated by reference to the subcontractor's claim, it is not advanced as trustee for the subcontractor. Compare the Scottish case of *Veitchi v Crowley Russell* [1972] S.C. 225 in which a contractor's obligation under the main contract to "pay over" sums due to subcontractors was merely "useful machinery enabling the subcontractor to enforce timeous payment of a debt due to him by" the contractor (at 230, *per* Lord Hunter).

On the contractor's insolvency, could the nominated subcontractor still use the contractor's name or obtain specific performance of cl.1.13 or cl.10(2)? The obvious analogy is with the right of an administrative receiver to use the borrower's name in proceedings to realise property caught within a charge. This right survives the borrower's entry into liquidation but is only available by reason of the security. Similarly a liquidator of an insured was ordered to co-operate with the insurer to obtain payment of money to which the insurer was entitled by subrogation: *Re Miller Gibb & Co* [1957] 2 All E.R. 266. But where the subcontractor only has a contractual right against the company, the liquidator has a discretion whether to co-operate and cannot be compelled to do so. An insolvency practitioner may decide to seek an injunction preventing the subcontractor from using the company's name or possibly do nothing and claim the benefit as soon as an award is issued. The best solution seems to be for the subcontractor to ask the liquidator for an assignment of the cause of action against the employer.

5. Breach of trust

Wrongful revocation

There are no reported cases on claims for breach of an English construction trust. Breach of a subcontract trust was found in *ESPL v Radio & General Engineering* (considered above). See also the Malaysian case of *Fawziah Holdings v Metramac* [2006] 1 M.L.J. 435, which concerned a project for the design, build, finance and operation of toll roads. The project company agreed with investors to open an account and pay into it on trust for the investors all moneys received in respect of "future contracts" relating to the works. The concession was terminated by consent for political reasons and a second concession agreement was entered into later. It was held that the project company was holding the second agreement on trust for the original investors and, if it had failed to pay receivables under it into the account, it would have been in breach of trust (para.67). **9–029**

There is also an Australian authority in which a finding of breach of trust at first instance was overturned on appeal: *Stork Electrical v Leighton Contractors* [2000] QCA 517. Leighton agreed to act as managing contractor to the State of Queensland for the construction of the Brisbane Conference Centre. The contract was subject to a guaranteed maximum price of $138 million. All sums payable to subcontractors were to be paid by the employer into a designated bank account and held by the contractor on the terms of a separate trust deed. The execution of the deed by Leighton was a condition of the managing contract. Aware of the trust arrangement, and in reliance on it, Stork entered into a subcontract for electrical work with Leighton.

After approximately 80 per cent of the work had been completed, the employer and the contractor varied the main contract by increasing the guaranteed maximum price and deleting the trust in favour of the subcontractors. The employer was no longer obliged to make future payments into the trust account as Leighton became directly responsible for payment of subcontractors. Stork claimed $2.3 million from the contractor, representing variations and losses resulting from delay, and asserted that the variation of the main contract and subsequent receipt of $45 million by the contractor on its own account constituted breaches of trust. The court heard the breach of trust allegation as a preliminary issue.

9–030 At first instance, Atkinson J. pointed out the co-existence of a contractual and fiduciary relationship. As a matter of contract, there was nothing to prevent the employer and the contractor amending their contract. Indeed, there was even an express term recognising their right to do so. But, as a matter of trust law, the contractor had allowed its own commercial interests to prevail over the fiduciary duty it owed to the subcontractors. It was no answer to a conflict of interest arising under a trust to point to rights ordinarily available under a contract, where, as here, Leighton held its contractual rights to payment against the employer in trust. The trust property consisted not only of the benefit of the bank account, it extended to the employer's promise to the contractor to make payments in respect of subcontractors' work directly into the account.

By a majority of two to one, the Queensland Court of Appeal reversed this decision. The majority were influenced by three factors:

(1) The managing contract provided that no term should be varied without the employer's consent. The court inferred that, by expressly allowing for its variation, the parties must have intended to reserve the right to revoke the trust. The managing contract was the source of the trust which depended on the contract for its continued existence. The trust property was therefore inherently flawed and vulnerable.

(2) The trust deed allowed the employer to terminate the trust two years after the issue of the final certificate or earlier should it so decide. This was referred to as an "early vesting date". The court inferred that this reflected an overall discretion in the employer that was consistent with the deletion of the trust by consensual amendment of the managing contract. Curiously, no one seems to have considered the possibility that the employer's power to terminate the trust before the end date could be of benefit to the subcontractors, a necessary protection of their rights to the fund. If the managing contract were terminated, through Leighton's default or insolvency, there would have to be some machinery for payment out of the account. It is also curious that neither Atkinson J. nor the Court of Appeal made any reference to the terms of the termination clauses in the managing or the subcontracts.

(3) The Court of Appeal was also impressed by a term of a direct agreement between the employer, contractor and subcontractor, which stated that the employer owed no duty to the subcontractor. The

majority considered that this negated any duty to maintain the existence of the trust until completion.

The Court of Appeal took a contractual approach to an equitable issue. As a matter of contract, to state that one party owes no duty to another may well, in the context of a chain of contracts, be sufficient to exclude privity of contract between them. But where they have already entered into an arrangement with proprietary consequences, it cannot be inferred that the parties have agreed to derogate from the trust in the absence of much clearer wording. If instead the court had taken the approach suggested in *Rafidain Bank v Saipem* [1994] C.L.C. 252 discussed at para.9–030 below, it might have held that the wording in the direct agreement was apt to exclude privity of contract but not to adversely affect the trust arrangement under which the subcontractor had become a beneficiary only a week before.

For this reason, the reasoning of the dissenting judge in the Court of Appeal seems preferable (Quick and Davis 2002). He considers the position from the point of view of the law of trusts, and notes that the trust embraced the benefit of the account and anything which might represent that benefit, including the contractor's rights against the employer. Similarly, in construing the terms of a trust, he would expect to find an express right of revocation or variation reserved in the trust deed before holding that the settlor could diminish the rights of the beneficiaries by varying the instrument creating the trust. It is hard to see how the power to vary the managing contract could amount to such a reservation, at least after the subcontractor had acquired an equitable interest in the trust property.

Misappropriation of money

If tracing is not an effective remedy, e.g. where money is paid in to an **9–031**
overdrawn account, the beneficiaries of the trust may have personal claims against the companies concerned and their directors for knowing receipt or knowing assistance. In *Caltong (Australia) Pty Ltd v Tong Tien See Construction* [2002] 3 S.L.R. 241, the directors of a contractor transferred S$985,000 to an associated company in breach of their fiduciary duties. The Singapore Court of Appeal made a tracing order in respect of the money. The liquidator of the contractor was able to prove that the associated company had purchased three properties with the money, one of which had been sold and the proceeds reinvested in the purchase of a further property. The court declared that the associated company was a constructive trustee of all three properties. The liquidator failed in a claim against the sole director of the associated company for knowing receipt and knowing assistance because he could not show that the director knew that the funds had been obtained through a breach of trust.

Consider the following example. An employer asks a funder to pay an amount representing retention withheld under a JCT contract to its parent company, which pays it into an overdrawn bank account and then goes into liquidation. Assume that the employer had no right of deduction against the amount and, on ordinary trust principles, could only have received the cheque as bare trustee for the contractor. The authorisation to the funder to pay the parent company was a breach of trust, and the employer and any of it directors and employees concerned with the making of the payment could be personally liable for knowing assistance. If the parent was aware of the breach of trust, or turned a blind eye to the obvious, or failed to make the enquiries an honest person would have made, it could also be liable to the contractor for knowing receipt, and the relevant directors and employees for knowing assistance. Where the employer held its right to retention from the funder as bare trustee, and the contractor gave notice of that fact to the funder, the funder may only be entitled to a good discharge for the payment by paying the contractor. A contractor in this position should consider giving notice to anyone liable to pay money to the employer which could represent retention.

6. Termination of trusts

Revocable trusts

9–032 A trust terminates either pursuant to an express power of revocation or when its purpose has been fulfilled. In *Re Old Inns* (1994) 13 A.C.S.R. 141, the employer went into liquidation a month before the expiry of the defects liability period. Two weeks later the architect resigned and as a result no certificate of making good defects could be issued. Although the employer had a duty to appoint a new architect the liquidator failed to do so and instead claimed the benefit of the account. The contract provided that the account was held on trust "except that in the event of the Builder determining his employment under this Agreement pursuant to clause 12.06 the rights and interests of the Proprietor in respect of such amounts shall be and are hereby transferred to and for the benefit of the Builder". The contractor terminated under this clause but the employer argued that it was not open to the contractor to terminate after having performed the contract, relying on *Greene v West Cheshire Railway* (1871) L.R. 13 Eq. 44. The court rejected the argument since:

- the defects liability period had not fully expired; even though only one per cent of the works remained outstanding, it was technically incomplete; and
- there was no objection to a contract providing that a notice of termination could be served even if the contract had been fully completed "so as to trigger certain other parts of the contract" (at 143).

Irrevocable trusts

9–033 Construction trusts are usually irrevocable and fulfilment depends on the performance of contractual obligations. In *Nev Mellon Electrical v AAPC* [2005] NZHC 391, the contractor went into liquidation shortly before completion. A new contract was entered into whereby the employer agreed to pay the contractor as trustee for 18 subcontractors the sum of $385,000 in the following stages: $200,000 up front, $100,000 on the issue of a certificate from the building inspector, and the balance once the subcontractors had completed the work to the employer's satisfaction. The second tranche of $100,000 was held in a trust account by the solicitors for the subcontractors; the balance was not funded but notionally held by the employer. A dispute arose and the employer obtained an injunction restraining payment out of the $100,000. The subcontractors issued proceedings claiming the employer had prevented them from completing the work so as to satisfy the inspector. The court refused to order security for costs against the subcontractors and directed that an expert be appointed to determine what work would be needed to comply with building control requirements.

Revocation of the trust depends on completion of the contract, and difficulties will arise where either or both parties become insolvent before completion. The termination clause in JCT contracts does not expressly deal with retention in this situation. Numerous cases of employer insolvency arose in the early 1990s after retention had been set aside. In some cases, receivers opted to "mothball" the project, awaiting an improvement in the market and approvals to changes of use. Contractors were apparently left without a remedy. Although their retention was protected, it was depreciating over time because the employer in receivership was entitled to the interest. The court might conclude that it was an implied term of the trust that where the contractor lost possession of the site on the employer's insolvency, practical completion should be deemed to have occurred at that moment, allowing part of the retention to be paid out to the contractor with the balance becoming payable once the period for rectifying defects had expired. Otherwise:

> ". . . it may well be that a Chancery judge will intervene to prevent the trustee-employer from unconscionably exploiting the strict contractual terms in its own favour well beyond what the parties contemplated when allowing the trustee-employer to have the benefit of the retention trust. This may enable the judge to impose a term that could not have been implied as a matter of contract at common law" (Hayton 1994a, at 29).

A possible solution is for the trustees to apply to the court under CPR Pt 64 for guidance or for extra powers under s.57 of the Trustee Act 1925 or the court's inherent jurisdiction: *Rafidain Bank v Saipem* [1994] C.L.C. 252. In that case, an Italian consortium as contractor agreed to build a pipeline for an Iraqi state-owned organisation as employer for about $500 million. The employer was named as engineer under the project contract. The contractor was to be paid from a trust account at Banca Commerciale Italiana in London on presentation of invoices to the trustee (Rafidain Bank) which had been approved by the employer in its capacity as engineer and certified by the Central Bank of Iraq. The project had been completed and the only remaining sum due to the contractor was the second half of its retention.

It was a condition of final payment to the contractor that it obtained clearance certificates from the Iraqi authorities in relation to income tax, social security and customs, as proof that the contractor had discharged its obligations to make these payments pursuant to the project contract. The contractor applied for the clearance certificates but before they were issued the Gulf War intervened, and the pipeline was destroyed by allied bombing.

Iraq passed legislation preventing payment to foreign contractors and international sanctions were imposed against it.

The trust account was funded by another Iraqi state-owned organisation from the proceeds of sale of oil to an Italian company (Saipem) linked with the contractor. In the absence of the clearance certificates, the employer would not approve the contractor's final invoice and the Central Bank of Iraq would not certify payment. On the contractor's application under RSC 85 as a beneficiary of the trust, the court directed Rafidain as trustee to pay the contractor its retention from the account, despite the absence of the requisite documents. The decision was upheld on appeal on different grounds. In the leading judgment, Hobhouse L.J. had to consider the interaction between the project contract, the finance agreement and the trust agreement. The trust agreement created both contractual and proprietary rights. He considered the contractor's claim in two stages: (1) Was the contractor entitled to payment from the account pursuant to the contractual obligations in the trust agreement? (2) If not, was it entitled to payment pursuant to its equitable proprietary rights in the fund? The answers were "no" and "yes" respectively.

In contract, the contractor argued that the mechanism for payment had broken down and that where a contractual condition had become impossible to fulfil, the court had jurisdiction to step in and provide a remedy. The argument failed since, although extremely unlikely, it remained a possibility that the Iraqi authorities would issue the clearance certificates. Even if this were not possible, the court would not intervene because the impossibility had not been caused by the employer. It was common ground that the employer was not in breach of the project contract. The trustee was in the same position as the issuer of a demand guarantee or a letter of credit. Provision of documents in the correct form was a condition of liability intended to protect the paying parties. The court rejected an implied term excusing the contractor from providing the documents. The trust agreement was part of the overall contractual matrix: provision of documents was not simply procedural but conditioned the contractor's right to payment.

9–034 The arguments which were rejected when put in contract terms were accepted when advanced by the contractor as a beneficiary under the trust. The contractor was exclusively beneficially entitled to the account. "It was an equitable title which came into existence as an interest in possession at the time that the proceeds of the sale of the crude were paid by Saipem AG into the account" (at 46). The finding that the contractor had a vested interest in property cast a different light on the matter. The property vested under the terms of the trust agreement. The trust was to pay the contractor, in other words "to discharge, *pro tanto*, the obligations of [the employer] under the project contract" (at 48).

As between the contractor and the employer, the retention was due for payment: the evidence was that the contractor had paid the local taxes. The court concluded that the duty to provide documents to the trustee was "part of the machinery of the administration of the trust, and not a qualification on the contractor's equitable proprietary right in the account" (at 49). The requirement for invoices approved by the employer as engineer and certified by the Central Bank of Iraq was a contractual term governing the exercise of the trustee's powers, not the existence of the trust or the interest of the contractor in the fund (at 51). To order payment to the contractor could not prejudice anyone. Even if it could, the contractor had given indemnities under the trust agreement which would cover the position.

Hobhouse L.J. referred to *Re New* [1901] 2 Ch. 534 as authority for the court's jurisdiction to enable the purpose of a trust to be fulfilled in this kind of case:

> "Where some event or development unforeseen, perhaps unforeseeable, and anyhow unprovided against by the settlor or testator, threatened to make shipwreck of his intentions: and it was imperative that something should be saved from the impending wreck. These are often referred to as the 'salvage' cases . . ."

What was an absolute bar to recovery in contract was only an administrative detail in trust. The case is an excellent example of the status of property in English law. With only a contractual right to payment, the creditor has an uphill struggle and will be defeated by clearly expressed contractual conditions to its release. Where the creditor also has a vested right in the fund from which payment will be made, the court will take a broader view and intervene to rescue the creditor (or rather its property) if that is the just result in all the circumstances. The case is exceptional, arising out of extreme facts, but shows how overlaying a trust on a contractual matrix can enlarge the court's jurisdiction to deal with what was essentially a contractual problem.

A developer may be required to establish a trust fund as security for performance of obligations under a waste management licence under the Environmental Protection Act 1990. In *Environment Agency v Hillridge* [2004] 2 B.C.L.C. 358, the licence holder went into liquidation and the liquidator successfully disclaimed the company's interest in the licence under s.178 of the Insolvency Act 1986. It was held that the disclaimer also divested the contractor of its interest in £367,000 which had been paid into a trust account. The Environment Agency was unable to claim the money because the trust deed provided that the account would be held as security for the purpose of satisfying expenses it incurred but expenses could only be incurred while the licence remained in force. The trust fund therefore vested in the Crown as *bona vacantia*.

Chapter 10

Retention Trusts

Many trust claims made in the industry concern the JCT retention trust. Common issues concern the constitution of the trust and the scope of the trustee's rights of recourse. In the new 2005 edition of the JCT forms, the right to have retention funded on request has been continued but the concept of nominating subcontractors has been dropped. Nevertheless, it is only possible to understand the nature of this trust by analysing the previous case law on nominated subcontract trusts. **10–001**

1. The nominated subcontract trust

The earliest case on the retention trust concerned an application by nominated subcontractors in the liquidation of a main contractor: *Re Tout and Finch* [1954] 1 All E.R. 127. The contractor was involved in the construction of flats for a local authority under an RIBA contract with quantities. Ten per cent retention was withheld. The subcontract was in the Green Form and provided as follows: **10–002**

> "If and to the extent that the amount retained by the employer in accordance with the main contract includes any retention money the contractor's interest in such money is fiduciary as trustee for the subcontractor [and if the contractor attempts or purports to mortgage or otherwise charge such interest or his interest in the whole of the amount retained aforesaid (otherwise than by floating charge if the contractor is a limited company), the contractor shall thereupon immediately set aside and become a trustee for the subcontractor of a sum equivalent to the retention money and shall pay the same to the subcontractor on demand; provided that upon payment of the same to the subcontractor the amount due to the subcontractor upon final payment under this sub-contract shall be reduced accordingly by the sum so paid]." (square brackets supplied)

A fiduciary is not necessarily a trustee in the full sense of the word: such a person can have obligations towards another's property even though it may not be vested in him. The nature and extent of a fiduciary's duties are variable and depend on the circumstances of each case. However, in this contract the words "fiduciary as trustee" are sufficiently clear to show that a trust is intended with the subcontractor as beneficiary.

There was no evidence in this case that the contractor had attempted to charge its retention; it had simply gone into liquidation before receiving it from the employer. Although that contingency had not occurred, the court held that the nominated subcontractors were entitled to a declaration that the contractor's rights to retention were held in trust for them and that the liquidator was bound to pass over the proportion due to them on receipt from the employer. The judge observed that:

> "On the face of it there are clear words used which are apt to create a trust which will operate by way of an equitable assignment of assets described as the contractor's interest in the retention money" (at 134, *per* Wynn-Parry J.).

The words in square brackets in the clause quoted above show that the trust was originally intended to prevent the contractor's creditors obtaining priority over the nominated subcontractors in respect of retention. The exception in favour of floating charge holders might have diluted the protection had the court not construed the first part of the clause as an effective assignment: see *MacJordan Construction v Brookmount Erostin* (1992) 56 B.L.R. 1. The sanction of accelerated payment never seems to have been used in practice and was dropped in later contracts, e.g. cll.4.29 of WC/2 and 4.22.1 of NSC/C, which also introduced the requirement to set aside a fund on request. In *Re Tout and Finch*, the contractor was already in liquidation and incapable of complying with an injunction to set aside a fund as its assets had become subject to the statutory trust in favour of creditors: *Ayerst v C & K (Construction) Ltd* [1976] A.C. 167. As the retention had not been paid to the contractor before its liquidation, the court could enforce the assignment by ordering retention to be paid direct to the subcontractors or by ordering the liquidator to "pass it on" as soon as it was received by him.

In *Harry Bibby v Neill Construction* [1973] E.G.D. 52 the main contract was in CCC/WKS/1 form (the precursor of GC/Works/1), and the subcontract was in the Green Form. The contractor went into liquidation before receiving the retention from the employer, the Ministry of Public Building and Works. The Ministry released the retention to the liquidator apparently before the proceedings were issued by the subcontractor. The Court of Appeal held, following *Re Tout and Finch*, that "the payment made by the Ministry to the liquidator in March 1970, was impressed in the liquidator's hands with a trust in favour of Harry Bibby". The report is unfortunately very brief but it seems the trust of the contractor's rights declared by the Green Form extended to the Ministry's cheque for the retention and the proceeds of the cheque held by the liquidator (see Ch.9).

What is the position where a subcontractor's retention is received by the contractor but not paid to the nominated subcontractor before the contractor's liquidation? At first sight, unless the employer had received notice of the equitable assignment, it could not be compelled to pay the subcontractor the same sum, i.e. to pay twice. Could the fact of nomination be actual or constructive notice? The question was considered in *Re Arthur Sanders* (1981) 17 B.L.R. 125 in which Nourse J. held:

> "Putting it at its lowest it seems to me to be clear that the employer requires and authorises the contractor to enter into a subcontract in that form and that the employer has notice of its contents. The subcontract therefore takes effect as an assignment to the subcontractor, made with

the authority and with the knowledge of the employer, of a due proportion of the contractor's beneficial interest in the retention moneys under clause 30(4)(a) of the main contract. In my judgment there can be no doubt that that is the effect of clause 11(h) of the FASS subcontract" (at 138).

Although the employer is fixed with knowledge of the terms of the Green Form or NSC/4, it may not know whether a subcontract incorporating them was in fact concluded: the contractor might have substituted its own terms and conditions or amended the standard form by omitting the trust clause. For this reason, a nominated subcontractor concerned to protect its retention is best advised to give notice to the employer of the assignment effected by the subcontract.

The ASI form of subcontract includes the following clause: "6.41: All amounts retained will be held in trust by the employer in a separate banking account as money due to the contractor pending satisfactory completion of the work, and will include such money due to the subcontractor". The reference to "money due to the contractor" seems to suggest that only the contractor is the beneficiary, and there is no sub-trust or assignment as in *Re Tout & Finch*. The form seems to be a simplified version of NSC/4.

2. Rights of recourse

The subcontract trust clause is subject to two equities: (1) any right of **10–003** recourse which the employer has over the whole retention, and (2) any right of recourse which the contractor has against the retentions of the nominated subcontractors.

If notice of assignment is given and the employer pays the subcontractor's retention to it direct, the contractor will have been deprived of its right of recourse. Clause 23 of NSC/4 gives the contractor a right of set-off in respect of loss and/or expense actually incurred provided it complies with certain conditions. The architect is involved only where the cross-claim arises out of the subcontractor's delay in completion. Even in that case, the architect may fail to notify the employer of the contractor's cross-claim. If the loss and expense is incurred as a result of a different breach neither the architect nor the employer would know of it unless notice were given by the contractor. In this situation, the employer should seek the contractor's confirmation that it claims no right of set-off against the subcontractor before releasing the money. In the event of a dispute between contractor and subcontractor, the employer should interplead. Interpleader proceedings enable the court to decide which of two or more claimants is entitled to property in the hands of a disinterested third party: e.g. *Drew v Josolyne* (1887) 18 Q.B.D. 590. The employer's right of recourse contained in JCT 98 reads:

> "Notwithstanding the fiduciary interest of the Employer in the Retention as stated in clause 30.5.1 the Employer is entitled to exercise any right under this Contract of withholding and/or deduction from monies due or to become due to the Contractor against any amount so due under an Interim Certificate . . ." (clause 30.1.1.2).

This right protects the employer in two ways: it may excuse it from having to set up a trust fund at all or, if an account is opened, it will enable the employer to make withdrawals from it without being in breach of trust. The expression "right under this Contract of withholding and/or deduction" could suggest that the employer's cross-claim must derive from an express right under the contract rather than at common law. Sums expressly deductible include liquidated damages; the cost of employing others to carry out an instruction if the contractor refuses to do so (e.g. cl.4.1.2 of JCT 80 applied in *GPT Realisations v Panatown* (1992) 61 B.L.R. 88); a premium for personal injury insurance taken out by the employer if the contractor fails to do so, e.g. cl.21.1.3 of JCT 80; or direct payments to nominated subcontractors, as in *Glow Heating v Eastern Health Board* (1992) 8 Const. L.J. 56. Claims for damages in tort are excluded. Damages for breach of contract also probably fall outside the scope of deductible claims although there are dicta to the contrary: *Rayack Construction v Lampeter Meat* (1979) 12 B.L.R. 30 at 38.

It is thought that the right of recourse given by the contract is exhaustive of the employer's rights of set-off against funded retention. There is an argument that "right under this Contract" means "under an express or an implied term" and, as the common law is implied unless excluded, it must apply even to funded retention. Although the words used might ordinarily be a restatement of the general law, this is unlikely here because, as trustee, the employer would normally have no rights against the retention, and the court will assume the parties had this in mind when using the expression "under the contract". *GPT Realisations v Panatown* (at 98) appears therefore to have been wrongly decided on this point. The right of recourse is an inherent weakness of the chose in action representing retention: it constitutes the employer as an active self-interested trustee rather than a beneficiary of the trust with the contractor: *Wates v Franthom* (1991) 53 B.L.R. 23; *Obaray v Gateway (London) Ltd* [2004] 1 B.C.L.C. 555; Hayton (1994a). This is in contrast to other contexts where a commercial trustee has been found to be a co-beneficiary in respect of a right of deduction: *Re Lewis's of Leicester* [1995] 1 B.C.L.C. 428.

10–004 If the employer holds retention on trust for the contractor, who in turn holds a proportion of its interest in the retention on trust for nominated subcontractors, can the employer exercise its rights of deduction against the whole retention or only against the contractor's own proportion? This question arose in *Re Arthur Sanders* (1981) 17 B.L.R. 125. In that case, a contractor had two contracts with the same employer. On the contractor's liquidation, one contract was virtually finished and retention of £11,086 was due and payable, of which £1,374 represented retention withheld against six nominated subcontractors. On the other contract, the contractor owed £98,155 to the employer. The contracts were both in JCT 63 form, which allowed the employer recourse against retention "for payment of any amount which he is entitled under the provisions of this contract to deduct from any sum due or to become due to the contractor". The liquidator conceded that the employer was entitled in principle to liquidation set-off of its claim against the retention (see Ch.18). The issue was whether the employer could make the set-off against the nominated subcontractors' proportion. At first sight this depended on the question of mutuality: if the contractor held the nominated subcontractors' portion as trustee, it would be held in a different capacity to the remainder of the retention and be unavailable for liquidation set-off.

Nourse J. denied set-off to the employer, analysing the position as follows:

> "In the present case the effect of the equitable assignment was to create a trust in favour of the subcontractor of the Company's equitable interest in the retentions. In other words, the position as between employer, contractor and subcontractor under the present RIBA Conditions and the FASS Subcontract is that the employer holds a due proportion of the retentions on trust for the contractor as trustee for the subcontractor. . . . First, it is not the retentions which are expressed to be subject to the right of the employer to have recourse thereto, but the contractor's 'beneficial interest' therein. In my judgment once a subcontract has been entered into the contractor no longer has a beneficial interest in the subcontractor's due proportion of the retentions. At that stage his only interest in that proportion is as a trustee for the subcontractor . . . Secondly, once that stage is reached I do not see how the proportion in question can really be said to be 'due' to the contractor at all. It may strictly still be payable to him under the terms of the main contract, but he must immediately pay it over under the subcontract. . . . to hold otherwise would necessarily involve the consequences that the subcontractors were deprived of the security which this elaborate scheme of things was clearly intended to give them at the very moment when they most needed it, that is to say on the insolvency of the contractor" (at 138–140).

The court seems to have reached the right result but for the wrong reasons. Liquidation set-off allowed the recourse against the main contractor's proportion of retention since there was mutuality between contractor and employer. But as between the employer and the nominated subcontractors, liquidation set-off was not available because the trust scheme only allowed the employer to set off against the nominated subcontractors' proportion of the retention in respect of claims against the contractor on the same project. In this case the employer's cross-claim arose under a different contract. Lack of mutuality between the employer and the subcontractors was not the issue in the case.

The purpose of the retention trust is to protect the contractor against employer insolvency or the subcontractors against contractor (and indirectly employer) insolvency. It is not intended to rewrite the contract. Nourse J. has not taken the employer's right of recourse into account in his analysis. This view is supported by a decision of the High Court of Hong Kong where an employer was allowed to set off against the whole retention in respect of losses arising from a nominated subcontractor's default. No question of insolvency arose. The court distinguished *Re Arthur Sanders* in the following passage:

> "The phrase 'any sum due or to become due to the main contractor' is almost a term of art in this contract. It simply covers all certified payments payable to the main contractor. I do not see how its meaning can be affected by any equitable assignment. To say that the assignor, main contractor, 'must immediately pay it over' seems to me with respect wrong. It ignores the provisions of clause 13 subject to which the assignment was made. . . . As its initial recipient, the main contractor has an interest in the whole fund. The interest in 'his' part is admittedly

> beneficial. But although he may hold other portions as trustee for particular nominated subcontractors, in no case is he simply a bare trustee. Clause 13 gives him the right to retain or set off for his own benefit. I therefore conclude that for the purposes of clause 30(4), the main contractor has a 'beneficial interest' in the whole retention fund. Accordingly in my judgment, the employer's right of recourse under clause 30(4) extends to the whole retention fund, and no valid distinction can be drawn between the main contractor's and the nominated subcontractor's proportions of it. Such recourse may be based upon a right to deduct arising under any term of the contract, e.g. clauses 2(1), 19(1)(c), 22 or 27(c). In each case the effect is the same. Up to the total amount of the permitted deduction, the employer's obligation to set aside ceases; as does *pro tanto* the relationship of trustee and beneficiary. The trust continues to apply only to the balance if any" (*Hsin Chong Construction v Yaton Realty* (1986) 40 B.L.R. 119 at 129, *per* Hunter J.).

In *Harrington v Co Partnership* (1998) 88 B.L.R. 44, considered later in this chapter, the Court of Appeal applied the reasoning of Nourse J. to the trust in the JCT 87 form. In so doing, the court again ignored the employer's contractual rights of recourse. The problems with JCT trust clauses arise because of a failure to work out the relationship between retention and set-off under the main and subcontracts. In a decision on the retention trust provisions in the Australian SC JCC A (1985) subcontract, it was held that the contractor's right of set-off against subcontractors' retention was "one of the terms of the trust qualifying the builder's obligations as trustee and limiting the subcontractor's beneficial entitlement": *KBH Construction v Lidco Aluminium* (1991) 7 B.C.L. 183 at 191, *per* Giles J.

3. Main contract retention trusts

10–005 JCT 63 introduced a trust of retention in favour of the main contractor. Clause 30(4) of this form reads:

> "The Employer's interest in any amount so retained shall be fiduciary as trustee for the Contractor (but without obligation to invest), and the Contractor's beneficial interest therein shall be subject only to the right of the Employer to have recourse thereto from time to time for payment of any amount which he is entitled under the provisions of this Contract to deduct from any sums due or to become due to the Contractor."

The fundamental difficulty is the apparent lack of trust property. In the Green Form quoted earlier, the "amount so retained" was identifiable as the main contract retention and the trust property consisted in the contractor's rights to that retention. In the JCT 63 clause, the "amount so retained" refers to the debt owed by the employer but the employer cannot have a right against itself. Nevertheless, the clause has been construed as imposing "an obligation on an employer to appropriate and set aside as a separate trust fund a sum equal to that part of the sum certified in any interim certificate as due in respect of work completed which the employer is entitled to retain during the defects liability period" (*Rayack Construction v Lampeter Meat* (1979) 12 B.L.R. 30 at 37).

The retention trust clause of JCT 98 runs as follows:

> "30.5 The Retention shall be subject to the following rules:
> .1 the Employer's interest in the Retention is fiduciary as trustee for the Contractor and for any Nominated Subcontractor (but without obligation to invest);
> .2.1 at the date of each Interim Certificate the Architect shall prepare, or instruct the Quantity Surveyor to prepare, a statement specifying the Contractor's retention and the Nominated subcontract retention for each Nominated Subcontractor deducted in arriving at the amount stated as due in such Interim Certificate;
> .2.2 such statement shall be issued by the Architect to the Employer, to the Contractor and to each Nominated Subcontractor whose work is referred to in the statement.
> .3 The Employer shall, to the extent that the Employer exercises his right under clause 30.4, if the Contractor or any Nominated Subcontractor so requests, at the date of payment under each Interim Certificate place the Retention in a separate banking account (so designated as to identify the amount as the Retention held by the Employer on trust as provided in clause 30.5.1) and certify to the Architect with a copy to the Contractor that such amount has been so placed. The Employer shall be entitled to the full beneficial interest in any interest accruing in the separate banking account and shall be under no duty to account for any such interest to the Contractor or any subcontractor."

JCT 05 has a similar clause although the references to nominated subcontractors are omitted. As payment of retention is deferred under the building contract, release of the equivalent amount to the employer under the funding agreement is usually withheld on the same terms, although the funding agreement may impose as a further condition a certificate from its surveyor that all defects have been made good. This is well understood in the industry and may be the reason for the request envisaged by cl.30.5.3. The rationale is that the employer should not be expected to fund a payment it has not received itself. If the parties deleted this sub-clause, the court would still give effect to the trust wording in the main contract and order an equivalent amount to be set aside. The sub-clause is "merely machinery for giving effect to the trust" (*Herbert Construction v Atlantic Estates* (1993) 70 B.L.R. 46 at 65). As a fiduciary the employer cannot use retention as part of its own working capital: *Wates Construction v Franthom* (1991) 53 B.L.R. 23.

Where the form is unamended, but no request is made to set money aside, it has been argued that the trust wording will extend to any right the employer has to "retention" under the funding agreement (Hayton 1994a). If it can be shown that the employer knows that a receivable under the funding agreement will represent the retention it agreed to hold on trust for the contractor, it is reasonable to conclude that the employer holds that chose in action on trust for the contractor, subject to its rights of deduction: *Pullan v Koe* [1913] 1 Ch. 9. Once payment is made by the funder to the employer, it will become subject to the trust, in substitution for the original chose, and the contractor will have tracing rights in respect of it.

In *Re Jartay Developments* (1982) 22 B.L.R. 134, the employer went into liquidation before having set aside retention. The court rejected the contractor's claim that the main contract trust clause was an assignment of the employer's rights under a development agreement. Unlike the position with nominated subcontractors, there was no express assignment in the building contract of the employer's rights under the development agreement, and it was not made a condition of the development agreement that the building contract include a trust clause. Nor could any assignment be implied:

> "The provisions for retentions under Clause 30 of the RIBA conditions have no reference to the retentions under the development contract. They take effect *de novo* as between [the contractor] and [the developer]. Moreover, as Mr. Hegarty for the liquidator pointed out, the provisions in the two contracts which deal with certificates and payments, retentions, practical completion and release of retentions are entirely different. The retentions were different in amount, being £30,000 under the development contract and about £46,000 under the building contract. In my judgment this is not a case where it can be said that [the developer] and [the contractor] must have intended that there should be an assignment to [the contractor], either in whole or in part, of [the developer's] contractual right as against [the fund] to the retentions of £15,000. It is clear to me that if I were to hold that that must have been their common intention I would be making for the parties a contract which they could have made, but did not make, for themselves" (at 142 *per* Nourse J.).

A development agreement often mirrors the building contract. For example, in *Banque Paribas v Venaglass* [1994] C.I.L.L. 918, a freeholder terminated a development agreement on the developer's insolvency. The bank was assignee from the developer of the benefit of the agreement. The termination clause obliged the freeholder to pay the value of the work carried out as quantified by an independent quantity surveyor. It was held that the *quantum meruit* approach was correct: the freeholder's liability was not limited to such amount of the development value of the site as had been released by the termination date.

10–006 The funding agreement is also likely to mirror the payment terms of the building contract: *Finnegan v Ford Sellar Morris (No. 2)* (1991) 27 Con. L.R. 41 at 51; contrast *Thompson Land v Salzer Constructions* [1998] VSC 111. The funder's approval of the building contract will be made a condition of the loan, as in the *MacJordan* case considered later. The only significant difference is the interposition of the funder's surveyor's approval as a condition of release of retention over and above the certificate of making good defects. The surveyor's approval is a restriction on the chose owed by the employer without negativing a trust of that chose. As soon as approval is given the chose would mature into a debt. If the employer had no rights of deduction, it would hold the debt as bare trustee for the contractor and there would be an implied equitable assignment as in *Re Tout and Finch*. If the contractor then gave notice of the assignment, the funder could only obtain a good discharge by paying the contractor. The same presumably applies where the surveyor's approval or the architect's certificate are wrongly withheld.

JCT forms impose no duty on the employer to invest funded retention. This means that the employer keeps any interest earned on it, even if retention is released in full at the end of the defects liability period. This is unjust, as not only does the contractor have to suffer withholding of its retention, but it also has to finance it. A fairer approach would be for interest to follow the retention, so that if the retention is released in full, the contractor would be entitled to the interest. If on the other hand, the employer had a cross-claim which could not be met in full by the retention, it should be entitled to the benefit of any interest required to meet the balance of the cross-claim. Under the Australian AS 2124–1992 form, the account is in the joint names of employer and contractor and withdrawals have to be sanctioned by both of them. Interest on the retention belongs to the contractor. It is interesting to note that this was the position in the predecessors of the JCT forms. For example, cl.25(d) of the RIBA contract (1931 edn) obliged the employer, on the architect's certificate, to open a trust account in joint names once the retention reached £1,000. The fund thereby created was to be held "together with all interest upon trust for the Employer as security for the due completion of the Works". The retention and accrued interest was then paid to the contractor on completion in two stages. This was expressly subject to the employer's right to any liquidated damages for delay. The clause also dealt with the situation where the employer became insolvent or repudiated the contract: in either case, the retention and accrued interest had to be paid to the contractor.

This clause, and indeed the contract as a whole, is refreshingly clear and shows how a standard form, while essential in an industry like construction, becomes progressively more unwieldy as time goes by. The only disadvantage was that the retention trust was an optional clause, whereas it is integrated within the JCT forms.

4. Management contract trusts

When the JCT introduced a form of management contract, it was decided to extend the protection of the retention trust to the management contractor and to all works contractors. It is possible for the trust to be limited to one particular group of works contractors to the exclusion of the others if the drafting is clear enough but if there is no express trust clause the court will not imply a trust simply because the subject matter is retention: *Herbert Construction v Atlantic Estates* (1993) 70 B.L.R. 46. **10–007**

As with JCT 80, retention is only funded under JCT 87 on request. In the unreported case of *HL Smith Construction v Albany Estates* (noted in Dean 1996), the contractor contended it had performed its function by passing on a request from a works contractor even though the employer had not opened the trust account. Despite the lack of privity, the works contractor obtained a mandatory injunction against the employer to set up the account. There were common directors between the employer and the management contractor and the court was satisfied that the employer had actual or constructive notice of the request.

The scheme is closely analogous to JCT 80. On the basis of the interlocking provisions of the management and works contracts and the extensive case law on the retention trust it might have been expected that, once an account had been set up, the employer would hold it (subject to its own rights of deduction) on trust for the management contractor, who in turn held it (subject to its rights of deduction) as sub-trustee for the works contractors as tenants in common, in proportions ascertainable from certificates issued under the management contract. According to the Court of Appeal in *Harrington v Co Partnership* (1998) 88 B.L.R. 44, however, this is not the case.

10–008 Harrington was a works contractor under WC/2, with John Lelliott as management contractor. Harrington's work was completed early on in the project and it was agreed that the defects liability period under its works contract had expired. The project had been practically completed but defective work by other works contractors meant that there had been no project-wide certificate of completion of making good defects. The latter certificate was a condition to the release of the second half of retention to the works contractors, including Harrington. The employer had set aside a retention fund which stood at nearly £300,000 when Lelliott went into administrative receivership. Under JCT 87, Lelliott's employment was automatically terminated. The architect certified under the management contract termination clause that the employer's loss following termination was just over £650,000. The employer exhausted the retention account in partial satisfaction of its claim. Harrington claimed directly from the employer in respect of approximately £20,000, as its proportion of the money which had been in the account.

The court at first instance decided that the employer's right of recourse was limited to retention withheld against the management contractor's fee, and could not be exercised against retention held for works contractors since such retention could never have been money due, or to become due, to the management contractor. This decision was upheld on appeal. In giving the judgment of the court, Morritt L.J. stated:

> "Down to the date of practical completion there were two parallel provisions for retentions, namely the retentions under the Management Contract pursuant to and in respect of the items specified in clause 4.6.2 and the retentions under the Works Contract pursuant to and in respect of the items specified in clause 4.23. The latter retentions never had been money due to the Management Contractor for they were specifically excluded from the interim certificates to be issued under clause 4.6 of the Management Contract. From the time the respective retentions were made they were held in one fund by the Employer in trust in the amounts of the respective retentions for the Management Contractor and the Works Contractor pursuant to clause 4.8.1 of the Management Contract. After practical completion the Management Contract retentions did become due by the Employer to the Management Contractor for the authority to retain them ceased at that stage and at the later stage of the certificate of completion of making good defects. Thus the right of set-off of the Employer under clause 7.4.4 was exercisable against those retentions. But in my view it is clear that such right was never exercisable against the Works Contract retentions. Those retentions had not been and never became 'money due to the Management Contractor'. They were held by the Employer in trust for the Works Contractor. By the time for the preparation of the interim certificate prescribed by clause 4.11 of the Management Contract the Works Contract retentions should have been released because the authority to retain them had lapsed pursuant to clause 4.23. In that event clause 4.3.2 could not be applied for the Employer would no longer hold the retention. But if for some reason the certificate of completion of making good defects had not been

> granted at the time when the certificate required by clause 4.11 was prepared it would make no difference. At all times since the Works Contract retentions had been made they had been held by the Employer in trust for the Works Contractor. The interim certificate required by clause 4.11 could not operate so as to make the Works Contract retentions due to the Management Contractor rather than the Works Contractor" (at 54).

Under the management contract the employer agrees to pay the management contractor the prime cost of the project and a management fee. The prime cost is defined as including all sums due to works contractors, which must include their retention. All sums payable to the management contractor are channelled through interim certificates issued by the architect. The employer has no right to pay works contractors direct, other than after termination, and even then there needs to be a contractual set-off against money due or to become due to the contractor. It follows that retention like all other payments to works contractors begins life as a sum due to the management contractor.

The employer's right of recourse is linked with the trust retention clause in the management contract which specifically states that retention in that context includes works contractors' retention, thereby ousting the contract definition of retention as that withheld against the management fee. The existence of the trust seems to have blinded the Court of Appeal to the ordinary contractual restrictions on release of retention. As no certificate of making good defects for the project had been issued prior to termination, no works contracts retention was due for release. This was a condition precedent and there was no allegation that the certificate had been wrongly withheld.

The court appears to have regarded the trust as freeing retention from its **10–009**
conditionality but there is no justification for this. The only machinery for release of works contract retention after making good defects of the project is by interim certificate under cl.4.11. This certificate can only be for money due to the management contractor in the first instance. It is true that, if employer and contractor confirmed that they had no rights of deduction, the works contractor could call for payment direct, the contractor stepping out of the picture as bare trustee (Hayton 1994a). But that did not happen here since the employer had a right of deduction under the main contract termination clause.

The effect of Lelliott's receivership was to automatically terminate the employment of the management contractor and all works contractors. In each case, the termination was without prejudice to the accrued rights or remedies of either party, which included their rights as beneficiaries under the retention trust, subject to other relevant terms of the management and works contract forms. Such terms included the automatic suspension of payment to the management contractor and the employer's right to recover termination losses by way of set-off. The termination clause in the management contract replaced the normal payment provisions, including those relating to retention, since the employer's set-off was to be made against "the total amount which would have been payable on due completion in accordance with this Contract" (i.e. the prime cost). As with JCT 80, the purpose of the trust was not to re-write the contract terms relating to retention but to change the status of payer–payee from that of debtor–creditor to trustee–beneficiary.

It is possible that the court may have confused the expiry of the defects liability period under the works contract with the defects period for the project as a whole. Had the employer been attempting to use its right of recourse to satisfy a cross-claim arising against Lelliott under a separate contract, it would have been right to order release of retention to the works contractors: *Re Arthur Sanders*. The court may have been misled by the approach of Nourse J. in that case, where he held that the proportion of retention attributable to nominated subcontractors could not be due to the main contractor. The court also rejected the employer's submission that the contractor's right to deduct a cash discount of two and a half per cent from all payments implied that retention must have been due to the contractor, perhaps through a misapprehension that retention becomes automatically due for release on the certificate of making good defects for the project, without the need for a further interim certificate.

This analysis is supported by the Scottish case of *Balfour Beatty v Britannia Life* [1997] S.L.T. 10 which concerned almost identical contractual provisions to those considered by the Court of Appeal in *Harrington.* The facts were also very similar except that retention had not been set aside in a separate account by the date of the management contractor's receivership. Two works contractors sued the employer for payment or the setting up of a trust account. Dismissing the claim the Court of Session held:

(1) "retentions" under cl.4.8 comprised retention in respect of the works contracts as well as the management contract;

(2) no trust had been constituted under Scots law at the date of the receivership;

(3) reading the contract provisions as a whole, the intention was that on determination of the management contract the terms as to payment, including the duty to fund retention on request, were superseded by the terms of the termination clause;

(4) accordingly the receivers were not obliged to ask the employer to set up a trust account;

(5) upon determination of the contract, any trust in favour of the works contractors terminated since the determination brought cl.7 of the management contract conditions into play, which made the protection of the employer's interests paramount;

(6) the employer's claims against the management contractor could be set off against the whole retention. Works contractors had no right to have their proportion of retention protected against such claims even if they related to liabilities of the contractor or of other works contractors.

Both cases can be read in the context of an earlier decision of the Court of Appeal, *Rafidain Bank v Saipem* [1994] C.L.C. 252, which is considered in Ch.9. The court ordered payment out of the trust account of the second half of retention to a contractor even though the contractor could not provide one of the documents required by the trust agreement. In that case the document was regarded as a formality rather than an equity qualifying the contractor's proprietary interest in the fund. The employer as engineer had issued a final acceptance certificate, had no cross-claim and apparently accepted that the document in question was merely evidence of something the employer already knew to be the case.

In *Harrington*, the court was naturally concerned to arrive at a just result and overrode the employer's equity. Admittedly, the contrary result would have been hard on works contractors, especially those who finish their packages early in the project. It is hard on innocent works contractors to be deprived of retention because of defaults by the management contractor or by other works contractors. That is, however, how the JCT retention scheme works: *Hsin Chong Construction v Yaton Realty* (1986) 40 B.L.R. 119. The position is analogous to a claim by a subcontractor pursuant to an American mechanics lien which may (depending on the particular statute) only succeed to the extent of any surplus owing to the contractor after the employer has set off the cost to complete. There is a potential conflict between the notions of "retention" and "trust". Retention protects the employer against the contractor's insolvency, in particular by making the issue of a making good defects certificate a condition precedent for its release. A trust protects the works contractors against the insolvency of the contractor and the employer but cannot alter the nature of the trust property as defined by the contract.

5. Mandatory injunctions

In practice, employers do not set aside retention into a separate account **10–010** unless requested to do so. Research suggests that employers regard such requests as insulting (Hopper 1996). If the employer refuses to open a trust account, the court has power to grant a mandatory injunction ordering it to do so. An application for such an under may be made *ex parte* in urgent situations, but otherwise it can only be made on notice, or on an application for summary judgment. The court requires evidence that the parties entered into a contract containing a trust clause, or conceivably that such a term was incorporated by a course of dealing (*Harry Bibby v Neill Construction* [1973] E.G.D. 52), that retention has been withheld, and that the employer has refused a request to fund it. The affidavit should also give all relevant details surrounding the application, e.g. a description of the works, the stage they had reached, the amount of the contract sum received on account, and any cross claims which had been raised by the employer, and disclose any special circumstances. In this regard:

> "It is ridiculous to suggest that the main contractor can only insist on the trust being set up if it can adduce evidence of some shakiness in the employer's financial position. If the main contractor had to wait till such evidence was forthcoming it would often by then be too late to take steps which would result in the fund being secured. Rather than requiring the main contractor to show that the horse is showing signs of bolting, the courts allow it to take steps to have the stable door shut while there is still no suggestion of anything being amiss. In asking for a trust fund to be set up, the main contractor is merely acting prudently" (*Concorde Construction v Colgan* (1984) 29 B.L.R. 125 at 135, *per* Rhind J.).

Even so, there are limits it seems, and injunctions were refused partly for lateness in *GPT Realisations v Panatown* (1992) 61 B.L.R. 88. It was an extreme case in that, of the three contracts between the parties, two had already reached practical completion and the other had been terminated.

The court has granted injunctions after practical completion before and this ought not to be a problem especially in view of the kind of relief being sought.

Termination ought not to have been regarded as a bar, as only the contractor's employment was terminated, and the termination clause did not suspend the employer's duty to fund retention, only its duty to pay sums due; but see *LEC Contractors v Castle Inn* [2001] 5 M.L.J. 510. The court seems to have been influenced more by the fact that the contractor was in receivership, refused to give an undertaking in damages, and was also dragging its feet in arbitrations against the employer. Against this, however, it might be argued that the insolvency of the beneficiary (and its consequential difficulty giving an undertaking in damages) could not have prejudiced the employer, as its property would have been preserved in the account pending the resolution of the dispute. The case seems to have come down to the court's perception that the application was, at heart, a tactical one. Further, as the injunction was refused in the end because the employer had rights of recourse exceeding the retention, *GPT Realisations v Panatown* is not persuasive authority on these issues.

There is no reported case on the position where an employer goes into administration before having set aside a retention fund. Under the procedure prior to the changes made by the Enterprise Act 2002, the court refused to impose a remedial constructive trust over the assets of a company in administration. "You cannot grant a proprietary right to A, who has not had one beforehand, without taking some proprietary right away from B" (*Re Polly Peck (No. 2)* [1998] 3 All E.R. 812 at 831, *per* Nourse L.J.). Although the contractor's right to have a trust funded can be specifically enforced, it is contractual not proprietary in nature.

10–011 An order for payment of retention to a joint account was set aside in *Zhong v Fuynam* (1996) 2 H.K.C. 342. The account was in respect of retention withheld under ten different contracts. The case is also authority that a retention trust injunction may be made by an arbitrator pursuant to Art.8 of the UNCITRAL Rules. The court has granted injunctions on the eve of the employer's formal insolvency: *Finnegan v Ford Sellar Morris (No. 2)* (1991) 27 Con. L.R. 41. If it turns out that the employer is genuinely unable to comply with the injunction, the court can always discharge the order leaving the contractor with other remedies such as winding up or personal claims against the directors (see Ch.20). In *MacJordan Construction v Brookmount Erostin* (1992) 56 B.L.R. 1 the court was concerned with an application against an employer who was already in receivership. In passing, Scott L.J. expressed the view that to grant an injunction where the employer was informally insolvent would be a preference of the contractor (see below and Ch.20).

The court will not grant an injunction if it is satisfied that the employer is entitled to exercise a right of recourse in excess of the retention for two reasons: (1) it would be pointless to set aside a fund for it to be immediately exhausted; and (2) if the employer exercised its right of deduction there would be no retention capable of being funded. Where an employer has claimed liquidated damages, the court has refused an injunction when the architect had certified non-completion under JCT 63 (*Henry Boot v The Croydon Hotel* (1985) 36 B.L.R. 41 *LEC Contractors v Castle Inn*), but not where the employer had given notice of non-completion under JCT 81 (*Finnegan v Ford Sellar Morris (No. 1)* (1991) 53 B.L.R. 38).

Where the employer only has an unsubstantiated claim for defects, an injunction will be granted: *Concorde Construction v Colgan* (1984) 29 B.L.R. 125; compare *ESPL v Radio & General Engineering* [2005] 2 M.L.J. 422, considered in Ch.9. In one case, where ordering an employer, who was a private individual, to open a trust account, the court directed that he could not exercise any right of recourse against the fund without an order of the court: *Tolent Construction v Kustow* (unreported, June 28, 1994). It seems to follow from the decision in *Harrington v Co Partnership* (1998) 88 B.L.R. 44 that the employer under JCT 87 would have to fund works contractors' retention in full notwithstanding any right of recourse it may have against the management contractor. As a request by one works contractor is deemed to be a request by them all, would the court discriminate between performing and defaulting works contractors when ordering the fund to be set aside, if satisfied that the employer's right of recourse against the contractor was not attributable to its default? This would be impracticable on an injunction application, and highlights one of the problems with the decision in *Harrington.*

In order to avoid setting up a fund, the directors of the employer may assure the contractor that it has funds available to pay retention as and when it became due. If the assurance is given dishonestly or recklessly, it may ground an action in deceit against the directors personally if it later emerges that the assurance was untrue. Other alternatives are to ask the employer to procure a bond from the funder, an assignment or attornment from the funder or a parent company guarantee from the employer, although only a demand bond would give the same protection as a properly funded trust.

6. Contractual right versus security interest

The nature of the contractual right to have retention funded was explored in *MacJordan Construction v Brookmount Erostin* (1992) 56 B.L.R. 1. This case concerned a contest between a contractor and administrative receivers of an employer over money standing in the employer's general bank account. Brookmount agreed with the local authority to develop land. Brookmount approached Generale Bank for funding, who agreed in principle, subject to three conditions: that the terms of the intended building contract be satisfactory to the bank; that a certified copy of the building contract be given to the bank after execution; and that Brookmount give as security a floating charge over its undertaking. All three conditions were satisfied. **10–012**

The contract with MacJordan was in the JCT 81 form, which included the standard retention trust clause. Before completion of the contract, Generale appointed administrative receivers to Brookmount under its floating charge, and MacJordan gave formal notice terminating its employment. The statement of affairs disclosed a shortfall under the bank's security of £2 million, and a claim by MacJordan for £1 million, which included retention of £110,000. The retention had not been set aside into a trust by the time the receivers were appointed. Brookmount had over £150,000 cash at bank with Barclays. It was this account which formed the subject of the dispute. Until it saw the statement of affairs, MacJordan was unaware of the cash at bank. On the face of it, the bank account fell squarely within Generale's floating charge over Brookmount's undertaking. The onus was on MacJordan to satisfy the court why it should grant an injunction setting aside £110,000 of the £150,000 in the account into a separate trust fund. In order to do this, MacJordan had to show that either a trust had been formed in some way before the receivership or that its right to have the money segregated was an equity subject to which the bank took the borrower's property by equitable assignment on the appointment of the receivers.

10–013 MacJordan put its case in three ways. First, it argued that the trust clause gave it an interest in a notional fund which took priority over the floating charge. The contractor raised the maxim that "equity looks on as done that which ought to be done". The problem for MacJordan was that the maxim was only effective against Brookmount, not against a third party like the bank which had given consideration for its security. It was true that Nourse J. had treated retention as notionally set aside in *Re Arthur Sanders* (1981) 17 B.L.R. 125, but that could not assist MacJordan since in *Re Arthur Sanders* it was the contractor who was insolvent not the employer-trustee (compare *G & T Earle v Hemsworth RDC* (1928) 140 L.T. 69).

MacJordan's second argument was that it had an equitable interest in the bank account at Barclays. The precise basis for the claim was not elaborated, and it had to be rejected because, apart from the rough parity between the amounts, there was no link between the retention and the bank account. (Compare the unsuccessful trust argument in *G&M Aldridge v Walsh* (1999) 169 A.L.R. 710.) Even if Brookmount had declared itself trustee of £110,000 of the £150,000, the trust would have failed for lack of identifiable subject matter. It might have been possible, however, for MacJordan to have argued that it had an equitable charge over the account under the principles explained in *Re Diplock* [1948] Ch. 465 (see Hayton 1994b).

It was the third argument that caused the court to pause. This was that the trust clause was an equity binding on Generale since it had notice of it before accepting the floating charge. Generale had specifically made it a condition of providing finance to Brookmount that it approved the form of the building contract and it must be taken to have known of the existence and legal effect of the retention trust clause. There was binding authority in the form of *De Mattos v Gibson* (1858) 4 De G. & J. 276 in support of the view that a person obtaining an equitable right aware of a prior equity must take subject to that equity (Clarke 1992).

10–014 The court accepted that, when the floating charge was granted, Generale's rights against Brookmount's property were subject to MacJordan's rights under the building contract, including the right to have retention funded. Funding the retention would have been an act in the ordinary course of Brookmount's business. The bank was, or ought to have been, fully aware of this possibility.

Unfortunately for MacJordan, on the appointment of the receivers, the floating charge crystallised and became a fixed charge on Brookmount's property, including the bank account at Barclays. In law, crystallisation took effect as an equitable assignment to Generale of all the property covered by the floating charge. It followed that, after the receivers' appointment, Brookmount had no cash available to it from which to fund the retention and the court would not make an order in vain. There were two further points: on crystallisation, the property caught by the floating charge became subject to the rights of preferential creditors who took priority over

Generale. It was possible that the money in the account would be required to pay preferential creditors.

Finally, and controversially, the court observed that to grant an injunction against an informally insolvent employer would be to prefer the contractor. This aspect has been heavily criticised (Moss 1992, Lightman and Moss 2007), on the ground that, provided liquidation has not intervened, the court is always ready to assist one creditor over another in perfecting its rights, following *Roberts Petroleum v Kenny* [1983] 2 A.C. 192. This point is considered further in Ch.18. The *MacJordan* case demonstrates that the value of retention trust clauses is lost unless enforced early on in the contract.

7. Registrability as a charge

The question whether the retention trust might be registrable as a charge under s.395 of the Companies Act 1985 is considered in Ch.9. **10–015**

Chapter 11

Pre-emptive Measures

Although this book concerns corporate insolvency, this is one area where it is necessary to consider aspects of personal insolvency law. The reason for this is that the criteria for granting an injunction restraining a creditor from presenting or advertising a winding up petition served on a company are very similar to those which govern applications to set aside a statutory demand served on an individual. However, there are differences in the procedures which need to be respected when making comparisons: *Re a Debtor (No. 544/SD/98)* [2000] 1 B.C.L.C. 103 at 116. This chapter sets out the general position. Specific problems arising from the adjudication procedure are considered separately in Ch.12. **11–001**

1. Statutory demands against individuals

Service of a statutory demand under s.268 of the Insolvency Act 1986 is an essential condition of the right to present a bankruptcy petition: *TSB Bank v Platts* [1998] 2 B.C.L.C. 1. If there is a defence to the debt on which the demand is based, the debtor has to apply to the court to set aside the demand. The hearing of the petition is not the right forum for this purpose: *Turner v Royal Bank of Scotland* [2000] B.P.I.R. 683. At the petition hearing, the debtor would have to show there had been a change of circumstances since the hearing of his application to set aside the demand, e.g. new legislation: *Re a Debtor (No. 27 of 1990)* [1996] B.P.I.R. 519. **11–002**

The rule of practice in *Turner v Royal Bank of Scotland* will not apply where there has been no hearing on the merits, e.g. because no application to set aside was made or because it was dismissed for procedural reasons: *Adams v Mason Bullock* [2004] EWHC 2910. The court will enquire why arguments relied on at the hearing of the petition were not raised before and may draw appropriate inferences: *West Bromwich BS v Crammer* [2002] EWCA 1924. Since a failure to apply to set aside a demand is not an abuse of process and raises no issue estoppel the court may feel bound to allow the debtor to present its defence on the hearing of the petition (Bamford 2006b).

The court has power under r.6.5(4) of the Insolvency Rules 1986 to set aside a demand served on an individual where:

(a) the debtor appears to have a counterclaim, set-off or cross demand which equals or exceeds the amount of the debt or debts specified in the statutory demand; or

(b) the debt is disputed on grounds which appear to the court to be substantial; or . . .

(d) the court is satisfied, on other grounds, that the demand ought to be set aside.

In the case of (a) and (b), the court will normally set aside the demand if in its opinion there is a genuine triable issue: *Practice Direction (Insolvency Proceedings) 1999* [2000] B.C.C. 927. The practice direction provides:

> 12.3 Where the statutory demand is based on a judgment or order, the court will not at this stage go behind the judgment or order and inquire into the validity of the debt nor, as a general rule, will it adjourn the application to await the result of an application to set aside the judgment or order.
>
> 12.4 Where the debtor (a) claims to have a counterclaim, set-off or cross demand (whether or not he could have raised it in the action in which the judgment or order was obtained) which equals or exceeds the amount of the debt or debts specified in the statutory demand or (b) disputes the debt (not being a debt subject to a judgment or order) the court will normally set aside the statutory demand if, in its opinion, on the evidence there is a genuine triable issue.

A judgment creates an issue estoppel, which means that it cannot be challenged on an application to set aside a demand. If at the time of the hearing of a petition, there is pending a *bona fide* appeal or application to set aside the judgment on which the statutory demand is based, the bankruptcy court adjourns the hearing of the petition until that application or appeal has been decided: *Royal Bank of Scotland v Farley* [1996] B.P.I.R. 638 at 641. If the debtor relies on a cross-claim which has been rejected by the court but which is the subject of an application for leave to appeal, the court will evaluate it and may set aside the demand: *Everard v Society of Lloyd's* [2003] EWHC 1890.

2. Industry examples

Cross-claims

11–003 For an analysis of the categories of claim made in the industry see Ch.3, and for adjudication cases see Ch.12. Cross-claims for snagging and other defects as well as direct payments and the cost of repairing an employer's chattel were insufficient to set aside demands in *Shalston v DF Keane* (2003) 19 Const. L.J. 290. The cross-claims fell £20,000 short of the demand and the court refused to interfere with the registrar's finding that a net sum of £60,000 was due to the claimant. Similarly, in *Howcutt v GS Property Developments* [2006] EWHC 3271 (David Richards J.), an employer's cross-claim based on misrepresentation was insufficient to set aside a demand served by a builder. There was an oral contract to build a house. Disputes arose which were settled by an agreement to pay a specific sum once the house was sold. After the sale it emerged that two of the disputed invoices representing a small proportion of the overall debt had concerned a project for a different employer and the builder reduced its claim accordingly. The employer unsuccessfully argued that the agreement to pay the specific sum was vitiated by the negligent misrepresentation.

Disputed debt

In *Re a Debtor (No. 10 of 1988, Aylesbury)* [1989] 2 All E.R. 39, Lovell **11–004** Construction served a demand on a householder for about £15,000, which was disputed on the grounds of quality and cost. However, she agreed that at least £2,500 was due. The court set aside the demand, taking the view that if part of the debt were disputed then the whole demand should be set aside. This view was later reversed: *Re a Debtor (No. 1 of 1987)* [1989] 1 W.L.R. 271. The correct procedure is for the debtor to pay the part which is admitted and apply to have the demand set aside on the ground that the rest is disputed.

Other grounds

In *Budge v AF Budge (Contractors) Ltd* [1997] B.P.I.R. 366, administrative **11–005** receivers served a statutory demand against a director claiming £1.75 million owing to the company on the director's loan account. It was held that the words "other grounds" in r.6.5(4) should be given a wide meaning. The debtor needs to show a substantial reason, comparable to those discussed above, as to why the demand ought to be set aside. The director argued that the demand was unjust because he was assisting the receivers to realise the maximum value of the assets for the benefit of the creditors by purchasing them through his own companies at the best price obtainable, backed by his personal guarantees. He personally held a licence from the Ministry of Defence which was a pre-requisite for continuing with the business which would lapse on his bankruptcy. It was held that the receivers had never promised not to pursue repayment of the loan and the court refused to set aside the demand.

An application to set aside a demand based on unpaid invoices in respect of certified sums due under the IFC form failed in *Shalston v DF Keane* (2003) 19 Const. L.J. 290. The employer argued that the demand should be set aside because it was entitled to a stay under s.9 of the Arbitration Act 1996. This was rejected because a demand did not fall within the definition of a "legal proceeding" brought in relation to the contract: see also *The City Hotel v Stephenson* [2003] NICA 47. The employer then argued that the demand would lead to a bankruptcy petition which would be a "legal proceeding". This was also rejected: see *Best Beat v Rossall* [2006] EWHC 1494, Park J. Firstly, the purpose of r.6.5(4)(d) was to prevent the injustice of allowing a petition to proceed that was bound to be struck out as oppressive and an abuse of the process: *Re a Debtor (Nos. 49 and 50 of 1992)* [1995] Ch. 66. Secondly, in this case, it would not be right to intervene at the demand stage because it could not be shown that the petition was bound to fail. Thirdly, on the facts, the registrar was right to disregard the possibility of an arbitration although the position might have been different had an arbitration been commenced before the hearing of application to set aside the demand (para.18).

A debtor cannot rely on sub-clause (d) by arguing that there are grounds to reduce the amount of the demand. In *Re a Debtor (No. 657/SD/91)* [1993] B.C.L.C. 180, a contractor owed the Inland Revenue £40,000 in respect of tax withheld by him from subcontractors (of which £15,000 was a judgment debt) but had a claim for up to £24,000 against the Revenue for a refund of tax withheld against his own earnings when working as a subcontractor. Ferris J. refused to set aside the demand on the grounds that he could not go behind the judgment, and that any overstatement of indebtedness in the demand was not a sufficient reason to set it aside.

3. Disputed claims against companies

General principles

11–006 Where a statutory demand or a winding up petition is served and the debt on which it is based can be disputed in good faith and on substantial grounds, the court will grant an injunction restraining further proceedings: *Mann v Goldstein* [1968] 2 All E.R. 769. In the case of the demand, the injunction is against the issue of a petition. Once a petition has been issued, the injunction restrains its advertisement (Oditah 1995).

Where the petitioner relies on a judgment debt, he is unquestionably a creditor even if the judgment is the subject of an appeal: *Re Dollarland (Manhattan) Ltd* [2005] All E.R. (D) 371. The court carries out a careful balancing exercise. In that case, there was no economic advantage to creditors in an administration and the company was wound up leaving it to the liquidator to decide whether to pursue the appeal, following *Re Douglas Griggs Engineering* [1963] 1 Ch. 19. Where the company satisfies the court that the petitioner's claim can properly be disputed it is unnecessary to go further and enquire into the solvency of the company. The rationale is that the petitioner has failed to establish that he is a creditor: *Mann v Goldstein* at 774. This reasoning does not apply where the company only advances a cross-claim: *Re Alexander Sheridan* [2004] EWHC 2072 at para.59.

Insolvency proceedings are a class remedy, not for the benefit of the petitioning creditor alone. Nor are they the correct forum for deciding whether the claimant's debt is due, prospective or contingent: *Stonegate Securities v Gregory* [1980] Ch. 576. It is an abuse of the process to use a winding up petition as the means of enforcing a disputed debt where the company has a "rational prospect of success": *Re a Company (No. 0012209 of 1991)* [1992] 2 All E.R. 797, 800. The court has jurisdiction to investigate and decide the dispute on the hearing of the petition and has occasionally done so (Paterson and Marks 2004). Insolvency proceedings are not regarded as a form of execution: they are of a different kind to the remedies ordinarily available to a judgment creditor: *Re Bayoil* [1999] 1 All E.R. 374 at 383.

Claims against employers

11–007 A petition was dismissed in *Re a Company (No. 12209 of 1991)* [1992] 2 All E.R. 797, as the contractor's debt was disputed on *bona fide* and substantial grounds. It was based on an unpaid application under JCT 81 which is normally payable within 14 days. In this case, the employer alleged an oral agreement varying the dates for submitting applications and that the application on which the demand was based was premature. It also made incentive payments and purported to accept a repudiation by the builder claiming consequential damages. Both aspects were contested by the contractor. There was evidence that the employer had net assets exceeding £100 million and that the contractor had cash flow problems. Hoffmann J. dismissed the petition on the ground that there was a triable issue on the debt. He expressed no view on thc cross-claim.

An injunction restraining presentation was granted in *Celtech International v Dalkia Utilities* [2004] EWHC 193. The proposed petition was based on a statutory demand by a contractor against an end user claiming £3.6 million in respect of the allegedly wrongful termination of a long-term agreement to design, build, finance and operate a combined heat and power plant. The contractor relied on a term entitling it to terminate in the event of the client's "material breach", in this case non-payment of sums due. David Richards J. considered that it was arguable: (a) whether the client's default amounted to "material breach" in view of the long-term nature of the contract; and (b) that, on its true construction, the termination clause did not entitle the contractor to the amounts claimed. The debt was genuinely disputed. See Ch.14 for other aspects of this case.

A petition based on unpaid certified sums was granted in *Re Clemence* (1992) 59 B.L.R. 56. The employer raised a counterclaim for defects which could have abated the contractor's claim, and thus disputed the petition debt, but for the fact that it was not properly quantified and, in any event, was for less than the claim. See also *RJBL Design v Hill Commercial Developments* (unreported, June 22, 2005) in which Mann J. restrained advertisement of a petition issued by a contractor against an architect. In *Medlock Products v SCC Construction* [2006] C.I.L.L. 2384, Judge Weeks Q.C. refused to grant an injunction restraining advertisement where the debt was based in part on an agreement recording the consensual termination of a subcontract under which the subcontractor was released from liability to complete the work or for latent or patent defects.

Claims against contractors

There are few English authorities regarding claims against contractors, but **11–008**
overseas cases provide some useful background (see para.11–017 below).

Contingent creditor's petition

The criteria to be applied where the contractor petitions on a contingent or **11–008**
prospective debt are not entirely clear (Lee Beng Tat 1993). Neither expression is a term of art. In the context of a winding up petition:

> ". . . the expression 'contingent creditor' means a creditor in respect of a debt which will only become due in an event which may or may not occur; and a 'prospective creditor' is a creditor in respect of a debt which will certainly become due in the future, either on some date which has been already determined or on some date determinable by reference to

future events": *Stonegate Securities v Gregory* [1980] Ch. 576 at 579, *per* Buckley L.J.

More recently, in *Customs and Excise v Broomco (1984) Ltd* (unreported, March 13, 2000), Neuberger J. stated that:

> ". . . a contingent debt is one which is dependent upon an event which is outside the party's control, in any event, it is not a debt which is dependent on an assessment of the outcome of the dispute between the parties as to whether it [is] owing. A prospective debt is one which is going to become payable but which is not yet payable."

How do these definitions apply to the industry?

The court has often stated that where the right to payment depends on the issue of a certificate, the contractor is a contingent creditor in respect of its work in progress until that event: see e.g. *Karl Construction v Palisade Properties* [2002] CSOH 350. There is similar authority in the context of a winding up petition: *Community Development v Engwirta Construction* (1969) 120 C.L.R. 455. On the other hand, Goode (2005, para.4–29) considers a contractor's uncertified payment claim to be a prospective debt. One of the problem areas is where the petition is based on a claim for damages for breach of contract. In a South African case, *Gillis-Mason Construction v Overvaal Crushers* [1971] 1 S.A. 524, a subcontractor was unable to fulfil its contract to supply crusher stone and the contractor was unable to obtain an alternative supply. Such supplies as were available were at rates exceeding those in the subcontract. The contractor was also at risk of failing to complete the main contract on time. Time was of the essence under the subcontract. The subcontractor accepted that it had repudiated the subcontract but relied on the contractor's duty to mitigate its loss. There was evidence that the subcontractor was insolvent. The court exercised its discretion and made a winding up order on the basis of the subcontractor's liability being contingent.

4. Cross-claims against companies

General principles

11–010 If a company has a genuine and serious cross-claim in an amount exceeding the petitioner's debt which it has been unable to litigate, then in the absence of special circumstances, the court ought to stay or dismiss the petition: *Re Bayoil* [1999] 1 W.L.R. 147. Although it was a shipping case, the facts of *Re Bayoil* have implications for construction contracts. A shipowner had a claim for freight under a charterparty, while the charterer had a counterclaim for damages arising out of delays caused by defects to the ship's engines. The charterer obtained security for its cross-claim from the owner's P&I club. Both claim and counterclaim were referred to arbitration. The arbitrator made an interim final award of $1.2 million in favour of the owner because, under well established case law, claims for freight are immune from set-off. The owner then served a statutory demand and presented a winding up petition.

At the hearing of the petition, the charterer admitted the debt but asked for the petition to be dismissed on the basis of its counterclaim. A winding up order was made at first instance but discharged on appeal. The court dealt with the appeal in the following way:

- The court has a discretion when hearing a winding up petition to dismiss it, adjourn it, make an interim order or any other order it thinks fit: s.125(1) of the Insolvency Act 1986.
- The discretion must be exercised judicially. For example, a judge would have to explain why he considered that the facts amounted to special circumstances. In this case, the court was satisfied that the charterer had a genuine and serious cross-claim.
- The charterer was unable to litigate the cross-claim because, under the charterparty, all disputes had to be referred to arbitration. It appears that the court construed "inability to litigate" strictly as inability to process through the courts (at 155).
- There were no special circumstances for making a winding up order. The following were insufficient: the finality and unappealablity of the interim final award; the charterer's security for its cross-claim; the charterer's potential insolvency; the absence of evidence that the award could be paid; and the charterer's failure to seek a stay of the interim award. Nourse L.J. stated: "The ability of a petitioning creditor to levy execution against the company does not entitle him to have it wound up" (at 155).

The last of these points is especially significant when considering a petition based on an adjudication debt (see Ch.12). In *Marchands Associates v Thompson Partnership* [2004] EWCA 878, a differently constituted Court of Appeal considered it was open to question whether inability to litigate the cross-claim was an essential condition (para.46). Nourse L.J. may just have been saying that where there was delay in bringing a cross-claim, the delay must not be such as to throw a real doubt on the genuineness of the cross-claim (para.123). In that case, Peter Gibson L.J. stated:

> "In the cross-claim cases . . . [it] matters not that the debt is one for which summary judgment would have been obtained or on which execution could be levied notwithstanding the cross-claim. A winding up order has more serious consequences and the Companies Court is entitled to adopt a different approach" (para.46).

Leave to appeal was given because of a possible defence of failure of consideration for the cheques on which the petition was brought (para.36). The court would not countenance a winding up petition as a substitute for orthodox execution. It could not be said that the parties had agreed that, if the cheques were not honoured, the respondents might present a petition in circumstances in which the court would not otherwise make a winding up order (para.56, *per* May L.J.). See also *Popely v Popely* [2004] B.P.I.R. 778 (para.124). *Re LHF Wools* [1970] Ch. 27 also concerned a petition based on a dishonoured cheque. In that case, the bank's judgment debt entitled it to a winding up order but the existence of a cross-claim made the matter one for the court's discretion. The Court of Appeal set aside the order.

The court will scrutinise the cross-claims as much as is necessary in order to form a view on them. In *Re Alexander Sheridan* [2004] EWHC 2072, for example, the court separately analysed eight cross-claims, enquiring in each case whether a genuine issue had been made out, and giving each a minimum monetary value. Even when added together, the cross-claims fell well short of the value of the claim, and a winding up order was made. At para.21, the court gave examples of questions it would not be prepared to decide. There included issues such as whether either party's terms and conditions had been incorporated to the contract, and what was or was not said at meetings, etc.

The requirement that the company had not been able to litigate its cross-claim was noted in *Re Mouse Corporation* [2001] All E.R. (D) 251. On the evidence, there was a genuine dispute in respect of the petition debt. In respect of the cross-claim it was reasonable for the company not to have resorted to litigation earlier, as the amount claimed was minimal and would have resulted in a breakdown of communications between the parties. See also *Alstom Transport v Elequip Projects* [2004] EWHC 2897; *Southern Cross Group v Deka* [2005] B.P.I.R. 1010, at para.28; and *Popely v Popely* [2004] B.P.I.R. 778, at para.124.

Construction cases

11–011 In *RWH Enterprises v Portedge* [1998] B.C.C. 556, an employer had a cross-claim for defects but failed on an application to restrain the presentation of a petition by an assignee of a debt from the contractor because the defects had been insufficiently particularised. It then filed further evidence which the court accepted gave rise to an arguable cross-claim which was greater than the assigned debt. The Court of Appeal refused an application to restrain advertisement of the petition on the grounds that:

(1) the evidence could have been submitted in support of the earlier application;

(2) the company had not been forthcoming about its own financial position; and

(3) no injustice would be done by allowing the petition to go for hearing as the company had already informed its bank of its existence.

An injunction sought by a subcontractor against a labour only sub-subcontractor restraining presentation relying on a cross-claim for defects was refused in *Re a Company* (No. 2966 of 2005) [2005] All E.R. (D) 176. The cross-claim had been prompted by an *ad hoc* retention of five per cent for defects imposed by the employer towards the end of the project, which the applicant was attempting to pass down the line to the petitioning creditor without sufficient evidence that its work had been defective. The final payment otherwise due was insufficient to cover five per cent of the sub-subcontract price and the subcontractor argued therefore that nothing was due. The subcontractor also presented a schedule of defects running to 182 pages. Warren J. held that the schedule did not amount to a genuine and serious cross-claim, disapproving in particular global figures claimed for overheads and supervision. The defects claim was only made after service of the statutory demand. This case is a good example of the court being prepared to evaluate a construction claim in some detail on an application for an injunction to restrain a petition.

It is an abuse of process to use the winding up procedure for the purposes of debt collection. In *Re a Company* (No. 006798 of 1995) [1996] 2 All E.R. 417, a petition was struck out with indemnity costs and an order made that wasted costs be paid by the petitioner's solicitor. The petitioner was a sub-subcontractor claiming a balance due on its final account. Meetings had taken place between surveyors but the sum claimed in the petition had never been agreed or even demanded from the subcontractor; nor had a statutory demand been served or admission made. On the evidence, the company was solvent. The facts were disputed but the court stated that "what they would show is that this is a company which—perhaps like other companies in the construction industry—chooses not to pay its debts until it is obliged to do so. The facts alleged demonstrate that, when obliged to pay by the threat or presentation of a winding up petition, the company appears to have no difficulty in finding moneys sufficient to satisfy the creditor" (at 429, *per* Chadwick J.).

The petitioner accused the debtor of getting up to its "usual tricks" of rejecting unsigned daywork sheets, disputing that signatures were authorised, or that the works were genuinely outside the scope of the contract. This is precisely the kind of claim that could now be taken to adjudication. Perhaps as a result there will be fewer abuses of the winding up procedure. **11–012**

An employer's petition against a contractor was struck out in *Penrith District Council v VP Developments* [2005] B.C.L.C. 607. The petition was based on an unpaid costs order in an arbitration. The contractor successfully established that it had substantial cross-claims in a different arbitration which was still ongoing. It was admitted that the contractor was insolvent, having entered into a company voluntary arrangement one of whose purposes was to allow the company to pursue its claims against the employer. The employer argued that the cross-claim should not be taken into account because it was brought by the company as trustee for the arrangement creditors whereas the costs order was made against the company in its own right. This was rejected on the ground that the company had a personal interest in both the order for costs and the claim in the arbitration.

Finally, in *Re a Company (No. 007020 of 1996)* [1998] 2 B.C.L.C. 54, the petitioner was a subcontractor who had obtained a default judgment on its claim for an agreed final account figure. The contractor cross claimed for liquidated damages by way of indemnity for claims made against it by the employer and in its own right under the subcontract. The Court of Appeal would have granted an injunction restraining advertisement but for the fact that the petitioner had already advertised it contrary to the contractor's understanding that the petition would not be advertised pending the hearing of the appeal. Instead the petition was struck out.

"Advertisement of a winding up petition against a construction company must be calculated to do very serious damage indeed to the business of that company. It is difficult to imagine that any employer would be willing to employ a construction company against which there is a pending petition which has been advertised" (at 62, *per* Chadwick L.J.).

The contractor's difficulty in that case arose from the fact that a judge had expressed the opinion that its cross-claim had already been included in the final account settlement.

5. International comparisons

11–013 A company on the verge of insolvency is in a volatile state. Exactly how a construction company makes the transition from informal to formal insolvency can be explored further by considering a few of the many overseas cases on statutory demands and winding up petitions. It is worth noting that in some jurisdictions, such as New Zealand, instead of seeking an injunction restraining a creditor from issuing or advertising a petition, the corporate debtor's remedy is to apply to set aside the demand on grounds very similar to r.6.5(4) set out above. Other jurisdictions have enacted statutes based on the Housing Grants, Construction and Regeneration Act 1996. Cases on statutory demands arising out of contracts falling within those statutes are discussed in Ch.12.

Claims against employers

11–014 In *Fletcher Development v New Plymouth Hotels* [1986] 2 N.Z.L.R. 302, a contract provided for release of retention in two stages: a payment of $20,000 13 weeks after practical completion, and another of $30,000 39 weeks after that date. The first tranche was certified due for release but no certificate was issued for the balance. Statutory demands were served for both tranches and the employer applied to restrain the issue of a petition relying on a cross-claim for defects.

The judge at first instance was initially minded to allow the petition to proceed in relation to the first tranche of retention but concluded that the injunction should be granted. This was because the dispute arose out of a building contract, the amounts at stake were very small compared with the overall contract sum (which had been paid on time during the contract), and because the contractor was using improper pressure to recover a debt. This decision was reversed on appeal on the ground that the employer's evidence of defective work was inadequate and that it had failed to disclose in its evidence that it was in receivership.

Similarly, in *Mine v Henderson Drilling* [1989] 1 A.C.S.R. 118, a contractor served a statutory demand in respect of payment for drilling work. The employer disputed liability to pay on the grounds that the drilling had been carried out at depths greater than specified; the contractor was not entitled to payment for the over-drilling; some work had not been authorised by the employer; and other work had had to be redone at the employer's expense. In refusing the injunction, the court was influenced by payments which had been made by the employer, the absence of criticism of workmanship in contemporary correspondence, and the fact that the employer had never threatened or issued proceedings. It also appeared that the employer was insolvent on its own evidence.

In *Primary Health v Avoca Residential* [2004] NZCA 220, the New Zealand Court of Appeal refused to set aside a demand on the ground of a cross-claim for delay. The evidence was that the parties had varied the contract to defer payment of a certified sum until after the sale of properties and that delay-related issues would be referred to an expert. As the expert had not reached a decision, and it remained uncertain whether the employer's cross-claim was valid, the demand would stand. In *Pacific Park Hotel v 3 Bald Men* [2005] NZHC 349, a contractor served a demand for its final account in respect of project management services. The employer argued that the contract was for payment on a cost reimbursable basis rather than for a fixed price. The court decided the issue on the set aside application in the contractor's favour.

A winding up order was made on a contractor's petition based on unpaid certified sums in *Re Jade Union Investment* [2004] HKCFI 166. The employer raised various cross-claims. The contractor had commenced an arbitration to ascertain what was due under its final account. Barma J., rejected the employer's argument that this was an implicit recognition that the petition debts could be disputed. The court accepted there could be a cross-claim based on direct payments to subcontractors. Although the contract provided for direct payment in limited circumstances, they did not apply to this case. But there was a dispute on the evidence whether the contractor had expressly consented to the payments being made. Even allowing for the direct payments however there was still a substantial sum owing to the contractor and an order was made. **11–015**

By contrast, an injunction was granted in *Club Marconi v Rennat* [1980] 4 A.C.L.R. 883, where a management contractor had agreed a guaranteed maximum cost. Any variations were to be charged at cost plus a four and a half per cent fee. The contractor's claim exceeded the maximum cost and the employer relied on an apparent absence of authorisation signed by the architect in respect of variations. Other claims for extras were not properly documented. The employer argued that until the contractor put forward a particularised claim it was impossible to ascertain the true position. Although there was evidence that the employer had suffered a liquidity crisis, it was not possible to conclude that that was the cause of non-payment.

In another Australian case, an injunction was granted where there was clear evidence of a dispute over the quality of workmanship and valuation. Although the court found it likely that a considerable sum would be found payable to the contractor at the conclusion of an arbitration, it held that winding up was not the proper forum for the dispute: *Patrick Carr v Marosszeky* [1982] 7 A.C.L.R. 59. **11–016**

In *Group Kildey v JM Kelly* [2005] QSC 264 a construction management agreement was entered into following the liquidation of the original contractor. The completion contract was itself delayed and the parties entered into a deed whereby the employer agreed to make further payments, the last on completion of outstanding works as defined in the deed. The construction manager served a statutory demand in respect of the final payment. The employer argued that the work had not been completed either at all or to the quality required. The schedule attached to the deed described some of the outstanding work in general terms and there was conflicting expert evidence as to whether it had been done. The demand was set aside.

Claims against contractors

In *Re Stonehenge Constructions* [1986] 2 N.Z.L.R. 302, a subcontractor orally agreed to construct an entrance road and car park. The contractor disputed payment contending that the subcontract was on a schedule of rates rather than a lump sum basis and that the subcontractor had already **11–017** been paid what was due to it. The contractor also relied on an oral pay when paid term. The evidence showed that the contractor had in fact been paid more on a rates basis than the amount of the subcontractor's petition debt and the court refused to grant an injunction restraining the issue of the petition. The Federal Court of Australia refused to set aside a statutory demand against a contractor in *Spencer Constructions v G. & M. Aldridge* [1997] FCA 681. An underpinning subcontractor claimed release of retention. The contractor disputed the debt on several grounds: the employer had terminated the main contract and agreed to assume direct responsibility for sums due to subcontractors; and in any event, there was a pay when paid clause in the subcontract and the contractor had not received any sums in respect of the subcontractor's retention. Neither contention was supported by the evidence. Even if these grounds could be established, there was no evidence that the subcontractor had released the contractor by an implied novation of the subcontract and the employer claimed to have paid the contractor in respect of the retentions.

In *Freemont v Natures View Joinery* [2006] NZHC 866, a supplier served a statutory demand in respect of supplies of concrete and aggregate. The contractor claimed seven weeks preliminaries as damages for failure to deliver the materials on time but there was no evidence that the supplier had agreed to deliver by specific dates and in any event it had been justified in stopping the contractor's credit for non-payment. The demand was set aside conditional on payment within 15 days.

In *John Holland v Kilpatrick Green* (1994) 14 A.C.S.R. 250, the court set aside a statutory demand claiming $1 million representing work done under a letter of intent where the contractor had obtained the main contract but had not engaged the claimant as its subcontractor. See also *Solarite v York* [2002] NSWSC 411 (statutory demand served by supplier against subcontractor set aside).

In *Re Yat Kwai Construction* [2003] HKCFI 268, a case before the Hong Kong Court of First Instance, an employer issued a winding up petition based on an order for costs made on an application for an injunction to remove the contractor from site. The petition was supported by the company's employees. The contractor raised a cross-claim for sums due. There was an action pending, brought by the employer claiming sums paid direct to subcontractors and employees, and damages for defects, delay, and repudiation. The contractor's cross-claim had been fully pleaded there even though it was acting without legal representation. The employer had not proceeded with the action for a year and a half before issuing the petition. There no evidence that the contractor was still trading or that it could pay its debts. There was a genuine cross-claim and no special circumstances why the company should nevertheless be wound up. The petition was adjourned to allow the supporting creditors to apply for legal aid.

In *Re Fortune Hill Engineering* [2003] HKCFI 455, a petition brought by a sub-subcontractor against a subcontractor was struck out. It was based on a statutory demand in respect of non-payment of 23 invoices. The Hong Kong Court of First Instance went through the invoices in detail and accepted the company's submissions that liability could be disputed in good faith: there was evidence that they used an incorrect unit price, claimed sums that could not be tallied with the quotation, duplicated each other, or did not have a job number. In *Malta Timber Products v N&P Constructions* [2004] 1 M.L.J. 119 a petition brought by a supplier against a subcontractor was dismissed on the grounds of unchallenged evidence that door panels were defective (leading to cross-claims by the contractor against the subcontractor for the costs of rectification) and an arguable case that the debt had been novated.

Chapter 12

Adjudication

Adjudication is a mandatory feature of all construction contracts falling within the Housing Grants, Construction and Regeneration Act 1996 (the Act), which came into force on May 1, 1998. Since then, there have been over 260 cases on the Act (Sheridan and Helps 2006b). A working knowledge of adjudication is now essential to the administration of construction projects. It is best considered in context as part of the reforms brought about by the Act rather than on its own. Most adjudicators are industry professionals rather than lawyers. Submitting disputes to one's peers was a feature of the law merchant, a body of law from which modern insolvency principles were developed. This chapter focuses on the interaction between adjudication and insolvency. To what extent has adjudication become a form of security in its own right? Has it altered the balance of insolvency risk struck by the standard forms? Is there a conflict between the policy considerations behind the Act and those of insolvency law? These are some of the questions that will be considered. **12–001**

1. The procedure

The intention of the Act is to provide a speedy procedure for deciding construction disputes on an interim basis: *Macob Civil Engineering v Morrison* [1999] B.L.R. 3. Either party can commence an adjudication at any time, even after acceptance of repudiation or the expiry of the limitation period, or while there are proceedings pending in court or by arbitration: *Connex v MJ Building Services* [2005] B.L.R. 201. An adjudication is begun by serving a notice identifying the nature of the dispute and the redress sought. Once an adjudicator is appointed, the claimant serves a notice of referral within seven days setting out its claim in detail and attaching any relevant documents. The other party then has the opportunity to answer the claim in writing and the adjudicator decides the dispute within 28 days of the referral to him or longer by agreement. In many cases there will be no need for a hearing. The adjudicator cannot make an order for costs (except for his own fees) unless the contract so provides or compel witnesses to appear. **12–002**

The procedure is most often used in claims for valuation or interim payment (Kennedy and Milligan 2005, 7). It has, however, been used in much wider contexts such as extension of time and loss and expense claims, disputed terminations (e.g. *All in One Building v Makers* [2005] EWHC 2943), and final accounts. Most types of claim can be adjudicated provided they concern a dispute arising from a construction contract as defined by the Act. Adjudication does not extend however to disputes arising under bonds and guarantees or finance documents unless they otherwise provide (see Ch.19). Compare the Australian case of *ACA v Sullivan* (2005) 21 B.C.L. 71 in which an employer unsuccessfully argued that a construction contract fell outside the Building and Construction Industry Security of Payment Act 1999 (NSW) on the ground that it "formed part of" a loan agreement.

2. Enforcement of adjudication decisions

12–003 By s.108(3) the adjudicator's decision is binding on the parties unless and until their dispute is finally determined in court, in arbitration or by agreement. "It is merely a decision that, at the present time and on the basis of the material then available to the adjudicator, a sum of money appears to the adjudicator to be due": *Herschel Engineering v Breen Property (No. 2)*, unreported, July 28, 2000 at para.7, *per* Judge Humphrey LLoyd Q.C. The decision has a temporary or provisional finality which the parties agree to respect but it does not have the binding force of a judgment.

In order to enforce an adjudication decision, the claimant applies to the court for summary judgment under the Civil Procedure Rules Pt. 24. The usual basis for such applications is that the defendant has no reasonable prospect of successfully defending the claim at trial. As a claimant seeking to enforce an adjudication decision will not necessarily be able to show that, a rationale is needed for allowing the summary process to be used for that purpose. The rationale appears to be that the parties have agreed to comply with the decision in the interim: to that obligation there can be no defence, unless the decision falls outside the adjudicator's jurisdiction (see Gould 2005). Provided the adjudicator answers the question asked of him his decision will be enforced even if it is wrong in law or based on an arithmetical error: *Bouygues v Dahl-Jensen* [2000] B.L.R. 522; *C&B Scene v Isobars* [2002] B.L.R. 93. There is a "temporary ouster of the court's jurisdiction": *Ballast v The Burrell Co* [2001] B.L.R. 529 at para.30.

12–004 The court has limited its role to two matters: whether the adjudicator had jurisdiction, and whether he acted in accordance with the rules of natural justice. The issue of jurisdiction involves four questions: does the contract fall within the Act? has a dispute arisen and what is its scope? was the adjudicator validly appointed? has he decided the question referred to him? On natural justice, the test is whether "the manner in which [the adjudicator] has gone about the task is obviously unfair": *Carillion v Devonport Royal Dockyard* [2006] B.L.R. 15 at para.85, *per* Chadwick L.J. In effect, the court is saying that the parties have agreed to treat the adjudication process as if it were an application for summary judgment on the merits: *Bouygues v Dahl-Jensen*, para.26. In taking this approach, the court accepts that injustice will result from time to time.

> "It is inherent in the scheme that injustices will occur, because from time to time, adjudicators will make mistakes. Sometimes those mistakes will be glaringly obvious and disastrous in their consequences for the losing party. The victims of mistakes will usually be able to recoup their losses by subsequent arbitration or litigation, and possibly even by a subsequent adjudication. Sometimes they will not be able to do so, where, for example, there is intervening insolvency, either of the victim or of the fortunate beneficiary of the mistake:" *Bouygues v Dahl-Jensen* [2000] B.L.R. 49, 55, *per* Dyson J., affirmed on appeal [2000] B.L.R. 522.

This is a strikingly direct statement with implications for insolvency law which have yet to be fully explored. Where both parties are solvent, and remain so until after the dispute has been finally determined, the policy of the Act only affects the question of cash flow. If the claimant loses at trial, the money awarded by the adjudicator can be repaid with interest. In that respect, an order for summary judgment of an adjudicator's decision is equivalent to an order for interim payment. Where insolvency intervenes, the "victim" may lack the funds to take proceedings for repayment, or be unable to provide security for the defendant's costs, or be denied permission to sue at all. If the adjudicator's decision is patently wrong, however, that fact may persuade the court not to order security. If the beneficiary becomes insolvent, the claimant is an ordinary unsecured creditor. As an adjudicator has no ability to order costs, he cannot order security for costs where the claimant is insolvent. Nor can he attach conditions to his decision to take account of either party's insolvency unless permitted by the contract. Repayment risk in construction is normally managed by the provision of a bond or an escrow account. A pre-existing performance bond may depending on its terms be sufficient to secure repayment in this context: compare *John Holland v Roads and Traffic Authority of New South Wales* [2007] NSWCA 140. An adjudicator lacks the power to order security of this kind or to defer payment of sums found due pending some future event: *Allied London & Scottish Properties v Riverbrae Construction* [1999] B.L.R. 346.

If the court refuses to order summary judgment, it may in theory order an interim payment on account of the amount claimed in the adjudication while the whole dispute is taken further in court. This option is only available where the contract does not contain an arbitration clause. The criteria for summary judgment and interim payment are different. An order for interim payment can be made if on a balance of probabilities at least a specific proportion of the claim will awarded at the trial. A claimant can serve a statutory demand under s.123 of the Insolvency Act 1986 or issue a winding up petition whether or not the debt is supported by an adjudication decision. A statutory demand may only be served in respect of a debt exceeding £750 which is due and payable. Issuing a winding up petition to 'enforce' an adjudication decision is a high risk strategy. The petition usually results in the freezing of the company's bank account and may simply push the debtor into liquidation (Ch.13). The debtor may be able to persuade the court to grant an injunction restraining the creditor from continuing with the petition. Even if it works and the decision is paid the petition cannot be dismissed if another creditor gives notice of support: see *Harwood Construction v Lantrode* (unreported, November 24, 2000). These aspects are discussed below.

The Technology and Construction Court encourages claimants to apply for summary judgment as the way to enforce an adjudication decision (T.C.C. Guide, 2nd edn, 2005). "Other ways of enforcing such decisions (such as, for instance, bankruptcy proceedings) are something of a blunt instrument and raise potential issues which have little or nothing to do with the decision which is at the heart of any enforcement application" (*Harlow & Milner v Teasdale* [2006] EWHC 54 at para.18, *per* Judge Peter Coulson Q.C. Once an adjudication decision is enforced by an order for summary judgment, the claimant has access to ordinary post-judgment remedies. For example, despite the fact that an arbitration was on foot in which the adjudication decision was being challenged, a charging order has been made final (*Harlow & Milner v Teasdale* (No. 2) [2006] EWHC 535), and an order for sale made in respect of the property the subject of the dispute (*Harlow & Milner v Teasdale* (No. 3) [2006] EWHC 1708).

3. Stay of execution

12–005 Unless the claimant is in liquidation, insolvency is not a bar to obtaining an order for summary judgment: *SL Timber Systems v Carillion* [2001] B.L.R. 516 at para.30. In what circumstances will the court protect the paying party against the risk that the claimant will be unable to repay an amount found due by an adjudicator? The main relief available is a stay of execution of the order for summary judgment. In this context the court has drawn a sharp distinction between informal and formal insolvency. To a lesser extent it has also discriminated between the various formal insolvency procedures.

Criteria on stay applications

12–006 RSC Ord.47 (preserved by CPR Pt. 50.2) gives the court a discretion to stay the execution of a judgment either absolutely or for such period and subject to such conditions as the court thinks fit if satisfied:

(a) that there are special circumstances which render it inexpedient to enforce the judgment or order, or

(b) that the applicant is unable from any cause to pay the money.

It is worth noting that even before the commencement of the Act, where the contract provided for adjudication in the event of a disputed set-off, the court would not normally usurp the function of the adjudicator by ordering a stay of execution of summary judgment pending the hearing of a counterclaim in an arbitration: *Tubeworkers v Tilbury Construction* (1985) 30 B.L.R. 67 at 79. There was no evidence of insolvency in that case.

The court has not defined "special circumstances" and each case is decided on its own merits (Helps and Sheridan 2006a). In the context of adjudication the following factors have been taken into account:

1. The policy of the Act is that decisions of adjudicators should be enforced by summary judgment: *AWG Construction v Rockingham* [2004] T.C.L.R. 6 at para.186. The fact that a decision is patently wrong is not a special circumstance warranting a stay: *Herschel Engineering v Breen Properties (No. 2)* at para.11.
2. Of prime importance is the strength of the evidence of the claimant's insolvency and the consequent extent of the repayment risk borne by the defendant. A generalised fear coupled with the existence of cross-claims which could not be set off against the adjudicator's decision are not enough: *Solland International v Daraydan Holdings* (2002) 83 Con. L.R. 109 at para.18. There must be a "real likelihood" of non-payment (*Herschel v Breen No. 2* at para.12) or "credible evidence" of insolvency (*Rainford House v Cadogan* [2001] B.L.R. 416 at para.10). Failure of the balance sheet test may not be sufficient: *Ale Heavylift v MSD (Darlington) Ltd* [2006] EWHC 2080.
3. The harm and prejudice that might be caused to the claimant if a stay were granted need to be assessed: *Herschel v Breen (No. 2)* at para.13. "To keep the claimant out of this money for several months would be

contrary to the plain intent of the 1996 Act" (*Herschel Engineering v Breen Properties (No. 1)* [2000] B.L.R. 272 at para.23, *per* Dyson J.).

4. "Evidence that some third party has taken action which puts the continued financial viability of the claimant at hazard must, I think, be evaluated seriously" (*Rainford House v Cadogan* at para.9, *per* Judge Richard Seymour Q.C.). Apart from the enforcement of security, examples could be the repossession of plant, termination of contracts or the calling of bonds (Ndekugri and Russell 2005, 405).

5. If the claimant has entered a formal insolvency procedure such as administrative receivership that is strong *prima facie* evidence of insolvency for the purpose of a stay application: *Rainford House v Cadogan* at para.12.

6. The position shown in audited accounts can be adjusted by reference to management accounts (e.g. converting a retained loss into an anticipated profit), especially if they are supported by evidence from the company's auditor: *JW Hughes Building Contractors v GB Metalwork* [2003] EWHC 2421; *SL Timber Systems v Carillion* [2001] B.L.R. 516 at paras.24–25 (dealing with summary judgment rather than a stay).

7. The existence of loans made to the company by the directors or by associated companies is material especially if the terms of repayment are unclear, e.g. whether they carry interest, or are repayable on demand, or represent an attempt to manipulate the accounts: *Wimbledon Construction v Vago* [2005] B.L.R. 374.

8. The willingness or otherwise of the company's bankers to continue or extend overdraft facilities is relevant as is the extent of any security taken over the company's assets: *JW Hughes Building Contractors v GB Metalwork* at para.43.

9. It is for the defendant to prove that the claimant will be unable to make any repayment on the final determination of the dispute. To that extent, the test is analogous to that for security for costs under s.726 of the Companies Act 1985 (*Herschel Engineering v Breen (No. 2)* at para.16; *Wimbledon Construction v Vago* at para.24). The claimant can bring into account prospective assets. This is not allowed when applying the balance sheet test under s.123 of the Insolvency Act 1986 (Ch.8). Alternatively, the relevant time is the date of the stay application, the onus being on the claimant to rebut any inference arising on the evidence that its position will not have improved by the expected date of repayment: *Rainford House v Cadogan* at para.11.

10. The nature of the claimant's business is relevant, e.g. a labour only subcontractor cannot be expected to own valuable fixed assets or plant and equipment: *Total M and E Services v ABB Building Technologies* [2002] C.I.L.L. 1857 at paras 48 and 53. The same could be said of most small contractors.

11. The financial position of the claimant must have deteriorated since the contract was entered into: *Herschel v Breen (No. 2)* at paras.18–19; *Total M and E Services v ABB* at para.50; *Wimbledon Construction v Vago* at para.39; *Michael John Construction v Golledge* [2006] EWHC 71 at para.79; *Ale Heavylift v MSD (Darlington) Ltd* at para.99.

12. Can the company's actual or potential insolvency be attributed to the non-payment of the sum awarded in the adjudication? See *Absolute Rentals v Gencor Enterprises* [2000] C.I.L.L. 1637; *Lovell Projects v Legg and Carver* [2003] B.L.R. 452 at para.42; *Wimbledon Construction v Vago*, paras.40–41; *All in One Building v Makers* [2005] EWHC 2943 at para.66; *Tera Construction v Lam* [2005] EWHC B1 at 9.
13. The conduct of the parties is important, especially "the diligence with which the applicant has pursued the substantive remedy": *AWG Construction v Rockingham* at para.186. Delays in the courts have much reduced since the Act came into force; expedition by the defendant will limit the extent of the repayment risk and enable the court to estimate the date at which to assess the claimant's solvency: *Ale Heavylift v MSD (Darlington) Ltd* at para.100.
14. The defendant's ability to pay the decision and its own financial position are crucial: *Total M and E Services v ABB*, paras.53–4. "A court might well come to the conclusion that there should be a stay if the result would be that the whole project would grind to a halt because the applicant main contractor was unable to pay the money and would have to go into liquidation": *Herschel v Breen (No. 2)* at para.13.
15. Credit ratings and status reports are "sometimes material" (*Herschel v Breen (No. 2)* at para.17) but are generally of limited value and unlikely to be determinative on their own: *JW Hughes v GB Metalwork* at paras.41–2; *Wimbledon Construction v Vago*.
16. A stay will not be granted merely because the payer has commenced an arbitration: *Absolute Rentals v Gencor Enterprises*; *Wimbledon Construction v Vago*; *Harlow & Milner v Teasdale (No. 3)* [2006] EWHC 1708. If the defendant has established a counterclaim which goes to the root of the claim, however, a stay will be ordered on the claim: *David McLean v Swansea Housing* [2002] B.L.R. 125 at para.24.
17. Some weight may be given to the merits of the dispute: *Baldwins Industrial Services v Barr* [2003] B.L.R. 176 at para.36.
18. Actions that might indicate cash flow problems such as requests for advance payments for materials may not be significant when assessing the likely position at the estimated time for repayment: *Wimbledon Construction v Vago* at para.34.
19. Any stay should be granted for a limited time only, requiring the successful party to return for extensions of time if necessary: *AWG Construction v Rockingham* at para.187.
20. A stay or order for security is a possibility where there is serious evidence of inability to repay in a case where the debtor has an application for summary judgment pending and a hearing is imminent: *Hillview v Botes Building* [2006] EWHC 1365 at para.33; *Alstom Signalling v Jarvis Facilities* [2004] EWHC 1285 at para.20.
21. A stay may be ordered where the claimant is a company registered outside the jurisdiction and has no branch in the UK: *McConnell Dowell Constructors v National Grid Gas* [2006] EWHC 2551. In that case the claimant was Australian but offered a bond as security for its repayment obligation. On that basis a stay was refused (para.54).

22. All of the above criteria are subject to the court's overriding objective of doing justice between the parties: *AWG Construction v Rockingham* at para.185.

Stay granted

In this context, a stay has only actually been granted in four cases: *Harwood Construction v Lantrode*; *Rainford House v Cadogan* [2001] B.L.R. 416 (receivership); *Baldwins Industrial Services v Barr* [2003] B.L.R. 176 (receivership); *Bouygues v Dahl-Jensen* [2000] B.L.R. 522 (liquidation). In lieu of a stay the court refused to order summary judgment in *Hart Investments v Fidler* [2006] EWHC 2857 (liquidation). It is significant that these are all cases of formal insolvency or, in *Harwood*, of a pending insolvency proceeding. The threshold for a stay in this context appears to be a high one: if the allegation is of informal insolvency, very good evidence will be needed to justify a stay. **12–007**

The Australian courts have reached a similar conclusion in relation to their construction payment legislation. The Australian equivalent of administration is a valid ground for granting a stay (*Grosvenor Constructions v Musico* [2004] NSWSC 344), as is probably a company deed of arrangement (*Brodyn v Davenport* (2004) 61 N.S.W.L.R. 421). Apart from cases of formal insolvency, it has been held that a "very high risk" of irrecoverability is required: *Herscho v Expile Pty* [2004] NSWCA 468; or that formal insolvency should be "imminent" or "very close": *Taylor Projects v Brick* [2005] NSWSC 571.

4. Adjudication and administration

Administration and adjudication have a lot in common. Both are statutory in origin. Both are concerned with cash flow: supported by administration through the moratorium on the enforcement of claims against the company; and by adjudication as a procedure designed to facilitate the recovery of claims by the company. Further, both are interim procedures. Administration allows a breathing space for the company to consider its position; adjudication is a means of recovering debts in advance of an expensive and time-consuming legal process. It is interesting therefore to consider the situation where claims are brought either by or against a company in administration. **12–008**

There are no specific rules regarding claims by a company in administration. If the company is the defendant, permission is needed under para.43, Sch.B1 of the Insolvency Act 1986 (or s.11 of the Insolvency Act 1986 where the administration began before September 15, 2003) from the administrator or the court to bring "proceedings" in court, arbitration or adjudication. The criteria are set out in *Re Atlantic Computers plc* [1992] Ch. 505 (see Ch.7). In the industry permission may be necessary in connection with claims to title of materials or plant, calls against on demand bonds or disputed claims to trust or escrow accounts. In other jurisdictions, the purpose of the adjudication may be to obtain a judgment which operates as an assignment to the subcontractor of sums due to the contractor from the employer: see *Belmadar Constructions v Environmental Solutions International* [2005] VSC 24.

In the context of adjudication in the UK, permission has been refused in the cases reported so far: *A. Straume (UK) Ltd v Bradlor Developments* (2000)

2 T.C.L.R. 409, [2000] B.C.C. 333; *Joinery Plus v Laing* [2003] B.L.R. 184; *Canary Riverside v Timtec* (2003) 19 Const. L.J. 283. These cases are interesting in drawing out the security function of adjudication. They also illustrate how the procedure can come into conflict with insolvency law.

Claims under the contract

12–009 At first sight, a claimant in administration has the best of both worlds: protection against creditor pressure and a relatively low cost and quick procedure for collecting its debts. In *Straume v Bradlor*, the contractor went into administration before completion of the works and served notices of adjudication claiming unpaid certified sums. The employer defended on the basis that nothing was due until the works were completed (relying on the suspension of payment in the termination clause) or that it was entitled to set off cross-claims for liquidated damages and the cost of rectifying defective work.

The employer referred its cross-claims to adjudication by serving a separate notice on the administrators. The contract was in the JCT 80 form as amended to comply with the Act. Having found that the employer needed permission of the court to bring an adjudication against the contractor, Judge Behrens refused to grant it on the ground that the notice duplicated the defence in the administrators' adjudication and was advanced for a collateral purpose. The facts are not fully set out in the judgment but it appears that the employer had not served the appropriate withholding notice entitling it to set off its cross-claims against the certified sums. By bringing a fresh adjudication, it was presumably hoping to improve its prospects of defending any enforcement proceedings the administrators might bring by asking the court to set off the two adjudication decisions and give a balance judgment. The court has since made it clear that it will not do such a balancing exercise: *Interserve v Cleveland Bridge* [2006] EWHC 741, discussed in Ch.5.

It appears that the certified sums represented work done before the administration order and that one certificate was issued before the order and the other the day after. It seems that the suspension of payment provision was not raised in argument. The administrators argued that to grant permission would be futile as the employer could only be an unsecured creditor in respect of its claims. In their view the effect of the administration order was (a) to prevent the employer invoking the adjudication procedure while preserving the contractor's right to do so; and (b) to enable the contractor to treat any resulting adjudication decision as having a final rather than a temporary effect (compare *Baldwins Industrial Services v Barr* at paras.27 and 35; and *Grosvenor Constructions v Musico* [2004] NSWSC 344 at para.35). It was held that the employer should not be allowed to evade the consequences of excluding set-off (and it seems of failing to serve withholding notices) "by a side door". However, this ignores the temporary and procedural nature of adjudication: set-off is not intended to be excluded but only postponed to a later certificate. In this case it seems that only retention would have been payable in future. Normally in an administration the common law of set-off applies to protect a debtor against having to pay the creditor in full while only being able to prove for a dividend in respect of its own debt. Here a combination of adjudication and s.111 of the Act removed this protection but that is not necessarily the end of the story.

The outcome of the adjudication in *Straume v Bradlor* is not known: the employer may have succeeded on the basis that the suspension of payment did not require a withholding notice. In this case, it seems that the employer had a cross-claim which qualified for equitable set-off but lost that protection because:

(a) he had failed to serve a withholding notice;

(b) an adjudicator only has jurisdiction to decide the dispute referred to him and cannot consider counterclaims as the court does (there is no equivalent of a balance judgment in an adjudication); and

(c) he was barred from pursuing his claim under a separate adjudication or action by s.11 of the Insolvency Act 1986.

If it is right that the policy of the Housing Grants, Construction and Regeneration Act 1996 is to improve cash flow rather than reallocate insolvency risk, a stay would be the just result where the claimant is in administration and the defendant has a genuine cross-claim.

Claims on dishonoured cheques

The position is more complicated if the claim is one which is normally enforced by the court independently of any cross-claims, e.g. if it is based on a cheque. In *Canary Riverside v Timtec International* (2003) 19 Const. L.J. 283 the court again refused an employer permission to begin an adjudication against a contractor in administration. The chronology is particularly important. On June 21, 1999, a contractor (Timtec) entered into a trade contract with an employer in connection with a development at Canary Wharf. On January 5, 2000, the site was re-opened after the Christmas shutdown and the employer received two invoices totalling £285,000 dated December 23, 1999 from Timtec. **12–010**

Under the terms of the trade contract, they were due for payment 30 days later. Some of Timtec's subcontractors failed to return to site after January 5 and little or no further work was done. On January 14, Timtec went into administration. On January 17, unaware of Timtec's insolvency, the employer issued a cheque for £285,000 and sent it to Timtec. On January 18, Timtec presented the cheque for special clearance. On January 19, the construction manager informed the employer that Timtec had gone into administration and the employer immediately stopped the cheque. On January 26, the employer terminated Timtec's employment and served two withholding notices which appear to have claimed an entitlement to suspend payment of the two invoices until after Timtec's works had been completed by another contractor.

On March 17, the administrators required the employer to honour the cheque and challenged the validity of the withholding notices on the ground that they were served out of time. This was based on the erroneous assumption (shared by both parties) that the invoices had been received by the employer on December 27, 1999. Timtec issued proceedings in court claiming payment under the cheque. On April 14, the employer issued an application for leave under s.11 to bring an adjudication against Timtec. On May 3, the day before the hearing of the employer's application for leave, Timtec served its court proceedings on the employer.

12–011 Pausing here, it is worth noting that the contractor's claim was not for payment of its invoices or for summary judgment of a decision that £285,000 was due but simply for payment of a stopped cheque. Arguments based on misrepresentation, suspension of payment, mistake of fact or the timeous service of withholding notices cannot amount to defences to such a claim; only proof of failure of consideration, invalidity or fraud would normally be sufficient. In this case the contractor had provided consideration for the cheque and the claim was not fraudulent. It was not argued that the proceeds of the cheque were subject to a constructive trust in the employer's favour: compare *Re Farepak* [2006] EWHC 3272 at para.39. The usual rule is for summary judgment to be ordered with no stay of execution.

Against that background, how should the court regard an employer's application to adjudicate his contractual cross-claims? The court (DKR Oliver Q.C.) upheld the decision of the registrar of the Companies Court and rejected the application but on grounds that are not entirely satisfactory. By analogy with *Straume v Bradlor*, it was held that the employer's cross-claims could be best decided by way of defence and counterclaim in the proceedings brought by the contractor. However, it is plain that they could not amount to a defence for the reasons given above and as a counterclaim they could only result in an unsecured judgment.

The court referred to the temporary finality of adjudication and considered that it would be more efficient for the cross-claims to be dealt with in litigation which could offer a final resolution. Oddly, it also held that adjudication was introduced to deal with disputes arising in the course of a contract whereas here there had been a termination. This is in conflict with other authorities: *Connex v MJ Building Services* [2005] B.L.R. 201. The other ground is an echo of the court's attitude to the enforcement of adjudication decisions themselves: that the appeal from the registrar was a true appeal in the sense that it had to be shown that he had exercised his decision on the wrong principles. Although both parties had acted in the mistaken belief that the withholding notices had been served out of time, the registrar had reached his decision by correctly applying the law to the facts before him.

12–012 This case concerned the interaction between principles governing adjudication, administration and bills of exchange. The issues could not be properly dealt with on an appeal of this kind. This is not such an unusual situation. The employer invoked its contractual rights as soon as it became aware of the contractor's formal insolvency. It is ironic that the employer issued the cheque some two weeks before the final date for payment only to find itself penalised for its efficiency. In the event the contractor's administrators penetrated the defences established by the termination clause. The upshot is that the employer had to pay the value of the cheque and prove as a creditor for the additional cost to complete as and when it was quantified.

If a cheque is issued in payment of a sum stated as due in a certificate, it is not open to the drawer to avoid liability by stopping the cheque where it appears from a later certificate that the payee had already been overpaid: *Isovel Contracts v ABB Building Technologies* [2002] 1 B.C.L.C. 390. This was not an adjudication case. The sub-subcontract, which was based on DOM/2 and entered into before the Housing Grants, Construction and Regeneration Act 1996 came into force, provided for errors in any valuation on which a certificate was founded to be corrected in later certificates (para.19). At the time the cheque was issued, the drawer only had an unliquidated and unquantified cross-claim for incomplete or defective work.

The court rejected a submission that there had been a failure of consideration, granted summary judgment and refused a stay of execution. It was alleged that the claimant had repudiated the contract and caused substantial losses as a consequence but neither feature amounted to the "exceptional circumstances" required for a stay in claims involving bills of exchange (para.26). The court (Simon Berry Q.C.) was impressed by the argument that the effect of a stay in these circumstances would be to extend r.4.90 of the Insolvency Rules 1986 (liquidation set-off) to companies in administration and thereby give an advantage to the defendant which was not available to the other creditors (see Ch.18). (Conversely it could be argued that to refuse a stay in this context would be to deprive the debtor of its common law rights of set-off which apply whether or not either party is in administration.) The court also took account of the purpose of the administration, to effect a more advantageous realisation of assets than on a winding up.

Submissions were made in support of a stay based on *Herschel v Breen (No. 2)* and *Rainford House v Cadogan* but the court did not find them helpful in this context and treated them as decisions turning on their own facts. However, an analogy can be drawn between a claim to enforce an adjudication decision and a claim on a dishonoured cheque in that in both cases the existence of cross-claims cannot afford a defence even if they would ordinarily qualify for set-off. There is as yet no reported case on the criteria for a stay application in the context of adjudication where the claimant is in administration. Perhaps the Isovel case will introduce an element of caution when considering such an application.

If the cheque has already been paid before the recipient enters administration, it may be too late to take any salvage action. In *Joinery Plus v Laing* [2003] B.L.R. 184, a subcontractor went into administration two months after successfully claiming £70,000 from Laing in an adjudication. Unfortunately, the adjudicator had reached his decision by applying the terms of a different contract between the parties. The subcontractor accepted Laing's cheque on account of its claims for loss and expense in the adjudication (almost £700,000) and then successfully applied to the court for a declaration that the decision was a nullity, leaving it free to commence a fresh adjudication in respect of the same claim. **12–013**

Laing wanted to make it a condition of any fresh referral that the £70,000 be repaid on the ground that there had been a total failure of consideration, "the payment having been made by Laing in consideration of the obligation to meet an adjudicator's decision which was invalid" (para.98). It was held, however, that the subcontractor would have succeeded on a claim for summary judgment in that amount even if it had not first pursued its claim in adjudication. It followed that Laing's claim would be met by a cross-claim in the same amount which would have been eligible for equitable set-off. Whether Laing applied for summary judgment or an injunction restraining the subcontractor from beginning a new adjudication, it would first have to obtain leave under s.11. Judge Anthony Thornton Q.C. applied the guidelines of *Re Atlantic Computers plc* [1982] Ch. 505. The main objective of the administration was to make it easier to collect the company's debts. The claim against Laing was one of the company's major assets and the court held that it would undermine the purpose of the administration to allow Laing's claim for repayment to proceed. Laing could not show that it was prejudiced by being unable to pursue its claim for repayment. Laing had also failed to enter into meaningful negotiations on the claim for loss and expense even though invited to do so by the subcontractor.

Whether the act of banking a cheque discharges the underlying debt depends on the intention of the party accepting it as determined objectively from the circumstances: *Stour Valley Builders v Stuart* (*The Independent*, February 9, 1993). In this case, the subcontractor had already challenged the validity of the adjudicator's decision before it received Laing's cheque. It also wrote to Laing saying that it was accepting the cheque on account before banking it. In the application under s.11, Laing had not put forward any reason for challenging the subcontractor's underlying entitlement to the £70,000. Indeed, it was made up of elements which were largely admitted by Laing before the adjudicator.

The question arises whether Laing would have been entitled to leave under s.11 if it had had a good claim for repayment on the merits. On the general approach of the court in this case, it seems unlikely. In conclusion it seems that the court will not intervene to protect a creditor once it has made a payment to the company. Creditors need to be alert to their rights in the run up to the company's insolvency.

5. Adjudication and liquidation

12–014 The court's permission is required under the Insolvency Act 1986 to bring an adjudication against a company in compulsory liquidation (s.130) or against an individual either subject to an interim order (s.252) or once made bankrupt (s.285). Where a petition for winding up has been issued, the company can apply to the court to stay the adjudication (s.126). The court will not normally grant summary judgment on a claim by a liquidator to enforce an adjudicator's decision unless he has previously carried out the accounting required by r.4.90 of the Insolvency Rules 1986: *Bouygues v Dahl-Jensen* [2000] B.L.R. 522 (see Ch.18).

Bouygues was followed recently in *Hart Investments v Fidler* (2006) 109 Con. L.R. 67. In that case the employer made a claim against a builder following a partial collapse of the structure. The builder was in liquidation and counterclaimed to enforce an adjudication decision it had obtained. Judge Peter Coulson Q.C. refused to enter judgment on the counterclaim in view of the effect of r.4.90 and the provisional nature of the adjudicator's decision. Where it is clear, however, that the debtor has no cross-claim of any kind against the claimant, summary judgment has been ordered in favour of a company in liquidation without a stay: *Fastrack Contractors v Morrison Construction* [2000] B.L.R. 168.

In *Harwood v Lantrode* (unreported, November 24, 2000, Judge Richard Seymour Q.C.) the claimant applied for summary judgment to enforce an adjudication decision two weeks before the hearing date of a winding up petition issued against it. The petitioning creditor was paid, but the petition remained alive because the defendant had served a notice in support of it. The claimant maintained that the petition would be dismissed. No evidence of the claimant's financial position was before the court. As a winding up order takes effect from the date of the petition, Judge Richard Seymour Q.C. granted a stay until the hearing which was to cease if the petition were dismissed. The stay preserved the *status quo* so that the terms of the mandatory set-off under r.4.90 could be operated if the winding up order was granted. If the claim were satisfied between the issue of the petition and the making of the winding up order the claimant would have to apply to the court under s.127 of the Insolvency Act 1986 for an order retrospectively validating the payment.

There have been no reported cases in this area but is hard to see why the claimant should be preferred in this way simply because it has the benefit of an adjudicator's decision.

6. Adjudication and receivership

It is often difficult for receivers to finance the cost of proceedings to recover debts owed to the company. If they go ahead and bring an adjudication hoping to recover their costs from the proceeds of the claim, there is a risk of personal liability for the adjudicator's fees if the company's claim fails. In *Faithful and Gould v Arcal* (unreported, June 1, 2001) an adjudication was brought by a company in administrative receivership. The adjudicator sought assurances from the receivers that they would be personally responsible for his fees. The receivers avoided making any express commitment but agreed to be bound by his decision. When he found against the company they refused to pay his fees but the court ordered summary judgment against the company and the receivers personally in respect of them. **12–015**

Administrative receivership is a form of enforcement of a floating charge. In legal terms, the appointment of a receiver is comparable to an equitable assignment of the assets comprised in the charge to the secured creditor. Building contracts often contain restrictions on assignment without consent. It is arguable therefore that an adjudication brought in the name of the company by a receiver under such a contract will be a nullity and any decision made by the adjudicator be beyond his jurisdiction. If so, summary judgment to enforce such a decision might be refused. This argument is considered in more detail in Ch.4. Otherwise, summary judgment may be granted but subject to a stay of execution pending trial of any counterclaim on condition that the amount in dispute be paid into court and that the claimant have leave to apply to lift the stay on providing security for repayment: *Rainford House v Cadogan* [2001] B.L.R. 416. In that case, administrative receivers were appointed to a contractor while an adjudication was in progress and after the contractor's employment had been determined by the employer for failing to proceed diligently with the work. The adjudicator made an order for payment to the contractor. The employer asserted a cross-claim to recover an overpayment and the amounts of direct payments made to subcontractors but had not served a withholding notice in respect of it.

The court distinguished *Bouygues v Dahl-Jensen* and held that different criteria apply in the case of a receivership. It was appropriate to enter judgment but it should be subject to a stay on the basis that:

> ". . . the statute is not concerned to reallocate the risk of having to endure the consequences of a trading partner becoming insolvent, but simply to address the question, on the footing that all parties are solvent, which party should hold the fund of money about which there is a dispute pending the resolution of that dispute." (para.9, *per* Judge Richard Seymour Q.C.)

It appears that no argument based on the suspension of payment contained in the termination clause was made. Normally the court considers a stay in this context because of the company's inability to repay the judgment sum. It might also regard the argument based on non-assignability mentioned above as a "special circumstance". An assignment splits the benefit and the burden of the contract. The charge holder takes the benefit (the claim) but leaves the burden (the contingent duty to repay) with the company. A stay might not be ordered if the charge holder were to offer an undertaking to the court to make any repayment subsequently ordered: compare the Australian case of *Main Roads Corporation v Samary Enterprises* [2006] VSC 144 at para.40. By invoking the adjudication procedure as part of the benefit transferred to the charge holder, the receivers may also be bound by the "pure principle of benefit and burden" discussed in Ch.4. To avoid these potential difficulties, a charge holder may delay appointing receivers until after an adjudication decision has been successfully enforced. The same may apply to a company considering administration.

The question of actual or potential insolvency can arise in respect of both parties. In *Baldwins Industrial Services v Barr* [2003] B.L.R. 176, the claimant went into administrative receivership after obtaining an order for payment in an adjudication but before applying for summary judgment. The defendant claimed there was a realistic prospect that it would succeed on the merits before a court or arbitrator. There was evidence that it had made losses in two of the previous three years and itself might be facing liquidity difficulties. Judge Frances Kirkham Q.C. granted a stay on terms proposed by the parties: it would last for one month only unless the defendant paid the amount ordered by the adjudicator into court within seven days and commenced its claim within one month. The stay did not apply to liability for the claimant's costs and adjudicator's fees.

7. Individual statutory demands

12–016 This section is a continuation of Ch.11, which deals with the criteria for applications to set aside a statutory demand served on an individual under r.6.5(4) of the Insolvency Rules 1986, and for injunctions restraining the issue or advertisement of a winding up petition against a company. From an adjudication perspective, these tests raise acute problems which have so far resulted in conflicting case law. Does an adjudication decision create a debt in its own right? Or is it a temporary resolution of a dispute in which the unsuccessful party agrees to act as if he were a debtor? Is such a decision properly a 'judgment or order' for the purposes of the *Practice Direction (Insolvency Proceedings) 1999* [2000] B.C.C. 927? If the creditor serves a statutory demand without first having obtained an order for summary judgment, can the bankruptcy court deal with challenges to the adjudicator's jurisdiction? How does the adjudication procedure relate to the criterion of inability to litigate in *Re Bayoil*? To what extent is *Re Bayoil* of relevance in personal insolvency? In considering such questions it is useful first to look at the general position. The cases disclose a number of scenarios which invite comparison with adjudication.

Analogies with adjudication

Settlement agreement

12–017 Firstly, a demand may be based on a compromise of a contractual dispute. This has occurred in several cases involving Lloyd's names. In *Re Debtors (Nos.4449 and 4450 of 1998)* [1999] 1 All E.R. (Comm) 149, a settlement agreement was entered into under which a sum was payable "free and clear of any set off, counterclaim or other deduction on any account whatsoever". Lloyd's then made a further proposal which was to remain open until December 31, 1996 but withdrew it before the time had expired and served a statutory demand based on the original settlement figure. In setting aside the demand, the court held that the no set-off provision could not bind the bankruptcy court: "Such a contractual provision cannot override the statutory rule" (para.19, *per* Carnwath J.). Although the settlement agreement could not be impugned, there was a genuine triable issue that the proposal had contractual effect and that Lloyd's were in breach of an implied obligation not to frustrate the conclusion of an agreement. As there was some doubt whether the damages would exceed the amount of the demand, the court based its decision on the ground that the debt was disputed because Lloyd's had agreed to assume responsibility for it in the event that the proposal was accepted.

In *Garrow v Society of Lloyd's*, reported as *Re a Debtor (No. 544/SD/98)* [2000] 1 B.C.L.C. 103, the demand was based on a judgment pursuant to a settlement containing the same no set-off clause. It had been established in previous litigation that this clause did not prevent the debtor proceeding by way of separate action and the debtor had, together with two hundred other names, issued proceedings before receiving the demand. He admitted the debt and his inability to pay but once again the demand was set aside.

(1) The court agreed that the proceedings issued by the debtor disclosed a genuine triable issue and was prepared to assume that damages would at least equal the demand.
(2) It was not appropriate to allow a petition to be issued and then suspended merely to preserve the limitation period for insolvency claims since there was no evidence of such claims in this case.
(3) The debtor could have brought an action some years previously but his delay could be justified as the claim was in the nature of a class action requiring common defences and was of a high degree of complexity.

> "Delay in putting forward a cross-claim may lead to an inference that it is not put forward in good faith, but only as a pretext in an attempt to stave off bankruptcy. However, there may be a satisfactory explanation for delay, and the practice direction recognises that failure to raise it in the original action against the debtor need not be fatal" (at 114, *per* Robert Walker L.J.).

At first instance Jacob J. thought it would be disproportionate to give effect to the no set-off clause in the context of an insolvency proceeding especially as the hearing of the debtor's action was likely to take place before the hearing of any petition. The Court of Appeal held that purely as a matter of construction the clause did not prevent the debtor's action being taken into account on the set aside application. The court was careful to avoid expressing a view whether it is possible to oust the court's jurisdiction by an agreement not to set up a cross-claim in opposition to a statutory demand (at 121).

These cases are closely analogous to the position in an adjudication. Both involve contractual disputes which are resolved through contractual processes. In the Lloyd's actions, they resulted in a final settlement, whereas adjudication is only an interim stage. *A fortiori*, the approach taken in the Lloyd's cases ought to apply to adjudication decisions. The question arises whether a distinction should be made on the ground that in an adjudication a third party resolves the dispute (even though named in the contract or appointed by an institution named in the contract). On one view, it should make no difference because the decision takes effect as if it were a contractual term agreed by the parties. On the other hand, the involvement of a third party might suggest that an adjudication decision is more than an agreement but less than a judgment or order. The crucial difference lies in the provisional nature of adjudication.

Cheques

12–018 The second scenario is where a statutory demand is based on a dishonoured cheque. The only defences to such a claim are fraud, invalidity or failure of consideration: *Nova (Jersey) Knit v Kammgarn* [1977] 2 All E.R. 463. In *Hofer v Strawson* [1999] 2 B.C.L.C. 336, the court refused to set aside a demand based on a dishonoured cheque. The drawer alleged a cross-claim for damages for misrepresentation under a share sale agreement of which the cheque represented part of the consideration. The court stated that:

> "... if the debtor, the writer of the cheque, does have a genuine counterclaim which may exceed the amount of the cheque, while it is appropriate that he should have to pay on the cheque, it is quite another thing to say that he should be liable to be bankrupted in respect of it in circumstances where he has a genuine cross-claim which may well exceed the amount of the cheque" (at 342, *per* Neuberger J.).

In that case, the court refused to set aside the demand because the cross-claim did not give rise to a genuine triable issue. A cheque is equivalent to cash; an adjudication decision is intended to improve the cash flow between the parties.

In *Nova v Kammgarn* at 479, Lord Russell stated: "The bill is itself a contract separate from the contract of sale." This can be compared with the view taken in some adjudication cases that the decision amounts to a debt in its own right. It appears to follow if that a demand based on a cheque can be set aside, so can a demand based on an adjudication decision. See also *Marchands v Thompson* and *Re LHF Wools*, discussed in Ch.11, in which winding up petitions based on unpaid cheques were stayed or struck out because of the company's cross-claims.

Freight

12–019 The analogy is even stronger between applications to enforce adjudication decisions and claims to recover freight payable under a charterparty. For example, in *Western Bulk Carriers v Li Hai* [2005] 2 Lloyd's Rep. 389, the court held that freight had to be paid in full fifteen days in advance even though both parties knew on the date the sum became due that part or all of it would have to be repaid owing to temporary defects in the ship. It is significant that the demand in *Re Bayoil* itself was based on a claim for freight which was supported by a final interim award of an arbitrator (see Ch.11).

Costs

The fourth comparison is between adjudication and a statutory demand based on an order of costs. In *Popely v Popely* [2004] B.P.I.R. 778, the Court of Appeal held that an order for costs was analogous to the stopped cheque in *Hofer v Strawson* and the claim for freight in *Bayoil*. **12–020**

In *Popely*, the debtor had a genuine cross-claim for damages for breach of contract which had been pursued in litigation before the costs order was made against him in a different action. The creditor argued that to allow the demand to be set aside would be to subvert the policy of "pay as you go" under the Civil Procedure Rules. This was rejected by the Court of Appeal. What was at issue was not the enforceability of the costs order but whether the debtor had satisfied the criteria for setting aside a demand. Insolvency proceedings were of a different order to ordinary litigation.

Further analogies

An analogy can be drawn between an adjudicator's decision and an individual statutory demand itself. Neither is considered a judgment or a final order for payment. A statutory demand is not a "legal proceeding" for the purposes of the Arbitration Act 1996: *Shalston v Keane*, discussed in Ch.11. In both cases, the debtor has to take action or risk losing the ability to challenge the claim. Obviously, there are differences: the decision is a contractual matter; the demand is based on statute. The decision is binding on the debtor, the demand will only have binding effect by limiting the debtor's room to manoeuvre on a petition hearing unless it is set aside beforehand. **12–021**

A further analogy is with liability for VAT. For example, under relevant tax legislation, where an amount of VAT has been assessed and notified it is deemed to be an amount due from the taxpayer notwithstanding any appeal to the VAT and Duties Tribunal: see e.g. *Re Arena Corporation* [2003] EWHC 3032. The situation is reminiscent of *Dawnays v Minter* [1971] 1 W.L.R. 1205, discussed in Ch.5; and also, *Pegram Shopfitters v Tally Weijl* [2004] B.L.R. 65 at para.1. The court was treating an interim certificate as if it were cash and making a final order for summary judgment. Here, it is inherent in the process that any order is temporary.

Another analogy might be an on demand bond. It was envisaged by Parliament that adjudication would embody a policy of "pay now, argue later" (*AWG Construction v Rockingham* [2004] T.C.L.R. 6, para.118), a policy frequently expressed in the context of applications to restrain calls against such bonds. This approach to adjudication has been sanctioned by the court: *RJT Consulting v DM Engineering* [2002] 1 W.L.R. 2344. In bond cases however the only widely recognised ground for avoiding immediate payment is that the demand was made fraudulently (see Ch.19).

Arbitration

Before the mandatory stay introduced by the Arbitration Act 1996, the court had a discretion under s.4 of the Arbitration Act 1950 whether to stay proceedings to arbitration. There were several cases under that section where the plaintiff resisting the stay was insolvent. In *Trustee of the Property of Alan Andrews v Brock Buildings* (unreported, November 21, 1996), there was a subcontract in the DOM/1 form which contained an arbitration clause. It was **12–022** terminated by the contractor on the ground of delay. The subcontractor disputed the termination and claimed £70,000 as the value of work done, materials on site and loss of profit. The contractor cross-claimed for damages of £60,000.

Before any proceedings were issued, the subcontractor was made bankrupt on a petition served by another creditor. The trustee in bankruptcy obtained legal aid and sued the contractor. The trustee argued that, if the proceedings were stayed to arbitration, he would not be able to pursue them as legal aid only applied to litigation. He also claimed, that, had the subcontractor been paid what he was due by the contractor, he would not have been made bankrupt. It would, therefore, be unjust to deprive him of a legitimate claim by staying the proceedings.

The Court of Appeal considered that these factors did not amount to sufficient reason within the section why the dispute should not be referred to arbitration. In exercising its discretion against the subcontractor, the court held that:

(1) A stay could be refused if the subcontractor could show a reasonable prospect of success in his argument that he was unable to prosecute arbitration proceedings because of the contractor's breaches: *Fakes v Taylor Woodrow* [1973] 1 Q.B. 436 at 446. This required the court to enquire into matters of causation, e.g. whether his insolvency resulted from wrongful actions by the contractor.

(2) It was not disputed that the subcontractor had a reasonable prospect of success on its claim, but the same could not be said of the argument that his insolvency had been caused by the contractor's breaches.

Judgments had been entered against the subcontractor several months before the termination, during which time he was receiving interim payments under the subcontract. Excluding the contractor's proof of debt, the subcontractor owed over £46,000 to his creditors. It is possible that the subcontractor would have been bankrupt therefore, even if the subcontract had been completed and he had been paid the agreed price. Also, there was no evidence that, even if he had not been made bankrupt, he would have had funds to conduct an arbitration. The claim was being pursued for the benefit of the creditors and it was for them to fund the arbitration if they so wished.

Conclusion

12–023 The question is: should the policy underlying the Housing Grants, Construction and Regeneration Act 1996 affect the way the court exercises its discretion? In *Re Bayoil* [1999] 1 All E.R. 374 at 383, Ward L.J. stated:

> ". . . a winding up order is a draconian order. If wrongly made, the company has little commercial prospect of reviving itself and recovering its former position. If there is any doubt about the claim or the cross claim, that seems to me to require that the court should proceed cautiously."

Although statutory adjudication is a remedy unique to construction, it would seem appropriate to adopt an approach to demands based on adjudication decisions similar to those based on settlement agreements and the other categories discussed above. If this is correct, it follows that a counterclaim which cannot be set off through the operation of the 1996 Act remains a cross-claim which can be taken into account for the purposes of an application to set aside a demand. This reflects what happens on the making of a bankruptcy order, when an account is taken and all claims and cross-claims are set off against each other (see Ch.18).

Procedural aspects

As explained in Ch.11, the court expects the debtor to raise any defences to the claim on an application to set aside the demand: *Turner v Royal Bank of Scotland* [2000] B.P.I.R. 683. If the demand is not set aside, the debtor can appeal but it is a true appeal rather than a rehearing of the original application and the court is limited in its power to review the decision below. The court has a residual discretion under r.6.25 of the Insolvency Rules 1986 to hear argument on the debt at the hearing of the petition but it will only be exercised as a matter of practice if there has been a change of circumstances after the unsuccessful application to set aside. The question arises what such change of circumstances might be in the context of adjudication. It seems likely to be a material change if in the interim the court has refused to order summary judgment on the ground that the adjudicator had no jurisdiction. Could it also be material that the position dealt with in the decision has been superseded by later valuations? **12–024**

Although the petition only concerns the debt asserted in the statutory demand, if the debtor puts forward a cross-claim the court is entitled to take account of any other claims of the creditor to see whether they qualify for equitable set-off against the debtor's cross-claim. If they do, only the balance of the cross-claim will be available to set against the petition debt: *TSB Bank v Platts* [1998] 2 B.C.L.C. 1. This could be a significant factor in adjudication cases as by the time of the hearing of the petition other rights to payment may have accrued in the creditor's favour. See also *Re a Company (No. 00962 of 1991)* [1992] B.C.L.C. 248.

Adjudication case law

Cross-claims

A demand based on an adjudication decision was set aside by Judge Behrens under r.6.5(4)(a) in *Parke v Fenton Gretton Partnership* [2001] C.I.L.L. 1712. It was served by a contractor in respect of a final account balance found due and owing by the adjudicator. The employer cross claimed for defects and delay asserting that no certificates of completion had been issued and that the works were incomplete. The cross-claims exceeded the value of the claim. The employer had issued proceedings in court and the contractor had served a defence to them before the hearing of the application to set aside the statutory demand. There was a genuine triable issue. **12–025**

Disputed debts

In *Oakley v Airclear Environmental* [2002] C.I.L.L. 1824, a contractor brought an arbitration against a named subcontractor for retention, discount, and damages. Two months later the subcontractor brought an adjudication to **12–026** recover sums due. Both claims were based on a subcontract in the terms of NAM/SC. After the adjudicator's appointment, but before service of the notice of referral, the contractor changed its position arguing that no contract had been formed and took no further part in either proceeding. The subcontractor obtained a decision from the adjudicator which confirmed its claim and served statutory demands on the two individuals trading as the contractor. The demands were set aside by Etherton J. on appeal.

(1) There was insufficient evidence to hold that a contract had been formed and the adjudication was a nullity.

(2) The contractors were not estopped from denying that a contract had been formed. It was not unconscionable of them to have changed their position when they did.

(3) The subcontractor now wanted to present its claim as a *quantum meruit* but that was not the basis on which the demands had been served.

The contractor had cross-claims arising from the subcontractor's conduct of the work and the threat of insolvency proceedings was not a proper way to resolve the issues. The court did not specify the particular grounds of r.6.5(4) relied on but it appears to have been subsection (b), that the debt was disputed.

An unsuccessful challenge to the adjudicator's jurisdiction was made in *Mohammed v Bowles* (unreported, February 1, 2002) although the court approached the issue in a different way. An employer obtained an adjudicator's decision against a builder for payment of £26,000 as damages for defects and delay. No further details of the claim are given in the report. When the employer served a statutory demand, the builder applied to set it aside on the grounds contained in subsections (b) and (d). He had been paid up to date and evidently had no cross-claim. The bankruptcy registrar characterised the issue before him as "whether the adjudicator's decision creates a debt that can form the basis of a statutory demand and, if so, the nature of that debt" (para.13). This was necessary because a statutory demand cannot be served in respect of an unliquidated claim. In effect, the bankruptcy registrar was being asked to decide between competing theories on the status of an adjudication decision.

The builder had from the start disputed the jurisdiction of the adjudicator. Before the registrar, he argued that the decision could not amount to a judgment or order within r.6.5(4) because adjudication is not a legal proceeding, relying on *Austin Hall v Buckland Securities* [2001] B.L.R. 272 at para.35. The builder had agreed to comply with adjudication decisions in the interim but (implicitly) only if they were validly made. He argued that the contract was for work at the employer's home and therefore fell outside the construction legislation. Secondly he argued that the original contract which included an adjudication clause had been replaced by a later contract without such a clause. There were also arguments based on natural justice and the apparent absence of a notice of non-completion to support the employer's claim for liquidated damages.

The employer relied on *Parke v Fenton Gretton Partnership* as authority that the decision created a debt in its own right which should be treated as if it were a judgment or order for the purposes of the practice direction. He argued that there was no reason to differentiate between contractual and statutory adjudications and that the evidence regarding the replacement of the contract was weak. The registrar refused to set aside the demand. He found that the parties had entered into a contract which contained an adjudication agreement. The adjudicator had already decided the question whether the contract had been replaced and it was not for the bankruptcy court to look behind the decision. He pointed out that the builder had not applied to the court for a declaration that the adjudication was a nullity. The registrar did not consider that the employer was under any obligation to take enforcement proceedings before serving a statutory demand. In any event, on the evidence, the registrar did not consider that the builder had put forward a genuine triable issue to dispute the debt and there were no other grounds on which the builder could rely.

Other grounds

Had it been necessary, the claimant in *Parke v Fenton Gretton Partnership* **12–027** [2001] C.I.L.L. 1712 would have relied on this ground, arguing that the existing defended action was inconsistent with the bankruptcy route. Judge Boggis Q.C. stated at 1713 that "... it cannot be right that an employer or main contractor can be made bankrupt when it is known that he has proper proceedings on foot which if successful will result in a payment to him."

Status of adjudication decisions

In applications to set aside statutory demands the court is unable to go **12–028** behind a judgment or order. The question arises: does an adjudicator's decision fall within this category? An adjudication debt is of an "unusual kind" (*Herschel v Breen (No. 2)* at para.7). The decision is not a judgment: *VHE Construction v RBSTB Trust Co.* [2000] B.L.R. 187 at para.55. As with cases on the definition of debt it is possible that the answer to this question will depend on the context. Adjudication is a proceeding for the purposes of s.11 of the Insolvency Act 1986: see *Straume v Bradlor* (2000) 2 T.C.L.R. 409, discussed above. This decision makes sense in the context of an administration where the aim of s.11 is to provide a breathing space or respite from creditor pressure. In the bankruptcy context the situation is not so clear.

(1) One aim of the set aside procedure is to deal with a debtor's contention that he does not owe the sum demanded. Challenges can be made to an adjudicator which cannot be made to a judge, e.g. that his appointment was invalid.

(2) Adjudication is unusual in its intentionally provisional nature.

(3) There is also the practical point that given the complexity of construction contracts as well as the law and practice of adjudication, having to open up an adjudication decision could make life very difficult for the bankruptcy court.

A judge treated an adjudicator's decision as if it were a judgment or order in *George Parke v Fenton* and his approach was followed in *Mohammed v Bowles*. Perhaps these cases rest on an analogy between an adjudication decision and an order for interim payment under CPR Pt.25. In *Maxwell v Bishopsgate Investment* (*The Times*, February 11, 1993) such an order was held to be sufficient to found a bankruptcy petition. See also *Cox v Bankside* [1995] 2 Lloyd's Rep. 437.

12–029 On the other hand there is authority for the proposition that adjudication is not a proceeding: *Austin Hall v Buckland Securities* [2001] B.L.R. 272 at para.35. In *David McLean v Swansea Housing* [2002] B.L.R. 125, the court observed:

> "An action to enforce an adjudicator's decision is an action to enforce the right or liability which has been upheld by the decision" (at para.17, *per* Judge Humphrey LLoyd Q.C.).

In other words, the decision does not create a new cause of action in its own right. On this view, a decision on its own, without the backing of an order under Pt.24, cannot be a judgment or order and it is open to the bankruptcy registrar to go behind it.

Some bankruptcy judges have been prepared to go behind adjudication decisions. The issue was not specifically addressed in *Oakley v Airclear Environmental* [2002] C.I.L.L. 1824, but Etherton J. embarked on a detailed analysis of the decision and declared it a nullity. By inference, therefore, the court did not consider itself bound by the decision for the purpose of the set aside application. Indeed, by asking whether the decision was made within the adjudicator's jurisdiction it performed the same function as a court hearing a summary judgment application. Further support for this view comes from *Galliford (UK) Ltd v Markel Capital* [2003] All E.R. (D) 303, in which it was held, in the context of a claim under the Third Parties (Rights Against Insurers) Act 1930, that an adjudicator's decision was not sufficient to establish liability so as to enforce an indemnity.

If an adjudicator's decision is a judgment or order, a disputed claim based on it has to go to the hearing of the petition. On balance, for the purposes of r.6.5(4), it seems unjust for this to happen in all adjudication cases especially where, as in *Oakley v Airclear Environmental*, the decision is a nullity. The set aside application seems to be the better forum to enquire into the decision's validity.

It can be also argued that the summary judgment of an adjudication decision is of a different kind from the judgment or order contemplated by the practice direction because the court will grant summary judgment of decisions which are patently wrong provided they were made within the adjudicator's jurisdiction. Pending resolution of the conflicts in the case law, the following appears to be the position:

1. The effect of an adjudicator's decision may be either to create a debt (e.g. by crystallising a claim for damages) or to reinforce a debt arising under the contract by obliging the debtor to pay it before any dispute over it has been finally determined.
2. A creditor can seek to enforce payment of the adjudication debt by serving a statutory demand without having first obtained summary judgment in respect of it.
3. If he does, he runs the risk that the decision is not a judgment or order within r.6.5(4), allowing the debtor to re-run before the bankruptcy registrar arguments which had been rejected by the adjudicator.
4. In that situation, the immunity from challenge of patently wrong decisions would not apply to applications to set aside demands in the bankruptcy court.

5. A personal statutory demand based on an adjudication decision may therefore be set aside if it can be shown that the adjudicator exceeded his jurisdiction.
6. If the decision has been enforced by an order for summary judgment, or is otherwise treated as a judgment or order, the debt cannot be disputed but the demand can still be set aside under the grounds contained in subsections (a) or (d).
7. It is possible that a demand could be set aside under subsection (d) if the court which granted summary judgment considered that the adjudicator's decision was patently wrong even though made within his jurisdiction.
8. If the debtor applied to the court for a declaration that the adjudicator lacked jurisdiction before the hearing of his application to set aside the demand, then the latter may be dismissed or adjourned pending the hearing of the former.
9. The same will apply where the debtor is actively pursuing substantive proceedings in relation to the issues heard by the adjudicator.

8. Company statutory demands and petitions

Injunction refused

In *Re a Company (No. 1299 of 2001)* [2001] C.I.L.L. 1746, a contractor applied for an injunction restraining a subcontractor from presenting a winding up petition based on a claim for a certified sum. After the final date for payment, the contractor had been informed by the employer that there were defects, and that unspecified materials had been used by the subcontractor. Although both allegations were denied, the contractor terminated the subcontract and engaged other subcontractors to complete the work. **12–030**

The court (David Donaldson Q.C.) refused to grant the injunction.

(1) By failing to serve a withholding notice within the time limit, the contractor had lost its right to dispute the debt on the grounds of abatement or set-off.

(2) Although evidence in support of the cross-claim was "somewhat meagre", the court appears to have accepted that it passed the test of "genuine and serious" and overtopped the claim.

(3) The "pay now, litigate later" policy of the construction legislation was not a special circumstance for making a winding up order. *Re Bayoil* concerned a similar regime.

(4) The contractor was able to litigate its cross-claim, in that it could have commenced an adjudication and probably obtained a decision before the hearing of its application for an injunction.

The finding that the contractor had been able to litigate its cross-claim was apparently based on the assumption that adjudication is a form of litigation. In *Medlock Products v SCC Construction* (unreported, July 13, 2006) Judge

Weeks Q.C., the court specifically relied on the lack of a withholding notice as support for its conclusion that the contractor's cross-claims were not genuine and serious. The absence of the notice could not be a special circumstance within *Re Bayoil* (para.22).

Another case in this area is also somewhat problematic. In *Guardi Shoes v Datum Contracts* [2003] C.I.L.L. 1934, the court refused an application by an employer to restrain the advertisement of a contractor's petition. The works had been completed but the employer withheld the final sum alleging defects and refused the contractor access to remedy them. The contractor had taken every step to recover payment: it had made a claim, obtained an adjudicator's decision, obtained summary judgment, accepted part payment by instalments, had served a statutory demand, and finally it had issued a petition. Conversely, the employer had not pursued its cross-claim until very late, or fully quantified it, and had pleaded short term financial difficulty as an excuse for non-payment of sums admitted due. Ferris J. held that the cross-claim was "not obviously without substance" but he was "not in the least convinced" that it would equal or exceed the petition debt and therefore dismissed the application.

The judgment could have ended there but Ferris J. concluded by saying that "the most important factor" was that the employer had been able to litigate its cross-claim but had failed to do so. For him it was "of crucial importance" that the employer had failed to serve a withholding notice in respect of its cross-claim. However, service of a notice clearly could not amount to litigation. It may be that the court had in mind the employer's failure to adjudicate its defects claim, treating adjudication as litigation for this purpose. It is questionable how much weight should be placed on a company's failure to serve a withholding notice in this context.

This case is a clear indication that the Companies Court expects the parties to a construction contract to use the adjudication procedure or risk being penalised if they seek its protection without having done so. The difficulty in practice is that the referring party defines the scope of the adjudication and it may be difficult for the responding party to bring in its cross-claim.

Injunction granted

12–031 In *Re Environmental Services* (14 November 2001, Hart J.) a sub-subcontractor issued a winding up petition against a subcontractor in respect of an unpaid invoice without having previously gone to adjudication, applied for summary judgment or served a statutory demand. The contract fell within the 1996 Act. The court was satisfied that the subcontractor had a genuine and serious cross-claim for delay and defects. The main contactor had made a claim against the subcontractor which the subcontractor intended to pass on to the petitioner. The most difficult area once again was the question of inability to litigate. The subcontractor had not taken proceedings on its cross-claim because of its mistaken belief that the petitioner's claim was not due until the end of the defects liability period.

On the court's construction of the contract, the claim was interim in nature and the subcontractor had failed to serve the requisite withholding notice in respect of its cross-claims. The subcontractor asked the petitioner to bear with it while it disputed the main contractor's claim. The subcontractor did not know the quantum of the claim being made against it by the main contractor until shortly before the hearing. The petition was issued while the parties were in discussion about the petitioner's liability for parts of the main contractor's claim. The quantum of the subcontractor's claim against the petitioner had increased in the months preceding the application to the court.

Hart J. was "narrowly satisfied" that the subcontractor had not had a reasonable opportunity to litigate its cross-claim "and, which may be a different test, has not acted unreasonably in not having litigated it as at the date of the petition". He agreed with the view expressed in *Re a Company (No. 1299 of 2001)* [2001] C.I.L.L. 1746 (see above) that the "pay now, litigate later" regime of the construction legislation was not in itself a special circumstance for making a winding up order. The court implied that 'litigate' in this context could mean "take proceedings in court, arbitration or adjudication" (pp. 14, 16 of transcript). The court restrained advertisement and dismissed the petition.

9. International comparisons

In Australia, the procedure under the Corporations Act 2001 is for a corporate debtor to apply to the court to set aside the statutory demand. There is now a significant body of case law in which demands based on adjudication decisions have been set aside on the basis of a *bona fide* dispute or genuine cross-claim (see Hayford 2005, 350). Similarly, an adjudication decision is not seen as "an accurate predictor of the outcome of a fully prepared hearing" for the purposes of an application for a freezing order: *Walter Construction v The Robbins Company* [2004] NSWSC 549 at para.30, *per* McDougall J. **12–032**

The position seems to be different in New Zealand. Under s.79 of the Construction Contracts Act 2002, the paying party cannot set off against a construction debt without having obtained judgment on the cross-claim. In *10 Gilmer Ltd v Tracer Interiors* [2005] NZHC 332, a contractor served a demand for the balance due under the last four of 12 payment claims. The employer disputed the amount claimed and asserted a right to liquidated damages but had not served the payment schedule required by the Act in time so as to prevent the claim becoming a debt due. It also contended that the contractor had not completed its maintenance obligations and provided guarantees. The employer did not file sufficient evidence of solvency and the court refused to set aside the demand on the basis that the employer had not shown a *bona fide* dispute.

The amount of a demand was reduced in *Jian Hua Property v Freemont Design & Construction* [2006] NZHC 77, on the basis that it included a claim for loss of profit, following a consensual termination, which fell outside the scope of the construction legislation. In *Freemont Design & Construction v Natures View Joinery* [2006] NZHC 866, a subcontractor served a demand on a contractor to enforce an adjudication decision. The contractor applied to set it aside arguing defects and delay but both grounds had been put in issue in the adjudication. There was a disputed termination under the main contract. The court refused to set aside the demand. It seems that the court treated the construction legislation as limiting the cross-claims that could properly be brought into account on the application to set aside. It may be significant that the contractor had not particularised its cross-claim.

10. Adjudication and insolvency risk

12–033 From the beginning, the court has taken a purposive view of the Housing Grants, Construction and Regeneration Act 1996. The judges want to make it work and have repeatedly denied that the policy of the Act is to transfer or reallocate insolvency risk as apportioned by the parties: *Total M and E Services v ABB Building Technologies* [2002] C.I.L.L. 1857 at paras.49 and 52; *Rainford House v Cadogan* [2001] B.L.R. 416 at para.9. The aim of the Act, as they see it, is to assist cash flow in the industry by preventing disputes from causing delays to payment. Adjudication is an intervention which allows the payment process to continue by temporarily resolving the dispute:

> "Those who consider and make policy for the building industry, including the government, have taken a general view over the years that a temporary balance should in appropriate circumstances fall in favour of those who claim payment, at the temporary expense if necessary of those who pay" (*Pegram Shopfitters v Tally Weijl* [2004] B.L.R. 65 at para.2, *per* May L.J.).

It is worth noting the repetition of "temporary". Similarly, the court views the withholding notice procedure as if it were something quite straightforward and legally neutral in effect. Consider these comments from the Court of Appeal in *Rupert Morgan Building v Jervis* [2004] B.L.R. 18:

> "The principal disadvantage of the statutory scheme from the client's point of view is that if he has overpaid he is at risk from insolvency of the builder. But the risk is one which he can avoid by checking the certificate and giving a timeous withholding notice (para.15, *per* Jacob L.J.). There is . . . nothing irrevocable about the section 111 process . . . It has no legal effect, even presumptively, on the true incidence of liability" (para.17, *per* Sedley L.J.).

While these views may be correct statements of the law, the question arises whether they accurately represent the nature of adjudication as it manifests in practice. They can also be contrasted with the quotation from *Bouygues v Dahl-Jensen* in para.12–004 above, and with the following:

> "The enforcement of an adjudicator's decision through the courts might put one party into liquidation or bankruptcy or save the other from a similar fate. An adjudicator's decision may be at least as important as a decision of a court making an order for a temporary injunction or for a payment on account:" *Austin Hall Building v Buckland Securities* [2001] B.L.R. 272 at para.43, *per* Judge Peter Bowsher Q.C.

One unintended consequence of the Act is that an adjudication decision may stimulate the provision of additional security. In *SGS Projects v Ross* [2005] EWHC 441, for example, such decisions became reinforced by the giving of solicitor's undertakings and the making of a charging order.

It is a theme of this book that security (whether for payment or for performance) appears in the construction industry in three ways: formal, contractual and procedural. It is the conjunction of these three types of security that matters rather than any single device. There are dozens of terms and procedural steps which individually may count for little but, when taken together, can give the parties to a construction contract substantial protection against insolvency (Davis 2001). Of these, one of the most important is the right of set-off. Any interference with rights of set-off has a significant effect on the overall balance of security between the parties.

If the contractor is insolvent, the employer may be able to obtain a stay of execution of summary judgment on the contractor's claim, but there appears to be no reported case in the nine years since the Act came into force of a stay being granted where the claimant is informally as opposed to formally insolvent. The question arises whether the court is applying too high a standard on stay applications because of the duty it feels to implement the policy behind the Act. Although failure to serve a withholding notice in time may appear to be a simple enough lapse, as a result of the court's approach to summary judgment applications inroads have been made into the balance of security effected by the standard forms. Consider for example *Northern Developments v J & J Nichol* [2000] B.L.R. 158 and *Re a Company (No. 1299 of 2001)* [2001] C.I.L.L. 1746, in which it was impossible to serve a notice as the events in question only occurred or came to the company's notice after the final date for payment. It seems likely that these cases need to be reconsidered in the light of *Melville Dundas v George Wimpey* [2007] 1 W.L.R. 1136 (See Ch.14).

The termination clause in the standard forms is an important informal **12–034** security. The case law on the construction legislation has revealed just how important is the suspension of payment on termination. The Court of Appeal in *Ferson Contractors v Levolux* [2003] B.L.R. 118, attempted to destroy the security offered by this term without giving proper reasons for its decision other than a brief reference to the policy of the Act. In holding that the suspension of payment provision does not require a withholding notice to be effective, the House of Lords in *Melville Dundas v George Wimpey* has reasserted the validity of contractual security. This case has shown that the Act has limits. The balance of insolvency risk achieved by the standard forms has been respected. Ironically, service of a withholding notice is the mirror image of receipt of a receiver's notice of appointment. The first confirms a debtor's right not to pay by setting off its cross-claim; the second aims to prevent the debtor acquiring any further rights of set-off after that date.

It is now essential for the parties to a construction contract to know how to operate the adjudication procedure. This is not a straightforward matter as the sheer volume of cases implies. The fact that many enforcement applications go over the same ground suggests that there remains a good deal of uncertainty especially in critical areas such as whether a dispute has arisen, its scope, and whether the adjudicator has acted within his remit. Moreover, what was intended as a "rough and ready" procedure "to provide a quick, easy and cheap provisional answer" has "developed into an elaborate and expensive procedure which is wholly confrontational . . ." (*AWG Construction v Rockingham* [2004] EWHC 888 at para.122, *per* Judge Toulmin Q.C.) Temporary finality is a paradox which is stretched to the limit when a creditor bases a petition for winding up or bankruptcy on an adjudication debt. As the court has stated, it is one thing to enforce an adjudication decision to foster cash flow but quite another to use it to force a person into formal insolvency. The cases reported so far show the bankruptcy and companies courts struggling to fit adjudication into the established criteria for setting aside an individual statutory demand or granting an injunction restraining the presentation or advertisement of a petition.

If an adjudication decision is interpreted as a judgment or order for the purposes of the *Practice Direction (Insolvency Proceedings) 1999* it means that a temporary decision reached after only a few weeks, on limited evidence, and by a person without legal qualifications, could lead straight to the hearing of a bankruptcy petition. It must be doubtful whether such a result was intended by the Act.

The other area of difficulty stems from the requirement in *Re Bayoil* that a debtor applying to restrain the presentation of a winding up petition must have been unable to litigate its cross-claim. In view of the nature of such an application, it is unsatisfactory that there is disagreement at Court of Appeal level as to whether this element is necessary. It has encouraged technical arguments which have led to confusion. In *Re Bayoil* itself, arbitration was not regarded as litigation for this purpose whereas in the construction cases discussed above, arbitration, adjudication and even a withholding notice have been interpreted as litigation. If the criterion were abandoned, the court could focus on the point at issue: is the cross-claim genuine and serious and does it exceed the amount of the claim? The court remains free to test the genuineness of the cross-claim by examining how the claimant has acted in relation to it. Active pursuit tends to support the view that it has merit; inactivity suggests otherwise; but such inferences can be rebutted by evaluating the debtor's reasons in either case.

To return to the questions asked at the beginning of this chapter, it does appear that adjudication and the withholding notice constitute valuable procedural securities which if skilfully employed can alter the balance of insolvency risk allocated by the contract. There is a conflict between the construction and the insolvency legislation which goes beyond the brake effected by the moratoria in some insolvency procedures on a creditor's ability to refer a dispute to adjudication at any time.

Chapter 13

Formal Insolvency

1. Introduction

Informal insolvency, the inability to pay debts as defined by s.123 of the Insolvency Act 1986, was considered in Ch.8. This chapter concerns formal insolvency procedures and how they work in the construction industry. There is little empirical research but it seems that construction insolvencies can pose special challenges to insolvency practitioners. There is, however, no necessary reason why any of the available informal or formal procedures cannot be used successfully in the case of a contracting company. In cases where the directors leave it too late or where the company has no viable business, there may be little that can be done. But in the absence of these factors, there is a range of possibilities. **13–001**

There are different procedures for individuals and companies. For an individual, the main alternatives are bankruptcy and individual voluntary arrangement. For a company, they are liquidation, administration, administrative receivership, and company voluntary arrangement (see generally Totty and Moss 1986, Goode 2005). This book focuses on corporate insolvency procedures. The use of administrative receivership is now in sharp decline as a result of the Enterprise Act 2002. The basic pattern of formal insolvency is found in the liquidation procedure and for that reason it is proposed to consider it first. Unless otherwise stated, references are to the Insolvency Act 1986.

2. Liquidation

Legal background

Liquidation is also known as winding up: **13–002**

> "The winding up of a company is a form of collective execution by all its creditors against all its available assets. The resolution or order for winding up divests the company of the beneficial interest in its assets. They become a fund which the company thereafter holds in trust to discharge its liabilities": (*Buchler v Talbot* [2004] 2 A.C. 298 at para.28 *per* Lord Hoffmann).

There are several different types: members' voluntary liquidation, creditors' voluntary liquidation, and compulsory liquidation. A members' voluntary liquidation is not strictly an insolvency procedure. It is most often used as part of a group reorganisation. The directors swear a statutory declaration that the company will be able to pay its debts in full within a maximum of twelve months after the start of the liquidation. The shareholders (members) then pass a resolution to wind up the company and appoint a liquidator. If it turns out that the company cannot pay its debts in full within that time, the members' voluntary liquidation will normally be converted into a creditors' voluntary liquidation.

In *Re William Thorpe* (1989) 5 B.C.C. 156, a contractor whose assets consisted of freehold property, debts and work in progress, went into members' voluntary liquidation. The directors estimated in their declaration that the company would have a surplus of assets over liabilities of £100,000. As a result of trading losses during the liquidation, the company incurred net liabilities of £600,000 and the court ordered that the company be placed in compulsory liquidation. The assessment of contingent and prospective liabilities poses special difficulties in this context (Simmons 1996). The directors can be liable for a fine or imprisonment if their declaration is not made on reasonable grounds: s.89(4) of the Insolvency Act 1986.

13–003 The court can make a winding up order where it is just and equitable to do so irrespective of insolvency: s.122(1)(g) of the Insolvency Act 1986. This may occur in cases of deadlock between the directors of a family company: see e.g. *Guerinoni v Argyle Concrete and Quarry Supplies* [1999] WASC 1050, where an order was refused partly in view of the petitioner's behaviour; and *Re Jayflex Construction* [2004] 2 B.C.L.C. 145. Under s.459 of the Companies Act 1985, the court may also grant relief on the basis that the affairs of the company have been conducted in an unfairly prejudicial manner. Both procedures were invoked in *Re Botherill Builders* (unreported, April 25, 2001, Rattee J.).

Creditors' voluntary liquidation is the most common form of winding up. It is initiated by the directors convening a board meeting at which they resolve that the company cease trading and call separate meetings of shareholders and creditors under s.98 of the Insolvency Act 1986. In practice these are usually held on the same day. The shareholders pass a resolution that the company be wound up and appoint an insolvency practitioner as liquidator. The directors prepare a statement of affairs for the creditors who either confirm the shareholders' nominee or make their own choice of insolvency practitioner as liquidator. Voting for this purpose is carried out by reference to the amount of the creditors' debts. In construction cases, this can be contentious since the directors may consider that a creditor's claim is invalid or the company has a cross-claim which equals or exceeds it. If the creditor's claim is unliquidated, it is the duty of the chairman of the meeting to place an estimated value on it for voting purposes. Not uncommonly, in the absence of firm valuation evidence or proof of validitythe estimate is set at a nominal sum.

Compulsory liquidations are commenced by the issue of a winding up petition against the company. This is usually filed by a creditor, but it is open to the company or the directors to do so. A petition is usually presented on the ground that a company is unable to pay its debts. This can be proved by failure to comply with a statutory demand for payment of a debt exceeding £750 or by showing that a company's liabilities exceed its assets. The procedure is quite simple. The petition is listed for hearing on a date about six weeks after presentation at court and is served at the registered office of the company. The petitioning creditor allows at least seven days after service of the petition before advertising it in the London Gazette. The advertisement must be placed at least seven days before the hearing.

The court is prepared to waive procedural defects in certain circumstances. Other creditors are entitled to serve notice on the petitioner indicating their intention to support or oppose the petition. If the petition is opposed, it is usually adjourned so as to allow time for submissions to be made. The consequences of a petition being filed are that disposals of property will be invalid from the date of filing if a winding up order is made. Hence, the company's cheques will be dishonoured immediately. **13–004**

On a winding up order being made, the official receiver assumes office as liquidator. If the company has assets, a meeting of creditors is convened to consider whether an insolvency practitioner should be appointed in the place of the official receiver. This also applies where there is cause for concern about the conduct of the directors or the possibility of claims against them and others. A compulsory liquidation follows the same course as a creditors' voluntary liquidation with the exception that in a compulsory liquidation no proceedings can be issued against the company without the permission of the court.

Once confirmed in office, the liquidator will:

- identify the company's property as defined by s.436 of the Insolvency Act 1986 and have it valued;
- deal with property claims by third parties, e.g. where goods are supplied subject to retention of title (Ch.7) or property is held in trust (Chs 9 and 10);
- check on the validity and registration of security granted by the company (Ch.2);
- invite creditors to submit details of their money claims (known as "proofs of debt") and either accept or reject them (discussed in the context of liquidation set-off in Ch.18);
- sell the company's property, by novation in the case of ongoing contracts (Ch.15);
- distribute the net proceeds of sale to the creditors in accordance with an order of priority known as "the statutory scheme" (see below);
- investigate the conduct of the directors and, if appropriate, file a report on their fitness to act as such in the future (Ch.21); and
- pursue claims to recover property of the company misappropriated in the run up to the liquidation (Ch.20).

It is a fundamental principle of insolvency law that ordinary unsecured creditors are treated *pari passu*, on the same footing: s.107 of the Insolvency Act 1986, r.4.181 of the Insolvency Rules 1986. In practice, the law has developed an order of priority of payment known as the statutory scheme:

1. Debts secured by a fixed charge and the costs of enforcing the charge are payable out of the proceeds of the charged asset. Any shortfall is an unsecured debt (category 5 below); any surplus is added to the company's property and applied in the following order.
2. The expenses of the winding up. Currently the liquidator's own expenses are not payable in priority to floating charge debts. The expenses will

have priority when s.176ZA of the Insolvency Act 1986 comes into effect, but even then not over the prescribed part (see below).

3. Preferential debts, now restricted by Sch.6 of the Insolvency Act 1986 to employment claims, contributions to occupational pension schemes, and levies on coal and steel production. Sums owed to HM Revenue & Customs, such as PAYE, VAT and deductions in respect of construction industry subcontractors, no longer have preferential status.
4. Debts secured by floating charges, with the exception of the "prescribed part", a proportion of floating charge realisations which now has to be made available for payment of unsecured debts: s.176A of the Insolvency Act 1986.
5. Unsecured debts.
6. Interest on preferential and unsecured debts.
7. Debts or other sums due from the company to its shareholders (e.g. unpaid dividends).
8. Any surplus is distributed to shareholders in accordance with their respective rights and interests.

Each class of debt has to be paid in full before the next class becomes entitled to share in the estate. The "prescribed part" is defined as a percentage of the company's net property after satisfying the preferential creditors in full: Insolvency Act 1986 (Prescribed Part) Order 2003 (SI 2003/2097). Where the net property is less than £10,000, the liquidator may allow 50 per cent as the prescribed part if he is satisfied that the cost of making a distribution is not disproportionate to the benefits. If the net property is in excess of £10,000, then 50 per cent of the first £10,000 and 20 per cent of the excess is available subject to a maximum prescribed part of £600,000.

When the liquidation process has been completed, the liquidator files a final account and return with the registrar of companies and the company is deemed to be dissolved three months later: s.201 of the Insolvency Act 1986. It is possible for the liquidator or an interested person to apply to the court under s.651 of the Companies Act 1985 for an order restoring the company to the register in certain situations, e.g. where an asset comes to light after dissolution. On dissolution, any property which has not been distributed by the liquidator passes to the Crown as *bona vacantia*. Such property automatically re-vests in the company if the dissolution is set aside and the company restored to the register.

Application to the industry

13–005 Where there are contracts which are not charged, or realisation is left to the liquidator, he carries out a review similar to that undertaken by administrative receivers (see para.13–012 below). A quantity surveyor is appointed to appraise the contracts and, if appropriate, employers are invited to accept novations (Ch.15). This rarely occurs in practice because novations are more conveniently arranged through administration or a company voluntary arrangement. A voluntary liquidator has power to trade under s.165(3) of the

Insolvency Act 1986 so far as may be necessary for the beneficial winding up of the company and may decide to complete ongoing contracts: see *Re Asphaltic Wood Pavement* (1885) 30 Ch. D. 216, and *Asphaltic Limestone v City of Glasgow* [1907] S.C. 463, noted in Ch.18. Liquidation trading requires the sanction of the court on a compulsory winding up: s.167 of the Insolvency Act 1986. If ongoing trading is a possibility, the liquidator is now more likely to apply for an administration order pursuant to para.38 of Sch.B1.

In jurisdictions such as Hong Kong which do not have an equivalent to administration, a provisional liquidator may be appointed to continue trading pending the agreement of a scheme of arrangement. For example, in *Re Tai Kam Construction* [2004] HKCFI 740, an approved contractor on two public works lists experienced cash flow difficulties and applied for the appointment of provisional liquidators after a creditor issued a winding up petition against it. There were two ongoing government contracts with up to eight months to completion. The company normally paid 92 per cent of receipts to sub-contractors and kept the balance for itself. It would benefit from the stay against the issue and continuance of proceedings that provisional liquidation would effect. There was a possibility of putting together a scheme of arrangement that would result in higher distributions to creditors than on a winding up.

An insolvency practitioner estimated that on a liquidation the preferential creditors might receive a dividend of 10 per cent, while a scheme might enable them to be paid in full together with a dividend of 20 per cent to ordinary unsecured creditors. The income forecast adopted in their estimate was regarded as conservative. The company's listings might assist in negotiating a sale of the shares to another contractor. One had already expressed interest. The prospective liquidators agreed to cap their fees in advance at a specific figure. On that basis, Barma J. concluded that a winding up order would certainly be made on the creditor's petition and that, on a balance of convenience, it was appropriate to appoint provisional liquidators.

By contrast, in *Re Cheery City Contractors* [2004] HKCFI 336, Kwan J. **13–006** refused to adjourn a winding up petition to allow the company to seek the sanction of the court to a scheme of arrangement. The company specialised in acting as a subcontractor for port works and site formation but was not on the list of approved contractors. The company's two major subcontracts were with the same contractor. Both had been terminated but the validity of the terminations was disputed by the company which had referred claims for the value of work in progress to arbitration. Both claims were resisted. A scheme had been approved by over 80 per cent of the value of admitted claims. The contractor's proof was only admitted at 10 per cent of its value.

The scheme provided for a loan to prosecute the claims but there was no fund to cover costs. Any fruits of the arbitrations would fall outside the scheme and the expected dividend to scheme creditors from the sale of the company's undertaking was minimal. Despite this the creditors' claims would be totally discharged, including apparently the counterclaims of the major creditor. The proposal was presented in a misleading way. Owing to the structure of the Hong Kong economy, there are many reported cases of insolvency applications concerning contractors. These two cases are illustrative of some of the practical problems which arise.

A provisional liquidator appointed over a house builder continued trading in the Australian case of *Re Avonwood Homes* [2002] VSC 147. On his appointment there were over five hundred houses in various states of completion; and deposits had been received on a further two hundred on which work had not commenced. With the authorisation of the court, the liquidator entered into an agreement with HIH General and Casualty which had provided warranty insurance cover to purchasers similar to the NHBC scheme in the UK (see Emden, 9th edition, IV, para.792). The insurer agreed to provide working capital to finance the repair and completion of properties covered by its policies and to indemnify the liquidator against subcontractors' claims. It was believed that, although some houses would be completed at a loss, the agreement would result in a greater return to the unsecured creditors. Completion of all houses was scheduled to take place within six months.

13–007 Unfortunately, before the work could be completed, the insurer itself became insolvent and it was necessary for the provisional liquidator to apply for the winding up of the builder. He was then appointed liquidator, but it appears he was unable to continue trading, progress payments from purchasers being insufficient to cover the company's costs. Several hundred houses were insured by a different insurer which refused to deal with the liquidator. In order to realise some benefit for the company, the liquidator granted a licence to another builder to use the company's plans and drawings under which a fixed fee was payable by the builder for each house completed, but there was no novation and it was up to the builder to negotiate separately with each purchaser. The insurer argued unsuccessfully that the liquidator's agreement with the builder was in breach of the company's policy obligation not to carry out rectification works without its consent.

In practice, the liquidator's role may be limited to selling the company's tangible property and collecting debts on completed contracts, by taking proceedings if necessary. A major difficulty is in funding the legal costs involved. In *Re Apollo Engineering* [2003] CSOH 329, the company, Apollo Engineering, was a sub-subcontractor to James Scott who were mechanical and electrical subcontractors for works on an explosives handling jetty. After the company went into compulsory liquidation, the parties referred disputes to arbitration in which the company advanced claims totalling £2.6 million and Scott counterclaimed for £1 million. The liquidator was removed after the creditors rejected his recommendation to accept an offer of settlement from Scott of £330,000. He retained £40,000 to meet any order for costs that might subsequently be made against him by the arbitrator. The company then agreed a voluntary arrangement after one of the creditors, who was also a shareholder, agreed to lend sufficient funds to enable the company to pay the preferential creditors and finance the arbitration.

It was a term of the arrangement that the supervisor would apply to the court to stay (or sist in Scottish terminology) the liquidation so that the arbitration could be conducted by the company's directors, without having to provide an indemnity for costs to the liquidator. James Scott opposed the stay on the ground that it deprived it of costs protection in the form of the liquidator's personal liability. In staying the liquidation, Lord Hamilton was mindful of the arbitrator's power to order security for costs. Another option would be for the liquidator to assign the claim for value or a share in the eventual proceeds.

13–008 Liquidators may lack the documentary evidence needed to prove the company's claim. The company may not have kept adequate records or they may have been lost or taken away by staff in the run-up to the liquidation. In *JB Building Services v Multiplex Constructions* [1999] QSC 179 a liquidator appointed over a steelwork subcontractor claimed sums due, retention and damages for repudiation and applied to the court for disclosure of documents. The contractor objected, contending the application was a "fishing expedition" and applied to strike out part of the claim as insufficiently particularised. Wilson J. refused to strike out but ordered that the particulars be filed in 14 days and the documents provided in a further 14 days. He went through each category and ordered disclosure of programming schedules, site diaries and variation summaries, in each case limited to specific periods. He refused to order disclosure of certain correspondence, quality assurance records, site manning registers, structural drawings and the drawings register, mainly on grounds of relevance.

If the company is part of a group, it may also be necessary to ascertain who is the correct claimant. In *W. Cook Builders v Lumbers* [2007] SASC 20, the Supreme Court of South Australia considered a small family group. Following a reorganisation, it consisted of the claimant (Builders) which carried out building work, W Cook & Sons (Sons), which specialised in joinery and carpentry, and Portrush Traders which employed all the staff and performed administrative functions for the group. There was a common bank account, and all internal transactions were conducted by journal entry.

The claim brought by the liquidator of Builders was for the balance of the cost of constructing a large house, i.e. mainly for sums payable to subcontractors who were creditors in the liquidation. There was no written contract but it was clear that Sons had made the original agreement with the employer, who was unaware that the work was mainly done by Builders. The liquidator argued that the benefit of the contract had been equitably assigned to Builders but failed as there was insufficient evidence of intention to assign.

Vanstone J. (dissenting) considered that it was open to the court below to find that this building contract was personal to the parties and therefore unassignable in any event (para.116). Builders could not sue in its own right as it was not licensed under state legislation. But the liquidator succeeded on an alternative claim for a *quantum meruit* based on unjust enrichment which could be advanced even without a licence. (For reasons unexplained in the judgment, Sons had admitted that no further payments were due from the employer.)

The case contains a useful discussion of restitution in the context of a construction contract. Compare the case discussed in Klein (2007), of a contractor who carried out refurbishment work at a pub for a licensee who absconded without paying for it. The brewery repossessed the pub together with the benefit of the builder's work but rejected any liability in restitution.

Leave is required to bring proceedings against the company if it is in **13–009**
compulsory liquidation: s.130 of the Insolvency Act 1986. In *Re B+B Construction* [2003] HKCFI 322 the company acted as a design and build piling contractor in connection with the construction of six 41–storey blocks of flats. When the superstructure was nearing completion, settlement to the foundations became apparent which the employer attributed to defects in construction and the falsification of the piling records. The employer's claim was estimated by the liquidators at $500 million. Creditors' claims in general exceeded $2.5 billion. The company had a contractor's all risks policy which indemnified it against legal costs up to $10 million. There was evidence that it also had the benefit of global third party liability insurance taken out by its ultimate parent, Bilfinger and Berger, in Germany with indemnity cover of up to $500 million. The employer argued that if its proof were rejected it would appeal to the court and that, in any event, the nature of its claim was outside the usual sphere of a liquidator in adjudicating proofs of debt. Kwan J. of the Hong Kong Court of First Instance agreed and granted leave to the employer.

A liquidator may apply for an order for the oral examination of a director under s.236 of the Insolvency Act 1986. This may be necessary where the books and records of the company are missing: see *Re Wing Fai Construction Co.* [2004] HKCFI 208. In that case there was also evidence that the company's computer systems had been "tampered with" before the liquidation. In *Re B+B Construction*, orders were made against some of the directors to enable the liquidator to investigate a transaction between the company and its immediate parent whereby a loan of $200 million was discharged and all of the company's plant and machinery sold.

Companies working in the UK construction industry which appear to have gone directly into liquidation include the insurer Builders Accident, which went into provisional liquidation in 1998, Declan Kelly (1990), Zimmcor, Clifford Barnett (1991), Nugent (1994), Fastrack (1999), Nomad AED, Bridgeway (2000), Protec (2004), Fast Track (employment agency) (2006), and Pluswall Facades (2007).

3. Administrative receivership

Effect of the Enterprise Act 2002

13–010 The appointment of a receiver has until recently been the most common means of enforcing a charge (Lightman and Moss 2007). An administrative receiver is a receiver appointed under the terms of a floating charge granted over the whole or substantially the whole of the assets and undertaking of the business (see Ch.2). As a result of amendments to the Insolvency Act 1986 made by s.250 of the Enterprise Act 2002, administrative receivership as a remedy is now only available where the floating charge was created before September 15, 2003: s.72A of the Insolvency Act 1986.

There are a few exceptions, notably where the charge was granted, among other things, in connection with project finance deals (where the debt is at least £50 million), public-private partnership projects, utilities, and urban regeneration projects, all of which must include step-in rights. The power to appoint an administrative receiver is not a step-in right for this purpose: *Cabvision v Feetum* [2006] Ch. 585. If a security granted before that date is a "qualifying floating charge" the holder now has the option of appointing an administrator in lieu of an administrative receiver. As administration has certain advantages for construction companies, this course is quite likely to be followed even where the holder is a bank. It follows from this that administrative receivership has virtually ceased to be used as a secured creditor's remedy in the industry.

There are three reasons, however, why it remains necessary to be familiar with it for the foreseeable future. Firstly, there are many charges in existence that were entered into before September 15, 2003. The advantages of administration may be outweighed in an exceptional case by the control afforded to the charge holder by a receivership. Secondly, the exceptions are in the context of major construction projects. Thirdly, a great deal of history, both social and legal, is bound up with the procedure, e.g. it provides the context for the development of the law of novation in the industry. Similarly, what is known as "receivership set-off" is in substance a term for the effect of equitable assignment of the benefit of the construction contract (Ch.18).

"Receivership set-off" will continue to apply where a floating charge is crystallised by the appointment of an administrator. Thus although the introduction of the "prescribed part" (see para.13–002 above) has lowered the charge holder's ranking in the statutory scheme, the charge itself remains an effective way of obtaining rights in the debtor's property as security for payment. The case law in this important area cannot be fully understood without a knowledge of the background. The law relating to receivers appointed under a fixed charge is not affected by the Enterprise Act 2002.

A "qualifying floating charge" is defined as a floating charge over the whole, or substantially the whole, of the company's property, which is created by a document that states that para.14 of Sch.B1 to the Insolvency Act 1986 applies, or which purports to empower the charge holder to appoint an administrator or an administrative receiver of the company. The charge holder cannot appoint an administrator if the charge is not enforceable or either a provisional liquidator or an administrative receiver has already been appointed. If he applies to the court for an administration order, the charge holder does not have to prove that the company is insolvent or about to become so (para.35). These aspects reflect the fact that administration in this case is the means of enforcing a security.

Legal background

Typically, the company is served with a demand for moneys due which is followed within hours by the appointment. Alternatively, the company may invite the charge holder to appoint a receiver. An administrative receiver has full power to carry on the company's business, including the right to bring or defend proceedings in the company's name and collect and get in the company's property: Insolvency Act 1986, Sch.1. Any surplus of the proceeds of sale over the debt plus interest is returned to the company which in theory is free to continue trading. **13–011**

In the case of an administrative receivership, the procedure usually leaves the company as a shell without assets and liquidation follows immediately. The court has jurisdiction to appoint a receiver, e.g. where a creditor has a charge but the document is defective in some way, but the vast majority of receivers are appointed out of court. The holder of a fixed charge takes priority under the "statutory scheme" over preferential creditors, whereas the holder of a floating charge is subordinated to the preferential creditors (see above). The charge will state that the receiver is the agent of the company.

This is an unusual use of agency designed to protect the charge holder. However, the agency ceases if the company enters liquidation: s.44 of the Insolvency Act 1986. Administrative receivers owe a duty to the charge holder, the company, and its guarantors, to obtain the best price but no general duty to the company's creditors: *Downsview Nominees v First City Corp* [1993] 3 All E.R. 626.

The holder of a floating charge has an inchoate interest in every class of asset described in the charge. This is perfected on the appointment of an administrative receiver by an equitable assignment to the charge holder of all the assets falling within the charge at that moment which takes effect by operation of law (Ch.4). The administrative receiver has power to deal with the assets by asserting the charge holder's title as assignee: *Biggerstaff v Rowatt's Wharf* [1896] 2 Ch. 93.

It is important that the charge holder gives notice of assignment as soon as possible to all those owing obligations to the company: see *Alstom Transport v Elequip Projects* [2004] EWHC 2897. This prevents third parties getting a good discharge by paying the company and also, broadly speaking, prevents debtors acquiring enforceable cross-claims against the charge holder as assignee after receipt of the notice (Chs 5 and 18).

Given their different functions, a receivership, whether under a fixed or a floating charge, can exist at the same time as the company is in liquidation. For example, a company might have granted a floating charge to its lending bank and separate fixed charges to project financiers over sites being developed. An unsecured creditor might petition to have the company wound up, the holder of the floating charge may appoint an administrative receiver and the holders of the fixed charges may each appoint a receiver over each site all at the same time. The exception is administration since there can be no administrative receivership or liquidation while an administration order is in force.

Application to the industry

13–012 Although primarily a security enforcement procedure, administrative receivership promotes business rescue since the best price is normally obtained by selling the business as a going concern. The perception of receivers by the industry has, however, largely been a negative one since they are primarily acting in the interests of the banks. Receivers may be appointed after other informal options have been explored and rejected. They were appointed to Conder, for example, in 1992 after attempts to raise working capital failed and the proposed sale of a subsidiary company fell through.

Receivership does not necessarily mean the loss of the name of the company. Bovis novated numerous contracts from Lelliott and formed a new Lelliott division retaining the services of John Lelliott as head of the division. When Sunley Turriff acquired Lilley Construction (Scotland) they preserved the Lilley name and livery and retained 300 of the 500 employees. Even where the company is broken up and its assets and contracts dispersed among a number of different purchasers, there is a chance that jobs will be saved. Where a significant package of contracts is novated to the same purchaser, the prospects are good. In a sense, receivership is a natural process of the industry. "Because of the nature of the building industry, if a company fails it is usually only money that is lost. The basic resources of a skilled labour force, plant and administrative expertise are dissipated to other companies with little or no disruption to the industry as a whole" (Upson 1987, 1).

The ideal scenario for a receiver is to sell the business or novate all the contracts to the same purchaser within a few days of the appointment. This occurred in the receivership of Farr Group in December 1990. The group had 40 current contracts, 34 of which were novated to Amey Construction within a couple of days. "Amey diverted dozens of senior staff to phone all 40 clients and accompany Farr contract staff to site to negotiate terms with the clients' representatives" (*Building*, 17 January 1992). Two hundred of the 400 staff were kept on as a result.

Unless he has already investigated the company and prepared a report on its financial position, a receiver's first action is to identify the company's property and have it valued. This exercise requires specialist advice because it involves issues of asset valuation, quantity surveying and insolvency and construction law. The receiver will therefore assemble a team including a surveyor, a valuer and a lawyer, while at the same time mobilising his own staff to visit the company's offices and sites.

Having taken possession of such books and records as the company may have kept (especially signed building contracts), the receiver establishes a system for logging correspondence, invoices, tender enquiries etc and attempts to reconcile the company's accounts. The receiver also ascertains the whereabouts of the company's motor vehicles, plant, equipment and other assets and arranges to schedule them and have them professionally valued. The surveyor will carry out an appraisal of the company's completed and current contracts to enable the receiver to decide which should be completed, sold or abandoned. The lawyer will advise on the validity of the receiver's appointment and any other legal problem areas. The receiver may also consider entering into new contracts.

The surveyor's contract appraisal is the key exercise (see Ch.16). Priority is **13–013** given to current contracts which are scheduled as short, medium and long term. A complete financial profile of each contract is then prepared showing the net amount, if anything, payable by the employer on completion compared with the cost to complete. The difference between the two represents the receiver's profit or loss as the case may be. Loss-making contracts are likely to be abandoned.

The receiver is aiming to sell the contracts (as a whole if possible) rather than to complete them himself but may be prepared to continue trading in order to preserve their value pending disposal. The surveyor's contract appraisal will ascertain the time and cost required to complete each contract. Marginal contracts may be completed in order to preserve value on other completed contracts with the same employer. The receiver will analyse claims and cross-claims in cost benefit terms and may conclude that it is cheaper to incur a small loss on one contract than to risk the uncertainty, delay and cost of litigation. There may be value remaining in completed contracts which only emerges from a study of the contract documents, e.g. *Powergen Retail v British Sugar* [2006] EWHC 316.

Once a decision has been made to dispose of particular contracts, the receiver decides the value he wants for them. Experienced receivers know which major contractors and subcontractors are interested in making acquisitions and may be assisted in this aspect by their professional advisers. It may be necessary to advertise the sale. Previous tenderers on contracts on which the company is involved should also be contacted. The directors and estimating staff will be able to assist in this connection. Once a list has been compiled, information needs to be assembled and disclosed to potential purchasers on a confidential basis.

After basic heads of terms have been negotiated, they need to be formalised into a binding agreement. The standard procedure is a novation. There are a large number of permutations to novation agreements (see Ch.15). The consideration is sometimes deferred or payable out of profits earned from the contract or the business, whichever has been sold. The possibility of purchaser default makes it particularly important for the receiver to be satisfied with the purchaser's solvency and reputation before formalising terms, otherwise a guarantor may be required. It is worth noting that construction contracts normally contain restrictions on assignment which will be binding on the insolvency practitioner (Ch.4).

Heads of agreement may not be fully comprehensive and there is usually scope for the lawyers for both parties to improve their clients' positions. There is a tension between the need for expedition and the desire for the best possible deal. The receiver may decide that the anticipated receiver's profit in a contract makes it worthwhile building out. The uncertainties in the contracting process mean that this is only done where there is a high probability that the profit will be recovered. The receiver will wish to avoid asking the charge holder to finance building out and will instead attempt to obtain advance payments from the employer in respect of labour and materials. In addition, the employer may be amenable to purchasing materials and entering into subcontracts direct. The receiver may also renegotiate the contract terms to remove or restrict the employer's right of set-off, liquidated damages, retention, maintenance obligations, the payment period and any other term affecting cash flow, profit and liability. All these factors are matters for negotiation depending on the circumstances of the case.

13–014 Receivers are wary of completing current contracts because of the risk of previous over-certification. In such cases, the architect reduces the gross value of the works shown in future certificates. As a consequence, receivers carefully analyse the accuracy of pre-receivership certificates and discuss the situation in detail with the employer. Difficulties are experienced with trade creditors regarding future supplies. These may only be available by paying cash on delivery or on receipt of orders, hence the need to negotiate advance payments from the employer. Problems are also experienced with office and site staff. Motivation is difficult as staff realise that they are working themselves out of employment. The promise of a completion bonus if targets are met alleviates the position.

If the company cannot be sold as a going concern, the receiver turns to the realisation of the value of completed contracts. This involves three assets: the collection of retention, the recovery of final account balances, and claims for loss and expense or damages for breach of contract. A large number of uncollected retentions is a sign of poor financial management. A cost benefit analysis has to be made comparing the investment required in terms of receiver's time costs and professional fees against the amount of the likely judgment and the prospects of enforcement. The absence of a signed contract may indicate that no contract was formed, which would entitle the receiver to recover a reasonable sum for the work done by the company prior to receivership without the risk of set-off by the employer. In view of the widespread use of letters of intent by employers and contractors, this is a significant aspect for receivers to consider. It is at this stage that insolvency practitioners encounter the "presumption against payment" referred to in Ch.3. Construction debtors will exploit the fact that the creditor's resources to enforce payment may be limited, especially if it is in liquidation.

If no interim funding is available, the company may go into liquidation. In *OBG v Allan* [2007] 2 W.L.R. 920 (considered in Ch.14), up to 90 per cent of a contractor's turnover was attributable to one employer. There were 88 contracts between them. The employer suspected it was being overcharged and suspended the company from its list of approved contractors. Work under existing contracts was revalued. This resulted in certificates showing sums due to the employer which would be set off against sums due for future work. At this time, the contractor was undercapitalised and experienced an immediate cash crisis. A subcontractor provided short term debt finance in return for an assignment of security over the company's assets held by a bank. Without cooperation from its major employer, however, the company could not survive and administrative receivers were appointed. When the employer refused to pay a sum the receivers calculated as necessary in order to avoid closing the company down, the company went into voluntary liquidation. Unlike *Re Harris Simons* (1989) B.C.C. 11 considered below, administration was not feasible because the company's major customer was not prepared to defer setting off its cross-claims for overvaluation.

Other construction companies entering receivership have included: Dunning (1989); Farr, Brims, Harry Neal, Rush & Tompkins (1990); Conder, Isis, Turriff, J. A. Elliott, Shepherd Hill, Locker & Riley, Allied Partnership, Graham Wood (1992); Lilley, Budge, McLaughlin & Harvey, Dove Brothers, Thompson Mechanical and Electrical, Lelliott, Tubeworkers, Rees Hough, Clayton Bowmore, Elliott Northern (1993); VAT Watkins, MF Kent, Kentz, Johnson & Bailey (1994); Donelon Tyson (1995); Rawlings (1997); Ruddy, Wolfe (1998); Porter, Beechdale Homes, Fearnley (1999); Ledwood, CJ Sims, MDA (2000); General Building Maintenance, Brunswick Group, Cox Brothers (2001); ASW (steel supplier), Swallow, Stenoak (2002); Elequip Projects, Melville Dundas, Bickerton (2003); Roberts and Partners (engineers) (2004); Dew, Curzon, (2006).

4. Administration

Legal background

Administrations commencing before September 15, 2003 are governed by ss.8–27 of the Insolvency Act 1986. Those commencing after that date are dealt with under Sch.B1 of the Insolvency Act 1986, an amendment added by s.248 of the Enterprise Act 2002. Under the original regime, a company could only enter administration by means of a court order. As from September 15, 2003, there are three ways in which an administrator may be appointed: by the court, by the holder of a qualifying floating charge (see para.13–010 above), and by the company or its directors. **13–015**

A company, its directors, or one or more creditors, may apply to the court for the appointment of an administrator. The court only appoints an administrator if satisfied that the company is, or is likely to become, unable to pay its debts and that administration is reasonably likely to achieve the "statutory purpose" set out in para.3 of Sch.B1 (see below). The applicant must notify any person of his intention to appoint an administrator who has appointed or is in a position to appoint an administrative receiver or who could appoint an administrator.

If the company wishes to appoint an administrator out of court, the directors swear a statutory declaration that the company is, or is likely to become, unable to pay its debts and that it is reasonably likely that administration will achieve the statutory purpose: para.27. In practice, almost all administrators are now appointed by the company out of court (voluntary administrations). This procedure cannot be used by the directors or the company if a winding up petition or administration application is pending, or an administrative receiver is in office, or if within the previous 12 months:

(a) an administration of the company at the instance of the company or its directors has come to an end;

(b) a voluntary arrangement has ended prematurely (e.g. because the company has defaulted in making payments under it); or

(c) a moratorium under Sch.A1 of the Insolvency Act 1986 has ended without a voluntary arrangement having been approved.

The directors or the company must give five business days' prior written notice of their intention to appoint an administrator to any holder of a qualifying floating charge and to other prescribed persons (such as a sheriff charged with execution against the company, a person who has levied distress against the company or its property, and the supervisor of a company voluntary arrangement). Although the holder of a qualifying floating charge can no longer prevent the appointment of an administrator by the court, it can prevent the appointment of an administrator by the company or its directors, if after receiving notice of intention to appoint out of court, it appoints an administrator itself (or, if appropriate, an administrative receiver).

Originally an applicant for an administration order had to show that the procedure was likely to achieve one or more of the following: the survival of the company and its business, the approval of a company voluntary arrangement, the sanctioning of a compromise under s.425 of the Companies Act 1985, or the more advantageous realisation of the company's assets than would be effected on a winding up. Administrations after September 15, 2003 have a single purpose expressed in terms of a hierarchy of three aims:

(1) The primary purpose is to rescue the company as a going concern.

(2) The secondary purpose is to achieve a better result for the company's creditors as a whole than would be likely on a winding up, e.g. a sale as a going concern. The administrator can seek to achieve the secondary purpose if he believes that the primary purpose is not reasonably practicable or that the secondary purpose would achieve a better result for the creditors as a whole.

(3) As a fallback, the administration can aim to realise the company's property in order to make a distribution to one or more secured or preferential creditors. This applies if the administrator believes that neither primary nor secondary purposes are reasonably practicable and no unnecessary harm will be caused to the interests of creditors as a whole.

In practice, the secondary purpose is the most commonly used.

Administration gives a breathing space for the company to achieve the statutory purpose; it is "a temporary measure which provides a gateway to a variety of alternative exit routes" (Goode 2005, para.10–21). An interim moratorium is imposed when the company files notice of intention to appoint an administrator at court which is made final when the administrator is actually appointed. Once appointed he takes over the day to day management of the company from the directors and reports to creditors within eight weeks. The procedure is intended to last a maximum of twelve months but the period can be extended by court application or creditor approval. The forum for distribution of dividends to creditors will normally be a company voluntary arrangement or a creditors' voluntary liquidation although distributions can be made in the administration if the court so orders: *Re GHE Realisations Ltd* [2006] W.L.R. 287.

Application to the industry

Administration offers various benefits to companies trading in the construction industry: **13–016**

- Proceedings against the company can only be commenced or continued with the consent of the administrator or permission of the court: para.43, Sch.B1 of the Insolvency Act 1986. Hostile claims divert resources away from productive work on other contracts which may themselves become subject to claims as a result. Administration breaks this vicious circle. Consent is also required to bring an adjudication against the company under s.108 of the Housing Grants, Construction and Regeneration Act 1996: *Straume v Bradlor Developments* [2000] B.C.C. 333; *Joinery Plus v Laing* [2003] B.L.R. 184 (Ch.12).
- Retention of title creditors are prevented from repossessing their materials: paras.43(3) and 111(1), Sch.B1 of the Insolvency Act 1986. This can be a useful bargaining point with an employer (Ch.7).
- Where the contractor's cash flow has been damaged through wrongful set-off by the employer, administration can provide the time to recover the amounts set off and improve cash flow: *Smallman Construction v Redpath Dorman Long* (1988) 47 B.L.R. 15.
- Administration relieves the pressure on companies to settle claims for less than they are worth. Realisations in the receivership of Mitchell Construction referred to in Ch.8 would probably have been greater had the administration procedure been available at that time.
- The statutory moratorium against claims gives the company the necessary protection and time in which to organise a company voluntary arrangement.
- It is possible that administration carries less stigma with licensing or registration bodies than other formal procedures, although Klein (2005) records that when TPT Fire Protection Services went into administration in 2004, it lost its approved contractor status with the Loss Prevention Certification Board. As a consequence, the company lost business but was able to obtain accreditation later under a comparable scheme.

It may be necessary for an administrator appointed over a contractor to make additional payments outside the terms of the contract to subcontractors or suppliers to ensure their continued co-operation, e.g. if they would otherwise be entitled to terminate. These might be justified under the Insolvency Act 1986 by reference to para.66 of schedule B1 (if the payment is likely to assist the achievement of the statutory purpose) or para.13 of schedule 1 (if necessary or incidental to the performance of his functions).

Pre-Enterprise Act cases

Pre-Enterprise Act cases required applications to the court for an administration order. The insolvency practitioner had to be satisfied that there was a real prospect that the statutory purpose of the procedure could be achieved. **13–017**

As so much of the contractor's value is locked up in long term contracts, this would be difficult if the company's contracts were terminated. It was desirable for the practitioner to know in advance whether the employer was prepared to co-operate and waive automatic termination or re-instate the contractor's employment to allow the company to continue trading during administration.

The second major difficulty was in funding the company's working capital. In most cases, inadequate working capital contributed to the company's failure and it was often difficult to persuade creditors to increase their exposure to give the administration a chance of success. A secured lender was only likely to do this where the company's activities had been thoroughly reviewed and detailed cash flow projections prepared. The court considered both aspects in *Re Harris Simons* (1989) B.C.C. 11.

> "The company carries on business as builders. Over the past four years there has been a spectacular increase in turnover, from £830,000 in the year to April 1985 to £17 million in the year to April 1987 and £27 million in the year to April 1988. Almost all of its increased turnover has come from one client, a property developer called Berkely House Plc with which the directors had a close relationship. Recently the relationship has turned sour. There are disputes over a number of contracts and Berkely House has purported to dismiss the company and require its employees to leave their sites. It is also withholding sums running into several million pounds which the company says are due and in respect of which Berkely House says it has cross-claims. The effect on the company's cash flow has been that it is unable to pay its debts as they fall due and several writs and a statutory demand have been served. If no administration order is made, the company cannot carry on trading. There is no debenture holder who can be invited to appoint a receiver. The company will have to go into liquidation more or less immediately. The workforce will have to be dismissed and the contracts and work in progress will become a tangle of disputes and probably litigation. The report of the proposed administrator says that in those circumstances it would be extremely difficult to sell any part of the business. If an administration order is made, the company will have what is usually called a breathing space but unless some sort of funding can be found, will continue to have serious respiratory problems with its cash flow. It has however been able to negotiate at least an armistice with Berkely House by which the latter will, conditionally upon the administration order being made, provide sufficient funding to enable the company to complete four current contracts on condition that it quietly removes itself from the other sites in dispute. It is hoped that the four remaining contracts will produce a profit and that it may thereby be possible to stabilize and preserve a business which can either survive or be sold to a third party. In the meanwhile, it may be possible to arrive at a negotiated settlement of the underlying dispute with Berkely House" (per Hoffmann J., at 12).

The court accepted that there was a real prospect either of the survival of the company and the whole or part of its undertaking as a going concern or a more advantageous realisation of its assets than would be effected on a winding up. There were several other construction cases in the early years of the administration procedure. In *WF Fearman* (1988) 4 B.C.C. 139, an insolvent contractor was involved on five or six sites in the London area. A practitioner supported the making of an administration order but had yet to complete his report. A quantity surveyor interviewed the managing director of the company and its employers and concluded that there was no prospect of continuing work on those sites. As a result, the proposed administrator changed his mind and was appointed provisional liquidator instead to safeguard the assets.

In *Re Goscott (Groundworks) Ltd* (1988) 4 B.C.C. 372, a contractor unable to comply with a statutory demand sought advice from an insolvency practitioner who advised it to cease trading. When a creditor petitioned to wind up the contractor, it applied for an administration order shortly before the Christmas shutdown. The directors hoped that it would be possible to complete contracts after the shutdown but this was insufficient reason to justify an order and a provisional liquidator was appointed.

Where there was clear evidence that the company had current contracts which were profitable and that, by continued trading in the short term, offers for the assets and goodwill of the company could realise more than would be available in a liquidation, the court was prepared to make an administration order. In *Re Cavco Floors* [1990] B.C.C. 589 Harman J. abridged time between presentation and hearing of the petition. Only about £13,000 was owed to the contractor's bank who declined to appoint an administrative receiver. No one could be prejudiced by the abridgement of time:

> "the directors (having been warned of the dangers of trading while insolvent) have said that they are not prepared to carry on the business of the company even for some two or three days during which, the evidence of Mrs Harvey makes it plain, it is vital that the company continues to perform its building contract; that the bank has withdrawn support and will not finance the business for that short time, and therefore that unless an administrator is appointed forthwith there is a serious risk that the company will suffer the substantial difficulties that arise in the building trade, which it is notorious are quick to be snatched [sic] by prime contractors when a subcontractor fails to perform according to his contract" (at 590).

In that case, the object of the administration was a better realisation than liquidation.

In *Re SCL Building Services* (1989) 5 B.C.C. 746, the court considered a building, mechanical and electrical engineering contractor. The company was insolvent and its bank had refused further credit. Its problems stemmed from financial assistance given to an associated company, of which nearly £800,000 was outstanding and thought to be irrecoverable. The practitioner's report:

> ". . . proceeded on the footing that the administrator will sell the business carried on as a going concern. The company was said to be concentrating its activities on two substantial contracts, one at St Vedast House in the City carried out on a day work basis averaging £100,000 per month, yielding a gross profit of £40,000, and another in Dulwich Village, there being £1 million of work to carry out within four months of 14 April, and a gross profit of £150,000 being anticipated on that contract. The Dulwich Village contract has now been mutually determined without that profit being realised. Mr. Goldstein reports that the company is now trading

profitably and is generating a net surplus of about £25,000 per month. He says he is cautiously optimistic about new work. He says that funding initially will be from the collection of book debts, but he says 'clearly the company can become self-financing in the near future'" (at 747).

Peter Gibson J made an administration order on the "better realisation than liquidation" ground, the evidence being insufficient to show a real prospect of the survival of the company and its business in whole or part as a going concern. The company was bound to go into insolvent liquidation even after a sale on a going concern basis and it would have to continue trading over a long period to restore it to solvency. There was no cash flow forecast, no evidence on the likely duration of the remaining contract nor of the likelihood of further work being obtained. There was no evidence of support from the Crown and the alleged support of trade creditors was not supported by the evidence. "At least a hope" was not enough.

More recently, an administration order was made in *Re Digginwell Plant & Construction* [2002] B.P.I.R. 299. Most creditors supported the administration but a minority favoured a winding up. In giving effect to the wishes of the majority, Neuberger J. asked the administrators to review the estimates of realisations given in the statement served under r.2.2 of the Insolvency Rules 1986. Some assets such as plant and equipment ought to fetch the same value whether sold through a company voluntary arrangement or a liquidation; others such as retention were likely to realise more if collected through a company voluntary arrangement. If, as the opposing creditors contended, the figures were too high, then the administrators were to refer the matter back to the court.

This procedure has been quite widely used with construction companies but there has been little empirical research. In the early days, it was possible to take advantage of a lacuna in JCT 80 whereby administration was not included as a termination event. Eclipse Copper, a fitting-out contractor, entered administration before Amendment 4 (July 1987) added administration to the termination clause. This enabled the administrators to complete some of the contracts and negotiate settlements with employers who had wrongly thrown the contractor off site.

In an early research paper comparing the administrations of Smallman, Harris Simons, CJ Pearce and Burlingway, there were voluntary arrangements with distributions to creditors after administration in two cases and a better realisation than on liquidation was achieved in the others (Grogan 1992). For three of the companies, a major cause of insolvency was the wrongful set-off of sums due, while for the fourth it was the rising cost of an arbitration. Survival and company voluntary arrangement were the grounds for the administration order in three cases with better realisation accompanying them in two cases and the sole purpose in one. The whole board of directors was retained in all cases together with the majority of employees. Only in one case was bank finance available during the administration. In the others, the company traded on credit from subcontractors and suppliers. In three cases retention was collected while in the fourth there was a need to insure against latent defects to obtain release of retention. In three cases litigation or arbitration was necessary.

The study concluded that administration had been effective as an insolvency procedure and that problems with collection of retention, retention of title, set-off and defects liability caused less difficulty than might have been anticipated. It is impossible to say from such a small survey but the proportion of companies successfully undergoing administration may be no better and no worse in construction than other industries. It is, however, more suited to the larger company able to bear the cost of the procedure.

Post-Enterprise Act cases

As a contractor can now go into administration voluntarily out of court, i.e. without the need for a court order, there have been few recent reported cases on the operation of the procedure in the industry. The directors need to apply to the court however if a winding up petition has been issued against the company and they wish the court to make an administration order instead: see *Re Redman Construction* [2005] EWHC 1850. **13–018**

In that case, a contractor experienced cash flow difficulties due apparently to pricing errors when tendering for work. A winding up petition was issued which had the effect of freezing its bank account. In support of his application for an administration order the director filed an affidavit sworn by a quantity surveyor which stated that the company had "current contracts with a value of £500,000 to finish and that our own job costing show all the company contracts could trade profitably". An insolvency practitioner also filed a report in support of the application stating that, on information received from the director, the estimated deficiency in an administration would be half that on a liquidation, assuming that the current contracts would be completed profitably and that book debts could be collected at the rate of £150,000 per month.

Lewison J. noted that the insolvency practitioner had exercised independent judgment in reviewing the company's cash flow and intended to engage an independent quantity surveyor on his appointment. The judge was reasonably satisfied than an administration order was reasonably likely to achieve at least a better result for the creditors than a winding up. However, he invited further submissions on the initial duration of the order and was not prepared to allow as much as ten weeks to elapse before the first meeting of creditors.

By contrast, an administration order was refused in *Re AMCD (Property Holdings) Ltd* [2004] All E.R. 125. The facts are not fully set out in the case summary but it appears that the company was a special purpose vehicle formed in order to manage construction projects for a developer. The current project was 95 per cent complete, with the properties already advertised for sale. The developer expected to make £2 million profit from the development. The assets of the company equalled its liabilities. A receivable owed by the developer was the company's sole asset and was due for payment on final completion. A creditor had petitioned to wind up the company but the debt was disputed. Lewison J. considered that neither of the tests for the appointment of an administrator had been made out. He was not satisfied that the company was insolvent or that there was a better prospect of recovering the debt from the developer through administration rather than liquidation.

A creditor has to apply to the court for an administration order. In *Thunderbird Industries v Simoco Digital* [2004] 1 B.C.L.C. 541, an order was refused on the ground that the creditor's debt was disputed. It arose out of a contract to supply digital radio and telecommunications equipment and is of interest to the construction industry because the creditor claimed among other things damages based on repudiation of the contract for late delivery or an anticipatory breach (see Ch.14). It therefore petitioned as a contingent or prospective creditor. Patten J. held that the criteria for winding up petitions applied, namely that contingent or prospective liability had to be established or agreed for the creditor to have the *locus standi* to petition. He therefore tried the status of the creditor as a preliminary issue holding provisionally that the creditor itself was in repudiation for cancelling the contract, the delay in delivery not being a repudiatory breach (para.15). Nor did the facts bear out an anticipatory breach based on a failure to obtain a software licence by a particular date and concerns about the supplier's solvency.

Conclusion

13–019 The most successful construction administration so far has probably been Smallman Construction. Smallman was a specialist steel erection subcontractor working on the Broadgate development in the City of London. It had a high concentration of work with one contractor who made large set offs against money due to the company. As a result the company experienced a liquidity crisis and was forced into administration. The administrator took proceedings against the contractor to recover the sums set off and was substantially successful. An aspect of the administration is reported at (1988) 4 B.C.C. 784. In the meantime, the company was able to continue trading and to win new work. The creditors were paid in full and a surplus returned to the shareholders. The case is a heartening example of how administration can work even in a difficult industry.

Other construction-related administrations have included the Ward Group (1992), a serial administration since the Ward Group had previously purchased Smallman from the administrators, Brignell (1992) whose contracts were novated to Amey, Cosslett Contractors (1993), Dean Jesmond, a cladding specialist, David Meek Plant (1992), Ellis, Team, Nico (1996), Brazier (1997), Maxim, Isovel Contracts, Bradlor Developments (1998), Niagara Mechanical Services (1999), Swift Structures, Christiani & Nielsen (2000), Joinery Plus (2001), Ballast Wiltshier, Sunley Turriff, Tendring (2003), Spectrum Projects, Lark, Loweth, Lilley, Capital Project Consultancy (project manager) (2004), Kelsey Roofing Industries, Bellwater, Benson, RC Group (2005), CAP Aluminium, Greenfield, Botes, Schmidlin, Britin, Coverite (2006), Scanmoor (2007). Other significant construction-related administrations have been ordered under special legislation: Railtrack under the Railways Act 1993, Metronet Rail under the Greater London Authority Act 1999. In Europe, by far the largest construction insolvency has been Philipp Holzmann AG (Fritz 2004).

5. Company voluntary arrangement

Legal background

13–020 A company voluntary arrangement (CVA) is a court-approved procedure enabling a company to propose a composition with its creditors whereby they accept a dividend in full settlement of their debts. There is no requirement that the company be, or about to become, insolvent. The directors make a proposal to an insolvency practitioner as nominee who files a report at the court stating whether a creditors' meeting should be called to consider it. All creditors entitled to vote on the proposal are bound by the arrangement, even if they had no notice of the meeting, provided that at least 75 per cent in value of creditors attending or represented by proxy at the meeting vote in favour of it. Once agreed, the arrangement takes effect as a contract between the company, the creditors and the supervisor. A CVA does not prejudice the rights of secured or preferential creditors. It is fundamental that the creditors are realistic when considering the company's proposal (especially in relation to the percentage of their debts to be written off), and that the company is realistic when proposing the dates by which sums will become payable.

There is no standard form of CVA although the Insolvency Rules 1986 set out the minimum it needs to contain (see Goode 2005, para.10–123). The arrangement will describe how payments to creditors will be funded, e.g. from the disposal or refinancing of assets, a management buy out, other external finance or future profits. Once appointed as supervisor, the insolvency practitioner's role will probably be limited to supervising the disposal or refinancing of assets, organising the payment of dividends and ensuring that the directors comply with undertakings given in the CVA. Day-to-day management remains with the directors.

Without a good core business and competent management, a company may have difficulty persuading its creditors to accept a CVA. A practical difficulty is that, while the proposal is being put together, the company may experience considerable creditor pressure. There is no statutory moratorium of creditors' claims, as in the case of administration, unless the company falls within the definition of a small company under s.247(3) of the Companies act 1985: Sch.A1, s.1A of the Insolvency Act 1986. This applies where a company fulfils two of the following three conditions: turnover below £5.6 million, balance sheet total less than £2.8 million, fewer than 50 employees. As a consequence, directors almost always place the company in administration in the interim while an arrangement is being negotiated. It is then for the administrator to propose the CVA. If the CVA is agreed it is common practice for the administrator to act as supervisor, performing both functions at the same time. The CVA may provide for example that realisations in the administration are paid from time to time by the administrators into a special account in the name of the supervisors to be applied on the terms of the arrangement. Such a term has been held to create a trust of the account in favour of the CVA creditors which will, depending on the terms of the CVA, survive the subsequent winding up of the company: *Re NT Gallagher & Son* [2002] 1 W.L.R. 2380.

Application to the industry

The long term nature of construction contracts give rise to practical **13–021** difficulties over the treatment of contingent and prospective debts for voting purposes. If the creditor's claim is rejected, and he is not bound by the arrangement, to what extent can he pursue and enforce his legal remedies against the company? Specifically, can he get paid in priority to the CVA creditors?

This issue arose in the non-construction case of *Re TBL Realisations* [2004] B.C.C. 81. When a bank went into administration, there was an outstanding action for damages pending against it. The court granted leave under s.11 of the Insolvency Act 1986 to the claimants to continue the proceedings. The administrators proposed a CVA. The claimants asked for their claim to be agreed for voting purposes only at £1.5 million but the chairman of the meeting convened to consider the proposal did not admit the claim or place an estimated minimum value on it for voting purposes. Although the claimants would have voted in favour, the chairman's actions meant that the claimants were not bound by the CVA as they were not "entitled to vote" in terms of s.3 of the Insolvency Act 1986.

Eventually, judgment in the action was given by consent in the claimants' favour for $575,000. The claimants argued that, not being bound by the arrangement, they were entitled to enforce the judgment in full against the company's assets. The administrators applied for directions as to what sum they should retain outside the CVA in respect of the judgment. Chadwick L.J. considered that there was no basis for treating the claimants more favourably than they would be treated if they were paid *pari passu* with the creditors of the CVA or the company were wound up. He demonstrated that the dividend they could expect under the CVA would always be greater than that receivable in a liquidation and directed the administrators to pay the claimants an amount equivalent to their CVA dividend. The administrators had wisely retained the full amount of the claim in the meantime and not paid it into the CVA trust account. In a recent case involving an individual voluntary arrangement, Kitchen J. granted a stay of execution against a creditor holding a judgment for interest who was bound by the IVA in respect of his debt: *El Ajou v Stern* [2006] EWHC 3067.

In *Wallace-Smith v Thiess Intraco* (2005) 218 A.L.R. 1, the Federal Court of Australia considered a proof of debt in respect of a contractor's contingent claim for damages for loss of profit in the context of a deed of company arrangement. The basic facts are given in Ch.17. In simplified form, a contractor went into receivership and a subcontractor (Thiess) served notice of intention to terminate the subcontract on the employer pursuant to a direct agreement. The employer served a step-in notice requiring the subcontractor not to terminate on the basis that future payments would be met. The subcontract was later terminated by agreement (but not through the subcontractor's acceptance of the contractor's original repudiation). The deed of company arrangement was funded by the employer and the contractor's parent. The supervisor accepted a proof in respect of unpaid progress payments of $7 million but rejected the proof for damages for loss of profit of $19 million. Although the deed of arrangement defined "claim" as including a contingent claim, it was argued that the direct agreement had extinguished the subcontractor's right to terminate. Alternatively, the right had been lost by affirmation or abandoned by consent under later agreements between the parties. As a consequence, the subcontract had never been terminated in response to the contractor's original repudiation and the claim for loss of profit could not have arisen. The court had to analyse the legal effect on the subcontract of the operation of the direct agreement. It was held that the right to terminate could be deferred or barred without being extinguished. The direct agreement took effect separately from the subcontract: a duty to continue imposed by the former need not extinguish a right to terminate the latter. The right to damages arose before the date for qualifying claims under the deed of arrangement.

See also *County Bookshops v Grove* [2003] 1 B.C.L.C. 479 (contingent creditor's claim admitted to proof in CVA), and *Bovis Lend Lease v Wily*

[2003] NSWSC 467, in which Bovis' claim for an overpayment, "back-charges," and liquidated damages of $500,000 was admitted to vote in the sum of $1. On appeal, it was held that the decision was vitiated by the failure of the chairman of the meeting to act impartially. However, the arrangement would have succeeded even if Bovis had been allowed to vote in the full amount of its debt, and the creditors' resolution for the deed of company arrangement was not invalidated (para.298). In *Simpson v Bowker* [2007] EWCA 772 a company supplying project management services to the oil and gas industry entered a CVA after a major client terminated a contract to review its supply chain and procurement procedures. The claim against the client was the company's principal asset. A director agreed to fund the claim on the basis that his costs would be met from the proceeds before they were paid to the supervisor. A settlement was reached by mediation but a dispute arose over the level of costs claimed by the director. The Court of Appeal held that although nothing would have been recovered but for the director's actions his entitlement was limited to that properly allowable on a true construction of the CVA. As a result he was not entitled to deduct the costs of the CVA itself, the costs of his own time incurred after he could no longer afford solicitors, or those of selling his house to fund the claim.

If the company has a substantial claim, but experiences cash flow problems and is unable to fund it, a CVA may be the way forward: *Re Apollo Engineering* [2003] CSOH 329, *Penrith District Council v VP Developments* [2005] B.C.L.C. 607. In *Re NT Gallagher & Son* [2002] 1 W.L.R. 2380, a civil engineering contractor entered into a CVA for this purpose. It was prompted by the alleged repudiation of a cabling contract with its principal customer Mercury Communications resulting in a claim against Mercury for £2.3 million. The aim of the voluntary arrangement was to allow the company to continue trading while pursuing its claim. The judgment sets out the main terms of the arrangement, one of which was that it would end on the settlement of the claim against Mercury.

The claim was referred to arbitration but had not been concluded two and a half years later when the company went into creditors' voluntary liquidation. At that time, the supervisors had retained approximately £575,000 but the company's post-CVA liabilities were £2.5 million and its overall total liabilities amounted to £5 million. The claim against Mercury was the company's principal asset. The liquidators applied for directions as to whether the claim was held on trust for the CVA creditors or was available for distribution to all the company's creditors, whether before or after the CVA was agreed. It was held by the Court of Appeal that the CVA operated as an accord and satisfaction as between the company and the CVA creditors who gave up their rights to enforce their debts, including the right to seek a compulsory liquidation. Although the CVA terminated on the company's entry into liquidation, the trust had been fully constituted and the supervisors held the claim and the retained funds on trust for the sole benefit of the CVA creditors, applying *Re Leisure Study Group* [1994] 2 B.C.L.C. 65.

In the Australian case of *Bovis Lend Lease v Wily*, a subcontractor specialising in plasterboard and ceiling partitions went into liquidation, then administration and later a deed of company arrangement (set out at para.102). The main purpose of the arrangement was to enable the company to pursue a claim for damages against Bovis of $7.5 million for delay and disruption (a figure which equated to the company's liabilities). Austin J. held that the arrangement should terminate as not being in the interests of the creditors as a whole and the company be returned to liquidation. Among his reasons were that the creditors had not been given adequate information on the claim against Bovis, the director and an associated company could cease funding the claim for any reason at any time, and the arrangement effectively prevented further investigations against possible insolvency claims.

An industry arrangement was also terminated by the court in *Bidald Consulting v Miles Special Builders* [2005] NSWSC 1235. A steel erector went into the Australian equivalent of administration and then agreed a deed of company arrangement with its creditors; but the arrangement was terminated on the ground that it had been obtained by providing materially false and misleading information to creditors. It is probably the most detailed judicial analysis of an arrangement in the construction industry.

When it went into administration, the company had 12 full-time employees and 50 subcontractors. The original proposal was that the directors would subordinate their own claims and inject $40,000 for distribution to creditors. The administrator would allow the directors to complete the ongoing contracts under an exclusive licence for a "pre-determined price." They would act through a new company which would be entitled to accept new work. The new company would be responsible for financing the ongoing trading and pay a royalty of $2000 per week. There were five current contracts, mostly at or near completion. It was estimated that under the arrangement, creditors would receive 57 per cent of their debts; whereas in a liquidation, a dividend of seven cents in the dollar would be paid; in both cases assuming that disputed creditors were entitled to prove. (When the company entered administration, it was stated that all creditors would receive 100 per cent of their debts.) This estimate was revised downwards in subsequent reports to creditors: by the time the arrangement was terminated, ordinary unsecured creditors could expect little or no dividend at all.

The report sets out the figures for work in progress and retention anticipated for each contract and analyses why in each case they were not realised (compare the case study in Ch.16). It was found that the directors had misrepresented the company's financial position by failing to inform creditors of counterclaims made by contractors, by including as collectable receivables sums which had already been paid, by inflating the value of stock, by failing to disclose known doubts over recoverability of retentions, and by exaggerating the amount of ongoing work. What was put into effect was not the proposal which was put to the creditors (para.269).

13–022 Suppliers giving credit to a construction company subject to a CVA take the risk that trading receipts will be insufficient to pay them and that, as a result of the CVA trading trust, the company's assets will not necessarily form part of its estate on a winding up. In practice, there is likely to be a considerable overlap between CVA creditors and post-CVA creditors: *Re N.T. Gallagher & Son* [2002] 1 W.L.R. 2380 at para.49. The question is: to what extent can the creditor rely on the feasibility of the company's proposal in deciding whether to extend further credit?

In *Heritage Joinery v Krasner* [1999] B.P.I.R. 683, the claimant was a CVA creditor who continued to trade with a contractor after a CVA was agreed, but lost a further £40,000 as a result by the time the contractor went into liquidation a year later. It was alleged that the indebtedness of the company as a whole had increased by over £700,000 over the same period. The claimant sued the insolvency practitioner who had acted as nominee and supervisor alleging a breach of a duty of care in reviewing the company's proposal and, in particular, in ensuring that it did not contain inaccurate information. The proposal had valued work in progress at £2.3 million and book debts at £620,000. After approving the proposal, the creditors requested that a report be prepared by independent quantity surveyors, who could only identify a book value for work in progress and book debts together of £1 million with an estimated realisable value of just over £400,000.

Owen J. struck out the claim. The nominee or supervisor owed no general duty. The claim could only proceed if he had made some negligent representation on which the claimant had relied and suffered loss as a result. In this case the claimant argued that the nominee had represented that the company had good prospects of trading out of its difficulties through the CVA and that extending further credit would not expose the claimant to further financial exposure. On the facts the only representation could have been made as nominee and concerned existing not future debts. But in any case the claimant could not show reliance as the creditors approved the continuation of the CVA and presumably the claimant continued to trade with the company after the quantity surveyor's report had been disclosed. It would not be just and reasonable to impose a duty of care.

Another issue has arisen in connection with direct payment. In *Hitachi Plant v Eltraco* [2003] 4 S.L.R. 384, a contractor was placed under judicial management (the Singaporean equivalent of administration) and agreed a scheme of arrangement with its creditors, who included various unpaid nominated subcontractors. The company's assets consisted mainly of receivables claimed from two employers on completed contracts. Two years later the architects on one of the contracts certified direct payment to the nominated subcontractors. The scheme administrators obtained an injunction preventing the employer paying the subcontractors which was upheld on appeal. The basis of the decision was that the scheme stated that realisations of the company's assets were to be distributed among the creditors in accordance with the scheme, and that the whole receivable from the employer was an asset for this purpose. The subcontractors had impliedly agreed not to accept any direct payment offered to them. The subcontractors had no right to a direct payment when the scheme was agreed and direct payment was, in any event, at the architects' discretion. The scheme did not have to deal expressly with the position. For cases on schemes of arrangement involving large construction companies in Singapore see *Wah Yuen Electrical Engineering v Singapore Cables* [2003] 3 S.L.R. 629 and *Re Econ Corp Ltd* [2004] 1 S.L.R. 273, discussed in Chan (2004). The court sanctioned schemes of arrangement for 25 companies making up a construction group in *Re UDL Civil Contractors* [2000] HKCFI 519. The basic terms were that preferential creditors were to be paid in full, while ordinary creditors would receive a small dividend partly in cash and partly in new shares. There would be a moratorium to allow the company's free assets to be sold although pending arbitrations would continue in order to quantify the relevant creditors' claims for dividend purposes. Some of the schemes were opposed by a major creditor whose claim was disputed and given a net value of nil for voting purposes. In overriding the creditor's wishes, Le Pichon J. stated at p.20 of the transcript:

> "There is a disputed claim, the value of which is sufficiently large to block the scheme. The disputed claim is valued at $0, an estimate made in good faith. If such disputed creditor has the right to vote for the full amount of his debt, he would be in a position to bring about the liquidation of the Company when, under the Companies legislation, he does not even have

locus to present a winding-up petition. That cannot be right."

The availability of administration out of court followed by a CVA is open to abuse. In the Australian case of *Re Paradise Constructors* [2004] VSC 92, an administrator was removed from office by the court. Among other things, it appears that he had not exercised any independent judgment in assessing the value of the company's principal asset, a claim against an employer, or in inquiring as to why the director was so keen on a deed of company arrangement. For other construction-related cases, see *Souster v Carman Construction* [2000] B.P.I.R. 371; *Re Arthur Rathbone Kitchens* [1998] B.C.C. 450; *Re Brelec Installations* [2001] B.P.I.R. 210; *Lomax Leisure v Fabric London* [2003] EWHC 307 considered in Ch.14.

CVAs have been used in the construction industry in the UK, both with and without the support of the administration procedure. Examples of successful CVAs without administration are:

- HLM, an architectural practice, where the CVA apparently worked as there were comparatively few creditors, the directors were prepared to invest in the company through a management buy-out, the buy-out would generate sufficient funds to finance a dividend, and the directors were prepared to reduce salaries and overheads. The company went into administrative receivership in 2004 and was the subject of a successful management buy-out (Hay and McCulloch 2004);
- Charles Gregory, and various subsidiaries, civil engineering contractors, which were bought by the Miller Group in July 1992. The creditors agreed to accept a dividend of 35 pence in the pound through a CVA. It appears that the sale was conditional on the agreement of a CVA and that the creditors were influenced in their decision by the assurance of payment of the dividend from the proceeds of sale. Miller's chairman was quoted as saying that he thought CVAs would become a growing trend in the industry; and
- Ebor, a Yorkshire construction group, which entered a CVA the term of which stated that secured and preferential creditors were to be paid in full and unsecured creditors would receive a dividend after agreeing to reschedule their debt. The CVA was prompted by the company's bank halving its overdraft limit and refusing a request for further facilities.

Construction companies which have used a CVA as an exit from administration include:

- Smallman Construction, which went into administration following wrongful set-offs by its employer. The administrators recovered the set-offs through litigation and the creditors agreed to a CVA. The administrators became the supervisors under the CVA and paid 100 pence in the pound to the creditors. They were also able to return to the shareholders an amount in excess of the shareholders' equity at the date of the administration order.
- SCL Building Services, where the company petitioned for an administration order based on the survival of the company, the approval of a CVA or a better realisation of assets than liquidation. The administration order was made only on the basis that it would enable a better realisation of assets. The CVA purpose was rejected because there was

no evidence in support from the main creditors, and one creditor with less than 10 per cent of the overall debts of the company opposed it. However, the administrators later successfully applied to the court to add a CVA as an additional purpose and the creditors later agreed. A first dividend of 60 pence in the pound has been paid. The final outcome is not known.

- Ellis Construction, where there was an anticipated return for creditors of 20 per cent. The grounds for the CVA over a liquidation were lower professional costs, greater flexibility to agree creditors' claims, and the ability to obtain higher rates of interest on realizations.
- Cool Technology, a specialist supplier of plant to the food industry (Stokes 2000). Following a management buy in, which was leveraged against the company's assets, the company went from a cash positive position of £300,000 to one of £20,000. After difficulties with fixed and discounted contract prices the company went into administration. A CVA was agreed whereby the business was sold and a dividend of 74 pence in the pound paid to ordinary unsecured creditors. The company had a profitable core business with 25 per cent of the UK market for its products. It had factored its debts even though it had no significant payment problems from clients. Ending the factoring arrangement saved double the company's bad debt provision.

6. Individual insolvency

The formal procedures available to an individual are bankruptcy and **13–023** individual voluntary arrangement. A bankruptcy petition can be issued by a debtor, a creditor or a supervisor under an individual voluntary arrangement. The minimum sum on which a petition can be based is £750. There are several different forms of statutory demand for debts owed by individuals.

A statutory demand served on an individual as a means of enforcement of an adjudication award is liable to be set aside on application under r.6.5(4) of the Insolvency Rules 1986, if the individual asserts that he has a cross-claim, even though it would not be sufficient to prevent summary judgment being entered against him (Ch.12). The court has power to dismiss the petition if it can be shown that the individual can pay his debts or has made an offer to secure or compound the petition debt which has been unreasonably refused: s.273 of the Insolvency Act 1986. Until the bankruptcy order is discharged, a bankrupt cannot incur credit exceeding £250 without disclosing his status (s.360 of the Insolvency Act 1986) or act as a company director (s.11 of the Company Directors Disqualification Act 1986).

A bankrupt is entitled to the "tools of his trade" (which include items such as computers) and other property of a personal nature (s.283(2) of the Insolvency Act 1986). As with liquidation, the creditors submit proofs of debt and, if there are sufficient assets, receive a dividend from the trustee. The bankrupt's estate automatically vests in the trustee in bankruptcy on his appointment without the need for any formal transfer documents: s.306 of the Insolvency Act 1986. The trustee has powers of disclaimer similar to those of a liquidator, in that he can disclaim onerous property, leaving the creditor to prove for damages.

Contracts often make bankruptcy a termination event. As with liquidation, any rights of set-off prior to bankruptcy are replaced by bankruptcy set-off which applies in all cases. This is wider than the general law and arises in respect of all mutual credits, mutual debts and other mutual dealings between the bankrupt and the other party (compare Ch.18). As from April 2004, most individuals will be discharged from bankruptcy after 12 months, although "culpable" bankrupts may now be subjected to a bankruptcy restriction order extending the period of bankruptcy by a further two to 15 years. The procedure is similar to disqualification proceedings and an undertaking may be accepted without the need for a hearing (see Ch.21).

An individual voluntary arrangement (IVA) is an increasingly popular alternative to bankruptcy. An IVA is, like a company voluntary arrangement, a court procedure enabling an individual to make a compromise with his creditors. The purpose of an IVA is to provide the machinery whereby a debtor can make a proposal to creditors and, if the proposal is accepted, enter into an arrangement which is binding on them and thereby avoid bankruptcy. The key difference between an individual and a company voluntary arrangement is that an individual can apply to court for an interim order before sending out proposals to creditors. The interim order has the effect of staying all proceedings against the debtor and is designed to allow the debtor a breathing space while an insolvency practitioner reports to the court on whether the proposal is such as to make it worthwhile summoning a meeting of creditors. If a meeting is held and more than 75 per cent in value of those voting are in favour, the IVA is approved and binds all creditors present at the meeting or who had received notice of it. An IVA is a practical way out for both debtor and creditors: the debtor avoids bankruptcy and the creditors stand to receive a higher dividend than they might have done on a bankruptcy.

Chapter 14

Termination

If a contractor fails to complete the works, it loses more than the balance of the contract sum. This is because of the extended termination clauses found in the standard forms. As well as the right to recover the additional cost to complete, the employer is given wide powers over the contractor's property to facilitate the completion of the works. These powers can mean that a contractor with a substantial book value becomes virtually worthless on the appointment of an administrator. A termination can have other important consequences. The contractor's failure to complete may have a knock-on effect on anyone else involved as well as the project itself. Termination creates conflict between creditors with proprietary rights or security interests and those with purely contractual rights against the insolvent company, who may have to choose between rights given by the contract and other rights available under the general law. **14–001**

1. Termination at common law

"Termination" is not a term of art with a fixed meaning: *Wallace-Smith v Thiess Intraco* (2005) 218 A.L.R. 1. In this chapter, it is used in its broadest sense to include discharge, determination of employment, acceptance of repudiation, release from performance—any way in which a contract comes to an end. In *Heyman v Darwins* [1942] A.C. 356 at 397, Lord Porter described a termination at common law in three ways: **14–002**

> "(1) renunciation by a person of his liabilities under it, (2) impossibility created by his own act, and (3) total or partial failure of performance. In the case of the first two, the renunciation may occur or the impossibility be created either before or at the time for performance. In the case of the third, it can occur only at the time or during the course of performance. Moreover, if the third be partial, the failure must occur in a matter which goes to the root of the contract. All these acts may be compendiously described as repudiation, though that expression is more particularly used of renunciation before the time for performance has arrived."

Renunciation

If there is no evidence of a clear refusal to perform, the test for renunciation is whether the person's actions would lead a reasonable person to conclude that it no longer intended to be bound by the contract. **14–003**

This also applies where a person intends to carry out the contract but in a way which is inconsistent with its obligations or requires the other person to do something it is not obliged to do, e.g. to accept price increases of materials (*Highness Electrical v Sigma Cable* [2006] SGHC 114, or renegotiate the payment terms following a receivership (*APC v Amey Construction*, [2004] CSOH 182). "But unwillingness and inability are often difficult to disentangle, and it is rarely necessary to make the attempt. Inability often lies at the root of unwillingness to perform. Willingness in this context does not mean cheerfulness; it means simply an intent to perform. To say: 'I would like to but I cannot', negatives intent just as much as 'I will not'": (*Universal Cargo Carriers v Citati* [1957] 2 Q.B. 401 at 437, *per* Devlin J.)

Repudiation "is not lightly to be inferred . . . it is necessary for the Court to find a clear and unequivocal refusal to perform. . . . an ambiguous statement will not do, and nor in my judgment will a statement which merely casts doubt, even grave doubt, on the party's willingness to perform": *Jaks v Cera Investment Bank* [1998] 2 Lloyd's Rep. 89 at 93, per Moore-Bick J. An example of renunciation is *Covington v Xiamen Shipbuilding* [2005] EWHC 2912 in which a shipbuilder entered into several contracts but almost immediately walked away from them to build "essentially three of the same vessels for another buyer".

Impossibility

14–004 This occurs where a person through an act or omission makes it impossible to complete its side of the bargain. Examples are where an owner sells a ship it has previously agreed to charter or where goods which a vendor has agreed to sell are seized by a sheriff before they can be delivered to the purchaser.

Failure to perform

14–005 The third category of termination, a failure to perform which goes to the root of the contract, is most commonly found in the industry. It may be useful at the outset to contrast the differing ways in which the employer and the contractor can fail to perform their respective sides of the bargain.

Repudiation by the employer

14–006 This may stem from failure to give access to site, to appoint a certifier, or to make interim payments. Much depends on the context. An employer may repudiate by purporting to accept a repudiation by the builder based on insufficient grounds: *Oxborough v North Harbour Builders* [2001] NZCA 331, *Mirimskaya v George Evans* (September 5, 2007, Richard Fernyhough Q.C.). Delayed access—beyond that allowed by the JCT form—was unsuccessfully relied on by a bondsman as a repudiatory event vitiating an advance payment bond in *Mercers Company v New Hampshire* [1992] 2 Lloyd's Rep. 365. In *Scheldebouw v St James Homes* [2006] B.L.R. 113 the employer dismissed the construction manager and appointed itself in its place, something which was not permitted under the contract. Like an architect, the manager holds the balance fairly between the parties: the loss of such protection is likely to go to the root of the contract. The employer preventing the proper issue of certificates is sometimes made an express termination event, e.g. cl.69.1 of FIDIC (4th edn).

Termination for non-payment in the absence of an express right is difficult: *Decro-Wall v Practitioners in Marketing* [1971] 1 W.L.R. 361. Construction contracts do not usually make time of the essence whether in relation to performance of the works (*Shawton Engineering v DGP International* [2006] B.L.R. 1) or to payment for them (*Dalkia Utilities v Celtech International* [2006] 1 Lloyd's Rep. 599 at para.130). Time was of the essence for payment in *Wallace-Smith v Thiess Infraco* (2005) 218 A.L.R. 1, but the unpaid subcontractor could not exercise its right of termination because of obligations to the employer under a direct agreement. If there are valid reasons for non-payment, such as failure to obtain the site manager's signature on invoices, a subsequent withdrawal of labour by the contractor will be repudiatory, as would failure to give the required notice before exercising a statutory right of suspension: *Tombs v Wilson Connolly* (2004) 98 Con. L.R. 44 at paras.48 and 57.

In *Stocznia Gdanska v Latvian Shipping* [2002] 2 Lloyd's Rep. 436 at para.75, it was stated by Rix L.J. that a non-repudiatory failure to pay can become repudiatory in time. However, the threshold seems to be a high one: the breach in question must be such as to deprive the contractor of substantially the whole benefit of the contract. Even a failure to pay three instalments coupled with an admission of informal insolvency was held not to constitute repudiatory conduct in *Dalkia Utilities v Celtech International* at para.134. See also *Multiplex v Cleveland Bridge* [2006] EWHC 1341 at paras.596–632 (abating payment for onsite costs, serving withholding notices for excessive sums, and issuing certificates showing negative values not repudiatory).

The few cases in which non-payment has been repudiatory seem to turn on unusual facts. In *Bradley (Cable Jointing) Ltd v Jefco Mechanical Services Ltd* (1988) 6 Con. L.D. 7–19, Mr Recorder Rich Q.C. found that a refusal to make an interim payment was repudiatory of an oral subcontract. Non-payment was held to be a repudiation by the employer in the Australian case of *Alucraft v Growcon* (1995) 11 B.C.L. 20. More recently, in *CJ Elvin Building Services v Noble* [2003] EWHC 837, a builder sued for payment of sums due as at the date it suspended the works and left site. The court made an award of £40,000 after making deductions in respect of incomplete or defective work. The case concerned an oral contract to carry out the work for a reasonable sum, to be paid in reasonable instalments, within a reasonable time. Although the contractor did not argue repudiation, the court held that the employer's actions in failing to pay the amount due and, more significantly, in seeking to impose new terms as to payment at a later stage of the works, were repudiatory. The repudiation was not accepted by the builder (leading the court to conclude that there had been a mutual abandonment of the works) but it reinforced the court's conclusion that the builder had been entitled to suspend.

> "Failure or refusal to pay sums due under a building contract can amount and often does amount to repudiatory conduct on the part of the employer. This will obviously depend on the terms of any construction contract . . . A refusal to honour payment obligations, at least insofar as it relates to a relatively sizeable sum of money due or the threat not to

pay further sums due in accordance with the contract must be capable of being repudiatory" (at para.91, *per* Robert Akenhead Q.C.).

Non-payment was also held to amount to repudiation in the recent case of *Mirimskaya v George Evans* (September 5, 2007, Richard Fernyhough Q.C.), para.55. The facts were unusual in that payment under the contract was to be made by stages in advance. If the contract specifically provides for termination for non-payment, however, it will be enforced by the court even if most of the sum due has been paid: e.g. *The Jotunheim* [2004] EWHC 671, a shipping case in which hire was payable monthly in advance "discountless and non-refundable".

Repudiation by the contractor

14–007 This occurs most clearly when there is an abandonment of the works. In *CFW Architects v Cowlin Construction* (2006) 105 Con. L.R. 116, a firm of architects entered into a "huge loss-making contract" (para.94) to design housing for service personnel. Eventually "it wanted out" and ceased work, arguing among other things that the contractor was in repudiation for non-payment and wrongful set-off. Neither plea was sustainable: the sums claimed were not then due and the alleged set-off was merely a proposal to settle a dispute. By ceasing work, the architects repudiated their engagement and had to pay damages of over £800,000. Ironically, the architects were initially engaged by another contractor who had become insolvent after its tender was accepted but before concluding a contract with the employer on the project.

In *Greenore Port v Technical & General* [2006] EWHC 3119, the contractor laid off its employees and allowed its insurance cover to lapse on a project as its available funds were exhausted. Jackson J. held this was repudiatory conduct which the employer accepted by engaging a completion contractor (para.175). The contractor went into administration immediately afterwards. Even if the contractor's conduct had not been repudiatory, the court would not have regarded the employer's actions in asking another contractor onto site as repudiatory, but merely as "recognising reality" (para.182).

It is more difficult to argue repudiation on the basis of delay or defects. A claim which relied on delay failed in *Shawton Engineering v DGP International* [2006] B.L.R. 1. The case concerned a design sub-subcontract under which the work was to be completed within a reasonable time. The subcontractor terminated in reliance on a notice it had served making time of the essence but the Court of Appeal held that the notice was inadequate to convey such an intention and, in any event, the sub-subcontractor was not in breach at the time. Repudiation can occur through the accumulation of breaches if they are such as to lead to the inference that they will lead to sub-standard performance: *Rice v Great Yarmouth Borough Council* (unreported, June 30, 2000, CA).

In *South Oxfordshire DC v Sita* [2006] EWHC 2459, it was held by David Steel J. that breach of an obligation to provide a surety bond did not amount to repudiatory conduct. It was not a condition precedent and the parties had not noticed its absence until a dispute arose (para.122). But the wrongful calling of bank guarantees without giving prior notice required by the contract after the contractor served a valid notice to show cause why the works should not be suspended for non-payment was held to be repudiatory conduct in *Kane Constructions v Sopov* [2005] VSC 237 at paras.800 and 807–8.

The principle in Woodar v Wimpey

The position is complicated by the principle that a wrongful termination based on a *bona fide* but mistaken interpretation of the contract will not necessarily be a repudiation if there is no intention to abandon it: *Woodar v Wimpey* [1980] 1 W.L.R. 277. The case arose out of the collapse of the Stern property group in the recession of 1974. Similarly, the seller of a car who asks for more than the agreed price on delivery in mistaken reliance on a term entitling it to charge its list at that time whatever the circumstances was not in repudiation and could keep the buyer's deposit on his failure to complete: *Vaswani v Italian Motors* [1996] 1 W.L.R. 270. The same applies to a termination based on a mistaken view that the term in question was part of the contract: *Design Company v King* (1992) 8 Build. L.M. 1. 14–008

Unless the exception in *Woodar v Wimpey* applies, if one person wrongly treats the other's conduct as repudiatory, it may find itself in repudiation entitling the other to damages: *Bedfordshire County Council v Fitzpatrick Contractors* (1998) 62 Con. L.R. 64; *CFW Architects v Cowlin Construction* (2006) 105 Con. L.R. 116; *Dalkia Utilities v Celtech International* [2006] 1 Lloyd's Rep. 599 at paras.145–151.

Consequences of repudiation

If one party is in repudiation, the other has the option either to accept the repudiation and claim damages or to affirm the contract. 14–009

Acceptance of repudiation

If the repudiation is accepted, the unperformed obligations of both parties are released and those of the defaulter are replaced by a liability in damages: *Photo Production v Securicor* [1980] A.C. 827. The accrued rights of both parties are preserved: "even a party in repudiation is entitled to keep what he has already earned": *Explora Group v Hesco* [2005] EWCA 646 at 85, per Rix L.J. In that case, a right to commission earned before but not payable until after termination survived an agent's repudiation. Contrast the case where a receiver of an earthworks subcontractor on a motorway project who repudiated the subcontract failed in a claim for a bonus payment as it had not been earned: *APC v Amey Construction* [2004] CSOH 182 at paras.38–44. Where a purchaser repudiated a contract for the purchase and construction of a house, he could not recover three stage payments totalling £50,000 from the vendor-builder as there had not been a total failure of consideration: *Clowes Developments v Mulchinock* (unreported, May 24, 2001, Mr. John Martin Q.C.). 14–010

Acceptance must normally be communicated by some unequivocal act, but inactivity can in context be sufficient:

> "Postulate the case where an employer at the end of a day tells a contractor that he, the employer, is repudiating the contract and that the contractor need not return the next day. The contractor does not return the next day or at all. It seems to me that the contractor's failure to return may, in the absence of any other explanation, convey a decision to treat the contract as at an end": *Vitol v Norelf* [1996] A.C. 800 at 811, *per* Lord Steyn.

Thus, in *Discain Project Services v Opecprime* [2001] EWHC 450, a contractor accepted an employer's repudiation by ceasing to do any further work (at para.57).

In *Manx Electricity Authority v JP Morgan* [2003] B.L.R. 477, the Court of Appeal considered that a demand under a bond could constitute acceptance. If the contractor's failure to return was caused by its insolvency, however, acceptance may not be inferred. If it later turns out that a repudiation was not in fact a breach, an acceptance may still be valid if there were at that time another repudiatory breach in existence. This applies even where the innocent party is not aware of the other breach unless the defaulter is prejudiced by lack of notice, perhaps because it could have remedied the breach: consider *Sheffield v Conrad* (1987) 22 Con. L.R. 108.

If a repudiation is not accepted, the contract continues. In *Munib Masri v Consolidated Contractors* [2006] EWHC 1931, for example, the claimant of an interest in an oil field concession obtained judgment even though he had at one time been in repudiation since his breach had never been accepted by the defendants.

Affirming the contract

14–011 As with acceptance, an affirmation is irrevocable, with the possible exception of an anticipatory breach (*Stocznia Gdanska v Latvian Shipping* [2002] 2 Lloyd's Rep 436 at para.99). Affirmation can be express or implied from an unequivocal act. Simply protesting about the repudiation and calling on the defaulter to change its position and honour the contract is not necessarily an affirmation and there may be a half-way house for the innocent person to occupy while it decides what to do. "The law does not require an injured party to snatch at a repudiation and he does not automatically lose his right to treat the contract as discharged merely by calling on the other to reconsider his position and recognize his obligations": *Yukong Line v Rendsburg* [1996] 2 Lloyd's Rep. 604 at 608, *per* Moore-Bick J. For example, continuing an agreement for the purpose of negotiating a reconstruction of it is not necessarily affirmatory: *Internet Trading Clubs v Freeserve* (unreported, June 19, 2001, Tomlinson J. at para.30). After affirmation, both parties retain previous causes of action and the contract remains alive for the benefit of them both.

Insolvency and repudiation

14–012 Can insolvency itself be a repudiatory act? The main difficulty is that at common law, insolvency, whether formal or informal, is not necessarily a breach of contract: *Re Agra Bank, ex parte Tondeur* (1867) L.R. 5 Eq. 160.

"The appointment [of administrative receivers] may be consistent with the firm intention to continue the contract rather than to abandon it, especially if it is profitable": *Laing and Morrison-Knudson v Aegon Insurance* (1997) 86 B.L.R. 70 at 91, *per* Judge Humphrey LLoyd Q.C. Nor is insolvency in itself an anticipatory breach: *Re Pinto Silver Mining* (1878) 8 Ch. 273. It is unlikely that a term will be implied allowing termination for insolvency: *Re Premier Products* [1965] N.Z.L.R. 50. It would be possible for the parties to agree not to become insolvent but the standard forms do not take this approach (compare *Cadogan Estates v McMahon* [2001] 1 A.C. 378).

If the insolvency practitioner can find a way for the company to continue performing, the employer can do nothing about it. As insolvency is usually progressive over time, it is crucial for employers to understand the warning signs and weigh them up as potential breaches. The following are typical: failing to pay direct labour, subcontractors or suppliers leading to disruption and delay; supervisory staff leaving the company and not being replaced leading to defective work; and requests for advance or accelerated payments. The employer needs to be careful: "going slow" by the contractor is not necessarily a repudiation: *Hill v London Borough of Camden* (1980) 18 B.L.R. 31.

Anticipatory breach

If the renunciation or impossibility occurs before the time for performance **14–013** has arrived, it is known as an "anticipatory breach". "So anticipatory breach means simply that a party is in breach from the moment that his actual breach becomes inevitable": *Universal Cargo Carriers v Citati* [1957] 2 Q.B. 401 at 438, *per* Devlin J. Acceptance of the breach would release both parties from further performance and entitle the innocent person to damages without having to wait until the time for performance has expired.

It is sometimes argued that insolvency is an anticipatory breach entitling the other party to terminate the contract (see the discussion in Wee, 2005). This could be so if the construction contract was personal to the parties or of a long term nature: *Re Asphaltic Wood Pavement* (1885) 30 Ch D 216. Commenting on this case in *Re Charge Card Services* [1986] 3 All E.R. 289 at 311, Millett J. observed that "the winding up no doubt amounted to an anticipatory breach of contract." An anticipatory breach can be accepted by conduct even where the act constituting acceptance would otherwise be a breach. Where the innocent party does not affirm, acceptance could be inferred from action incompatible with continued performance or a simple failure to perform further: *Vitol v Norelf* [1994] 1 W.L.R. 1390. If the contract excludes the common law, and provides for automatic termination and other remedies on the appointment of an administrative receiver to the contractor, the employer loses any right to treat the receivership as an anticipatory breach: *Perar v General Surety* (1994) 66 B.L.R. 72.

A recent industry example is *HSS Hire Services v BNB Builders Merchants* [2004] EWHC 2013. A tool hire company obtained damages against a builder's merchant for the anticipatory breach of a licence agreement. The agreement was for five years and allowed the merchant to run a tool hire agency in its branches in the north of England. A year into the agreement, the merchant agreed to sell its business. The purchaser had its own tool hire business already and did not want to continue the existing arrangement. Under the licence agreement, the hire company had the power to terminate on any change of control of the licensee which was defined as an event of default. The repudiatory act consisted of three telephone calls on the same day in which the hire company was told of the impending sale and that the future of the agency would be up to the purchaser, was informed by the purchaser that it did not wish to continue with the agency, and notified the merchant of the purchaser's intention. The merchant wanted the licence agreement to continue until after the sale had taken place in order that the purchaser would be liable for damages to the hire company. The purchaser wanted to achieve the opposite result, leaving the merchant with liability for the damages. In the end, both were liable: the builder's merchant for its repudiatory breach and the purchaser for wrongful interference with the licence agreement.

Breach as cause of insolvency

14–014 Wrongful termination by one person can lead to the other's insolvency. If it can be proved that the insolvency was the natural and probable consequence of the breach, then in principle the costs of the relevant insolvency procedure are recoverable as damages. A major problem is that there are likely to have been other causes of insolvency, such as under-capitalisation. In *Dalma Formwork v Concrete Constructions* [1998] NSWSC 472 it was held that non-payment of progress claims of $500,000 neither caused nor materially contributed to the administration of a subcontractor. Rolfe J. concluded that: "There were too may other factors at work to come to that conclusion. In my view a substantial portion of the problem, if not the whole of the problem, stemmed from the payment of management and hire fees [to other group companies] and the failure to recover pre-paid fees." Even if the costs of the procedure are irrecoverable, the court might penalise the wrongdoer, e.g. the exemplary damages awarded against the employer in *Egan v State Transport Authority* (1982) 31 S.A.S.R. 481, considered in Ch.6.

In *Bentley Construction v Somerfield* (2001) 82 Con. L.R. 163, a contractor claimed damages representing sums withheld by its own debtors as a consequence of the employer's breaches of contract in deliberately 'starving' it of payments in order to force it to cease trading. Once rumours spread of the contractor's financial difficulties, its debtors postponed payment as a form of self-protection or in the hope that they would never have to pay. Judge Richard Seymour Q.C. struck out the claim. It was possible that non-payment with intent to damage the contractor could amount to the tort of using unlawful means to cause harm to the economic interests of another but, even accepting that the facts here amounted to the tort, sums owed to the contractor by third parties were irrecoverable from the employer as damages (paras.26–28).

Claims of this kind may founder either because they are difficult to fit within established remedies or through funding difficultes. In *Monaveen v ABB Service* [2006] WASC 263, a subcontractor claimed that unlawful withholding of payment by the contractor forced it to accept amendments to the subcontract harmful to its interests and that until its entry into receivership it was effectively controlled by the contractor and its credit relationship with suppliers was destroyed. Eventually the claim was struck out for want of prosecution. In *Trustees of the Roman Catholic Church v*

Hughes Bros [2000] NSWCA 296 the employer validly excluded the contractor from site and took over the works after a winding up petition was issued against the contractor by a formwork subcontractor working on the project. In so doing, the employer relied on an express termination clause in the main contract. The employer had the works completed and claimed $4.8 million as the additional cost to complete over and above the original contract sum. This claim was undisputed but controversially the court upheld the contractor's cross-claim for damages in the same amount, thereby cancelling it out. Priestley J.A. held that "one principal cause" of the termination was the employer's own failure to pay substantial prolongation claims made by the contractor. Although *bona fide* at the time, this failure was "wrong to a substantial extent." The non-payment was a cause (but not the only cause) of the contractor's cash flow problems which "materially contributed" to the issue of the petition (para.50). It followed that as well as liability for prolongation accrued due before the termination, the employer also had to compensate the contractor for its liability for the additional cost to complete (owed to the employer under the termination clause). Surprisingly, the argument that the chain of causation was broken when the employer validly served notice to repossess the works was rejected. Eleven years after the termination, a net sum was found due to the contractor of about $2 million.

Invalid receiverships

In a case concerning the invalid receivership of a contractor, the company unsuccessfully claimed as damages from the receivers the difference between the value of its business on the date of their appointment and the actual realisations: *OBG v Allan* [2007] 2 W.L.R. 920. Lord Hoffmann stated that the only possible causes of action were the tort of procuring a breach of contract or the tort of causing loss by unlawful means. Neither was established in this case. First there had been no breach of contract which the receivers could have procured. Second they had neither used unlawful means nor intended to cause any loss. They had acted in good faith throughout. Nor could they be liable in conversion as that tort applied to chattels rather than contractual rights. **14–015**

Far from wishing to prevent the performance of an obligation, the receivers were willing to cause the company to perform it provided it had the working capital to do so. The company was already insolvent when the receivers were appointed and it was inevitable that its contracts with the employer would have been terminated in due course either from liquidation or abandonment. It could not be proved therefore that, but for the appointment of receivers, the company would have continued trading or, in the absence of a claim of negligence against the receivers, obtained a better value for its property without the receivers being in place.

2. Termination under the contract

To avoid the need to prove repudiation, construction contracts include an express term allowing the parties to terminate on various grounds. Termination events can be wider or narrower than, or the same as, those at common law. They can include ordinary and repudiatory breaches, events **14–016** which are not breaches at all, something not happening (e.g. *Total Gas v Arco* [1998] 2 Lloyd's Rep. 209), the insolvency of a non-party (e.g. a parent company), and termination at the option of either party. A termination of employment is equivalent to the acceptance of repudiation, in the sense that it is a termination of future performance rather than of the contract as a whole, leaving existing rights fully enforceable, e.g. in adjudication: *Northern Developments v J&J Nichol* [2000] B.L.R. 165 at para.35.

Procedural requirements

14–017 Any person wishing to terminate under the contract must do so without undue delay but in practice this can be months or, it seems, even years: *Laing and Morrison-Knudson v Aegon Insurance* (1997) 86 B.L.R. 70. A person relying on a contractual termination clause needs to act in accordance with its requirements, e.g. as to the statement of grounds, period of notice, method of service etc, or risk being in repudiation itself: *Hill v London Borough of Camden* (1980) 18 B.L.R. 31. Where the contract lays down specific periods for the giving of notices, it can be a repudiation if notice is given prematurely: *Afovos Shipping v Pagnan* [1983] 1 W.L.R. 195. In *RWE-Industrie-Loesungen v Thyssen* [2006] EWHC 2111, a notice relying on administration as a termination event was valid because a previous notice had been too ambiguous to amount to a repudiation.

Particular care is required where the employer wishes to serve notice but has agreed to the assignment of the benefit of the contract to a third person: *Linden Gardens v Lenesta Sludge* [1994] 1 A.C. 85 at 105. If the contract allows termination only after a certificate, a person may be in repudiation if the certificate is invalid: *Nelson Carlton v Hatrick* [1965] N.Z.L.R. 144. The same might apply where the contract requires notice to show cause why it should not be terminated, but it is not given, or is insufficiently connected to the notice of termination in terms of its content or timing: *Architectural Installation Services v James Gibbons Windows* (1990) 16 Con. L.R. 68. If the default referred to in the notice to show cause has been remedied, the contractor may be able to obtain an injunction restraining the employer from serving the notice of termination: *Robert Salzer Constructions v Elmbee* (1991) 10 A.C.L.R. 64; compare *Concord Trust v Law Debenture Trust Corporation* [2005] 1 W.L.R. 1591 at para.26. In *NextCall Telecom v BT* [2000] All E.R. (D) 2371, Lloyd J. refused an injunction to restrain a proposed contractual termination of a calls and access service for non-payment of invoices for future services.

Termination may be automatic, automatic for some grounds but on notice for others, on notice only, on notice to the other contract party and a third person, e.g. a beneficiary under a warranty or direct agreement, on notice only after notice to show cause, or on notice after a certificate from a third person. Termination clauses often confer rights wider than the common law to the party with greater bargaining power.

Accrued rights

14–018 Termination under a contractual provision does not prevent the person terminating from recovering an accrued unpaid stage payment as a debt even if the buyer obtains no benefit under the contract: *Stocznia Gdanska v*

Latvian Shipping [1998] 1 All E.R. 883. In that case there was no failure of consideration, as the contract was for the design as well as the construction and delivery of a number of ships. Although several contracts were terminated before delivery of the vessels, the builder had carried out design and construction work in relation to them.

A contractor who becomes insolvent and repudiates before completing the works still remains entitled to payment for work done before the termination. In *Coba Industries v Adams* (1987) 15 B.C.L.R. (2d) 68, the contract was informal but allowed the builder to invoice monthly in arrears. When the employer accepted the builder's repudiation, about $800,000 was outstanding. The employer could have had the works completed to the original design using an alternative contractor but instead opted to abandon the project. To avoid paying the contractor, it argued that, despite the agreement to make progress payments, the contract was entire and the contractor was due nothing. The argument was rejected and the matter referred back to the trial judge to deal with issues concerning set-off and quantification of loss.

Where a contractor terminated the contract for non-payment, an employer was still entitled to make a call under an on demand bond in respect of unliquidated damages arising from breaches by the contractor before the termination: *Geraldton Building v Christmas Island* (1995) 11 B.C.L. 23. Accrual of rights prior to termination can be compared with the position on a disclaimer. In *Groveholt v Hughes* [2005] EWHC 48, a liquidator disclaimed a development agreement and a novation agreement. A creditor failed in a claim for sums due because they had not accrued by the date of the disclaimer. A provision in a termination clause which excludes an entitlement to accrued rights may be unenforceable as a penalty: *Integral Home Loans v Interstar Wholesale Finance* [2007] NSWSC 406.

An indemnity from the purchaser in an asset sale agreement has proved useful to an employer facing a claim under a termination clause from the contractor's insolvency practitioner. In *Lomax Leisure v Fabric London* [2003] EWHC 307, a building contract was terminated when the contractor entered a company voluntary arrangement. The employer engaged a completion contractor but, before the works could be completed, the employer went into administration. The administrator entered into an asset sale agreement under which the purchaser took an assignment of the employer's rights to apply for relief against forfeiture of a lease (reported as *Re Lomax Leisure* [1999] 3 All E.R. 22), and agreed to carry out and complete all building contracts entered into by the employer before the date of the agreement "which then remained to be performed in whole or in part", and to indemnify the employer against all claims made in relation to them. It was held that the purchaser was liable not only in respect of the completion contract, which it was in its own interests to fulfil, but also for any residual liability of the employer to the original contractor. This was established in arbitration at nearly £100,000 in respect of the value of work done before the termination. It appears from *Re Lomax Leisure* that the asset sale agreement included an agreement to assign the lease once the works were completed. One stage payment was due to the completion contractor when the application for an administration order was made.

Excluding the common law

14–019 The general rule is that clear words are necessary in order to exclude the common law. It follows that if a contract says nothing about the common law, its terms are in addition to and not in substitution for it: *Gilbert-Ash v Modern Engineering* [1974] A.C. 689. Compare the position in Australia. In *Tan Hung Nguyen v Luxury Design Homes* [2004] NSWCA 178, for example, a term permitting an employer to terminate where the contractor was "unable or unwilling to complete" was held to exclude the common law of repudiation. Occasionally the court has found an implied exclusion of the common law but this is very rare in English law: *Lockland Builders v Rickwood* (1995) 77 B.L.R. 38. It follows that words such as "without prejudice to the parties' rights and remedies at common law" are "legal verbiage" (*Architectural Installation Services v James Gibbons Windows* (1990) 16 Con. L.R. 68 at 73, *per* Judge Peter Bowsher Q.C.); Carter (1990, 107). The danger of including them is that, if common law rights are preserved in one context, e.g. the power to terminate, the court might construe the remainder as excluding the common law. This is the "argument from redundancy" criticised by Lord Hoffmann in *Beaufort Developments v Gilbert-Ash* (1998) 88 B.L.R. 1 at 10.

In *Perar v General Surety* (1994) 66 B.L.R. 72, the Court of Appeal observed that cl.27 of JCT 81 reserved common law rights when setting out termination events but did not repeat the reservation in a sub-clause conferring post-termination rights. The court concluded that the post-termination rights were exclusive of common law and amounted to a complete code. (Compare *Dalkia Utilities v Celtech International* [2006] 1 Lloyd's Rep. 599 at para.21.) This problem has been rectified by cl.27.8 of JCT 98 (now cl.8.3.1 of JCT 05) which preserves the common law in respect of the whole termination clause.

It has been held that the preservation of common law rights makes it clear that the termination clause offers an alternative to acceptance of repudiation: *Tern Construction v RBS Garages* (1992) 34 Con. L.R. 137 at 145; *Mazelow v Herberton Shire Council* (2002) 18 B.C.L. 272. In context, it can be regarded as keeping alive the innocent person's right to elect to affirm the contract or accept the repudiation even after operating the termination clause: *Laing and Morrison-Knudson v Aegon Insurance* (1997) 86 B.L.R. 70. This is a key issue in construction insolvency since so much depends on the successful completion of long term contracts. An express power to terminate in the event of the "breach of any of the terms of this Agreement" may be construed as "any repudiatory breach" (*Explora Group v Hesco* [2005] EWCA 6, *per* Rix L.J. at para.87).

Termination and/or repudiation

14–020 Where the termination event is a repudiatory breach, and the contract does not exclude the common law, could the innocent person both terminate under the contract and accept a repudiation? The two remedies are not inconsistent although the damages recoverable may be different: *Financings v Baldock* [1963] 2 Q.B. 104. The problem is that, on one view, in order to terminate under the contract, the innocent person has to rely on the termination clause, i.e. affirm the contract, thereby disabling itself from accepting the repudiation. Thus, in *Johnstone v Milling* (1886) 16 Q.B.D. 460 a claim for damages for anticipatory breach failed as a tenant had previously treated a lease as being in existence by relying on its terms in terminating it.

In *Laing and Morrison-Knudson v Aegon Insurance*, a subcontractor went into administrative receivership before completion. The management contractor terminated "the subcontract work" pursuant to an express term and claimed damages from the subcontractor's bondsman representing the cost of completion. The termination clause allowed the contractor to take possession of the subcontractor's plant and materials but did not confer any right to compensation for loss caused by the termination. The contractor argued that its reliance on the clause constituted the acceptance of a repudiation which had preceded the insolvency, and claimed full repudiation damages.

It was held that termination under an express clause was neither an acceptance of repudiation (because the clause provided for the termination of the works not the contract), nor an affirmation of the contract (because the contractual rights were expressly without prejudice to the parties' common law rights). It was a neutral event, a holding action to allow the innocent person to consider its position: "clearing the decks to enable [the contractor] to be able to do that which [the subcontractor] was not going to do" (at 112, *per* Judge Humphrey LLoyd Q.C.). The court held the defendant bondsman liable because it was asked to assume that at the time of the termination, the subcontractor was in repudiatory breach; the repudiation was accepted by the statement of claim in the action; and, as a consequence, the contractor was not limited to the relief allowed by the termination clause but could recover full repudiation damages.

A similar approach was adopted by the Court of Appeal in *Stocznia Gdanska v Latvian Shipping* [2002] 2 Lloyd's Rep. 436, although *Laing and Morrison-Knudson* was not referred to:

> "I do not think that the use of a contractual mechanism for terminating the contracts is inconsistent with reliance on repudiatory conduct for effecting a common law acceptance of an anticipatory breach. Where contractual and common law rights overlap, it would be too harsh a doctrine to regard the use of a contractual mechanism of termination as unequivocally ousting the common law mechanism, at any rate against the background of an express reservation of rights" (*per* Rix L.J. at para.88).

In *Laing and Morrison-Knudson*, the bondsman argued that the contractor's loss was incurred as a result of the contractual termination which had removed the subcontractor's right to continue work, rather than the repudiation which was not accepted until long after the loss had been incurred. This reasoning was not accepted by the court since it became necessary for the contractor to incur the cost to complete as soon as the subcontractor repudiated. The subcontractor remained in repudiation long after the contractual termination of the works. The fact that the repudiation was not accepted until after the loss was incurred was immaterial. (See also the discussion in (1998) 15 Build L.M. 6, and generally van Deventer 1993, 311–319). The notice of termination in *Laing and Morrison-Knudson* only referred to the termination clause not the common law and the event relied on (receivership) was not a repudiation.

In *Kennedy v Collings Construction* (1991) 7 B.C.L. 25 at 39, a notice of termination under an express clause also referred to the builder's repudiation and some of the termination events were also repudiatory. It was held to be an effective acceptance of repudiation. This seems also to have been the case in *Bovis v Whatlings Construction* (1995) 75 B.L.R. 1, where the House of Lords spoke of repudiation damages in the context of a termination under an express term.

If the employer writes saying it is having the works completed by someone else in view of the contractor's failure to perform, the court may in context treat the employer's letter either as an acceptance of repudiation or a notice of termination: *Gibbs v Tomlinson* (1992) 35 Con. L.R. 86 at 118. A contractual notice asserting immediate termination, although the contract requires 30 days advance warning, can still amount to an acceptance of repudiation: see *Internet Trading Clubs v Freeserve* (unreported, June 19, 2001). In that case the other party alleged that the server of the notice was itself in repudiation but to little effect "for there is no principle that a party himself in repudiatory breach may not accept his contracting partner's repudiatory conduct as terminating the contract" (per Tomlinson J. at para 29).

14–021 The position is more difficult where the breach relates to payment rather than performance. In *Dalkia Utilities v Celtech International* [2006] 1 Lloyd's Rep. 599, the contractor successfully invoked a clause allowing it to terminate for 'material breach' where the employer had failed to pay three outstanding invoices. The case concerned a long-term contract for the provision and operation of a combined heat and power facility. The employer became cash flow insolvent, missed three instalments of the annual charge, and invited the contractor to agree a six-month moratorium. The contract allowed for termination for formal insolvency and also in the event of material breach of the employer's payment obligations. The contractor served a notice of termination on the latter ground (which was held to be effective: para.102), but argued further that the notice took effect as acceptance of repudiation (there being a dispute on the level of compensation available under the termination clause). It was held that the non-payment was not repudiatory conduct, and that even if it had been, the notice of termination did not amount to acceptance. Christopher Clarke J. stated *obiter* that such a notice could also constitute acceptance of repudiation if it merely exercised the right to terminate without stating the ground or, where a contractual termination clause was referred to, it was evident from the context that the party was not relying on it exclusively (paras.143–4).

If the termination event is not a repudiatory breach, it is crucial to examine the contract carefully because the innocent person will be limited to such relief as the clause allows (or which has already accrued due), which might be less than the damages recoverable on a repudiation: *Thomas Feather v Bradford* [1953] 52 L.G.R. 30; *Explora Group v Hesco* [2005] EWCA 646 at para.88; *Stocznia Gdanska v Latvian Shipping* [2002] 2 Lloyd's Rep. 436 at para.64.

If the parties go to the trouble of specifying certain events as entitling them to terminate the contract, does that mean that they must have intended them to take effect as conditions (as opposed to warranties or intermediate terms)? If so, it would mean that the occurrence of any of these events would be a breach of condition and give rise to an election to accept a repudiation or affirm the contract. In *Stocznia Gdanska v Latvian*

Shipping Rix L.J. at paras.79–81 saw no reason why a right to rescind a shipbuilding contract following non-payment of an instalment of the price should not have precisely that effect.

Effect of subsequent insolvency

An employer cannot reduce sums payable to a contractor under a termination at will clause if the contractor becomes insolvent after the termination: *Chiemgauer Membran v New Millennium Experience Company* [2001] C.I.L.L. 1741, *per* Geoffrey Vos Q.C. The employer terminated the contract without cause pursuant to an express right to do so. After termination, but before the quantification of the contractor's claim for loss and damage, the contractor filed for bankruptcy under German law. The employer argued that the contractor would have become insolvent during the performance of the contract. In that event, the contract would automatically have terminated and the contractor would not have made any profit. The court compared the position on a repudiation. In assessing damages it had to be assumed that the contract would have been performed according to its terms by the innocent party. The right to damages vested before the supervening insolvency and the same principles applied to termination at will. The insolvency of the contractor could not affect the question of damages since its insolvency was not inevitable, predestined or bound to occur at the date of the termination. The contractor could therefore recover any direct loss and/or damage which had been caused to it by the termination. This case may need to be reconsidered in the light of *Golden Strait Corporation v Nippon Yusen* [2007] UKHL 12. See also *Koch Hightex v New Millennium Experience Company* [2000] C.I.L.L. 1595 (Ch.19). 14–022

The court has jurisdiction to make a declaration as to whether the party is entitled to terminate the contract although in *Midland Land v Warren Energy* [1997] C.I.L.L. 1222, it declined to do so on the basis that it might encourage a flood of applications. The court was satisfied that the buyer under a gas supply agreement was solvent on the balance sheet basis under s.123(2) of the Insolvency Act 1986. The seller wanted to be certain in advance that a termination for insolvency under the contract would be valid.

3. The standard forms

What is being terminated?

Ever since termination clauses were introduced, a distinction has been made between terminating the contract and terminating the contractor's right to continue work on site. The distinction is normally recognised by the court, most recently in *OBG v Allan* [2005] B.L.R. 245 at para.66 (referring to cl.63 of ICE 5th edn), but there are exceptions: see *Lomax Leisure v Fabric London* [2003] EWHC 307 at paras 4–8. Examples of the former include clauses which set out defined events and then declare the contract void or give the employer power to avoid it should any of those events occur: e.g. *Munro v Wivenhoe and Brightlingsea Railway Company* (1865) 12 14–023

L.T. 656. The contract is terminated under MF/1 and GC Works/1 (2nd edn).

Examples of the latter fall into three groups. First, the JCT forms state that the contractor's employment under the contract is terminated: see the comparative table in Totty and Moss at H6.02. A variant of this approach is core clause 90.1 of NEC3 which refers to the termination of the contractor's obligation to provide the works. Secondly, the ICE forms entitle the employer to enter upon the site and expel the contractor from it. Thirdly, many older cases allow the employer to take the works "out of the contractor's hands" and have them completed by others: e.g. *Pauling v Mayor of Dover* (1855) 10 Ex. 753. There is no substantial difference between these expressions: the intention is to give the employer power to terminate the contractor's right to continue the works without avoiding the contract. The use of the word "employment" suggests that the contractor loses both the right and the duty to continue work but is not released from its other liabilities under the contract. Important consequences flow from this, since subsequent non-performance of work on site cannot be repudiatory if the contractor's right to continue has been terminated: *Perar v General Surety* (1994) 66 B.L.R. 72. This has an impact on the question whether there has been a default for the purpose of liability under a bond or an insurance policy or a limitation defence: *Burns & Dutton v Yule* (1969) 8 D.L.R. (3d) 683, *McPhail v Cunninghame District Council* (1985) S.L.T. 149.

Automatic termination

14–024 Some forms make termination automatic on insolvency but optional in relation to other events, or automatic on some insolvency events but not for others. Automatic termination might help an employer who pays a certificate in ignorance of the occurrence of an insolvency event. As the termination suspends the employer's duty to pay, it may be able to recover the payment as made under a mistake of fact. On the other hand, automatic termination removes any chance of accepting the contractor's conduct after the insolvency event as a repudiation, at least as far as it concerns the completion of the works: *Perar v General Surety* (1994) 66 B.L.R. 72. It is arguable that automatic termination would not affect the employer's right to accept a repudiation which occurred before the insolvency event: *Laing and Morrison-Knudson v Aegon Insurance* (1997) 86 B.L.R. 70 (which concerned a termination on notice).

In *Samuel Properties v London Borough of Richmond* (unreported, 22 July 1983), Judge John Newey Q.C. stated:

> "I think that if a contract, whether it be for building or for anything else, provides for automatic termination in a certain eventuality, termination as a result of that term is in accordance with the contract and not in breach of it."

It is possible, however, that the court would not uphold a term providing for automatic termination if satisfied that it was activated by an event within one of the parties' control: *New Zealand Shipping v Société des Ateliers* [1919] A.C. 1 at 9, Carter (1990 97–8). If so, it would take effect as a term giving a right of termination to the innocent party. Conceivably, this could be the case in the event of a voluntary liquidation, administration or receivership where the appointment is made at the borrower's request. It has been suggested that it is "just conceivable" that an automatic termination clause could constitute a preference under s.239 of the Insolvency Act 1986 (Totty and Moss at H6.02). This possibility is considered in Ch.20. Automatic termination on informal insolvency suffers from the problems inherent in the automatic crystallisation of a floating charge (Lightman and Moss 2007). How can a third party know when the event has occurred? What happens if the contractor manages to trade out of its difficulties? In view of these and other potential problems, provision for automatic termination on informal insolvency is perhaps best avoided.

Automatic suspension

The 2005 edition of the JCT forms has introduced a new concept: the automatic suspension of the contractor's duty to carry out the works and the employer's duty to pay under cl.8.5.3 (the former only in the event of employer insolvency). This is effectively the suspension or freezing of the contract. It applies on the occurrence of any of the formal insolvency events listed in cl.8.1 and will continue until either the employer or the contractor serves notice of termination. As well as the suspension, a formal insolvency event has the effect of activating the post-termination payment regime of cll.8.7.4 and 8.7.5, whether or not a notice of termination is served. The financial consequences of the automatic suspension are not articulated but will presumably either be the subject of an agreement whereby the other party agrees not to terminate or fall within the post-termination losses recoverable under cl.8.5.3. **14–025**

Insolvency events

Under JCT 2005 each party agrees to notify the other "if he makes any proposal, gives notice of any meeting or becomes the subject of any proceedings or appointment relating to any of the matters referred to in clause 8.1" (cll.8.5.2 and 8.10.2). These words could refer to the preparatory steps for a company voluntary arrangement, liquidation or administration, or the appointment of a provisional liquidator. **14–026**

In *Martyn Rose v AKG Group* [2003] 2 B.C.L.C. 102, the court was asked to construe a clause in a shareholders' agreement which included as an insolvency an event where "any person takes any step (and it is not withdrawn or discharged within 30 days) to appoint a liquidator". It was held that the issue of a winding up petition was a step towards an insolvency event within the clause. The petition was presented against the company by a director claiming damages for constructive dismissal and was alleged to be a deliberate tactic to extract a speedy settlement, exploiting the director's knowledge of the terms of the shareholders' agreement. The agreement included a duty to notify in similar terms to the JCT form but there was no sanction in the event of a failure to notify. The wording is similar to the prohibition in para.43, Sch.B1 of the Insolvency Act 1986, that once an administration has commenced "no step may be taken to enforce security" See Goode 2005, para.10–54 on this expression).

An event of default can occur even where insolvency proceedings are later withdrawn. In *The Law Debenture Trust Corporation v Elektrim Finance* [2005] EWHC 1999, the events of default under a guarantee included proceedings initiated "under any applicable bankruptcy, reorganisation or insolvency law". An application was made in Poland for the bankruptcy of the guarantor but later withdrawn. The guarantor argued that the debts on which it was based were the subject of a *bona fide* dispute and there was evidence that a petition once withdrawn was of no effect under Polish law. Nevertheless, Hart J. held that an event of default had occurred (paras 57–61).

It sometimes happens that the parties provide for an insolvency event which is conceptually impossible. In *Martyn Rose*, the agreement provided that an insolvency event should occur if a court of competent jurisdication made an order for the 'dissolution' of one of the parties. The court cannot make an order for dissolution under English insolvency law. In the Court of Appeal, Blackburne J. (with whom Peter Gibson L.J. agreed) decided that the word could only sensibly mean liquidation (para.36) while Arden L.J. considered it could only refer to a possible order by a foreign court (para.49).

The standard forms range widely in the scope of insolvency events giving rise to termination. Some are restricted and limit the events to bankruptcy or liquidation. Others are more comprehensive and include events short of formal insolvency e.g. simply "becoming insolvent". Nineteenth century contracts commonly included "insolvency" as a termination event: e.g. *Davies v Mayor of Swansea* (1853) L.J. Ex. 297. This applies even now to FIDIC (4th edn) as well as one-off contracts: *RWE-Industrie-Loesungen v Thyssen* [2006] EWHC 2111.

The Australian Cole Report referred to a term entitling a contractor to terminate "where it suspected on reasonable grounds that [a subcontractor] was insolvent or unable to pay its debts as they fell due" (Cole, 2003, Vol.8, Ch.12, Appendix A, para.105). This approach can be useful where an employer fears that a contractor may be insolvent and likely to default but cannot otherwise terminate the contract without risking liability for damages. An Australian case concerned a subcontract which allowed the contractor to remove the works from the control of the subcontractor on notice on the subcontractor "becoming insolvent." The contractor served a notice but on a different ground not available at the time. Nevertheless, it was held that the contractor had validly terminated since the subcontractor had been informally insolvent at the date of the notice. It was irrelevant that the contractor was unaware of the fact: *Minion v Graystone* (1990) 2 A.C.L.B. 7. The court has generally upheld such clauses: *Byblos Bank v Al-Khudairy* (1986) 2 B.C.C. 549 at 560–4. The widest term in a standard form is probably cl.63.1 of FIDIC (4th edn):

> "If the Contractor is deemed by law unable to pay his debts as they fall due, or enters into voluntary or involuntary bankruptcy, liquidation or dissolution (other than a voluntary liquidation for the purposes of amalgamation or reconstruction), or becomes insolvent, or makes an arrangement with, or assignment in favour of, his creditors, or agrees to carry out the Contract under a committee of inspection of his creditors, or if a receiver, administrator, trustee or liquidator is appointed over any substantial part of his assets, or if, under any law or regulation relating to

reorganisation, arrangement or readjustment of debts, proceedings are commenced against the Contractor or resolutions passed in connection with dissolution or liquidation or if any steps are taken to enforce any security interest over a substantial part of the assets of the Contractor, or if any act is done or event occurs with respect to the Contractor or his assets which, under any applicable law has a substantially similar effect to any of the foregoing acts or events, or if the Contractor has contravened Sub-Clause 3.1 [assignment and subcontracting], or has an execution levied on his goods . . ."

Although intended for use on international projects, the FIDIC contract is construed in accordance with English law. Questions arise on the adequacy of some of the descriptions, e.g. an administrator under the Insolvency Act 1986 is appointed to the company rather than its assets. The termination clause in the current (1999) edition of the Red Book refers to the making of an administration order but in practice, following the Enterprise Act 2002, administrations are almost always commenced out of court. Other possible events are the receipt of a statutory demand under s.123 Insolvency Act 1986 and the dishonouring of a cheque; but relying on such events may backfire on the employer. The more technical the event and the further away it is from being repudiatory at common law, the stricter will be the court's construction of the clause. A provision which includes as termination events procedures having a similar effect under overseas law to those named, is likely to be upheld by the court: *Merrill Lynch v Winterthur* [2007] EWHC 893 at paras 34–5.

The JCT forms tend to have a comprehensive list of events but omit the **14–027** appointment of a receiver under a fixed charge. In the JCT Constructing Excellence Contract (2006), however, either party can terminate the contract on notice if the other "becomes insolvent or has a liquidator, receiver, manager or administrative receiver appointed". It is not clear whether the choice of events reflects a view within the JCT that administration should now be supported in principle and no longer give rise to the right to terminate or whether the draftsman thought that administration might fall within the term "manager". The term "insolvent" would no doubt catch many administrations, but not necessarily all. The company or its directors have to declare that insolvency is actual or impending but this requirement does not apply if the appointment is made by the holder of a qualifying floating charge (Ch.13).

At any rate this approach contrasts with ICE (6th edn) in which the only insolvency event relevant to a company is liquidation. 'Administration' has been added as an insolvency event but (it seems) on the assumption that the contractor is an individual. The court may, however, construe the term as applying to any legal person acting in the capacity of contractor. When dealing with individuals, the clause has maintained the receiving order as an event, even though the concept was abolished with the repeal of the Bankruptcy Act 1914 by the Insolvency Act 1985. It sometimes happens that a termination clause in a contract between companies refers to insolvency events that can only happen to individuals. In such a case, the court may, by applying ordinary principles of construction, decide that the parties intended to refer to analogous procedures affecting companies: *Doheny v New India Assurance* [2004] EWCA 1705.

Some clauses require an architect's certificate of sufficient cause to terminate following an insolvency event. It has been held that:

"The fact that the contract could be fully and adequately completed by the trustee may well (in the absence of some ulterior motive) be good reason why the architect would not in the circumstances execute such a certificate. For that reason it seems to me the architect would first have to determine whether the contract could be completed by the trustee and hence the need for his certificate" (*Casson v Laing Construction* (1974) 18 C.B.R. 133 at 142, *per* Andrews J., affirmed on this point at (1975) 19 C.B.R. 89).

Under NEC3, if one party wishes to terminate, it has to notify the other of its reason as well as the project manager. The project manager then issues a termination certificate under cl.90.1 "if the reason complies with this contract". By clause 90.3, the employer's right to possession of the site and other remedies "are implemented" immediately after the certificate is issued. This form uses the present tense throughout. The clause seems to mean that the certificate is a condition precedent to the post-termination remedies.

Under ICE (7th edn), the employer can terminate on notice on the contractor's formal insolvency, but needs an engineer's certificate before relying on the effects of informal insolvency, such as abandonment of the site, suspension of the works or failing to proceed with due diligence. Unlike the JCT forms, there is no express prohibition against serving a notice "unreasonably or vexatiously" but there may be an implied obligation on the employer not to serve notice of termination if this would be acting unfairly or unreasonably: *Balfour Beatty v Docklands Light Railway* (1996) 76 B.L.R. 42. In an insolvency situation, the employer may prefer to rely on an event of default independent of an insolvency event. For example, in *OBG v Allan* [2007] 2 W.L.R. 920, (facts set out in detail at [2005] B.L.R. 245), the contractor went into receivership and left site when it became clear that interim funding would not be forthcoming. The employer repossessed the site on the engineer's certificate that the contractor had abandoned the works under cl.63 of ICE (5th edn). Clause 63.1 of FIDIC (4th edn.) similarly allows the employer to terminate if the engineer certifies that in his opinion the contractor has repudiated the contract.

Consensual termination

14–028 Where it is recognised by both employer and contractor that the contractor will not be able to complete, the parties sometimes agree to terminate the contract: e.g. *Leyland Motors v Napier Harbour Board* [1930] N.Z.L.R. 113 at 118, *Crouch Mining v The Scottish Coal Co* [2003] CSOH 217. If a payment is made by a contractor to get out of a contract and the payment is influenced by a desire to improve the employer's position on the contractor's liquidation, it may have to be repaid by the employer as a preference (see Ch.20). It was the consensual termination of contracts which led to the investigation of Norwest Holst Ltd under s.165(b) of the Companies Act 1948 (DTI 1981). Most consensual terminations take place as part of a novation (Ch.15).

Termination on notice

14–029 Termination on an employer's insolvency is on notice under JCT 80 or FIDIC (4th edn). The contractor has no express power to terminate in the event of the insolvency of the employer under JCT 81, GC Works/1 or ICE

(5th edn.). Employer and contractor are given reciprocal rights to terminate on notice on the insolvency of the other under ACA 82 (3rd edn.).

JCT contracts provide that the notice must not be given "unreasonably or vexatiously" (although this requirement has been dropped in JCT 05). This has been held to involve an ulterior motive of oppressing the other party (*John Jarvis v Rockdale* (1986) 36 B.L.R. 48), or causing disproportionate disadvantage to it (*Reinwood v Brown & Sons* [2007] C.I.L.L. 2413). It is probably not unreasonable to terminate under the contract even if this increases or fails to reduce loss: Opeskin (1990, 314); *Thomas Construction v Grafton Furniture* [1988] 2 S.A. 546 at 560. How might this provision apply to an insolvency event? It would be reasonable for a contractor to terminate its employment if its employer were insolvent and unable to make any further payments under the contract, as in *Comco Constructions v Westminster Properties* (1990) 2 W.A.R. 335 at 344, where the contractor terminated its employment on the employer having execution levied against it. But if the employer through its insolvency practitioner were able to continue the contract and honour all its payment obligations, it might be unreasonable for the contractor to terminate, especially as it would not have had the right to do so under the general law. If the employer were in administration, the court might consider it unreasonable or vexatious for the contractor to terminate in view of the purpose of the administration procedure and the fact that the contractor as a creditor of the employer, actual or contingent, has an interest in the outcome of the procedure.

In Australia an express power to remove the contractor from site by reason of insolvency is subject to an implied duty to exercise it reasonably: *Hughes v Trustees of the Roman Catholic Church* (1994) 10 B.C.L. 335. It would usually be reasonable to terminate for insolvency but not in all cases, e.g. where a winding up petition has been issued vexatiously. The implied term as to reasonableness imposes a duty on the employer to enquire about the surrounding circumstances before exercising its power. "Examples can be multiplied. A contractor may be in the process of having the proceedings against it disposed of by agreement . . . [or] where the [employer] has engineered or encouraged the commencement of the proceedings against the contractor" (at 362, *per* Priestley J.A.). In that case, the court found that the power had been exercised reasonably. The petition had been issued by unpaid nominated subcontractors and statutory demands had been served. The contractor argued that its inability to pay had been caused by the employer but this was not supported by the evidence.

Waiver and withdrawal of termination

Where termination is not automatic, the right to terminate must be exercised within a reasonable time of the event relied on, otherwise the employer may be taken to have waived it: *Marsden v Sambell* (1880) 43 L.T. 120. What amounts to a reasonable time will depend on all the facts of the case. **14–030**

JCT contracts make automatic termination subject to re-instatement by agreement with the insolvency practitioner. The employer should be wary of re-instatement being inferred from all the circumstances where this is not intended. This may occur where an insolvency practitioner is allowed to retain possession of the site after his appointment and is likely where the insolvency practitioner is allowed to continue the contract to the knowledge of the employer. If a notice of termination is expressly subject to withdrawal on fulfilment of a condition, ceasing work after the condition has been satisfied will be a repudiation: *Ellis Tylin v Co-Operative Retail Services* [1999] B.L.R. 205, 216, 220. This could occur where a receiver persuades an employer to withdraw a termination notice if it can obtain a bond in support of the completion of the works. In *Robin Ellis v Vinexsa International* (2003) 93 Con. L.R. 92, where a contractor remedied a breach following a notice to show cause served under IFC 84 but defaulted a second time, it was held that the employer could rely on the original notice and terminate the contractor's employment. The breach in question was withdrawal of labour from site.

4. Subcontracts

14–031 One of the major risks to contractors arising of employer insolvency is liability to subcontractors. A common way of managing this risk is to insert a clause in the subcontract allowing the contractor to terminate it on termination of the main contract. As a result, the contractor's inability to give access to the subcontractor will not be a breach of the subcontract. As a further way of reducing its loss, the termination clause may limit the compensation payable to the subcontractor. Such transfer of risk involves a narrowing of the subcontractor's rights at common law. The court requires clear wording in order to achieve such a result. In practice, this can only be achieved by the harmonisation of main and subcontract termination clauses.

To the layman, there is no real difference between the methods of termination adopted in construction contracts: terminating the contract, terminating the contractor's employment, or excluding the contractor from site without avoiding the contract. The particular formula seems to have little effect on the consequential rights conferred by the contract. If those rights mirrored or were wider than the common law, the court might be willing to treat these approaches as having the same effect. Since termination clauses in subcontracts often cut down the subcontractor's common law rights, however, subtle differences in approach between main and subcontract termination clauses have been construed in favour of the subcontractor. It is important to remember that the main function of a subcontract termination clause in this context is to allow the contractor to deny the subcontractor future access to site without being in repudiation of the subcontract.

Under cl.63(1) of ICE (5th and 6th editions), the employer is entitled in certain circumstances to enter the site and expel the contractor "without thereby avoiding the contract or releasing the contractor from any of his obligations or liabilities under the contract . . ." The FCEC form of subcontract allows the contractor to terminate the subcontractor's employment on notice "if the main contract is determined for any reason whatsoever". The compensation allowed to the subcontractor after termination excludes loss of profit. The court has refused to regard the employer's entry on site as a "determination of the contract." As a result, it will be a repudiation of the subcontract entitling the subcontractor to full repudiation damages: *ER Dyer v Simon Build, Peter Lind Partnership* (1982) 23

B.L.R. 23. In *Iezzi Constructions v Currumbin* (1994) B.C.L. 408 a contractor terminated the main contract where the employer was insolvent. The contractor then repudiated a subcontract by denying the subcontractor access to the site. The repudiation was accepted. The contractor could not rely on a pay when paid clause as a defence to a claim for a *quantum meruit* following the termination. On its true construction, the clause related only to progress payments payable while the primary obligations under the contract were still alive and could not apply to a claim for a *quantum meruit*.

The JCT forms use the concept of "termination of employment". For example, cl.31.2.1 of NSC/4A provides that if the employment of the contractor is determined under the main contract then the employment of the subcontractor thereupon also determines. The subcontract also limits the subcontractor's rights to compensation. If the main contract is repudiated by the employer, it will not be treated as a termination of the contractor's employment. It follows that the contractor will also repudiate the subcontract entitling the subcontractor to full repudiation damages: *Scobie & McIntosh v Clayton Bowmore* (1990) 49 B.L.R. 119. Although it might be assumed that acceptance of repudiation would terminate the contractor's employment, since the greater includes the lesser, the need for exceptionally clear words to exclude the common law enables the court to take a literal approach.

In *Milburn Services v United Trading Group* (1995) 2 Con. L.R. 130, a **14–032** subcontract provided: "In the event that the main contract is terminated by the employer for any reason attributable to the contractor, then the contractor hereby undertakes to reimburse, on demand, all costs and expenses incurred by the subcontractor as a result of such termination". The failure to provide for termination meant that the subcontract was repudiated by the contractor on the same day as the employer's repudiation of the main contract since the contractor could no longer give access to the subcontractor. One solution may be to avoid all of the expressions historically used in construction contracts (expulsion, determination, and the like) and follow shipping practice. In *Aktieselskabet v Mobil North Sea* [2001] 2 Lloyd's Rep. 127, for example, a charterparty for the hire of an anchor handling vessel was terminable by the charterer on notice in the event that their own charter for an off-shore drilling unit was 'terminated'. David Steel J. held that 'termination' in that context simply meant coming or being brought to an end, however it occurred, i.e. irrespective of fault. This is the approach taken by cl.10.1 of the JCT Constructing Excellence Contract (2006).

In the case of NEC3 the termination clause is stepped down into the subcontract in identical terms. There is no specific right allowing the contractor to terminate the subcontract in the event of a termination of NEC3. By cl.90.2 of the subcontract, however, the contractor may "terminate for any reason", and once it issues a certificate of termination, the suite of post-termination remedies becomes available, including the right to instruct the subcontractor to leave site. The right is so wide that it would appear to include a termination under NEC3 even if caused by the contractor's default. But it is not clear how this general right relates to the specific grounds set out in the clause. Could the contractor exercise the right simply because it suspected the subcontractor was in financial difficulty or must one of the specified insolvency events have occurred? There is a tension between the contractor's desire for absolute power and the subcontractor's wish to define the limits of that power.

A peculiarity of DOM/1 and NSC/4 is that neither form allows the subcontractor to terminate its employment on the insolvency of the contractor. The forms are inconsistent in this respect, as the subcontractor's employment is terminated on its own insolvency (on notice under DOM/1 and automatically under NSC/4). There is no obvious justification for the absence of reciprocal rights. A domestic subcontractor is denied loss and expense where its employment is terminated on termination of the contractor's employment under the main contract. This apparently unreasonable provision is mirrored in NAM/SC. It is hard to understand this distinction between domestic and nominated subcontracts. The termination would not affect the subcontractor's accrued rights: *Westralian Farmers v Commonwealth Agricultural Service Engineers* (1935) 54 C.L.R. 361.

In practice, subcontractors may not exploit the fact that they are no longer obliged to continue working on site unless they want to get out of the contract or to re-negotiate their rates. From the point of view of an insolvency practitioner appointed over an employer, this can make it more difficult to rescue the project. Even if the employer is already the assignee of the benefit of existing subcontracts, this will be of little use where the subcontractors are no longer obliged to perform. In this situation, however, the automatic termination of subcontracts may assist the employer in approaching the subcontractors direct without risk of liability in the tort of interference with contract: compare *Remm Construction v Allco* (1990) 53 S.A.S.R. 471 discussed in Ch.6.

In summary, the following questions are worth bearing in mind:

- Do main and subcontracts use the same terminology?
- Does the subcontract accurately reflects the processes of the main contract?
- Does the subcontract anticipate a main contract repudiation as well as contractual termination?
- Can the subcontract termination procedure be activated whoever terminates the main contract?
- Take care when using an engineering subcontract form with a building main contract form and vice versa.
- Can a subcontract termination can be activated even if the main contract termination is disputed?

5. Post-termination rights

14–033 The consequential rights given by termination clauses are of very long standing and have generally been upheld by the court. They derive from nineteenth century building leases and railway contracts, e.g. *Roach v Great Western Railway* (1841) 1 Q.B. 51. Historically, the main benefit to the employer has been the major change in its payment obligation: the duty to pay is suspended and then postponed until after the final account of the completion contractor has been agreed. The suspension supports two further changes to the employer's duty to pay. First, it is made contingent on a net amount being due to the contractor after setting off the cost to complete against the outstanding balance of the contract sum. Second, to the extent that the employer makes direct payments, the duty to pay the contractor is converted into a right to pay subcontractors and suppliers and to set off equivalent amounts against the contractor (see Ch.17). Issues concerning the fate of plant and equipment on termination are considered in Ch.6, and goods and materials in Ch.7. For completion options see Chs 15 and 16. The range of consequential rights is as follows:

1. to repossess the site;
2. to make alternative arrangements for completion of the work by engaging a completion contractor;
3. to suspend further payments to the contractor until after the works have been completed and a final accounting exercise has been carried out;
4. to use the contractor's plant, equipment and materials for the completion of the works;
5. to use designs whose copyright is vested in the contractor or others;
6. to call a demand bond or, once loss is established, to enforce a surety bond;
7. to forfeit a security deposit, trust account or escrow account;
8. to set off the cost to complete and losses following termination against the balance of the contract sum and any other monies due or to become due to the contractor;
9. to pay subcontractors, suppliers and leasing companies direct and set the payments off against money due to the contractor;
10. to compel the assignment or novation of all contracts entered into by the contractor with others relating to the works;
11. to sell materials and plant after the works have been completed and set off their value against the loss caused to the employer by the termination;
12. to require the contractor to remove unwanted items, such as site accommodation, or to sell them if the contractor fails to do so;
13. to forfeit extracted material which would otherwise belong to the contractor;
14. to deem money already paid to the contractor as having been received in full and final satisfaction of all claims under the contract; and
15. to deduct liquidated damages from sums due to the contractor until the works are finally completed.

In the absence of agreement, a claim to enforce post-termination rights can be brought by an adjudication: *Orange v ABB* [2003] B.L.R. 323. Adjudication can also be used in order to recover the cost to complete following a termination: *Bracken v Billinghurst* [2004] 2 T.C.L.R. 4.

6. Possession of the site

A contractor is entitled to possession of the site while it carries out the work. **14–034**
If its employment is terminated it can no longer carry out the work. In the employer's view, it follows that the contractor must leave the site. The

contractor may apply to the court for an injunction preventing the employer from removing it or the employer may seek an injunction ordering the contractor to leave. Such orders are treated as specific performance of the contract. When hearing applications for specific performance, the court pays particular regard to the nature of the project and the reasons for termination.

Specific performance

14–035 Outside insolvency, the court has often refused specific performance of construction contracts on the following grounds: damages would be an adequate remedy; the works to be done were not sufficiently defined; the court could not supervise them; the employer should not be forced to continue if it wished to abandon the project; the balance of convenience or the merits were against the applicant; or the court could not form a view on them without a full trial. Even so, the court has a discretion to order specific performance of a building contract and will do so where it thinks fit: *Wolverhampton Corporation v Emmons* [1901] 1 K.B. 515.

During the nineteenth century, orders for specific performance were consistently made in two situations: (1) in consideration of the sale of land on which to lay track, railway companies promised to build roads or bridges for the landowner connecting the severed parts of the estate; and (2) in consideration of the construction of houses on its land, an owner promised to convey an interest in the land to the builder on completion. In the first case, the works were part of the consideration for the grant of the land. In the second, the grant of land was consideration for the works (Jones and Goodhart 1996). The same would apply to a sale of land where the vendor agreed to lay drains and sewers on her own land for the benefit of the land being transferred: *Carpenter's Estates v Davies* [1940] Ch. 160.

In the ordinary situation where the works are not connected with a grant of land by or to the builder, it is hard to lay down any general principles. The court has refused to grant an injunction ordering the contractor to leave site following termination of its employment: *London Borough of Hounslow v Twickenham Garden* [1971] Ch. 233. Most later decisions have gone the other way, and the criteria for an injunction have since been lowered, making it easier for the employer to remove the contractor in this situation (Lightman and Moss 2007). Where the works are ongoing, however, the case will be decided on its merits.

In *Channel Tunnel Group v Balfour Beatty* (unreported, November 27, 1991, Evans J.), the contractor threatened to suspend part of the works unless it was paid in respect of a substantial variation. At first instance, the court made it clear that, had the contractor not given an undertaking to give at least 14 days notice of any cessation of work, it would have granted an injunction restraining the contractor from suspending the work, i.e. ordering it to continue. Suspension would have "vast financial consequences" for the employer for whom damages would not have been an adequate remedy. The work in question was well defined and the injunction would be effective in stopping the suspension being instructed at management level. The Court of Appeal would have granted an injunction in this case had it not concluded that it lacked the jurisdiction to make it: (1992) 56 B.L.R. 18, 41. The House of Lords acknowledged that the injunction would have been equivalent to an order for specific performance, but the employer failed on jurisdictional grounds: (1993) 61 B.L.R. 38.

The law on specific performance was reviewed by the House of Lords in *Co-Operative Insurance v Argyll Stores* [1997] 2 W.L.R. 898. A distinction was drawn between ordering a person to carry out a contract "to achieve a result" and "to carry on activities" such as running a business. A construction contract could fall within the former category and therefore remain capable of an order of specific performance if justified by the circumstances. However, a seven year outsourcing agreement might fall within the latter: see *Vertex Data Science v Powergen* [2006] EWHC 1340 in which Tomlinson J. refused an injunction restraining a party from acting on a notice of termination it had served.

Contrast a non-insolvency case in which a mandatory injunction in aid of a supply contract was refused. In *Comtec Cable Accessories v Datwyler* (unreported, December 12, 2000), Datwyler agreed to supply fibre optic cable to Comtec who had agreed to supply it to a customer who was building a national telecommunications network. The order was for four hundred kilometres of cable to be supplied by December 29, 2000 but by early December only 48 kilometres of cable had been delivered. Comtec sought an injunction for the delivery of a further 88 kilometres of cable by the end of the year. On the evidence:

(1) there was a world wide shortage of the fibre;

(2) Datwyler was only a distributor although its parent company was a manufacturer of such cable and there were common directors;

(3) since May the price of cable had increased substantially and Datwyler could make a greater profit by selling to other customers above the fixed price agreed with Comtec;

(4) Datwyler was having difficulty getting supplies from the Far East and had no significant stock it could appropriate in order to comply with an injunction; and

(5) supplies to customers other than Comtec were being reduced *pro rata*.

Sachs J. refused the injunction, saying that on the evidence he was satisfied that Datwyler had discharged the burden of showing that it would be impossible to comply with it.

The contractor's licence extends to re-entry after completion to the extent necessary to complete its remaining obligations to the end of the defects liability period. In *Wiltshier Construction v Parkers Developments* (1996) 13 Const. L.J. 129, an injunction was granted on unusual facts restraining an employer from serving notice of termination of a management contract which relied on a notice which had been held to be invalid.

Insolvent contractor

If the contractor is insolvent, two questions arise: Can the employer obtain an order that the contractor complete the works? Can the contractor force the employer to continue the contract and even prevent the employer from re-entering the site? The court is understandably reluctant to intervene in such situations: "Commercial life would be subjected to new and unjust hazards if the court were to decree specific performance of contracts normally sounding **14–036** only in damages, simply because of a party's insolvency" (*Anders v O/Y Lovisa Stevedoring* [1985] S.T.C. 301 at 306, *per* Goulding J.).

In *Macleod v Alexander Sutherland* (1977) S.L.T. 44, a contractor bought land and covenanted with the vendor to carry out works on it. This is the reverse of the situation in *Carpenter's Estates v Davies* referred to above. The contractor went into receivership and the court refused to order the receiver to complete the works as it would involve expenditure for which the receiver might become personally liable.

This case can be compared with *Manchester & District Housing Association v Fearnley Construction* (2001) 81 P. & C.R. DG2, in which the contractor agreed to carry out building works on its own land and to sell the property to the association once they had been completed. Before completing the work, the contractor went into administrative receivership. The receivers made it clear that the contractor would not be completing the work. The association claimed specific performance of the builder's obligation to convey the land and an abatement of the purchase price in respect of damages for non-completion. The contractor then went into voluntary liquidation. It was argued by the liquidator (and the bank who had a charge over the property) that, as the obligation to convey only arose on completion of the building work, it could not arise. The conditionality of the agreement meant that the association had not acquired the equitable interest in the land needed for specific performance. The material obligations (to do building work and to convey the land) were so intertwined that one could not be enforced without the other. Finally, it was argued that to grant specific performance with an abatement of the purchase price would subvert the statutory scheme for payment of creditors *pari passu* in a liquidation.

Mr K. Garnett Q.C. granted an order for specific performance and ordered an inquiry as to the amount of the abatement. He was impressed by the principle that a person should not be entitled to take advantage of his own wrong; here, the contractor would be relying on its own breach in relation to the building work to avoid having to transfer the land. The court distinguished other authorities on the question of severability. Having held that the contract "was no longer conditional in the sense argued for" and that the association did have an equitable interest, specific performance was ordered.

If the insolvency practitioner can satisfy the court that the contractor has the resources to complete the works, are there circumstances in which the contractor might obtain specific performance of the employer's obligations? As the employer's obligation is primarily to pay certified sums, the position ought to be simpler than an order to complete the works. An order against the employer is conceivable if it could be shown that the contractor could only obtain a grant of property from the employer or a third party after it had completed the work. This is analogous to relief from forfeiture (see para.14–038 below).

Insolvent employer

14–037 The court is not likely to order a contractor to work for an insolvent employer, at least in the absence of a secure mechanism for payment. If the receiver of the employer decides not to complete the project, specific performance will not be ordered against him: *Munroe v Wivenhoe & Brightlingsea Railway* (1855) L.T. 655. The court will not grant specific performance if it would mean forcing an employer to accept a building or a contractor it no longer wishes to have. If the property market is such that the receiver decides to suspend the project pending an improvement in the situation, the position is less clear. A contractor can improve its prospects of retaining possession of the site by electing not to terminate its employment or deciding to affirm the contract if the employer is in repudiation. In this situation contractors sometimes claim to be exercising a "builder's lien". In English law, however, there is no lien whether possessory or non-possessory. In the US and Canada, contractors have rights to a lien in certain circumstances but this affects title to the land and does not confer any possessory right (Odams 1996, Reynolds 1996).

Relief against forfeiture

Relief is available only where the rights under forfeiture are proprietary or possessory rather than contractual: *On Demand Information v Michael Gerson* [2002] 2 W.L.R. 919. Relief was granted in *Underground (Civil Engineering) Ltd v London Borough of Croydon* [1990] E.G.C.S. 48, where the contractor was to be entitled to a 125–year lease within one month after practical completion. The contract allowed the employer to re-enter and take possession of the contractor's plant and materials if the contractor failed to complete within 12 months or such extended period as the contract allowed. The contractor failed to complete in time because it had ceased work on learning from the employer that the site was to be compulsorily purchased. Nevertheless, the employer re-entered when only three weeks' work was outstanding. The court held that the termination clause was not a penalty but did grant relief from forfeiture. **14–038**

> "I am persuaded by counsel for the corporation that in an ordinary building contract the licence granted by the building owner to the builder is for the benefit of the owner as opposed to giving the builder any kind of 'beneficial' right or interest in the land. For that reason I do not consider that a builder in such a case would have a possessory or proprietary right such as would give the court jurisdiction to grant relief: the builder would have a 'mere' licence. In other words, the requirement in the authorities binding on this court that the jurisdiction to grant relief from forfeiture arises only in relation to contracts concerning the transfer of proprietary or possessory rights is not satisfied in an ordinary building contract. There are a number of features in this agreement which distinguish it from an ordinary building agreement. . . . The company went into occupation of the land with a view to becoming a long leaseholder of it. It had an insurable interest in the building. It had the right to specific performance of the corporation's obligation to grant the lease. It had the right to use the agreement as security for financial arrangements. It was required to observe the provisions of the lease as if it had been granted. . . . By reason of the factors just referred to I take the view that the company was granted sufficient interest in the land and building thereon to satisfy the 'possessory or proprietary interest' requirement and that the concept of relief from forfeiture applies in this case" *per* Mr Thomas Morison Q.C.

An application for relief against forfeiture was refused in the Australian case of *Westminster Properties v Comco Constructions* (1991) 5 W.A.R. 191.

The contract was in the JCCB 1985 form which allows the contractor to terminate its employment if the employer "has an execution levied against it" together with the usual insolvency events. The court considered that execution "has at least the potential to adversely affect the ability of the proprietor to meet its obligations under the contract" (at 194, *per* Malcolm C.J.). After terminating, the contractor had a lien on materials the property in which had passed to the employer until all moneys due to the contractor had been paid. This was not the forfeiture of a possessory right. Even if it were, it would be relief against that provision rather than against termination of the contractor's employment.

There was no reported case of relief being granted for loss of the contractual right to perform. The contractual term was neither "the exaction of a forfeiture nor the imposition of a penalty" (at 197). If performed, the contract would not result in the acquisition of an interest in land, only its improvement by the aggregation of chattels. Termination was to protect the contractor against the employer's insolvency by avoiding the obligation to continue working at the risk of not being paid. The motive of the builder in opting to terminate on this ground was irrelevant.

The court held that the contractor was under no duty to act fairly in exercising the power. As a consequence, there was no scope for an argument based on unconscionability and no equity to grant relief. This was the case even though the contractor knew, at the date of termination, that the employer had satisfied the writ of execution. The contractor gave no warning of its intent to terminate nor did it make any enquiries about the writ of execution, it simply decided that to continue the contract would be "commercially unsound". The contractor was under no duty to investigate the employer's financial circumstances (at 201). The court conceded that the distinction between an ordinary chose in action and a possessory or proprietary right was sometimes difficult to draw (at 205). The court distinguished between a forfeiture (the loss of an interest in property as a result of a failure to perform a covenant), and a penalty (a contractual provision which allowed one party to require the whole price to be paid even though it vastly exceeded the actual loss sustained).

It is worth comparing the question of relief from forfeiture with a power to terminate which has to be exercised on reasonable grounds or the situation where a contract is nearing completion ahead of programme and, but for the termination, the contractor would have become entitled to an early completion bonus. It is possible that the power of a contractor to resist termination by rectifying a default following service of a notice by the employer could displace any claim there might otherwise have been for relief against forfeiture: see the discussion in *Western Bulk Carriers v Li Hai* [2005] 2 Lloyd's Rep. 389. Such a power is contained in the anti-technicality clause found in modern charterparties which mitigates against the exercise of an owner's right to withdraw the ship from hire in the event of small amounts not being paid. Compare also this aspect of shipping law with the modern right of a contractor to determine its employment for non-payment.

7. Assignment of subcontracts

14–039 It is important for the employer to have direct access to subcontractors on the contractor's insolvency. Construction contracts often provide that after termination the contractor is obliged to assign to the employer the benefit of any contracts with subcontractors or suppliers. This could be useful to the employer as until these contracts are terminated the subcontractors or suppliers are bound to perform them. This device is only likely to work where the subcontractor has been paid up to date and has no other claim against the contractor at the date of receipt of notice of assignment from the employer. The device will not work where the subcontract automatically terminates on termination of the main contract or has a non-assignability clause.

In that context it is worth noting *ANC v Clark Goldring and Page* [2001] B.C.C. 479, in which a non-assignability clause was held not to survive the termination of the agreement. The clause prevented assignments by franchisees of a parcel collection and delivery service without the prior written consent of the franchisor. Consent was not to be unreasonably withheld provided the franchisee was not in breach at the time and the proposed assignee was prepared to pay the assignor's costs of the assignment, agree to be bound by the agreement, and sign a specific undertaking to comply with the restrictive covenants. (This provision could be interpreted as a conditional agreement to novate.) The court heard two claims together, both brought by assignees of insolvent franchisees. One franchisee had entered a company voluntary arrangement, the other a creditors' voluntary liquidation. In both cases the assignment was on the basis that a percentage of the proceeds of a successful claim would be paid to the company. The Court of Appeal held both assignments valid because on its true construction the intent of the agreement was to give a franchisee freedom to assign, provided the franchisor was protected against unfair competition as well as incompetence on the part of the assignee, by new enforceable undertakings being put in place. Once the agreement had come to an end such a prohibition on assignment served no useful purpose.

In the PFI context, the principal contract may provide for the assignment of the benefit of subcontracts to the employer on the contractor's default. This provision is intended to apply to smaller subcontractors for whom step-in agreements are impracticable. When negotiating the principal contract the contractor may argue that, in return for agreeing to the assignment of subcontracts on its default, it should be released from liability in respect of the work done under them. In answer to this the employer may argue along the following lines: although the assignment would give the employer a direct right, the contractor had to continue to be responsible for the insolvency risk attached to the subcontracts, i.e. that the subcontractors would be unable to satisfy a judgment obtained pursuant to the assigned claim. In any case there may be a gap in the overall risk which would not be covered if the contractor were given a release. For example, every assignment is subject to equities and the subcontractor may put up a defence that the matters complained of were instructed or approved by the contractor.

If necessary, perhaps the employer could give an undertaking to the contractor to re-assign the benefit of the subcontracts if the employer did not wish to rely on them. The damages received from the subcontractors would go to reduce the contractor's liability and the employer would have been doing the contractor's work for it in assuming conduct of the proceedings at no cost to the contractor. It is worth asking, by analogy with name-borrowing procedures, whether the principal contract needs to incorporate a term that the contractor will co-operate in the provision of documents and witnesses.

Before Amendment 11 (1992), JCT contracts provided that the employer could assign the benefit although the subcontractor was given the right to object to a further assignment: e.g. cl.27.4.2.1 of JCT 80. This reflected the purpose of the clause, namely to enable the employer to assign the benefit of the subcontract to the completion contractor. The Australian JCC-1994 forms supplement compulsory assignment by making the employer the contractor's attorney, allowing it to execute the assignment on the builder's behalf.

As the benefit of contracts with third parties falls within the wide definition of "property" in s.436 of the Insolvency Act 1986, the enforced assignment on bankruptcy or liquidation is likely to contravene the *pari passu* rule. The position would be different if before bankruptcy or liquidation the contractor had declared a trust of the benefit of its subcontracts to the employer (Ch.9). Still more problematic are terms which enforce a novation following a contractor's insolvency. As novation requires the consent of employer, contractor and subcontractor, it is not possible in the main contract to enforce a novation without the subcontractor's consent (Ch.15). As the identity of the replacement contractor is not known until after the contractor's default, and the terms of the proposed novation are usually not prescribed, the agreement may be void for uncertainty. One solution is to require the subcontractors to enter into direct agreements with the employer at the inception of the project with draft forms of novation annexed.

8. Liquidated damages

14–040 After the works have been completed by an alternative contractor, can the employer claim liquidated damages to the date of completion from the insolvent contractor? The answer is usually "no" because it would be beyond the contractor's power to stop damages running and within the power of the employer to continue them by delaying completion. In *British Glanzstoff v General Accident* [1913] A.C. 143, the date for completion under the completion contract was one month before the date for completion under the original contract but the works were not completed until after the latter date. It was held that the termination clause allowing the employer to re-enter the site after the contractor's bankruptcy was incompatible with an entitlement to liquidated damages, which could only apply where the works had been finished by the original contractor (see also *Chanthall Investments v FG Minter* [1976] S.C. 73; Burke 1986, 84–85).

Where the works are completed by another contractor following an acceptance of a repudiation, "time ceases to have relevance. Damages thereafter flow from the repudiation resulting from non-performance and the need to provide for substitute performance": *Bovis v Whatlings Contractors* (1995) 75 B.L.R. 1 at 9, *per* Lord Jauncey; *Greenore Port Technical & General* [2006] EWHC 3119. In other words, the employer can only recover liquidated damages up to the date of the repudiation. As Judge Humphrey LLoyd Q.C. pointed out in *Tower Housing v Technical & General Guarantee* (1997) 87 B.L.R. 82 at 94:

> "The revenue predicted by the contractual rate might not have materialised for reasons unconnected with the determination or it might in fact be less than the contractual rate used. Even if the rate were representative of loss of return on capital employed it would have to be justified as being the actual loss caused to be recoverable under clause 27.6.6.1."

The terms of both original and completion contracts are crucial, however, and can in context allow the employer to recover liquidated damages even if the contract is completed by another person. For example, where the works were completed by the contractor's guarantor, and the agreement between the guarantor and the employer provided that the original contract was to remain in being as if the completion contract had not been made, the employer was entitled to deduct liquidated damages from retention: *Re Yeadon Waterworks* (1895) 72 L.T. 832. See also *Baylis v Mayor of the City of Wellington* (1886) 4 N.Z.L.R. 84; *Williamson v Murdoch* [1912] W.A.R. 54; Kennedy-Grant (1999, 449).

9. Suspension of payments

A general power to suspend payment in the event of any breach by a **14–041** subcontractor was held to be a penalty in *Gilbert-Ash v Modern Engineering* [1974] A.C. 689. But one of the most valuable rights given to an employer after termination is the right to suspend payment to the contractor of sums which are already due and payable: *Thomas Construction v Grafton Furniture* [1986] 4 S.A. 510 at 519–520, affirmed in [1988] 2 S.A. 546. This right prevents an insolvency practitioner from arguing that the cost to complete and any consequential losses could not exceed a given proportion of the claim and obtaining summary judgment or an interim payment. The suspension of payment only relates to sums payable by the employer; if the contractor were liable for liquidated damages before termination, the employer could recover them even before the cost to complete was ascertained: *Tower Housing v Technical & General Guarantee* (1997) 87 B.L.R. 82 at 94. JCT 05 provides for suspension of payment in two scenarios: following the automatic suspension of the works on the occurrence of an insolvency event and after the termination of the contractor's employment.

The effect of the suspension on existing debts is not absolutely clear. On one view an existing debt is extinguished by the termination clause and replaced by a right to have an equivalent amount credited to the final account; on another the debt remains in being as part of the unpaid balance of the contract sum against which the cost to complete is set off but is deferred pending the taking of the account. In practice it may not matter which view is correct: see *Jackson v Laurieston Homes* [2005] CSOH 7 at para.18.

There are several exceptions. First, it has been held that payment is not suspended under the clause where automatic termination occurs after practical completion: *Emson Eastern v EME Developments* (1992) 55 B.L.R. 114. Second, there is an implied term in JCT 80 that where a contractor goes into administrative receivership and the employer abandons the project rather than engaging a completion contractor, the suspension of payments under cl.27 should come to an end: *Tern Construction v RBS Garages* (1992) 34 Con. L.R. 137. The employer is liable thereafter to pay previously certified sums. This situation is dealt with by cl.27.7 of JCT 98. Third, cl.27.6 of JCT 98 provides that the suspension does not apply to sums which accrue due 28 days or more before the termination which the employer has "unreasonably not paid".

In *Jackson v Laurieston Homes* a creditor issued proceedings against a contractor and obtained an arrestment against a certified sum due for payment by the employer. The contract incorporated JCT 98 with contractor's design. Several months later the employer terminated the contractor's employment, leaving the certified sum unpaid. Having obtained judgment against the contractor, the creditor sued the employer to enforce the arrestment. It was held that, as between itself and the creditor, the employer could not rely on the arrestment as a ground for not having honoured the certificate. As a consequence it could not rely on the suspension of payment and had to pay the creditor direct. Contrast the Malaysian case of *Binamin v Way Soon Construction* [2001] MLJU 111 in which the court refused to grant a garnishee order in respect of retention under a subcontract as the subcontract had been terminated and the right to payment of the retention had been suspended pending the taking of accounts. See also *Pierce Design International v Johnston* [2007] EWHC 1691 discussed below.

"Construction contracts"

14–042 The court has often said that the Housing Grants, Construction and Regeneration Act 1996 is intended to improve cash flow in the industry, not to interfere with substantive rights. In *Melville Dundas v George Wimpey* [2007] 1 W.L.R. 1136, the Act was considered for the first time by the House of Lords. It was held by a majority of three to two that the suspension of payment provision was a good defence to a claim for payment of a "sum due" under the Act even though the employer had not served a withholding notice by the final date for payment. Before considering the reasons for the decision, it useful to summarise the progress of the case in the courts below.

It concerned a valid termination by an employer following the contractor's entry into administrative receivership. A certified sum was due for payment but it had not been outstanding for 28 days or more before the receivership and was therefore caught by the suspension of payment under cl.27 of JCT 98 (with contractor's design). At first instance the receivers failed in their claim to the certified sum on the ground that ss.109–111 of the Act were "concerned with, and directed at, cash-flow questions, arising during the course of a continuing, non-determined construction contract" ([2005] S.L.T. 24 at para 24, *per* Lord Clarke). In other words the Act was not intended to regulate the position after a termination. In any event s.110(1) provided that the parties were free to agree the length of the period between the date on which a sum became due and the final date for payment. The suspension of payment was the exercise of such freedom of contract. However, the decision was reversed on appeal to the Court of Session reported at [2006] B.L.R. 164.

The court's reasoning was as follows. First, the receivership resulted in the termination of the contractor's employment but the contract remained in being. The Act continued to apply, as did cl.30, under which the final date for payment was 14 days after the contractor's application, which had expired a few days before receivers were appointed. No notice under s.111 had been served. Second, cl.30 (payment) was not made subject to the operation of cl.27 (termination), nor could suspension of payment have retrospective effect so as to alter the final date for payment of sums accrued due. Third, on the employer's case, it was not possible to tell from the termination clause when the final date for payment might be. The court accepted that, but for the Act, the receivers' claim would have failed.

Speaking for the majority in the House of Lords, Lord Hoffmann emphasised the security function of suspension of payment. Neither the Act nor the preparatory materials (the Latham Report (1994) and the DTI's consultation paper 'Fair Construction Contracts') refer to suspension of payment. The Act is procedural in nature. It is unlikely to have been Parliament's intention to remove this valuable security by implication. Where the right to suspend payment arises on a termination after the final date for payment, it is not possible to serve a withholding notice. The law does not compel performance of what is impossible. For the minority, Lord Neuberger took a simple approach based on the literal words of the Act: ". . . if a statute provides that a person 'may not withhold payment' after a specified date has passed, it appears to me that a contractual provision that he may do so must be ineffective" (para.64). If the court gave precedence to such a provision, ss.109–111 of the Act could be "rendered a dead letter" (para.69). The clarity of the Act admitted of no exceptions.

Different perspectives are at work here. If one starts with the Act it does appear at first sight, before looking at the contract, that it is intended to override anything the parties may decide. If one starts with the contract it is evident that the termination clause is intended to protect the employer against the consequences of the contractor's insolvency. It may be said that Lord Hoffmann is seeing through a perspective based on insolvency law (and its equitable background), while Lord Neuberger takes the viewpoint of construction (and its common law heritage). When the point at issue in this case was considered at a meeting of the Society of Construction Law seven years ago, the majority of those present inclined to Lord Neuberger's approach and this may represent received opinion in the industry (Davis 2001, 19). Archetypally, the literal approach belongs to Saturn and his children; but one which operates more deeply, and resorts to original solutions in aid of 'the just result', may belong to Hermes (see Ch.22).

Insolvency arguments

Some of the arguments based on insolvency were novel. Lord Hoffmann stated: **14–043**

> "Mr Howie [for the receivers] said that to allow the employer *any* security in the form of an unpaid instalment payment would be to allow him to profit from his own wrong. But the security arises, not from the terms of the contract but from the law of bankruptcy set-off. . . . It is in any case artificial to speak of the employer profiting from his own wrong when the contractor has no further interest in the matter and the issue is one of priority between the employer and the contractor's other creditors" (para.13).

The reference to bankruptcy set-off is not easy to follow. Obviously, it applies only where one of the parties becomes bankrupt, which is not the case here. Lord Hope expressed himself in similar terms, holding that suspension of payment "applies the principle of compensation in bankruptcy [bankruptcy set-off in Scottish law] to all cases where the employer determines the employment of the contractor by giving the employer the right to withhold payment of liquid debts making up the account" (para.34). Perhaps the idea is that bankruptcy set-off is the conceptual model for suspension of payment or is an analogy for the clause's security function or that suspension of payment is in theory at least a legitimate preparatory step towards bankruptcy set-off which deserves the court's protection. Or the thinking could be that liquidation set-off, which is practically identical to bankruptcy set-off, is in the background whenever a company becomes 'heavily insolvent' as in this case, even if all claims are dealt with in a receivership or administration.

Lord Hoffmann then seems to direct his mind to the situation in this case in which the claim brought by the receivers was in the name of the contractor but in right of the charge holder, who appointed them, as equitable assignee of the claim (see Ch.18). On the merits the question is: why should the charge holder benefit from the impossibility of serving a withholding notice in time at the expense of the employer who bargained for suspension of payment at the outset? Put in these terms the merits lay with the employer.

14–044 "Upon insolvency, liability to make an interim payment therefore becomes a matter which relates not to cash flow but to the substantive rights of the employer on the one hand and the contractor's secured or unsecured creditors on the other" (para.11, *per* Lord Hoffmann). If this is not a dispute about cash flow, then textual linguistic analysis of the statutory language is beside the point. Section 111 and the suspension of payment provision are concerned with different matters: facilitation of payment and security for payment. To make the latter subject to the former would be "to write it out of the contract" (para.18). It would be absurd to impute an intention to parliament to nullify suspension of payment "by the device of providing a notice requirement with which the employer can never comply" (para.20). Otherwise "the parties' freedom of contract" would be "curtailed by a mere piece of machinery" (para.22). The mischief addressed by s.111 was withholding of stage payments without notice, not the situation which arose in this case (para.41, *per* Lord Hope).

The response of the minority on the insolvency arguments was to contextualise the dispute as a purely contractual matter. Lord Mance stated that bankruptcy set-off and suspension of payment were entirely different concepts: one statutory, the other contractual (para.50); the Act was conclusive as far as the terms of the contract were concerned. He did not refer to the security function of the termination clause. Lord Neuberger was of the opinion that, had Parliament intended to exempt suspension of payment from the notice requirement under s.111, it would have legislated to that effect, just as it exempted certain formal insolvency events from the ban on pay when paid under s.113 (para.79). This is the "argument from redundancy" criticised by Lord Hoffmann in *Beaufort Developments v Gilbert-Ash* (1998) 88 B.L.R. 1 at 10. He also drew support from the proposal in "Fair Construction Contracts" that a trust be introduced as a payment mechanism into construction contracts. He inferred an intention behind this proposal that payment ought not to stop merely because of insolvency (para.80). It seems weak however to pray in aid a proposal that was never formally developed or carried through.

The whole exercise of imputing intention to Parliament is notoriously difficult. The 1996 Act was a compromise not so much between the political parties as between the constituent elements of the industry. The fact that suspension of payment on termination was not considered by the DTI or the legislature could be used as an argument either way. But Lord Hoffmann's concern that a procedural statute ought not without express provision to be allowed to negate a substantive right, including a contractual right functioning as a security, is surely justified.

Construction arguments

Many arguments were presented based on interpretations of the Act. They included the following **14–045**

- It was doubted whether s.111 ceased to apply in the event of a termination of the contractor's employment. Lord Hoffmann gave as an example a contractor's right to notice under cl.27.2 where his employment had been terminated for default. Lord Neuberger also thought that ss.109–111 applied to final payment under a construction contract (para.76).
- Lord Hoffmann rejected the submission that the effect of the suspension of payment was to extend the final date for payment until after the taking of the final account after the works had been completed by an alternative contractor. He considered that the concept of a final date for payment applied only to interim payments (para.21).
- Lord Hoffmann did not accept the idea that suspension of payment had the effect of making a "sum due" cease to be due for the purposes of s.111 (para.21). This submission was also rejected by Lord Neuberger (para.72).

Commentary on Melville Dundas v George Wimpey

The split decision reveals a real conflict between the perceived policy behind the Act and the legitimate expectations of the employer in protecting its position after a termination, especially if caused by the contractor's insolvency. The right to treat suspension of payment as a form of security goes back to Brunel's days: *Ranger v Great Western Railway* (1854) 5 H.L.C. 72 at 94. *Melville Dundas* respects its security function and stands as a necessary corrective to the over-literal application of the 1996 Act. The argument based on bankruptcy set-off relied on by Lord Hoffmann and Lord Hope is, however, somewhat strained. Other possible arguments I canvassed in my paper to the Society of Construction Law were: **14–046**

> "To the extent that it is necessary to harmonise the termination clause with the Act, suspension of payment could be regarded as a standing withholding notice of such sum or sums as may be due to the contractor in the event of a termination. Alternatively, the suspension of payment can be regarded as an inherent limitation of all receivables arising under the contract, so that every sum becoming due for payment for the purposes of the Act is conditional on the contractor's employment not having terminated before payment. Alternatively, if the suspension of payment precedes the final date for payment of a certified sum, no dispute can arise to be referred to an adjudicator as the parties have agreed that no action can be taken to recover the receivable until the contractual set-off has been operated and, where the contract so provides, a further certificate issued" (Davis 2001, 19).

Lord Hoffmann adverted to the first of these points when he implied that a notice of termination had the same effect as a withholding notice in giving the contractor the information it needed to decide whether to refer a dispute to adjudication. If termination were automatic on an insolvency event, the information would be within the contractor's knowledge without a notice. But perhaps the second suggestion, which borrows the "flawed asset" theory from finance law, appears the most convincing. Rather like *Bouygues v Dahl-Jensen* [2000] B.L.R. 522 or *MacJordan Construction v Brookmount Erostin* (1992) 56 B.L.R. 1, this case invites the question: is it a construction case or an insolvency case? But polarising the area of law which this book is calling "construction insolvency" can lead to confusion.

What are the implications of the case on previous case law on the Act? In *KNS Industrial Services v Sindall* (2001) 75 Con. L.R. 71, a subcontractor's employment under DOM/1 was terminated after an alleged right to payment accrued but before a dispute was referred to adjudication. Judge Humphrey LLoyd Q.C. commented:

> "If s 111 applies (which I doubt since clause 29.6 is part of a typical self-contained code applicable when the subcontractor is in serious and irreparable default) then that is the time when notice of intention to withhold might be given. There was therefore no need to give a notice in respect of the sums allowed by the adjudicator. The adjudicator appears prudently to have anticipated the inevitable" (at para.25).

It appears that an adjudicator had upheld the suspension of payment provision but this is not clear from the report. There was discussion whether, if the subcontractor's employment were terminated after the adjudicator's decision, the contractor could avoid complying with the decision by relying on the suspension of payment. This would be on the basis that it had a reasonable prospect of defending the claim. The judge did not give a clear answer but decided the issue on the basis of the particular wording of the subcontract.

> "To take an extreme instance, it would mean that in the event of an insolvency payment in full would have to be made to the liquidator, despite the clear wording of clause 29.6.3, with no prospect of recovery of that amount whether as an overpayment or by way of loss or damage under clause 29.6.4 except as an unsecured creditor. Seen as a contractual intention this result would be devoid of any commercial sense and absurd, just as it would be if there had been a termination for culpable default. In my judgment the answer is clear. Clause 38A.7.2 expressly provides that 'the parties shall, without prejudice to their other rights under the Contract, comply with decisions of the Adjudicator . . .' Therefore other rights under the contract which were not the subject of the decision remain available to the relevant party. If therefore by the time an adjudicator makes a decision requiring payment by a party the contract has been lawfully terminated by that party (or that party has real prospects of success in supporting that termination) or some other event has occurred which under the contract entitles a party not to pay then the amount required to be paid by the decision does not have to be paid" (para.28).

The reference to "some other event" could perhaps include a formal insolvency event which triggers the availability of a "pay when paid" clause which complies with s.113 of the Act. This reasoning treats the suspension of payment as a structural limitation on the subcontractor's rights, a role it has played since the nineteenth century. It is noteworthy that the court carefully reserved the application of the suspension to lawful terminations or those having a real prospect of success.

In *Fersons Contractors v Levolux* [2003] B.L.R. 118, the Court of Appeal was concerned with an unlawful termination and not surprisingly held that the suspension could not apply. Dicta in that case, which appear to be contrary to the decision in *Melville Douglas*, are no longer persuasive. In *The Construction Centre Group v The Highland Council* [2003] CSOH 114, a contractor obtained summary judgment to enforce an adjudicator's decision (reported at [2002] B.L.R. 476) but then went into receivership. The employer invoked cl.63 of ICE (5th edn) and expelled the contractor from site. It then appealed unsuccessfully against the summary judgment relying among other things on the suspension of payment in cl.63. The argument was rejected as defeating the intention of the parties "ascertained as it must be against the relative statutory background" (at para.15, *per* Lord Hamilton). The Law Lords in *Melville Douglas* were unanimous that the suspension related to "any payment" including payment of debts accrued due before the termination. But presumably the employer would have to apply to the court for a stay of execution of any summary judgment obtained by the contractor before the termination. If the termination was for formal insolvency a stay would probably be granted on that ground in any case.

The suspension of payment will not protect the employer under a JCT form in respect of debts accrued due more than 28 days before the termination which the employer has "unreasonably not paid" (see above). In *Pierce Design International v Johnston* [2007] EWHC 1691, an employer under JCT 98 (with contractor's design) failed to pay the VAT element of five interim valuations and also abated sums due without serving withholding notices, before terminating the contractor's employment on the ground that it had failed to proceed regularly and diligently with its obligations. It was held by Judge Peter Coulson Q.C. that the non-payment was unreasonable because it was not supported by withholding notices. It is not clear from the report whether any explanations for the abatements were offered at the time. Unlike the situation in *Melville Dundas v George Wimpey*, it was within the employer's power to serve the notices long before exercising its right to terminate. The contractor obtained summary judgment for the balances due.

It appears from the report that, as at the date of termination, the employer had a cross-claim for liquidated damages in excess of the claim, and there were also allegations of defects. The validity of the termination was disputed by the contractor. The court assessed the question of reasonableness by reference to the procedural requirement for notices rather than the substantive merits of the employer's cross-claims, which were not explored. The JCT termination clause "gave a limited benefit to the contractor;" it was "a short-cut to payment" (para.35) pending the ascertainment of the final cost to complete (and the validity of the termination if challenged). The court considered that its approach would not result in a windfall to a contractor's creditors in the event of insolvency because "an insolvent contractor is not entitled to enforce its right to any further sums following its insolvency," citing *Bouygues v Dahl-Jensen* [2000] B.L.R. 522. It is worth remembering that that case concerned liquidation set-off. If the contractor were in receivership or administration, there is no bar on it seeking to recover debts due for more than 28 days before termination, although the employer may seek a stay of execution in those events (see Ch.18).

Cheques

14–047 What happens if termination occurs between the issue of a cheque and its payment? If the employer stops the cheque, it is apparently arguable that it would be unjust to allow the contractor the benefit of the normal rule that there is no defence to a claim brought on a cheque other than fraud or failure of consideration: *Willment Brothers v North West Thames* RHA (1984) 26 B.L.R. 51 at 64. If the cheque is issued or paid after (but in ignorance of) automatic termination, perhaps the court had in mind the possibility of a claim for the money as having been paid under a mistake of fact. It is not, however, open to the drawer to avoid liability by stopping the cheque simply because it appears from a later certificate that the payee has been overpaid: *Isovel Contracts v ABB Building Technologies* [2002] 1 B.C.L.C. 390. In that case the court rejected a submission that there had been a total or partial failure of consideration. The sub-subcontract provided for errors in a valuation on which a certificate was founded to be corrected in a later certificate. At the time the cheque was issued the drawer had only an unliquidated and unquantified cross-claim. The court granted summary judgment and refused a stay of execution. The claimant was in administration but this was not regarded as an "exceptional circumstance" justifying a stay in claims involving bills of exchange (para.26). Adjudication cases such as *Herschel Engineering v Breen Property* (unreported, July 28, 2000, Judge Humphrey LLoyd Q.C.) and *Rainford House v Cadogan* [2001] B.L.R. 416 were not regarded as helpful in this context being treated as decisions turning on their own facts (see Ch.12).

10. Security deposits

14–048 The contractor may have to deposit a sum of money with the employer as security for performance of the contract: *Official Assignee v Mayor of City of Wellington* [1885] 3 N.Z.L.R. 159; *Goodman v Napier Harbour Board* [1939] N.Z.L.R. 97; *Amman Aviation v Commonwealth of Australia* [1988] 92 A.L.R. 601 at 606, 626 and 649. This may be in addition to other forms of security which have been provided, e.g. bonds and guarantees. Security deposits are an effective form of security to employers: compare *Public Bank v Perbadanan* [1980] 1 M.L.J. 214 and *Kratzmann v University of Queensland* [1982] Qd. R. 682. They are a feature of the Australian standard forms. In the UK a cash deposit is more common in support of a counter-indemnity to an insurance company in respect of a surety bond than as security for performance of the contract. Occasionally the forfeiture of a deposit has been held to be a penalty: *Bysouth v Shire of Blackburn* [1928] V.L.R. 562 at 574; Beale (1988).

It is important to specify how an advance payment is to be taken into account. In *John Dee v WMH (21) Ltd* [1997] B.C.C. 518, affirmed [1998] B.C.C. 972, the contract provided for a down payment and two kinds of monthly payments, one in advance and the other in arrears. The contract was silent on how the down payment was to be taken into account. It was held that in context it was not a payment on account of the other types of charge but a kind of security deposit repayable only on completion or termination of the contract.

11. Copyright

Outside insolvency, the issue is likely to be whether a work qualifies for copyright protection under the Copyright Designs and Patents Act 1988 or whether copyright has in fact been infringed. In insolvency, the questions turn on the ownership of the work and the extent to which third parties have acquired rights in it (Thomas 2004). Copyright subsists independent of registration in plans and drawings, models for buildings and buildings themselves (artistic copyright) and in reports, explanations on plans and drawings and computer software (literary copyright), but not in the construction process. An employer who pays for the work will become the owner of it but he does not acquire an interest in the copyright in the absence of specific agreement, e.g. outright assignment, a licence or by way of security. However, he will usually have an implied licence to use the plans etc for the purpose for which they were prepared and in accordance with them. Similarly a contractor has an implied licence in respect of work created by a subcontractor and so on (Wheeler 1991). The contract may provide expressly for the survival of certain obligations after a contractual termination, e.g. the support and maintenance of software: *Harbinger v GE Information Systems* (2000) 1 T.C.L.R. 463. **14–049**

The RIBA form of agreement between client and architect (SFA/92) gives the employer the right to copy the architect's design where he has completed the design and all his fees have been paid, but it does not explain the consequences of non-payment. One writer considers that payment is a condition precedent to copyright under this form (Delemore 1994, 95, 107). The same point arises under the CIOB Facilities Management Contract (1999) under which the facilities manager grants an irrevocable copyright licence to the client "subject to the client having paid all sums due" under the agreement. It is not clear whether the licence is irrevocable once granted even if the client stops paying or whether its irrevocability is conditional on the client continuing to pay. The position is clearer in SFA/99 which expressly allows the architect to suspend the licence for non-payment on giving seven days notice. "Use of the licence may be resumed on receipt of outstanding amounts" (cl.6.2.3). There is also an absolute non-assignability clause. This is very valuable in this context. The ACE Conditions (2nd edn, 1998) allow the engineer to revoke the licence for non-payment on seven days' notice (cl.7.1). There is no equivalent protection for the consultant under the CIC (2007) form.

In *Devefi v Mateffy Perl* (1993) 113 A.L.R. 225 an engineer was awarded damages for breach of copyright. His appointment was in the Australian ACE form which granted the employer an express licence to use his drawings for the purpose of completing the project and prohibited either party from assigning the agreement without the other's written consent. Shortly before entering liquidation the employer sold the site and purported to assign the appointment, including the express licence, to the purchaser, warranting that it had paid the engineer up to date even though there were progress payments outstanding. When he learned of the transfer the engineer continued to provide supervision on site, reserved its rights in relation to its copyright, proved in the liquidation of the employer for its unpaid invoices and claimed damages from the purchaser for breach of copyright.

It was held that the clause restricting assignment applied to the express licence with the result that the purchaser could not rely on it as an assignee.

An implied licence would be inconsistent with the express terms of the agreement and could not be inferred from the engineer's conduct in reserving his proprietary rights pending completion of the development. Damages for breach of copyright were also awarded in *Jones v London Borough of Tower Hamlets (No. 2)* [2001] R.P.C. 23, but only for a small aspect of the design; the architect lost on most of his arguments when he sued the employer after the design and build contractor became insolvent. There was apparently no claim based on an implied licence.

How is an implied licence affected by the insolvency of the licensee? In *Hunter v Fitzroy Robinson* (1977) 10 B.L.R. 84, an architect was owed £46,000 for design work to an existing building which remained outstanding when the employer went into receivership. The receiver sold the building and its associated business to a purchaser who engaged other architects to complete the project. The architect failed in an application to prevent the new firm using part of his original design. It was strongly arguable that the original employer had an implied licence which had been assigned to the purchaser. Even if the assignment were subject to the architect's claim for payment, he could suffer no loss by allowing the building to be completed and could pursue his claim for payment at the trial (at 93).

The case highlights the passive nature of copyright. The architect could only try and prevent his design being used. He could not assert his debt as a claim against the new owner; he could only use it as a defence to a claim brought by the purchaser based on the assignment, but there was no need for the purchaser to bring such a claim. Even if the architect recovered damages for infringement at the trial, he could still not recover his original debt. By refusing the injunction, the court prevented the architect from using copyright as a commercial bargaining counter to recover a pre-receivership debt. Had the application been brought by the new owner (e.g. for delivery up of the designs themselves), the position might have been different. Also, had there been a non-assignability clause in the architect's retainer, he could have required payment of the pre-receivership debt as a condition of an assignment to the purchaser. A similar situation arose in the receivership of Land & Property Trust before the site had been sold, although the issue was settled between the parties (Wheeler 1994).

14–051 *Ng v Clyde Securities* [1976] 1 N.S.W.L.R. 443 is an Australian case on similar facts. An architect submitted a proof of debt for unpaid fees in the liquidation of a developer but a dividend was unlikely. He therefore sued the mortgagee of the development, who had gone into possession, in an attempt to use his copyright as a lever to recover his pre-liquidation debt but failed. Once granted the licence was irrevocable and it had passed to the mortgagee pursuant to the developer's implied right to assign.

> "The withdrawal of the licence would not merely affect the future activities of the licensee, but, by preventing the completion of a building, would render valueless what might be an enormous past investment in the building. Looking at the matter in terms of business efficacy, I find it unthinkable that an owner would agree to a licence revocable if a possibly temporary difficulty prevented him from paying his architect at the agreed time. Unless an architect expressly stipulated for such a devastating right of revocation to enforce actual payment, it is more reasonable to regard him as giving the licence in return for a debt recoverable, if unpaid, by ordinary litigious processes. He is essentially selling something, viz, his plans and a

licence to build in accordance with them, in return for a promise of future payment, and the ordinary basis of a sale is that it gives the vendor a right in the event of non-payment to sue for recovery of the purchase price, not a right to deprive the purchaser of the enjoyment of the object sold, or to complain of the use by the purchaser of the article sold prior to payment for it" (at 446, *per* Wootten J.).

A similar situation arose in *Torpey Vander Have v Mass Constructions* (2003) 19 B.C.L. 288 although in that case the mortgagee, who exercised its power of sale to the defendant who had the development completed, could not prove that the licence had passed to it as it failed to bring its security in evidence. The effect of a repudiation of the architect's retainer on a copyright licence of this kind has not been formally considered by the English court, but *dicta* suggest that the view in *Ng v Clyde Securities* may well be followed: see *Stovin-Bradford v Volpoint* [1971] Ch. 1007 at 1018. The licence will probably be regarded as a right vested in the licensee which neither a repudiation nor a termination under the contract can destroy. In *High Mark v Patco Malaysia* (1984) 28 B.L.R. 129, a turnkey contract was terminated at the completion of the design stage but before work had commenced on site. The court granted an injunction to the contractor restraining the employer from using drawings prepared by consultants engaged as subcontractors and from entering into direct contracts with them. The position might have been different had the construction work already been under way. In *Re Mercury Developments* (July 5, 2007, Lewison J.) there was a restriction in the construction contract which gave the employer permission to use designs solely for the completion of the works. There was also a collateral warranty from the designer without any such restriction. On the employer going into administration, it was held that the administrators could transfer a licence to use the designs to a purchaser of the site without having to obtain the contractor's consent. The warranty and the construction contract had to be construed separately.

From a practical point of view, infringement of copyright in this area is perhaps not as serious as in others: the designer is unlikely to be able to prevent the building being constructed since damages would normally be an adequate remedy (*Hunter v Fitzroy Robinson* (1977) 10 B.L.R. 84), and will probably be limited to a fair fee for the licence (*Charles Church v Cronin* [1990] F.S.R. 1). The same may well apply to claims concerning computer software source code: see s.27.4, Standardisation of PFI Contracts (SoPC), Version 4 (March 2007). For example, in *Psychometric Services v Merant International* [2002] F.S.R. 8, a purchaser of computer software obtained an interim injunction requiring the supplier to hand over the source code so it could continue to develop the software with an alternative supplier despite the original supplier's claim for unpaid fees. The purchaser was in financial difficulty and could not provide security against the release of the code. The agreement between the parties entitled the purchaser to switch suppliers on the basis that the original supplier would be released, but it was silent regarding the source code. On the balance of convenience, an injunction was granted because otherwise it was likely that the purchaser would go into liquidation causing substantial losses to employees, investors and customers, as well as the original supplier. If the injunction were granted, the supplier would suffer no additional loss whereas the purchaser may well prosper and become able to pay whatever sum was due.

Difficulties may arise where the software has been created by another group company. In *SCI Games v Argonaut Games* [2005] EWHC 1403 an agreement to develop software was terminated and the client demanded delivery up of the software. It had however been developed by an associated company of the developer named in the contract and administrators appointed to the associate refused to hand it over. David Young Q.C. refused an application by the administrators to strike out a claim against them for interfering with the contract by failing to procure the delivery up. Of interest to construction insolvency is the potential implication of a contract between the two associated companies containing terms back to back with the development contract, including an express duty to hand over software on a termination. For an analogous situation in which a trade mark was registered unsuccessfully as a lever to obtain payment, see *Ball v The Eden Project* [2002] 1 B.C.L.C. 313. A further analogy could perhaps be drawn with the improper registration of a caution against the title to a building site.

12. Final accounts

14–052 It may be several years before an insolvency practitioner will know whether there will be a balance payable in favour of the contractor. In one case a receiver had to wait three years before the contractor's final account was agreed. The account showed a balance due to the contractor in respect of retention but this was successfully claimed by a prior assignee: *Earle v Hemsworth RDC* (1929) 140 L.T. 69. A delay of a different order was experienced in *AES Barry v TXU Europe* [2005] 2 B.C.L.C. 22, in which a power purchase agreement was terminated on the supplier going into administration. Disputes arose between the operator and the administrator over the calculation of the early termination payment and the operator unsuccessfully applied for leave under s.11 of the Insolvency Act 1986 to refer them to the Commercial Court. The operator was forced to await the implementation of a scheme of arrangement. NEC3 (2005) deals with the question of delay by requiring the project manager to certify within 13 weeks of termination a final payment to, or from, the contractor (cl.90.4). Unless the works are close to termination, the certified sum will be based on a forecast of the additional cost to complete (cl.93.2).

The standard forms differ in their approach to the ascertainment of the employer's loss. Broadly, they take two different approaches. Under the first, the employer's losses are added to the amount already paid to the contractor and then both are deducted from the amount which would have been payable to the contractor had it completed the contract in accordance with its terms (cl.27.4.4 of JCT 80). Under the second approach, the employer's losses are added to the amount already paid to the contractor and both are deducted from the value of the contractor's works as at the date of termination (cl.57(2) of GC/Works/1). The second approach may be vulnerable to attack as a penalty because it fails to bring into account the balance of the contract sum: *Corporation of the City of Adelaide v Jennings Industries* (1984) 156 C.L.R. 274 at 294. Also, where the contract is to build and operate, a termination provision entitling the contractor to recover unearned operating charges may be held to be penal: *Dalkia Utilities v Celtech International* [2006] 1 Lloyd's Rep. 599 at para.123. See also *Integral Home Loans v Interstar Wholesale Finance* [2007] NSWSC 406.

The law of penalties is an anomaly of the common law and "the courts are predisposed, where possible, to uphold contractual terms which fix the level of damages for breach": *Alfred McAlpine v Tilebox* [2005] B.L.R. 271 at para.48, *per* Jackson J. The usual measure of damages for failure to complete building works is the difference between the cost to complete and the balance of the contract sum: *Mertens v Home Freeholds* [1921] 2 K.B. 526; *Ventura v Svirac* [1961] W.A.R. 63; *APC v Amey Construction* [2005] CSOH at para.14. The contract sum must be adjusted by reference to omissions or variations instructed during the works: *Greenore Port v Technical & General* [2006] EWHC 3119 (para.191).

The question arises whether these provisions contravene the *pari passu* rule. Where the contractor's property is used as payment for the cost to complete, the procedure is confiscatory because the employer would always have had to pay the completion cost whether the contractor's employment were terminated or not. This has been described as "too greedy an approach to take on a termination clause" (Carter 1990, 117). This is the reason why standard forms require a notional final account to be drawn up of what would have been due to the contractor had it completed the works. The liquidator is not entitled to re-write the contract and, subject to the *pari passu* rule, is bound by its terms: *Re Scheibler, ex parte Holthausen* (1874) L.R. 9 Ch. App. 722 at 726. The position seems to be therefore that no challenge can be made to the employer's set-off provided it is restricted to non-confiscatory items, e.g. expense flowing from the termination. Similarly there is nothing objectionable in the suspension of payment provision. These issues are reviewed in the South African case of *Thomas Construction v Grafton Furniture* [1988] 2 S.A. 546. **14–053**

If the parties exclude the common law and intend the termination clause to be a "comprehensive code" of their rights and liabilities after an insolvency termination, it is necessary for the clause to deal with the financial consequences: *Perar v General Surety* (1994) 66 B.L.R. 72; *Thomas Feather v Bradford* [1953] 52 L.G.R. 30. Where the common law has not been excluded, and the termination clause fails to make adequate provision for the financial consequences, it may be supplemented by the court ordering damages for repudiation: *Laing and Morrison-Knudson v Aegon Insurance* (1997) 86 B.L.R. 70. Whether or not the common law has been excluded, the court may enable a party to recover its loss, whether it was responsible for the termination or not, by "filling a gap" in the termination clause by construing the contract as a whole: *BMBF (No. 12) Ltd v Harland & Wolff* [2001] 2 Lloyd's Rep. 227.

In that case a termination clause in a shipbuilding contract provided that, in the event of default by the builder, the employer could cancel the contract and recover all sums previously paid, in which case the builder would be entitled to keep the part-completed vessel; or take possession of the ship and complete it in accordance with the contract. If the cost to complete exceeded the amount of outstanding instalments, the builder would be liable for the excess. In either case the owner could make a call under a letter of credit but, if it elected to complete the vessel, it had to account to the builder for any of the proceeds which were not used to complete it. The owner decided to terminate (not on grounds of insolvency although it had concerns about the builder's financial standing), and elected to complete the vessel. The builder contended it was already complete and claimed payment of the final instalment of 20 per cent due on delivery. The owner disputed liability to make any further payment.

14–054 The builder obtained an interim arbitration award in its favour which was confirmed by the Court of Appeal. To hold otherwise would have been to provide the owner with an "unwarranted windfall" where, as in this case, the cost to complete was less than the outstanding instalment (para.77). Central to the court's reasoning was the conclusion that, if it opted to take possession of the vessel, the employer had to complete it "in accordance with this contract". By saying that the builder had to compensate the owner if the cost to complete exceeded the outstanding instalments, the contract implied that the outstanding instalments remained at least notionally due but that they were not payable if the cost to complete exceeded them. If the cost to complete were less, it followed that the owner had to pay them (para.77). If that were not the case on a simple construction of the words used, the court would have implied a term to that effect.

The court also construed the whole termination regime as enabling an accounting to take place "which broadly ensures that neither party pays more nor gets more than contemplated under the original bargain" (para.52, *per* Potter L.J.). Under that scheme, the owner could draw on the letter of credit for interim funding of the cost to complete, and set off any liquidated damages already accrued against the last instalment, but it still had to pay the last instalment that was due. The owner was protected by a right to payment from the builder on demand of any loss not compensated by the letter of credit. The fact that this future liability was unsecured must have been a major factor in the employer's mind in deciding not to release the final instalment. The common law had not been excluded and the owner would have been entitled to damages had the builder been in repudiation (para.49).

In *Lomax Leisure v Fabric London* [2003] EWHC 307 the building contract was terminated when the contractor entered into a company voluntary arrangement. The contractor issued arbitration proceedings against the employer, which was itself in members' voluntary liquidation, and obtained an award of an extension of time together with the value of work done before termination. The employer recovered this amount under an indemnity given by a purchaser of its assets and, although the report is silent on the point, presumably the contractor was paid as a result. See also *OBG v Allan* [2005] B.L.R. 245 at para.66.

Where the general law is not excluded, the employer is entitled to abate the amount which would have been payable to the insolvent contractor by the value of any defective work: *Lintest Builders v Roberts* (1978) 10 B.L.R. 120, affirmed (1980) 13 B.L.R. 38. An employer who wrongfully repudiates a contract is still entitled to abate the contractor's claim by the value of defective work carried out before the termination: *Slater v Duquemin* (1992) 29 Con. L.R. 24; *Doidge v Rahim Tadj-Saadat* (unreported, July 21, 1999, Judge Richard Havery Q.C.).

In JCT Practice Note 24 it is stated that the reference to verification of accounts within a reasonable time in cl.27.4.4 of JCT 80 means agreement with the insolvency practitioner or his representatives (at 33). In *Kennedy v Collings Construction* (1991) 7 B.C.L. 25 at 43, the court allowed a set-off for rent, the cost to complete, and a bank charge. In *Ferguson v Sohl* (1992) 62 B.L.R. 95 a completion contractor finished the works for less than the original contract sum after the original contract had been repudiated. Despite this, the Court of Appeal allowed the employer's claim for an over-payment before the repudiation.

In assessing damages for repudiation, the court takes into account that a business has spare capacity during a recession. In *Western Webb Offset*

Printers v Independent Media [1995/6] C.I.L.L. 1122, the Court of Appeal allowed the innocent party to recover its gross profit without making any reduction for labour costs and overheads. In *OTV Birwelco v Technical & General* (2002) 84 Con. L.R. 117, Judge Anthony Thornton Q.C. ordered the contractor as beneficiary under a surety bond and the surety company to appoint a quantity surveyor to value the costs to complete and other losses incurred by the contractor following the repudiation of a subcontract immediately before a subcontractor's liquidation. It is desirable to measure the works performed by the insolvent contractor as soon as it leaves the site but existing records may be sufficient for the court to make a reasonable assessment of the cost to complete: *Greenore Port v Technical & General* [2006] EWHC 3119 at para.199.

13. Deemed settlement

Some contracts provide that payments previously made to the contractor **14–055** shall be deemed to be the full value of its work executed to the date of termination and accepted by the contractor in full and final satisfaction of all claims: *Davies v Mayor, Aldermen and Burgesses of Swansea* (1853) 22 L.J. Ex. 297; *Goodman v Napier Harbour Board* [1939] N.Z.L.R. 97. In *Roach v Great Western Railway Company* (1841) 1 Q.B. 51, this was to be the position even if no payments had been made at all. A clause of this type has been held to be a penalty (*Bysouth v Shire of Blackburn* [1928] V.L.R. 562), and is not found in the standard forms. For a deemed settlement clause in a New Zealand standard form, see Kennedy-Grant (1999, 448–9).

A term that on termination for insolvency the contractor should accept all sums previously paid together with all sums then payable in full satisfaction of its claims was upheld in *Thiess Watkins White v Commonwealth of Australia* (1998) 14 B.C.L. 61. Under the Australian NWPC3 (1981) form, on the contractor's insolvency the employer has the option of taking over the works or cancelling the contract. Under the former, there is an accounting under which the employer gives credit for all sums received on account of its loss, including proceeds of bond calls or sums owed to the contractor. But if the contract is cancelled, the employer becomes entitled to forfeit all cash deposits and bonds without having to account for the excess they may represent over its actual loss.

> "That may work to the advantage of the [employer], but it will work to its disadvantage if it thereafter discovers that the extra cost of completing the work exceeds the amount forfeited. There is no later accounting between them. In this way the [employer] and the contractor agree upon a means by which there can be an immediate end to their relationship. There will be a clean break in which the contractor knows where it stands and the [employer] takes the risk that it will be worse off than if it had taken over the work rather than cancel the contract. The result may be arbitrary but it is understandable that the bargain of the parties should include it" (at 76, *per* Giles J.).

14. Validity of termination clauses

In practice, the validity of a termination clause having effect on bankruptcy **14–056** or liquidation is taken for granted (*Re Sneezum, ex parte Davis* (1876) 3 Ch.D. 463 at 471; *Shipton v Micks, Lambert & Co* [1936] 2 All E.R. 1032;

Scott Barnes v Premium Credit [2001] B.C.C. 27 at para.57). However there is little direct authority and the question probably still remains open for argument (Totty and Crystal 1982).

The general principle is that there cannot be a valid contract that a man's property shall remain his until his bankruptcy and, on the happening of that event, go over to someone else and be taken from his creditors: *Money Markets v London Stock Exchange* [2002] 1 W.L.R. 1150; *Fraser v Oystertec* (2004) B.C.C. 233. The issue is whether the termination clause has the effect of divesting the contractor's estate of property in breach of the *pari passu* rule or simply limits the contractor's interest under the contract. "Property" is defined by s.436 of the Insolvency Act 1986 as including "money, goods, things in action, land and every description of property wherever situate and also obligations and every description of interest, whether present, or future or vested or contingent, arising out of, incidental to, property".

As a thing in action, an ordinary contract right would fall within this definition: *Re Walker, ex parte Barter* (1884) 26 Ch.D. 510. A building contract is clearly property for the purpose of the statutory definition because it may be disclaimed by a liquidator as onerous property under s.178 of the Insolvency Act 1986. But has the termination clause made the contract into a flawed asset, i.e. contingent for its existence on the absence of insolvency? "The general distinction seems to be that the owner of property may, on alienation, qualify the interest of his alienee by a condition to take effect on bankruptcy; but cannot, by contract or otherwise, qualify his own interest by a like condition, determining or controlling it in the event of his own bankruptcy, to the disappointment or delay of his creditors:" *Whitmore v Mason* (1861) 2 J. & H. 204 at 210, *per* Lord Hatherley. On this principle, a clause terminating a lease on the tenant's liquidation has been held valid: *Civil Service Co-Operative Society v Trustee of McGrigor* [1923] 2 Ch. 347.

An employer under a construction contract grants possession to the contractor rather than an interest in the land. This has been analysed as a contractual licence: *London Borough of Hounslow v Twickenham Garden* [1971] 1 Ch. 233. Thus there is no alienation of property in Lord Hatherley's terms, and the idea of a contingent contractual right seems more appropriate. Similarly, relief against forfeiture is usually denied in the case of an ordinary construction contract as no right of property has been forfeited: *Westminster Properties v Comco Constructions* (1991) 5 W.A.R. 191. As Oditah comments:

> "in 'ordinary contracts' it is difficult to identify who is the owner of what. So long as there are unperformed obligations by both parties, they are both creditors or 'owners' of each other's obligations. There is therefore simply no occasion for invoking the rule that an owner of property could limit his grantee's interests. Rather acceleration and rescission clauses are built-in limitations on each party's entitlement to the other's unperformed obligations" (Oditah 1992, 499).

In other words, the contractor's right to perform continues only as long as the employer has no right to terminate its employment or opts not to exercise that right: *Laing and Morrison-Knudson v Aegon Insurance* (1997) 86 B.L.R. 70 at 112. This raises the question of the effect of *British Eagle v Air France* [1975] 1 W.L.R. 758. The "decision remains very difficult to understand. . . . If one were to pursue *British Eagle* to its logical end many contractual self-help remedies, particularly those encountered in building contracts, will not survive the insolvency of the builder" (Oditah 1992, 466). There is a line of authority holding that direct payment clauses are valid as an inherent limitation on the contractor's right to payment (Ch.17). But there is another, and more persuasive, line which holds them invalid, since in substance they acknowledge a sum due to the contractor which is subject to set-off in respect of amounts paid direct to subcontractors. When applied to termination clauses, the former approach appears more convincing. "The distinction between clauses that forfeit and clauses that determine is very subtle indeed and hard to defend" (Bridge 2003, 34). Goode (2005, para.7–11) argues that as a matter of policy express termination clauses operating on insolvency ought to be invalidated, leaving the solvent party to rely on termination for default.

15. Suspension

The common law does not recognise a right in the contractor to respond to non-payment by suspending work: *Canterbury Pipelines v Christchurch Drainage Board* (1979) 16 B.L.R. 76. A contractor unsuccessfully attempted to rely on the civil law concept of *exceptio* at first instance in *Channel Tunnel Group v Balfour Beatty* (unreported, November 21, 1991, Evans J.) on the ground that, unusually, the proper law of the contract was stated to be the common principles of English and French law. **14–057**

Section 112 of the Housing Grants, Construction and Regeneration Act 1996 introduced a right of suspension for non-payment into construction contracts. The right to serve a suspension notice only arises where there has been no effective withholding notice served by the paying party (see Ch.5). Thus an unpaid contractor takes the risk when invoking s.112 of an adjudicator finding that the notice was effective. The JCT main contract forms now have a contractual right to suspend work. The ICE form does not provide for contractual suspension, leaving it to the Act to provide this right. At least seven days' notice of intention to suspend has to be given.

By s.112(4) the period of suspension is disregarded in computing the length of time taken to carry out the works, i.e. the contractor's time for completion is extended by an equivalent period. But there is no entitlement to additional money. The DTI proposes to remedy this *lacuna* by amending the Act to entitle the unpaid contractor to recover the costs of suspension and remobilisation as loss and expense and to an extension of time for remobilisation (DTI 2006, 10, 24). This proposal was the one most strongly supported by respondents to the DTI's consultation paper (at 46).

16. Checklist

Consider the contract: **14–058**

- does it have a termination clause which covers the situation?
- does it preserve common law rights?
- what procedural requirements have to be followed?
- is there time to follow them?

- does the termination clause confer adequate compensation rights?
- is someone else's permission needed before the notice of termination can be served?
- what effect will the termination have on subcontracts or associated contracts?

What is the common law position:

- how are common law rights affected by the contract?
- is the termination event relied on a repudiatory or other breach of contract?
- how much time has gone by since the breach occurred?
- could you already have affirmed the contract?
- what documents are available to support your position?
- what oral evidence could be given to support your contentions?
- could you have accepted repudiation already informally, e.g. at a meeting, in a letter on another topic, by issuing proceedings, by not continuing your side of the contract etc.

Keeping options open:

- what rights have already accrued (on both sides)?
- is it better to wait until further rights accrue due?
- are the breaches remediable or not?
- can a letter terminating under the contract be widely expressed so as also to act as acceptance of repudiation?
- what are the knock-on effects of terminating under the contract or accepting repudiation as far as bonds, guarantees, insurance and warranties are concerned?

Chapter 15

Novation of Contracts

The leading work on the law of contract devotes nearly 40 pages to assignment but only one to novation (Chitty 2004). In practice they are both important. The law developed in a series of cases involving the dissolution of partnerships and the transfer of business between insurance companies. The issue was whether liability for a debt had been transferred. In *Rouse v Bradford Banking* [1894] 2 Ch. 32 novation was described as "a substitution of debtors" (at 53, *per* Lindley L.J.). The authorities mainly concern situations of debtor and creditor, in which the creditor has already performed its obligations. A novation of a construction contract has to deal with unperformed obligations on both sides. As with the law of assignment and security, it is sometimes difficult to apply the principles from these debt cases to the complex terms found in construction contracts (von Laun 2004). **15–001**

1. Function of novation

Novation is used in the industry in a wide variety of contexts. Apart from insolvency situations, it is the means of transferring contracts entered into by the employer with consultants or nominated subcontractors to a design and build or main contractor. Novation is also provided for in step-in agreements and direct warranties between funders, employers, contractors and subcontractors which restrict contractual rights of termination. A party may have to give prior notice to the funder beforehand who may reserve the right to novate the contract through a substituted entity. Novation is also a way to distribute contracts among companies on a group reorganisation or a business sale, or to transfer contracts on the incorporation of a partnership. In the insolvency context, novation is the standard procedure for transferring contracts to a purchaser or to a new company set up by the directors of the insolvent company. Novation arguments commonly arise where one of the parties becomes insolvent or is not the owner of the major group asset. **15–002**

2. Novation and other processes

It may be useful at the outset to compare novation with other processes such as assignment, subcontracting, dissolution, subrogation, and joint liability.

Assignment

15–003 Assignment differs from novation in three important respects:

(1) Assignment is a transfer of rights under a contract which continues to exist after the assignment. Novation brings an existing contract to an end and creates a new one in its place: *Scarf v Jardine* (1882) 7 App. Cas. 345 at 351;

(2) Assignment can only transfer the benefit of a contract. Under a novation with all parties' consent the burden can also be transferred: such a transfer is not an assignment of the burden but a novation of the contract: *SVI Systems v Best & Less* (2001) 187 A.L.R. 302, para.105; and

(3) Consideration is not generally required for an assignment but is necessary on a novation as a new contract is being formed. Consideration is normally implicit in a novation agreement.

Subcontracting

15–004 A subcontract is the delegation of work to another by a separate contract. The subcontract does not release the contractor from liability for that work under the main contract. The main contract is not terminated or the benefit assigned (compare *British Energy v Credit Suisse* [2007] EWHC 1428, para.23). Nor does the subcontractor assume any contractual liability direct to the employer as there is no privity. A subcontract is not a substitute for part or whole of the main contract. Consider *Storford v Poole Harbour Yacht Club* (unreported, November 13, 1996, Clarke J.) in which an arrangement whereby part of the restoration work to a classic yacht was given to another firm was held to be a subcontract by the engineering contractor rather than a novation by the owner. One of the reasons was that the owner's project manager lacked the authority to contract direct with the other firm even though he was involved in agreeing the subcontract price.

Dissolution

15–005 The dissolution of a construction company transfers its property to the Crown as *bona vacantia* but the Crown does not assume the company's obligations or accept any active duties regarding the property. If the company is restored to the register under s.651 or s.653 of the Companies Act 1985 (which will become a single procedure when the Companies Act 2006 comes into force), its property is transferred back to it together with any causes of action, although prior arbitrations are not preserved: *Morris v Harris* [1927] A.C. 252. Dissolution has the effect of substituting the Crown as owner of property but without releasing the company or its debtors from liability in the event that the company is restored. It therefore lacks the essential elements of a novation. In *Orchidway Properties v Fairlight Commercial* [2002] EWHC 1716, it was held that the dissolution of a contractor was not a repudiation of a joint venture agreement it had with a developer. Under the agreement the developer was to obtain planning permission and the contractor would carry out the building work. Profits were to be shared equally. The contractor's name was struck off the register for failure to file accounts. The developer later obtained planning permission but sold the land and kept the profits for itself. On the contractor's restoration to the register, it issued proceedings against the developer for its share of the development profit. Jacob J. refused to strike out the proceedings on the ground that under s.653 of the Companies Act 1985 the contractor "is deemed to have continued in existence as if its name had not been struck off". If during the period of dissolution, "something which could be regarded as a repudiation happened" then it was possible that the company, when restored, might have lost the rights it formerly had but that was not the situation here. It was possible that the joint venture agreement had become frustrated by the dissolution, but in that event the restored company would be able to claim against the developer under s.1(3) of the Law Reform Frustrated Contracts Act 1943.

Subrogation

If A owes a liability to B which is discharged by C, in certain circumstances C is entitled by subrogation to enforce B's rights against A. In order to allow C to sue in its own name, B may legally assign its claim against A. Alternatively, C may issue proceedings in B's name in exercise of its rights of subrogation. A typical example is where an insurer issues proceedings in the name of an insured against a third party whose actions caused the loss. The insurer has an equitable or proprietary interest in the insured's right to damages: *Lord Napier and Ettrick v Hunter* [1993] A.C. 713 at 738. This process is different from novation in that it concerns the enforcement of a contract, e.g. an insurance policy or a guarantee, rather than a substitution of one contract by another. Subrogation "is a remedy, rather than a cause of action, founded in equity and natural justice not in contract, designed to prevent unjust enrichment" (*Liberty Mutual v HSBC Bank* [2002] EWCA 691 at para.43, *per* Rix L.J.). **15–006**

Joint liability

It is theoretically possible for a party to be added to an existing contract as co-obligor without releasing the original obligor, so that a contract between A and B becomes one between A/C jointly and B. Such an arrangement would be "a strange one in practice" and require clear evidence: *The Tychy (No. 2)* [2001] 2 Lloyd's Rep. 403, at para.76. See *Connex v MJ Building Services* [2005] B.L.R. 201; *Far East Consortium v Airedale* [1991] HKCA 305; *Star-Trans v Norske-Tech* [1996] A.D.R.L.J. 62. **15–007**

3. Criteria for novation

Definition

"Novation is the substitution of a new contract for an old by the agreement of all parties to the old and the new": *Tito v Waddell (No. 2)* [1977] Ch. 106 at 287, *per* Megarry V.C. There are two aspects to substitution. The first is **15–008** where the parties to an existing contract agree to cancel it and substitute a new contract in its place: compare *Try Build v Blue Star Garages* (1998) 66 Con. L.R. 90. The second is where they agree that one of them will be released from its obligations and a new contract formed between the survivor and the newcomer: "the process by which a contract between A and B is transformed into a contract between A and C" (*Linden Gardens v Lenesta Sludge* (1992) 57 B.L.R. 57 at 76, *per* Staughton L.J.). Most novations following insolvency are of this second type. Many of the cases concern implied rather than express novation.

Elements of novation

15–009 In order to establish a novation, "what the Plaintiff has to prove is conduct inconsistent with a continuance of his liability, from which conduct an agreement to release him may be inferred": *Rouse v Bradford Banking* [1894] 2 Ch.32 at 54, *per* Lindley L.J. A recent reformulation of the test is "whether that inference [of novation] is necessary to give business efficacy to what actually happened" (*Evans v SMG Television* [2003] EWHC 1423 at para.181, *per* Lightman J.).

Is there an intention to replace one of the parties?

15–010 "*Novatio*" under Roman law required evidence of an intention to novate and the substitution of one liability for another: *Wilson v Lloyd* (1873) L.R. 16 Eq. 60; *Olsson v Dyson* [1970] 120 C.L.R. 365; *SVI Systems v Best & Less* (2001) 187 A.L.R. 302, para.109. Much turns on the facts. An agreement between an employer and a contractor that work under a JCT 80 contract would be "carried out" by an associated company of the contractor was not sufficient to evidence a novation, even though it was the associate who procured a surety bond in support of the building contract: *WJ Harte Construction v Scottish Homes* [1992] S.C. 99. The associate was merely acting as the contractor's agent. This is sometimes referred to as 'informal subcontracting': *Smith v Charles Building Services* [2005] B.C.C. 513 at para.10. See also *CS Geotechnic v Neocorp Innovations* [2005] SGHC 116. By contrast, an exchange of faxes between a vessel operator and a container operator agreeing that their slot charter would be "taken over" by a subsidiary of the container operator to whom future invoices should be rendered did amount to a novation: *The Tychy (No. 2)* [2001] 2 Lloyd's Rep. 403. The faxes, when construed against the background of earlier discussions on substitution, gave rise to an inference that the subsidiary was intended to replace the parent as contracting party. There was no comparable commercial matrix in *WJ Harte Construction*. Even if the faxes were ambiguous the parties' conduct afterwards would have estopped the vessel operator from denying that a novation had taken place (para.80).

In *Rossco Civil Engineering v Dwr Cymru* (unreported, July 15, 2004, Recorder Dermod O'Brien Q.C.) a contractor succeeded in enforcing an adjudication decision by relying on estoppel rather than novation. The contractor began trading as a partnership of two individuals who later transferred their business to a limited company. An adjudication was commenced by the contractor in the company's name, and the employer took part without making any objection even when the question of possible misnomer was raised by the adjudicator. On the contractor winning the adjudication, the employer argued it had never traded with the company. It was held that the arrangements fell short of the criteria for a novation: the partners had not notified the employer of the change although work was later invoiced by the company; more significantly there was no release of the partnership from its liabilities. But there was a common understanding at least by the time of the adjudication that the company was the contracting party on existing projects (para.66). In *Le Grys Building Services v Sealand Associates* (unreported, March 29, 1990, noted in (1994) 11(1) Build. L.M. 9) the court inferred a novation from the cumulative effect of an oral agreement, a series of changes on site, and changes to accounting procedures. A contractor was set up by an employer as a project vehicle. A subcontractor alleged an oral agreement with the director of the employer whereby the subcontractor would be substituted as contractor. Following this, the contractor's employees left site, the subcontractor put up its own name boards, the subcontractor ceased submitting daywork sheets, the contractor ceased keeping site records, and the subcontractor's applications for payment stopped claiming zero rating for VAT, as had previously been the case. The contractor went into liquidation six months later. It was held that the subcontractor was entitled to recover its final invoice from the employer direct pursuant to a novation of the main contract.

See also *Quarmby Electrical v Trant* [2005] EWHC 608, in which Jackson J. held that an oral novation had occurred in respect of four contracts between an electrical subcontractor on the verge of compulsory liquidation and a new company set up by a director of the subcontractor. It was immaterial that certificates approving electrical work done after the novation were issued by the director on headed notepaper of the insolvent company (at para.25). A novation argument may depend entirely on the court's evaluation of the evidence. In *Daly and Daly v Sheikh* (unreported, March 7, 2002, Gray J.), house owners originally contracted with a limited company and failed in a claim that their contract had been orally novated in favour of the company's sole director. The director had asked to be paid in cash but that did not of itself indicate a novation. The court examined the conduct of the parties after the alleged novation and found that aspects of the claimants' actions, e.g. attempting to make an insurance claim against a policy taken out by the company, were inconsistent with their contention. After evidence of forgery emerged, the case was retried before Pitchers J. who concluded that a novation had occurred: see the summary reported in [2004] EWCA 119. In the light of the new evidence Pitchers J. placed special weight on the absence of any invoices from the company and the fact that "the contract was not reflected in the company's records, for there were next to no records at all" (para.32, *per* Rix L.J.).

This decision was affirmed on appeal. It was established that the director had lied in a number of respects and the householder's evidence that the director had asked to switch the company's contract to himself personally was to be preferred. Pitchers J. took a different view on the request to be paid in cash. The money was not accounted for by the company and must be treated as having been appropriated by the director to his own use consistently with his personal novation of the contract (paras.52–3). "If then the benefit of the contract had gone to [the director], there was nothing improbable in the burden going as well" (at para.63, *per* Rix L.J.). On oral novation and novation by conduct in a sale of business context see *Carbofuels v Dampskibs* (unreported, July 11, 1996, Morison J.); *MRS Distribution v DS Smith* [2004] S.L.T. 631.

Is there an undertaking from the purchaser to the employer?

15–011 Although the purchaser may undertake to an insolvent company to discharge its liabilities to others the court normally expects this to be expressly communicated to the other contract party. The practical problems in this area are illustrated by comparing two construction cases. In *Chatsworth v Cussins* [1969] 1 All E.R. 143, the Court of Appeal considered a building contract where, after practical completion, the contractor assigned all its assets including the contract to a purchaser who undertook to discharge all its liabilities. The purchaser then changed its name to that of the contractor. On defects appearing in the works, the employer issued a writ against the purchaser in the mistaken belief that it was the original contractor. The purchaser admitted it had given an undertaking to the contractor to discharge all its liabilities but refused to accept liability as it had made no direct promise to the employer. The court held the purchaser liable to the employer on the basis of an implied novation. From the brief report it seems that the decision was made on the basis of unusual facts and at an interlocutory stage when the matter was not fully argued. The original contractor was effectively unable to enforce the undertaking against the purchaser. Lord Denning M.R. said novation was "very easy to infer" (at 144), but there was no evidence of consent or that the original contractor had been released.

The court reached the opposite conclusion on similar facts in *Westminster City Council v Reema Construction (No. 2)* (1990) 24 Con. L.R. 26, which concerned a defects claim by a local authority. The contractor became informally insolvent and hived down its assets to a purchaser and subsequently went into compulsory liquidation. The council claimed against the purchaser on the basis of an implied novation, an implied contract or an implied term that the purchaser would fulfil the unperformed obligations of the insolvent contractor. The claim failed. Although there was an express obligation in the hive down agreement that the purchaser would discharge the contractor's burden in the defects liability period in order to collect the remaining receivables which it could then keep outright, there was no direct agreement with the council who imagined it was dealing with the insolvent contractor throughout. It could not be inferred that the purchaser had given an undertaking to the council or that the council had accepted any undertaking: compare *Re European Assurance* (1875) 1 Ch. D. 334. The court would not impute to the council notice that it was dealing with a different company simply because correspondence from the purchaser showed a different company number. It is interesting to note that before formal novation agreements became the norm, insolvency practitioners appointed over contractors used assignment coupled with an undertaking as the means of disposal of ongoing contracts.

Is there evidence of consent?

15–012 The previous issues—of an intention to novate, and a promise by the purchaser to be bound—are connected to a third question: have all the parties to the alleged novation consented to it? This requirement is evident from *Finning v Inveresk* (unreported, May 16, 2007, C.A.). In that case an operator of a paper mill entered into long-term plant hire agreements in respect of five trucks which provided for payment of damages for early termination. The operator sold the mill and invited the purchaser to novate the plant hire agreements. The purchaser agreed to pay hire charges arising after the sale of the mill but would not assume any other liabilities. The purchaser then closed the mill down and the hirer repossessed the trucks. It was held by the Court of Appeal that the operator remained liable to pay the damages for early termination. There had been no novation because the purchaser had not consented to discharge the operator's liabilities. The assumption of responsibility for certain hire charges could only amount to a "part novation". The court is sometimes asked to infer consent from the fact that an accounting process is established between the purchaser and the surviving party: *The Tychy (No. 2)* [2001] 2 Lloyd's Rep. 403, at para.62. Direct payment by the employer to the purchaser was not sufficient to evidence novation in *Fairfax Gerrard Contracts v London Fire and Emergency Planning Department* [2004] All E.R. (D) 152. A sole trader agreed to do maintenance work at fire stations under a measured term contract. He tendered on rates which were 35 per cent below those in the PSA Schedule of Building Works, "apparently far below any other tender" (para.8). Three months later he entered into a factoring agreement in an attempt to deal with cash flow problems. The concept of the agreement was that the trader would become the factor's agent for the purposes of the maintenance contract. The trader was to invoice the factor, less a 2.75 per cent discount, who would pay 70 per cent of the discounted sum to the trader and invoice the whole amount to the employer. On payment by the employer the factor would account for the balance to the factor less discount, interest and charges. Notice was given to the employer whose accounts department altered the payee's name on its computer system to that of the factor. The employer never saw the factoring agreement itself and was unaware of the agency between the trader and the factor.

With its invoices the trader had to give the factor evidence that the work had been completed. The employer's surveyor was sympathetic to the trader and was prepared to assist him to obtain regular payment from the factor by signing "job tickets" which had endorsed on them the date of completion of work and the trader's value for it, even though the value was not an agreed amount. The factor's invoices were based on the job tickets but these in turn were based on the trader's self measurement (which sometimes claimed dayworks rates, i.e. higher than those allowed by the PSA) instead of the surveyor's certificates as the measured term contract required. About a year after entering into the factoring agreement the trader went bankrupt. The factor sued the employer for unpaid invoices. It was held that the employer's action in signing the job tickets was insufficient to establish consent to a novation in favour of the factor. Its surveyor did so only to facilitate the trader's cash flow by payment from the factor. The agency was never disclosed to the employer. The employer never agreed to deal with the factor whose invoices were totally ignored by it: compare *Lorentzen v White Shipping* (1942) 74 Ll. L. Rep. 161. Payment was only made to the factor at the direction of the trader. The factor never claimed to be an assignee. Although not referred to in the judgment, it may be that the factor was employing agency as a device to avoid the effect of a non-assignment clause in the maintenance contract, e.g. cl.3.1 of MTC 98. In another case on a similar form of factoring agreement, the factor was refused leave to claim against the debtor's contract party as an undisclosed principal: *P&O Ferrymasters v Radicon* (unreported, May 22, 2001, Jack J.). See also *Alfred McAlpine Construction v Forum Architects* [2002] B.L.R. 378.

What is the effect on security?

15–013 The court is not likely to infer a novation where the circumstances are inconsistent with it, e.g. if it would mean the creditor losing the benefit of a security. For example, novation was refused where a life assurance company claiming to have been released had granted a charge over its assets securing payment of an annuity (*Re Endowments Society* (1870) L.R. 5 Ch. App. 118) and where a company had provided a cash deposit securing its performance of a contract that still remained executory (*The Aktion* [1987] 1 Lloyd's Rep. 283).

4. Contingent novation

15–014 A contract may provide for its novation to a named party or class of person in certain specific events. In *British Gas v Eastern Electricity*, *The Times*, November 29, 1996, a gas supply agreement allowed either party "to assign any or all of its rights and obligations hereunder to an affiliate". Both parties agreed, and the court confirmed, that these words took effect as conferring a right to impose a novation on each other. If the novation took place without obtaining the consent of the other party in advance, the original party remained fully liable for all claims whether occurring before or after the novation. But where prior written approval (which was not to be unreasonably withheld) was obtained, the original party would be released as far as post-novation breaches were concerned. As between the original party and the affiliate, the affiliate covenanted to be bound by the gas supply agreement from the date of novation and the original party confirmed it would remain liable for pre-novation breaches.

In addition, either party had the power to terminate on the insolvency or a change in control of the other. British Gas planned a de-merger which would result in a change in control of its subsidiary which was party to the gas supply agreement. This would entitle Eastern to terminate the agreement. Before the de-merger took place, British Gas asked Eastern to consent to a novation to an affiliate. As the market price of gas had fallen considerably below the rates set out in the supply agreement, Eastern refused, intending to invoke the termination clause as soon as the de-merger took place. It was held by the Court of Appeal that its refusal was unreasonable. It was for British Gas to prove that the withholding of approval was unreasonable. All the circumstances had to be taken into account. It was not in dispute that the nominated affiliate possessed the necessary technical and financial ability to perform the contract. Eastern argued that where the parties have stipulated for a general right to terminate a contract, the court should be slow to place a fetter on that provision. The court held that the primary if not the sole purpose of the power of approval was to enable the remaining party to ensure that the party seeking approval was replaced by a satisfactory substitute able to sustain the contract for the remainder of its term.

Eastern's objection was unreasonable because it was based on an extraneous purpose, namely to force the original British Gas subsidiary to remain an unwilling party to the contract solely to enable Eastern to terminate it. It was wrong to allow Eastern to use its power to withhold a novation for such a purpose. At first instance, Colman J. said that it would be repugnant to suggest that "if one of them was about to make a composition with its creditors, it was precluded from preserving the agreement by assigning it to a contractworthy party" (unreported, November 19, 1996 at 19). Both the clauses dealing with assignment and termination were intended to provide a measure of protection with regard to the creditworthiness of the proposed replacement contractor. If Eastern were right, it:

> "would produce the unsatisfactory result that if a party anticipated that due to impending insolvency it would have to make an arrangement with its creditors or that an administrative receiver might be appointed, but had another party willing to take over the contract, the opposite party would be justified in withholding approval of the assignment to that other party, however commercially suitable the proposed assignee might be, solely on the ground that, if the agreement were not assigned, it would probably be possible to terminate it in the future by exercising the right which could be expected to accrue under clause 17(1)" (p.8).

Under the gas supply agreement, it was agreed that neither party would exercise its power to terminate on the appointment of an administrator or administrative receiver provided that within seven days of the appointment the insolvency practitioner personally guaranteed the payment of any charges in respect of the gas supply that fell due after his appointment. The case is interesting in several ways:

1. As an example of the effect of a fall in the market on the parties' attitudes to the contract terms: compare *Forth Shipbuilding v Tonnevold* (1923) 14 Ll. L. Rep. 554.
2. In showing the persistence of loose and confusing language even in major contracts. On its true construction the contract concerned mutual options to novate rather than assign.
3. In showing the unintended consequences of the interaction between the novation and termination clauses. The novation clause anticipated a transfer to another company in the group. This could be one formed specifically for the purpose as part of a reconstruction to avoid formal insolvency.
4. It was open to either party to invoke the termination clause provided a specified event had occurred. The presence of an ulterior motive was irrelevant. The same applied to the operation of the novation clause by substituting a suitable affiliate. But one party could not prevent the other from operating the novation clause if its nominated affiliate was otherwise suitable, in order to be able later to invoke the termination clause for the ulterior motive of getting out of a bad bargain.

Compare *Rhodia International Holdings v Huntsman* [2007] EWHC 292 (Julian Flaux Q.C.), in which a purchaser of a business was held liable to indemnify the vendor in respect of sums payable under an energy supply contract. The purchaser had agreed to use reasonable endeavours to obtain the supplier's consent to a novation to the special purpose vehicle company used by the purchaser. The supplier asked for a parent company guarantee as a condition of the novation but the purchaser refused to give it and the vendor remained liable for supplies made after the sale. The judge held that its refusal was in breach of the sale agreement.

5. Statutory novation

15–015 A novation can be effected by statute in many ways. The burden of a bond or insurance policy can be novated without the beneficiary's consent under Sch.2C of the Insurance Companies Act 1982. A company reconstruction scheme can take effect as a statutory novation of debts: *Wight v Eckhardt* [2004] 1 A.C. 147. Novation has occurred where a company which was incorporated by a private Act became insolvent and was re-incorporated: *Earl of Jersey v Great Western Railway* (1893), reported as a note to *Fortescue v Lostwithiel and Fowey Railway* [1894] 3 Ch. 621. A statute may reorganise local government so that one local authority's contracts are taken over by another: *McPhail v Cunninghame* (1985) S.L.T. 149.

In *McGregor Navine v British Railways Board* [1986] 1 F.T.L.R. 100, a contractor learned of the statutory novation of its employer five years after the event when it commenced arbitration proceedings. It argued that the original employer was estopped from denying that it was the proper respondent in the arbitration. Bingham J. rejected the contractor's argument on the ground that it could not show that it had been prejudiced in any way. It is worth noting that the statute in that case, the Transport Act 1968, provided that the substitution applied "as respects anything falling to be done or not after the transfer date". On the facts, it appears that the causes of action arose after that date, otherwise presumably the contractor would have been at liberty to proceed against the original employer. There was no evidence that the novatee was any less creditworthy than the original employer, even though, as the result of a privatisation, the employer had sold its shares in the novatee to a private company. The court did not, therefore, have to consider the consequences of a statutory novation to a company with a higher credit risk.

Statutory novation is similar to the civil law concept of universal succession with the exception that arbitration proceedings begun by the first company can be continued for the benefit of the second: *Eurosteel v Stinnes AG* (2000) C.L.C. 470. The process of universal succession is recognised by the English courts as being a special case, different from the dissolution of a company or the assignment of the benefit of a contract: *SEB Trygg Holding v Manches* [2005] 2 Lloyd's Rep. 129.

6. Different forms of novation

Novation of debts

15–016 In its simplest form novation occurs when with the consent of A as creditor B is replaced as debtor by C (Fig.15.1). If C owes B a sum equal to or greater than B's debt to A, a novation could occur where A accepts C as debtor in the place of B: Halsbury, 4th edn, 9(1), para.1037. This is novation rather than assignment since a new contract is formed between A and C which extinguishes C's liability to B (Fig.15.2). These situations assume that A owes no further obligations to B. In the nineteenth century cases, A may have supplied goods to B or be a client of B as a solicitors' firm or an insurance company. The release of B comes before A's acceptance of C in its place: *Re United Railways* [1960] 1 Ch. 52 at 85. Under a construction contract, the parties owe each other mutual obligations, and a novation has to take account of the benefit and burden of both A and B.

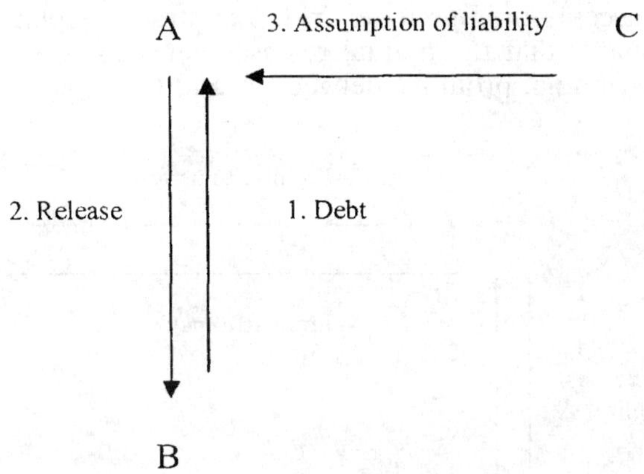

Fig.15.1

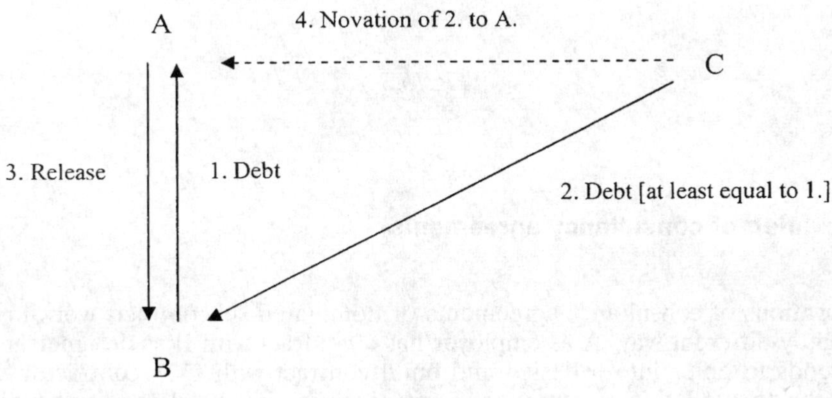

Fig.15.2

Novation of construction contracts

Figure 15.3 assumes a straightforward novation whereby one contractor is substituted for another. This time, as between A as employer and B as contractor, two releases are required to terminate the old contract. There are four stages: **15–017**

(1) The employer releases the contractor from liability.

(2) The contractor releases the employer from liability.

(3) C as purchaser promises the employer to complete the contract.

(4) The purchaser accepts the employer's promise to pay for the work.

Stages 1 and 2 terminate the old contract; stages 3 and 4 create the new one. In consideration of its release, the contractor arranges for the purchaser to assume its responsibilities; and in consideration of its release, the employer accepts the purchaser in the contractor's place. The correct analysis is probably that the mutual releases between A and B come first followed by the mutual promises between A and C.

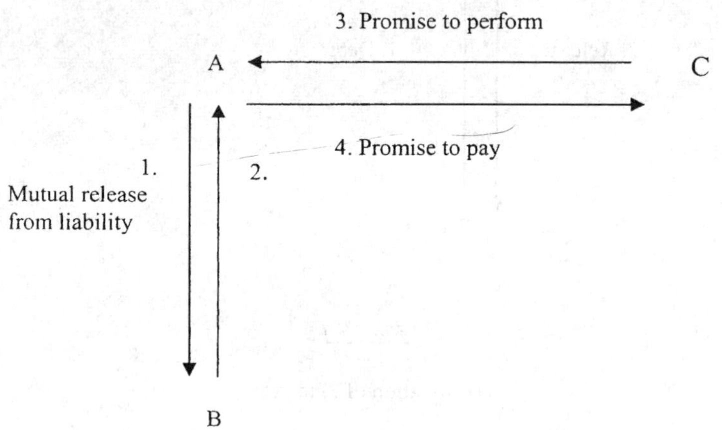

Fig.15.3

Novation of consultancy agreements

15–018 Novations of consultancy agreements or nominated subcontracts work in a slightly different way. A as employer has a contract with B as designer and intends to enter into a design and build contract with C as contractor. B agrees to novate its contract to C on execution of the design and build contract and C agrees to accept a novation of the design contract in that event. The novation agreement is indicated in dotted lines in Fig.15.4. Here there are three main stages:

(1) execution of the design contract which B agrees to novate to C on execution of the design and build contract in the form of an agreement annexed to the design contract;

(2) the execution of the design and build contract in which C agrees to accept a novation of the design contract from B in the same form; and

(3) a novation between A, B and C with the same four steps as in Fig.15.3.

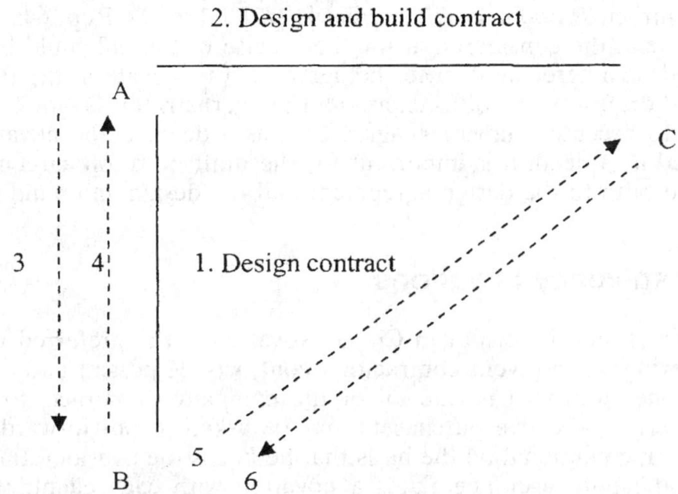

Fig.15.4

In this context, novation is a way of merging one contract into another, although the novated design contract will take effect as a new subcontract for which C will be vicariously liable to A. It has been pointed out that novation agreements drafted by employers sometimes omit stage 3 from Fig.15.4. In other words, although the employer is released, the designer is not (McNicholas 1993). On the face of it, this means the employer could sue the designer or the contractor for breaches in connection with the design although its cause of action against the designer would be limited to claims accrued before entering into the design and build contract. This is presumably the employer's intention. It could have been intended to apply to work carried out by the designer for which the contractor does not assume responsibility, e.g. planning matters. It could also be extra informal security against the risk of the contractor becoming insolvent before paying any award of damages for failures in the design. **15–019**

It has been argued that the court could infer a release either as the common intention of the parties derived from all three agreements or on the ground that the arrangement falls within the situation in Fig.15.2 (McNicholas 1993). The first possibility would depend on the construction of the three documents. The second seems less likely since it is an example of inferred novation, whereas the example in Fig.15.4 is an express novation. In the absence of rectification, the court is likely to assume the parties intended the designer to remain potentially liable to the employer. In *Baxter Clark & Paul v Tulloch Construction* [1999] G.W.D. 37–1789, the Scottish Court of Session refused summary judgment to an architect claiming fees on an abortive project on the ground that it had not proved either the terms of its original appointment to a charity wanting to promote a housing development, or of a novation to the design and build contractor (who happened to own the proposed site). It seems that, because the project never proceeded, the precise arrangements between architect, client and builder were never formalised. In principle Lord Penrose was unwilling to infer a novation releasing the client from liability (stage 4 in Fig.15.4) simply because a construction contract is entered into.

Could the lack of a release avoid a novation for want of consideration from the employer? The court is concerned to find consideration for the new contract: *Rasbora v JCL Marine* [1977] 1 Lloyd's Rep. 645 at 650. In this context, the consideration for the release of the old could be supplied by the design agreement since the agreement to novate in the form of the annexed draft was one of its express terms. Perhaps this is, however, a good reason to execute a novation agreement as a deed. If the novation is not executed as a deed, it is important for the draft novation agreement to be annexed both to the design agreement and the design and build contract.

7. Insolvency novations

15–020 The background is set out in Ch.13. Novation is the preferred vehicle for transferring an insolvent contractor's contracts. If possible, the insolvency practitioner wants to novate all of the company's contracts to the same purchaser. Prospective purchasers may be asked to put forward two bids: the first unconditional on the basis that he keeps the consideration whether or not the purchaser negotiates a novation with each client; the second conditional where the price allocates specific sums to individual contracts which only become payable on novations being achieved. Once informal agreement is reached, the terms are expressed in a sale agreement which is kept private between the insolvency practitioner and the purchaser, which sets out the consideration and the scope of the purchaser's obligation to procure the novations. A draft form of novation agreement is often included as a schedule to the sale agreement. The purchaser then approaches each individual client with the aim of negotiating a novation on the terms of the draft agreement. If clients impose more onerous terms in the novations than anticipated by the sale agreement, the purchaser may attempt to renegotiate the price with the insolvency practitioner.

8. Consequences of novation

15–021 A novation can release a guarantor from liability: *Commercial Bank of Tasmania* [1893] A.C. 313; *Housing Guarantee Fund v Yusef* [1991] V.R. 17. Many guarantees anticipate this and preserve the guarantor's liability in that event. Novation did not effect a release in *De Montfort Insurance v Lafferty* [1997] S.C. 335. It appears, however, that all the novation did was to make a new party liable for payment to the contractor without discharging the existing employer; otherwise, the contractor's rights and obligations were unaffected. See also *Manx Electricity Authority v JP Morgan* [2003] B.L.R. 477. A novation may provide for the apportionment of liabilities as between the outgoing and incoming party. In *Crouch Mining v The Scottish Coal Co.* [2003] CSOH 217 the parties to a mining contract decided to terminate it by consent. The contractor had obtained excavating, earth moving and haulage plant for the works under two finance leases and it was agreed that the leases be novated to a subsidiary of the employer so the plant could continue to be used. By the novations it was agreed that sums due under the finance leases would be apportioned on a time basis, so that those parts attributable to the period before the date of the termination agreement would be borne by the contractor and those accruing after that date would be paid by the employer's subsidiary. If the plant had simply been hired there would have been no difficulty. But the finance leases provided for "balloon payments" and the employer argued that these should be apportioned even though they fell due for payment after the date of the termination agreement. One of the leases, for example, was for 60 months, at a monthly rental of just over £20,000 for 59 months and a final balloon payment of £250,000. Lord Clarke held that on the true construction of the novation agreements the employer's subsidiary was liable for the balloon payments.

By reason of the express termination clauses in the standard forms (Ch.14), formal insolvency usually terminates the contractor's employment. Novation agreements sometimes reinstate the employment before effecting a mutual release between employer and contractor. This is not strictly necessary and can reactivate an employer's duty to make a direct payment: *Construction Award No. 9 (1988)* [1995] 2 Con. L. Yb. 103. Among other things, it was reinstatement that led the arbitrator in that case to construe the novation as a variation of the original contract. The facts are given in Ch.17. The incoming contractor may also, on signing a novation agreement, immediately become liable in damages to the employer in respect of breaches of contract by the insolvent contractor. This possibility is considered in the next section.

9. Liability for pre-novation breaches

Whether a novation takes effect only as from the date of the novation agreement or has retrospective effect, as if the purchaser had been named as a party in the original contract, depends on all the circumstances: *Lorentzen v White Shipping* (1942) 74 Ll. L. Rep. 161 at 165. The issue is analogous to the question whether the scope of a guarantee covers pre-existing as well as future debts: consider *Egan v Static Control Components* [2004] 2 Lloyd's Rep. 429. **15–022**

In "inception" cases the position ought to be the same where the surviving party is in breach before the novation. Logically it should be liable for the loss actually suffered by the newcomer rather than the damages which the original contracting party would have suffered. In this respect novation differs from assignment. Thus in *Yarm Road v Costain* (unreported, July 30, 2001), a subcontract in the FCEC blue form entered into before the Housing Grants, Construction and Regeneration Act 1996 came into force was novated after the Act came into force. It was held by Judge Richard Havery Q.C. that the novation was a new contract falling within the Act, entitling the new subcontractor to bring an adjudication against the contractor even though in theory it could rely on pre-novation breaches committed before the Act which could only arise from the provisions of the Act.

Some liabilities, such as delay and cost overrun, are normally accepted by the employer; but others, such as liability for defects, may be shared with or wholly allocated to the incoming contractor. The hazards of construction, and the possibility of a decline in the quality of work immediately before an insolvency, make it important that this risk be properly appraised. To an extent, it may be apportioned between the major subcontractors in the form of collateral warranties to the employer, but these may be unavailable or insufficient. For all these reasons, novation agreements in the industry commonly provide that the incoming contractor agrees to be liable to the employer as if it had been named as a party to the original contract from the inception of the project: e.g. the terms set out in *Yarm Road v Costain*. The effect of such a provision was considered in *W&J Leigh v CBI Nederland* (unreported, June 20, 1985, Otton J.). The case is significant in that it explores the interrelationship between novation, assignment, termination, suretyship and direct payment. The facts are particularly important.

The facts in *Leigh v Nederland*

15–023 The dispute arose out of a specialist subcontract for the painting of oil storage tanks in the Netherlands. Both contractor and subcontractor were Dutch companies. The specification required the subcontractor to obtain the paint from an English supplier; and the subcontract provided that the English supplier should give a guarantee of the subcontractor's performance. (The subcontractor was unable to procure a bond to support its own performance.) From the outset, the contractor was concerned to avoid any risk that, in the event that it enforced the guarantee, it would remain liable to make further payments to the subcontractor. In order to address this concern, all three parties entered into a direct agreement whereby, in consideration of its guarantee, the supplier was given the option of being substituted in place of the subcontractor in the event of its default, subject to satisfying the contractor that substitution was necessary to ensure completion of the work and to minimise the supplier's loss.

In the event of substitution, both contractor and supplier agreed to be bound by the terms of the subcontract as if the supplier had been the original party in the place of the subcontractor. The contractor agreed to make all further payments due under the subcontract direct to the supplier whether in respect of work carried out by the subcontractor before or after substitution. The subcontractor agreed to make no claims against the contractor (effectively a release expressed in negative form), but there was no equivalent term releasing the subcontractor from liability. In effect, the direct agreement gave a guarantor the right to perform in lieu of paying damages and allowed a contractor to pay a supplier direct to the extent that sums due to a subcontractor at the date of substitution had not been paid. In a separate side agreement, the subcontractor promised, if the supplier became liable under its guarantee, to assign to it all rights to further payment under the subcontract.

About a year after starting work, the subcontractor entered into a factoring agreement whereby all its debts, including those arising under the subcontract, were assigned to International Factors. The contractor was notified of the assignment and was instructed to pay the factor direct by an endorsement on the reverse of the subcontractor's invoices. A few months later, the subcontractor admitted to the supplier that it was insolvent and unable to complete the subcontract. Pursuant to its agreement with the supplier, the subcontractor "surrendered all its rights" under the subcontract to the supplier. In reliance on the admission of insolvency, the supplier exercised its option to be substituted under the direct agreement. The contractor exercised its power to cancel the subcontract while reserving all its rights against the subcontractor, which went into liquidation. The contractor authorised the supplier's substitution and the supplier arranged for the work to be completed by a replacement subcontractor. At this point, the factor demanded payment of three invoices issued by the subcontractor shortly before the termination. The supplier issued its own invoices for the same sums and asked for payment pursuant to the direct agreement. The contractor admitted that the sums were due and payable but found itself in the invidious position of defending proceedings by the factor in the Netherlands and by the supplier in England for the same sums—the very situation it feared would happen.

The English court had to construe the subcontract and the side agreement (both of which were governed by Dutch law) and the direct agreement (which was governed by English Law). The facts were straightforward and the court had little difficulty in finding that both the termination of the subcontract and the substitution had been validly effected. The issue was the effect of the direct agreement on the contractor's pre-substitution liabilities. The contractor argued that, construing all three documents together, the parties had agreed, as from the date of any substitution, that any sums due to the subcontractor at that time would become payable to the supplier. However, between signing the direct agreement and the substitution, the subcontractor had assigned its debts to the factor. As a consequence, at the date of the substitution, all outstanding sums were payable to the factor, thereby restricting the supplier's entitlement to payment to such sums as it could earn through performance of the work.

Decision and commentary on the case

Otton J. held that: 15–024

1. The combined operation of the direct agreement and the termination clause in the subcontract disentitled the subcontractor from any further payment. "In my judgment, [the subcontractor] is only entitled to receive such amount by which the contract price exceeds the cost to the contractor of completing the work, less payments already made on account. However, in the event of substitution . . . the cost to the contractor of completing the work is the amount which remains to be paid under the [subcontract] and, accordingly, in a situation such as occurred here, [the subcontractor's] entitlement must be nil" (p.21 of the transcript).
2. As an assignee, the factor could be in no better position than the subcontractor. The rights assigned to the factor were subject to all of the provisions of the subcontract and the direct agreement and were defeated by the events which happened.
3. Under the direct agreement, the supplier acquired rights against the contractor which were independent of the subcontractor's rights against the contractor. Sums due ceased to be payable to the subcontractor. Instead, the contractor assumed a direct obligation to pay them to the supplier. Since a burden cannot be assigned, the whole arrangement took effect as a novation of the subcontract.
4. Even if the finding of novation were incorrect, and the supplier's rights to payment were acquired by assignment, the supplier's claim took

priority over that of the factor since: (a) the assignment to the supplier was first in time and first to be notified to the debtor and therefore took priority; and (b) the subcontractor could not by its unilateral act (the assignment to the factor) affect its own rights and obligations under the subcontract and the direct agreement. The factor's rights were inherently flawed and were destroyed by the consequences of the subcontractor's insolvency.

The court observed that, in the event of default by the subcontractor, the contractor had both the power to cancel the subcontract and the right to authorise the substitution of the supplier as subcontractor by way of novation. The remedies were cumulative rather than alternative. The invoices were not equivalent to debts arising from delivery of goods; they were claims for payment in respect of work done in accordance with the terms of a construction contract under which all payment was conditional on the contract not being cancelled before completion through the subcontractor's default. In the case of all three invoices, the notice of cancellation of the subcontract preceded the due date for payment. The cancellation of the contract determined the rights of the subcontractor, and any assignee of the subcontractor, to be paid any outstanding instalments (p.11). By virtue of the termination clause this was an implied suspension of payment after cancellation.

This case is unusual in a number of respects: the coupling of a guarantee with an option to novate by an inferior party in the contract chain; and the claim under the novation being for recovery of debts rather than payment of damages. Even so, it is a valuable authority and provides a legal foundation for modern step-in agreements. It could also be argued that it provides authority for the proposition that a novation is not dependent upon the mutual release of obligations as between the two existing parties. In this case, the emphasis was upon the contractor and the supplier being mutually bound to each other (that is, to form a new contract) rather than a mutual release as between contractor and subcontractor. The side agreement between the subcontract and the supplier may have had no legal effect. By the time it was executed, all three parties had laid down a contractual series of consequences in the event of the subcontractor's default, under which the subcontractor's rights against the contractor ceased to be enforceable and the supplier acquired fresh independent rights. Arguably, the subcontractor had nothing to assign to the supplier. Significantly, however, the side agreement could not be construed as having in some way altered the legal effect of the direct agreement, for the simple reason that to do so would have required the consent of the contractor. The subcontractor's consent to the novation was given in advance by its execution of the direct agreement.

Blyth & Blyth v Carillion

15–025 *Leigh v Nederland* can be compared with *Blyth & Blyth v Carillion Construction* (2001) 79 Con. L.R. 142, in which the novation of a consultant's appointment to a design and build contractor was not contingent on the consultant's default but available at any time at the employer's option. The case is significant because the court rejected the contractor's claim for damages arising out of a pre-novation breach by the engineer even though the novation agreement provided that the engineer should be liable to the contractor as if the contractor had been named as a party to the appointment from the inception.

The facts

In April 1998, Carillion entered into a JCT contract, governed by Scottish law, to design and build a leisure centre in Edinburgh. The contractor assumed responsibility for any design work previously done by the employer and agreed to correct any inaccuracy in the employer's requirements (on which the JCT contract was based) at its own cost. In May 1998, the employer entered into a deed of appointment with the engineer, Blyth & Blyth, with effect from the date on which the engineer had commenced work 18 months before. The engineer agreed to carry out its obligations with all proper professional skill, care and diligence and to use reasonable endeavours to see that the employer suffered no loss or expense. A form of novation agreement was attached to the deed which could be activated at the employer's option. **15–026**

In June 1998, all three parties entered into a novation agreement which apparently provided that the original appointment was not terminated, the employer retaining rights against the engineer under a separate duty of care letter. Under cl.3.4, the contractor required the employer's consent before suspending or terminating the novated appointment. Clause 3.5 enabled the employer to step in after a termination to "reverse the novation". By cll.4 and 5, the engineer accepted liability to the contractor in respect of past or future breaches of the appointment and agreed to carry out the appointment and be bound by its terms as if the contractor had originally been named as a party in place of the employer. The agreement was a mixture of terms found in novations and collateral warranties.

The engineer sued for unpaid fees (we are not told whether they were incurred before after the novation), and the contractor counterclaimed for breaches of the appointment before the novation. The engineer's breach consisted of an error in the original information to tenderers by which the amount of steel reinforcement needed for the project had been underestimated. The error was repeated in the employer's requirements which became part of the JCT contract. During the work, the contractor incurred additional costs of reinforcement which were irrecoverable from the employer because the contractor had agreed to bear the cost of correcting any inaccuracies in the employer's requirements. The contractor claimed these costs from the engineer pursuant to the novation. It was assumed by the court, without deciding the issue, that a competent engineer would not have made such an error. The employer was not involved in the case because it had suffered no loss through the engineer's mistake. There were no defects in the work attributable to the engineer's design error: the contractor was not passing on to the engineer a claim made against it by the employer.

The issues

There were two main issues: (a) was the agreement a novation? (b) did it enable the contractor to recover the loss claimed? **15–027**

The contractor argued that the agreement took effect as a simple novation which required the court to substitute "contractor" for "employer" in the original consultant's appointment. The engineer's error was a straightforward breach entitling the contractor to claim the additional cost of reinforcement as damages. The engineer pointed out that substitution would result in absurdities, e.g. the recitals would read: "The contractor proposes to enter into a building contract with a main contractor." It would also place the engineer in a conflict of interest between his duties to the employer and to the contractor. One of the services provided by the engineer was the evaluation of tenders. It could not have been the intention of the parties that the engineer should owe a duty to the contractor to evaluate the contractor's tender.

The engineer argued that the intention of the parties was to provide the contractor with recourse against the engineer in the event of a claim by the employer arising out of negligent design. The claim was one which only the employer could bring, and the employer had reserved the right to sue the engineer in respect of such matters. The agreement was never intended to protect the contractor from its own pricing errors. Finally, according to the appointment, the engineer had to provide services to the satisfaction of the employer, but there was no evidence that the employer had been dissatisfied with its performance. The engineer might have a defence of waiver if the contractor were to dispute this. In the light of these submissions, the contractor did not pursue its claim that the agreement was a novation. Instead, it argued that the agreement constituted the contractor as the "creditor in the obligation" owed by the engineer, without altering its content, namely to provide services to the employer. On this interpretation, the contractor should be treated as having contracted with the engineer for the provision of services to the employer, so that if they were not provided, the engineer would be liable in damages to the contractor in respect of any loss caused to it.

The decision

15–028 This subtle argument was rejected by the court: as far as past breaches were concerned, the agreement took effect as an assignment of the employer's benefit of the appointment to the contractor. As a result, the contractor could only recover damages in respect of loss suffered by the employer. In this case, the employer suffered no loss because the contractor had agreed to bear the cost of any errors in the employer's requirements. The contractor protested that it had only agreed to assume responsibility for such errors in the belief that it could transfer the risk to the engineer by novation. The court pointed out that the contractor had no right to the novation: as the documents were drawn in this case, novation was only available at the employer's option. To allow the contractor to succeed would involve "the retrospective recasting of the scope of the performance or duty owed by the consultant".

Commentary

15–029 The decision has been heavily criticised in the industry on the ground that it was open to the court to substitute "contractor" for "employer" *mutatis mutandis*, i.e. so far as the context so admitted. On this approach, the absurdities referred to resulted from a literalistic approach which, bearing in mind the established practice of novation of consultants' appointments in the industry, cannot have reflected the parties' intentions. It could also be argued that the reservation of rights against the original engineer is not an impediment to novation: see *Leigh v Nederland*. It is interesting to note that *Leigh v Nederland* was not referred to in *Blyth & Blyth*. Against this line of reasoning, the decision can be supported on a number of grounds:

1. Damages would have been recoverable by the contractor had it not agreed, by way of amendment to the JCT standard form, to assume liability for errors in the employer's requirements. The contractor caused the problem by failing to think through the legal consequences of this amendment on its rights under any novated appointment from the engineer.
2. The nature of this novation is different in quality from that in which a replacement is found for one of the original parties. It follows the pattern in Fig.15.4 rather than Fig.15.3 above. As such, it more closely resembles a merger of contracts than a traditional novation. It could be argued that the contractor chose an inappropriate vehicle to carry out its intentions; too much was left to the interpolation of the court (see Cullen 2005, von Laun 2004).
3. More fundamentally, it could be argued that the "inception" approach is only viable in simple cases, reflecting its origin in the novation of debts. As the effect of a novation is to transfer the burden of a contract, it is reasonable for the court to expect a higher degree of clarity of the parties' intentions than was demonstrated in this case.
4. Underlying the decision may have been a feeling of repugnance at being asked to treat a professional relationship as a freely transferable form of property.

New standard forms

This final point is implicit in a Liability Briefing published by the **15–030**
Construction Industry Council (2004). The CIC objects to the inception approach on the ground that part of the engineer's burden is to act in accordance with the interests of the employer. This factor informs the whole relationship: the terms of the appointment as well as how they are implemented. It is not feasible to "switch" loyalties during the project to acting primarily in the interests of the contractor after an arbitrary date. The CIC also points out that it would be wrong to expose the engineer to a greater loss to the contractor than it would have been liable for to the employer. Nevertheless, the CIC has produced a new form of novation agreement (CIC/NovAgr) in which the engineer remains liable to the employer in respect of pre-novation work but warrants to the contractor that it has carried out its pre-novation work in accordance with the appointment. Compare *Aquatec-Maxcon v Barwon Regional Water Authority (No.6)* [2007] VSC 127.

By contrast, the City of London Law Society (2004) has issued a form of agreement which follows the inception approach but deals with the problem raised in *Blyth & Blyth* by including a warranty by the engineer that it will be liable to the contractor for any loss arising out of pre-novation breaches, even where the loss claimed by the contractor would not have been suffered by the employer. It is not clear what effect *Blyth & Blyth* will have on novation in insolvency situations. It is already common practice to prepare a schedule of the liabilities undertaken by the new contractor. It is possible that the case will be restricted to design and build situations. Nevertheless, it is valuable in highlighting the potential complexities involved in using novation as a vehicle for transferring obligations in the industry.

Chapter 16

Completion Contracts

Where a contractor becomes insolvent, a way has to be found to have the works completed. The employer has a range of options: see SBCC Insolvency Practice Guide (1991); JCT Practice Note 24 (1992); and RICS Construction Insolvency Information Paper (1997), which has some useful flow charts. Although these guides have not been updated to take account of later editions of the standard forms and the changes made by the Enterprise Act 2002, they remain useful. **16–001**

1. Overview

The employer's options for completing the works include tendering, negotiation, novation, as well as other methods. **16–002**

1. **Tender** The employer could send the works out to open tender or invite the original tenderers to bid for the completion contract: *City of Moncton v Aprile Contracting* (1977) 17 N.B.R. (2d) 678; *Kamlee Construction v Town of Oakville* (1960) 26 D.L.R. (2d) 166; *CJ Pearce Developments v Oakbridge* (unreported, January 14, 2002, Judge Anthony Thornton Q.C.).
2. **Negotiation** The employer could approach the original second highest tenderer and negotiate a contract with it. Or the employer can ask contractors working on adjacent sites or a contractor with whom there is an ongoing working relationship: *Bank of East Asia v Scottish Enterprise* (unreported, June 19, 1992, OH); *CFW Architects v Cowlin Construction* (2006) 105 Con. L.R. 116. Or invite only one contractor to quote: *Avonwood Homes v Jaffer* [2003] VCAT 443; *Greenore Port Technical & General* [2006] EWHC 3119.
3. **Self-build** The employer could complete the work itself using its own resources. To take an historical example, in 1855 the contractor engaged to build the Saltash Bridge, CJ Mare, seriously underestimated his bid and went bankrupt, just as the first of the bridge's main trusses were beginning to take shape. Brunel himself took charge and engaged labour directly completing the bridge three years later (Brindle 2005, 179).
4. **Direct agreement** The employer could enter into direct agreements with subcontractors either through step-in rights or by making a new approach to them: *Gee Walker & Slater v Société Generale* (unreported, October 27, 1999, CA); *Triodos Bank v Dobbs* [2004] EWHC 845;

Starelec v Kumagai Gumi [2002] QSC 137; *Nev Mellon Electrical v AAPC* [2005] NZHC 391 discussed in Ch.9; *Braspetro Oil Services v FPSO Construction* [2005] EWHC 1316; *Wallace-Smith v Thiess Infraco* (2005) 218 A.L.R. 1.

5. **Continue** Allow the insolvent company through its insolvency practitioner to complete the contract: *Forth Shipbuilding v Tonnevold* (1923) 14 Ll. L. Rep. 554; *McIlwee v Foley Brothers* (1916) W.W.R. 5.
6. **Novation or assignment** The employer could agree a novation with the insolvency practitioner who introduces a new contractor or allow the insolvency practitioner to assign the benefit of the contract to another contractor and appoint the assignee as the agent of the insolvent contractor for the purpose of completing the works: *W&J Leigh v CBI Nederland* (unreported, June 20, 1985, Otton J.) discussed in Ch.15.
7. **Framework contractor completes** If the contract falls within a framework agreement, the employer may prefer not to novate but to terminate and transfer the work to another framework contractor (Leftly 2006).
8. **Surety completes** The employer may allow the guarantor or bondsman to complete the works or to procure a novation to its preferred contractor. This rarely happens in the UK: *Greenore Port v Technical & General* [2006] EWHC 3119 at paras.184–189.

The same care is needed when procuring a completion contract as any other: there are cases where completion contractors have defaulted: e.g. *Mertens v Home Freeholds* [1921] 2 K.B. 526; *Vigers v Swindell* [1939] 3 All E.R. 590; *Stanley Brown v Maryland Casualty Co* 442 S.W. 2d 187 (1969); *Samuel Properties v London Borough of Richmond* (unreported, July 22, 1983, Judge John Newey Q.C.); *Triodos Bank v Dobbs* [2004] EWHC 845, and FG Minter Ltd (information supplied by the late Len Mann). The JCT has recommended its own Form of Prime Cost Contract (1992) in cases where the employer prefers a negotiated contract with a replacement contractor (Practice Note 24, p.21). For a practical example see "Carry on Contracting" (*Building*, January 22, 1993), which concerned Callendar Square, Falkirk. In that case the original contract was a management contract, the completion contract was design and build, and the original design team's conditions of engagement were novated to the incoming contractor. The design team would have preferred a completion contract based on construction management.

Special care is needed in defining the scope of a completion contract, especially the extent to which the incoming contractor accepts responsibility for latent defects. In *CJ Pearce Developments v Oakbridge* (unreported, January 14, 2002, Judge Anthony Thornton Q.C.) a roadworks contractor went into liquidation before completing an access road for a proposed development. In the tender documents for the completion contract, the employer's requirements included an obligation to complete the access road. In its contractor's proposals the successful tenderer stated that the road would "be taken on and completed". The parties entered into a JCT 81 contract. After the road was completed, it needed remedial work in respect of defects arising from work carried out by the original contractor. An arbitrator held that the completion contractor had assumed full contractual responsibility for the defects. This finding was reversed on appeal. Reading the employer's requirements and the contractor's proposals together, there was no clear assumption of responsibility. This led the court to adopt a narrow construction of the words "taken on" in the contractor's proposals, i.e. to continue but without responsibility for latent defects. This view was supported by the factual background. It was possible to define the work left incomplete but the completion contractor had no means of assessing or pricing the risk of assuming responsibility for the work it was taking over. The fact that the court had to become involved in a detailed examination of the contract documents including the drawings makes it particularly important that, if the parties do intend a completion contractor to assume legal responsibility for the quality of existing work, an express obligation is clearly set out. This case can be contrasted with *Monavon Construction v Davenport* (2006) 108 Con. L.R. 15 which concerned an oral completion contract on the basis of cost plus 20 per cent. Although the parties seem to have made no effort to define the extent or the quality of the work done by the original contractor, Judge Anthony Thornton Q.C. at para.31 found that the completion contractor agreed to check the previous work "using reasonable methods of inspection and would remedy and complete any defective work that was discovered by a reasonable inspection." The builder's contention that it had assumed no obligations regarding the original contractor's electrical work carried out to first fix stage was rejected (at paras.38–40).

2. Step-in agreements

It is common for the financier on a project to demand the right to step in and exercise the employer's rights under the main contract in certain events, primarily if the contractor claims the right to suspend or terminate its performance: see especially *Wallace-Smith v Thiess Infraco* (2005) 218 A.L.R. 1, discussed in Ch.17. Some elements have become standard, although the drafting is often the subject of detailed negotiation (Fox and Tott 1999, Ch.9). The step-in may be for a limited period and the agreement will provide for its termination or step-out (Tan 2004). In the context of the right to appoint an administrative receiver, "step-in rights" are defined in Sch.2A para.6 of the Insolvency Act 1986 as rights which entitle a project financier to "assume sole or principal responsibility under an agreement for carrying out all or part of a project or . . . make arrangements for carrying out all or part of a project" (see *Cabvision v Feetum* [2006] Ch. 585). In practice the phrase is used to denote any kind of enforcement action relating to a project whether based on a security interest or contractual right. The primary aim of step-in agreements on a major project is to maintain the integrity of the project and the anticipated revenue stream from which the project loans will be repaid (Scriven *et al.* 1999, Ch. 29). **16–003**

There is little case law on such agreements. In *Braspetro Oil Services v FPSO Construction* [2005] EWHC 1316 (Cresswell J.), step-in rights were reserved in an agreement between a contractor and an end user. However, on the contractor experiencing financial difficulties, the end user preferred to enter into direct payment agreements with individual suppliers rather than enforce its step-in rights (see Ch.17). In *Triodos Bank v Dobbs* [2004] EWHC 845 (Lewison J.), step-in rights were not reserved by the bank at the inception but acquired as a condition of a refinancing of a developer. By that time, two contractors in succession had gone into receivership and a third was threatening to terminate for non-payment. The bank was advised by its own surveyor that the project would cost up to £500,000 more if a fourth contractor had to be engaged, even though the present contractor had been the highest tenderer and was working on cost plus 3.5 per cent profit and 3.25 per cent for overheads. Under the refinancing, the employer was given an increased facility. The construction contract was varied by increasing the contract sum, converting it into a fixed price contract, and permitting the bank to make direct payments to the contractor on receipt of approvals from the bank's surveyor. Sums due to the contractor were guaranteed by the bank which was given step-in rights. The precise nature of these rights is not set out in the report, other than to say that if the bank terminated the finance agreement, it could take the employer's place as the person entitled to give instructions to the contractor. Importantly, if the bank appointed a receiver over the employer's assets, it accepted an obligation to exercise its step-in rights (para.54). The contractor was given a second charge over the site and a floating charge over the undertaking of the employer. Under a deed of priorities, the contractor would receive the first £10,000 per plot and other benefits up to a maximum amount after which the bank would take priority.

Eventually, the bank appointed administrative receivers who opted to sell the site rather than build out. The bank succeeded in its claim against a director of the employer under his personal guarantee and resisted the director's own claim for damages of over £16 million except for a claim for breach of contract in failing to exercise its step-in rights for a period of two months only for which nominal damages were recoverable. The obligation to step in was subject to the condition that the bank could not be required to increase its overall funding of the project: compare *Gee Walker & Slater v Société Generale* (unreported, October 27, 1999, CA), discussed in Ch.17. The rights simply entitled the bank to give instructions to the contractor but, by the date of the receivership, the contractor had not been paid for many months. Had the contractor terminated on the ground of non-payment, the bank's step-in rights would have vanished. The bank would not have been obliged to take legal action against the contractor even if there was anything it could have done. It was highly unlikely that the bank could have persuaded the contractor to carry on working without reaching a settlement of its claims for a larger amount than was eventually agreed. In addition, the outstanding work falling within the scope of the contract was relatively minor and could not sensibly be done until after other work outside the scope of the contract had been done.

3. Completion by insolvency practitioners

16–004 This may occur where a relatively small amount of work is outstanding and there is a likelihood of significant profit arising from the conversion of work in progress into debt. Funding the work can be a major problem. In *Carrello v Benchmark Debtor Finance* [2003] WASC 140, an earthmoving contractor went into administration under s.436A of the Corporations Act 2001. It had previously factored its debts but the factoring agreement terminated on the administration. The administrator met the factor who agreed to finance future trading but a dispute emerged later as to whether this was a continuance of the original agreement or, as the administrator maintained, an agreement to fund the company which would among other things facilitate the recovery of debts already factored. The dispute was not suitable for resolution on the factor's application for summary judgment in respect of receivables arising from continued trading.

Completion of the contract can only be achieved by an insolvency practitioner who is able to inspire confidence in the employer and the contractor's staff, as well as the subcontractors and suppliers. It has been seen that formal insolvency events are not in themselves breaches of contract. However, as almost all construction contracts contain termination clauses, it will in practice be impossible for an insolvency practitioner to complete the works unless the employer agrees to reinstate the contractor's employment or waives the termination by allowing the company to continue. If these hurdles can be overcome, the insolvency practitioner may attempt to re-negotiate the contract by providing for weekly or fortnightly payments or by limiting or excluding the employer's right of set-off. Care is required in these negotiations as the employer may be entitled to treat such attempts at re-negotiation as repudiatory. Repudiation arguments are very common in this context, especially in a falling market: e.g. *Forth Shipbuilding v Tonnevold* (1923) 14 Ll. L. Rep. 554, analysed in the second edition of this book.

Amendment 11 (1992) to JCT 80 introduced an interim procedure whereby an employer can agree terms on a temporary basis with a receiver while considering its options. This is now contained in cl.27.5.3 of JCT 98. No particular terms are specified except that "any right of set-off which the employer may have shall not be exercisable in respect of any payment due from the employer to the contractor under such interim arrangement". It should be noted that abatement for defective work performed under the interim arrangement has not been excluded (see Ch.5). This clause has been dropped from JCT 05, although the terms may well be agreed informally with the insolvency practitioner. In *Melville Dundas v Hotel Corporation of Edinburgh* [2006] CSOH 136, a contractor was engaged to fit out a shell constructed by another builder. A dispute arose as to which contractor was responsible for cracking to external glazing and whether the cost of remedial work was covered by the employer's works insurance. When the fit-out contractor went into receivership, the works had been completed save for snagging items and the problem with the glazing. The receivers agreed the final account on the basis that retention of £20,000 would be released on the issue of a certificate of making good defects once the snagging items were corrected and that a further £90,000 would be separately withheld on the glazing issue. In consideration of the employer's agreement to pursue the other contractor and its insurer the receivers agreed not to take steps to recover the £90,000. On receipt of any compensation from those sources the employer was to pay it to the receivers. If the whole sum had not been paid by July 31, 2004, the employer would make the payment "except to the extent that it has been established by our agreement or any court action that we are liable". None of these events occurred by that date and the receivers argued that the sum was due and payable. The employer asserted a set-off in respect of various cross-claims for the cost of rectifying latent defects and for consequential losses. It was held that the parties' agreement in relation to the sum of £90,000 had excluded the employer's rights of set-off by necessary implication and imposed conditions for the release of the money which had been fulfilled. The receivers were entitled to summary judgment (para.22). See also *Powell v General Electric* [2005] EWHC 644, (terms of payment out of a retention account in respect of warranty claims under a share sale agreement) and *Mawdsley's WL Inc v Mawdsley's GNS Ltd* (unreported,

March 1, 2007, Stuart Isaacs Q.C.), which concerned a retention escrow account used as a payment mechanism in respect of scheduled debts transferred under a sale of business agreement. It is worth noting that JCT Practice Note 24 advises employers to consider "retaining funds in excess of the contractual retention until the defects have been rectified but taking into account any performance bond that may be available and obtaining an undertaking from the insolvency practitioner that funds paid to him in respect of the contract will be applied to completing the works" (p.20).

4. Completion by guarantors

16–005 In North America, and in some guarantees offered by US and Canadian insurance companies in the UK, the guarantor offers or has the right to procure completion (McDevitt 1985, Scott and Reynolds 1994). This is to the guarantor's advantage because it can control the selection of the completion contractor, the agreement of the cost to complete and the timing of the completion contract. It also enables the guarantor to spread the period over which it has to outlay the cost to complete. Many employers are not prepared to cede control of the works in this way, apprehensive lest they minimise cost at the expense of quality. In *Greenore Port v Technical & General* [2006] EWHC 3119, it was held by Jackson J. that the employer's refusal of an offer from the bondsman to complete the works at the original contract sum was reasonable (para.189). Nevertheless, completion by guarantors has its advocates in the UK. In the late 1990s, bonds became available in high value PFI projects for 50 per cent, 80 per cent or even 100 per cent of the contract price, under which the bondsman was given the right to step in and complete the works or procure completion by another contractor. Stebbings (2000) stated that such bonds "have been used to replace the letters of credit required by monoline insurers to cover completion risk and to supplement parent company guarantees". As the guarantor has no better rights against the employer than the contractor has, it may find itself in dispute with the contractor's bank or assignee or the employer in relation to receivables which become payable on completion, particularly retention: *Royal Bank of Canada v Wilson* (1963) 4 C.B.R. 300, *Re Yeadon Waterworks* (1895) 72 L.T. 538, *Alexander v Administrator Transvaal* [1974] 2 S.A. 248.

5. Novation by insolvency practitioners

16–006 The majority of novations in the context of construction insolvencies are those negotiated by the insolvency practitioner (Ch.15). In the course of negotiations the parties need to work out the intended allocation of risk under the new contract. If the old contract is used as a basis for the new, any revisions should be clearly drafted and included as a schedule to the novation agreement. It will usually be necessary to revise the date for completion and to extend the newcomer's time for completion by reason of the delay resulting from the insolvency. The parties may also take the opportunity to make changes relating to:

- pricing provisions
- the scope of the works

- liability for liquidated and ascertained damages already incurred
- availability of plant and materials on and off site
- retention of title claimants
- existing patent and latent defects
- past and continuing breaches
- subcontractors' claims
- willingness of subcontractors and suppliers to novate their contracts
- enforceability of bonds and guarantees
- the Transfer of Undertakings (Protection of Employment) Regulations 2006
- availability of the professional team for novations (if design and build).

JCT Practice Note 24 and SBCC Insolvency Practice Guide both annex specimen forms of novation agreement. The contractor acts through its insolvency practitioner who will normally wish to be a party to the novation, especially if the contractor has continued trading while the novation was being negotiated. This is to enable the insolvency practitioner to be released from any personal claims which the other parties may have and to take the benefit of any indemnities and warranties which have been negotiated (Fig.16.1).

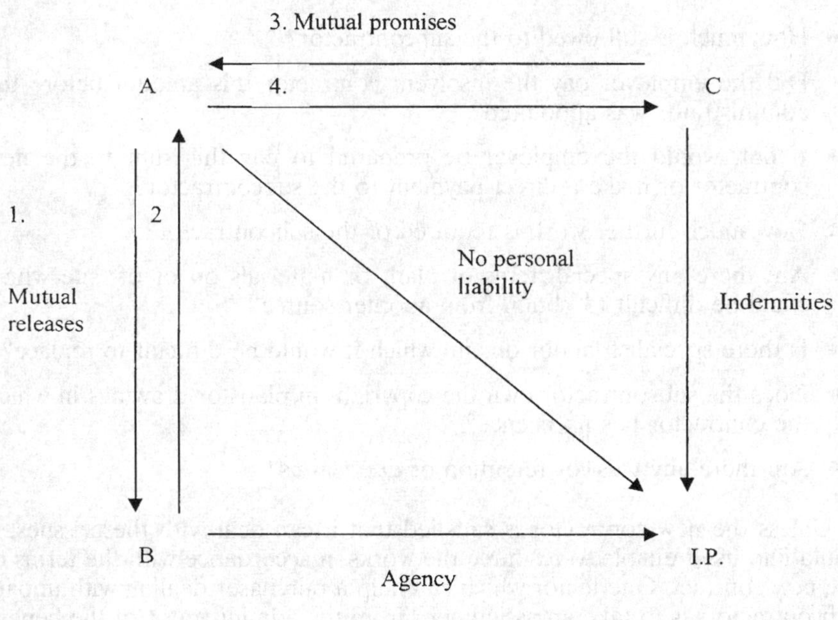

Fig.16.1

Where a contractor has a number of ongoing contracts at the date of an administration, and some of them are bonded, one of the administrator's priorities will be to have the bonds discharged by novating the contracts thereby releasing any security the contractor may have given to the bondsman such as a cash deposit. The bondsman may be prepared to offer some of the deposit to the purchaser if it agrees to take on all uncompleted contracts and assist the bondsman in getting its existing bonds released. The administrator will try to prevent this by making it a term of the negotiations that the purchaser does not make any direct approaches either to the bondsman or the employer. The suggestion is sometimes made that an existing bond be novated by substituting the purchaser for the insolvent contractor as joint and several obligor. In practice, new bonds are normally issued.

The insolvency surveyor's review may reveal that the contractor has been working without a binding contract. There may be a letter of intent or a payment undertaking from the employer or in simple cases an implied promise to pay arising from a request to carry out work. All of these give rise to a receivable, e.g. a claim in quasi-contract for a *quantum meruit*. The risk of misrepresentation by the receiver or a member of his staff makes it important in this context to agree to sell only such title to the receivables as the company may have.

6. Subcontractors

16–007 As the major part of a project is carried out by subcontractors, it is important that a prospective purchaser from a contractor in administration is aware of their position. Questions of particular relevance as far as subcontractors are concerned are:

- How much is still owed to the subcontractor?
- Did the employer pay the insolvent contractor this amount before the administrator was appointed?
- If not, would the employer be prepared to pay this sum to the new contractor or make a direct payment to the subcontractor?
- How much further work is required of the subcontractor?
- Are there any special items of plant or materials on or off site which could be difficult to obtain from another source?
- Is there specialist labour on site which it would be difficult to replace?
- Does the subcontractor own the copyright in plans or drawings in which the contractor has no licence?
- Are there any trust or retention of title claims?

Unless the new contractor is satisfied that it can deal with these issues, it could find itself unable to resource the works in accordance with the terms of the new contract. One factor which can help a purchaser dealing with unpaid subcontractors is to take an assignment from the administrator of the benefit of the subcontracts. This can be included in the novation agreement itself. By virtue of the assignment, a subcontractor would owe the new contractor a duty to carry out work under the old subcontract while only being able to look to the insolvent contractor for payment. In practice, of course, the subcontractor would be likely to cease work in the absence of a promise of payment by the new contractor but, as assignee of the benefit of the subcontract, the new contractor does have a certain hold which it may be able to use to its advantage. This would only assist the new contractor in cases where the old contractor had reached a binding contract with the subcontractor which has not automatically terminated on the main contract termination. If work were being done under a letter of intent, the subcontractor would normally owe no obligation to continue.

In deciding which subcontractors should be approached with a view to novation, the new contractor will probably disregard those whose works are neither specialist nor significant, whose materials have already been fixed or whose works are completed. The same would apply to trades in plentiful supply on the market at the time. Having identified those subcontractors whose services are still required, the new contractor will then negotiate a cost to complete using such commercial pressure as is available to avoid paying the amount left unpaid by the insolvent contractor. Subcontractors seek to recover their unpaid debt by enhancing their rates and the new contractor may be prepared to accept some enhancement as the price for retaining a particular subcontractor or supplier.

7. Mitigation of loss

Relevant criteria

Following a termination, if the employer fails to act reasonably in minimising its loss, its claim for damages will be calculated as if it had acted reasonably: *Sotiros Shipping v Sameiet Solholt* [1983] 1 Lloyd's Rep. 605. An employer would not recover damages for any part of its loss flowing from the breach which could have been avoided by taking reasonable steps. But if reasonable steps are taken, the employer can recover any additional expense incurred in taking them. The standard required of the employer in these circumstances is not a high one since the contractor is the wrongdoer: **16–008**

> "The law is satisfied if the party placed in a difficult situation by reason of the breach of a duty owed to him has acted reasonably in the adoption of remedial measures, and he will not be held disentitled to recover the cost of such measures merely because the party in breach can suggest that other measures less burdensome to him might have been taken" (*Banco de Portugal v Waterlow* [1932] A.C. 452 at 506, *per* Lord Macmillan.).

See also *Popular Homes v Circuit Developments* [1979] 2 N.Z.L.R. 642; *Goodman v Napier Harbour Board* [1939] N.Z.L.R. 97 (where the contract gave the employer "uncontrolled discretion as to price and method to employ any person" to complete the works). It is always possible that the completion contractor will complete for less than the original contract sum: *Ferguson v Sohl* (1993) 62 B.L.R. 95. A claim for reduction of damages on the ground of failure to mitigate is difficult to pursue unless the plaintiff has been obviously unreasonable. There need to be strong facts for an insolvency practitioner to have a fair prospect of success:

> "Now, when a contractor gets into difficulties which culminate in bankruptcy, and the employer is in consequence put to the extreme inconvenience and annoyance of having himself to complete the work, I think the

employer should be allowed a large discretion in the way in which he completes it, and that the contractor, in the absence of fraud or extreme negligence, cannot complain if the work be carried on in an uneconomical manner" (*Fulton v Dornwell* (1885) 4 S.C. 207 at 210, *per* Williams J.).

In that case, the contractor's trustee had not brought sufficient evidence to show that the cost to complete incurred by the employer was unreasonable. If it had been unreasonable due to "an extravagant and largely unnecessary remedial scheme", the employer might have been able to recover from its professional team the damages it could not claim against the insolvent contractor for failure to mitigate: *Equitable Life v Kenchington Ford* [1996] C.I.L.L. 1163.

"Cost plus" contracts

16–009 "Cost plus" is appropriate for emergency work where speed is more important than economy or where the employer is unclear precisely what work needs to be done (Capon 1990, 17). In *Kamlee Construction v Town of Oakville* (1960) 26 D.L.R. (2d) 166, a contractor was engaged to construct a storm relief sewer but left site before the works were completed. It appears from the report that the contractor experienced financial difficulties without becoming formally insolvent. Within a week, the employer invited tenders to complete the work and received one offer of a fixed price and another at cost plus 15 per cent. The second offer was accepted. On completion it was found that the works had cost substantially more than the fixed price offer. The original contractor argued that the employer had failed to mitigate its loss. The contractor's submission was rejected on a number of grounds: completion was urgent as winter was approaching; the cost plus contractor had available resources in the locality; and the employer's decision was taken on the engineer's advice that the likely final account on a cost plus basis would be close to the fixed price bid. The fact that the engineer's estimate proved to be completely out of line with the result did not mean that the employer had acted unreasonably.

In *Samuel Properties v London Borough of Richmond* (unreported, July 22, 1983, Judge John Newey Q.C.), after a contractor went into receivership, the employer appointed a new contractor as caretaker on the basis of cost plus 10 per cent but the completion contractor also went into receivership and had to be replaced by a third before the works were completed. The employer was in joint venture with a local authority and it was a term of their agreement that the employer would act with diligence and take appropriate steps to complete or procure the completion of the works. It was held that the employer had complied with this duty in selecting the defaulting second contractor. The employer had worked with the contractor before and had no reason to doubt an encouraging bank reference which properly reflected the bank's views at the time. "If [the employer] had called for a company search, I do not think that it would have altered the position. Many development and building companies are heavily dependent upon their banks and have to rely upon them to act reasonably," *per* Judge John Newey Q.C. In *Kraft Construction v Guardian Insurance* (1984) 57 A.R. 118, the contractor was held to have acted reasonably in hiring an alternative subcontractor on a cost plus basis in view of the "knock on effect" on the project of the failure of a significant subcontractor and the inactivity of the guarantor. Compare *Multiplex v Cleveland Bridge* [2006] EWHC 1341, at paras 114 and 137 (Jackson J.) and *Greenore Port v Technical & General* [2006] EWHC 3119, in which one of the factors persuading Jackson J. that a cost plus completion contract was reasonable was that the replacement contractor had neither the abilities nor the experience to enter into a lump sum fixed price contract (para.198). See also *Monavon v Davenport* considered at para.16–002, above.

Other forms of mitigation

In *City of Moncton v Aprile Contracting* (1977) 17 N.B.R. (2d) 678 it was held **16–010** that it was not unreasonable for a local authority to send the works to competitive tender rather than engaging an alternative contractor on a cost plus basis. See also *Canadian General Insurance v Dube* (1982) 39 N.B.R. (2d) 484 at 492. It was reasonable for an employer to obtain only one quotation for a completion contract for a house in circumstances where the demand for building services caused by the Sydney Olympics led to a shortage of supply and the employer had a deadline by which he needed to move in: *Avonwood Homes v Jaffer* [2003] VCAT 443. In that case it was stated that "a second builder has to be cautious in relation to the work that has gone before, making adequate allowance to ensure any risks of unsatisfactory work are covered. This means that the margin for profit and risk on completion contracts will be far higher than that placed on normal contracts to carry out the whole of the domestic building works" (*per* Mr Roger Young, at para.7.29).

In *OTV Birwelco v Technical & General* (2002) 84 Con. L.R. 117 the court ordered the beneficiary under a surety bond and the surety company to appoint a quantity surveyor to value the cost to complete and other losses incurred by the contractor following the repudiation of a subcontract immediately before a subcontractor's liquidation. The surety challenged the report on the grounds that the contractor had not surveyed the work on the date of termination and had failed to keep adequate records of labour and material costs for each item of the work. It was held that the absence of a survey was immaterial as site representatives for the parties had agreed a schedule of incomplete and defective work a few days before the termination. Judge Anthony Thornton Q.C. allowed the claim on the basis that the costs were a reasonable estimate of the cost to complete, without any additional work or betterment (para.137). He also allowed the contractor's claim to recover consultancy fees and overheads in dealing with the bondsman's queries on the ground that the contractor had provided sufficient information with its demand under the bond (para.150). The employer will be expected to give details of the additional cost to complete, especially where it is considerably more than the outstanding balance of the contract sum and includes extras or expenses incurred as a result of damage to the works or theft after the termination: *Tower Housing v Technical & General Guarantee* (1997) 87 B.L.R. 82 at 94. In *CFW Architects v Cowlin Construction* (2006) 105 Con. L.R. 116, the court assessed the damages flowing from a repudiation by an architect of its engagement with a contractor. Judge Anthony Thornton Q.C. held it was reasonable to engage a small firm to complete the design despite the large amount of work outstanding and the resulting delays since it had previously been employed to check the original architect's designs and had some familiarity with the project. The period of four weeks between the repudiation and the engagement of the new firm was also reasonable. The contractor recovered losses in respect of mobilisation, winter working, liquidated damages levied by the employer, prolongation, head office overheads, additional fees of the replacement architect over and above those which the original architect would have earned (e.g. in rectifying errors), other additional professional fees, and price increases. The contractor obtained a much longer extension of time under the main contract than it was entitled to and this reduced its claim for repudiation damages. Compare *Payzu v Saunders* [1919] 2 K.B. 281, a non-construction case where a refusal to accept an offer of a substitute contract was held to be unreasonable.

Failure to mitigate

16–011 An insolvency practitioner may argue that an employer has failed to mitigate its loss by refusing his offer to complete the contract. In order to succeed on a mitigation argument, an administrator may have to undertake to meet any loss caused by the termination, even if it continued to accrue after the contractor resumed working on site, and to take account in the proposal of any change in circumstances following the termination: *McIlwee v Foley Brothers* (1916) W.W.R. 5; *Avonwood Homes v Jaffer* [2003] VCAT 443. One standard form gives the employer a choice in the event of the contractor's insolvency of terminating the contract or of giving the insolvency practitioner "the option of carrying out the contract subject to his providing a guarantee for the due and faithful performance of the contract up to an amount to be agreed": cl.13 of Model Form A/1976/1978. If the second option is followed and the termination clause is invalid (or invalidly invoked), the demand for the guarantee could amount to repudiatory conduct by the employer. It will normally be reasonable to require a bond or a guarantee as a condition of allowing the contractor to continue.

In *Bank of East Asia v Scottish Enterprise* (unreported, June 19, 1992, Court of Session) the defendant employer engaged a contractor to design and build three factories for £500,000 under a deferred payment arrangement. The contractor went into receivership shortly after the date when the majority of the deferred consideration fell due for payment. The employer refused to pay relying on a set-off of its cross-claim for defects and the cost to complete. Of particular interest is the rigorous approach taken by the court in disallowing aspects of the completion contractor's cost on the ground that the employer had failed to mitigate its loss. The failure to mitigate was in the context of defective work but would seem to have applied equally to incomplete work. Separate quantity surveyors were appointed by the receivers and the bank to whom the contractor had assigned the contract receivables. Their combined evidence, which was accepted by the judge, was that it was unreasonable of the employer to have agreed a negotiated contract with its usual contractor instead of sending the works out to four contractors on competitive tender, and the employer's claim was reduced by 7.5 per cent as a consequence. The rates in the original contract were increased by seven per cent in negotiations between the completion contractor and the employer. Since the tender price index had actually fallen during the relevant period, this increase was disallowed.

8. Case study

by Neil Burton*

Background

In an ideal world, the investigating team appointed to a contractor collates the relevant information on its contracts before insolvency occurs so that a strategy for each contract and an assessment of the collectability of debts can be made in advance. However, in practice the team often has limited access to the key staff (estimators, surveyors and contracts managers), and the details have to be taken from management accounts and debtor ledgers, which can be very inaccurate or omit the essential information. Obtaining the right information and interpreting it correctly is critical if the course of an insolvency is to run smoothly and the recovery of assets is to be maximised. **16–012**

Base data

Management accounts are normally taken from a rolling series of figures, with profit and loss projections taken from tender estimates, adjusted for reserves and accruals. This does not give an appropriate view of a contract on which a decision can be made. For this purpose, a snapshot or "freeze-frame" approach needs to be taken. If the company cannot or will not provide the basic information, then this should sound double warning bells. Key information on a contract-by-contract basis is needed, as set out below for both contracts in progress (CIP) and completed contracts (CC). **16–013**

1. **Estimated final account** This should be a realistic assessment of the total amount that will be received on the contract, net of any discounts. Amounts assessed relating to claims for loss and expense or damages for late completion should be clearly identified and allowed for within the figure.
2. **Value of work done** This should be assessed on the basis of the cumulative gross value certified or applied for, plus a reasonable assessment of work in progress (WIP) between the certificate and the snapshot date. It should be noted that WIP can be negative, and often is on design and build contracts, if the stage payments are front-end loaded. An allocation between fixed and floating charge assets can be undertaken if the WIP figure is known.
3. **Sums previously paid** This should be the cumulative total paid as at the snapshot date. If a large sum will become due for payment in the near future, i.e. shortly after the snapshot date, this should be taken into account in considering when a decision should be taken on a particular contract.

© Neil Burton, Burton Marriott Ltd, 16 Crosthwaite Court, Stewart Road, Harpenden AL5 4RN. Tel: 01582 765853, Email: *burton@burtonmarriott.co.uk*.

4. **Completion dates** For CIPs, a realistic anticipated completion date is required so that this can be looked at in comparison to the amount of work still to be done. It is also valuable in assessing the value of claims for loss and expense or the amount of damages for late completion. For CCs, the actual completion date is needed to give a view of when the defects liability period might expire.
5. **Retentions** Although desirable, it is not normally essential to identify retentions separately. The exception is for main contractors where nominated subcontractors are involved as their retention may be held by the client in trust. In these cases the amounts should be separately identified and deducted from any balances shown due.
6. **Client name and contract** Details of the client and the project enable a view to be taken as to the grouping of contracts and debts with a particular client and work type.
7. **Other information** If it is readily accessible other information should also be obtained such as:
   - form of contract;
   - date and number of last certificate;
   - estimate of costs to complete;
   - warranties and guarantees; and
   - bonds.

Care must be taken not to take too much time at the early stages obtaining information which is desirable rather than essential, otherwise the initial consideration of the key issues will be delayed.

Presentation of findings

16–014 The tabular presentation of key statistics enables a clear review of a portfolio of contracts to be undertaken. Typical figures for a small- to medium-sized main contractor are set out in Figs 16.2 and 16.3.

A. Contracts in progress

A *Client and contract*	*B* *Estimated final account*	*C* *Value of work done*	*D* *Previously paid*	*E* *Value to complete (B-C)*	*F* *Completion date*
1. Local authority school extension	2,000	100	0	1900	Aug 2000
2. Housing association (20 units refurbishment)	1,200	1,000	500	200	Sept 1999
3. Housing association (30 units new build)	1,500	750	600	750	March 2000
4. Manufacturer new warehouse	1,000	200	0	800	March 2000
		2,050 (1,100)	1,100		
Balance due		950			

Fig.16.2

A *Client and contract*	*B* *Estimated final account*	*C* *Previously paid*	*D* *Balance (B–C)*	*E* *Completion date*
5. Local authority sports facility	2,000	1,800	200	April 1999
6. Housing association 10 new build	600	500	100	June 1999
7. Developer office block	1,900	1,400	500	Sept 1998
8. Manufacturer new wordshop	1,300	1,100	200	Jan 1999
		Total balance	1,000	

Note.
1. Assumes no nominated subcontractors involved.
2. Figures are exclusive of VAT.
3. Figures are rounded to thousands only for case of presentation.

Fig.16.3

Insolvency practitioner's options for contracts

From the basic statistics presented for the contracts, various possible options can be explored. It is important to remain mindful of common clients for both CIPs and CCs where there will be a risk of set-off between one and another. In the example given it will be important to ensure there is no linkage between the contracts in these three groups: (1) contracts 2, 3 and 6, (2) contracts 1 and 5, and (3) contracts 4 and 8. **16–015**

Contracts in progress

- **Contract 1** With a distant completion date, a large value to complete and a nominal amount outstanding, this contract will either be abandoned or novated as part of a package if there is sufficient profit in the value to complete. **16–016**
- **Contract 2** If detailed investigations and negotiations ensured that the £500,000 outstanding were definitely due, then with a close completion date and only £200,000 of work to do, this may be a prospect for completion by the insolvent company or a novation to a third party for a sensible consideration.
- **Contracts 3 and 4** With only nominal amounts outstanding and significant amounts of work to complete over an extended period, these contracts will either be abandoned or novated for nominal amounts as part of a package.

Completed contracts

Contracts 5, 6 and 8 look fairly straightforward in terms of reasonable balances of final account and retentions outstanding for a relatively short period of time. Debt collection for these, on the assumption there are no **16–017** major defects, should be a relatively simple case of agreeing final accounts and reasonable client contra charges.

Contract 7 is more difficult in that a significant amount is shown as due and has been for some time since completion. A detailed investigation may reveal claims and counterclaims, defective work or a difficult client. Key company staff may need to be retained to assist with the collection of this debt.

Arrangements for debt collection can include incentivised deals with existing staff, sale of contract debts for a lump sum or a percentage of recovery, and the appointment of third party agents on hourly rates or percentage based fees. Care needs to be taken in structuring any arrangements for debt collection to allow for the long time scale that the process takes when a company is no longer trading.

Realisable assets

16–018 Basic book values for contract debts are not recovered on a pound for pound basis in insolvency situations. Clients have a duty to mitigate loss and substantiate the amounts they are seeking to deduct from monies due to an insolvent company. However, there are many items which legitimately reduce the asset value. These include but are not limited to:

- excess completion costs;
- additional professional fees;
- absence of warranties;
- inability to pursue claims;
- inability to defend counterclaims;
- enhanced costs of rectifying defects;
- set-off between contracts; and
- negotiable settlements.

A statistical analysis of main and subcontractor's debts and collectability using data from insolvencies handled by my firm shows that, over a 10–year period, recoverability in the range of 5 per cent to 69 per cent was achieved, with an average rate of 19 per cent. In the case study, Fig.16.4 sets out a good result representing a return of 23 per cent to 38 per cent (figures in thousands):

	Balance due	*Recoverable*
CIP	950	250–350 (assuming novation)
CC	1,000	200–400
TOTALS	1,950	450–750

Fig.16.4

Chapter 17

Direct Payment

Any disruption to cash flow has a potential knock-on effect for the project. Payment may be delayed by a contractor for a number of reasons: deliberately so as to earn more interest, through the operation of a pay when paid policy, under pressure from its bank to apply certified sums in reduction of an overdraft, or as a result of formal insolvency. In any of these situations, the project may be delayed through subcontractors suspending work in retaliation or through their own lack of working capital or even repossessing materials and plant and terminating their subcontracts. In an attempt to manage these risks, employers include direct payment clauses in main contracts. At first sight, they operate by allowing the employer to bypass or leapfrog the contractor, but in reality they allow the employer to make payments to subcontractors with one hand and take an equivalent amount from the contractor with the other. In legal terms, the effect of these clauses is not to divert payment but to convert the employer's duty to pay into a right, or rather two rights: to pay subcontractors direct and then set off an equivalent amount against sums due to the contractor: see e.g. s.31.7.3, Standardisation of PFI Contracts (SoPC), Version 4 (March 2007). It was reported that subcontractors were paid direct after the contractor on a schools PFI project went into administration (Leftly 2003). There are, however, many forms of direct payment. Depending on how the contract is structured, the power or the duty on the employer to pay direct may represent an inherent limitation on the contractor's right to payment. **17–001**

1. The nature of direct payment

Where the contractor is solvent

The fact that construction work is carried out using chains of contracts gives rise to the idea that payment is linear. Subcontractors often complain that certified sums are not being "passed on" to them. The FCEC form of subcontract even uses this expression (see Ch.9). The image is of payment as a thing to be divided by the contractor between itself and all the subcontractors, and then sub-divided among the sub-subcontractors and so on down the line. In law, a right to payment is a chose in action enforceable by proceedings against the debtor. There is nothing to be "passed on": compare *Veitchi v Crowley Russell* [1972] S.C. 225 which held that a **17–002** contractor's obligation to "pay over" to subcontractors sums identified as due to them in an interim certificate as a condition of entitlement to future certificates was part of the machinery of payment and did not create a trust in their favour. When the contractor's right to be paid is converted into a credit balance in its bank account, the contractor is solely beneficially entitled to it.

Even though they are linked in a number of ways with the main contract, subcontracts set up an autonomous right to payment against the contractor which is unrelated (other than in amount) to the contractor's rights against the employer. For example, in *Schott-Kem v G Percy Trentham* (unreported, May 15, 1985) a nominated subcontractor claimed about £50,000 from the contractor and also sought a declaration that, under the main contract, the contractor was owed at least £125,000 by the employer. The contractor defended on the basis that the subcontractor had been paid everything that was due to it. There was no unpaid certified sum outstanding. The Court of Appeal rejected the subcontractor's application. Its difficulties:

> "were essentially inherent in the nature of the original contractual arrangements into which the subcontractor—presumably with its eyes open—originally entered. These contractual arrangements seem to me clearly, carefully and deliberately designed so that the building owner will not be exposed to any kind of direct contractual obligation to the subcontractor" (*per* Slade L.J.).

Where a trust is used, a subcontractor has both contractual and equitable proprietary rights as explained in Ch.9. By contrast, direct payment clauses are purely contractual and do not normally confer an actionable right on the subcontractor. They operate down the chain by giving the employer power to calm any disruptions to payment. Trust rights usually operate up the chain by conferring equitable rights in property as an informal security for payment. In addition, each contract in the chain is regarded as a separate entity: *Hampton v Glamorgan County Council* [1917] A.C. 13. An employer can therefore only obtain a good discharge by paying the person with whom it is in contract. If it pays a person further down the line it remains liable to pay the same sum to its own contracting party.

17–003 Where the contractor is solvent, a direct payment provision will be effective provided that the debt owed to the contractor is greater than or equal to the amount of the direct payment and there are no other restrictions on the employer's rights of set-off. For example, in *Lovell Projects v Legg and Carver* [2003] B.L.R. 452 a right of recourse following a direct payment to a subcontractor could not be exercised against a sum payable to the contractor pursuant to an adjudication decision in the absence of a valid withholding notice (Ch.5). In that case, the direct payment had been brought to the adjudicator's attention and he was regarded as having taken it into account in reaching his decision on the amount due to the contractor. (See also *Rainford House v Cadogan* [2001] B.L.R. 416 at para.5.) The reverse applied in *Parsons Plastics v Purac* [2002] B.L.R. 334 in which a cross-claim by a main contractor for the additional cost to complete and direct payments to a subcontractor's suppliers was held eligible for set-off against an adjudicator's decision. Although the contract provided for the service of a withholding notice as a condition to the exercise of set-off rights, that provision was expressly subject to another term which preserved the common law. The contract did not fall within the Housing Grants, Construction and Regeneration Act 1996 (see Ch.12).

The question whether a withholding notice is required in order to effect a set-off following a direct payment after an insolvency termination needs reconsideration in the light of *Melville Dundas v George Wimpey* [2007] 1 W.L.R. 1136 considered in Ch.14. In that case it was held that the operation of the suspension of payment provision did not depend on the service of a withholding notice. That provision operates automatically whereas direct payment is usually a matter of discretion, but in both cases it may be impossible for the employer to serve a withholding notice before the final date for payment. If so, it would seem to follow that a direct payment set-off does not require a withholding notice. In any event the suspension of payment will already be in force and the employer will not need to rely on direct payment set-off in order to resist a claim for an interim payment. The set-off will be made as part of the final account process.

Even if there is a valid clause permitting direct payment while the contract is still in being, the conditions must be satisfied. In *Re Jade Union Investment* [2004] HKCFI 166, payments were made to subcontractors even though the circumstances anticipated by the clause had not occurred. The employer had to argue that the contractor had expressly consented to the payments.

Where the contractor is insolvent

Some kinds of formal insolvency change the beneficial ownership of the contractor's property, including the right to be paid the value of work carried out by subcontractors. There are difficulties here whether or not the contract contains a direct payment clause. Take first the situation where there is no express right to pay direct. In *Re Holt, Ex p. Gray* (1888) 15 L.J.Q.B. 5, a contractor was instructed to spend a provisional sum of £137 and the items were supplied and fixed before the contractor went bankrupt. At that time, the £137 had not been certified for payment and the supplier asked the employer to pay direct. On the supplier giving indemnities to the architects and the employer against any claim by the contractor's trustee, the architects issued a certificate and the employer paid the supplier. It was held that the employer was liable to pay the same sum to the trustee. Lord Coleridge C.J. said: **17–004**

> "It seems clear to me that, without any real dispute, this is an attempt on the part of the architects to interfere with the division of the bankrupt's estate and with the bankruptcy laws" (at 7).

Cave J. considered that the architects' action in certifying payment to the supplier was "a pure piece of impertinence". Several points call for comment. No authority was cited for the decision on this aspect of the case, which suggests that it was the first time that the court had had to consider whether a direct payment could infringe the pari passu rule. The goods appear to have been fixed to the building by the time the contractor went bankrupt: if so, the employer did not have to make any payment to the supplier as the supplier had lost title to the chattels when they became converted into land on incorporation (see Ch.7). The case is sometimes cited as authority for the proposition that an employer can make a direct payment to a subcontractor or supplier if the contract so provides. It would be more accurate to say that the case decided that an employer cannot pay a supplier direct where the contractor is bankrupt as it would amount to a distribution of the bankrupt's assets in a manner contrary to insolvency law. There is nothing in the judgment to support the view that the direct payment would have been valid if the contract had sanctioned it in the event of the contractor's bankruptcy; the substance of the decision is, if anything, to the contrary. Nevertheless, in the absence of insolvency, a properly drawn direct payment clause avoids the risk of the employer paying twice for the same work. In *Vigers Sons & Co v Swindell* [1939] 3 All E.R. 590, the subcontractor failed in its argument that an employer was liable to pay under an order placed by the architect because it was held that the employer had not authorised the architect to place the order, nor had she ratified the order after learning of it. The contractor went into liquidation several months after the contract was formed and was replaced by one of the contractor's former directors who agreed to continue on the same terms. The new contractor was not involved in placing the order with the subcontractor. Although the subcontractor might have had a cause of action against the architect for breach of warranty of authority, the architect was insolvent. It appears from the report that the completion contractor also became insolvent or at least received money from the employer, which included a sum destined for the subcontractor, and misapplied it.

2. Construction of direct payment clauses

Contractual set-off

17–005 Normally, the only way in which an employer will be able to pay a subcontractor and be released from paying the contractor the same sum is by an express term in the main contract. A direct payment clause gives a dual right to pay direct and to set off the amount paid against money due or to become due to the contractor. This is an example of contractual set-off in the strict sense as the contract is conferring a right of set-off where none exists under the general law. The position is therefore different from *Gilbert-Ash v Modern Engineering* [1974] A.C. 689 where a failure to follow contractual set-off machinery was not fatal as the set-off was saved by the general law which had not been excluded. Here the general law is not excluded but it does not permit this type of set-off. Direct payment is sometimes stepped down the contract chain, e.g. permitting a sub-subcontractor to apply to the contractor for payment: *Marplan v Hanhyo* [2001] M.L.J.U. 458.

Strict construction

17–006 Because this device interferes with cash flow and is an exception to privity of contract, it is strictly construed by the court: *Milestone v Yates Brewery* [1938] 2 All E.R. 439. That case concerned the RIBA Standard Form (1909 edn) which included the following term:

> "The provisional sums mentioned in the specification for materials to be supplied, or for work to be performed by special . . . tradesmen or for other work or fittings to the building shall be paid . . . to and in favour of such persons as the architect shall direct, and the sums so expended shall be payable by the contractor without discount or deduction or . . . by the employer to the said . . . tradesmen."

The contractor went into liquidation after having completed the majority of the work and having received payment of certified sums, part of which represented work done by nominated subcontractors, but before having paid the subcontractors. The liquidator claimed the balance of the contract sum but the employer argued that it was entitled to pay the subcontractors direct and that no further sum could become due to the contractor. The architect had issued a certificate to the contractor but then proceeded to issue certificates for the same work in favour of the nominated subcontractors. It was held that the certificates in favour of the subcontractors were invalid and the employer was liable to the liquidator on the ground that the direct payment clause was to be strictly construed as giving the employer the right to elect between them. By paying the contractor, the employer had elected not to exercise the right to pay the subcontractors direct. *Milestone* was followed in *Cone Textiles v Mather & Platt* [1981] 3 S.A. 565. The right to certify in favour of either contractor or subcontractor was removed in later editions of the standard forms. In *Hobbs v Turner* (1900) 17 T.L.R. 83, (1901) T.L.R. 235, the Court of Appeal had some difficulty in ascertaining the identity of payer and payee and held that the contractor had acted as the employer's agent in entering into the subcontract. The court in *Milestone* referred to an earlier case of *British Investment Trust v Foundation* (unreported, December 15, 1930), which evidently concerned a similar type of clause, although it appears that the RIBA form was not used. Maugham J. considered how best to approach the matter in the following passage:

> "Further, I think that a number of circumstances must be borne in mind in considering the operation of such a clause. It is plain that there may be disputes between the contractor and the tradesman in which the building owner may have no concern. It is plain that the terms of credit between the contractor and the tradesman may be of a special kind. In this case, as in most cases, the contractor is, in the first instance, paid on the certificate only a percentage of thc total amount due. In the first case, he is paid 80 per cent, then perhaps another 10 per cent after a period of maintenance, while the tradesman may, and very often would, be entitled to the whole of the amount due to him from the contractor. Further, I think that it is not unreasonable to remember that the contractor may be at a particular moment in very urgent need of money to be paid on his certificates, partly by reason of the fact that he is being paid only in part for the work which he has done, and partly in consequence of unforeseen circumstances. All these grounds lead me to think that a clause entitling the building owner to pay a subcontractor, with whom he has no contractual relation, for work done and materials supplied ought, I think, to be strictly construed" (quoted in *Milestone* at 442).

This passage is the genesis of the way in which direct payment clauses have developed since the 1930s. Maugham J. has recognised that the contractor may dispute the subcontractor's entitlement to be paid, perhaps because of defective work entitling the contractor to abate the subcontractor's payment. This factor is now recognised in the standard forms and the contractor is given an opportunity to justify why he has not paid the subcontractor, e.g. cl. 5.4 of FIDIC (1st edn, 1999) and 59(7) of ICE (7th edn). The case also acknowledges the importance of cash flow, the absence of privity and the fact that the terms as to credit in the main contract and subcontract may not be back to back. In *Milestone*, and possibly also *British Investment Trust*, the contractor had gone into liquidation. The court did not have to consider whether a payment would infringe the *pari passu* rule as the liquidator succeeded in his claim.

Policy considerations

17–007 Direct payment clauses arose out of provisional sums and prime cost sums inserted in bills of quantities which reflected the role played by specialist subcontractors in nineteenth century contracts, especially in mechanical and electrical works. The rationale was that, having chosen the subcontractor, the employer should have a right to pay it direct. The importance of specialist subcontractors is even greater now than it was then and an obvious policy reason behind direct payment clauses is the need to ensure that these subcontractors perform their works on time. In construing clauses of this kind, the courts have over the years taken account of what are strictly considerations of public policy rather than principles of law. For example, in *Re Wilkinson, Ex p.Fowler* [1905] 1 K.B. 713, the court upheld a direct payment clause on the bankruptcy of the contractor on the grounds that the clause benefited the employer as much as the subcontractor, promoted the satisfactory performance of public works contracts, enabled the employer to make contracts more advantageously as subcontractors and suppliers knew there was a reasonable probability of payment, and placed the employer in a better position when inviting tenders on future projects.

It can be inferred from this case that the major policy consideration was that the clause fostered competition between subcontractors and benefited the employer by ensuring a good spread of competitive tenders. In English case law the predominant public policy consideration is that it is desirable that the employer should be protected. In other jurisdictions, public policy lays the emphasis on protecting the rights of those who actually carry out the work by granting a charge or lien on the land and on moneys payable to the contractor as security for payment. Until it was repealed in 1988, a similar position applied in New Zealand under legislation which applied to sums due to suppliers, subcontractors or the contractor's employees. It did not apply to government contracts but, as a concession, they included a right to pay direct at the government's discretion. In *HM Att-Gen v McMillan & Lockwood* [1991] 1 N.Z.L.R. 53, the New Zealand Court of Appeal upheld the judge at first instance who had declared direct payment provisions to be void as infringing the *pari passu* rule but disapproved the judge's conclusion that so long as the legislation remained in force the clauses could not be considered contrary to public policy. The court considered that the direct payment clauses were:

> ". . . sensible commercial provisions which were given particular significance during the wages protection legislation era by the desire to provide

subcontractors under Crown contracts with a measure of the protection they had under that legislation in respect of private contracts. But in circumstances where the Crown was not bound by the wages protection legislation, so where Parliament in expressing the public interest did not give statutory protection to such subcontractors, it would not be right to elevate those commercial concerns into public policy considerations" (at 62, *per* Richardson J.).

It was not a matter of balancing different public policy considerations as the court was dealing with the *pari passu* rule which is a legal principle. In the context of public policy in commercial contracts where both parties are solvent, however, the court approved the approach taken in *Re Wilkinson*. As the right to pay direct arises only through some default of the contractor, there was no reason on policy grounds why the contractor should be protected.

Insolvency aspects

It is sometimes argued that an administrative receiver's statutory duty to pay preferential creditors in priority to floating charge holders under s.40 of the Insolvency Act 1986 overrides an employer's rights under a direct payment clause. A possible answer is that the charge holder takes the receivable subject to equities which in this context includes the employer's contractual right of set-off, so that it can never be an asset "coming to the hands of the receiver" under the section (compare Totty and Moss, H6.03). This argument avoids having to resolve the issue whether the contractor's right to payment in this situation is conditional or is absolute subject to set-off. **17–008**

It has also been suggested that direct payment clauses are contrary to the spirit of the administration procedure (Totty and Moss, H6.03). The exercise of set-off rights clearly damages the financial position of a company in administration. Also set-off has a security function and the Act focuses on the functional aspects of a security rather than its strict legal classification (Bridge 1991). Nevertheless, the Insolvency Act 1986 identifies the devices which are to be treated as security for this purpose even though they do not give rise to an equity of redemption and set-off is not included among them. It is possible however that administrators will derive some benefit from the adjudication procedure: see *Lovell Projects v Legg and Carver* [2003] B.L.R. 452 referred to above.

3. Discretionary direct payment

There are two types of discretionary direct payment clause in common use. The first applies during the contract where the contractor fails to honour payment obligations to subcontractors and suppliers. This clause is frequently restricted to nominated subcontractors. The second type of clause applies after termination of the contract or the contractor's employment where direct payment is one of a bundle of rights conferred on the employer. **17–009**

During the contract

Three approaches can be identified. The first permits the employer to pay subcontractors from the debt owed to the contractor as if the contractor had assigned its rights to payment to the subcontractors. An example is the **17–010** form of government contract used in New Zealand set out later in this chapter. The second category, and probably the most common in practice, is where the employer pays the subcontractor from its own resources and then sets off the payment against money due to the contractor. A typical example is cl.27(c) of JCT 63 which provides:

> "Before issuing any certificate under clause 30 of these Conditions the Architect may request the Contractor to furnish to him reasonable proof that all amounts included in the calculation of the amount stated as due in previous certificates in respect of the total value of work, materials or goods executed or supplied by any nominated subcontractor have been duly discharged, and if the Contractor fails to comply with any such request the Architect shall issue a certificate to that effect and thereupon the Employer may himself pay such amounts to any nominated subcontractor concerned (to which amounts the Employer may add an amount for any value added tax which would have been properly due to the nominated subcontractor) and deduct the same from any sums due or to become due to the Contractor."

Other variants entitle the employer to make the deduction from "any sums due or which become due" (ICE 7th edn, FIDIC 4th edn) or "from the next certificate due to the contractor" (*Re Wilkinson*), or by being "taken into account by the Architect in the Final Certificate": *Hitachi Plant v Eltraco* [2003] 4 S.L.R. 384. The employer's right of deduction has been replaced by the contractor's duty to repay in FIDIC (1st edn, 1999). The third approach is that taken by JCT 80 (replicated in JCT 98 but omitted from JCT 05). Clause 35 of JCT 80 states that once the architect has issued his certificate:

> ". . . the amount of any future payment otherwise due to the Contractor . . . shall be reduced by any amounts due to Nominated Subcontractors which the Contractor has failed to discharge . . . and the Employer shall himself pay the same to the Nominated Subcontractors concerned . . ."

What does "reduction" mean in this context? It seems to point towards the conditional nature of the contractor's right to payment rather than to confer a distinct right of set-off, as if the reduction operates automatically after the architect's certificate of non-payment. Compare the Australian AS4303–1995 subcontract which gives the contractor power to make a direct payment "on behalf of" the subcontractor to sub-subcontractors, the amount paid becoming "a debt due" to the contractor under the subcontract: quoted in *Brodyn v Davenport* (2004) 61 N.S.W.L.R. 421, at para.68.

On termination of the contract

17–011 Clause 25(3)(b) of JCT 63 provides:

> "In any case, the Employer may pay any supplier or subcontractor for any materials or goods delivered or works executed for the purpose of this Contract (whether before or after the date of determination) insofar

as the price thereof has not already been paid by the Contractor. The Employer's rights under this paragraph are in addition to his rights to pay nominated subcontractors as provided in clause 27(c) of these Conditions and payments made under this paragraph may be deducted from any sums due or to become due to the Contractor."

Under JCT 80, a similar right is given to the employer but it cannot be exercised where the contractor has become bankrupt or gone into liquidation. As an alternative to set-off, the direct payment is also "recoverable from the contractor by the employer as a debt", presumably to establish a right to submit a proof. The right to pay direct on termination was removed in its entirety from JCT 80 by Amendment 11 (1992) only to be partially reinstated by Amendment 13 (1994). Direct payment was then permitted on an insolvency termination except on bankruptcy or liquidation or the filing of a petition alleging insolvency which is subsisting. This remains the position under JCT 98 although post-termination direct payment rights have been omitted altogether from JCT 05.

Neither ICE nor FIDIC provides for direct payment on termination. Clause 57(1)(d) of GC Works/1 Ed 3 provides simply that "the Authority may pay to any subcontractor or supplier any amount due to him which the Project Manager certifies as included in any previous advance to the Contractor. The amount so paid shall be forthwith recoverable by the Authority from the Contractor". The Singapore SIA form takes a different approach. In its first edition, by cl.32(8)(c) the employer is deemed to make the direct payment as agent for the contractor and has the option to deduct an equivalent amount from sums to become due to the contractor, otherwise the payment "shall be deemed to be a part of the cost of completing the Works" (Wallace 1986, 603). SIA 2005 gives the employer a discretion to make a direct payment within three months before the issue of the final certificate and to have the payment taken into account in that certificate.

4. The effect of bankruptcy and liquidation

There are two distinct lines of authority on the validity of direct payment clauses on bankruptcy or liquidation. It is proposed to start with the arguments for their validity by examining the English cases. **17–012**

Arguments for validity

The earliest case is *Re Holt, Ex p. Gray* (1888) 15 L.J. Q.B. 5 discussed at para.17–004 above. In that case the contract did not contain a direct payment clause and the court invalidated a direct payment made after the contractor's bankruptcy. The first case where the validity of such a clause was questioned was *Re Wilkinson, Ex p. Fowler* [1905] 2 K.B. 713 where a contractor was to be paid by monthly instalments on the certificate of an engineer. The contract also required the contractor at his own cost to provide all materials, machinery and plant which might be necessary for the completion of the works. Clause 54 of the contract provided: **17–013**

"At each and every certificate in which the engineer shall deem proper to include a sum or sums for machinery, the contractor shall, upon

> measurement being made, produce to the authorised officer a receipt showing that he has paid the machinery makers the net sum to be included, notwithstanding that he has not at the time of paying of such machinery makers received the said sums from the council. If the engineer shall have reasonable cause to believe that the contractor is unduly delaying proper payment of the firms supplying the machinery, he shall have power if he thinks fit to order direct payment to them and shall deduct from the next certificate issued to the contractor the money so paid, provided that no payment in the manner referred to shall be held to relieve the contractor from any of his liabilities under this contract."

The court considered that the payments could be made direct notwithstanding the bankruptcy on the public policy grounds mentioned earlier and because:

> ". . . [the clause] amounts to an authority given by the contractor—that is to say, by the bankrupt in this case—to the engineer representing the council to dispose of money, which would otherwise come to the bankrupt, in a certain way under certain circumstances. It is an authority which, in my opinion, it was not competent for the bankrupt to withdraw, and it was never contemplated that he should withdraw it; and indeed, it is not contended on behalf of the trustee that the authority was one that could be lawfully withdrawn. It is an authority, therefore, which the bankruptcy of the contractor did not annul" (at 720, *per* Bigham J.).

The idea seems to be that the employer has "a power coupled with an interest" (Oditah 1992, 477). It is significant that: (a) no argument was made based on the *pari passu* rule or bankruptcy set-off; (b) the case of *Re Holt, Ex p.Gray* was not cited in argument; and (c) the trustee conceded that the authority given by the direct payment clause was irrevocable. Given that the effect of the concession was to accept that the contract could disturb the realisation and distribution of the bankrupt's property in the absence of a security interest, it is questionable whether this case was correctly decided.

It was followed, however, in *Re Tout & Finch Limited* [1954] 1 All E.R. 127, in which the court considered cl.21(c) of the RIBA form which stated as follows:

> "Before any such certificate is issued to the contractor he shall, if requested by the architect, furnish to him reasonable proof that all nominated subcontractors' accounts included in previous certificates have been duly discharged, in default whereof the employer may pay such accounts upon a certificate of the architect and deduct the amount so paid from any sums otherwise payable to the contractor . . ."

17–014 The court considered an application by a nominated subcontractor in the winding up of a contractor for a declaration that the employer was entitled to make a direct payment to the subcontractor of the balance remaining unpaid of amounts included in previous certificates representing its work. The judge dealt briefly with this issue, holding that the case was on all fours with *Re Wilkinson*. The only argument put forward by the liquidator was that the certificate referred to in cl.21(c) could only be interim and not final. In summarising the effect of the clause, Wynn-Parry J. commented that:

> "... the council has a right—and the matter is entirely one for the council—to pay such accounts on a certificate being duly given by the architect, and, as mere necessary machinery, to deduct the amount so paid from any amounts otherwise payable to the company" (at 133).

These words suggest that the judge was not referred in argument to liquidation set-off or conditionality. This decision has been relied upon by the UK Government as validating the direct payment provision on termination in GC Works/1 (HMSO 1974). *Re Tout and Finch* is of limited value because it concerned an entitlement to a direct payment of retention which the judge held in any event to be the subject of an equitable assignment. The employer was bound to pay direct because the subject matter of the assignment did not constitute property of the company in liquidation.

The English cases have been followed in Australia. In *Re CG Monkhouse Properties* [1968] S.R. (N.S.W.) 429, the New South Wales Court of Appeal considered a direct payment clause in virtually identical terms to JCT 63. The court rejected a claim that payments to nominated subcontractors constituted preferences and stated as follows:

> "This is not a case where the building owner paid the subcontractor out of moneys which were then due or would certainly become due to the building company. If it were, then there might be much to be said for the submission made on behalf of the appellant; but it is fundamental to this case that the moneys, the subject of the claim, were not due to the builder and could not, on the terms of the contract, become due so long as cl.21(c) of the contract operated. The right of the builder to receive the certificate from the architect and his right to be paid on that certificate is governed under this contract by cl.25, and cl.25 specifically makes it clear that the builder is not entitled to any certificate or to any payment except subject to cl.21(c) of the contract. That being so, the payment made by the building owner cannot be described as a payment made out of moneys for the builder. It is a payment made out of the building owner's own moneys which, if the contract were strictly carried out, would never become due to the builder" (at 431–432, *per* Jacobs J.A.).

This case was followed by the Supreme Court of Western Australia in *Gericevich Contracting v Sabemo* [1984] 9 A.C.L.R. 452 which sanctioned direct payments to the subcontractor's employees following the contractor's liquidation on the ground that the employer's debt to the contractor was limited to the balance, if any, remaining after the direct payments had been made. The court held that the contractor's property capable of disposal could only be ascertained after compliance with the contract terms affecting the debt, i.e. the debt was conditional. See also *Victorian Railway Commissioners v Williams* (1969) 44 A.L.J.R. 32. The Irish High Court adopted a similar approach in *Glow Heating v Eastern Health Board* (1992) 8 Const. L.J. 56, which is discussed later.

Arguments against validity

17–015 The other stream of authorities which invalidate direct payment clauses operating on a contractor's bankruptcy or liquidation comprises cases decided in South Africa, Canada, New Zealand, Singapore, Northern Ireland and Hong Kong. These will now be considered in turn.

In two cases injunctions were obtained in the South African courts by judicial managers appointed over a contractor restraining an employer from making direct payments to nominated subcontractors. In both cases, the parties had used a standard form of building contract which was in substantially the same terms as JCT 63. In *Norman Kennedy v Norman Kennedy Ltd* [1947] 1 S.A. 790 the court upheld the injunction. Although there was no privity of contract and the court followed *Re Wilkinson* in holding that the contractor's authority to the employer could not normally be revoked, it exercised its discretion under the South African Companies Act against the nominated subcontractors on the grounds that they had no legal right to payment, the employers had not appeared at the hearing to object to the granting of the injunction, and the court paid great regard to the submissions of judicial managers as court appointees who spoke in the interests of the general body of creditors. This case was overruled by the South African Court of Appeal in *Wire Industries v Certes* [1953] 2 S.A. 531 on the ground that although there was no privity of contract, the subcontractor had a material interest that the employer should not be restrained from paying direct which the court would protect.

In *Administrator, Natal v Magill Grant & Nell* [1969] 1 S.A. 660 a liquidator applied for directions when an employer claimed to set off sums paid after the commencement of the liquidation to two nominated subcontractors. The court refused set-off on the following grounds:

(1) The absence of privity of contract meant that the subcontractors could not compel the employer to pay them direct.

(2) The authority given to the employer was not automatically terminated upon insolvency or liquidation of the contractor.

(3) The main contractor was not merely a conduit for payment of money due to nominated subcontractors.

(4) The contractor's right to payment was not contingent on itself paying the subcontractors.

(5) The set-off would disturb both the realisation of assets and distribution to creditors contrary to the *pari passu* rule.

The court left open the question whether, had the set-offs been made before liquidation, they would also have been invalidated but it was conceded by counsel for both parties that the set-offs would have been valid. In a powerful dissenting judgment, Wessels J.A. stated:

> "The amount of the Administrator's indebtedness in the circumstances postulated would, therefore, not only depend upon the valuation of 'all the work done up to' the date of the valuation in terms of the contract, but also (1) upon the performance by the contractor of the further contractual obligation above referred to, and (2) the payment by the

Administrator to a nominated subcontractor of the amount due to him, such payment being made pursuant to an election made by the Administrator in terms of the provisions of clause 21(b). . . . Pending the exercise by the Administrator of his contractual right to elect to make a payment to a nominated subcontractor, the defaulting contractor would, in my opinion, have no legally enforceable claim based solely on a valuation of the work done by him. On the proper construction of clause 21, sub-para. (b) in effect provides for an alternative 'manner' in which the Administrator may perform the contractual obligation imposed upon him by clause 2 of the contract between the parties. In the circumstances postulated in clause 21 of the conditions of contract the Administrator makes a payment in terms of the contract when he exercises his right of election and makes a payment to the nominated subcontractor . . . The true effect of the payment made pursuant to an election to make such payment is to reduce pro tanto the amount due to and claimable by the contractor in terms of the contract" (at 674).

In other words, Wessels J.A. considered that the contractor had only a conditional right to payment and, as the condition was never fulfilled, the direct payments were not made from the property of the contractor but from the employer's own assets.

A similar approach was taken in the Canadian case of *AN Bail v Gingras* **17–016**
[1982] 2 S.C.R. 475 although *British Eagle* was not cited. In *HM Att-Gen v McMillan & Lockwood* [1991] 1 N.Z.L.R. 53, the New Zealand Court of Appeal had to construe the following clauses in a government contract:

"19.10 The [Architect] shall not be bound to certify that any payment is due to the Contractor until the Contractor has satisfied him that payment has been duly made of all sums due and payable by the Contractor in respect of: (a) Wages to persons employed on the Works; (b) Progress payments or other sums due to subcontractors; (c) Sums due to any person for services supplied or for Materials, Plant, or prepared work (or cartage thereof) incorporated in the Works or used in connection therewith or brought upon the Site or placed on or near thereto for the purposes of being used in or upon the Works; (d) Premiums in respect of policies of insurance of any nature required in terms of the contract. 19.11 The Minister may at his discretion and notwithstanding the exercise by him of all or any of the other powers conferred on him by the contract pay to any employee of the Contractor or to any subcontractor, supplier, or other person to whom any moneys as specified in the last preceding clause are due [by the Contractor] the whole or any part of such moneys as if such persons were a lawful assignee of the Contractor in respect of such moneys. Any such payment may be made out of moneys then due or accruing due to the Contractor and the Minister shall have no further liability to the Contractor in respect of any amount so paid."

By a majority, the court declared these clauses void as infringing the *pari passu* rule. The reasons were:

(1) As work is done the entitlement of the contractor and the associated obligations of the Crown accrued, and those obligations existed before the time for payment arrived.

(2) The assignment deemed by cl.19.11 assumed that the contractor had property in those moneys.

(3) As at liquidation, the company had an existing chose in action, measured by the value of the work done under each contract and as yet unpaid, even though the time for payment had not arrived.

(4) As a result of the *pari passu* rule and the decision in *British Eagle v Air France* [1975] 2 All E.R. 390, it was not open to the employer to make payments out of moneys due to the contractor and the clauses were therefore void.

(5) The English and Australian cases were distinguishable on the ground that the direct payments were not made out of moneys which were due or to become due to the builder nor were they payments on behalf of the builder.

(6) It was not a matter of balancing public policy considerations as the *pari passu* rule applied absolutely on liquidation.

The distinction between these decisions and the English and Australian cases is perhaps more apparent than real: it is hard to see any difference between a payment made "out of moneys due" to the contractor and a set-off "against moneys due" to the contractor, as the latter is merely a deemed payment or discharge by set-off and is equally inconsistent with the *pari passu* rule. Bridge (2003) criticises the decision in *McMillan & Lockwood* arguing that the contractor never acquired a property right subject to divestment because the employer's power to elect, in certain circumstances, whether to pay the contractor or the subcontractors was a basic limitation on the contractor's right to payment under the contract. Much depends on how the contract is structured. In *Glen Eight v Home Building* [2005] NSWSC 907 the contract was explicit: the employer had power "to elect to pay direct to the subcontractors instead of to [the contractor] (which direct payment will constitute a *pro rata* discharge of the obligation of [the employer] to pay the [contractor] under this contract)."

17–017 In *Joo Yee Construction v Diethelm* [1990] M.L.J. 66 the High Court of Singapore heard an application for directions issued by a liquidator appointed over a contractor. The employer wished to make direct payments to four nominated subcontractors and the liquidator sought a direction whether they could validly be made. After reviewing the authorities, Thean J. concluded that the proposed payments would contravene the *pari passu* rule. He declined to follow the English cases on the ground that the *pari passu* rule had not been raised in argument and that, had Bigham J. been alerted to the principle, he would not have considered the contractor's authority in *Re Wilkinson* to be irrevocable. It has been noted that retention trust cases were not cited in argument on the scope of the decision in *British Eagle* (Powell-Smith 1991); however, they do not seem relevant to this issue. Under a trust or an assignment (in the case of a subcontractor) the contractor loses its beneficial interest in the debt. In the normal situation where a subcontractor is seeking a direct payment, the contractor still has the beneficial interest in the debt owed by the employer representing the certified sum.

These decisions were followed by the Court of Appeal of Northern Ireland in *Mullan v Ross* (1996) 86 B.L.R. 1. The case concerned an application by an ordinary subcontractor for a direction in the liquidation of a contractor that the employer could make a direct payment pursuant to cl.27.4 of JCT 81. The court refused to authorise the direct payment, holding that the receivable formed part of the contractor's property and was payable to the liquidators. The English and Irish cases were distinguished, the court preferring the other line of cases culminating in *Joo Yee Construction*. Although the contractor went into administrative receivership over three months before it entered voluntary liquidation, the receivers were not joined as a party to the application. Presumably the benefit of the main contract was either not charged or had already been released from the security.

The High Court of Hong Kong followed the decision in *Mullan v Ross* in *Golden Sand v Easy Success Enterprises* [1999] 2 H.K.C. 356. Over a year before it went into compulsory liquidation, the contractor agreed with the employer and a number of nominated subcontractors that the employer should pay the subcontractors direct. The agreement was evidenced by contemporary correspondence. The court seems to have held that the arrangement was an equitable assignment to the subcontractors of relevant proportions of future certificates and therefore payments falling due after the liquidation could not be the contractor's property. Interestingly, the evidence was that the parties did not intend the agreement to affect any of their existing rights and obligations. It is possible that the arrangement amounted to no more than an agreement by the contractor that the employer should act as its agent in the payment of the subcontractors, in which case it would, on the court's own analysis of the authorities, have been invalidated by the *pari passu* rule.

Summary of the current position

There are therefore two lines of authority: England, Australia and the Irish Republic, on the one hand, and South Africa, Canada, New Zealand, Singapore, Northern Ireland and Hong Kong on the other. The English cases were both decisions at first instance and in neither case was the possible conflict with the *pari passu* rule argued. *Re Wilkinson* rests on a concession that the authority given to the employer to pay direct was irrevocable even on the contractor's bankruptcy. The decisions are unsatisfactory and should not be followed. Only the Australian decisions (and the dissenting judgment of Wessels J.A. in the *Magill* case) grapple with the real issue: is the contractor's property a debt subject to reduction by set-off following direct payment or only such amount as is left after the direct payment and set-off have been made? It seems immaterial whether the direct payment is made out of the debt owed to the contractor (as in *McMillan & Lockwood*) or made out of the employer's own funds and then set off against a debt due to the contractor. In other words, the issue is whether the debt owed by the employer is absolute subject only to contractual set-off or conditional so that it cannot arise if the contract conditions governing its accrual are never fulfilled. **17–018**

A similar question was considered by the House of Lords in *British Eagle v Air France* [1975] 2 All E.R. 390. The issue was whether the claim against Air France was the property of British Eagle or the International Air Transport Association (IATA). The court had to rule whether the liquidator was bound by a clearing house arrangement whereby British Eagle and

Air France agreed that debts arising between them should only be dealt with through the medium of IATA. With some hesitation, the House of Lords decided that the clearing house arrangement was void as against the liquidator of British Eagle. Philip Wood has argued forcefully that *British Eagle* is just one in a long line of cases holding that a creditor cannot help himself to a debtor's property after insolvency unless he has a charge or unless the debt owed by the employer is a "flawed asset" (Wood 1989, 214–232). In other words, it will only become payable if there are no unpaid subcontractors at the commencement of the liquidation or there are unpaid subcontractors but the employer elects not to pay them direct (Bridge 2003, 29). No doubt there are circumstances where a flawed asset arrangement would be valid in the event of liquidation. But a close reading of the cases on direct payments does not support a construction that all the employer owes is a conditional debt. Reading *British Eagle* with these clauses in mind, it does seem to be their intention to allow the employer to "help itself" to the contractor's property and pay one of the contractor's own creditors.

Most contracts have discretionary clauses permitting a direct payment both during and on termination of the contract. The question arises whether the former could be operated where the latter is invalidated. There could be difficulties because first, it is not necessary for a clause or contractual arrangement to be operative only on insolvency to infringe the *pari passu* rule; and secondly, as the contract has provided what is to happen in the event of termination it is thought that the employer's direct payment rights may be restricted to those contained in the termination clause in that event.

17–019 In view of the absence of modern English case law, and the conflict between the two lines of authority, the position could be summarised thus:

1. A direct payment clause, whether operated during the contract or after termination, which has the effect of paying one particular group of creditors from the property of the contractor, will, if operated after bankruptcy or liquidation, offend against the *pari passu* rule because the money ought to be distributed rateably among all the contractor's creditors. This is the case whether the clauses provide for payment by the employer from its own resources and subsequent set-off against money due to the contractor or payment from money due to the contractor.

2. Whatever the merits of the public policy considerations in *Re Wilkinson*, they must yield to the *pari passu* rule. For considerations of public policy to prevail over the rule, they would have to be enshrined in statute: *Farrier-Waimak v Bank of New Zealand* [1965] N.Z.L.R. 426; *Panorama Development v Fitzroya Investments* [2003] 1 S.L.R. 93 (discussed in Ch.18).

3. Even if expressed to be irrevocable, an authority given by a contractor to an employer to pay direct and set off will be defeated by the *pari passu* rule. In *British Eagle*, notice to the clearing house of any credit or debit for clearance was said to "constitute an irrevocable authority to Clearing House to clear the same and for that purpose to collect or pay (as the case may be) the amount thereof in accordance with the Regulations and current clearing procedure and to make all necessary sets off in that behalf and to pay any ultimate balance due as a result of

the clearance effected." Despite this irrevocable authority, the House of Lords on a majority of three to two, decided that the clause was not binding on the liquidator (see Prentice 1983, Oditah 1992).

4. To regard the contractor's right to payment as conditional or contingent on the operation of the direct payment clause as was held in *Monkhouse* would be wrong as that would be applying the very term in the contract which offended the *pari passu* rule.

In view of current uncertainty, the prudent draftsman would still include the right to pay direct in the event of liquidation or bankruptcy but before exercising such right an employer should seek an indemnity from the subcontractor, secured if necessary, for the return of the payment if the employer is forced to pay the same amount to the liquidator. If the contractor's obligations had been guaranteed, it is advisable either to obtain the guarantor's approval beforehand or legal advice that the direct payment will not affect the guarantor's liability. In *Doe v Canadian Surety* (1937) 1 S.C.R. 1 a guarantor was discharged from liability partly because the employer had made direct payments to subcontractors with the contractor's consent. To avoid any problems over ownership of materials or equipment whose value is included in the direct payment, a form of agreement should also be prepared in which the subcontractor gives a warranty as to title and agrees that title will pass to the employer on payment unless the goods have already been incorporated.

5. Mandatory direct payment

So far this chapter has considered contracts which allow an employer to make a direct payment to a contractor at its discretion. But there are occasions when direct payments are mandatory: under the main contract, under a direct warranty, by a collateral contract taking effect as a primary payment undertaking or a step-in agreement, by a guarantee, or a trust, or an assignment, or an escrow account, by a court order for payment of damages or costs or for the attachment of debts, and finally pursuant to statute. **17–020**

Main contract

In *Glow Heating v Eastern Health Board* (1992) 8 Const. L.J. 56, the main contract contained a mandatory direct payment clause which operated where a contractor could not prove it had discharged sums due to nominated subcontractors from previous certificates. The subcontract was based on the Green Form but also provided that all sums received by the main contractor in respect of the subcontract work were to be held in trust. On the contractor's entry into liquidation, the liquidator decided to complete the works. Before the liquidation, a payment of £6,617 was certified and made to the main contractor who dissipated it. The subcontractor had no tracing remedy but successfully claimed a direct payment from the employer under the main contract in the same amount. In effect, the employer compensated the subcontractor for the main contractor's **17–021** breach of trust. The liquidator challenged the consequential set-off against the contractor's retention in respect of the amount of the direct payment but the court held that the effect of the direct payment clause was to impose

> "a contingent liability on an asset of the main contractor, the monies in the retention fund, namely, a liability to suffer a reduction in the event of a specified default on the contractor's part. The liquidator, in my opinion, took the retention fund subject to this liability" (at 61, *per* Costello J.).

The absence of privity was no defence to the employer in view of *Re Tout & Finch*. However, in that case, the employer had not yet made the payment and was abiding the court's decision as to whether to pay the liquidator or the nominated subcontractors. In this case, payment had already been made in accordance with the main contract. Where direct payment is a mandatory consequence of the contractor's inability to prove prior payment to subcontractors, there is perhaps a stronger case for the "flawed asset" theory mentioned above (Capper 1998).

Standard form warranties

17–022 There has long been a practice for specialist subcontractors to enter into direct design warranties with the employer. In return for the warranty, the employer may undertake to pay the subcontractor to the extent that the contractor fails to do so. Like direct payment clauses these forms have changed over the years and it can be useful to know how they have developed.

The warranty for use with JCT 63 was known as the "grey form". The employer's undertaking was amended in NSC/2 and NSC/2A which were introduced to accompany JCT 80. This was necessary because the decision in *British Eagle v Air France* [1975] 2 All E.R. 390 led the JCT to remove the employer's duty to make a direct payment where the contractor was in bankruptcy or liquidation. NSC/2 provides:

> "7.1 The Architect/The Contract Administrator and the Employer shall operate the provision in regard to the payment of the Subcontractor in clause 35.13 of the Main Contract Conditions. 7.2 If, after paying any amount to the Subcontractor under clause 35.13.5.3 of the Main Contract Conditions, the Employer produces reasonable proof that there was in existence at the time of such payment a petition or resolution to which clause 35.13.5.4.4 of the Main Contract Conditions refers, the Subcontractor shall repay on demand such amount."

Although this appears to be a comparatively simple procedure, problems arise in practice. First, is the clause intended to apply on the presentation of a winding up petition rather than the making of an order? Reading the clause literally, the employer could make a direct payment, ascertain later that a petition had been issued before the payment was made, even though it was later withdrawn, and then demand the return of the payment, thereby stultifying the operation of NSC/2 at a time when it was most needed:

compare *Law Debenture Trust Corporation v Elektrim Finance* [2005] EWHC 1999 at para.60. Perhaps the problem would be remedied when dealing with the following certificate. Second, JCT 80 provides that the employer is only obliged to make the direct payment to the extent that future payments fall due to the contractor. This may never happen, e.g. where the architect has over-certified, and could work unjustly against a subcontractor which has carried out work since the last certificate. Third, in view of the limited fund available, if more than two subcontractors are unpaid they will presumably share *pro rata*. On a substantial project, there could be numerous nominated subcontractors who are owed significant amounts. The employer's undertaking would be of limited value to them.

The employer's undertaking only arises where the architect has certified **17–023** that the contractor has failed to provide reasonable proof of prior payment. What happens where the architect fails to issue the certificate? Can the employer rely on the absence of the certificate as a defence to a claim by the subcontractor? An example of this type of situation is reported in *Construction Award No. 9 (1988)* [1995] 2 Con. L. Yb. 103. After the contractor went into receivership, the architect refused to certify under cl.35 of JCT 80 that the contractor had failed to pay an amount attributed to a nominated subcontractor in the previous interim certificate. The contractor then went into compulsory liquidation. Between the petition and the winding up order, the main contract was novated and a further interim certificate issued. The contractor was only released from liabilities arising after the date of the novation and the employer agreed not to deduct from any sums due to the incoming or the insolvent contractor any amounts unpaid to nominated subcontractors. The subcontractor brought and won an arbitration against the employer under NSC/2 claiming the amount of the direct payment. The employer relied on cl.35 under which the duty to pay direct ceases if at the date when it "would otherwise be made" there is a petition to wind up the contractor. This argument was rejected on the ground that, had the architect issued his certificate promptly after receiving the subcontractor's request, payment would have been due under NSC/2 several weeks before the petition was issued. The employer was in breach of NSC/2 in failing to procure that the architect operated cl.35 and should not be allowed to profit from its own wrong. The employer also argued that the receivership had activated the employer's post-termination rights which replaced cl.35 and released the employer from its obligations under NSC/2. The arbitrator disagreed and held that the novation took effect as a reinstatement and variation of the original contract. This was an unusual finding based on the specific terms of the novation (which are not set out in full in the award), and made it unnecessary for the arbitrator to consider the effect of the termination clause.

NSC/2 fails to deal with the situation where the contractor is in receivership and liquidation at the same time. For example, if administrative receivers are appointed before the winding up commences, the set-off following direct payment to the subcontractor will not be made from property of the company under the liquidator's control, but from the receivables assigned to the charge holder on the receiver's appointment: *Buchler v Talbot* [2004] 2 A.C. 298. If the contractor were to go into liquidation before the direct payment, it would seem wrong to deprive the subcontractor of the benefit of it. Against this, a liquidator may argue that the assignment to the debenture holder is for the purpose of security and the contractor has a contingent interest in any property which is not required to discharge the secured indebtedness. It would be a preference over other creditors for a subcontractor to be paid from (or for an employer to set off against) property which it later emerged was not needed to discharge the security. The answer may be that it is a question of timing: the charge holder is entitled to the benefit of all the property falling within the charge until the security is paid off. If that means that the employer has access to a receivable for the purpose of set-off which it would not have had in the event of the contractor's liquidation, that is merely the consequence of the differing natures of receivership and liquidation: *Hargreaves v Action 2000* [1993] B.C.L.C. 1111.

These forms—along with the concept of nomination of subcontractors—have been discontinued by JCT 05. The nearest equivalent is a subcontractor collateral warranty for use with funders, SCWa/F. This provides for a completion contract between funder and subcontractor to arise on service of a notice by the funder under which the funder assumes liability for payment of any sums not paid by the contractor before the notice was served (see Ch.16).

Collateral contract

17–024 There have been several recent cases of direct payment arising out of one-off arrangements. These can be negotiated at the inception of the contract or as the work proceeds.

At the inception

17–025 Occasionally, a subcontractor may be able to replace the payment mechanism in the subcontract with an independent payment undertaking from the employer. This occurred in the Scottish case of *Brican Fabrications v Merchant City Developments* [2003] B.L.R. 512. The facts here are particularly significant. Merchant engaged Circle Construction as main contractor for the refurbishment of a market building. Brican were specialist steel fabricators and welders and had not worked with Circle before. When they were asked to tender, they obtained a trade reference to the effect that Circle were "only good for £20,000", which was less than 15 per cent of the subcontract sum. Brican therefore chose not to respond to Circle's invitation. The employer was concerned at the lack of progress in letting the steelwork subcontract and contacted Brican direct. A meeting was arranged to which Circle was not invited. Brican made it clear that they were not prepared to enter into a subcontract with Circle unless all payments were made direct by Merchant. The employer was in a very weak bargaining position as the steelwork was on the critical path: unless work started immediately there would be serious implications for the project. The employer therefore agreed to pay direct on receipt of the subcontractor's VAT invoice and Brican began work on site the following day.

A standard form of subcontract was entered into some weeks later but the payment terms were left unamended and did not reflect the agreement Brican had made with the employer. The works proceeded and eight interim payments were made direct to the subcontractor. Less than a year after the subcontract was entered into and just before completion of the steelwork subcontract, the contractor was placed in compulsory liquidation.

The subcontractor made a claim for payment of £43,000 under its final account excluding retention but including VAT. The employer refused to pay on the basis that its agreement with Brican was simply to deduct and pay direct from certified sums due to Circle such amount as Circle instructed them was due to Brican. The direct payments had been made as paying agent on behalf of Circle whose authority had been required as a condition of each payment and deduction. The arrangement was a payment mechanism intended to provide comfort to Brican rather than an independent source of payment. It was collateral to Circle's payment obligations under the subcontract and did not impose an obligation on Merchant.

The Court of Session enforced Brican's claim for payment on the following grounds:

(1) An oral agreement for direct payment had been reached subject only to the consent of Circle which was later obtained. The agreement was either made by all three parties or by Merchant and Brican with Circle's consent as a condition subsequent but the precise legal analysis did not affect the outcome of the case.

(2) The factual background, and in particular the relative bargaining positions of the parties, justified the finding that the employer had given an unconditional payment undertaking to the subcontractor irrespective of its ability to recoup payments made from sums otherwise due to the contractor.

(3) The court below had been in error in beginning its analysis with the forms of main and subcontract. The order of events was: main contract, direct payment agreement, assent by Circle to the direct payment agreement, subcontract. It was not intended that the subcontract should supersede the direct payment agreement; it was just a way of implementing it by providing a framework for ascertaining sums due.

(4) The payment obligations of the employer were not affected by the liquidation of Circle even though its employment was automatically terminated as a result.

> "While the contractual mechanism for valuation may have fallen with that contract, the continuing availability of that mechanism was not, in the circumstances of this case, a condition precedent to the right to payment" (para.20, *per* Lord Hamilton).

If necessary, the court was prepared to imply a term into the direct payment agreement that, in the event of a breakdown of the valuation mechanism in the subcontract, amounts payable should be valued on the basis of the subcontract bills. This aspect of the case invites comparison with the termination of the retention trust where again the contract fails to provide any machinery for payment out to the beneficiaries (see Ch.10). The employer protested that to construe the direct payment agreement as a primary obligation might expose it to liability to pay both contractor and subcontractor for the same work. This aspect is dealt with briefly by the court but presumably the employer's ability to set off an amount equivalent to the direct payment against sums otherwise due to the contractor would depend on the terms of the contractor's consent to the direct payment agreement itself and the consequent removal of the contractor's rights and obligations as to payment in connection with the steelwork package. There was no direct payment clause in the main contract operative either during the works or after termination. Under the subcontract, Brican's employment automatically terminated on Circle's liquidation. There was a pay when paid provision in the subcontract termination clause.

17–026 What was the scope of the direct payment agreement in this case? Could it also include liability for damages in the event of a breach of the subcontract by Circle? In argument, Lord Hamilton considered that the agreement would be limited to the value of work done: compare *Bouygues v Shanghai Links* [1998] 2 H.K.L.R.D. 479. In conclusion, the employer's argument that the direct payment agreement was intended to avoid delay in payment rather than secure payment was not accepted. The arrangement was not varied or superseded by the terms of the subcontract but stood apart from it. It is worth comparing the outcome of this case with that in *Stork v Leighton Contractors* [2001] A.C.L. Rep. 430. In the courts below, there was an issue whether the direct payment agreement contravened the *pari passu* rule. The sheriff had held that it could not because the only debtor-creditor relationship was that between Merchant and Brican. The issue was not however raised in the Court of Session.

Where a contractor enters into a step-in agreement as part of a large property or PFI transaction, it is always a question of construction as to the extent to which the contractor acquires a right to payment enforceable against the funder. In *Gee Walker & Slater v Société Generale* (unreported, October 27, 1999), a contractor completed a housing development for an employer under a JCT form. After the end of the defects liability period, the developer's bank appointed receivers to the unsold part of the development. The contractor terminated its employment and obtained an arbitration award against the developer which it sought to enforce against the bank pursuant to a step-in agreement entered into by all three parties under which the contractor agreed to give fourteen days notice to the bank before terminating the building contract. The bank had an option whether to serve a counter-notice on the contractor requiring it to continue its obligations under the contract. If a counter-notice was served, the contractor agreed to accept the bank's instructions as if it had been named as employer under the building contract and the bank agreed to pay all sums due or to become due under the contract. If no counter-notice were served and the contractor exercised its right of termination, the bank was obliged to exercise a discretion reserved to it by the credit agreement (between the bank and the developer) and pay direct to the contractor all amounts certified by the bank's surveyor (appointed under the credit agreement) as required by a particular clause of the credit agreement in respect of work done before the termination.

17–027 It was held that the bank was not liable to the contractor because by the date of termination the developer's facility had already been exhausted. The relevant terms of the credit agreement are not set out in the judgment but it appears that it placed a limit on the bank's liability for direct payment. In this case, the facility was limited to £2.5 million or 70 per cent of the value of the development from time to time remaining unsold. It was apparent, the court observed, that the developer would have had to make a significant capital contribution of its own and this may be one reason for the terms of this particular step-in agreement. The critical factor seems to have been that after the facility was exhausted the bank's discretion to make direct payments under the credit agreement terminated. The case illustrates the danger from the contractor's point of view in importing into contracts such as step-in agreements the terms of finance agreements. Although it seems not to have been a material fact, the judgment records that the bank had terminated the employment of its surveyor under the credit agreement six months before the receivership and did not replace him.

In a direct agreement, the employer may undertake to ensure the performance of the contractor's obligations as from the date of the step-in but not to indemnify the subcontractor against losses caused by the contractor's default: *Wallace-Smith v Thiess Infraco* (2005) 218 A.L.R. 1. In that case, the Government of Victoria entered into a long term franchise agreement with National Express to operate part of the state tram and train system. National Express entered into an infrastructure maintenance service agreement with Thiess containing terms back to back with the franchise agreement. The government took a charge over the undertaking of National Express as security. On the withdrawal of support by the UK parent of National Express, it defaulted in payment to Thiess and the government appointed receivers and managers under its security. Thiess served notices of default relying on both events as entitling it to terminate its contract. The government served a notice under its direct agreement with Thiess, requiring it to continue to perform on the basis that it would be paid from that time onwards by the receivers. National Express went into administration and later agreed a deed of company arrangement. The supervisors under the arrangement accepted a proof of debt from Thiess in respect of the progress payments outstanding as at the date of default but rejected a proof for damages for loss of profit on the basis that such a claim depended on the termination of the contract which had never actually happened because of the effect of the direct agreement. The Federal Court of Australia ruled by a majority that the proof should be accepted as a contingent claim (see Ch.13).

During the contract

In *Greenore Port v Technical & General* [2006] EWHC 3119, direct payments were made to concrete and steel reinforcement suppliers pursuant to an agreement between employer and contractor which was recorded in two variation orders (para.21). They were a "temporary expedient" and "treated by the parties as payments on account towards [the contractor's] lump sum entitlement" (para.197, *per* Jackson J.). The underlying contract was in the form published by the Institution of Engineers of Ireland (3rd edn). By contrast, in *Sydenhams (Timber Engineering) Ltd v CHG Holdings* [2007] EWHC 1129 it was held by Judge Peter Coulson Q.C. that the claimant had a direct contract with the employer and had never been a subcontractor (to a contractor that had since gone into administration). But in any event the heads of claim were covered by a direct payment agreement made expressly with the employer following the claimant's suspension of the work for non-payment. As in *Brican Fabrications v Merchant City Developments* considered above, the claimant was wary of contracting with the builder proposed by the employer, considering the builder was under-resourced for the project, and had been careful in making its position clear when negotiating the contractual arrangements. **17–028**

Braspetro Oil Services v FPSO Construction [2005] EWHC 1316 is an unusual example of *ad hoc* direct payment agreements being used in connection with construction work in the oil and gas industry. There were two construction contracts between a special purpose vehicle company and FPSO for the conversion of a crude carrier and a crane platform into floating storage and floating production units respectively. The contractor entered into step-in agreements with the end-user (Braspetro) which also conferred rights of supervision and the approval of all progress certificates. Taking both contracts together, direct payments totalling $250 million were made pursuant to 1,500 side letter agreements. Although the background facts were complicated, the side letters themselves were very brief. They were between Braspetro, FPSO and the supplier or subcontractor in question and provided that, in consideration of the supplier continuing to provide its services:

> ". . . the parties hereto agree that in the event [contractor] fails to make any payment when due under the Purchase Order [end user] confirms an irrevocable commitment upon first written request from [supplier] to make payment directly to [supplier] subject always to aggregate of any and all such payments not exceeding . . ."

The letter continued by conferring on Braspetro a right of recoupment from FPSO of the direct payment in the following terms:

> "[Contractor] acknowledge and agree that any payment made by [end user] hereunder shall as between [contractor] and [end user] be regarded as payment by [end user] to [contractor] which may be recovered (subject to the settlement and reconciliation of all claims, costs and expenses due to either party which are hereby reserved) by [end user] from [contractor] including, by way of deduction from any sums due to [contractor] from [end user] under the provisions of the Supervision agreement" (para.120).

The court held that these words were sufficient to enable the end-user Braspetro to recover the amount of direct payments from FPSO but that the agreement had not excluded FPSO's rights under the general law to set off against such claims any cross-claims they may have in respect of the work. It was conceded by FPSO that all of the direct payments were made by Braspetro on behalf of FPSO (para.220). It was held that the side letters gave rise to a debt on the part of FPSO in respect of moneys paid by Braspetro following a conforming written request from the supplier (para.224). It appears that the court concluded that the side letters gave rise to a primary obligation although there was no discussion on whether they amounted to an indemnity rather than a guarantee.

It is interesting to note that Braspetro chose to have the work completed by making direct payments to suppliers and keeping the original contractual structure in place as an alternative to invoking its own step-in rights. Exactly why the suppliers were not being paid by FPSO is not explored in the case. The suppliers were protecting their interests by refusing to deliver equipment or provide further services pending payment or by charging interest on overdue sums (para.85). Perhaps it was not clear whether the circumstances justified the exercise of step-in rights. It appears that the exercise of such rights by the end-user on other projects had led to disruption and to costly litigation. Before the direct payment regime was introduced, FPSO and Braspetro had agreed a tied account system whereby Braspetro would set up an escrow account from which suppliers would be paid against documentation signed by both Braspetro and FPSO. However, the system was only intended to facilitate payment of milestones to FPSO. At this point, the estimated cost to complete the works already exceeded the unpaid balance of the contract sum, which meant that it was very unlikely that another contractor would make an offer to novate (para.104). The remaining milestone payments lasted only until the end of March 2000 by which time the project funds were exhausted while significant amounts were still needed to complete the project. At this point the tied account system ceased and the direct payment letters began to be sent out. FPSO denied that the direct payment system involved any liability on its part to pay such amounts to Braspetro. For details of Braspetro's successful proof of the quantum of its claims to recover the direct payments see *Braspetro Oil Services v FPSO Construction* [2007] EWHC 1359.

Other forms of direct payment

An arrangement to pay a subcontractor direct may in context be interpreted as a secondary guarantee: *Actionstrength v International Glass* [2003] B.L.R. 207. However, in *Ballast v Laurieston Properties* [2005] CSOH 16, an undertaking that "all future payments will be paid directly from the JV account" was construed as a letter of comfort. Alternatively a direct payment system may be clothed in the language of trust law: *Stork v Leighton Contractors* [2001] A.C.L. Rep. 430. Payment may also be made from an escrow account established by the employer: *Bouygues v Shanghai Links* [1998] 2 H.K.L.R.D. 479. Claims involving trusts and escrow accounts are discussed in Ch.9. In *PJ Davidson v Hanson Quarry Products* [2005] EWHC 298, a contractual joint venture entered into a main contract with the Highways Agency for work to the M27 motorway. The arrangement between the venturers was that payment would be made to one of them (Stenoak) who would account to the other (Hanson) for the proportion attributable to its part of the work. When Stenoak went into administrative receivership, Hanson agreed to complete the work and the employer agreed to pay it direct. The joint venture agreement was terminated two weeks later. **17–029**

Attachment of debts

If a subcontractor obtains a judgment against a contractor, it can enforce it by attaching a debt owed to the contractor by issuing a third party debt application (formerly known as garnishee proceedings) under CPR Pt 72. This is a two stage process: in the first stage, the subcontractor obtains an interim order which states an amount that the third party has to retain out of what he owes the judgment debtor. The order fixes a date for the hearing at which the court considers any objections and makes the order final or discharges it or decides the issue between the parties. The crucial factor is that any attachment must have been completed before the start of a winding up, otherwise it cannot be relied on and the subcontractor will remain an unsecured creditor: s.183 of the Insolvency Act 1986. **17–030**

In *Wilson v Metropolitan Property* [1975] 2 All E.R. 814, the Court of Appeal refused to allow a subcontractor the benefit of attachment. This case was one of several arising out of the collapse of the Stern Group in the recession of the early 1970s. The contractor was a subsidiary whose parent company had gone into voluntary liquidation. The creditors of other group companies had agreed on a six month moratorium of their debts to enable a scheme of arrangement to proceed. The subcontractor refused to participate in the scheme and obtained a garnishee order nisi. The contractor went into voluntary liquidation and later the garnishee order was made absolute. The Court of Appeal held that the order should not have been made absolute as it conferred a preference on the subcontractor (see Ch.20). The court also approved *Hudsons Concrete v Evans* (1961) 105 Sol. J. 281, where the facts were similar, although there was no resolution or winding up petition, only an originating summons seeking the sanction of the court to a scheme of arrangement.

A third party debt order will only be made in respect of a debt which is "due or accruing due" even though it may not be immediately payable. Under the traditional lump sum building contract with interim payments payable under a certificate, no debt can arise for the purposes of attachment until a certificate has been issued: *Dunlop & Ranken v Hendall Steel* [1957] 3 All E.R. 344. Uncertified work in progress does not constitute a debt in this context. It has also been decided that, where a subcontractor sought a garnishee order against retention under the main contract after it had been terminated, retention was not a debt due or accruing due: *Grant Plant Hire v Trickey* (1961) 105 Sol. J. 255; *Binamin v Way Soon Construction* [2001] MLJU 111. The contract had the usual suspension of payment on termination. Retention would only become a debt if, after the cost to complete had been ascertained and set off against the balance of the contract sum, there were found to be a net balance payable to the contractor. Viewed in the context of attachment applications, these decisions make sense, but so far as they purport to hold that no debt can exist before a certificate is issued, they are inconsistent with decisions of the Court of Appeal in other contexts: *Earle v Hemsworth RDC* (1928) 140 L.T. 69; *Drew v Josolyne* (1887) 18 Q.B.D. 590. See generally Ch.3.

Third Parties (Rights against Insurers) Act 1930

17–031 A person who suffers loss may be able to claim direct against the other party's insurers under the 1930 Act, e.g. *Galliford v Markel Capital* [2003] All E.R. (D) 303, which concerned a claim by a contractor against a structural engineer pursuant to the ACE Conditions, which incorporated the CIC adjudication procedure. After the engineer went into voluntary liquidation, the contractor brought an adjudication under which the engineer was found liable for £722,000 as damages for defective design. The engineer was insured against claims resulting in "legal liability for damages" awarded against it. By an endorsement, the policy specifically included loss "consequent upon an adjudicator's award" unless the engineer had agreed to accept the adjudicator's decision as final. Rather than seek summary judgment to enforce the adjudicator's decision, Galliford issued proceedings against the insurer under the 1930 Act. The case turned on the legal status of the adjudicator's decision. Galliford considered that it acquired rights under the 1930 Act as soon as the engineer passed the resolution for voluntary winding up. Following *Post Office v Norwich Union* [1967] 2 Q.B. 363 the court held that, although the contractor acquired a cause of action against the engineer on the date of the negligent act, it could not assert any rights against the insurer until liability had been established so as to give rise to an indemnity. (It has since been held that a claimant under the Act does acquire the insured's rights on the date of its formal insolvency and is entitled to obtain a copy of the policy although the rights are inchoate or contingent until the establishment of liability: *Re OT Computers* [2004] Ch. 317.)

In holding against the contractor, the court considered that an adjudication decision could not establish liability for the purposes of the Act. It was not equivalent to a judgment or an arbitration award but created a contractual obligation enforceable by summary judgment. The court also rejected the contractor's submission that the policy endorsement had overridden the effect of an adjudication under the general law. On its true construction, the policy did not expressly provide that an adjudication decision would crystallise the insurer's liability. The contractor then applied for summary judgment against the engineer but failed, the court holding that no contract had been formed (see Ch.12).

Assignment

In Ch.4 it was seen how one of the functions of assignment is to deal with **17–032**
creditor pressure. Where the creditor is a subcontractor, it may bargain for an outright assignment of sums due or to become due to the contractor under the main contract. If the assignment is effective, the employer will only obtain a good discharge by paying the subcontractor. Assignment can therefore operate as a direct payment authorised by the contractor. If the assignment is validly made before the contractor goes into liquidation, it is binding against a receiver who would have to remit the payment to the subcontractor if the employer paid the receiver by mistake: *Ashby Warner v Simmonds* [1936] 2 All E.R. 697; *Kon Struct v Storage Developments* (1990) 6 B.C.L. 171; *Golden Sand v Easy Success Enterprises* [1999] 2 H.K.C. 356.

As the effect of the assignment is to remove the assigned property from the ownership of the contractor, a subsequent payment to the subcontractor cannot infringe the *pari passu* rule. In the event of assignment before a liquidation, however, it is more common for the liquidator to challenge the assignment itself as a preference and claim the payment from the subcontractor on that ground. This type of claim is considered further in Ch.20. It is not uncommon for arrangements to be made for the direct payment of subcontractors which fall short of an assignment: see *Re Right Time Construction* (1990) 52 B.L.R. 117, where payments were invalidated as post-petition disposals. Similarly, an arrangement whereby the contractor is paid direct by a funder may be for administrative convenience and have no effect on an employer's liability to fund retention, even if the payments are made against invoices issued to the funder by the contractor: *Finnegan v Ford Sellar Morris (No 2)* (1991) 27 Con. L.R. 41. In *Bowden v John Laing* (unreported, May 12, 2000, CA) an entrepreneur who was providing finance to a brickwork subcontractor decided to become involved in its management at a time when it was experiencing financial difficulty. The financier unsuccessfully alleged he had reached an oral agreement with the contractor for payment direct of materials delivered to site. In *Rogersons Development v The Housing Corporation* (unreported, October 14, 1994, noted in (1995) 12(1) Build. L.M. 4) the employer, a housing association, went into liquidation after practical completion but before paying the last stage payment and retention. The builder sued The Housing Corporation who had been funding the development against a mortgage over the site. The corporation had failed to inform the builder of its decision taken before practical completion to discontinue funding the employer but this could not give rise to an estoppel; nor could the builder base a claim on an implied assignment by the employer of its rights against the corporation since, on the employer's liquidation, it became liable to repay to the corporation all the sums it had received.

Direct payment orders

17–033 The court's power to order direct payment of damages and costs by a third party (now known as a Pt 20 defendant) to a claimant is another valuable procedural security. In *Re-Source America v Platt Site Services* (2005) 106 Con. L.R. 15, the claimant was an owner of a warehouse which had been damaged by fire caused by the negligence of the defendant, a subcontractor working for the third party contractor who was ultimately responsible for the fire. The subcontractor was a small company with limited insurance cover. The contractor was fully insured but there was doubt in the subcontractor's mind whether the contractor's insurer would admit liability. Each party was concerned to manage insolvency risk. The claimant saw the contractor as a more secure source of payment than the subcontractor. The subcontractor was concerned lest it pay the claimant but be unable to enforce its indemnity against the contractor. The contractor paid damages to the claimant who passed them on to its US parent company and ceased trading. The contractor appealed on quantum and was partially successful but unable to obtain repayment from the claimant. The case concerned the contractor's unsuccessful application against the subcontractor for repayment of part of the damages.

This situation could arise in adjudication cases where the court at trial orders repayment of sums paid under an adjudicator's award. The court was puzzled why the contractor had taken no steps against the claimant, e.g. by applying to have its name restored to the register and then issuing winding up proceedings or applying to the court for the appointment of a receiver to seek repayment from the US parent or approaching the parent company itself. On appeal, the contractor argued that: (a) it had been acting as the subcontractor's agent in making the direct payments: or (b) was only liable to pay direct to the extent of its liability to indemnify the subcontractor. The court analysed the various orders which had been made and rejected the appeal. The claimant had supported the applications for direct payment because it did not want to run the risk of the subcontractor's insolvency intervening between receipt of the money from the contractor and payment to the claimant. Judge Anthony Thornton Q.C. stated:

> "Thus, the intention of a direct payment order, whose effect is to bypass an intermediary in a payment chain, is to regulate which of the other

parties in that chain should avoid the loss flowing from the insolvency of another party in the chain. This intention is achieved since the direct order will exclude the party in the middle from both an entitlement to receive and an obligation to pay the relevant payment" (para.45).

See also *Mayer v Harte* [1960] 1 W.L.R. 770 on the direct payment of costs (a building case), *Gemma Ltd v Gimson (No. 2)* [2005] B.L.R. 163 (directors of an insolvent claimant builder liable for costs awarded against their company) and *Plymouth and SW Co-operative Society v Architecture, Structure and Management* (2006) 111 Con. L.R. 189 (indemnity insurers liable as non-parties for costs of unsuccessful defence by insured designer). Contrast *Taylor v Pace Developments* [1991] B.C.C. 406 in which the director of an insolvent defendant developer was held not to be personally liable for his company's costs of defending action.

6. Conclusion

Overseas jurisdictions have enacted legislation with the specific aim of protecting subcontractors and employees by conferring rights of direct payment against the employer in the event of financial default by the contractor. These were reviewed in the second edition of this book. The same questions keep recurring: Is the employer liable for damages payable by the contractor or only for the contract sum? Is the employer's liability limited to sums outstanding to the contractor when the request for direct payment is made? Can the subcontractor claim direct for non-payment during the contract or only after the contractor's formal insolvency? Can the subcontractor claim statutory priority over secured or judgment creditors of the contractor? **17–034**

Relevant statutes include: French Law No.75–1334 of 31 December 1975 (see Thomas 1997, Malinvaud 2006); the Contractors' Debts Act 1997 (NSW) (Merity 2002); the Building & Construction Industry Security for Payment Act 2002, Pt 3, Div 4 (Victoria) (Stephenson and Harrison 2003, 8); the Hong Kong Employment Ordinance and cases under it such as *Re Finbo Engineering* [1998] 2 H.K.L.R.D. 695 and *Pysogea v Rightfairs Development* [1991] 1 H.K.C. 341 discussed in the second edition of this book; the Industrial Relations Act 1996 (NSW) s.127 (e.g. Cole Report, 2003, Vol.8, Ch.12, App.A, paras.177–192), and the Building and Construction Industry Security for Payment Act (Singapore) (see Ng 2006).

As a matter of commercial practice, the usefulness of direct payment clauses is self-evident (UN 1988, 32). In 1997 the European Commission recommended that subcontractors should have the right to direct payment in "cases of unjustified non-payment by the principal contractor". During the 1990s it was increasingly argued that the *pari passu* rule should yield to a public policy favouring contractual mechanisms which promote the integrity of a project (McGaw 1992). Sir Michael Latham considered that employers' reluctance to make direct payments could be overcome by introducing a secondary trust in favour of the first line of subcontractors into all construction contracts by statute (Latham 1994). He also recommended that construction contracts be exempted from the rule in *British Eagle* through an amendment to the Insolvency Act 1986. This was by analogy with the exception made in favour of market contracts in the

Companies Act 1989 (McCormack 1997). The government accepted that a trust would overcome the problem caused by *British Eagle* and therefore opposed any amendment to the Insolvency Act 1986 but was not prepared to introduce legislation on trust funds without further consultation (DOE 1995). Ever since the Housing Grants, Construction and Regeneration Act 1996 came into force, subcontractors' organisations have been lobbying to make the construction industry a special case by reversing the effect of *British Eagle* in relation to direct payments but without success. There are no current government initiatives in this area: direct payment is not mentioned in DTI (2006). Nor has the Contracts (Rights of Third Parties) Act 1999 improved the position of subcontractors in this context since it only applies where the parties intend the direct payment clause to be enforceable by the subcontractor and the beneficiary is sufficiently identified: compare *Avraamides v Colwill* [2006] EWCA 1533. The position may be different where direct payment is mandatory under the main contract (Bridge 2003, 30). It is interesting to note that, notwithstanding a decline in the use of direct payment clauses in standard forms, there has been an increase in the number of reported cases involving one-off direct payment agreements. This suggests that the subject remains commercially relevant. In July 2007 the Office of Government Commerce announced that public sector clients "may wish to consider paying (but not necessarily employing) major sub-contractors and suppliers directly upon authorisation from the lead contractor that the work has been properly carried out" (OGC 2007, para.15). Direct payment on the largest government contracts will in effect be achieved through the use of the project bank accounts discussed in Ch.9.

Chapter 18

Set-off in Insolvency

18–001 The question of set-off is one of the most important in insolvency law. Whether formal insolvency makes any difference to the ordinary position (see Ch.5) depends on the procedure concerned. This chapter reviews the effect on set-off rights of administrative receivership, liquidation, administration and company voluntary arrangement. In each case a brief summary of the law is followed by reference to construction cases and industry-related issues.

1. Administrative receivership

18–002 The effect of the appointment of an administrative receiver (or an administrator following the changes made by the Enterprise Act 2002) is to crystallise the floating charge under which the appointment is made (Ch.13). At that moment, the charge becomes fixed on the assets included in the charge. On one analysis the assets are assigned in equity to the charge holder and the administrative receiver is entitled to claim them on the charge holder's behalf. It follows that set-off where one party is in receivership depends on the law of assignment. Thus, although administrative receivership is in decline as a formal insolvency procedure, the case law remains of value when considering the rights of an assignee of the benefit of a construction contract (Ch.4).

The charge holder, or the receiver on its behalf, must give notice to the debtor to prevent further acquisition of set-off rights. Letters sent by receivers on their appointment sometimes say that a debtor cannot rely on any right of set-off which arises after the date of the appointment. Strictly, this is inaccurate as the relevant moment from the debtor's point of view is receipt of the notice. For example the debtor can set off a cross-claim for legal set-off which arises between the appointment and receipt of the notice even though the mutuality has been destroyed because, owing to the statutory origins of legal set-off, mutuality is by reference to the legal title to the two claims. "The question is whether it is unconscionable for the debtor to rely on the right of set-off otherwise available at law when the equitable title to one of the debts is in someone else" (Derham 2003, para.11.08).

Giving notice is beneficial to the assignee for two reasons. First, after receiving notice, the debtor can only obtain a good discharge by paying the assignee. Where the assignee is the holder of a floating charge, this is unimportant as the assignor will be under the control of the receiver who acts as its agent and is entitled to use its name for the purpose of collecting in the charged assets. Secondly, the debtor cannot raise as a defence to the receiver's claim any new equities arising after the date of receipt of notice of appointment: *Business Computers v Anglo-African Leasing* [1977] 1 W.L.R. 578. It is as if a line had been ruled under the claim after notice was given. This is of crucial importance to an understanding of a debtor's right of set-off against a claim by a receiver.

"Subject to equities"

18–003 An equity is any defence or remedy which a debtor has against an assignor at the date of receipt of notice of assignment: *Roxburghe v Cox* (1878) 17 Ch. D. 520. Equities in construction cases can be divided into four types: a right to avoid a contract, a right to have a dispute referred to arbitration or adjudication, non-assignability clauses, and set-off and abatement (Oditah 1991).

Rights to avoid a contract on the ground of mistake, misrepresentation, fraud, duress or undue influence are all equities binding an assignee. An employer successfully defended a claim brought by an assignee of its contractor in *Wakefield & Barnsley Banking Co v Normanton Local Board* (1881) L.T. 697. A dispute arose between the contractor and employer over a contract to build a reservoir where the employer alleged that certain work was defective and incomplete. The dispute was settled on the basis that the employer was to take immediate possession of the site and pay an agreed sum on a particular date. The contractor assigned this sum as security to its bank and gave notice to the employer. When the employer failed to pay, it was sued by the bank as assignee. After the settlement, the employer discovered that the contractor had colluded with the engineer in the issue of fraudulent certificates. It appears from the report that the contractor had removed stone from the reservoir and substituted concrete. It was held that the employer had a good defence to the claim because the settlement agreement had been obtained by fraud (Tettenborn 1987).

A contractual right to have disputes referred to arbitration is also an equity: *Rumput v Islamic Republic of Iran* [1984] 2 Lloyd's Rep. 259. An insurer wishing to exercise rights by subrogation under a contract containing an arbitration clause will be restrained by injunction from doing so other than by arbitration in accordance with the terms of the contract: *The Jay Bola* [1997] 2 Lloyd's Rep. 279. The same point would also apply to transfers of rights by statute: *Through Transport v New India Assurance* [2005] 2 Lloyd's Rep. 378. In all these situations, what the transferee obtains is "a chose in action whose precise scope is determined by the contract under which it arises and which is inherently subject to certain incidents, in this case, a requirement that it be enforced by arbitration" (*Through Transport*, at para.22, *per* Moore-Bick J.). This principle now extends to adjudication under s.8 of the Housing Grants, Construction and Regeneration Act 1996 (see Ch.12). The effect of a non-assignability clause in a construction contract on the right of a receiver to claim under it in exercise of the charge holder's rights as assignee is considered in Ch.4.

18–004 The final group of equities consists of rights of set-off and abatement which have arisen or are in existence at the date of receipt of notice of assignment. The question when a claim comes into existence is not entirely straightforward (Grantham 1989). The easiest conceptually are cross-claims for legal set-off and abatement. The law is clear that both must be in existence before receipt of the notice. In the case of abatement, the right to make a claim for defective work accrues when the work is carried out: *Lintest Builders v Roberts* (1980) 13 B.L.R. 38. A claim for legal set-off must be liquidated or ascertainable with certainty and payable at the time the defence is filed: *Stein v Blake* [1996] 1 A.C. 243 at 251. The position is different with equitable set-off where, provided the cross-claim "impeaches" the claim, it will be allowed against a receiver even though it arises after the date of the notice (Derham 2003, paras 17.22, 17.82). This is best illustrated by considering the facts of cases where equitable set-off has been allowed against an assignee. The plaintiff contractor in *Young v Kitchen* (1878) 3 Ex. D. 127 was an assignee. The court had little difficulty in holding that the employer was entitled to equitable set-off because the cross-claim had arisen before the assignment was made (see Ch.5). In the leading case of the *Government of Newfoundland v Newfoundland Railway Company* (1888) 13 App. Cas. 199, the Privy Council considered a claim by assignees of moneys due to a contractor under an agreement to construct 340 miles of railway within five years. Thereafter it was to maintain and operate it in return for a subsidy of $180,000 per annum in half-yearly payments for a period of 35 years "such annual subsidy to attach in proportionate parts and form part of the assets of the said company, as and when each five-mile section is completed and operated, or fraction thereof". In addition to the subsidy, the employer agreed to grant 5,000 acres of land per mile of track completed "upon completion of each section of five miles of railway, or fraction thereof." After five years' work, the contractor had only completed 85 miles of track. The government had granted land and paid the subsidy as each five-mile portion had been completed. The contractor failed to complete the work but the assignee claimed the balance of the subsidy and land grants. It was held that the employer was entitled to an equitable set-off of its counterclaim for losses caused by the non-completion.

> ". . . the obligation to construct the whole is so intimately connected with the obligation to pay for a portion, as to give rise to a forcible argument that one is a condition precedent to the other; so intimately that their Lordships have serious difficulty in disengaging them, and can only do so by modifying the language of part of the contract" (at 211, *per* Lord Hobhouse).

The right to each payment and portion of land was dependent or conditional on the completion of five-mile portions of track. Not only did the cross-claim flow out of the dealings giving rise to the claim, but it was inseparably connected with them and "impeached" the plaintiff's demand. Significantly, the assignment occurred four years before the contractor's breach. This case was followed in *John Dee v WMH (21) Ltd* [1997] B.C.C. 518 at 530.

A contractual set-off is likely to be effective even if made after the notice provided that the cross-claim arises out of a pre-notice obligation. Consider the Australian case of *Main Roads Construction v Samary Enterprises* [2006] VSC 144 in which a contractor obtained summary judgment for six certified sums against an employer which the employer did not honour. The contractor served a statutory demand but, before the hearing of the employer's application to have the demand set aside, the contractor went into receivership and then liquidation. After the summary judgment, the supervising officer issued a certificate reducing the amount previously shown as due to the contractor by deductions for liquidated damages and the cost of dealing with defective and incomplete work. It also reflected the fact that some works had been omitted by consent. The employer successfully applied for a stay of execution of the judgment, even in respect of a balance payable to the contractor, pending the hearing of the employer's counterclaim, on provision of a bank guarantee. Habersberger J. granted the stay on the basis that the assignment of the judgment sum to the bank on the crystallisation of the charge was subject to the later adjustment of the contract sum (para.36). In this case, the adjustment was by a certificate issued after the assignment but in respect of events occurring before it.

18–005 There are many cases where disputes have arisen following a sale and lease back or charge back of commercial property. In two Canadian cases, the consideration for the land was partly in cash, part by assumption of an existing first mortgage and the balance left on a second mortgage to the vendor. In *Coba Industries v Millie's Holdings* [1975] 6 W.W.R. 14 the whole agreement was subject to the vendor taking a lease under which the rent was double the amount payable under the two mortgages. The vendor assigned the second mortgage some weeks later. Before taking the assignment, the assignee was aware of the vendor's arrangement with the purchaser. The purchaser gave the vendor 12 postdated cheques for the mortgage money which were handed over to the assignee. When the vendor defaulted in payment of rent under the lease, the purchaser stopped the mortgage cheques. It was held that there was a fundamental connection between the vendor's obligation under the lease and the purchaser's obligation under the mortgage such that the price for the building had been determined by the cash flow to be generated by the lease. "In cases where equitable set-off is justified, the assignee takes an impaired title" (at 29, *per* Macfarlane J.A.). Set-off was not limited to the arrears of rent owed at the date of receipt of notice of assignment but included damages flowing from a repudiation of the lease which occurred some months later. Because of the very close link between the lease and the mortgage obligations, even rent and other sums accruing due after notice of assignment was received could be set off. This can be contrasted with other authorities where rent becoming due after assignment was held not capable of set-off against an assignee.

In *Mercantile Bank of Canada v Leon's Furniture* (1989) 42 Bus. L.R. 1, a receiver was appointed over a manufacturer under a fixed charge on book debts which were owed by a retailer. The contract allowed the retailer a volume rebate, an advertising allowance, warranty and service entitlements, and the manufacturer always unquestioningly accepted back any damaged goods. The receiver claimed the book debts but refused to allow the rebate or perform any of the manufacturer's obligations. The manufacturer accrued liabilities under warranties in its accounts at the time that products were sold. It was held that the receiver was not entitled to collect the receivables without allowing for the discount and the value of the other obligations even though the discount itself was not payable until after the year end. The claim and cross-claim were so closely bound together as to make it unconscionable to allow one and exclude set-off of the other. In all these cases there was a close nexus between claim and cross-claim, much more than the simple fact that they both arose out of the same transaction.

These cases are examples of equitable set-off where the criterion of impeachment is present. In some cases where the English courts have allowed a cross-claim on the basis of an equitable set-off, there is no obvious nexus with the claim apart from the fact that both arose out of the same contract or transaction: *Bankes v Jarvis* [1903] 1 K.B. 549; *Morgan v Martin Johnson* [1949] 1 K.B. 107; *Hanak v Green* [1958] 2 Q.B. 9. Where the debt is contractually conditional on the performance of another obligation, the receiver will be unable to recover it without performing the obligation.

Receivership trading

It is often necessary for a receiver to continue trading to preserve the company's goodwill while a buyer is found or to convert work in progress into book debts. A receiver appointed over a contractor may decide to build out where there is a comparatively small amount of work still to be done. It is of concern to the receiver that receivables arising from trading during the receivership are not reduced by set-off of cross-claims arising before or during the receivership (e.g. this is the reason for cl.27.5.3 of JCT 98). Equally, those trading with a company which goes into receivership are concerned to preserve their rights of set-off against debts which become payable to the company in receivership through trading with the receiver. Unless the position is altered by agreement after the receivership, a receiver who continues to provide services under a pre-receivership contract is entitled to the benefit of any clause excluding set-off in that contract, even in respect of sums accruing due to the company after the contract has been terminated: *John Dee v WMH (21) Ltd* [1997] B.C.C. 518. **18–006**

The position was altered by agreement post-receivership in *Alstom Transport v Elequip Projects* [2004] EWHC 2897. Elequip had agreed to supply two items of equipment for use in tilting trains. By the time it went into administrative receivership, both items were ready for delivery but only one had been paid for. In their notice of appointment the receivers required customers to confirm among other things that future deliveries under existing orders would be paid for free of set-off and accepted without any warranty as to quality. On October 17, Alstom agreed a price of £730,000 with the receivers for the item not yet paid for which also covered all other liabilities as at October 1, payable as to £500,000 on October 20 and the balance on October 20, and arranged to collect the equipment from the supplier's premises. The agreement became binding on October 20, when the schedule of equipment was agreed. The same day the receivers told Alstom that they could only collect the goods if they counter-signed the notice of appointment agreeing to its terms. Alstom signed the letter imagining it related to future orders. On delivery, Alstom found that parts were missing from both items of equipment. They had already paid the £500,000 but claimed a set-off for defects which exceeded the balance of £230,000. The receivers conceded the value of the missing parts only as far as the equipment not paid for at the date of the receivership was concerned and claimed the net sum of £86,000. When this was not paid they threatened winding up proceedings. Alstom obtained an injunction restraining them from presenting a petition on the basis that it was seriously arguable that the parties had made an unconditional agreement on October

17, before Alstom countersigned the notice of appointment. On that assumption, the agreement of October 17, stood alone and Alstom's rights of set-off in respect of cross-claims arising under that agreement had not been excluded. Crucially, Hart J. also found that Alstom had an arguable set-off against the £86,000 in respect of the parts missing from the equipment which had been paid for pre-receivership. This was because the agreement of October 17 had made payment of the £500,000 a condition of the right to collect both items of equipment.

Where a receiver allowed the company to continue trading by delivering goods pursuant to a pre-receivership obligation, it was held that the debtor was entitled to legal set-off of a cross-claim which it had before the receiver's appointment: *Rother Iron v Canterbury Precision Engineers* [1974] Q.B. 1. Where a receiver realised a charged asset by selling it to a pre-existing creditor of the company, however, it was held that the pre-existing debt could not be set off against the price of the asset: *Felt and Textiles v Hubrich* [1968] N.Z.L.R. 716. In the former case, the receiver had incurred the post-receivership debt by delivering goods without previously agreeing that the purchaser would not make a set-off against the price. In the second case, the purchaser freely contracted in the knowledge that the receiver was selling an asset in the enforcement of the charge for the benefit of the debenture holder.

In a further case, a tenant lent money to its landlord to finance the construction and operation of a building and mortgaged the debt to its bank: *West Street Properties v Jamison* [1974] 2 N.S.W.L.R. 435. The bank appointed a receiver who went into occupation of the premises. The landlord claimed rent from the receiver who was allowed legal set-off of the loan which had been charged to the bank. This case can be contrasted with *Robbie v Witney Warehouse* [1963] 1 W.L.R. 1324, where a receiver succeeded in a claim against a pre-receivership debtor of the company who had bought another's claim against the company after receiving notice of appointment. These cases are not wholly logical in their reasoning. Although the concept of mutuality has generally been relied on, the courts appear to be applying a doctrine of unfairness and to look carefully at the facts in each case without applying dogmatic rules. If a receiver continues to trade, receivables through trading are probably subject to set-off rights acquired in the course of the post-receivership trading: compare *Rendell v Doors & Doors* [1975] 2 N.Z.L.R. 191. This is notwithstanding the fact that as soon as the receivables are created, they automatically fall within the (then) fixed charge over book debts and there is therefore no mutuality between the debtor and the creditor-assignee (Derham 2003, paras 17.23, 17.81). From a debtor's point of view, it is always desirable to reach an express agreement with a receiver before continuing a contract post receivership, otherwise a set-off problem may well arise.

2. Liquidation

18–007 Where one of the contracting parties goes into liquidation, the general law or the parties' own contractual set-off arrangements are replaced by a mandatory set-off applied by r.4.90 of the Insolvency Rules 1986, amended by the Insolvency (Amendment) Rules 2005 (SI 2005/527) as from April 1, 2005. Quotations from the rule in this section are taken from the new version.

Relevant parts provide:

(1) This Rule applies where, before the company goes into liquidation there have been mutual credits, mutual debts or other mutual dealings between the company and any creditor of the company proving or claiming to prove for a debt in the liquidation.
(3) An account shall be taken of what is due from each party to the other in respect of the mutual dealings, and the sums due from one party shall be set off against the sums due from the other.
(4) A sum shall be regarded as being due to or from the company . . . whether: (a) it is payable at present or in the future; (b) the obligation by virtue of which it is payable is certain or contingent; or (c) its amount is fixed or liquidated, or is capable of being ascertained by fixed rules or as a matter of opinion.
(8) Only the balance (if any) of the account owed to the creditor is provable in the liquidation. Alternatively the balance (if any) owed to the company shall be paid to the liquidator as part of the assets except where all or part of the balance results from a contingent or prospective debt owed by the creditor and in such a case the balance (or that part of it which results from the contingent or prospective debt) shall be paid if and when that debt becomes due and payable.

Rule 4.90 was considered in *Bouygues v Dahl-Jensen* [2000] B.L.R. 522, an important case on adjudication (Ch.12). As the argument in that case was far-reaching, it is convenient to use it as a framework for discussing liquidation set-off in general.

Bouygues v Dahl-Jensen

In this case it was held by the Court of Appeal that summary judgment ought not to be granted to enforce an adjudicator's decision where the claimant is in liquidation and the other party has cross-claims which might qualify for set-off under r.4.90. The facts are revealing. Dahl-Jensen was the mechanical services subcontractor on a project on which Bouygues was the contractor. The subcontract provided for adjudication and arbitration. Retention of five per cent was withheld, of which half was to be released thirty days after the completion certificate under the construction contract and the remainder after the certificate of making good defects under the project agreement. Over a year after commencing work, Dahl-Jensen's employment was terminated for failing to proceed with diligence and they left site. Bouygues arranged for the works to be completed by others although, by the hearing of the appeal in July 2000, the subcontract works had not been finally completed. Dahl-Jensen referred claims for delay and disruption, additional work and wrongful termination to adjudication. Bouygues then referred its cross-claims for overpayment, liquidated damages and post-termination losses to adjudication by a separate notice. The parties agreed that the cross-claims should be treated as a counterclaim in Dahl-Jensen's adjudication. 18–008

The adjudicator held that Dahl-Jensen's employment had been validly terminated and, after considering each element of the claim and counterclaim, awarded Dahl-Jensen £200,000. In doing so, he inadvertently gave credit for the whole retention even though it had not fallen due. Had he not done so, the decision would have been in favour of Bouygues for payment of £150,000. Dahl-Jensen had gone into voluntary liquidation the day before the adjudicator issued his decision. The liquidator applied to the court for summary judgment to enforce the decision. Although the adjudicator had made a mistake, it was made in connection with the disputes referred to him rather than a dispute falling outside his jurisdiction. He did not purport to decide that Dahl-Jensen were entitled to release of their retention. Dyson J. therefore ordered summary judgment: [2000] B.L.R. 49. He did not deal with Bouygues' claim for declarations that £150,000 was due and that the decision was void; nor did he consider Dahl-Jensen's application to stay Bouygues' claims to arbitration.

As r.4.90 had not been urged on the court by counsel for Bouygues, the summary judgment was upheld in the Court of Appeal subject to argument on a stay of execution. The liquidator's counsel opposed the stay because it presupposed that the liquidator would not deal with Bouygues' proof of debt in the ordinary way. Peter Gibson L.J. pointed out that counsel was appearing for the company in liquidation and was presumably in a position to inform the court of the liquidator's intentions as regards the proof, but the liquidator's counsel maintained he had no instructions.

Chadwick L.J. asked the liquidator's counsel to explain of what value summary judgment would be to the liquidator. He pointed out para.23(2) of the Scheme for Construction Contracts, under which an adjudication decision did not inhibit the power of the court or an arbitrator to come to a different conclusion after hearing full argument and the evidence of both parties. Until that process had been completed, there could be no balance capable of enforcement by the liquidator since, by virtue of *Stein v Blake* [1996] 1 A.C. 243, the claim and counterclaim merged on the company's entry into liquidation. Nevertheless, the liquidator's counsel maintained that she could rely on the summary judgment as a judgment in her favour. Chadwick L.J. pressed him, and enquired how she could do so in any practical sense. If she issued a winding up petition based upon it there would be an outcry. If she tried to execute the judgment by sending in the sheriff or obtaining a third party debt order, there would be a similar outcry. Peter Gibson L.J. enquired what suffering would be caused by the grant of a stay. Counsel for the liquidator then conceded the stay but argued that it should only continue until the liquidator placed a value on Bouygues' proof and not until the outcome of any appeal to the Companies Court. Chadwick L.J. pointed out that an appeal to the Companies Court in the event of a rejection by the liquidator of Bouygues' proof was all part of the assessment process whereby the amount of the claim and cross-claim which had merged on liquidation would be ascertained. As a result, the court granted a stay of execution until the expiry of Bouygues' time for appeal against the liquidator's adjudication on its proof or the outcome of any appeal, if lodged.

Mutual dealings

18–009 The requirement for "mutual dealings" in r.4.90(1) is normally satisfied in a construction contract as each party owes obligations towards the other: *Willment v NW Thames* (1984) 26 B.L.R. 51 at 62. This was assumed in

Bouygues v Dahl-Jensen to have been satisfied by the claims in the two adjudication notices. A claim for damages for conversion brought by a contractor against an employer is not a dealing for the purposes of this rule: *Smith v Bridgend County Borough Council* [2002] B.L.R. 160. Berg (2002 at 23) argues that such damages ought to have been admitted for liquidation set-off on the basis that there were mutual dealings in that case: namely, the signature of the building contract between the parties and the employer's wrongful sale of plant owned by the contractor. He makes the point that conversion damages were admitted for liquidation set-off in *Gye v McIntyre* (1991) 171 C.L.R. 609 and *Lord v Great Eastern Railway* [1908] 2 K.B. 54 (reversed on appeal but not on this point), neither of which are referred to by Lord Hoffmann in his speech in *Smith v Bridgend Borough Council*.

The liquidator has a duty to apply r.4.90 where the creditor has a right to prove in the liquidation whether or not a proof is actually submitted: *Stein v Blake* [1996] 1 A.C. 243 at 253. In *Bouygues*' case, the proof of debt was submitted shortly before the hearing in the Court of Appeal. Bouygues had included an element of loss in respect of its cost to complete in its cross-claim in the adjudication, thereby putting the liquidator on notice of it on her appointment.

Taking the account

Rule 4.90(3) states that an account shall be taken of what is due from each party to the other and a set-off effected. This is mandatory and self-executing and the parties cannot contract out of it: *National Westminster Bank v Halesowen Presswork* [1972] A.C. 785. The account is taken by the liquidator as at the date the company went into liquidation, i.e. the resolution or winding up order. Since only the balance is provable, it is not possible for the liquidator to assign the debt owing to the company without taking into account a debt owed by the company: *Farley v Housing and Commercial Developments* (1984) 26 B.L.R. 66. The balance can however be assigned by the liquidator before the account is taken: *Stein v Blake* at 258. In *Bouygues*' case, although the cross-claim was unliquidated and/or contingent, in that it could not be ascertained until after the work had been completed by the replacement subcontractor, it qualified as a debt for the purpose of liquidation set-off. Under r.13.12(3), "debt" is defined very widely and includes a liability which is "present or future, whether it is certain or contingent, or whether its amount is fixed or liquidated, or is capable of being ascertained by fixed rules or is a matter of opinion". Liquidation set-off is therefore much wider than the general law. This is normally done on affidavit evidence. Under r.4.86, the liquidator has a duty to "estimate the value of any debt which, by reason of its being subject to any contingency or for any other reason, does not bear a certain value". It was assumed without argument by the Court of Appeal in that case that the extra cost to complete and associated losses flowing from the termination fell within r.4.90. If the proof is rejected, the creditor has 21 days in which to appeal to the Companies Court under r.4.83. **18–010**

As it is rare for a liquidator to continue trading in the construction industry, the usual components of liquidation set-off where the contractor goes into liquidation are certified sums, work in progress and loss and expense owing to the contractor and the employer's claims arising out of the completion contract. It is not unusual for the cost to complete to exceed the balance of the contract sum resulting in a net debt owed to the employer. If the employer has to arrange for a completion contractor to finish the works, it could take some time before the liquidator can take the account (see Ch.16). If retention is held in a trust account, only such sum as remains after the employer has exercised its right of recourse will be taken into account under r.4.90(3): see *Obaray v Gateway (London) Ltd* [2004] 1 B.C.L.C. 555, discussed in Ch.9. In the Australian case of *Silvia v Brodyn Pty Ltd* [2007] NSWCA 55, a concrete subcontractor obtained an adjudication decision in its favour after having repudiated its subcontract but before entering administration and later a deed of company arrangement. Under Australian law the equivalent of liquidation set-off applied to proofs of debt under the deed. The contractor made a substantial claim which was assessed at nil by the administrator. It was held that it ought to have been largely accepted and set off against the adjudication decision, leaving a balance provable by the contractor under the deed.

The Insolvency Rules 1986 allow a creditor to prove in the liquidation for a contingent liability owed by the company. If the contingency occurs after the start of the liquidation but before the account is taken the full debt can be proved: *Ellis v Dixon-Johnson* [1924] 1 Ch. 342 at 357. If it does not, the claim is estimated and the liquidator may make a distribution on that basis even if later events prove that the estimate was too low. Where a contingent liability is owed to the company, the new r.4.90(8) provides that it may also be set off but any balance due from the other person is recoverable only when it becomes due and payable. "In other words, the acceleration is limited to what is necessary to exhaust the set-off rights of the company in liquidation" (Goode 2005, para.8–39). The change addressed the mischief illustrated by *MPS Constructions v Rural Bank of New South Wales* (1980) 4 A.C.L.R. 835. In that case, a contractor went into liquidation and the liquidator decided to complete the contract in order to release retention from a trust account. The account was held by both parties on trust for the employer subject to completion by the contractor. After the works were completed, the employer refused to release the retention relying on set-off of a prior separate debt owed by the contractor. The court upheld the employer's set-off. At the date of the liquidation, the contractor's right to the retention was contingent and there was no provision allowing the liquidator to value it as if it were a "sum due" or to allow it in full on the occurrence of the contingency.

18–011 Where a contractor is in financial difficulty, the fact usually becomes known on site some time before the contractor becomes formally insolvent. Employers feel it prudent in such circumstances to delay payment and occasionally stop cheques before payment after learning of the contractor's liquidation. It has been held that, because of the liquidation set-off provision, the liquidator cannot obtain judgment by suing on the cheque because, by virtue of r.4.90, the employer's contingent claim has to be brought into account: *Willment v North West Thames RHA* (1984) 26 B.L.R. 51; *Re Jason Construction* (1972) 17 C.B.R. 158. As the completion contractor commences work, defects may be found in the works which will constitute additional contingent liabilities requiring valuation and proof at a later date. The employer may also sustain additional losses as a result of the termination, e.g. loss of rent.

The contractor may owe sums to subcontractors which have been certified together with the value of uncertified work done since the last valuation date. A subcontractor would also be entitled to losses flowing from the contractor's breach of contract which could include the cost of removing plant and equipment and materials from site (assuming the subcontractor is not engaged by the completion contractor), and loss and expense caused by the termination. If one of the standard forms has been used, only a nominated subcontractor is entitled to loss and expense following the termination; whether nominated or not, the subcontractor would be entitled to any loss and expense which had been incurred before the termination. The certified sum may not have been immediately payable but the contractor's liquidation accelerates the debt to make it payable immediately. Other claims will be unliquidated and require valuation by the liquidator. In the case both of subcontractors and suppliers, the liquidator may reduce their proofs of debt on the ground that they had acted unreasonably in refusing offers of engagement from the completion contractor.

Liquidators should be aware of two peculiarities in the industry: the entire contract and the letter of intent. If the contractor is entitled to payment only on completion of the works (with no express or implied provision for progress payments), there will be no sum due to set off against the employer's claim. Generally, only small contractors operate on entire contracts. The potential injustice of this rule is mitigated to an extent by the doctrine of substantial performance but this will only apply where the works have been practically completed. Where the value of work in progress justifies the cost of obtaining advice, the liquidator may be prudent to investigate whether a contractor or subcontractor has been working under a letter of intent. If so, it is possible that the employer or contractor as the case may be would not be entitled to prove for damages as a result of the failure to complete. And, more importantly, the liquidator could be entitled to claim payment in the form of a reasonable sum under a *quantum meruit* against which the employer would have no right of set-off, although it would have a right of abatement: *Farnsworth v Garrard* (1807) 1 Camp. 38. Each letter must be carefully examined because, although called a letter of intent, it may in fact be a contract.

Only balance is provable

Under r.4.90(8), only the net balance after the set-off is provable in the **18–012** liquidation or payable to the liquidator as the case may be. It would be unjust to force a debtor to pay sums due to the company while restricting it to a dividend in respect of sums owing by the company. The account can be taken by way of appeal against rejection of proof in the Companies Court or by litigation or arbitration which allows both claim and cross-claim to be decided in the same proceedings: see *Re B + B Construction* [2003] HKCFI 576 discussed in Ch.13. Usually the liquidator will sue and the debtor will put in a defence and counterclaim. Although technically they have merged, the claims are treated as if they still had a separate existence for this purpose.

In the *Bouygues* case, the Court of Appeal held that the concept of temporary finality which applies in ordinary situations under s.108(3) of the

Housing Grants, Construction and Regeneration Act 1996 could not apply where one party was in liquidation. In argument, Chadwick L.J. pointed out to counsel for both parties the tension that seemed to exist between the construction and the insolvency statutes. The purpose of liquidation set-off is to do justice between the parties. The rights conferred by the construction legislation are procedural in nature and have to yield to r.4.90, which gives a substantive right of security for payment: *Stein v Blake* [1996] 1 A.C. 243 at 251. Bouygues were committed to appeal because it was on the basis of their intention to appeal that they obtained a stay of execution from Dyson J. below. In the ordinary case, where a liquidator applies for summary judgment to enforce an adjudication decision, an injunction restraining him might be appropriate since summary judgment will, in the absence of agreement, not be an appropriate way of applying r.4.90. In this case, however, Bouygues took the initiative and were the first to issue proceedings in court claiming a declaration that the adjudicator's decision was void. It was in response to this that the liquidator sued to enforce the decision.

It is unusual for a liquidator to force a debtor to pay notwithstanding its assertion of a substantial cross-claim. The closest analogy is *Re Cushla* [1979] 3 All E.R. 415, in which HM Revenue & Customs paid a VAT refund to a liquidator unaware that the company in liquidation owed debts to other government departments. The Commissioners applied to the Companies Court who ordered the liquidator to repay the VAT refund as money paid under a mistake. Peter Gibson J. stated, at 423, that it would be "shocking to the sense of propriety of any fair-minded man that the liquidator should retain these moneys for the benefit of the creditors generally". It seems likely therefore that, had the liquidator of Dahl-Jensen been able to enforce the order for summary judgment, she would have been liable to repay it to Bouygues if it were later established that Bouygues' cross-claims overtopped Dahl-Jensen's claim. This would be an extension of *Re Cushla*, under which the payment was made by mistake. The claim against Bouygues was the main asset of the company and it is unlikely that the liquidator would have made an interim distribution to creditors before dealing with Bouygues' cross-claim. If she had done so, however, the question arises whether it would be too late for Bouygues to claim repayment once the liquidation set-off had been ascertained. This would be unjust but there appears to be no mechanism to unravel the fact that a distribution had been made other than to try and make the liquidator personally liable in some way.

Where one of the parties to an adjudication goes into liquidation, the effect of r.4.90 should be drawn to the adjudicator's attention. The other party should then check whether it has any cross-claims which are not being brought in the adjudication but which can (and should) be taken into account under r.4.90. A draft claim is needed on which to base a proof of debt. The proof should be served on the liquidator as soon as possible, even in outline form, as this may be sufficient to persuade him not to enforce an adjudicator's decision made in favour of the company. If necessary, it may be worth seeking an injunction restraining the further progress of the adjudication or an undertaking from the liquidator not to apply to enforce any decision before having placed a value on the client's proof of debt and allowed any appeal to the Companies Court to run its course.

Executory contracts

Assume a contractor goes into liquidation and has two contracts with the same employer. The first is front-end loaded (see Ch.8) and 75 per cent complete. The cost to complete would exceed the eventual receipts. The second contract is not front-end loaded and the cost to complete is less than the anticipated receipts. Subject to the effectiveness of any termination clause, the liquidator has power to complete the second contract and disclaim the first: *Asphaltic Limestone v City of Glasgow* [1907] S.C. 463. This process is known as "cherry-picking". By failing to complete the first contract, the liquidator is not barred from recovering the full value of the second on completion (Goode 2005, para.8–44). The employer could in such circumstances apply to the court for an order rescinding the contract and the court may in its discretion consider that it is just to do so under s.186 of the Insolvency Act 1986. Each case depends on its facts but where the liquidator is able to demonstrate an ability to complete the court will not grant rescission as of course. Rescission is perhaps more likely where there is a significant amount of work still to be done or the two contracts are so closely connected as to make it inequitable to allow the liquidator to enforce one if he is not prepared to procure the company's performance in the other. **18–013**

Where a liquidator continues a contract but is unable to satisfy the maintenance obligations, the employer is entitled to prove for its costs in doing so. Where the employer is entitled to prove, it is entitled to liquidation set-off: *Stein v Blake* [1996] A.C. 243 at 253. This situation arises with long-term contracts. In the leading case of *Re Asphaltic Wood Pavement* (1885) 30 Ch. D. 216, the contractor agreed to pave a street and keep it in repair for two years and, if during that time the employer gave notice, to maintain the street for a further fifteen years for an agreed fee. Before the work was completed, the contractor went into liquidation. The liquidator completed the works but was unable to ensure that the company would perform its maintenance obligations. The liquidator's claim to payment was therefore defeated by the employer's set-off of its damages claim as a contingent liability of the contractor. The principles underlying this case were explored in *Re West End Networks* [2004] A.C. 506 which concerned a liquidator's claim for a VAT credit of £7,000 against HM Revenue & Customs and a subrogated cross-claim in the liquidation of £11,000 by the Secretary of State in respect of redundancy payments made from the National Insurance Fund. The difficulty was that the liability to repay VAT existed as a debt before the company went into liquidation but the liability in respect of employment rights was incurred afterwards. Lord Hoffmann stated:

> "It is sufficient that there should have been an obligation arising out of the terms of a contract or statute by which a debt sounding in money would become payable on the occurrence of some future event or events. The principle has typically been applied to claims for breach of contract where the contract was made before the insolvency date but the breach occurred afterwards . . . or claims for indemnity by a guarantor where the guarantee was given before the insolvency date but the guarantor was called upon and paid afterwards" (para.9).

It made no difference whether the debt was created by contract or statute, or whether the statute created a contingent liability which existed before insolvency but fell due for payment and was paid only afterwards (para.19). The Secretary of State had a debt arising out of a statutory obligation which existed before the insolvency date which fell squarely within r.4.90 and had to be set off against the liquidator's claim, leaving the Secretary of State to prove for the shortfall.

See also *Panorama Development v Fitzroya Investments* [2003] 1 S.L.R. 93, in which a developer entered into contracts for the sale of units whereby the purchase price was payable by instalments as the construction of the development proceeded. In the event of delay to completion, the developer agreed to pay liquidated damages to the purchasers, alternatively to allow the purchasers to set them off against any unpaid instalment. The developer went into liquidation shortly before completing the work. At that time completion under the contracts of sale was already delayed and liquidated damages were payable, but no instalment was due. After the liquidator had the building work completed, the final instalment of the price fell due which the liquidator claimed from the purchasers. They paid only the balance after setting off liquidated damages accrued both before and after the liquidation. The High Court of Singapore held them entitled to do so. The court applied *Re Asphaltic Wood Pavement*. In addition, the terms of the contracts of sale were prescribed by housing legislation and could not be regarded as contravening the *pari passu* rule (para.134). By that legislation, any instalments received by the developer had to be paid into a project account which would not form part of its property available for distribution to creditors on a liquidation; the fund had to be applied for the purposes of the contract of sale. That meant that, if the liquidator had chosen not to complete the development, the fund would have been available to compensate the purchasers in priority to other creditors of the developer. Although the word "trust" is not used, it appears that the terms of the contracts of sale were also the terms of a statutory trust.

3. Administration

18–014 Service of a notice, e.g. making time of the essence or accepting a repudiation, is not prohibited by s.11 of the Insolvency Act 1986: see *Re Olympia and York* [1993] B.C.L.C. 453. It ought to follow that a company's entry into administration has no effect on the parties' rights of set-off, at least in respect of equitable or contractual set-off: see *Electro Magnetic v Development Bank of Singapore* [1994] 1 S.L.R. 734. In *Smith v Bridgend County Borough Council* [2002] B.L.R. 160, equitable set-off was denied to an employer against a claim by a contractor in administration, not because of the status of the contractor but due to the fact that the contractor's claim was for damages in conversion (for criticism, see Berg 2002, 21).

As regards legal set-off, Derham (2003, at para.6.10) argues that, as it applies only to money claims which are enforceable by action, and actions against a company in administration cannot be brought without the consent of the administrator or leave of the court, it cannot be used in this situation. Nor is set-off the enforcement of a security for the purposes of the section. In *Morrison-Knudson v Australian National Railways* (1996) 22 A.C.S.R. 262 an administrator appointed to a contractor under the Australian Corporations Law (which is analogous to the English procedure although the timetable for holding creditors' meetings is much shorter) applied for directions whether a payment he had received was subject to a valid set-off. Both claims were liquidated.

The contractor's claim was for a sum due under an agreement with the client to maintain 25 trains over a period of 12 years. The cross-claim was for a sum due under a subcontract whereby the client undertook to carry out some of the obligations of the contractor under the maintenance agreement. The client's set-off claim was denied because there was a clear no set-off provision in the maintenance agreement. Otherwise, equitable set-off might well have been allowed. Under the maintenance agreement the creditor's claim for payment was mainly in respect of work done by the debtor under the subcontract. In addition, payment under the subcontract was made conditional on receipt of payment under the maintenance agreement. The client had paid the sum due under the maintenance agreement in respect of which it was cross-claiming and it would appear to be unjust to deprive it of its "return share". Alternatively, the client could have claimed a legal set-off as it seems that both claims were liquidated subject to the objection expressed by Derham above.

Because of the difference in policy underlying administration and liquidation, r.4.90 did not originally apply to administration: *Isovel Contracts v ABB Building Technologies* (2002) 1 B.C.L.C. 390. The rationale was that an administrator had very limited powers to make distributions to creditors. By Sch.B1, para.65(2) of the Insolvency Act 1986, a new power has been introduced as from September 30, 2003 to make distributions to general creditors if authorised to do so by the court. If the administrator gives notice of intent to make a distribution, r.2.85 will apply which in effect imposes the same set-off regime as applies to companies in liquidation under r.4.90. Thus, where the administrator makes a distribution to unsecured creditors, rules regarding set-off in insolvency have been harmonised, whether the company is in administration or liquidation. The set-off applies in that situation to claims owed by and to the company as at the start of the administration. At that time it may well not be known whether distributions will be made by the administrator. The question arises: what happens to a cross-claim arising between the start of the administration and service of the notice? It has been suggested that if the cross-claim cannot be subject to administration set-off, that the creditor only has a right to a dividend, unless it can persuade the administrator to treat it as an "expense" of the administration (Turing 2005, 166). Even tht may not afford total protection, e.g. if there are insufficient assets to meet all expenses in full (Lightman and Moss 2007, para.20–044). **18–015**

4. Company voluntary arrangement

A voluntary arrangement is treated as a kind of statutory contract or "statutory binding" between the debtor and each of its creditors. Like a contract, a voluntary arrangement can expressly modify common law rights of set-off. Thus, if the debtor tried to improve its position after an arrangement has been sanctioned by taking an assignment from another creditor bound by the arrangement, it would probably find itself unable to resist payment to the supervisor since its cross-claim would of necessity be subject to the terms of the arrangement. Where the assigning creditor is not **18–016** bound by the arrangement the position is more complicated. If the creditors approve a CVA as the exit route from the administration, it is for them to decide as a body when voting on the administrator's proposal how to treat their rights of set-off.

Chapter 19

Bonds and Guarantees

Bonds and guarantees have been required in connection with construction work for centuries (Salzman 1952, Simpson 1966, 403). They provide an informal security for performance by the contractor and occasionaly by the employer (for the distinction between formal and informal security see Ch.2). There is an enormous range of documents: many are drafted specifically for individual projects; there are some standard forms but even they tend to be amended by the parties. Although these documents are short, they often cause confusion. There are a number of reasons for this. Mainstream construction law concerns contract and tort whereas the law relating to guarantees is derived from less familiar principles of equity. The case law has arisen from commercial spheres such as banking or international sale of goods which have their own terminology. This has led to a plethora of terms used in different contexts to describe the same thing. The industry has persisted in the use of the conditional bond, a form of obligation which is otherwise largely obsolete. Bonds and guarantees are often dealt with last in the procurement process and may not be properly integrated with the other contract documents. Compromises during negotiations can leave them in an ambiguous state. **19–001**

1. The three variables

Bonds and guarantees can be considered by reference to three variables: the form in which they are expressed, the commercial function they are intended to perform, and the legal obligation they contain (*Attaleia Marine v Bimeh Iran* [1993] 2 Lloyd's Rep. 497 at 502). It is important in this context to make a distinction between primary and secondary obligations. A primary obligation is one in which the person undertaking the obligation (the obligor) is liable to the person benefiting from it (the obligee) without reference to the liability of any other person. An example is an indemnity by which an obligor promises to make a payment on the occurrence of a specific event. An obligation is secondary where its enforceability is contingent on a breach of an obligation owed to the obligee by a third person. This is a suretyship obligation or guarantee. Consider the following statements. The obligation is primary in statements 1 to 6, and secondary in 7 and 8. **19–002**

1. I promise to pay you up to £1 million on 1 June (single bond).
2. I promise to pay you up to £1 million if you ask me in writing (on demand bond).

3. I promise to pay you up to £1 million on receipt of your written demand accompanied by an arbitration award or a judgment in your favour for the amount of your demand (documentary demand bond).
4. I promise to pay you the cost of reinstating the works if they are damaged by fire (insurance).
5. I promise you that I will perform my contract with Peter (collateral warranty).
6. I promise to pay you up to £1 million on condition that if I perform my contract with you my promise is void (conditional bond with primary obligation).
7. I promise to pay you up to £1 million on condition that if Peter performs his contract with you my promise is void (conditional bond with secondary obligation).
8. I promise that my son Peter will perform his contract with you (parent company guarantee).

The court has also referred to hybrid obligations: *General Surety v Francis Parker* (1977) 16 B.L.R. 16. These arise where primary and secondary obligations feature in the same document or where it mixes terminology associated with both. The court then has the difficult task of making sense of apparently contradictory language. Where the obligation is ambiguous, the court has sometimes been influenced when construing it by the form in which it is expressed: a letter, a formal contract document or a bond. These documents can contain any form of obligation. In practice, a letter is the form preferred by banks and usually contains a primary obligation, whereas contracts and bonds are used for secondary obligations, but this is not necessarily so. The banking letter is an anomaly: it could be classed as a single bond but for the fact that it is not usually executed as a deed; it could be regarded as a contract but for the apparent absence of consideration. It appears to be either a contract between the bank and the obligee, the consideration being implied as the obligee's promise to enter into the construction contract (*Jaks (UK) Limited v Cera Investment Bank* [1998] 2 Lloyd's Rep. 89) or an autonomous payment undertaking not requiring consideration (Goode 2004, 72; Bailey 2003, 247, n.37). The fact that a bond is a deed means it can be enforced by the beneficiary even if it is not a party, e.g. *OTV Birwelco v Technical & General* (2002) 84 Con. L.R. 117. In that case a surety bond was sealed by the subcontractor as co-obligor in its trading name rather than its registered name. It was held that this did not prevent the bond being executed as a deed to enable the beneficiary to sue. The execution by the surety was not tainted as a result (paras.57–8).

In construing a document, the court will take account of its commercial function. Bonds and guarantees perform both general and specific functions (Ch.2). The most common general function is protection against insolvency: a primary obligation is a source of cash flow to finance the completion of the project, while a secondary obligation is a source of compensation once the project has been completed and the obligee's loss ascertained. The other general function is protection against default: in this context a primary obligation allows the obligee to call for payment on account of its loss without delay ("pay now, argue later"), whereas the beneficiary of a secondary obligation has to wait until liability has been proved and quantum of loss established. Specific functions range between obligations of performance in general and payment in particular. Performance obligations include the completion and maintenance of the works, the achievement of required efficiency and output levels, the duty to enter into a contract following a successful tender, and statutory duties under the Highways Act 1980. Payment obligations concern advances, retention, stage payments, liquidated damages and customs duty.

There is little uniformity in the titles given to bonds and guarantees. Broadly, those containing primary obligations are called "on demand" bonds or demand guarantees, while secondary obligations tend to be called default bonds or suretyship guarantees. The range of expressions used is set out in Fig.19.1. "Performance bond" is perhaps the most confusing as it is used freely to describe both types of obligation: bankers use it to describe a primary obligation, contractors use it for secondary obligations. Issuers are described as obligors, bondsmen or guarantors. Those receiving bonds and guarantees are called obligees or beneficiaries. The person on whose behalf the document is issued is known as the principal debtor or the account party.

Primary obligation	*Secondary obligation*
on demand bond	surety bond
demand guarantee	conditional bond
bank guarantee	default bond
standby letter of credit	parent company guarantee
documentary demand bond	guarantee
single bond	insurance bond
payment undertaking	suretyship guarantee
perfomance bond	perfomance bond

Fig.19.1

2. Primary obligations

A construction contract contains primary obligations: for example, the contractor's duty to carry out the work and the employer's duty to pay for it. On international sale of goods contracts, the means of payment is often by letter of credit issued by the buyer's bank. The credit is paid on the seller presenting documents to the bank. Since it does not depend for its enforceability on the liability of a third person, the credit is a primary obligation. The bank takes an indemnity from the buyer for the amount of the credit and may require a cash deposit or some other form of security. **19–003**

In the 1970s, employers on international construction projects began to require security for performance in the form of a primary obligation from the contractor's bank (Pierce 1993). This obligation was expressed in the form of a letter in which the bank promised to pay up to a fixed amount on receipt of the employer's first written demand without making any enquiry as to the position under the contract. These letters were originally called performance bonds. Although primary in obligation, they are secondary in function since unlike letters of credit they are not intended as the means of payment but as a source of compensation should the contractor fail to perform. Nevertheless, in the earliest reported case on these documents, Lord Denning M.R. equated primary obligations of this kind with letters of credit: *Edward Owen v Barclays Bank* [1978] 1 Q.B. 159. In other words, function was subordinated to obligation.

> "The first principle which the cases establish is that a performance bond, like a letter of credit, will generally be found to be conditioned upon the presentation of one or more documents, rather than upon the actual existence of facts which those documents assert. If the letter of credit or bond requires a document asserting that goods have been shipped or that a contract has been broken, and if such a document is presented, the bank must pay. *It is nothing to the point that the document is untruthful, and that the goods have not been shipped or the contract not broken*" (*IE Contractors v Lloyd's Bank* (1990) 51 B.L.R. 1 at 7–8, *per* Staughton, L.J., emphasis added).

The bank may be liable to pay on receipt of a simple demand but it is common for more to be required, for example an assertion that the contractor is in breach or a statement of the nature of the breach. Although these additional requirements are sometimes referred to as conditions (CUP 1994 refers to a "conditional demand bond"), they impose little extra burden on the employer, especially where the document provides that statements by the employer are conclusive evidence of their own validity and that the amount claimed is legally payable: *Bache v Banque Vernes* [1973] 2 Lloyd's Rep. 437. In that case, Lord Denning M.R. famously equated the effect of the conclusive evidence clause with his idea of an interim certificate being equivalent to cash (at 440).

19–004 Provided the issuer's liability depends on the presentation of a document, it will remain primary in character. So a requirement for a demand to be accompanied by a certificate of a third person, e.g. an engineer, will not alter the fundamental nature of the obligation, even if the third person has to state that the contractor is in breach and give relevant clause numbers and details of the factual background: *GUR Corporation v Trust Bank of Africa* (unreported, October 26, 1986, Leggatt J., noted in Andrews and Millett 2005, 525 and 553). The issuer's obligation is primary even where the demand has to be accompanied by a copy of a court judgment or arbitration award (see Fig.19.2).

Some standard forms of guarantee contain primary obligations, e.g. those annexed to recent JCT forms in respect of advance payment, retention and off-site materials, similar documents annexed to FIDIC (1999), World Bank standard bidding documents, and contracts published by the Institution of Chemical Engineers. The I Chem E Red Book (2nd edn) gives the parties the option of requiring different documents to be served with the demand, ranging from a statement of breach to an arbitration award. In its demand, the employer has to state that it has given the contractor 14 days written notice of intention to claim under the bond. The International Chamber of Commerce has developed a sophisticated set of Uniform Rules for Demand Guarantees (ICC No.458) to accompany its model forms (ICC No.503). The rules can be incorporated by reference into the guarantee, e.g. FIDIC (1999). See *Bateman Project Engineering v Resolute* (2002) 18 B.C.L. 41 for a construction bond securing obligations under a target cost

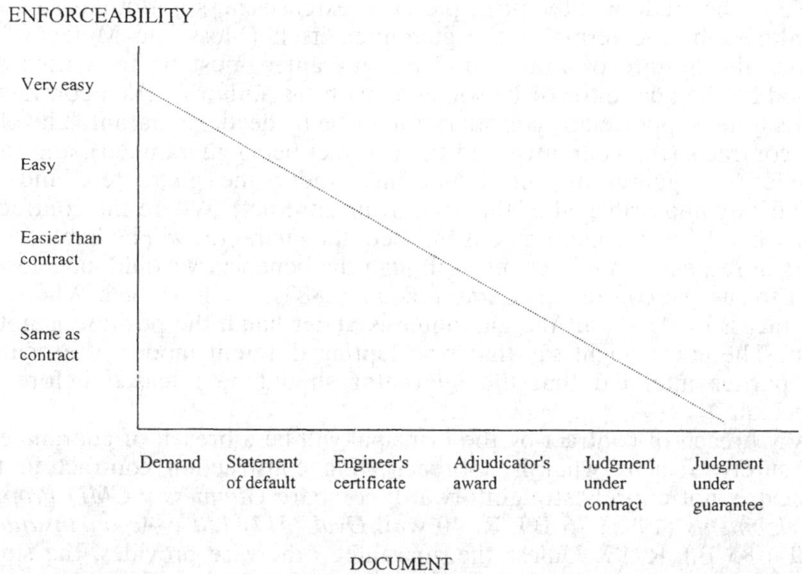

Fig.19.2

pain-gain share arrangement incorporating these rules. The main innovation is Art.20 by which the beneficiary, when making a demand, has to state that the contractor is in breach and describe the nature of the breach. An ICC bond can be enforced even where a breach has not occurred but Art.20 is intended to encourage the honest and fair use of such documents. Another ICC publication, ISP 98, deals with standby letters of credit (Goode 2004, 1015–1029).

3. Secondary obligations

Under an open contract of guarantee, all that is required is that there be some form of words which the court can construe as a "contract to answer for the debt, default or miscarriage of another" (Halsbury, 4th edn, 20(1), para.101). In modern English, the guarantor's obligation is to see to it that one person (the principal) does something for another person (the beneficiary) or to perform the principal's obligation if he does not: *Moschi v Lep Air* [1973] A.C. 331. If the guarantor fails to do this, he is liable in damages to the beneficiary. The guarantor's primary duty is not to pay damages in the event of the principal's default but to ensure the performance of the principal's obligations, unless the guarantee expressly limits the guarantor's obligation to the payment of damages. **19–005**

General principles of suretyship

A guarantor's liability is secondary to that of the principal, contingent rather than actual, unless and until the principal defaults ("the accessory principle"); and a guarantor is liable to the same extent as the principal is **19–006** liable to the creditor ("the principle of co-extensiveness"). Both aspects can be altered by the terms of the guarantee itself (Moss and Marks 1999). Under the Statute of Frauds 1677, a guarantee must be in writing and signed by the guarantor or by someone with his authority. As a contract, it needs to be supported by consideration or be by deed. A guarantee involves two contracts (the guarantee and the contract being guaranteed), and three people (the guarantor and beneficiary under the guarantee, and the beneficiary and principal of the underlying contract). Where the contract is under hand, but the guarantee is by deed, the guarantor will be liable for 12 years in respect of a breach, even though the beneficiary would have lost its right to sue the contractor: *Carter v White* (1883) 25 Ch. D. 666. Where the contract is by deed, but the guarantee is under hand, the position is not so clear. The court might say that by adopting different modes of execution the parties intended that the guarantor should be released before the principal.

Any breach of contract by the principal will be a breach of guarantee by the surety. Exactly what is a breach of a construction contract in this context is not entirely straightforward: compare *Guinness v CMD Property Developments* (1995) 76 B.L.R. 40 with *Oval (717) Ltd v Aegon Insurance* (1997) 85 B.L.R. 97. Unless the guarantee otherwise provides, the surety becomes immediately liable without any need for the beneficiary to serve a demand. The beneficiary will not usually take action against the guarantor unless the principal fails to remedy the breach. An award of an arbitrator appointed under the contract is not binding on the surety unless the guarantee so provides: *Re Kitchen, ex parte Young* (1881) L.R. 17 Ch. D 668; *Ards BC v Northern Bank* [1994] N.I. 121.

It appears that a guarantee will be construed in the same way as any other contract. Where there is a dispute concerning the scope of the guarantee, it will not be construed against the beneficiary. To the extent that the guarantee attempts to exclude rights implied at common law, however, its terms will be construed strictly. This appears to be the conclusion of Arden L.J. in *Egan v Static Control Components* [2004] 2 Lloyd's Rep. 429 (at para.37). In that case, a director gave a personal guarantee to a creditor in respect of "the price of all trade goods that you may supply" to his company. Nine months later, the company went into administrative receivership at which time it owed the creditor £112,000, of which only £14,000 represented the value of goods supplied after the date of the guarantee. The director argued that, on its true construction, the guarantee only applied to the £14,000. The Court of Appeal held him liable for the whole amount. On a director's guarantee for future rather than past supplies see also *Vadasz v Pioneer Concrete* (1994) 62 S.A.S.R. 150.

It is sometimes difficult to ascertain what exactly has been guaranteed. This question not only relates to the nature of the guarantor's obligation but also concerns defences available to it. For example, in *Try Build v Blue Star Garages* (1998) 66 Con. L.R. 90 a football club became insolvent owing a contractor £1.6 million. The contractor withdrew from site for non-payment but later returned and completed the work after entering into an agreement with the employer and a third party, Blue Star, whereby the debt was rescheduled. As part of the agreement, Blue Star provided a guarantee to the contractor. On the employer's default under the rescheduling agreement the contractor sued the guarantor. One of the defences raised was that the sum claimed represented excessive valuations by the contractor under JCT 81, giving rise to cross-claims for abatement. The defence failed because the guarantee was given in respect of sums admitted due in the rescheduling agreement rather than sums claimed as interim valuations. Further, the guarantee expressly excluded any right of cross-claim by the guarantor and treated demands served by the contractor as conclusive evidence that the amounts claimed were correct in the absence of manifest error, i.e. obvious mistakes or arithmetical errors rather than any question of valuation.

Exoneration of the surety

The surety is entitled to be relieved from liability (exonerated) under the **19–007** guarantee to the same extent as the principal has defences to liability under the contract. In *Langford Concrete v Finlay* [1978] 1 N.S.W.L.R. 14, a director of a contractor gave a guarantee to a subcontractor for payment "of all moneys which are now payable or may in the future become payable". It was held that the director could rely on abatement to reduce the subcontractor's claim. It was not necessary for the contractor to be joined as a party in light of its liquidation. The existence of a right of set-off in the principal debtor (the contractor in *Langford Concrete v Finlay*) when the beneficiary's claim arises also limits the payment obligation falling on the guarantor: *BOC v Centeon* (1999) 63 Con. L.R. 104 at 120. Although not formally decided, it seems that English law will not follow *Cellulose Products v Truda* (1970) 92 W.N. (NSW) 561, and will allow the guarantor the benefit of the principal's cross-claims even if they cannot be set off: *National Westminster Bank v Skelton* [1993] 1 W.L.R. 72. That case decided that if a director charges his home by way of legal mortgage to a bank as security for payment for a loan to his company, he will not be able to resist a claim for possession by relying on a cross-claim for damages vested in the company as he could have done had he given an unsecured personal guarantee. Excluding set-off by the guarantor can render a secondary obligation virtually the equivalent of an on demand bond.

A surety will be relieved from liability in certain cases by reason of the creditor's conduct. If the creditor alters the obligation which the surety has guaranteed without the surety's consent, he risks releasing the surety altogether: *Holme v Brunskill* (1878) 3 Q.B.D. 495. The case concerned a lease of a sheep farm in Wales. There was a guarantee for the redelivery of the flock of sheep in good condition at the end of the lease. Without the guarantor's knowledge, the tenant surrendered one of the fields in return for a reduction in rent. Even though the variation made no substantial difference to the lease, the guarantor was wholly discharged from liability.

> ". . . if it is not self-evident that the alteration is unsubstantial, or one which cannot be prejudicial to the surety, the Court . . . will hold that in such a case the surety himself must be the sole judge whether or not he will consent to remain liable notwithstanding the alteration, and that if he has not so consented he will be discharged" (at 505–6, *per* Cotton L.J.).

This principle is very much alive today. A guarantor was recently discharged in *Marubeni v The Mongolian Government* [2005] 2 Lloyd's Rep. 231 because of alterations to the original contract through the compromise of disputes, rescheduling of payment obligations and the alteration of security rights that were not insubstantial and were prejudicial to the beneficiary. The underlying contract was for the supply of equipment for a cashmere processing plant for $19 million payable by 12 equal half-yearly instalments. There were two reschedulings of payment by way of refinancing packages. Similarly, a guarantee in respect of all liabilities "under or pursuant to" a loan agreement which permits the bank to vary the loan agreement without vitiating the guarantee will still be released if, on its true construction, the variation is a replacement outside the scope of the original agreement: *Triodos Bank v Dobbs* [2005] EWCA 630. But where further construction works are added by way of a new agreement rather than a variation of the original one, a guarantee may remain enforceable in respect of the original works without extending to the new work: *RWE-Industrie-Loesungen v Thyssen* [2006] EWHC 2111.

19–008 Unless this "no-variation" defence is excluded, the beneficiary runs the risk that the guarantee will be unenforceable. This applies especially to documents which are drafted by the parties, rather than by their lawyers, perhaps as a result of a deterioration in the debtor's financial position: see for example *St Microelectronics v Condor Insurance* [2006] 2 Lloyd's Rep. 525. In that case, a supply contract provided for payment within 55 days. This was supported by a guarantee of payment of sums falling due under those terms within a particular period. The debtor experienced cash flow problems and agreed with the creditor to make two advance payments in return for the creditor's agreement not to require cash with order in respect of future supplies. Christopher Clarke J. stated that, where the debt guaranteed is payable within a specified time, a guarantor can be discharged if the creditor supplies goods on terms that the price is payable immediately, or where the contract is varied so as to require the debtor to pay earlier, unless such a variation was obviously incapable of prejudicing the guarantor (para.36). The rationale is that in both cases the obligation guaranteed was not that contemplated by the guarantee. In this case, it was not that payments had been made before the expiry of the credit period because it was not a requirement of the guarantee that the debtor should wait until then before making any payments. The problem was that, in order to ensure future supplies without having to pay cash in advance, the debtor had undertaken a binding obligation to pay before the expiry of the credit period. As a consequence, the creditor failed in its application for summary judgment against the guarantor. It is also arguable that the guarantor could be discharged if the creditor obtains premature payment by threatening to commit what would be a breach of the underlying contract (para.52).

Normally, the rule in *Holme v Brunskill* is expressly excluded by the guarantee. In *Lloyds TSB Bank v Hayward* [2005] EWCA 466 the guarantor escaped on the basis that, although the rule had been excluded in the guarantee, it had been reinstated in a side letter written by the bank in discussions with the debtor on rescheduling payment obligations. Further areas of concern are cases where guarantors have been released through the beneficiary giving additional time to the contractor to pay or to perform (*General Steam Navigation v Rolt* (1859) 6 C.B. (N.S.) 550; *Greenwood v Francis* [1899] 1 Q.B. 312); or where the employer releases retention early, giving up an asset against which set-off could have been made, and increasing the likelihood of a claim against the guarantor: *Calvert v London Dock Co* (1838) 2 Keen's Rep. 638.

Other examples of the surety being discharged are the making of direct payments to subcontractors where this is not allowed by the contract (*Doe v Canadian Surety* [1937] S.C.R. 1), paying for materials on site without asking the contractor for proof it had paid for them (*Administrator-General of SW Africa v Trust Bank* [1982] 1 S.A.L.R. 635), and the novation of the contract where the contractor is released absolutely from liability (*Commercial Bank of Tasmania* [1893] A.C. 313; *Housing Guarantee Fund v Yusef* [1991] V.R. 17; but contrast *De Montfort Insurance v Lafferty* [1997] S.C. 335; *Wittmann (UK) Ltd v Willdav Engineering* [2007] EWCA 824, para.22). It is also possible for a surety to be discharged if the creditor enters into a voluntary arrangement with the debtor (*Johnson v Davies* [1999] Ch. 117) or makes deliberate overpayment to the debtor (*RWE-Industrie-Loesungen v Thyssen* [2006] EWHC 2111, at para.47). If the bond imposes a duty on the bondsman to complete the work, or procure completion through another contractor, and the employer has the works completed without notifying the bondsman of the original contractor's default, there may be grounds for the bondsman to claim release from liability: see the Canadian cases of *Marigold Holdings v Norem Construction* [1988] 5 W.W.R. 710, and *Frasergate v Western Surety* (1998) 38 C.L.R. (2d) 119 discussed in Van de Leigh (1999). **19–009**

In practice, these protections to sureties conferred by equity in the nineteenth century are usually excluded by the express terms of the guarantee. As with any attempt to exclude the general law, however, the words used must be clear and unambiguous: *Trafalgar House v General Surety* [1996] A.C. 199 at 208. An act which benefits the contractor will not necessarily benefit the surety. The protection given to sureties originates from nineteenth-century cases where the guarantee was given gratuitously, e.g. by another family member. The equivalent in the modern commercial context is a parent company guarantee. The issuers of surety bonds are fully paid for their services and there is an argument that their protection should therefore be reduced on the ground that they have priced for the risk that the contingency occurs: *Citadel v Johns-Manville* [1983] 1 S.C.R. 513, an idea noted with approval in *Mercers Company v New Hampshire* [1992] 2 Lloyd's Rep. 365 at 377.

Subrogation, indemnity and contribution

If the surety carries out the principal's obligation, he is entitled to all the rights the creditor had against the principal. In other words, the surety is subrogated to the creditor's rights (see Ch.15). If the creditor held security to support his rights, then the surety is also subrogated to the creditor's security. Arguably subrogation also arises in favour of the issuer of an on demand bond (Ward and McCormack 2000). As against the principal, the surety has a right of indemnity to the extent he has discharged the principal's obligation. The surety may take security in respect of the indemnity. For example, in *Re Rudd and Son* (1986) 2 B.C.C. 98,955 a bank issued a surety bond to a local authority in support of a builder's obligations to carry out roadworks. The bank had a mortgage over land securing all moneys owing by the builder. On the builder's liquidation, the local authority enforced the bond. It was held by the Court of Appeal that the bank's security covered the builder's contingent liability under its counter-indemnity. **19–010**

If there is more than one surety for the same obligation, the surety who discharges the obligation is entitled to look to the other for a contribution. The proportion varies depending on the terms of the guarantees. This is worth bearing in mind where an employer has the benefit of a parent company guarantee and a surety bond: if the employer chooses to enforce only against the bondsman, who meets the claim in full, the bondsman can call on the parent company for contribution, e.g. *Stimpson v Smith* [1999] 2 W.L.R. 1292. Such rights can be excluded or postponed, e.g. until after the creditor has been paid in full, but clear words would be needed: *Liberty Mutual v HSBC Bank* [2002] EWCA 691. The bond in that case was not intended to be called upon except in the event of the customer's insolvency. The customer went into liquidation and the bank appointed receivers under its fixed charge.

Where the guarantor undertakes a performance obligation and also indemnifies the employer against all losses flowing from breaches by the contractor, to what extent can the indemnity expose the guarantor to a wider liability than the guarantee obligation set out earlier in the clause? This depends in each case on the words used. The court has sometimes construed an indemnity in this context as simply mirroring in financial terms the guarantor's obligation to procure performance by the contractor: *Western Credit v Alberry* [1964] 2 All E.R. 938. In *Lumley General Insurance v Oceanfast Marine* [2001] NSWCA 479 on demand bonds were issued to an employer in respect of various contracts to build tugboats. A counter-indemnity was given to the bondsman by an associated company of the builder. On both builder and associate going into administration, the employer sustained a loss of approximately $15 million. The bonds were called and yielded compensation of $5 million. The question arose as to what the employer and the bondsman could claim by way of proof of debt in the two administrations. At first instance, it was held that only the employer could prove. But on appeal, it was held that in the administration of the builder the bondsman could prove for $5 million, and the employer for $10 million; and in the administration of the associated company the bondsman could prove for $5 million under the counter-indemnity. The "rule against double proofs" did not apply.

4. Parent company guarantees

19–011 A parent company guarantee is a contract between a parent company and a beneficiary by which the parent guarantees the performance of one of its subsidiaries under a separate contract between the subsidiary and the beneficiary. The term is commercial rather than legal since the guarantee may be given by an intermediate parent or the ultimate holding company and the words used can make the parent's liability wider than that of the subsidiary. It is sometimes the case that a guarantee issued by an insurance company is less onerous than a parent company guarantee. This is partly because surety companies have developed a practice of requiring notice of breaches of the guarantee within a set period after the breach and of imposing strict deadlines for the issue of proceedings. It is commercially difficult for a parent company to justify giving a guarantee of its subsidiary's performance which is of a lower standard of obligation than the construction contract. Many forms used in the industry impose a higher obligation, e.g. by making the parent liable even where part of the construction contract becomes unenforceable. A short letter can be sufficient evidence of a guarantee from another group company, e.g. *Planned Storage Systems v DPM Design* (2002) 87 Con. L.R. 23; contrast *Ballast v Laurieston Properties* [2005] CSOH 16. But a promise in a bidding document signed only by the subsidiary without authority to bind its parents that they would "guarantee all funding" to the employer "outlined in this document" was insufficient: *Carlton Communications v The Football League* [2002] EWHC 1650 (Langley J.).

Although at first sight it may seem advantageous to ask for a guarantee from the parent or the ultimate holding company in the group, this will not necessarily be effective if the only assets of the guarantor are shares in its subsidiaries. Where a subsidiary becomes insolvent, the interests of the guarantor as shareholder are subordinated to the interests of the creditors, with the guarantor receiving only what is left after all creditors have been paid in full. The answer is to obtain a guarantee from a company within the group which owns significant assets but it can be difficult to ascertain where control and ownership of assets really lies. The expression "parent company guarantee" tends to assume the simple model of a holding company owning 100 per cent of the shares in its subsidiaries, but with a major project it is likely that the contractor will be a member of a large group of companies. If a multinational is involved, there may be hundreds of companies within the group. Such a group has a molecular structure rather than the familiar rake or pyramid. Conversely, the parent will remain liable under the guarantee even if it sells the shares in the subsidiary unless it obtains a release from the beneficiary: *RWE-Industrie-Loesungen v Thyssen* [2006] EWHC 2111.

A parent company guarantee reduces the effect of abusive or unfair treatment of a subsidiary by other companies in the group. Muscat (1996) has identified four ways in which a subsidiary can be mistreated. The first is "subservience" where the subsidiary acts to its detriment in the interests of the holding company, another group company or the group as a whole. A subsidiary's interests may be sacrificed in favour of a policy of maximising the profit of the group; there may be a policy of transfer pricing which obscures the real cost of transactions between group companies (e.g. providing services to another group company at less than market value or leasing equipment from the other group company for more than its rental value); a business opportunity won by the subsidiary might be diverted to another group company; its assets may be mixed with those of other group companies without adequate records being kept to enable them to be separated later; its assets may be transferred and re-transferred at convenient times; and it may be subject to bogus service charges or forced loans at uncommercial rates. The detriment can be a reduction in the profitability or the net asset value of the subsidiary.

There is no presumption, however, that transfer of assets between group **19–012**
companies is of itself abusive. In *Hsin Chong Construction v Henble* (unreported, May 12, 2005 CFI (HK), noted in Suen and Cheung 2007, 131), a contractor claiming in respect of unpaid certified sums and prolongation applied for a freezing order against the employer in the amount of its claim and estimated legal costs. It appears that the employer was part of a group of companies. In refusing the order, Reyes J. stated that there was nothing surprising or unusual in transfers of the proceeds of sale of residential units to other group companies for use as working capital as they simply gave rise to inter-company debts. It was possible that

transfers could be attempts to evade liability to the contractor but there was no evidence of the employer's intention to act in such a way.

The second kind of mistreatment is under-capitalisation where the subsidiary is set up with an inadequate or a "creditor-proof" financial structure. Instead of taking a shareholder's risk by injecting equity, the holding company might finance the subsidiary through debt in the form of secured loans from itself, or the subsidiary may own no property but take everything on lease from the holding company terminable on the subsidiary's insolvency. Thirdly, there is isolation in an "integrated economic enterprise" where a business is sub-divided into a number of separate legal units. For example, vertical or horizontal integration can be abused by separating functions or assets to an uncommercial degree and isolating them in specific subsidiaries. Finally, there is misrepresentation, a group persona situation where the group gives the false impression that creditors are dealing with the holding company or that the holding company is prepared to back the subsidiary. By contrast, some construction groups expressly constitute subsidiaries as trading agents for the holding company, although this may not be clearly communicated to outsiders.

In *WJ Harte Construction v Scottish Homes* [1992] S.C. 99 an employer agreed to the contractor's request that the works be carried out by one of its associated companies. The associate was named as co-obligor in a surety bond provided to the employer. The associated company went into liquidation and the contract was terminated but the original contractor objected on the basis that there had been no novation and that it remained entitled to payment for the work done. At first instance, the contractor failed, the naming of the associate in the bond being especially determinative. On appeal, the contractor succeeded on the basis that the associate had acted as its agent in carrying out the work. Merely executing a bond in relation to the same work did not of itself amount to a novation of the underlying contract under Scottish law.

19–013 It is probably more common for the employer to ask the contractor to work for one of its associated companies. In *EC Gransden v Ballard* [2001] N.P.C. 80, this occurred one month after works commenced. The contractor agreed to the change of party on condition that the original employer (Ballard) guaranteed the associate's performance. On the associate's liquidation, Ballard disputed liability on the ground that the guarantee had been executed by the wife of its sole director without authorisation but was held liable to the contractor.

A parent company guarantee recognises the existence of a group of companies as an enterprise in its own right even though the law still focuses on individual entities within the group, e.g. *Adams v Cape Industries* [1990] B.C.L.C. 479. It also expresses the commercial reality for which the law has yet to evolve a framework. Suing a parent can force a quick settlement, especially if the timing is right, e.g. issuing proceedings just before the parent intends to sign an agreement with underwriters for a rights issue. A creditor may have little or no knowledge about the parent's affairs, and the proceedings may be a "shot in the dark", but they can be devastatingly successful. Apart from proceedings, simply alerting the parent to the subsidiary's predicament can stimulate a change of attitude by the subsidiary's directors. A dissatisfied trading partner might also consider a claim in tort against the parent, e.g. *Stocznia Gdanska v Latvian Shipping* [2002] 2 Lloyd's Rep. 436, in which a parent was found liable for indirectly inducing a subsidiary to repudiate its contracts with a shipbuilder. There are also statutory claims which a liquidator appointed over an insolvent subsidiary can bring against the parent (Ch.20), but these are speculative options and more problematic than a direct remedy against the parent in contract, hence the popularity of parent company guarantees.

5. Conditional bonds

There are two kinds of bond: single and double. A single bond is an undertaking to pay a sum of money without any conditions. Single bonds have largely become obsolete. A double bond consists of two parts: first, an obligation to pay a sum of money; second, a condition which contains the real agreement between the parties (Halsbury, 4th edn, Vol.13 at para.90). The precedent given by Emden (1st edn, 1882) contains only one condition, performance by the builder in accordance with the contract. **19–014**

Approaches to construction

> "The obligatory part of a bond, being for the benefit of the obligee, is always construed most strongly against the obligor, but the condition, being for the benefit of the obligor, is construed most strongly in his favour" (Halsbury, 4th edn, Vol.13 at para.177). **19–015**

In *Fairclough v Cigna Insurance* (unreported, September 11, 1991), the conditions of the bond were full performance by the subcontractor or payment of damages by the surety "on written notice by the Main Contractor to the Surety of default by the Sub-contractor (such notice to provide full comprehensive and irrefutable evidence in substantiation of the default)". Judge James Fox-Andrews Q.C. held that these words changed the ordinary standard of proof of balance of probability to that of "irrefutable evidence", which the court suggested (without specifically holding) meant the criminal burden of proof "beyond all reasonable doubt".

Double bonds are normally "conditioned for" the performance of another obligation which the bond is intended to secure, so that the bond will be void if the condition is performed: *Tins Industrial v Kono Insurance* (1987) 42 B.L.R. 110. If the bondsman is the same person as the contractor, the bond will take effect as an indemnity. If, as is now almost always the case, the bondsman is a third person such as a surety company (or the contractor and surety company are made jointly and severally liable as bondsman), and the condition of the bond is the proper performance of the building contract, it will contain a secondary obligation and take effect as a guarantee: *Trade Indemnity v Workington Harbour and Dock Board* [1937] A.C. 1. Such a guarantee is often called a surety bond (Scott and Reynolds 1994). The relation between a bond and a guarantee is shown in Fig.19.3.

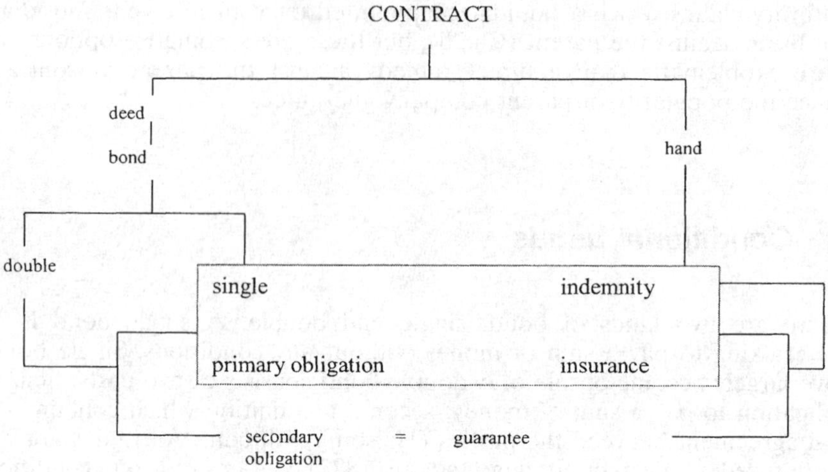

Fig.19.3

Disputes have arisen where the parties have used a conditional bond for a primary obligation. In a case involving an advance payment bond issued to an employer, of five judges who considered the document, one construed it as a guarantee of the underlying building contract, two as an on demand bond, while the remainder (who constituted the majority in the Court of Appeal) thought it was a guarantee by the bondsman of the contractor's obligation as co-obligor under the bond to earn the amount of the advance payment: *Mercers Company v New Hampshire* [1992] Lloyd's Rep. 365. In that case, the employer paid the contract sum in advance in order to avoid liability for VAT which was about to be extended to refurbishment contracts. The bondsman, jointly and severally with the contractor (Rush & Tompkins), promised to repay the advance of £4.5 million, on condition that if the advance were "liquidated in accordance with the terms of [the contract] and faithfully employed for the purpose of [the contract]" then the bond would be void. The contractor carried out work worth £1 million before going into receivership and the employer demanded immediate payment of the balance of £3.5 million.

19–016 The bondsman defended on two grounds: first that the document was a secondary obligation and the employer had to prove loss; second, that it should be discharged from liability since the contract had been varied by consent when possession of the site was deferred for longer than the contract allowed. It was held that delay in giving the contractor access to the site was not a variation but a simple breach which did not affect the employer's rights under the bond. Bonds of this kind are still being used in the industry. A primary obligation was also contained in a conditional bond in *Balfour Beatty v Technical and General Guarantee* (1999) 68 Con. L.R. 180.

To the layman, the layout of a surety bond gives the impression of enforceability without proof of loss. Thus, in *Perar v General Surety* (1994) 66 B.L.R. 72, a contractor working under JCT 81 became insolvent and the employer made a claim under a conditional bond. The claim failed because insolvency, although a termination event under the contract, is not in itself a breach of it (Ch.14). A breach would only result if, the contract having been completed and the losses arising from the termination ascertained, the contractor failed to pay any net balance due. The accounting exercise had not taken place by the time the claim was made (effectively overruling *Northwood v Aegon Insurance* (1994) 10 Const. L.J. 157). The position is different, however, where there are pre-existing breaches of contract before the intervention of insolvency: *Nene Housing Society v National Westminster Bank* (1980) 16 B.L.R. 22.

It has been argued that surety companies are keen on conditional bonds as their language and structure increase the prospect of avoiding liability (Wallace 1986). There have been some cases in which the bondsman has avoided liability on technical grounds, e.g. failure to notify the bondsman of all breaches within one month of their coming to its attention: *Oval (717) Ltd v Aegon Insurance* (1997) 85 B.L.R. 97. But it seems more likely that the conditional bond has survived because of the conservatism of the construction industry and because, on a deeper level, "conditional bond" accurately represents the psychological relationship between employers and contractors.

One of the current problems with conditional bonds arises from the way **19–017** the conditions relate to each other. The norm is to make the bond void on the performance of any of the conditions, i.e. they are to be construed disjunctively. Where only two conditions are inserted, namely performance of the contract or payment of damages in lieu, this makes sense. As was seen in the discussion on secondary obligations above, an obligation to indemnify in this context is normally the mirror image of the guarantee of performance. But where a third condition is added, uncertainty may arise as to its intended effect on the other two.

The third condition tends to deal either with the expiry of the bond or the effect of the contractor's insolvency. The question of expiry of guarantees of construction contracts is considered later in this chapter; but it is worth noting here that if expiry becomes a condition, there is scope for confusion between the substance of the obligation and its duration. If a contractor's employment is terminated for insolvency, there will normally be no breach of the bond until a failure by the contractor to pay any sum found due to the employer after the works have been completed by another contractor: *Perar v General Surety* (1994) 66 B.L.R. 72. A surety bond is not intended to provide access to immediate cash and, provided there is no problem arising from the expiry clause, there is nothing repugnant in requiring the employer to wait until after the completion contract has been finished before making a claim under the bond.

In an attempt to improve on their position, some beneficiaries have inserted as a third condition that the bondsman pays damages attributable to insolvency (which is defined in the bond as a contractual default) or complies with an adjudication procedure in the bond whose purpose is to ascertain losses caused by insolvency before finalisation of the accounts of the completion contract (Ch.16). Such provisions need careful drafting. In some cases they may add nothing because they have not displaced the accessory principle (described in para.19–006 above). In others, they may even benefit the bondsman, e.g. if he can establish that the claim accrued before insolvency. If the conditions are construed disjunctively, the question arises as to whether the bondsman could avoid part of its liability overall by performing the third condition. In practice, if the whole document is a secondary guarantee, the court may take a robust approach to construction and say that performance of the third condition (satisfaction of damages flowing from an insolvency termination) cannot have been intended to discharge accrued losses from prior breaches. In *Laing and Morrison-Knudson v Aegon Insurance* (1997) 86 B.L.R. 70 it was unsuccessfully argued that the loss claimed under the bond resulted not from the works contractor's default or its insolvency but from the management contractor's decision to terminate the contract.

Standard forms

19–018 The industry received a shock in 1994 when the Court of Appeal in *Trafalgar House v General Surety* (1994) 66 B.L.R. 42 construed a bond in the ICE (5th edn) form as a primary obligation. The decision was later overruled by the House of Lords: [1996] A.C. 199. Following this case, the Association of British Insurers (ABI) decided to produce a new guarantee in the form of a contract document rather than a conditional bond. Old habits die hard, however, and the document was entitled a "Guarantee Bond" (issued 1995, amended 2002). One of the problems with the ABI bond is that it does not resolve the perceived difficulty caused by the *Perar* decision referred to in the previous section. Employers have therefore made amendments to the form. In *Tower Housing v Technical & General Guarantee* (1997) 87 B.L.R. 82, such amendments did not work and the employer failed in a claim for summary judgment against the bondsman following the receivership of the contractor. The bond provided that the surety would:

> ". . . in the event of a proven breach of the contract by the contractor and/or in the event of the determination of the contractor's employment under the contract for reasons of insolvency whether such determination is automatic or otherwise . . . satisfy and discharge the net damages sustained by the employer as established and ascertained pursuant to and in accordance with the provisions of the contract, after taking into account all sums due or to become due to the contractor thereunder and all retention monies held, provided that nothing therein contained shall oblige the employer to await completion of the works prior to making any proper demand hereunder."

For reasons which are not explained in the judgment, the employer issued proceedings against the bondsman before the completion contract had reached practical completion and the additional cost to complete had been quantified. It may be that, as a housing association, the employer lacked access to funds to bring the works to completion without a contribution from the bondsman. The proviso did not enable the employer to recover before the works had been completed since no "proper demand" could be made under cl.27 of JCT 81 until that had happened. The proviso could only refer to a sum due to the employer under some other provision of the contract. If an employer needs help with cash flow to fund the completion contract, it should stipulate for an on demand bond or a hybrid bond entitling it to a payment on account. Compare *Paddington Churches v Tower & General Guarantee* [1999] B.L.R. 244 in which it was held that the reference to determination in the bond did not accelerate the bondsman's liability, which remained conditional on the employer's statement under cl.27.

The ABI bond imposes a secondary obligation to pay damages in the event of a breach by the contractor. Its purpose is to serve as a financial long-stop, primarily in the event of insolvency (ABI 2002). It is in the form of a deed but is expressed as a contract rather than a bond. It is interesting to note the ways in which it favours the issuer by cutting down obligations found in an open contract of guarantee. First, the obligation guaranteed is not to perform the contract in the place of the contractor but to pay damages in lieu, and there is a maximum cap on liability. Second, there is a question on the wording whether and to what extent the beneficiary has to pursue its remedies under the contract before claiming under the bond (Pike 2004). This would be a derogation from the general law which requires clear language. Even so, given that the bond is a device for managing insolvency risk, ambiguity in this area is undesirable. Third, the expiry provisions attempt to ensure that the guarantor is released on expiry (anticipated as practical completion or earlier sectional completion) unless there has been both a breach and notification of a claim before that event. Under the general law, depending on the precise words of the expiry provision, the guarantor would remain liable for the whole limitation period: *National House-Building Council v Fraser* [1983] 1 All E.R. 1090; compare *BCCI v Simjee* [1997] C.L.C. 135, CA. In *Econ Piling v Aviva General Insurance* [2006] SGHC 76 there was no expiry provision and the court construed the bond as perpetual.

The ABI explanatory guide (2002) is at pains to stress that the bond will be an effective source of compensation for an employer following a contractor insolvency once it has had the works completed and the accounting process in the termination clause has taken place, provided that "a claim in writing containing particulars of such breach" is made before the bond expires. The guide states that where expiry is defined as practical completion under the contract, "expiry under the bond will not occur", citing *City of Glasgow District Council v Excess Insurance (No. 2)* [1990] S.L.T. 225. But the ABI guide does not mention that bondsmen sometimes argue the opposite: *De Vere Hotels v Aegon Insurance* [1998] C.I.L.L. 1346. In practice, bonds are often the last project documents to be agreed and are dealt with under considerable time pressure. It is not uncommon for expiry to be defined by reference to a longstop date or to an event occurring under another contract, e.g. a subcontract bond might expire on practical completion under the main contract. These are perfectly reasonable terms, but they expose the beneficiary to the risk that the bond might expire before the occurrence of the default which it is intended to guarantee.

The obligation of the bondsman under the ABI bond is to satisfy the **19–019** damages suffered by the beneficiary up to a fixed amount. Unless the bond provides otherwise, "damages" will include costs awarded to the beneficiary. In *Ards BC v Northern Bank* [1994] N.I. 121, the bonded sum was £5,848. An arbitrator awarded the beneficiary £2,227 damages with costs of £9,823. It was held that the beneficiary was entitled to recover the full bond value, leaving it to prove in the liquidation of the principal debtor for the unpaid balance of its costs.

In contrast to the ABI bond, the document attached to ICE (6th edn) has retained the form of a conditional bond. This bond is interesting in containing an arbitration agreement whose ambit is any dispute or difference between employer and contractor concerning the date or otherwise as to the withholding of the defects correction certificate. In September 1999, a new form of bond was issued for use with ICE (7th edn). Under this form, the surety is liable to pay any sum certified by the engineer under cl.65(5) which has remained unpaid for 28 days. If the surety disputes the certificate, it can refer the matter to adjudication in accordance with cl.66 as if it had been a party to the contract. The surety agrees to be bound by the adjudicator's decision. The form is therefore an unusual indemnity to pay against documents and proof of default.

FIDIC (4th edn, 1987) has several standard forms of guarantee. It is curious, given that this form is intended for use internationally, that the draftsman has chosen the English conditional bond form. Both the FIDIC performance guarantee and the performance bond contain secondary obligations. In the first, it is a condition of the guarantor's liability that the employer obtains an award against the contractor, an exception to the normal law of guarantees. The performance bond follows American precedents in apparently making the guarantor's liability conditional on the employer having performed its obligations under the contract; and entitling the guarantor to complete or obtain bids from completion contractors. Under this bond, the employer loses a certain amount of control. Such factors may explain why, according to Bertrams (2000, 373), these forms have hardly been used in practice. FIDIC (1999) has a new suite of documents, of which only the parent company guarantee (although describing itself as a primary obligation) and surety bond are secondary obligations, the latter incorporating the Uniform Rules for Contract Bonds published by the International Chamber of Commerce (ICC No.524). These rules are being increasingly used in a wide range of jurisdictions, notably Japan. Other forms with secondary obligations are those used in connection with the MF/1 and G/90 main contracts, and issued by FASS, CCS and CECA for use with subcontracts. The Engineering and Construction Contract published by the ICE (NEC3, 2005) has optional clauses in relation to performance securities but no standard forms are provided.

6. Hybrid obligations

19–020 A guarantee may contain hybrid obligations if it mixes terminology associated with primary and secondary obligations. For example, in *Esal Commodities v Oriental Credit* [1985] 2 Lloyd's Rep. 546, the document stated: "We undertake to pay the said amount [$487,300] on your written demand in the event that the supplier fails to execute the contract in perfect performance . . ." The issuer argued that it was a secondary obligation. In construing it as a primary obligation, the court was influenced by the function of the document, holding that:

> "if the performance bond was so conditional, then unless there was clear evidence that the seller admitted that he was in breach of the contract of sale, payment could never safely be made by the bank except on the judgment of a competent Court of jurisdiction and this result would be wholly inconsistent with the entire object of the transaction, namely to enable the beneficiary to obtain prompt and certain payment" (at 549, *per* Ackner L.J.).

See also *IE Contractors v Lloyd's Bank* (1990) 51 B.L.R. 1; *Airport Authority Hong Kong v American Home Assurance* [2000] HKCFI 161, noted in Soo 2001); *Roehampton Developments v FAI General Insurance* [2000] WASC 235, *American Home Assurance v Hong Lam Marine* [1999] 3 S.L.R. 682. In *United Trading v Allied Arab Bank* [1985] 2 Lloyd's Rep. 554, Ackner L.J. stated that "to delay payment under such documents strikes not only at the proper working of international commerce but also at the reputation and standing of the international banking community" (at 561). Wording such as that used in *Esal Commodities* has been used in illustrative forms provided to customers by some of the clearing banks.

In *Marubeni v The Mongolian Government* [2005] 2 Lloyd's Rep. 231, the guarantee was issued by a foreign government rather than a bank and stated that the guarantor "unconditionally pledges to pay to you upon your simple demand all monies payable under the Agreement if not paid when the same becomes due . . ." The guarantor also "pledged" the performance of all the other terms of the agreement and indemnified the beneficiary against cost and damage occasioned by failure to pay or to perform any other term. There was no financial limit in the guarantee. The starting point adopted by the court was that the guarantee was not a banking instrument, either in terms of its self-description or the nature of its issuer (para.30). Banking cases on similar wording such as *Esal Commodities* were not helpful precedents (para.28). It was held by the Court of Appeal that the document constituted a secondary obligation, with a primary obligation in the form of the indemnity against cost or damage (compare *Canmer v UK Mutual* [2005] EWHC 1694 at para.50). The question arises whether the guarantee could still have been construed as a secondary obligation if it had been issued by a bank, especially as it had no financial limit, which is very unusual for a banking instrument.

Another kind of hybrid obligation occurs where the same document contains primary and secondary obligations in different clauses. *Harmon v Cigna Insurance* (unreported, April 16, 1992) concerned a conditional bond for £22 million which contained the following additional clause: **19–021**

> "Notwithstanding the foregoing, Obligee may demand 5% of the value of the bond subject to written notice of 10 days to the Principal specifying the reasons for the calling of the bond, with an additional 14 days (after the expiration of the initial 10 day notice period) for the right of the Principal to begin remedy."

Although at first sight a primary obligation, the clause was construed as secondary in the light of its reference to "remedy". The court reached the same conclusion in *TBV Power v Elm Energy* (unreported, November 21, 1995) which concerned a conditional bond for £3.8 million. After setting out the conditions of the bond, there were two provisos. The first stated that, if the employer served a written demand stating that a sum of money was due pursuant to a certificate issued under certain clauses of the contract, the bondsman's obligation would be to discharge the amount stated in the certificate either on the expiry of the time limit for serving an adjudication notice or, where a notice was served, on the issue of the adjudicator's decision. The obligation under the bond would not become null and void until after all payments due under this proviso had been made. The second proviso contained an arbitration agreement similar to that found in the ICE bond. The employer made a demand under the first proviso for the whole of the bond value. The court concluded that, construing the bond as a whole, the first proviso did not remove the bondsman's right under the conditions to make the bond null and void by paying damages. By including an arbitration agreement in the bond, the parties had recognised the possibility that such damages could be less than the bond value.

> "With the possibility that Seaboard's [the bondsman's] liability to pay damages in a sum less than the amount of the bond, a requirement that Seaboard should make full payment now and then seek repayment of some or all of the moneys at a later date does not suggest a construction that the parties intended . . . The absence of any provisions in the bond for repayment militates against [it] being other than a contract of guarantee" (*per* Judge James Fox-Andrews Q.C.).

See also the New Zealand standard form of bond TP/Wks 1 (Kennedy-Grant 1999, 411). In contrast, a proviso in a surety bond issued in support of a time charter obliging the surety, in the event of any default and on written demand, to pay the penal sum within 30 days, was held at first instance to constitute "a true on-demand performance bond": *Maridive & Oil Services v CNA Insurance* [2002] 2 Lloyd's Rep. 9. In these examples, what appears at first sight to be a hybrid obligation is resolved by the court into either a primary or a secondary obligation.

The bond in *TBV Power v Elm Energy* can be contrasted with the retention bond issued by the Civil Engineering Contractors Association (CECA) for use with GC and PC/Works/1 with Quantities (1998) Sub-contract. This form begins as a conditional bond under which the sub-contractor and the surety are jointly and severally bound to the contractor in a specific sum (a secondary obligation). However, cl.3 sets out a primary obligation to pay the contractor up to the whole of the bond value on receipt of its written demand. If the demand is for the whole bond value, the contractor can deduct retention from future progress payments. The bond states that it will be discharged on the fulfilment of the conditions of the secondary obligation or on the satisfaction of a demand made under the primary obligation. Although likely to cause confusion to subcontractors, there is no reason why a document cannot contain both kinds of obligation, and there may be good commercial reasons why the contractor would choose to enforce the secondary obligation first. The primary obligation could be abused since it is for the whole retention rather than gradually accruing as the work proceeds. In theory a contractor could call the bond in full at an early stage of the subcontract and then start withholding retention in the normal way. The contractor would be forced to issue proceedings for an interim payment to recover some of the bond proceeds but this may be impractical and the subcontractor may have to wait until agreement of its final account before obtaining a refund.

19–022 A default bond sometimes contains a primary obligation activated on the principal's insolvency so as to entitle the beneficiary to demand up to a fixed amount as an interim payment on account of the surety's liability. The employer may be required to apply the money for the purpose of the contract by paying it into a trust account and reporting to the surety periodically as to how the money has been spent. Alternatively, the default bond may include an expert procedure available to the beneficiary at its discretion enabling it to obtain provisional payments on account. The procedure may thus take effect as a primary obligation: *Odebrecht v North Sea Production* [1992] 2 All E.R. (Comm.) 405.

A similar process is at work in a guarantee which, after setting out a secondary obligation, constitutes the guarantor a "primary obligor" and goes on to say that it shall be liable to the beneficiary as if it had been the principal debtor: see *MS Fashions v BCCI* [1993] Ch. 425. It is a question of construction in each case whether this wording imposes a collateral indemnity obligation on the issuer independent of its duty as guarantor, e.g. *Raytheon v Space Cargo* (unreported, July 27, 2000, Jack J.); *Wittmann (UK) Ltd v Willdav Engineering* [2007] EWCA 824, para.22. Such a term is found in the form of parent company guarantee included with the CECA subcontract referred to above. In *Gold Coast v Caja de Ahorros* [2002] 1 Lloyd's Rep. 617, a refund guarantee securing repayment of stage payments under a shipbuilding contract was enforceable on service of a certificate from the buyer's bank stating: the amount of the stage payments made, the date of such payments, that the buyer was entitled to a refund under the contract, and that the builder had not made the refund. The report stated that the bank had provided all the finance for the transaction which was secured by an assignment of the contract together with the refund guarantees. It appears that the demand was served by the bank as agent for the buyer, rather than as assignee, and the Court of Appeal proceeded on the basis that the bank had taken legal advice and had reasonable grounds for issuing the certificate in good faith (para.8). Tuckey L.J. stated:

> "It might be unusual for a bank to undertake such a task but a first-class bank will obviously have to do so conscientiously in the knowledge that it could expose itself to the risk of being sued if it does not. The bank does not, of course, have to issue the certificate if it does not feel able to do so, in which case any call under the refund guarantees would have to await resolution by arbitration or settlement of the underlying dispute" (para.22).

Whether the obligation was primary or secondary depended on whether the bank, as signatory to the demand could satisfy itself on the merits of the buyer's claim! One wonders what the arrangements were between the buyer and the bank regulating the issue of the certificate.

7. Retention bonds

Retention is a special feature of the industry (ch.3). In return for its early **19–023**
release or payment gross without deduction, contractors often provide a retention bond. The purpose of such a bond is said to be:

> "to allow the contractor to realise his profit at the earliest moment so long as he continues to fulfil his contractual obligations, and secondly that the purchaser is entitled to reverse the position at any moment at his discretion if he has cause to object to the contractor's performance. *It must be emphasised that the rights and obligations of the parties are not affected by either the giving or calling of the bond*" (I Chem E Guide, 1980 at 47, emphasis added).

The sentiment is understandable—even desirable—but it does not reflect the legal position. In law the substitution of a bond for a contractual term represents a shift from bilateral agreement to unilateral obligation.

1. Unless the contract clearly states otherwise, the proceeds of a bond call belong absolutely to the employer, subject to an implied duty to give credit for them when agreeing the contractor's final account: *Anaconda Operations v Fluor Daniel* [1999] VSCA 214. They will not necessarily revert to the status of retention for the purpose of release at practical completion and the making good of defects.

2. Retention gradually increases as the relevant percentage, say five per cent, is withheld from the gross value of monthly certificates and it will take some time before the employer owes a significant debt against which it can set off a cross-claim. If retention is not withheld, and the retention bond is for five per cent of the contract sum from the start, the employer is better off receiving a bond.

3. Retention bonds are normally expressed as primary obligations, enforceable on presentation of a statement by the employer that the contractor is in default under the contract even though the contractor may have performed satisfactorily. Had retention not been bonded, the contractor might have been able to obtain an interim payment or even summary judgment in respect of retention. While the employer might be ordered to make an interim payment in an amount equivalent to the proceeds of the bond call, it is less likely since the court prefers not to interfere with primary obligations, even where the relief is directed to the proceeds.

4. If the contract limits the employer's right of recourse against retention, for example, to rights of deduction rather than rights of set-off under the general law, and retention is bonded, the employer may argue that its right to make a demand under the bond is unfettered. Although the bond is a substituted obligation it does not necessarily follow that restrictions in the contract will also apply to the bond: *Costain International v Davy McKee* (unreported, November 25, 1990, CA).

5. The contractor can be prejudiced if the terms of the bond do not accurately reflect the contract. This is especially so with reduction and expiry provisions. For example, a bank may refuse to reduce the bonded sum where there is no requirement under the contract to issue the certificate required under the bond, or where the bond purports to refer to a certificate issued under the contract but misdescribes it. If the bond has a dispute procedure, the contractor may find itself having to pay for the continued existence of the bond, and the cost of the dispute procedure, and remain on risk longer than it should have been.

6. On a major project, retention may be bonded in tranches, as it reaches pre-agreed levels. As a result, there may be more than one retention bond. This opens up the possibility of delays in reduction and expiry, and also problems in enforcement, especially where the terms of the bond, or the identities of the bondsmen, are different. It may be arguable that they reduce (or are to be called) *pro rata* or consecutively.

7. If retention is withheld, the employer owes the contractor a conditional debt which is defeasible by its own rights of recourse. If retention is bonded, the employer has a contingent asset in the form of the right to call the bonds. If a bond is called, the contractor becomes a contingent

creditor of the employer in respect of a claim for repayment under the contract. If the employer is insolvent at the time the call is made, the directors could become personally liable by creating the contingent debt in respect of retention. A claim might be framed in fraudulent trading, wrongful trading or misfeasance (Ch.20).

It has been held in Australia that evidence that a demand was made to pressure a contractor to settle a dispute will not vitiate a primary obligation or amount to fraud allowing the contractor to obtain an injunction: *Wood Hall v Pipeline Authority* (1978) 141 C.L.R. 443. Where the contract provided for a bond instead of retention and the contractor procured a bank guarantee but went into receivership before completing the works, it was held that the employer was entitled to set off against bond moneys amounts representing direct payments made to subcontractors and that the employer was obliged to pay any surplus to the contractor rather than the bank: *Australian Conference v Mainline* (1978) 141 C.L.R. 335. Contrast *Tradigrain v State Trading Corporation of India* [2006] 1 Lloyd's Rep. 216, discussed later in relation to the counter-indemnity.

8. Tender Bonds

The tender process on a construction project may take many months and **19–024** involve both employers and tenderers in considerable cost. Tender bonds, or bid bonds, compensate the employer for losses sustained if the contractor fails to follow through the tender process to the end. The form of bond varies widely but usually allows the client to call it in the following situations: if the contractor withdraws its tender without the employer's consent; the contractor is the successful tenderer but fails to enter into a formal contract; or the successful tenderer enters into a contract but fails to provide a performance or payment bond in accordance with it (Jones 1990). The usual reason for withdrawal of tenders is that a contractor realises it has made a serious pricing error. In an extreme case, the error could lead to insolvency if the contractor has to enter into a contract at its tender rates.

If the contractor experiences financial difficulties between the submission and acceptance of its tender, it may find itself with inadequate cash cover or asset value to support the performance bond. In that event, the contractor may be able to persuade the employer to accept an increased retention or reach some other arrangement whereby no call is made on the bid bond. Can a call be made against a tender bond if the employer fails to enter into the contract by reason of insolvency? As a call will not be prevented in the absence of clear and established fraud, a contractor ought to insert as a condition of the bond that the employer must have remained willing and able to enter into a contract. Article 6 of the Uniform Rules for Demand Guarantees (ICC No. 458) goes some way to tackling this problem by providing that the bond expires "in the event of the beneficiary expressly deciding that he does not intend to place a contract".

The amount stated in the bond may be a specific sum or a percentage of the tender price (between one and five per cent) subject to a maximum sum. Bid bonds are usually primary obligations. It has been suggested that the sum covered by a bid bond could be viewed as the "agreed price for the privilege of being permitted to tender" (Capper 1990). Where a bid bond provides that a performance bond must be procured if the tenderer is successful, it is important to ensure that the latter comes into effect only when the former has expired. Otherwise, a contractor may find its bonding capacity exhausted because of unreturned bid bonds on projects it has no hope of winning. It has been known for a tender bond to be called to compensate an employer for losses allegedly incurred on another contract. If a bank issues a bid bond, it will not necessarily issue the replacement performance bond, e.g. if the nature of the risk alters in the meantime. As with on demand performance bonds, tender bonds have historically been a creature of international contracting. However, with changes in procurement methods, and perhaps as a consequence of the 1990s recession, they are now more common on projects in the UK. One of the earliest was required in connection with the Midland Metro project (*Construction News*, May 28, 1992).

9. Advance payment bonds

19–025 Advance payments are sought to cover mobilisation of plant and equipment, e.g. items of high capital value which have to be designed and manufactured specifically for the project. They can also cover the cost of transportation and housing for foreign workers and, where necessary, the cost of stockpiling materials in advance of need. There may be commercial reasons for making an advance which benefit the employer, e.g. to avoid VAT (*Mercers Company v New Hampshire* [1992] 2 Lloyd's Rep. 365). Whatever the reason, unless the employer retains some control over the advance it may be diverted to some other use or simply paid into the contractor's overdrawn bank account. The bond protects the employer against abuses of this kind.

Some of the difficulties inherent in advance payment bonds appear from *TTI Team Telecom v Axarte* [2005] EWHC 762. In that case, a specialist software supplier received an advance payment of £1 million on the start date of the contract which provided for payment against five milestones. The milestone payments were due on agreed dates rather than on stages of the work being achieved. In return, the supplier procured an advance payment bond from a bank in favour of the client. The contract was silent as to how the advance payment would be earned by performance or "repaid" but provided that the bond would only be enforced if the agreement were terminated. The bond was in the on demand form and was to reduce on presentation of certificates to the bank signed by both parties. In practice, this never happened. Payment was to be made against the client's certificate that the supplier was in breach and that the amount claimed represented "the extent of the supplier's liability to repay the said advance payment".

The supplier was entitled to five days advance notice of intention to enforce the bond which was expressly subject to ISP 98 (ICC No.590). The customer terminated the agreement and served notice of intention to draw down the whole of the bonded sum. The supplier applied for an injunction restraining the customer from calling the bond, arguing that as the agreement did not provide for the repayment of the advance, the bond could not be properly called since the client would not be in a position to serve the relevant certificates. However, the draft bond annexed to the contract stated that it was intended "for the fulfilment of [the supplier's] obligations under the agreement". As such it was available in respect of any breach by the supplier and the application was refused. Judge Anthony Thornton Q.C. reasoned that, because of the advance payment, the supplier would have received in stage payments a significantly greater sum than the value of the services provided at any time during the work. This imbalance would correct itself as the work proceeded unless the contract were terminated beforehand.

10. The counter-indemnity

Under a contract of indemnity, there is an undertaking to pay if a person suffers a loss or incurs a liability: *Yeoman Credit v Latter* [1961] 1 W.L.R. 828. There is no need to show who caused the loss or why or how it was caused, only that it was caused and was of the kind for which the indemnity was given: *Gulf Bank v Mitsubishi* [1994] 2 Lloyd's Rep. 145. Broadly speaking, an indemnity exposes the issuer to wider liabilities than a guarantee, does not give rise to common law defences, has a different effect on assignment and limitation, and is likely to be easier to enforce than a guarantee. **19–026**

Where a bank issues an on demand bond, it may require its customer to provide a cash deposit which can be drawn down in case the bond is called unless the contractor's net worth is such that an indemnity is sufficient and the bond is given against a special credit facility. Alternatively the indemnity may give the bank the right to call for a cash deposit if the principal is in breach of one of its terms or even on demand at any time on account of its contingent liability, e.g. *Mitsubishi Heavy Industries v Gulf Bank* (1997) C.L.C. 597, *Technical & General Guarantee v Patterson* (unreported, February 12, 2003, L Henderson Q.C.). Thus in *HCC International Insurance v Conway* [2006] EWHC 3646 a counter-indemnity given by a director of a contractor entitled the bondsman to demand that the whole of the bond amount be deposited with it "as collateral security for the bond." The bondsman was authorised to apply the deposit to reduce any liability under the bond, with any surplus being returned to the director. The contractor went into liquidation and the bondsman made a demand under the counter-indemnity. It was held by Cox J. that the counter-indemnity created a simple debtor-creditor relationship. It was a contract to provide cash security on demand. Although analogous to JCT clauses entitling a contractor to have retention funded on request considered in Ch.10, there was no evidence here that the deposit was to be held on trust. In granting summary judgment to the bondsman for the value of the bond, the judge stated that he was making an order for payment of a debt and not for specific performance of the obligation to provide the deposit.

On an international contract, local law may require the bond to be issued by a bank based in the country of performance of the works (the issuing bank). This is put in place by a chain of indemnities: after the contractor has given an indemnity (which may be secured by a charge over a cash deposit or some other property), its bank gives an indemnity in the form of a primary obligation to the issuing bank which then provides the bond to the employer (Fig.19.4). On a large project, the indemnity given to the issuing bank may have been syndicated to a group of participating banks (Kronfol 1983). The parties to a joint venture or a consortium agreement may agree to provide a counter-indemnity to a bank providing bonds to the employer on the basis that their liability should be several, e.g. one joint venturer might be liable for 70 per cent of a demand and the other for 30 per cent. If either failed to pay its relevant proportion, the bank could not then call on the other to make up the difference.

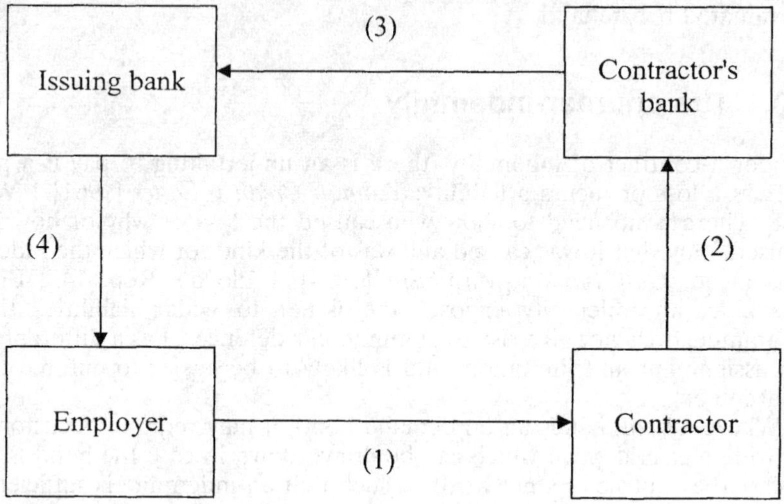

(1) Construction contract
(2) Counter-indemnity
(3) Indemnity/performance bond
(4) Performance bond

Fig.19.4

19–027 Indemnities sometimes oblige the contractor to pay on demand any sum which the bank has paid which was "properly due" or "in accordance with" the primary obligation. But some indemnities do not have this protection and expressly provide that the bank will be entitled to enforce the indemnity on demand even if it is not clear whether a valid demand has been made: *Technical & General Guarantee v Patterson* (unreported, February 12, 2003, L Henderson Q.C.); *Bollore v Banque Nationale de Paris* [1983] H.K.L.R. 78; contrast *Royal Bank of Scotland v Dinwoodie* [1987] S.L.T. 82. In *Liberty Mutual v HSBC Bank* [2002] EWCA 691 admiralty bonds were issued in default form by local banks backed by an indemnity from HSBC. As well as taking a general indemnity and a fixed charge over book debts, HSBC required the customer to procure in its favour a surety bond from Liberty in respect of each transaction. An issue in the case was whether HSBC could enforce the bond provided by Liberty simply by proving payment under its counter-indemnity to the local bank or whether it had to prove that the local bank had paid after judgment had been entered against it by the ultimate beneficiary. On the construction of the form of bond provided by Liberty in that case, the latter construction was held to be the correct one.

Compare this with *Wahda Bank v Arab Bank* (unreported, June 16, 1999, CA) in which the contractor's bank refused to honour a claim under a counter-indemnity given to an issuing bank in support of four performance bonds provided to a Libyan government agency. The counter-indemnity was governed by Libyan law. The agency had issued proceedings against the issuing bank in Libya which had been dismissed. It was held by the Court of Appeal that the contractor's bank was entitled to refuse to pay since the evidence was overwhelming that the contractor had fully performed the contract some years before, the demand had no basis and could not be made honestly. But where a Saudi bank honoured a call by the Saudi government under a performance bond and the contractor argued the contract had been completed three years previously, the court refused to give the contractor's parent leave to defend on the bank's application to enforce the parent's guarantee of the contractor's counter-indemnity: *Banque Saudi Fransi v Lear Siegler* [2007] 2 Lloyd's Rep. 47.

A bondsman who agrees to issue bonds on behalf of various companies **19–028** in a group can protect itself further by requiring them to agree to subordinate any claims for subrogation or proof they may have against each other (whether arising out of their liability to the bondsman or not) until after the bondsman has been fully indemnified. Such an arrangement will not infringe the *pari passu* rule: *Re SSSL Realisations* [2005] 1 B.C.L.C. 1.

The chain of indemnity in Fig.19.4 is demonstrated by *Tradigrain v State Trading Corporation of India* [2006] 1 Lloyd's Rep. 216. The case concerned a contract for the sale of goods but the principles apply equally to a construction contract, reading buyer as employer and seller as contractor. The buyer called a performance bond but the seller obtained an injunction in Switzerland preventing its bank from indemnifying the issuing bank. Arbitrators appointed under the contract rejected the buyer's claim and held that the call under the performance bond was unlawful. Christopher Clarke J. applying *Cargill v Bangladesh Sugar* [1998] 2 All E.R. 406, held it was an implied term of the contract that the buyer would account to the seller for the proceeds of the bond retaining only the amount of any loss suffered through the seller's breach. The proceeds of the bond were recoverable by the seller as a debt. The court expressed the view that, as the seller's bank had not indemnified the issuing bank, the seller would be under an obligation, on receipt of the money from the buyer, to pay the issuing bank since the performance bond was issued ultimately at their request (para.35). If the seller is insolvent when it receives the bond proceeds from the buyer, the question arises whether its bank or the issuing bank would have a proprietary claim to the moneys. At first instance in *Cargill v Bangladesh Sugar* [1996] 4 All E.R. 563 at 571, Morison J. considered that a trust would arise in favour of the issuing bank.

11. Disputes

Unfair calling

The separation of an on demand bond from the underlying contract opens **19–029** up the possibility of its being used unfairly. The question arises: will the court grant an injunction restraining the issuing bank from honouring a demand? Normally, an applicant for an injunction has to show three things: that there is a serious issue to be tried (i.e. that there is a cause of action), that damages would not be an adequate remedy and that, on a balance of convenience, it would cause less harm to grant the injunction than to preserve the *status quo*: *American Cyanamid v Ethicon* [1975] 1 All E.R. 504. Satisfying these tests is not sufficient in the case of demand bonds since the courts have chosen to equate them with letters of credit which, as autonomous obligations, must be honoured unless it can be shown that the demand was fraudulent: *Edward Owen v Barclays Bank* [1978] 1 Q.B. 159. The burden of proof is a high one: it is not sufficient to show a strongly arguable case of fraud; the applicant must establish that the only realistic inference from the facts is that the demand was fraudulent and that the bank was aware of the fraud: *GKN Contractors v Lloyds* (1985) 30 B.L.R. 48; *United City Merchants v Royal Bank of Canada* [1983] 1 A.C. 168; *United Trading v Allied Arab Bank* [1985] 2 Lloyd's Rep. 554. Such a high criterion is virtually impossible to satisfy.

The position may be different where the application is to restrain the beneficiary from making a demand. In *Themehelp v West* [1995] 4 All E.R. 215, the Court of Appeal upheld an injunction restraining a demand being made under a demand guarantee. The facts were unusual in that the fraud alleged concerned a misrepresentation inducing the underlying contract. The fraud did not relate to the guarantee or to the anticipated demand. Injunctions were also granted preventing the beneficiary from receiving payment in *Kvaerner v Midland Bank* (1998) C.L.C. 446 and *HLC Engenharia v ABN Amro* [2005] EWHC 2074 considered later. If there is evidence that the beneficiary will dissipate the proceeds the court may make a freezing order in lieu of an injunction restraining a demand: *Czarnikow-Rionda v Standard Bank* [1999] 1 Lloyd's Rep. 187.

Is it possible to rely on grounds other than fraud as a basis for an injunction against the beneficiary? The court has consistently refused to imply a term in the underlying contract that a demand will only be made under the bond where there is evidence of default or when there is reasonable and just cause. The court has also refused to imply any term into the bond itself: *Ermis v Banque Indosuez* (unreported, February 26, 1997, Thomas J.). The court has upheld an implied term of the contract that the beneficiary will account to the contractor for any excess of the bond proceeds over its actual loss, but this does not affect the principle of "pay now, argue later" or give the contractor any right to an injunction restraining payment in the meantime: *Cargill v Bangladesh Sugar* [1996] 4 All E.R. 563; affirmed [1998] 2 All E.R. 406.

19–030 It remains a possibility, however, that the *Cyanamid* principles will be sufficient where an injunction is sought on the ground that the bond has expired (*Gibraltar Homes v Agroman* (unreported, Gibraltar CA 15/96, Sir Brian Neill). *B+B Asia v Standard Chartered Bank* [1998] HKCFI 969); *Lorne Stewart v Hermes*, (unreported, October 22, 2001, Garland J.)); where there is an arguable case that the engineer is threatening to interfere with the underlying contract (*Press Construction v Penspen*, (unreported, April 16, 1996, Judge Michael Kershaw Q.C.); or where it can be shown that the beneficiary would not be able to repay the bond proceeds after the dispute between the parties has been resolved (*Bristol Meci v Ericsson* (unreported, October 25, 1996, CA)). In bond cases, damages are often not an adequate remedy to the contractor. This is because bond calls are comparatively rare and the contractor's reputation could be damaged if a bond call became widely known: *Hawker Siddeley Power v Peterborough Power* (unreported, May 9, 1994, Judge Peter Bowsher Q.C.). Invitations to tender may require contractors to state whether any bonds have been called against them. Bond insurance is available from the Export Credits Guarantee Department against the risk of unfair or abusive calls (see *http:// www.ecgd.co.uk*).

The contractor can sometimes rely on the bank not to honour a demand where there is a question over its validity. In *Balfour Beatty v Technical & General* (1999) 68 Con. L.R. 180, the beneficiary sought summary judgment against a bank under a demand guarantee. In what seems a refinement of the usual criteria, the Court of Appeal stated that if the evidence were powerful but not sufficient to show fraud, then judgment would either be entered with a stay of execution or refused until the other party's counterclaim under the contract had been fought out. In that case, a bond was given in support of a subcontract in the FCEC form which allows for termination on liquidation. The contractor terminated in reliance on an oral admission of liquidation from one of the directors of the subcontractor three days before the creditors' meeting. Although the point was not argued in the case, it is possible that the termination was premature (although perhaps hard for the subcontractor to dispute it in view of the director's admission). But the subcontractor relied on a requirement of the bond that the demand must be accompanied by a statement that the subcontractor was in default and that a specific sum was due and payable to the contractor. The Court of Appeal agreed that liquidation would not be a breach in most instances, although Waller L.J. was "not sure . . . whether on the terms of this contract that is right" (at 184). It seems the court thought that liquidation on the facts of this case would amount to an anticipatory breach. Nevertheless, until the work had been completed and the final account agreed, there was no specific sum due and payable under the subcontract. As the bond stated that the contractor's documents were conclusive evidence of the facts they asserted, they had to be accepted at face value and there was no arguable case of fraud. See also *Solo Industries v Canara Bank* [2001] 1 W.L.R. 1800.

The question arises: is it right to protect the interests of the issuing bank **19–031**
in all cases, e.g. even if the contractor suffers an injustice? Cases such as *Kvaerner v Midland Bank* and *Lorne Stewart v Hermes* (paras 19–041 and 19–038 below) show the court is fully aware of the tension between policy and justice in this area, although both cases have been criticised. In his research into Australian case law, Bailey (2003) reviews five possible situations in which an injunction could be granted, in addition to fraud: where there is no underlying contract (e.g. it is void for illegality); the demand is defective; the facts disclose unconscionability; the demand would be a breach of the underlying contract; and possibly lack of good faith. He makes the following proposal:

> "that the position of the law should be this: the bank is not entitled vis-à-vis the contractor (i.e. its customer) to pay the principal, and to enforce its counter-indemnity against the contractor, in circumstances where the bank is, at the time of payment, in possession of information which demonstrates clearly that the demand for payment made by the principal was unlawful and it can be said that the bank is, or that it ought to be, cognisant of this information and its meaning" (at 283).

He suggests that whichever ground is relied on, its existence should be the only realistic inference which can be drawn from the facts. Such a test might redress the balance in favour of the innocent contractor without unduly prejudicing the bank's position. "Unconscionability" as a ground for an injunction is being developed by the courts of Singapore. For example, an injunction was granted restraining a beneficiary from receiving payment in *Newtech Engineering v BKB Engineering* [2003] 4 S.L.R. 73. It appears that the beneficiary called the bonds with an ulterior motive of assisting its own flagging cash flow rather than in response to a default by its contract party. There was also a high risk of the beneficiary being unable to refund the bond proceeds.

The contractor may seek to protect itself against an unfair call by requiring the beneficiary to serve a copy of a judgment or award on the bondsman. The potential problems in restricting a beneficiary's rights to enforce a primary obligation are illustrated by *Sirius v FAI General Insurance* [2005] 1 All E.R. 191 (side letter with a letter of credit) and the Australian case of *Bachmann v BHP Power* [1999] 1 V.R. 420 (contractual restriction on converting standby credits into cash). Injunctions continue to be granted however where the contract is clear enough, e.g. *Rejan Constructions v Manningham Medical Centre* (2003) 19 B.C.L. 451.

Some jurisdictions have enacted legislation which can be invoked in this situation. In *Boral Formwork v Action Makers* [2003] NSWSC 713 a call under a standby letter of credit in excess of an agreed amount was declared unconscionable and ordered to be withdrawn pursuant to the Australian Trade Practices Act 1974. Section 51 of that Act provides that a company "must not, in trade or commerce, engage in conduct that is unconscionable." The call was made by administrative receivers appointed to an English supplier as beneficiary of a standby credit procured by an Australian contractor in support of a contract to purchase scaffolding components. Under the credit, the supplier had to state that the amount claimed was due and that a demand on the contractor had remained unsatisfied. The receivers called the whole amount of the credit even though the contractor had notified them that some of the goods were defective and had to be rectified and that the costs of rectification would be claimed from the supplier. The undisputed amount due would be paid. The receivers served a demand on the same date as making a call under the credit without responding to the contractor's claim in respect of the rectification costs. When the contractor protested, the receivers replied that it would be an unsecured creditor in a future liquidation of the supplier, and that no dividend was anticipated. Austin J. held that on a true construction of the supply agreement the supplier was under a duty to make an allowance for the defective goods. It followed that the receivers' statement in their call under the standby that the whole sum was due was false; and the statement that a demand remained unsatisfied was misleading. Even allowing for the principle of autonomy which applied to standby credits, their conduct was unconscionable, especially as they were fully aware of the repairs carried out by the contractor and had "acquiesced" in them.

Dispute resolution clauses

19–032 The presence of a dispute resolution clause in a bond can affect its construction: see *TBV Power v Elm Energy* (unreported, November 21, 1995) discussed earlier in connection with hybrid obligations. Disputes arising under bonds and guarantees are decided by the court since there is usually no arbitration clause in the bond, or if there is, it is limited in scope, as with the ICE bond (see Moss and Marks (1999) for precedents with ICC arbitration clauses).

In theory, it is open to an employer to sue a guarantor in court while at the same time arbitrating against the contractor to recover the same loss but there is a risk of inconsistent findings and wastage of costs. In *Alfred McAlpine v Unex* (1994) 38 Con. L.R. 63, the court refused to intervene to stay such an action pending the outcome of an arbitration. In *Alstom Combined Cycles v Aegon Insurance* (unreported, May 1, 2001, Judge Richard Seymour Q.C.), it seems that the judge stayed actions against the parent company and the guarantor pending the outcome of an arbitration brought against the employer by the contractor. One benefit of issuing the proceedings, however, was that the employer obtained undertakings from both parent and guarantor to abide by the award of the arbitrator. By contrast, in *Babcock Rosyth Defence v Grootcon* [1998] S.L.T. 1143, a parent company guarantee contained an arbitration agreement in terms of ICE (5th edn) while the underlying contract provided for disputes to be tried in the Scottish courts. On the facts, the contents of the guarantee were not sufficient to import the arbitration agreement into the contract.

Contractors often argue that on demand bonds should not be enforced pending the determination of the underlying dispute. In *Gold Coast v Caja de Ahorros* [2002] 1 Lloyd's Rep. 617, the contract provided that if the buyer rescinded the contract "subject to any arbitration" the builder should be liable to repay stage payments or the buyer could make a demand under refund guarantees. The guarantee was to remain in force until 21 days after a final award in arbitration proceedings started by the buyer or the builder. The issuing banks refused to honour a demand on the basis that the instrument was a default bond and an arbitration was ongoing. It was held that the words "subject to any arbitration" did not postpone the enforcement of the bond until after an arbitration but simply meant "without prejudice to the builder's rights to go to arbitration".

Arbitration

Some bonds and guarantees provide that disputes under them are to be **19–033**
referred to arbitration, e.g. most recently *Film Finance v Royal Bank of Scotland* [2007] EWHC 195. The guarantor may also agree in advance to have its dispute referred to an arbitrator appointed or to be appointed under the contract. Disputes under bonds and guarantees tend to focus on the beneficiary's entitlement to call, which in turn is likely to depend on the issue of documents under the bond or the contract. For example, in order to make a valid call, an employer may have to serve with its written demand a certificate of the engineer that the contractor is in breach. From the contractor's perspective, it may be possible to argue that the certificate was fraudulent or that the engineer's independence has been compromised. As such certificates are issued for the purposes of the bond, there is a certain logic in hearing this dispute by an arbitrator appointed under the bond. Other things may also depend on the issue of a certificate by the employer's agent, e.g. the increase or reduction in the bonded amount or the date of expiry of the bond. In such cases, a dispute may arise as to whether the contractor is entitled to the certificate, which a bond arbitrator could decide.

In *American Home Assurance v Hong Lam Marine* [1999] 3 S.L.R. 682 the Singapore Court of Appeal refused leave to appeal against an arbitrator's award made in a dispute between a bondsman and a ship owner concerning four bonds procured by a shipbuilder. A major issue was whether the bonds constituted primary or secondary obligations. This was held to be the "epitome of a 'one-off' case" (para.30) which suggests that bond arbitrations will be difficult to appeal against. It appears that the full bond wording is not set out in the judgment. Presumably it included an arbitration agreement.

Adjudication

19–034 In October 1995, the ICE issued a draft form of bond for consultation with a provision for adjudication where the bondsman disputes a claim. The purpose of the bond as explained in the guidance notes was to provide security against default in general (financial longstop) and protection against cash flow problems in particular. The adjudicator's jurisdiction is limited to deciding whether an event of default has occurred and/or the amount of the employer's loss. Both informal and formal insolvency are included as events of default. The document is not expressed as a bond in the traditional way. The adjudicator's decision is final for the purpose of the bond only, leaving it open to the parties to have their dispute heard in another forum after the bond has been paid. Since the reference to an adjudicator takes place after a call has been intimated, there could be more than one adjudication under the bond. The bond enables an employer in theory at least to obtain payment of a sum representing a future loss provided that the sum is claimed in good faith. The bond contains a provision that set-off is not allowed against a bond claim unless it has been certified by the engineer. In contrast to the NJCC form, it appears that claims are possible under this form of bond in respect of breaches occurring before expiry, even where the claim is made after expiry. The bonds issued with the sixth and seventh editions of ICE did not follow the format of this draft.

The form of subcontract bond published by the Confederation of Construction Specialists (1992) also contains an adjudication provision. The bond is conditional on the subcontractor's failure to remedy a default after service of two notices from the contractor. The adjudicator's jurisdiction is to decide on the basis of documents only whether the subcontractor has rectified the default and, if not, the amount payable by the guarantor. The adjudicator's decision is binding on the parties until the dispute is referred to arbitration or to the court. In an international case noted by Dixon *et al* (2005) an on demand performance bond incorporated an adjudication procedure in London under the CEDR Rules. The contract provided for ICC arbitration in Geneva. Shortly before the bond was due to expire, a call was made in its full amount. No reasons were given for the call. The contractor referred the demand to adjudication which was dealt with on documents only. In view of the fact that the employer had made no previous complaints of the contractor's performance, the adjudicator decided that nothing was due under the bond and the call could not be honoured. Apart from overcoming the hurdle posed by the fraud exception considered earlier, Dixon argues that the use of adjudication in this context would reduce the cost of construction as the need to make a provision in the tender for the bond value will be reduced.

Pre-arbitral referee

The International Bar Association has issued Illustrative Forms of Demand Guarantee which approach the problem of unfair calling from a different perspective (IBA 1992). The forms require the beneficiary to state that the principal is in default and to set out the nature of the breach. The bank's obligation to honour the call is deferred until either the principal confirms that it does not object to the demand or the beneficiary applies to the International Chamber of Commerce for a pre-arbitral reference on the validity of the call. The bank must then defer payment until the ICC gives its decision or until the beneficiary gives a counter-guarantee, if sooner. The bank is not concerned with the reference but only with documents. As well as constituting a source of ideas, the IBA forms have been used on high risk projects (Marston 2002). **19–035**

Reference to an expert

Bonds also sometimes contain an expert procedure, especially in connection with oil and gas projects: *Odebrecht v North Sea Production* [1992] 2 All E.R. (Comm) 405. **19–036**

12. Commercial factors

Expiry

In the construction industry, it is common for a guarantee to make express reference to expiry on one of the following: a fixed date, the issue of a certificate under the contract, or an event anticipated by the contract. If the guarantee is a secondary obligation and expires on one of the events given above, the beneficiary can sue the guarantor after expiry in respect of a prior breach: *National House-Building Council v Fraser* [1983] 1 All E.R. 1090. To make expiry a true cut-off point, the guarantee would have to say that after expiry the guarantor ceased to be liable to the beneficiary absolutely, even in respect of accrued causes of action, unless the beneficiary had already issued proceedings. In *Alstom Combined Cycles v Aegon Insurance* (unreported, May 1, 2001, Judge Richard Seymour Q.C.) the employer brought two actions, one under a surety bond and the other under a parent company guarantee, to recover the same loss of about £1.6 million as liquidated damages. One of the conditions rendering the bond null and void was the issue of the defects correction certificate. As this had been issued, Aegon argued that it was released from liability in respect of liquidated damages even though the action against it had been commenced before the certificate was issued. It was held (without referring to *NHBC v Fraser*) that the certificate could not affect previously crystallised claims (para.20). Alstom conceded that, had it not issued the proceedings before the certificate was issued, it would have had to repay Aegon (para.19). **19–037**

In *De Vere Hotels v Aegon Insurance* [1998] C.I.L.L. 1346 the surety provided a conditional bond for £1.6 million in support of a contract in JCT 81 form. The surety's liability was to expire on the issue of the statement of practical completion of the works. Any proceedings to enforce the bond had to be brought within six months after the date of practical completion named in the statement "and thereafter shall be absolutely barred". The contractor went into receivership before practical completion and the employer had the works completed by another contractor. Proceedings were issued more than six months after practical completion of the completion contract. On a preliminary issue, Judge Humphrey LLoyd Q.C. held that the employer was not barred from claiming under the bond since the proviso could only refer to practical completion under the original contract. As the contractor's employment terminated on its receivership, practical completion could never occur. The employer was under no obligation to enter into a completion contract or to do so on the same terms and with the same practical completion mechanism as the original contract. In addition, the completion contract did not include the whole of the works under the original contract. This case was followed in *Hong Kong Housing Society v China Insurance* [2000] HKCFI 359, where the bond was enforceable on demand. In *Associated British Ports v Hydro Soil Services* [2006] EWHC 1187 a contractor was obliged to procure a parent company guarantee in a form annexed to the contract. That form stated that the guarantee was to expire on the issue of a defects correction certificate. The guarantee actually provided had a fixed expiry date. The employer protested. After the expiry date had passed and defects had appeared in the works the employer sought an order for specific performance against the contractor to procure a guarantee from its parent in the contractual form. Judge Richard Havery Q.C. accepted that the employer had not waived its right to the guarantee in that form but refused to order specific performance (para.360). No reasons were given.

When issuing a primary obligation, a bank usually insists on a fixed expiry date, partly for ease of administration and partly to control its capital adequacy ratio, but the contract may require the bond to continue until practical completion or later. One solution is to insert a fixed date in the bond but require the contractor to procure the renewal of the bond or its replacement within a certain period before its expiry for as many times as is necessary until completion has been achieved. Were the contractor to refuse, the employer could treat the contractor's refusal as a breach of contract and call the bond. If so, and the contract is nearing completion or it is obvious that the employer is the net debtor, the contractor may immediately issue proceedings for repayment under the contract on the ground that, although technically in breach in failing to renew the bond, the employer's damages would be nominal. The employer occasionally stipulates for liquidated damages in respect of this breach but it is hard to see how they can be a genuine pre-estimate of loss. Where an employer instructs the bondsman to extend the period covered by a bond or pay, the court may regard such conduct as fraud: *Harbottle v National Westminster Bank* [1978] Q.B. 147. An "extend or pay" ultimatum is given in connection with all kinds of bonds, but particularly bid bonds where a prospective employer wants to keep all the tenderers in the frame and play them off against each other. If the contractor is obliged to keep a bond in force until practical completion and is threatening to allow it to expire, the employer may call it but place the proceeds on deposit until a replacement bond has been provided (Scriven *et al.* 1999, 213). The forms of primary obligation annexed to FIDIC (1999) allow the beneficiary to serve a demand where the secured obligation has not yet been performed and the contractor has in breach of contract failed to extend the period of the guarantee.

As in the case of express termination clauses, it may occasionally be necessary to serve a second demand in order to enforce a primary obligation: *Maridive & Oil Services v CNA Insurance* [2002] 2 Lloyd's Rep. 9. *OTV Birwelco v Technical & General* (2002) 84 Con. L.R. 117 arose out of a classic construction insolvency. Cash flow problems led a subcontractor to divert resources to another project. Labour shortages on site led to delays and defects and consequently the subcontractor abandoned the works and its conduct was treated as a repudiation by the contractor. It was a condition of the subcontract bond that "if a Final Certificate shall be issued pursuant to the provision of the Main Contract then upon the date stated therein this obligation shall be null and void". After the subcontractor's repudiation was accepted, the contractor engaged the subcontractor's staff and had the work completed at a cost exceeding the bond value. It then served a demand for the whole bond value together with supporting details. The surety asked for a great deal of further information and the claim had not been dealt with by the time a final certificate was issued under the main contract. The contractor issued proceedings against the surety nearly two years later. **19–038**

The surety argued that its liability under the bond ceased on the issue of the final certificate. The court had to decide, among various possible events, when the surety's obligation to compensate the contractor arose: e.g. on the subcontractor's default, when the contractor incurred loss, when the subcontractor failed to compensate the contractor, on service of the demand, as soon as the contractor proved its loss, on the bondsman's admission of liability, on the date such admission should have been made, on the issue of proceedings, or on judgment being entered against the bondsman (para.84). The main contract was I Chem E Red Book (2nd edn, 1991) which provided for the possibility of several final certificates being issued. This term was stepped down into the subcontract (Yellow Book) under which final certificates would be issued by the main contractor's contract manager. The court had to decide whether this meant that the bond expired on the issue of the first final certificate, or the last to be issued, or the issue of the final certificate which related to the subcontract works. The court accepted the first option, taking a literal view of the bond wording, but the certificate could not afford the surety any defence because its liability had crystallised on receipt of the contractor's demand accompanied by its evidence.

The question arises whether the beneficiary would have lost its rights under the bond if an expiry event occurred between notification of default and the actual incurring of the cost to complete. The default would amount to a breach of the first condition of the bond, i.e. performance by the subcontractor. Would the beneficiary be entitled to a declaration from the court to that effect, especially if it was obvious that the quantum of the claim would not be ascertainable before the occurrence of an expiry event? If the conditional bond is a secondary guarantee, a breach of the underlying contract ought to be actionable against the guarantor within the appropriate limitation period of the bond. The second condition (payment of damages by the surety) and the third (issue of a final certificate under the main contract) deal with different matters. A failure of the first condition ought not to be saved by the occurrence of the third but can be compensated by the second; otherwise, the guarantee is limited to an indemnity.

In *Lorne Stewart v Hermes* (unreported, October 22, 2001, Garland J.), the court granted an interim injunction restraining the bondsman from paying and the contractor from receiving £1.6 million pursuant to an on demand bond given in support of a subcontract. The bond provided for expiry on a longstop date or 40 days after the date of termination of the subcontractor's employment. The demand had to state that the long-stop date had not occurred. On the facts, the demand was actually served on the long-stop date and was invalid. Normally, where a demand is invalid, the court will not become involved because the bank or bondsman will refuse to honour it. As the application for the injunction concerned the demand's technical validity, rather than fraud, the court applied the ordinary *Cyanamid* criteria to the application. The report does not say whether the long-stop date was defined in the bond, the subcontract or the main contract.

Reduction

19–039 It may be necessary to provide for the reduction of the bonded amount before expiry for a number of reasons. These depend on the purpose of the bond: see previous sections dealing with retention and advance payment. In *Hunslet Transportation v Seaboard* (unreported, July 29, 1997, CA), a subcontractor procured a surety bond in favour of a contractor as security for the supply of railway equipment. One of the conditions of the bond was the delivery of 37 sets of bogies. It provided for the reduction of the bonded amount by 1/37th on delivery of each set. It was held that, although it might make the reduction provision more difficult to operate, "delivery" in this context was not limited to physical delivery of the equipment but meant transfer of possession in accordance with the contract, e.g. on the dates programmed, together with spares and operating manuals. In another case, it was apparent that words dealing with the reduction of the bonded amount had been omitted. The court held there was an issue of construction which could not be decided on an application for summary judgment: *Imperial Square v Aegon Insurance* (1998) 62 Con. L.R. 59.

Assignment

19–040 If the guarantee is assigned but the underlying contract is not, the assignee will not be able to pursue a claim. This is because a creditor cannot convert one obligation into two: the original contract duties owed to himself and the guarantor's duties owed to the assignee. There is no English authority but the principles are set out in the Australian case of *Hutchens v Deauville Investments* (1986) 68 A.L.R. 367. An assignment of a contract will not necessarily assign a guarantee issued in relation to it. It is important to deal specifically with the assignment of the guarantee.

It remains an open question whether the assignment of an on demand bond vests a right in the assignee to make a demand under the bond on its own account, or the power to call on the assignor to make the demand, or whether it merely passes the right to the proceeds of a successful call. The only English case in this area appears to be *HLC Engenharia v ABN Amro* [2005] EWHC 2074. A local authority entered into a PFI contract with a special purpose vehicle company. The SPV as employer then agreed a turnkey contract with a contractor, who procured an on demand bond in its favour. The employer assigned the bond by way of security to the bank providing finance to the project. There were problems with the project but the employer confirmed to the contractor that it was entitled to a full extension of time and an expert engaged by the bank accepted that the contractor bore no responsibility for defects in the works. Disputes arose between the local authority and the employer. The local authority purported to terminate its agreement and the employer went into administration. There was evidence that the bank requested the employer to enforce the bond but the employer refused. The bank then served a demand as assignee in the full amount of the bond. The court granted an injunction *ex parte* restraining the bondsman from paying and both bank and employer from receiving money under the bond. Judge Peter Coulson Q.C. considered that sufficient case had been made for the purposes of the *ex parte* application that there was a serious issue to be tried as to the validity of the demand. The beneficiary named in the bond admitted there were no grounds for a claim under it. If the beneficiary's demand was a condition precedent, no valid demand could be made at all. The court did not consider other potential arguments such as:

- that the assignment was subject to equities, one of which was that at the minimum the beneficiary's endorsement of the facts relied on by the assignee was required when making the demand;
- that the credit agreement which charged the benefit of the bond could not override the contractor's right to have the bond operated in good faith against the background of the employer's express and implied obligations under the building contract: consider *De Mattos v Gibson* (1858) 4 De. G.& J. 276 (Ch.10);
- that the degree of trust needed as between employer and contractor over the enforcement of the bond meant that only the fruits of a call once made could be assigned. In civil law jurisdictions an assignment of a primary obligation only passes the right to the proceeds, as is the case with assignments of letters of credit under the Uniform Customs and Practice (Bertrams 2004).

The court accepted that fraud was the only inference that could be drawn from the facts. It was reasonable to infer on the evidence that the bank was seeking to use the bond to reduce its financial exposure on the project. The balance of convenience was overwhelmingly in favour of the injunction. The bond was not close to expiry. This decision can be compared with the Australian case of *Boral Formwork v Action Makers* [2003] NSWSC 713 considered earlier. In that case a call by administrative receivers under a standby letter of credit was declared unconscionable on the facts. It seems that no reliance was placed on the fact that the call was in effect that of an assignee, the holder of the floating charge who appointed them.

Fraud is also an equity binding an assignee. In *Banco Santander v Banque Paribas* [2000] 1 All E.R. (Comm) 776, the beneficiary of a deferred payment letter of credit (whereby payment became due 180 days after presentation) discounted the letter and obtained immediate payment from Banco Santander, assigning its rights under the letter to the bank. Unfortunately it later emerged that the letter had been procured by fraud and the bank could not therefore make a valid claim under the letter of credit. Unless an argument based on conditional benefit were available (see Ch.4), an assignment would not impose on the assignee a duty to account to the contractor for the excess over the employer's loss: see *Pan Ocean v Creditcorp* [1994] 1 W.L.R. 161 at 165.

Link with the contract

19–041 As an autonomous obligation, a primary obligation ought to refer to the contract only so as to distinguish it from other obligations. Care is necessary where the document uses terms which are defined in the contract. The contract sometimes contains a term restricting the employer's right to call the primary obligation. For example, it may lay down a notice procedure whereby the contractor is given the opportunity to remedy an alleged default before a call can be made. Where the employer fails to follow such a procedure before making a call, it is conceivable that the court would grant an injunction restraining the employer from making a demand, although the facts would probably have to be exceptional.

In *Kvaerner v Midland Bank* [1998] C.L.C. 446, a contractor agreed to supply materials and design services for the construction of a chemical plant in Indonesia. The contract provided that if the contractor defaulted and the employer gave 14 days written notice of its intention to call a standby letter of credit specifying the details of the default, then the beneficiary could draw down under the credit. The beneficiary made a claim under the credit wrongly stating that the notice had been served. The contractor obtained an injunction against the bank restraining payment and against the beneficiary from receiving payment, which was upheld *inter partes*. The injunction was varied so as not to preclude the service of a further compliant demand. Cresswell J. stated:

> "In the wholly exceptional case where a demand under a performance bond or standby credit purports to certify that a written notice has been given as required by the underlying agreement when it plainly has not been given, the court will, in the exercise of its discretion, grant an injunction to restrain the beneficiary from maintaining the demand accompanied by what is in fact a false certificate. To grant an injunction in such a case is not inconsistent with the general principles set out above. It is, in my view, clearly arguable in the present case that the only realistic inference is that the demand was made fraudulently and it is, in my view, further arguable that it is, in the circumstances, dishonest to maintain the demand. I emphasize that this is a wholly exceptional case for the reasons that I have identified."

A standby letter of credit is very similar to an on demand bond although it may be more easily assignable and therefore present a greater risk to the contractor (see Andrews and Millett 2005, 573–5). Where a prior notice is served but fails to give the level of detail of the beneficiary's claim required by the bond, the court has refused to grant an injunction on the fraud exception: "to be mistaken or unduly sanguine does not amount to fraud in the sense in which it is used in this branch of the law" (*Lorne Stewart v Hermes*, unreported, October 22, 2001, *per* Garland J. at para.36). (Or even untruthful, according to Staughton L.J.: see the quotation from *IE Contractors v Lloyd's Bank* in para.19–003 above.)

In *Lorne Stewart* the court restrained payment under the bond on the ground that the demand was invalid. Garland J. was satisfied that the subcontractor had *locus standi* to apply for the injunction:

> "If Hermes paid money out in a situation where, in effect, no requirement for payment has been made, they clearly owe a duty to [the subcontractor] not to expose them to liability under the guarantee" (para.30).

The notices were simply part of ongoing correspondence; they did not assess the beneficiary's loss nor were they restricted to alleged defaults of the subcontractor. They were also served six months before the demand under the bond. Garland J. considered that, to comply with the bond, the notice of default ought to refer to the relevant clause of the contract which had been broken and be "reasonably close in time" to the demand. This is an echo of the case law on termination under which the court requires some connection in both content and timing between a notice to show cause and a notice of termination under an express clause. The case appears to be in conflict with *Ermis v Banque Indosuez* (unreported, February 26, 1997) in which Thomas J. held that an account party did not have *locus standi* to seek an injunction restraining a bank from paying where the demand was non-compliant. However the identity of the obligor may be significant: in *Lorne Stewart* the guarantee was issued by an insurance company rather than a bank. It is also worth noting ongoing litigation in Australia in which an injunction has been granted restraining calls under on demand bonds pending an appeal on the question whether the parties had entered into the contract whose obligations were to be "secured" by the bonds: *PRA Electrical v Perseverance Exploration* [2007] VSC 74. It was common ground that if the appeal were successful, the bonds would not be enforceable. Even though Smith J. concluded that the prospects of success on the appeal were not strong, he accepted there was an arguable case. The contractor relied on the adverse commercial consequences that would ensue if the calls were not stopped: damage to its reputation, reduction in future bonding capacity, damage to prospects of winning new work. There was also a "real concern" over the beneficiary's ability to repay the bond proceeds if the appeal were to succeed.

"Calling the bond"

In *Workington Harbour v Trade Indemnity (No. 2)* [1938] 2 All E.R. 101, it **19–042** was held that, where the contractor is in breach, the beneficiary of a conditional bond can obtain judgment for the entire bond value as long as some loss could be proved, the judgment standing as security for the recovery of damages for future breaches. This was an exception to the normal rule whereby fresh proceedings have to be brought if a cause of action arises after the first action. In *Bold v BGK Metals* (unreported, May 21, 1997, noted in Moss and Marks 1999) it was stated that the court will only grant a declaration as to a current breach and give judgment for loss which can be proved. Future breaches have to be pursued in separate proceedings. A declaration of liability under a parent company guarantee (with no financial order as loss had not been quantified) was granted in *RWE-Industrie-Loesungen v Thyssen* [2006] EWHC 2111.

In *Manx Electricity Authority v JP Morgan* [2003] B.L.R. 477, a contractor (an Enron subsidiary) procured a bank guarantee for £12 million under a contract to design and build a power station. The guarantee incorporated the Uniform Rules for Demand Guarantees (ICC No.458). The contractor withdrew from site and went into administration. The employer made a demand on the guarantee which was rejected by the bank as non-compliant.

The facts are worth careful study. The employer wished to have the work completed by novating subcontracts to a subsidiary. It therefore entered into a settlement agreement whereby the administrators consented to the novations. The agreement recorded a mutual release of claims as between employer and contractor which was expressly stated not to constitute a waiver of the employer's rights against the bank pursuant to the guarantee or the demand. After all the subcontracts had been novated, the contract would be regarded as terminated. At this point the employer served a second demand on the bank in identical terms to the first save that the employer confirmed that its losses exceeded the amount of the guarantee.

19–043 The employer then issued proceedings against the bank which argued it had been discharged from liability as a result of the settlement agreement. The bank applied to strike out the claim insofar as it concerned the second demand on the ground that, after the settlement, the employer could not in good faith serve a demand accompanied by the required certificate that the contractor was in present, actionable breach of contract. Tomlinson J. agreed with the bank and struck out that part of the claim. He considered that the contractor's abandonment of the site in December 2001 was an anticipatory breach and that there was no existing breach in October 2002 when the second demand was served. By that time, by reason of the settlement agreement, the original contract had ceased to exist.

The Court of Appeal rejected the judge's analysis and considered the contractor to have been in actual repudiatory breach and that it was "plainly arguable" that the employer's initial notice of intention to call on the guarantee was sufficient acceptance of repudiation. It was irrelevant that the contract had ceased to exist by the time the second demand was made. Termination of the contract was the necessary consequence of acceptance of repudiation. The court rejected the idea that a performance guarantee could expire at the very moment when the beneficiary needed to call upon it. The bank sought to rely on the terms of the settlement agreement but the parties had agreed that, for the purpose of the strike out application, the legal effect of the agreement would be dealt with at the trial.

The bank appears to have argued that, as the guarantee was given in support of performance (either physical or by payment of damages), it must be released from liability if performance were no longer possible. It seems ironic that the bank should have taken this point because it appears to involve doing what banks have constantly argued is not permitted, namely making a link between the facts asserted in demands and what has actually happened. It also seems to say that, as between itself and the beneficiary, it should be released by reason of an event occurring as between beneficiary and contractor. This would not normally be so with a first demand guarantee and in any event the employer would in this case be able to rely on the proviso that no alteration to the underlying contract should discharge the bank from liability.

Implied duty to account

The question of accounting for the excess of the bond proceeds over actual loss arose in *Siporex v Comdel Commodities* [1986] 2 Lloyd's Rep. 428 at 436. But *ENS v Derwent Co-Generation* (1998) 62 Con. L.R. 141 is the first reported case in which the court has considered a claim for repayment of the proceeds of a performance security (letters of credit) on the ground that the default asserted in the demand did not exist. The contract sum under a turnkey power contract was £97 million. The employer was entitled to draw down under the credits on presentation of a certificate that the drawing: (1) represented amounts due and owing; (2) was made as a result of the contractor's default; (3) which had not been cured after notice had been given; and (4) within the time limit allowed by the contract. The certificates were signed by the project manager who was an alternate director of the employer. The defaults were alleged defects. Under the contract, the contractor was liable for defects which may "appear or occur" during the defects liability period. It was held that this could not apply to items in a list of outstanding defects attached to a taking-over certificate (at 150–151). Judge Richard Havery QC concluded that the employer had to account for the moneys drawn down: "the burden will be on them to do so" (at 178, 182), relying on *Cargill v Bangladesh Sugar* [1998] 2 All E.R. 406 at 416. Much of the judgment concerned the defects issue but it is of interest in the way it deals with the burden of proof and the consequences of not preventing payment under letters of credit. It is also worth noting *Wollongong City Council v FPM Constructions* [2004] NSWSC 523 in which a contractor brought an arbitration against the employer to recover the proceeds of a call under a demand guarantee. It unsuccessfully argued that it should not have to provide security for costs as claimant in the arbitration as the employer was adequately protected by the bond proceeds. **19–044**

Procedural requirements

Under an open contract of guarantee, the guarantor is liable immediately a breach occurs of the underlying contract. However, the guarantee may provide that the guarantor's obligations only arise on service of a notice from the beneficiary. The guarantee may oblige the beneficiary to notify the guarantor within a certain period of any breach of the underlying contract which comes to the notice of the beneficiary. This apparently onerous provision was upheld as a condition precedent in *Clydebank v Fidelity & Deposit Company of Maryland* [1916] S.C. 69. This applies to all "non-performance or non-observance" and is not restricted to the particular event giving rise to the claim. For example, where a contractor working under JCT 81 went into receivership and the employer had the works completed by an alternative contractor, and the receiver refused to pay the net sum found due after the agreement of the completion contractor's final account, the bondsman could still resist payment of this sum on the ground that it had not been notified within one month of the original contractor's failure to complete by the date for completion: *Oval (717) Limited v Aegon Insurance* (1997) 85 B.L.R. 97. There are a number of reasons why a guarantor might require such notice, and where it is expressly made a condition precedent to liability in the bond, the court will uphold the **19–045** condition. The notice requirement was not unfair under the Unfair Contract Terms Act 1977. Even if the Act could apply, the term was held reasonable.

Government contracts

19–046 HM Treasury has stated that bonds are not always necessary on government contracts and are no substitute for a detailed risk assessment of the project and an appraisal of the capabilities and financial resources of the available contractors (CUP 1994). In response to pressure from the industry to ban the use of on demand bonds with government contracts, the Department of the Environment set up an inter-departmental working group to carry out research and recommend best practice. In its report, the working group recommended that on demand bonds should only be used for specific purposes, e.g. advance payments or retention. Instead of relying on bonds, departments should normally depend on effective pre-qualification and vetting procedures. The report includes model forms of performance bond, retention bond, advance payment bond and parent company guarantee (DOE 1996). Neither publication is mandatory and government departments retain a discretion over the use of bonds and guarantees. In the context of PFI projects, see s.24, Standardisation of PFI Contracts (SoPC), Version 4 (March 2007) which provides: "Under PFI, where the majority of projects are financed on a limited recourse basis and the Contractor is not paid if the Service is not delivered, such extensive direct comfort [i.e. guarantees, indemnities and collateral warranties] will not normally be necessary or appropriate." The "Contractor" in that context is the special purpose vehicle entering into the concession agreement with the government body. The section goes on to give some guidance on the type of comfort normally expected.

Subcontracts

19–047 Subcontract bonds and guarantees are derived from a number of sources: adaptations from main contract precedents, the contractor's own form, the subcontractor's preferred form, and occasionally one of the standard forms (e.g. the retention bond attached to the JCT Standard Building Subcontract Conditions 2005). On a major project, subcontract bonds can have a high value and require careful consideration. The issues which arise are analogous to those concerning the relationship between the main contract and the subcontract. These include: (1) whether subcontract bonds are properly back to back with bonds which the contractor has provided to the employer; (2) whether reduction and expiry provisions are properly tied in to significant events under the main contract or whether they depend on certificates, events or dates relating only to the subcontract; and (3) whether they are freely assignable. It may be necessary for the contractor to assign the benefit of subcontract bonds to the employer or allow them to be charged to project funders.

Special issues arise in connection with management contracting. In one case, on the insolvency of a works contractor, the management contractor had the works completed at considerable extra cost and made a claim under a surety bond. The bondsman defended arguing that, as the management contractor could only be liable to the employer to the extent that it recovered damages from the works contractor, the management contractor had suffered no loss and therefore had no claim under the bond. Judge Humphrey LLoyd Q.C. rejected this argument. If the management contractor had not yet recovered the additional cost of completion from the employer, the bondsman would be liable. If recovery had been made, the management contractor could recover from the bondsman provided that the employer asserted a claim against the management contractor: *Laing Management and Morrison-Knudson v Aegon Insurance* (1997) 86 B.L.R. 70.

Personal guarantees

A personal guarantee may be required by a bondsman in support of a bond **19–048**
or guarantee given under a building contract. The director's guarantee in this situation may be to pay the bondsman on production of a receipt of payment to the beneficiary which may constitute conclusive evidence of the director's liability: *De Montfort Insurance v Lafferty* [1997] S.C. 335. The use of a primary obligation in this context meant that the bondsman was able to recover even though it had compensated the employer for post-termination losses under JCT 63 before the architect had certified the sum payable. Similarly, in *De Montfort Insurance v Cooke* (unreported, February 18, 1999, Garland J.) a director was held liable to a bondsman under a guarantee to pay on demand any sum or sums which the bondsman might pay or be called upon to pay under a bond issued to IATA. Under the guarantee a notice that the bondsman "has paid or will pay or may pay" a sum in consequence of having entered into the bond was to be treated as conclusive evidence of the director's liability. See also *Technical & General Guarantee v Patterson* (unreported, February 12, 2003, L Henderson Q.C.) and *HCC International Insurance v Conway* [2006] EWHC 3646 discussed in para.19–026 above.

A director may give a personal guarantee as a temporary measure. In *Singer & Friedlander v Thomas* [2003] EWHC 861 a director provided his personal guarantee on a short term basis until a chattel mortgage could be put "in place". His company went into receivership and a dispute arose on the meaning of the words "in place". The director escaped liability by showing that the mortgage had been executed even though other matters such as deeds of release and priority had not been dealt with. As the receivership occurred after the provision of security, the guarantee lapsed before any liability under it could arise.

Where directors gave a personal guarantee to the NHBC as a condition of the company being admitted as a probationer to the National Register of House-Builders, they were found liable when the company defaulted under its obligations under the NHBC agreement: *National House-Building Council v Fraser* [1983] 1 All E.R. 1090. Guarantees may also be required from directors of subcontractors as a condition of obtaining exemption under the tax deduction scheme discussed in Ch.21.

Joint ventures

The principal might be a corporate or a contractual joint venture. If **19–049**
corporate, the employer may require a parent company guarantee from each of the shareholders. If contractual, parent company guarantees may be

required from the parent of each of the companies comprising the principal. In each case, the employer needs to be clear whether each guarantor is liable for any default or has a limited responsibility, e.g. for a specific part of the works. Even if not mentioned in the guarantee, these matters need to be dealt with in the consortium agreement by indemnities between the members. If the joint venture is contractual, and the members are jointly and severally liable to the employer, the employer may be prepared to accept some limitation on its recourse, e.g. if there are three members in the consortium, the employer may accept that the liability of their respective parents shall each be limited to one third of the consortium's total liability.

If a member of the consortium is the ultimate holding company of a group, the employer may dispense with the requirement for a group guarantee. Alternatively it may require a guarantee from the company in the group which owns most assets or cross-guarantees from all of the group companies. If there are co-guarantors, it is useful for the employer to reserve the right to reach a settlement with one without affecting its rights to recover the balance against the others. If the parent company guarantee provides for co-guarantors, but not all of them execute the document, the guarantee may be unenforceable if, on its true construction, it was a condition precedent to its coming into effect that all the guarantors should sign it: *James Graham v Southgate Sands* [1986] Q.B. 80.

It is common for a contractor and a developer to form a joint venture, each providing specialist services to the project. In *Wolsey Securities v Abbeygate* [2007] EWCA 423, the contractor guaranteed to the developer (who funded the work) that the joint venture company would perform its obligations under the agreement. The venture was unprofitable and the company went into liquidation. The developer sued the contractor under the guarantee for moneys lent to the joint venture company but failed on the ground that funding had been provided under a separate facility letter to the company which fell outside the scope of the guarantee in the joint venture agreement. On appeal, the developer succeeded on the ground that the joint venture obligations had to be interpreted in the light of the facility letter.

This case can be compared with *Nearfield v Lincoln Nominees* [2006] EWHC 2421 in which a developer borrowed £3 million from a bank and lent it to its joint venture partner to lend to a special purpose vehicle company for the purpose of acquiring an office building for redevelopment. The joint venturer agreed to procure that the SPV would repay the loan on demand. The project made a loss and the developer called in the loan. Peter Smith J. held that the joint venturer assumed an obligation to see to it that the loan was repaid which was not displaced by the terms of the joint venture agreement and it was therefore liable to the developer. An argument that an arrangement amounts to a guarantee sometimes arises in the context of direct payment: see *Ballast v Laurieston Properties* [2005] CSOH 16.

Chapter 20

Insolvency Claims

The underlying policy of insolvency law is that creditors should be treated equally by receiving the same percentage of what is owed them: s.107 of the Insolvency Act 1986. This is known as the *pari passu* rule (Ch.13). Although there are many exceptions, which often deprive ordinary unsecured creditors of any recovery, the rule is the primary basis for a wide range of claims available to a company which has entered a formal insolvency procedure, unjust enrichment being another (Goode 2005, Armour and Bennett 2003). Although relatively few claims are brought in practice, reflecting difficulties over funding and evidence (Milman and Parry 1997), their existence influences the way contracts are drafted as well as the conduct of directors and lenders in dealing with companies in financial difficulty. This chapter focuses on ways in which companies and individuals working in the construction industry may find themselves entangled in an insolvency claim. **20–001**

1. Fraudulent trading

Civil liability for fraudulent trading arises where "in the course of the winding up of a company it appears that any business of the company has been carried on with intent to defraud creditors of the company or creditors of any other person or for any fraudulent purpose": s.213 of the Insolvency Act 1986. The court may declare that any persons who were knowingly parties to the carrying of the business are liable to contribute to the company's assets. Only the liquidator can take these proceedings. Liability is not restricted to directors but extends to any participators in the fraud. There are no reported cases in English law involving fraudulent trading in the construction industry but a case brought under the Singaporean equivalent of s.213 provides a good illustration. In *Tong Tien See Construction v Tong* [2002] 3 S.L.R. 76 a contractor traded while insolvent for five years. By manipulating its accounts, changing its accounting methods, and transferring losses to an associated company by raising sham invoices, the company was able to maintain the highest solvency rating under the Singapore building control system (which required a minimum net worth of $5 million). This enabled it to obtain a regular flow of government contracts and long-term credit from subcontractors. The principal director, Mr Tong, is described as "a hot-tempered, traditional Chinese businessman who ruled his family with a strong arm". Family members were placed in positions of authority in the company and associated companies in the group. Three directors were made liable for fraudulent trading in the sum of $53.3 million. They were also liable for this **20–002** amount on the grounds of misfeasance and conspiracy to injure by unlawful means. The court allowed the liquidator to trace company money misapplied by the directors into property and other assets bought with it (see Ch.9).

Although the notion of carrying on business suggests a pattern of activity over a period of time, fraudulent trading can result from a single act or transaction: *Re Gerald Cooper* [1978] Ch. 262. For example, if a contractor calls a demand guarantee provided by a subcontractor, it assumes a contingent liability in the form of a duty to account to the subcontractor for the excess of the bond proceeds over its actual loss (see Ch.19). If the directors know when they authorise the call that the contractor will be unable to meet the contingent liability, it is conceivable that they could be made liable for fraudulent trading: consider *Boral Formwork v Action Makers* [2003] NSWSC 713 below (call under standby credit by administrative receivers). Another example might be where a labour only subcontractor engages workmen on a self-employed basis and absconds before paying them. It may be harder to establish liability in this context following the decision in *Morphitis v Bernasconi* [2003] 2 B.C.L.C. 53, in which the Court of Appeal approved *Re Gerald Cooper* but held that it did not necessarily follow that a business was being carried on with intent to defraud creditors simply because a fraud on a creditor was perpetrated in the course of carrying on business. In that case, the business was being carried on to protect former directors from penalties to which they would otherwise have been exposed under s.216 of the Insolvency Act 1986 (see para.20–013 below). In *Leong Seng v Chan* [2007] SGHC 9, for example, a claim for fraudulent trading against three directors of a piling contractor failed. It focused on the non-payment of one supplier over a period of four months during the year before the company was wound up. The company had paid all other creditors before and after this period and disputed liability to the supplier on legal advice. It had since obtained supplies from other sources. It was only when the supplier sued the company to judgment that it became insolvent on the cash flow basis. Until then, although it was insolvent on the balance sheet basis, it was supported by its bank overdraft and directors' loans. There was no evidence of dishonesty.

2. Wrongful trading

20–003 "Wrongful trading" was introduced by s.214 of the Insolvency Act 1986, which provides that the court can order a director to make such contribution to the company's assets as it thinks proper where it can be shown that a company has gone into insolvent liquidation and at some time beforehand the director "knew or ought to have concluded that there was no reasonable prospect that the company would avoid going into insolvent liquidation." Unlike fraudulent trading, it is not necessary to prove dishonesty. A director will not be liable if he can show he has taken "every step with a view to minimising the potential loss to the company's creditors . . . as he ought to have taken": s.214(3). A director is judged not simply by his own skill and experience but also by the knowledge, skill and experience of a reasonably diligent person performing his function in the company: s.214(4). The court looks to see whether the director acted properly to the best of his own ability (subjective test) and then whether he acted as a person carrying out his function in the company ought to have done (objective test). The greater the director's responsibility within the company, the greater is the risk of liability. A higher standard is expected from a director of a large company with sophisticated accounting procedures than a director of a small company in a modest way of business: *Re Produce Marketing* (1989) 5 B.C.C. 569. Wrongful trading uses the balance sheet test as the criterion of insolvency: s.214(6). The test can be difficult to apply where an unliquidated claim has been made against the company (Ch.8).

In *Re DKG Contractors* [1990] B.C.C. 903, the court considered a groundworks subcontractor whose directors and shareholders were a Mr and Mrs Gibbons. Mr Gibbons began business as a sole trader. They formed the company in 1986 and it was contended that he continued to run his own business in parallel with the company, supplying it with labour, materials and plant for which he rendered invoices. The company became informally insolvent in February 1988. Liquidation became an inevitability two months later. Between May and November, 16 creditors obtained judgment and there were ten visits from the bailiff. The company went into liquidation in December 1988 owing creditors over £160,000. During the previous ten months, it had paid Mr Gibbons over £400,000. No proper accounts were kept. The court rejected Mr Gibbons' claim that the company was dormant between 1986 and 1988. During 1987, it used its own headed notepaper on which tenders were submitted and correspondence entered into with main contractors who paid the company gross of tax in reliance on a tax exemption certificate in Mr Gibbons' name until the company obtained its own certificate in January 1988 (see Ch.21). Both directors were ordered to contribute to the company's assets a sum representing credit incurred after the end of April 1988. They were also liable for misfeasance and preference. This was an extreme case in view of the fact that the directors took no independent advice. See also *Re Brian D Pierson (Contractors) Ltd* [2002] 1 B.C.L.C. 275. A contractor may hope that new work or perhaps work of a more profitable kind will enable it to trade out of its difficulties, e.g. as in *Re Redman (Builders) Ltd* [1964] 1 W.L.R. 541, where a director of a small contractor kept the creditors at bay "with a cheque here and a promise there" (at 543), but the scope for such evasive action has been cut down by s.214. Other situations which might give rise to wrongful trading in the industry arise from the nature of the trading vehicle or the funding structure, e.g. joint ventures, lottery funded projects and charitable trusts (Davis 1988).

There is as yet no reported example of wrongful trading by an employer, but it is interesting to compare *Australian Securities and Investments Commission v Edwards* [2005] NSWSC 831. In that case a director of an employer was found liable under the Australian Corporations Act 2001 for failing to prevent the company from incurring debts to the contractor when he knew, or a reasonable person in his position would have known, that there were reasonable grounds for suspecting that the company was insolvent or would become so by incurring the debts. It appears likely that he would have been liable for wrongful trading had it been an English case.

The company, Murray River Ltd, was a special purpose vehicle set up pursuant to a contractual joint venture. One of the venturers held a 36–year lease on a lakeside property which was run as a tourist club; while the other had expertise in property development. The project was for a 142–unit apartment hotel on the site at a construction cost of approximately $15 million. The defendant was a director of the developer as well as the company. After a detailed analysis of the evidence Barrett J. held that the company was insolvent when the contractor began work on the project and at all times thereafter (para.211).

The director had allowed work to go ahead without obtaining construction finance. Problems had arisen through the need to increase the term of the lease to 99 years, the refusal by both joint venture partners to provide guarantees, lack of appropriate valuations on the basis of the extended lease, the absence of an executed fixed price building contract, lack of a formal management agreement with a recognised resort operator, lack of pre-sales or capital from a fully subscribed prospectus, among other things. The builder began work on the strength of a letter of intent. The employer was able to obtain short term finance to honour the first two progress payments but defaulted on four others totalling $2.5 million. As a result the builder suspended work. It appears that it was only then that the builder asked who was funding the project (para.132). One of the outstanding matters was the provision of a bond by the employer. It seems that finance was being sought on the basis of unrealistic assumptions or a lack of market awareness and therefore took longer than anticipated causing the need for the work to start prematurely. The joint venture agreement did not oblige either party to give a guarantee or make loans. There was evidence that the director had asked the builder to "slow down" but never to stop work. He gave the impression "that the various elements necessary to secure the necessary funding were within grasp. It was always just a matter of a short time until all would be well" (para.258). Although the builder's remuneration was for a *quantum meruit*, payment certificates were issued by the employer's surveyor. They were accepted by the court as evidence of the timing and amount of the "debts incurred" for the purposes of the Corporations Act. In the end the director was disqualified for ten years but no financial penalty was sought against him: [2006] NSWSC 376.

3. Preference

20–004 By s.239 of the Insolvency Act 1986, a preference occurs if the company does or suffers anything to be done which has the effect of putting a creditor into a better position in the event of the company's liquidation than he would have been in if the action had not been carried out. The company must have been "influenced in deciding to give it by a desire" to produce the preference: *Re MC Bacon* [1990] B.C.C. 78. As with transactions at an undervalue, it must be shown that the company was insolvent at the time of the preference or became so as a result. The claim can only be brought in respect of a preference made within six months before the "onset of insolvency" (or two years where the creditor is a connected person). A claim can be brought by an administrator or a liquidator.

Payments to creditors

20–005 In *Re DKG Contractors* [1990] B.C.C. 903, over £400,000 was paid to one of the directors in the ten months before the company went into voluntary liquidation in respect of services rendered to the company. As he was a connected person, the burden of proving a preference was reversed. The court was prepared to accept that some payments "may well have been influenced by commercial considerations such as the advantages of completing rather than abandoning the contracts" (at 910, *per* Judge John Weeks Q.C.). However, the desire to prefer was present. The company had been insolvent when the payments were made. The director was ordered to repay the money concurrently with an order in the same amount for misfeasance. See also *Leong Seng v Chan* [2007] SGHC 9, in which a director of a piling contractor failed to shift the burden of proving that cash payments received from the company were not preferences. A preference claim failed in *Leun v Sigma Cable* [2006] SGHC 86, which concerned the assignment of retention by a nominated subcontractor to a supplier by way of part payment of sums due. When the retention fell due for release, the supplier claimed direct against the contractor who interpleaded. The liquidators of the subcontractor argued the assignment was a preference under s.99 of the Singapore Bankruptcy Act which is in very similar terms to s.239. Although the supplier had a long term trading relationship with the subcontractor, the evidence was that it would not forbear to sue unless some payment were forthcoming. It also threatened to seek payment direct from the employer which would harm the subcontractor's reputation at a difficult time. The assignment was offered in immediate response to an ultimatum to pay or face legal action. Notice of assignment was given by the subcontractor. The supplier continued to make supplies for a year after the assignment but only on a *pro forma* basis. The court held that the assignment was in the subcontractor's commercial interests: "The assignment helped it to retain its principal supplier, and that, in turn, enabled it to carry on its projects and collect payment", at para.12, *per* Choo Han Teck J. Presumably other sums as well as the retention would accrue due on completion.

Although the criteria for a preference are different from English law, it is worth looking at several Australian cases. In *Kel Builders v Brett Nash Electrics* [2001] QSC 178 a liquidator appointed to a contractor succeeded in part in a preference claim against an electrical subcontractor. Under s.588 of the Australian Corporations Law, a creditor has a defence if at the time of the transaction, among other things, he had no reasonable grounds for suspecting that the company was insolvent. On the evidence, over a four year trading relationship, the contractor had consistently disregarded the subcontractor's terms of payment. So much so that the court accepted that such behaviour could not reasonably suggest that the contractor was insolvent. It was only after its licence was revoked and the subcontractor served a statutory demand that the subcontractor ought to have suspected insolvency. The preferences were limited to payments received after that time. In *Wily v Eastern Elevators* [2003] NSWSC 377 a preference claim failed in part as a lift subcontractor was able to show it had threatened not to install the lift to site or to enter the source code into the control panel without payment. In *Thompson Land v Salzer Constructions* [2001] 3 V.R. 305 a liquidator of an employer's parent company failed in a claim that six payments to a design and build contractor were preferences. Three of the payments were by the parent and three by a bank funding the project. It could not be established that they discharged any indebtedness of the parent to the contractor; they simply discharged the liability of the employer. The payments by the bank were all made at the direction of the parent.

In another case arising from the liquidation of Thompson Land, preference claims were successful against four trade contractors: *G&M Aldridge v*

Walsh [1999] VSCA 179. Several months before an order to wind up the employer was made, the trade contractors consulted a solicitor to recover what appear to have been sums due under final accounts. An agreement was made whereby the employer acknowledged specific sums due to each trade contractor and paid each a "deposit" of about five per cent and gave them units in a property fund as security for the balance. On the employer's default, the units were sold but realised minimal value. It was held that the payments were not made in the ordinary course of business and were preferences. The unusual aspect of the case was that they were made from assets falling within a fixed charge whose value was less than the debt secured by the charge but the charge holder had for reasons unknown failed to enforce its security. As the relevant assets were not available for distribution to unsecured creditors it is hard to see why the payments were held to be preferences. See also *County Construction v Hart* [2004] NSWSC 313.

Termination clauses

20–006 Totty and Moss comment that it is just conceivable that "automatic termination provisions or similar clauses" could be a preference (at H6.02). Automatic termination is less common than termination on notice and has potential disadvantages as well as advantages for an employer (Ch.14). Such terms are often regarded as informal security for performance and are long-established. It would thus be very difficult to prove that their inclusion was influenced by a desire to prefer the employer as opposed to the legitimate aim of protecting the employer against the contractor's insolvency. Some unusual surrounding circumstances would be needed. Perhaps there could be a preference where the employer is connected and the contract is entered into shortly before the contractor goes into liquidation. The employer might then get the benefit of fixed materials and work in progress without having to pay for them by raising a termination set-off.

Direct payments

20–007 Preference arguments often arise in connection with direct payments. There have been several cases in Australia on this issue. In *Re CG Monkhouse* (1968) 69 S.R.(N.S.W.) 429, an Australian case which concerned a direct payment made within six months before the contractor went into voluntary liquidation, the terms of the contract were similar to JCT 63. The liquidator argued that the subcontractor had been preferred on the ground that the payment had been made "on behalf of" the contractor. In rejecting the liquidator's claim, the court stated that "the payment made by the building owner cannot be described as a payment made out of moneys for the builder. It is a payment made out of the building owner's own moneys which, if the contract were strictly carried out, would never become due to the builder" (at 432, *per* Jacobs J.A.). The rationale for the decision was that the contractor only ever became entitled to such sum as remained after the direct payment had been made.

In a later decision, *Gericevich v Sabemo* [1984] 9 A.C.L.R. 452, the court rejected a preference claim on similar grounds. By contrast in *Analogy v*

Bell Basic Industries (1996) 12 B.C.L. 291, a direct payment by a contractor (Leighton) to a sub-subcontractor (Boral) was held to be a voidable preference at the suit of the liquidator of the subcontractor (Analogy). Boral withdrew from site on the ground of non-payment by Analogy of $450,000. Analogy claimed to be owed $650,000 by Leighton for work done before March 1989 and $130,000 for work done during March. Leighton wanted Boral to return to site and finish its work. An agreement was reached between the three of them whereby Leighton agreed that $100,000 was due to Analogy for the work done in March and agreed to make a further payment of $200,000 on account of Analogy's disputed claims on condition that Boral immediately returned to site. Analogy agreed to allow Boral to contract directly with Leighton for the balance of the work. Analogy executed an authority directing Leighton to pay these sums to Boral and Leighton undertook to Boral to make the payments in accordance with that direction. Leighton paid $100,000 to Boral who returned to site and completed the work. Boral claimed payment of the $200,000 but Leighton replied saying that payment depended on Analogy proving an entitlement under the subcontract for at least that sum. A receiver and manager was then appointed to Analogy, followed shortly afterwards by a liquidator. The court analysed the position as follows.

> "In the arrangement Boral had a promise from Leighton that Leighton would pay to Boral $300,000 of Analogy's indebtedness to Boral in return for Boral's promise to remobilise and complete the work. For its part, Analogy had an express or implied promise from Boral that Boral would receive the payments from Leighton in reduction of Analogy's indebtedness to Boral. The consideration for that promise was Analogy's agreement to forego its entitlement to be paid $100,000 by Leighton, and to permit Leighton to make the payment direct to Boral" (at 292, *per* Anderson J.).

It followed that the payment of $100,000 was made from "Analogy's money" and constituted a preference. The same could not apply to the $200,000 as it was treated as an advance for the specific purpose of payment to Boral and fell within the principle in *Barclays Bank v Quistclose* [1970] A.C. 567 (see Ch.9). In addition, Leighton was indebted to Boral for that amount. The criteria applied in these cases are not the same as under s.239 but the issue whether a payment is in substance made by or at the direction of the insolvent company would be relevant in English law. The differing outcomes of the preference claims reflect in part different approaches towards the construction of direct payment clauses (see Ch.17).

Construction trusts

Preference is sometimes raised as an argument where a company declares itself trustee of property shortly before becoming insolvent. In two cases decided before the commencement of the Insolvency Act 1986 such claims were rejected: *Re Kayford* [1975] 1 W.L.R. 279, *Re Chelsea Cloisters* (1981) 41 P. & C.R. 98. Some aspects of these decisions may no longer be correct (Anderson 1992). **20–008**

To what extent could a construction trust be vulnerable to such a claim? It is necessary to decide what action amounts to the preference: entering into the contract containing the trust provisions, voluntarily setting up a fund on request, complying with the court order to do so, or making payments from the trust account in accordance with the contract. The only real prospect of preference in this area consists in the action of setting aside the fund. As the test is subjective, and a mixed motive could be sufficient, the possibility that setting aside retention could be a preference cannot be completely ruled out: compare *Barnes v Premium Credit* [2001] B.C.C. 27, para.49.

If an employer has half a dozen contracts with different contractors using the same JCT form, has the funds to set aside retention in respect of them, is asked to do so by all of the contractors, but does so only for one of them, it could be inferred that the employer was influenced by desire to place that contractor in a better position than the others on a liquidation. There is a tension between the *pari passu* rule and the right of a creditor to use every available legal procedure to obtain payment before the debtor goes into formal insolvency. In *John Holland Construction v Majorca Projects* (1996) 12 B.C.L. 135 a judge awarded summary judgment to a contractor but stayed the drawing up of the order because of concern about the employer's solvency and the risk of giving a preference to the contractor. The decision was reversed on appeal since otherwise the contractor would be hindered "in its legitimate desire to obtain and retain payment of a debt due from a debtor whose financial position was admittedly doubtful" (at 137, *per* Brooking J.A.). Some authorities in the commercial context suggest that preference arguments in respect of a retention trust are not likely to succeed: *Re Lewis's of Leicester* [1995] 1 B.C.L.C. 428, *Re Branston & Gothard* [1999] B.P.I.R. 466. But there are contrary dicta in other cases: *MacJordan Construction v Brookmount Erostin* (1992) 56 B.L.R. 1 at 18, *Re Farepak* [2006] EWHC 3272 at para.52.

4. Transactions at an undervalue

20–009 The court has power to set aside a transaction entered into at an undervalue under s.238 of the Insolvency Act 1986. The section applies where the company receives no consideration or the value given by the company is significantly greater than that received. The company must have been insolvent at the time or have become so as a result but this is presumed where the transaction is with a connected person. An administrator or liquidator can bring the claim. There is a defence that the transaction was entered into in good faith for the purpose of carrying on the company's business and there were reasonable grounds for believing that it would benefit the company. It must have taken place within two years before the start of the insolvency procedure. The court has power to make such order as it thinks fit to restore the *status quo*. The liquidators of the subcontractor in *Leun v Sigma Cable* (considered in para.20–005 above) also argued that the assignment of retention was a transaction at an undervalue. They failed on the ground that it was made in god faith and for the purpose of enabling the subcontractor to continue trading. There were reasonable grounds for believing that the assignment would benefit the company.

Claims under this head involve an analysis of the transaction and the value of the consideration passing both ways. In *Buildspeed Construction v Theme* [2000] 4 S.L.R. 776 a novation of a building contract was held to be a transaction at an undervalue under analogous legislation in Singapore. The novation took place six weeks before the appointment of provisional liquidators at a time when the contractor was insolvent and was made with a new company owned and operated by the directors of the insolvent contractor. The consideration provided to the contractor consisted of a release from further performance and from liability for defects and for delays occurring after the novation. In return the insolvent contractor transferred the right to complete the contract, the value of an interim certificate issued the day after the novation, and retention. In working out the profit the new company could expect to earn by completing the work the court admitted expert evidence and made allowances for the costs of insurance and providing a new performance guarantee and the fact that costs had fallen since the contract was entered into. It appraised the likelihood that the employer would deduct the amount of direct payments from the interim certificate and reduced its value accordingly. It also estimated the likely delays which would have occurred but for the novation and reduced the retention by an estimate for liquidated damages. After quantifying the consideration on both sides, it emerged that full consideration was not given. The court declared the novation to be a transaction at an undervalue and ordered an account.

In *Lewis v Doran* [2005] NSWCA 243, a liquidator failed in a claim that a restructuring amounted to misfeasance or an "uncommercial transaction" under Australian legislation (broadly analogous to a transaction at an undervalue). The case concerned a family-owned construction group. The transaction concerned a debt of $4.1 million owed to Doran Constructions. Originally it was owed by Doran Holdings and was repayable on demand; after the restructuring it was owed by Doran Australia and deferred for six years. Doran Holdings had assets; Doran Australia did not, other than shares in Constructions. Both Doran Constructions and Doran Australia later went into liquidation; and the liquidator of Constructions claimed the debt from Holdings and/or the directors. He argued that the aim of the restructuring was to protect Holdings from pending claims against Constructions, one by a subcontractor, another by an employer, since if the claims succeeded Constructions would have had to demand payment of the whole debt.

The subcontractor's claim was for a final account; the contractor had a **20–010**
cross-claim for defects and delay. The contractor did not accept the subcontractor's claim but agreed to pass it "up the line" for consideration by the architect, who rejected it. The contractor then settled its own claims with the employer. Part of the global settlement figure related to the subcontractor's work but, after setting off its cross-claim, the contractor argued that nothing was due. The dispute was referred to arbitration in which the subcontractor was successful. On another project the contractor claimed damages for unlawful termination as well as prolongation and disruption costs. The employer asserted a cross-claim for defects. The contractor argued that they were defects of design for which it was not responsible. Both parties' claims were referred to arbitration but the contractor took no further part after it went into liquidation and the employer obtained a substantial award in its favour. In the action against the directors, it was held that the subcontractor's claim was not regarded as a "present and substantial financial threat" and played no part in the rationale for the restructuring. It was unliquidated and Constructions had a *bona fide* counterclaim for a greater sum which was only rejected some

years later. Nor was the employer's claim the "driving factor". At the time the directors thought that Constructions was the net creditor as between itself and the employer and their belief was not unreasonably held. The restructuring was carried out on accountants' advice in order to separate the property companies in the group (under Holdings) from the construction companies so as to make it easier to obtain finance for the former.

The case is especially interesting in its analysis of the question whether Constructions was insolvent at the time of the restructuring. The test was commercial rather than balance sheet insolvency. The normal signs of insolvency were absent (para.74). On the restructuring and for three years afterwards the company met all its debts as they fell due. In so doing it relied on continuing financial support from Holdings. Holdings had guaranteed Constructions' overdraft. It was in Constructions' interests to facilitate the restructuring so that Holdings could find it easier to borrow. It could not be said that Constructions suffered a detriment as a result. If Constructions had called for payment of the debt, Holdings could have put the debtor company in funds to pay it. Consideration may be provided by a third party under a separate contract. If it consists of a promise to pay instalments under a contract which is terminable on insolvency, and insolvency was likely to occur as at the date of the transaction, the consideration may however be given a nil value: *Phillips v Brewin Dolphin* [2001] 1 W.L.R. 143, para.26. This situation could arise if a contractor assigns the benefit of a contract as a part of a transaction involving a corporate group.

In addition the court can set aside a transaction in fraud of creditors under s.423 of the Insolvency Act 1986. This is similar to a transaction at an undervalue. It must be shown that the purpose of the transaction was to put assets beyond the reach of the claimant and was intended to prejudice the interests of the claimant. A successful claim was brought in *Pena v Coyne (No. 1)* [2004] 2 B.C.L.C. 703, which involved the transfer of a property at an undervalue. One of the issues was how to take account of improvements (presumably building works) that had been made by the transferee after the transaction. See also *Re Ayala Holdings* [1993] B.C.L.C. 256.

5. Misfeasance

20–011 A misfeasance occurs where a director or other person concerned in the promotion, formation or management of the company "has misapplied, or retained or become accountable for, money or other property of the company, or has been guilty of any misfeasance or breach of fiduciary or other duty in relation to the company": s.212 of the Insolvency Act 1986; Oditah (1992). The court has power to order that person to repay, restore or account for the money or property misapplied with interest, or to contribute such sum to the company's assets by way of compensation as it thinks just. The claim does not create any new cause of action which could not have existed before the insolvency: *Re B Johnson & Co (Builders) Ltd* [1955] 1 Ch. 634 at 647. Its purpose is to provide a relatively quick and economical remedy in the liquidation. It applies to anyone involved, even informally, in the running of the business.

Many claims concern the misappropriation of money. *West Mercia Safetywear v Dodd* [1988] B.C.C. 250 concerned a person who was a director of a parent and a subsidiary which both had accounts at the same bank. The director guaranteed the parent's overdraft and was advised that, in view of the financial difficulties of both companies, the bank accounts should not be operated. Nevertheless he transferred £4,000 from the subsidiary's account to reduce its debt of £30,000 owed to the parent, reducing his guarantee liability accordingly. The payment was a misfeasance and the director was liable to repay it to the liquidator with interest. One of the directors in *Re DKG Contractors* considered above in connection with wrongful trading and preference was held liable in misfeasance. The company received over £400,000 in the ten months preceding the liquidation. Instead of paying the money into the company's bank account, the director paid cheques drawn in favour of the company into his personal account, transferred money from the company's account into his own, drew cheques on the company's account in his favour, and drew cheques to cash and kept the money. In further breach of duty the director acted as a labour-only subcontractor to his own company which meant that "the general creditors were competing on unfair terms with one creditor, who was always likely to be paid ahead of the rest" (at 908, *per* Judge John Weeks Q.C.). He was ordered to repay the £400,000 to the liquidator. In *Re DKG Contractors*, it was held that the payments were in breach of duty because they were not authorised by the company's articles of association. Ratification of the payments by the shareholders was not possible because at that time the company was insolvent and the directors had failed to keep the company's assets intact for the benefit of creditors. Similarly, in *Covich Contractors v Covich* [2006] NZHC 873 directors of an earthmoving contractor withdrew cash from the company's account for personal purposes. They alleged that the withdrawals were to pay subcontractors but could not produce receipts. The directors did not have a fixed salary but took sums as advances from the company as they needed them. The court held that the advances were repayable on the company's liquidation.

The failure to distinguish between personal and company property is evident in the spectacular case of *Tong Tien See Construction v Tong* [2002] 3 S.L.R. 76 noted earlier in the section on fraudulent trading. Large sums were transferred to an associated company on the basis that it was a subcontractor but the transactions were not at arm's length. Company property was treated as the personal assets of the principal director, Mr Tong, and his family, who bought and built houses in their own names with company money. Mrs Tong would transfer company money to her own bank account, keep the interest earned, and transfer the principal back. "They needed a continuous stream of new projects to feed the debts of the old ones . . ." (at para.56, *per* Tay Yong Kwang J.C.). In another Singapore case, the directors of a contractor were held liable in misfeasance for writing off debts owed by them (or by companies controlled by them) to the company at a time when the company was insolvent: *Chip Thye Enterprises v Phay* [2004] 1 S.L.R. 434. As in *Tong Tien See Construction*, the company was family owned and had a subsidiary whose affairs were not properly distinguished from those of the parent. "Letters addressed to one would be responded to by the other. Payments for invoices directed at [the company] would be settled by [the subsidiary] and vice versa" (at para.8). The directors also sold a property and used the proceeds to pay dividends to themselves as shareholders out of capital (another misfeasance) rather than discharging the company's debts to nominated subcontractors. "Why should we use [our] own money to pay them?" the principal director asked rhetorically (at para.55). "The [company] could not pay its creditors without disposing its assets. It did dispose of its assets . . . but not to pay its unsecured creditors" (at para.57). Similarly, in *Discain Project Services v Opecprime* (unreported, December 11, 2001), the director of a property development company paid a contractor from whichever of his group companies happened to be in funds regardless of its legal liability to pay (paras.30 and 37). This was not an insolvency case but the director may have been liable in misfeasance if any of the paying companies went into liquidation.

A common construction misfeasance is the use of company resources to construct, extend or repair the directors' homes: *Halls v O'Dell* [1992] 2 W.L.R. 308, *Kenna & Brown v Kenna* [1999] NSWSC 533. In the absence of insolvency, if the directors adopt this practice they cannot complain as against each other that it is unfairly prejudicial conduct justifying a winding up order on the just and equitable ground under s.122 of the Insolvency Act 1986: *Re Jayflex Construction* [2004] 2 B.C.L.C. 145. Another misfeasance concerns the diversion of contracts from the company to the directors or to companies controlled by them: e.g. *Schott Kem v Bentley* [1990] 3 All E.R. 850. That case concerned a plumbing contractor with a special expertise in glass drainline pipework. The directors submitted artificially high tenders to prospective clients, following them up with lower unsolicited tenders on their own behalf. As time went by, they stopped bidding on behalf of the company and switched all enquiries to their own company, removed materials from site and appropriated payments in respect of labour supplied by the company. The Court of Appeal awarded substantial interim payments against the directors on account of claims for damages for breach of contract, the return of money paid under a mistake of fact, money had and received, and damages for conspiracy to defraud and the misuse of confidential information. In *Ball v Eden Project* [2002] 1 B.C.L.C. 313, a director registered a trademark in his own name in order to "hold the company to ransom", in a way analogous to the use of copyright as a lever to extract payment discussed in Ch.14. It was held that in registering the mark in his own name and for his own benefit the director was in clear breach of duty to the company. In *Blue Station v Kamyab* (unreported, February 6, 2007, David Donaldson Q.C.), a former director of an employer had to repay £100,000 to the company as he could not substantiate an agreement that he received the money as reimbursement after paying the builder on one of the company's projects. In *White Constructions v White* [2005] NSWCA 173 a contractor in liquidation failed in various misfeasance claims against its former directors. The action was funded by one of the creditors, an employer on a major project in which the contractor had been involved, who had a judgment debt of over $33 million. It was argued that the directors stripped the company of its assets in order to prevent the creditor from enforcing its judgment. But it could not be shown on the evidence that they knew at the time of the relevant transactions that the creditor would have a valid and substantial claim or that the company would not be in a position to meet it. Equally, none of the alleged divestments—book entries in group accounts, cessation of work following a merger, a share sale agreement to take advantage of tax losses, levy of management fees for group services, elimination of inter-company balances by set-off—amounted to breaches of duty. Nor could the company show that it suffered loss as a result.

Failure to differentiate between personal and company property is also apparent in *Roache v Culloo* [2005] IEHC 448 in which directors of a construction company purchased land in their own name but, after the development made a loss, maintained that everything had been done in the name of the company. They were disqualified for five years, and there was a specific finding of misfeasance against them.

6. Post-petition disposals

Any disposition of property by the company after a winding up petition has been issued against it is void unless validated by the court: s.127 of the Insolvency Act 1986. An application for validation can be made before or after the disposition. In general, a disposition for value in good faith and without notice of the petition will normally be validated unless there are grounds for believing that the payment was an attempt to prefer the beneficiary: *Denney v John Hudson* [1992] B.C.L.C. 901; *Re Gray's Inn Construction* [1980] 1 All E.R. 814. The application of the relevant principles to the industry was reviewed in *Re Luen Cheong Tai Construction* [2003] HKCFI 933. The court validated six payments to a subcontractor made after a petition was issued against a main contractor, which mostly represented subcontract work properly carried out and certified after the petition for which the contractor had been paid by the employer. The subcontract had been negotiated at arm's length. The subcontractor maintained that it was unaware of the petition but the court viewed this with "reasonable suspicion" since there had been a change in the dealings between the parties immediately afterwards. As a condition of the subcontractor's agreement to be involved with the project, an account had been set up in the joint names of contractor and subcontractor into which the employer made monthly payments. An agreed percentage was paid out as interim payments pending the taking of the final account. However, shortly after the winding up petition was issued a new account in the contractor's sole name was opened to receive the relevant funds from the employer from which the subcontractor was paid. The court held that the payments were made in the ordinary course of business and had benefited the contractor and its creditors by keeping the project afloat until it was nearly completed, thereby reducing the company's exposure to damages for early termination. The contractor had retained more than it was contractually entitled to and the subcontractor was an unsecured creditor to that extent. Finally the court felt that the subcontractor was virtually in the position of a post-liquidation creditor. Payments for hire of plant and equipment were validated under an equivalent Australian provision in *Sheahan & McGill Constructions v Piber Contractors* (1990) 3 A.C.S.R. 405. In that case the creditor was not aware of the petition and had enabled the company to continue working and realise work in progress. See also *Wreckair v Emerson* [1992] 1 Qd. 700. **20–012**

A validation order was refused in respect of payments made into an overdrawn current account and loan account between the date of the petition and the date of advertisement in *Re Tain Construction* [2003] 2 B.C.L.C. 374. There was evidence that the director of the contractor knew or must have known of the company's insolvency and of the existence of the petition. There was evidence that as guarantor of the company's indebtedness he intended to prefer the bank over and against HM Revenue & Customs. It could not be said that the payments to the bank had been for the benefit of creditors generally as the director had decided not to undertake further work and was completing existing contracts and collecting book debts. Direct payments to nominated subcontractors after presentation of a petition to wind up the contractor were invalidated in *Re Right Time Construction* (1990) 52 B.L.R. 117. The section could also invalidate a retention trust whether set up voluntarily or pursuant to a court order: compare the family law cases of *Re Flint* [1993] Ch. 319, *Treharne & Sand v Forrester* [2004] B.P.I.R. 338. Perhaps the court had this problem in mind in *Finnegan v Ford Sellar Morris* (1991) 53 B.L.R. 38 where an injunction was granted on terms that it would not be enforced for a period of time in case the employer was about to enter formal insolvency (Blackler 1998, at 768).

7. Use of prohibited names

20–013 By ss.216 and 217 of the Insolvency Act 1986, a director can be made personally liable for acting in relation to a company whose name is the same as a company (of which he was also a director) which has gone into insolvent liquidation within the preceding 12 months or is a name which is so similar as to suggest an association with that company. This is intended to address the so-called "phoenix syndrome" discussed in Ch.8. The common use of terms like "building" or "engineering" in company names in the industry might well expose many directors to this type of claim. A director was held liable in *Ricketts v Ad Valorem Factors* [2004] 1 B.C.L.C. 1. There, the company in liquidation was called Air Component Company Ltd while the other company was Air Equipment Company Ltd. Although this was not a phoenix case, and there was no evidence that creditors had been misled by the similar names, the Court of Appeal considered the section applied. In dealing with claims, the court enquires into all the circumstances in which the names are likely to be used, e.g. types of product, locations of the business, types of customers (para.22). Significantly, it was held that the provision could apply to group companies. The court considered that "the similarity between the two names must be such as to give rise to a probability that members of the public, comparing the names in the relevant context, will associate the two companies with each other, whether as successor companies or, as here, as part of the same group" (para.30, *per* Simon Brown L.J.). Similarly, "MPJ Contractors" was a prohibited name in relation to a director who had formerly acted for "MPJ Construction": *Archer Structures v Griffiths* [2004] 1 B.C.L.C. 201. In that case, the director argued that his liability should be limited to such sum as remained due to the claimant after applying liquidation set-off under r.4.90 of the Insolvency Rules 1986 (see Ch.18). This argument was rejected on the ground that s.216 had imposed a joint and several liability on the director before the company went into liquidation. The rule applied only to the company's liability. It might also be added that r.4.90 is concerned only with proof of debt. In this case the claimant would only wish to prove in the liquidation if it could not recover in full against the director.

Chapter 21

Directors and Employees

Once formed, a company lies dormant until animated by others. Only then can it become known, through its place of business, products, property, and the motives and actions of individuals which the law is prepared to attribute to it: *Meridian Global Funds v Securities Commission* [1995] 3 All E.R. 918. In the context of insolvency, those most relevant are directors and employees. 21–001

1. Directors

A director can be described in a number of ways: *de jure*, *de facto*, managing, non-executive, alternate, nominee, shadow, as well as by function in the company, e.g. contracts, development, finance. A *de jure* director is a person properly appointed as a director by the company. A director *de facto* acts as if he had been appointed and undertakes functions that only a director can perform: *Re Hydrodam* [1994] B.C.L.C. 180. A non-executive director also owes active duties to the company: *Re Continental Assurance* [1996] B.C.C. 888. 21–002

A director owes duties to the company rather than its shareholders, creditors or employees. His duty is to act in good faith in the best interests of the company. It demands honesty and the amount of care, skill and diligence which an ordinary man might be expected to take in his own affairs, but no greater degree of skill than can reasonably be expected from a person of his knowledge and experience: *Re City Equitable* [1925] 2 Ch. 407. Under English law the duties expected of a director have historically been lower than in other jurisdictions (Wheeler and Wilson 1998). They have now been codified by ss.171 to 177 of the Companies Act 2006, which are expected to come into force on October 1, 2008. The Act imposes duties to promote the success of the company, to exercise independent judgment, to avoid conflicts of interest, among others.

Duties to creditors

To what extent does the position change when a company becomes insolvent? The Companies Act 2006 does not deal with this situation. In *West Mercia Safetywear v Dodd* [1988] B.C.C. 250 the Court of Appeal approved an Australian case in which it was stated: 21–003

> "But where a company is insolvent the interests of the creditors intrude. They become prospectively entitled, through the mechanism of liquidation, to displace the power of the shareholders and directors to deal with the company's assets. It is in a practical sense their assets and not the shareholders' assets that, through the medium of the company, are under the management of the directors pending either liquidation, return to solvency, or the imposition of some alternative administration" (*Kinsela v Russell Kinsela* (1986) 4 N.S.W.L.R. 722 at 730, *per* Street C.J.).

Where a company is informally insolvent, the directors owe a duty to the company to take the creditors' interests into account but English law has not yet evolved a duty on the directors which is owed to the creditors themselves.

Shadow directors

21–004 Several insolvency claims can be made against a person other than a properly appointed director. For example, a fraudulent trading claim can be brought against any participator in the fraud and a misfeasance claim made against any person involved in the management of the company (Ch.20). The Insolvency Act 1986 extends liability for all claims which can be made against a director to a shadow director, who is defined by s.251 as "a person in accordance with whose directions or instructions the directors of the company are accustomed to act (but so that a person is not deemed a shadow director by reason only that the director acts on advice given by him in a professional capacity)". The concept of shadow directorship applies to construction companies in several ways. Where the contractor receives so much of its work from one particular employer that it effectively receives instructions from it, the employer and its directors could find themselves in the position of a shadow director. This example could apply to any other party in the contractual chain. Overdependence on one client was identified in Ch.8 as a cause of insolvency and is not uncommon where a contractor wishes to grow its business. In theory a parent may be a shadow director of other companies in the group although in practice this would require the active participation in the subsidiary's ordinary day to day decision making. A parent is normally regarded as an entirely separate entity from its subsidiaries and is not liable for their debts: *Adams v Cape Industries* [1990] Ch. 433. Hence the widespread use of parent company guarantees (Ch.19).

Liability in tort

21–005 Although English law has not developed a general duty to creditors so as to allow them to sue directors direct, certain causes of action are available to the creditors in tort or by statute. A director can become liable in the tort of deceit where he makes a representation which he knows to be false, or is reckless as to its truth, intending another person to act on it, and the person does so act on it and incurs loss. In *Thomas Saunders v Harvey* (1989) 30 Con. L.R. 103, a director of a subcontractor was held liable in deceit and negligent misstatement for confirming to a contractor that its proprietary flooring met with a certain specification. It became evident after installation that the flooring did not conform and that the representation had been false. The director was liable even though the representation had been made on behalf of the company in his capacity as managing director: see now *Standard Chartered Bank v Pakistan National Shipping* [2003] 1 A.C. 959. Similarly, in *Wong v Ratesharp* [1994/5] C.I.L.L. 1001, a director was held liable for damages in deceit for representing that his company had the expertise and skilled people for the work whereas it had only just been formed and had no working capital, and for falsely telling the employer that work to a particular stage, which triggered a further payment in advance, had been done when it had not. Compare *Convent Hospital v Eberlin* (1989) 14 Con. L.R. 1, where a claim in deceit against a director of a contractor failed because, although there had been a fraudulent misrepresentation, it was not an inducing cause of the contract. There had been a similar representation by the contractor's quantity surveyor which had been relied on but it could not be proved that the director had authorised it and he could not be held vicariously liable for torts which he had not authorised. The false representation was that the contractor had procured a performance bond. The contractor later went into receivership. The architect was found liable to the employer for failing to ensure that the bond had been provided but failed in its claim to pass on liability to the director.

If the director gave negligent rather than fraudulent advice, he would only be liable to a customer of the company who acted on the advice and suffered loss if objectively he assumed personal responsibility for the advice and the customer reasonably relied on his assumption of responsibility: *Williams v Natural Life Health Foods* [1998] 2 All E.R. 577. In that case, the House of Lords refused to award as damages the loss suffered by the plaintiffs following the liquidation of a company they had formed to take up a franchise from the defendant company. Compare also *Jarvis v Castle Wharf Developments* (2001) 17 Const. L.J. 430. A director can be made liable in the tort of trespass to goods for misapplying the property of another. This could happen where an unpaid supplier removes goods which had been fixed to the building where it had no contract with the landowner entitling it to enter for that purpose. Although the act is that of the supplier, the directors can be held liable in certain circumstances. This would normally require proof that the director expressly directed or procured the tortious acts: *Mancetter Developments v Garmanson* (1986) 2 B.C.C. 98,924. Where a director signs an order or a cheque without using the correct name of the company, he can be made personally liable under s.349 of the Companies Act 1985 to the addressee for the amount concerned: e.g. *Rafsanjan v Reiss* (1990) 7 C.L.D. 7.30.

In *Treadwell v Dawkins* (unreported, May 24, 2000, Nelson J.), the sole director of an employer was held liable for damages in deceit to the sole director of a contractor claiming as assignee after his company went into liquidation. The director of the employer had represented that funds were in place to finance construction work. In reliance on that representation, the contractor entered into a JCT design and build contract and suffered a loss of nearly £100,000 after it transpired that no funding was, in fact, available. The contractor was short of work and over-reliant on the contract to maintain its solvency; but it would not have undertaken the work without being satisfied that funding was in place. The fact that the director's motive for making the representation may have benign, in the sense that he hoped that it would shortly become true, was not relevant. A director can become liable for tortious acts committed in the course of his employment in three ways: if he himself commits the tort, if he assumes a personal liability, or if he procures the company to commit the tort. In *Treadwell*, the contractor accepted that representations were made by the employer rather than the director personally. This removed the first two grounds. It was clear to Nelson J. that the director's representation was both knowing and deliberate and could properly be described as procuring. It was also held that in arranging finance, the director was acting on behalf of an associated company of which he was also sole proprietor rather than in the course of his employment with the employer.

More recently in *McGarvey Construction v Shanks* [2007] CSOH 77, the court refused to strike out a claim by a contractor in damages for fraudulent misrepresentation against a director of the employer which had become insolvent owing an unsatisfied judgment debt to the contractor. The alleged representations were that the employer was developing the site, that it was in partnership with a well known housebuilder who was providing the finance for the development, and that the contractor would be working for both employer and housebuilder. The contractor had previously worked for the housebuilder but not the employer which was a shell company. In reliance on the representations, the contractor refrained from requiring a bond from the employer securing payment under the contract. See also *Contex Drouzhba v Wiseman* [2007] 1 B.C.L.C. 758. In *Arnhem Technology v Joiner* (unreported, January 31, 2000), a purchaser was asked by a director of the vendor to make advance payments into an account in his name for administrative reasons. On the vendor going into liquidation, Park J. rejected a claim by the purchaser for recovery of the payment from the director as money had and received on the ground that the arrangement had not displaced the director's role as agent of the company and the payment had been received by him in that capacity.

Statutory relief

21–006 Where a director or other officer of the company is found liable in proceedings in respect of negligence, default, breach of duty or breach of trust, he may yet be relieved of liability under s.727 of the Companies Act 1985 if he "has acted honestly and reasonably, and that having regard to all the circumstances of the case (including those connected with his appointment) he ought fairly to be excused. . ." (re-enacted by s.1157 of the Companies Act 2006). This relief was sought, but refused, in the wrongful trading cases discussed in Ch.20. Relief was granted in *Re D'Jan of London* [1993] B.C.C. 646, in which the court found that "conduct may be reasonable for the purposes of s.727 despite amounting to lack of reasonable care at common law" (at 649).

Agency

21–007 In exceptional cases, a shareholder can be made personally liable for a debt of an insolvent company if it can be shown that he entered into the contract as undisclosed principal for the company: *Hyundai Engineering v Prince Jefri Bolkiah* [2005] B.L.R. 416. In that case, Prince Jefri, brother of the Sultan of Brunei, failed in an application to strike out a claim by a contractor pursuant to an ICE design and construct form entered into with his company as employer. The contractor had suspended work and determined its employment for non-payment; the employer was then placed in compulsory liquidation in Brunei. The consent necessary to create an agency relationship could be implied from the surrounding circumstances. In this case, the employer did not own the site; nor was the development commissioned from a client; nor was the work in the ordinary course of its own business as a general contractor. The employer had no ability to operate the development commercially after it was completed. The terms of the construction contract did not impliedly exclude the principal's liability to be sued. The contractual terms would have worked if enforced against the undisclosed principal. There was some discussion of the insolvency termination clause. There might be a question whether the insolvency of the principal, by then disclosed, would be an event of default entitling the contractor to determine. The court thought this unlikely since the principal would not fall within the definition of employer. There was also no reason why an undisclosed principal of the employer should be unable to take the benefit of a performance bond in the same way as an assignee could take the benefit of a construction contract (paras.31–33).

2. Disqualification

Company Directors Disqualification Act 1986

The Act (as amended by the Insolvency Act 2000 and the Enterprise Act **21–008**
2002) gives the court power to disqualify any person from acting as a director or being concerned in the promotion, formation or management of a company. Where it is satisfied that the conduct of a director of an insolvent company makes him "unfit" to be concerned in the management of the company, the court must make a disqualification order of between two and 15 years. The application has to be made within two years after the start of the formal insolvency. The criteria of unfitness include breach of duty, misapplication of money or other property of the company, the extent of the director's responsibility for a transaction at an undervalue, the company's failure to maintain proper records, and failure to comply with obligations to provide information to insolvency practitioners. The primary purpose of the legislation is not to punish the individual but to protect the public. The power to disqualify is not fundamentally penal: *Re Lo-Line Electric Motors* [1988] Ch. 477 at 486. Incompetence or negligence can be sufficient for disqualification.

The Court of Appeal has issued guidelines on the period of disqualification. Two to five years is appropriate where the case is not very serious. Six to 10 years would apply for serious cases, and disqualification for over 10 years should be reserved for particularly serious cases, e.g. where the director had previously been disqualified: *Re Sevenoaks Stationers* [1990] B.C.C. 765. There could be an analogy between non-payment of Crown debts and an employer's non-payment or failure to make provision for retention: see *Re Stanford Services* (1987) 3 B.C.C. 326 at 334. Contravention of a disqualification order makes a director personally liable for all the debts of the company incurred after the contravention: s.15 of the Company Directors Disqualification Act 1986. He will also commit an offence punishable by a fine or imprisonment. In *Re H Laing Demolition Building Contractors* [1998] B.C.C. 561 the court refused to strike out disqualification proceedings on the ground that, on the evidence, it was possible that the respondent had been either a shadow director or a *de facto* director of the company in liquidation. Although not formally appointed as such, the respondent had become a signatory on the company's bank mandate. He was a director of a large contractor (Miskin) which was interested in acquiring the business of the company and actually provided a guarantee of the company's bank borrowing before formally acquiring its book debts and business. It was a case of serial insolvency as the contractor itself went into receivership several years later.

The Company Directors Disqualification Act 1986 (as amended by s.6 of the Insolvency Act 2000) allows the Secretary of State to accept an undertaking from a director in lieu of disqualification proceedings by which he agrees not to act as a director for a defined period without permission of the court. Normally a schedule of facts is attached to the undertaking which sets out the grounds of the director's unfitness to act (Walters and Davis-White 2005). The vast majority of disqualifications are now made in this way. A search of the register of disqualified directors can be made online at *http://www.insolvency.gov.uk*.

Industry cases

21–009 The grounds for disqualifying a director of a construction company are not usually industry-specific. For example, in *Re Carecraft Construction* [1993] 4 All E.R. 499 a builder carrying on business as a sole trader formed five different companies all of which went into liquidation a couple of years later. No accounts or annual returns were filed. Nor were returns made for National Insurance or PAYE. Crown debts were allowed to accrue, in some cases from the date of incorporation. No proper books of account were kept, and a sanguine view was taken of cash flow difficulties which arose six months before the company went into liquidation. The case proceeded on agreed facts and a disqualification order was made for the minimum period of two years.

The context was significant in *Re Grayan Building Services* [1995] B.C.C. 554 in which a disqualification order of two years was made. The company worked as subcontractor on three sites for the same contractor whose terms included a pay when paid clause. The company did not operate a pay when paid system with its sub-subcontractors. On two of the contracts, the main contractor agreed to certify payment on a fortnightly basis in return for a financing charge. On one contract where the company had a substantial loss and expense claim, the contractor was not paid by its client and therefore relied on its pay when paid clause. On the company's entry into liquidation, the contractor entered into direct contracts with the sub-subcontractors. Shortly before the liquidation, the directors made substantial payments into the company's overdrawn bank account which they had personally guaranteed. Preference proceedings were brought by the liquidator which were settled. Another payment to an associated company was declared a preference. The directors had caused the company to trade for six months after the point when they knew or ought to have known that it was bound to go into liquidation. The company wrote to the sub-subcontractors six months before liquidation informing them it was in financial difficulty. Similar problems over the following months were confirmed in the report distributed at the creditors' meeting. The contractor was only making payments on condition that the company paid the sub-subcontractors. The directors failed to keep accounting records which would enable them to allocate overheads and costs to particular contracts. Arden J. made no disqualification order but her decision was reversed on appeal. One of the relevant facts was the extent to which the directors had incurred credit after "the point of no return". The company had substantial claims against the contractor and believed they would be met but that was not an adequate reason to continue taking credit from subcontractors and supplies.

In *Official Receiver v Barnes* [2001] B.C.C. 578, the court disqualified a director of a subcontractor for four years primarily for failing to account to the Revenue for tax deducted from payments made to the company's self-employed workforce over a period of 18 months. The company was only able to trade by using these deductions as working capital. It must have been clear to the director that the decision to withhold payment was no mere temporary expedient. Significant sums were being withheld by main contractors and the resolution of such disputes had taken a long time. The company was balance sheet insolvent over the whole period. It was only by continuing to carry out work under their subcontracts, thereby denying the main contractor the opportunity of terminating or raising counterclaims, that the company had any prospect of recovering its claims from which to pay the Revenue. The director made no attempt to secure the Crown's agreement to this course of action. The company undertook seven contracts over two and a half years, each of which involved a major construction project. In five of these, it experienced difficulty in recovering payment from the contractor; but in four the company recovered payments equal to or in excess of the amount claimed. This above average level of dispute was attributed to the recession and the practice of "subbie bashing" by main contractors to assist their cash flow. The recoveries made in respect of the five disputed contracts were all achieved after the company had gone into administrative receivership and compulsory liquidation.

A director of four companies involved with damp-proofing, glazing, heating and plumbing was disqualified for ten years in *Re T & D Services* [1990] B.C.C. 592. The main grounds were that the companies had been funded by non-payment of Crown debts and there were preferences and the sale of a building at an undervalue to the director. The director withdrew substantial sums from the company's account, ostensibly to pay wages and buy materials, but this was not verifiable from the company's records. Likewise, a director of a building company who ignored an investigating accountant's report and wilfully misinterpreted a bank's willingness to extend an overdraft facility as evidence of the company's solvency was disqualified for three years in *Re GSAR Realisations* [1993] B.C.L.C. 409. In *Official Receiver v Zwirn* [2002] B.C.C. 760, a director of a double glazing company was disqualified for 11 years after five successive companies, of which he had been director, had gone into insolvent liquidation. Each had used the same trading name. Shortly before the end of each company's trading life the assets were sold to the next company, which traded from the same premises, of which the director was the lessee. The court observed that: "Honest creditors have been plagued by the phenomenon of phoenix companies for over 100 years" (at para.10, *per* Gabriel Moss Q.C.). In *Re Skyward Builders* two directors of a large construction group were disqualified: the first (Mr Broad) for 11 years by Blackburne J. (unreported, February 18, 2000); the second (Mr Mullarkey) for six years by John Randall Q.C. [2002] All E.R. (D) 367. Mr Broad had been a director of 76 companies of which 33 had gone into insolvent liquidation or receivership. Mr Mullarkey had been director of 56 companies of which 27 had become insolvent. See also *Kavanagh v Kelly* [2005] IEHC 421, a disqualification case involving directors of a company concerned with the supply of contract labour in relation to cabling and laying of telecommunication services. See Ch.8 for recent Australian research into the phoenix syndrome and Ch.22 for imaginal reflections.

3. Employees

21–010 As with directors, there is no all-embracing definition of an employee. Whether a person is employed or self-employed has a number of consequences. Only an employee renders an employer liable to contribute a levy to the Construction Industry Training Board or to claims under the Employment Rights Act 1996 for unfair dismissal, redundancy, etc. On a construction insolvency, the distinction between an employee and a self-employed person is relevant in three areas: the right to prove in a liquidation as a preferential creditor, the Transfer of Undertakings (Protection of Employment) Regulations 2006, and the tax deduction scheme operated in the industry. On employment law as it affects the construction industry, see Ryley and Goodwyn (2000).

Preferential debts

21–011 A preferential creditor takes priority over other unsecured creditors and floating charge-holders: s.386 of the Insolvency Act 1986. Where the assets are insufficient to meet them in full, preferential debts abate rateably: s.175 of the Insolvency Act 1986. Schedule 6 of the Act lists categories of debts which are accorded preferential status. By virtue of s.251 of the Enterprise Act 2002, with effect from September 15, 2003, sums owed to the Crown in respect of unpaid PAYE and VAT ceased to have preferential status. This includes sums due in respect of deductions which should have been made from sums payable to subcontractors working in the construction industry (formerly Category 1). Category 5, however, remains in place. This includes remuneration owed to an employee in respect of the whole or any part of the period of four months before the commencement of a formal insolvency procedure subject to a maximum of £800, together with accrued holiday pay, and money advanced to pay either of the above claims which would otherwise have been preferential debts. For the purposes of Category 5, the Act does not define an employee, but it does define remuneration as a sum "paid as wages or salary (whether payable for time or for piece work or earned wholly or partly by way of commission) in respect of services rendered to the debtor". On its face, the Act therefore excludes self-employed workmen and labour-only subcontractors.

Money advanced to pay wages and used for that purpose will be a preferential debt to the extent that the employees' preferential claims have been reduced: *Re Primrose Builders* [1950] Ch. 561. Thus, in *CW & AL Hughes, Re* [1966] 1 W.L.R. 1369, a contractor obtained an overdraft to operate a wages account. When the contractor went into voluntary liquidation, it was found that part of the overdraft represented payments to labour-only subcontractors made within four months before the winding up resolution. It was held that the liquidator was correct in refusing to treat the payments as being made "on account of wages or salary" within s.319(4) of the Companies Act 1948. Occasionally the employer pays the contractor's workforce direct. In *Greenore Port v Technical & General* [2006] EWHC 3119, it appears that only net wages were paid leaving it to the contractor to account to HM Revenue & Customs for PAYE and National Insurance contributions (para.107).

Transfer of Undertakings

Under the Transfer of Undertakings (Protection of Employment) Regulations 2006 (replacing the 1981 Regulations for transfers after April 6, 2006), when a business is sold the purchaser takes over responsibility for existing contracts of employment. An example of how the Regulations can apply to the industry arose in *Rolfe v Amey Construction* (unreported, November 13, 1992). Following the appointment of administrative receivers to Farr plc, 33 out of its 39 contracts were novated to Amey. Some of Farr's employees were not taken on by the purchaser and applied to an industrial tribunal for compensation for unfair dismissal. It was held that there had been a relevant transfer under the Regulations entitling the employees to claim compensation from Amey. The determining features were that: 21–012

- There had been an express assignment of goodwill.
- The reason why six contracts were not novated was not because Amey did not want to novate but because employers refused to accept a novation.
- Disruption was kept to a minimum by Amey's agreement to pay subcontractors direct.
- Before entering into the sale agreement with the receivers, Amey had offered employment to key site and head office staff.
- Amey took over part of Farr's premises under a separate agreement.

In the context of an insolvency the scope of the purchaser's liability will depend on the relevant insolvency procedure (see generally Lightman and Moss 2007).

The Construction Industry Scheme

The self-employed are taxed under Sch.D of the Income and Corporation Taxes Act 1988 which entitles them to defer payment of tax. Employees are taxed under Sch.E by which tax is deducted under the PAYE system. The self-employed have a cash flow advantage over the employed. Self- 21–013 employment has historically been high in the construction industry. Schedule D is open to abuse if the tax-payer absconds without paying the tax. In order to deal with widespread evasion of income tax, the Finance Act 1971 introduced a system whereby contractors have to deduct tax before making payments to a subcontractor unless the subcontractor obtains a certificate from the Inland Revenue entitling it to be paid gross. The system is contained in the 1988 Act as amended and the Income Tax (Subcontractors in the Construction Industry) Regulations 1993. It applies to all payments to subcontractors relating to construction operations. Under s.560 of the 1988 Act, a contractor is any person carrying on a business which includes construction operations.

The definition of subcontractor is wide enough to include the self-employed and labour-only subcontractors. It is even possible that a direct payment by an employer to a subcontractor could fall within the scheme (Ch.17). "Gross payment certificates" CIS 5 and CIS 6 are only issued to subcontractors whose turnover exceeds certain levels. This can adversely affect a subcontractor's cash flow since the labour element of its payments will be reduced by 23 per cent (Sadler 1999). Even if the subcontractor does not qualify under the scheme, and has to be paid net of tax, it has to obtain a registration card from the Revenue in order to be entitled to be paid at all. A contractor is liable to a penalty if payment is made to a subcontractor without a card. This requirement is intended to address the problem of "the lump" (see Bibliography) by giving the Inland Revenue access to information as to who is working in the industry and what they are earning. A new scheme is due to be introduced in 2007 whereby contractors will be required to declare that all subcontractors included in their monthly return to HM Revenue & Customs are genuinely self-employed: Income Tax (Sub-contractors in the Construction Industry) Regulations 2005, Beneyworth (2007).

There are several insolvency implications of the scheme. First, tax not deducted within 12 months before the start of the insolvency procedure is no longer a preferential debt (see para.21–011 above). Second, if an insolvency practitioner continues trading and pays a subcontractor gross, there is a risk that, if the subcontractor later defaults, the company could become liable to pay the deduction to the Inland Revenue, unless it can be shown that the payment was made in good faith and the practitioner exercised reasonable care in making it. If the court finds that insufficient care has been exercised, it is possible that the deduction could be a pre-preferential claim in the insolvency procedure. Third, under s.565 of the 1988 Act, it is a condition of entitlement to an exemption certificate that the subcontractor must have complied with its tax obligations, although "minor and technical" failures are excused: *Hudson v JDC Services* [2004] S.T.C. 834, *Barnes v Hilton Main Construction* [2005] S.T.C. 1532.

In *Gorge Fabrications v Wilson* (September 27, 1999, Special Commissioner Paul W de Voil), a subcontractor failed in an appeal against Inland Revenue's refusal to grant a certificate. The company had entered a voluntary arrangement under which a corporation tax liability of £4,000 was treated as a non-preferential debt in respect of which a payment of 25 pence in the pound was made, leaving £2,927 unpaid. The company argued that it was unfair to deny a certificate on this ground because, as a result of the CVA, the unpaid tax was no longer payable and could not be paid without unfairness to other non-preferential creditors. In addition, the PAYE and NIC debt of £30,000 had been treated as preferential and paid in full, and similar payments falling due after the voluntary arrangement was entered into exceeding £55,000 had been made. The tribunal advised the company to make another application in six months time at the end of the next qualifying period.

Who is an "employee"?

There is a substantial body of case law on the relevant criteria for deciding **21–014**
when a person working in the construction industry is an employee (Benneyworth 2007, 57–67). There are two fundamental questions: Must the work be done by the individual or could he provide a substitute? Is the individual both entitled to further work from the employer and obliged to accept it? Other criteria include: the amount of control the person has over how he does his job; whether the person supplies his own equipment; how long the person has been working for the contractor; whether the person runs his own business from separate premises; the degree of risk of non-payment undertaken; and whether the person tenders on a competitive basis. Leaflet CIS 349 sets out the criteria for an employee as interpreted by HM Revenue & Customs.

Chapter 22

Law into Myth

This book began by contemplating an image. In order to stay alive to the phenomena of construction insolvency rather than closing them down by too much legal definition, we called on the ancestors, metaphors, and perspectives at work in the industry. In this final chapter I would like to deepen the intervening legal analysis by placing it against the background of myth. I use "myth" not in the popular sense of misconception or falsehood but to refer to a basic pattern of the imagination. It seems to me that the legal concepts and procedures considered in this book evoke the myths of four gods: Saturn, Athene, Dionysos, and Zeus, who are traditionally linked with earth, air, water and fire respectively. At the outset it may be helpful to say a few words about myth in general. **22–001**

1. Two kinds of thinking

One of the insights of the psychologist C. G.Jung is to speak of "two kinds of thinking: directed thinking, and dreaming, or fantasy-thinking. The former operates with speech elements for the purpose of communication, and is difficult and exhausting; the latter is effortless, working as it were spontaneously, with the contents ready to hand, and guided by unconscious motives" (Jung 1998, 116). **22–002**

The legal method is a particularly strong example of directed thinking. The approach is conceptual, structured, much concerned with categories and cause and effect. A proposition has to be supported by authority; it must be tied as it were to the known. This kind of thinking values logic and order, and proceeds through the intentional development of an argument. It tends to be slow and can be ponderous. By contrast, Jung characterises fantasy-thinking as associative: images pile on images, feeling on feeling. Ideas rise and fall of their own motion, as if independent of the thinker. There is no criterion of relevance, either to external reality or a particular purpose. Instead, what is valued is the free flow of the process, the sense of pleasure and refreshment that it brings, the shock of the new, and a feeling of being involved in a drama not entirely of one's own making. The contrast is between literal and metaphorical; factual and poetic; in sum, between law and myth.

One of the things I have learned from writing this book is the need to understand the legal method. By "understanding" I am not referring to the techniques of the lawyer; I mean the need to "see through" the method to its mythical background. "To enter myth," argues James Hillman, "we must personify; to personify carries us into myth" (1976, 16). "What archetypal pattern is like my present behavior and fantasy? Who am I like when I do and feel this way?" he asks. This is a call to education, or "counter-education" as it been called, in the imaginative traditions in which the classical gods and goddesses are initiators and guides as well as subjects. These include what survive of their myths as told by poets and re-imagined in art forms such as pottery, metalwork, sculpture, painting and drama, and the hermetic arts of astrology and alchemy. The strange thing is that myths once played a significant part in legal education. Raffield (2004) gives a wonderful account of revels in sixteenth-century inns of court in which the lawyers took roles such as "knights of Athene". Participation was compulsory because poetic drama was a model for the values of the law and the attributes needed to practise it.

Mythos means story, and at its simplest a myth is a story of the gods—of their encounters among each other and with humankind. Who are the gods for us? "A God is a manner of existence, an attitude toward existence, and a set of ideas" (Hillman 1976, 130). The gods are personifications but not allegories. "Allegory only presents what consciousness already knows" (Shearer 1998, 154). If imagination is the background to all that we do, think and feel, then we can be seized at any time by mythic images with their own power to move and shock us even for a moment. James Hillman, who developed Jung's ideas into the new field of archetypal psychology, says that falling in love with images is the beginning of "psychological faith" in the reality of imagination (1976, 50). "Instead of reducing meaning to a definition, myths amplify and complicate. They are the path of richness. Myths add information to phenomena and offer insights. They provide images, puzzles, humour. . . . In a curious way, myths provide more objectivity than do models of thought" (Hillman 1995, 102–3).

In my own case, I was attracted by the metaphorical language used by the law in connection with insolvency. For many years it was just a vague curiosity, a hunch that there was more to the technical terms than met the eye. Then I began to collect examples and turn them over in the mind like pebbles. A word like encumbrance for example turns out to refer to the Old French *combre*, a river barrage formed by blocking the flow of water with felled trees. Seeing the image in the word in this way warms the imagination: slowly other connections are made (see Ch.1), and a pattern starts to emerge. Reading works on myth such as those by Kerényi (1951) and Graves (1960), on which the versions in this chapter are based, led me to the Greek god Kronos, known to the Romans as Saturn, and to some interesting reflections on the themes of this book seen through the saturnine perspective.

2. Saturn and his children

22–003 Ancient images portray the god as an old man with a cloak pulled over his head, carrying a sickle. Sometimes he is shown seated with his head resting on his hand, the pose of melancholy. Klibansky calls him the "most sinister of the gods," citing his frightening eyes, severe and menacing appearance, and unusual rigidity (1964, 197). Abû Ma'šar, a ninth-century Arabic astrologer, says that Saturn:

> "presides over . . . owners of land, works of construction . . . measuring things, division of estates . . . bitter poverty; over those who enslave men and rule, . . . bondage, imprisonment, distraint, fettering, caution, pondering, reflection . . . old men; over fear, reverses of fortune, loss, deaths . . .

fathers, misers; over those covered with shame . . . over people who count things . . . matters of boredom" (quoted in Klibansky 1964, 130).

Another writer, Alcabitus, accords the faculty of distinguishing to Saturn. In medieval art he was shown as a peasant working in the fields. Renaissance images drawing on astrological traditions show him as a cripple (Plate 4), prisoner or beggar. Particular trades came to be associated with him such as accountants, treasurers, carpenters, stonemasons, grave-diggers, latrine-cleaners, knife-grinders and "men who serve writs". Geometry and measuring of all kinds belonged to him, including time (hourly rates). He was a deep thinker, much concerned with making order. He was called *tekton sophos*, wise builder of cities; he invented agriculture and coin-minting. Cold and dry, yet he had a special relation to water, including death by drowning. The zodiacal constellation Aquarius, the Water Bearer, is traditionally a palace of Saturn.

Saturnine figures in literature include Faust, especially as he embarks on a massive project of land reclamation at the end of Goethe's poetic drama, and Lear dividing his kingdom in the opening scene of Shakespeare's play, rewarding his two daughters Goneril and Regan with Cordelia's share, when she cannot perform as he expects (an image of direct payment perhaps). We might recall too T.S. Eliot's poem "The Love Song of J Alfred Prufrock", who measured out his life with coffee spoons, and Goya's horrific painting of Saturn eating his children.

Geometry and melancholy, earth and water: is Saturn the god to whom we can return construction insolvency? We can find out more by telling his myths.

Every night Ouranos (starlit sky) mated with Gaia (deep-breasted earth), but he so hated the children she bore for him that he took grim pleasure in pushing them back into the darkest folds of her womb. Gaia let out her suffering in deep groans until her pain became unbearable. She created within herself a sickle of steel with sharp teeth and asked each of her sons to help her punish Ouranos for shaming her so. All were silent except for Kronos, her last-born, who promised to do her bidding. When his father came that night, Kronos lay in wait for him. As Ouranos slept, Kronos castrated him with the sickle and threw the genitals with his left hand behind his back into the sea. The waves carried them for a long time but eventually from the foam was born the goddess Aphrodite.

After this deed Kronos became lord of the Titans. One story told of him is that he lay with Philyra, daughter of Okeanos, in the form of a stallion so as to deceive his sister-wife Rhea. Their son was Chiron the centaur who became a teacher, musician and healer. But Philyra rejected Chiron at birth and prayed to the gods to be changed from her present state. She was metamorphosed into a lime tree.

Gaia told Kronos that his fate was to be dethroned by one of his sons. As a result he was constantly on the alert and swallowed each of his children as they emerged from the womb of Rhea. This caused Rhea grief beyond endurance and, on advice from Gaia and Ouranos, she gave birth to her sixth child Zeus in secret substituting an enormous stone wrapped in swaddling clothes for Kronos to swallow. Zeus grew up under Gaia's protection and, on reaching manhood, he hatched a plan to release his siblings. He obtained an emetic potion from Metis the Titaness and mixed it with Kronos's drink. He vomited up the stone, followed by Rhea's five children, who became the Olympian gods Hestia, Demeter, Hera, Hades, and Poseidon. Zeus then released the Cyclops, Kronos's brothers, from Tartarus. They vowed to fight on the side of Zeus in the ensuing war with the Titans.

Zeus threw chains around Kronos and took him to Tartarus, the deepest part of the underworld. There he ordered a bronze wall to be constructed, finished with impenetrable gates. There Kronos languishes, defeated for all time, alone in the eternal darkness. But others say he was exiled to the Isles of the Blest at the ends of the earth where he reigns in peace from the Tower of Kronos.

These are the bones of the Greek myth of Kronos, archetypal image of failure. Saturnus was an ancient god of central Italy associated with the winter solstice. As a working god, he manured and ploughed the fields, and carried out the winter sowing. He was synonymous with abundance and ruled Italy during the Golden Age.

> "In the temple of Saturn near the Capitol the State treasury was kept, as well as the standards of the legions which were not on campaign. The god's effigy was bound with woollen strips which prevented him from leaving Roman territory. His bands were untied during the Saturnalia" (Larousse 1968, 205–6).

The weights and measures used in the market places were also kept in his temple.

The Orphic philosophers revered Chronos as god of Time. They saw him as the architect of the world. The similarity of the name led to his being identified with Kronos. Chronos was imagined as a bond that was thought to encircle the cosmos. The bond was sometimes interpreted as a snake biting its own tail; it was also associated with the river, whose god was Okeanos, that ran like a band around the cosmos, washing the stars as it went (Onians 1951, 248–51).

Kronos, Saturnus, Chronos—three gods who form the archetypal pattern known as Saturn. This assembly of fragments, persons, places, events, and emotions constitutes the mythic background. If we now return to the themes of this book, and hold them lightly against the myths of Saturn, what do we notice?

Burdened with debt

22–004 First, it is apparent that the god has a particular attitude towards money. In the Saturnian world view money is associated with power maintained by force. Selby says that: "Debt brings about a power relationship and creates a 'bond' (the word is significant) that is often unequal and constraining" (1997, 3). He adds that debt has a "highly dangerous capacity to bind the future and impose the will of the creditor on the debtor" (68–69). This is precisely Saturn's intention in swallowing his children.

In Saturn's myth, however, he is also in the position of the debtor, powerless and defeated. He is often portrayed as lame, hobbling with a crutch. We use phrases such as "crippling debt", "debt burden", and "hopelessly insolvent". In Ch.3 it was suggested that in the construction industry, rights to payment are crippled by conditionality: dependent on certificates, on payment to the payer, on the contract not being terminated. Until final completion the contractor only ever has a conditional, provisional right to payment. Nothing is ever absolutely acquired, everything is contingent on perfect performance. When Brunel withholds payment to ensure a contractor's good behaviour (Ch.1), Saturn swallows another child. The story is told of a party trick Brunel used to play for his children in which he would appear to swallow a coin only to produce it from behind his ear. Unfortunately one day he actually swallowed the coin and it became stuck in his throat. After suffering for several weeks he designed a device himself whereby he was strapped to a board and turned upside down, and the coin came back out. A very saturnine tale!

In Renaissance books of emblems, a figure called *Debito* appears. In a contemporary guide, the *Iconologia* by Cesare Ripa, he is called a bankrupt or debtor and described in these terms:

> "A sad and melancholy young man; with ragged clothes, and a green bonnet upon his head; having fetters on his arms and legs like round rings; and in his mouth a basket; with a scourge in his [right] hand, whereon hang leaden bullets; a hare laying before his feet. This figure is formed partly out of natural things, and partly out of the present and ancient use of shame, wherewith debtors are punished" (Ripa website).

We are only now losing the stigma that for centuries attached to insolvency. The Latin word *debita* means both debt and duty; the German *Schuld* implies debt and guilt. Debt has power to enslave, as with debt bondage. The melancholy and shame attributed to debtors is a sign of Saturn's presence.

In *The Fall of Hyperion* (1819) John Keats describes the temple of Saturn, attended by his priestess Moneta. In calling her Moneta (= money) Keats evokes the god's temple in Rome. The poet goes up to the priestess, and asks the reason for her extreme sadness.

> Deep in the shady sadness of a vale
> Far sunken from the healthy breath of morn,
> Far from the fiery noon and eve's one star,
> Onward I look'd beneath the gloomy boughs,
> And saw what first I thought an image huge,
> Like to the image pedestal'd so high
> In Saturn's temple; then Moneta's voice
> Came brief upon mine ear. "So Saturn sat
> When he had lost his realms"; whereon there grew
> A power within me of enormous ken
> To see as a god sees, and take the depth
> Of things as nimbly as the outward eye
> Can size and shape pervade.

Perhaps money mediates Saturn in our lives: whenever we are obsessed, possessed, depressed by money (or its absence) the god is near. Elsewhere Keats describes Saturn as "unsceptered". There is no sense of heroic rescue, no plan for recovery. These belong to different myths. Power has passed away from him forever yet the sense of timeless isolation his presence evokes in the poet cultivates an inward eye for the depth of things as real as sense-perceptions. A paradox: loss of power externally and growth of power internally. Powers of different orders. Writing these words I see the eyes of Saturn's children sitting silently in his dark mouth.

Bringing something literal to the right myth subtly changes perception. A blocked account used to secure payment on performance of conditions becomes a police cell, a place of languishing while evidence is considered. The cell turns into a stagnant pool dense with uncollected leaves. The image is of dead things. Saturn is often viewed negatively and his philosophy of restraint and frustration is not going to be popular, but it needs to be remembered that Saturn is the most contradictory of the gods; he manifests in images of abundance as well as deprivation; and that the limitation he imposes is a negative way to other gods. James Hillman (2005) puts forward a powerful case that Saturn needs Hermes and vice versa, that serious problems occur when one dominates the other. Saturn is the *senex*, the principle of age with associations of rigidity; Hermes is the *puer*, priniciple of youthful transformations: two faces of the same mirror.

Building and ruling

22–005 Saturn is not the only god associated with construction but his traits certainly appear in the industry's conservatism, its careful planning and costing of work (estimators, quantity surveyors, bills of quantity), a certain unease with women, tremendous conflicts over money, legalistic inclinations, obsessions with time, internal lack of communication, preoccupations with property. Contractually, security and control are carried to pathological excess. Even the word "contracting" in the sense of shrinking or shrivelling up implies the god.

> "The concern with structure and abstraction makes him the principle of order, whether through time, or hierarchy, or exact science and system, or limits and borders, or power, or inwardness and reflection, or earth and the forms it gives" (Hillman 2005, 43).

Contractors work with Saturn's element—earth. In a sense, like Saturn the farmer they cultivate the land and increase its value. According to the Twelve Tables, one of the earliest systems of law promulgated in Rome in the fifth century B.C.E., building materials belonging to another became part of the land on annexation and could not be recovered until the building fell down. The rule exists today in English law in modified form (Ch.7). The image is of bricks as seeds planted in the soil.

There is also Saturn's image as Chronos, Father Time. Contractors are paid in arrears. We could see credit, that Nicolas Barbon loved so much (Ch.1), as an image of our ability to distinguish between present and future, to know time as an idea. Construction work involves programming the sequence of trades in great detail culminating in a fixed date for completion. Failure to complete on time results in liquidated damages, measured by days or weeks of delay. Time in this linear sense gives rise to expressions such as "cut-off" or "longstop" dates, or the rather grim "drop-dead" date. But Chronos circulates, flowing like the river of life. This difference in time is between material and spiritual perspectives and responds to the paradoxical nature of Saturn himself.

In Ch.3 evidence was quoted from a parliamentary inquiry into the practice of withholding five per cent of interim payments until completion (retention). Subcontractors said they felt powerless to recover their due. One said he almost had to beg for its return. With Saturnian deceit, the employer may allege non-existent defects or withhold payment for no reason. The contractor repeats the archetypal pattern by doing the same to subcontractors, a castration of the son by the father, for Kronos is both father and son. The series of contracts between employer-contractor-subcontractor is usually imagined as a chain but they could be understood as generations (Ouranos–Kronos–Zeus). We remember Nicholas Barbon rebuilding his father's house, and the fear of debt in Marc Brunel's household (Ch.1). I wonder whether, when main contractors emerged as a new industry entity in the mid-nineteenth century, they assumed the characteristics of employers like Barbon and engineers like Brunel when dealing with subcontractors.

To protect the contractor against the risk of non-payment of retention, a contract may require the employer to set aside an equivalent amount into a trust account. Placed against Saturn's myths, this is like swallowing two children, a double blocking. One wall is built by the employer (retention) and another by the contractor (trust). Both parties are saturnine, both are in Tartarus, the place to which we can return "risk management". **22–006**

Subcontracts often "incorporate", *mutatis mutandis*, the terms of the main contract ("the sins of the father"). Many a contractor has begun life as a subcontractor. The tone of contract correspondence can be childish and petulant, protesting or dismissive. Contractors often have soaring ambition and show a child-like eagerness for money and the things it can buy. I also pick up from the "sub" of subcontractor a hint of repression, as if the subcontractors are complexes threatening the contractor: submission, subjection, subordination.

The characteristic qualities of the titans are boundless pride and violence (Lopez-Pedraza 2000, 5–14). A titan would not think twice about exploiting another's weaker commercial position, whatever the contract may say—"predatory commerce" as Hillman calls it (1995, 43). This could be a way of appreciating the aggression and humiliation felt between contractors and subcontractors in fights over money. In this context, the wounding inflicted by delaying or evading payment goes right to the heart of the subcontractor's being. It is repudiating the maxim that a labourer is worthy of his hire and, somewhere within this macho industry, there lurks an equation between money and masculinity. Contractors can be titanic when they build, reckless of the effect on the earth's ecosystems. Projects on a vast scale requiring enormous amounts of energy, organisation, and the impersonal deployment of resources are commonplace. Thomas Moore speaks of "the tyranny of the usual Saturnian ego, which always wants to build and rule" (1989, 161).

The industry shuts down for two weeks over Christmas. Christmas obscures the Saturnalia, the god's winter festival, during which the normal establishment was reversed, with servants becoming masters. The law courts did not sit. "Encumbering togas were removed and [people] ate at ease in tunics" (Larousse 1968, 207). Possibly we are doing this now with dress down days, when ties are optional.

"Not pleasant to read"

Many gods are implicated in law, law-making, and justice. In the Greek world there are Zeus, Metis, Themis, Dike, Apollo, Hestia, Saturn, and others—each with a different pattern. *Perhaps we need an archetypal jurisprudence* **22–007** *which carefully and lovingly differentiates them*. In this book I am focusing on Saturn partly because he seems to be significant for insolvency and construction as well as law, and partly because methods of distinguishing and assimilating cases resonate with the myths of this god.

Immersion in legal study is an initiation into Saturn. Intuitions and insights arrive like taps from a prison cell. This has been reported since at least the sixteenth century. Peter Goodrich observes: "The study of law has always traveled under the sign of Saturn, and the sages both of common and civil law have seldom paused to doubt the depressing character of legal study" (1995, 1). He quotes William Fulbecke writing in 1599: "The books of law . . . are not pleasant to read, the words or terms are harsh and obscure, dull, and coldly prosaic, the style no whit delightful, the method none at all" (at 2). By becoming adept in the law, a person becomes a child of Saturn. But that means he or she will be consumed by the god. And with mythical accuracy that is what Fulbecke concluded: that law is addictive and consumes the student from within (Goodrich 1995, 4).

Every phenomenon brought to the court's attention is assessed by reference to established principles. The new is always judged against the pattern of the old. The common law is the yardstick: once a dispute is decided, the judgment is assimilated (devoured) by the common law, and so the cycle continues. A tenth-century prayer to Saturn (thought to derive from a Greek source) invokes the god in these terms:

> "O Master Saturn: Thou, the Cold, the Sterile, the Mournful, the Pernicious; Thou, whose life is sincere and whose word sure; Thou, the Sage and Solitary, the Impenetrable; Thou, whose promises are kept; Thou who art weak and weary; Thou who hast cares greater than any other, who knowest neither pleasure nor joy; Thou, the old and cunning, master of all artifice, deceitful, wise, and judicious; Thou who bringest prosperity or ruin, and makest man to be happy or unhappy! I conjure Thee, O Supreme Father, by Thy great benevolence and Thy generous bounty, to do for me what I ask" (quoted in Hillman 2005, 68).

These epithets have a distant strangeness to them. They show an ancient appreciation of archetypal complexity. We can sense a strong feeling in them, recollect Dionysius of Syracuse from Ch.1, and notice how the prayer speaks of a god "whose promises are kept", as if he images security in himself. The god is addressed as "weak and weary", with "cares greater than any other". His metal is lead. Words associated with legal security devices reflect this aspect. "Charge" for example is derived from the Latin word *carricare*, to load. As well as burdening a property with a financial liability, a charge may accuse a person of crime or sin. Mortgage means dead pledge.

22–008 I suggested in Ch.3 that conclusive evidence clauses found in various contexts are informal security devices. They can be seen as the modern secular equivalent of the classical oath, whose function ". . . is to guarantee that a statement is absolutely binding, whether it be a statement about something in the past or a declaration of intent for the future" (Burkert 1989, 250). Oaths were religious acts accompanied by animal sacrifice and, of course, invoked the gods. (When the gods swore oaths they did so in the name of Gaia.) Walter Burkert comments further:

> "Not without irony, Plato shows how Protagoras, who doubts the existence of the gods, cannot do without temples: he make the sophist assert, 'When

someone has finished with my instruction, if he agrees, he pays me what I ask and the matter is finished; if not, he has to go to the temple and swear on oath how much my instruction seems worth to him, and he deposits that sum' (328). Entirely archaic here is the fact that the oath signifies an act of self-determination: the debtor determines under oath the amount of the sum to be repaid." (at 253)

In this context, swearing an oath protected the debtor. A modern conclusive evidence clause is sometimes for the benefit of both parties but more often than not is inserted to protect the creditor. The difference is significant as the laws of the Mediterranean countries favour the debtor even today (Wood 1997, 1998).

Saturn rules over the winter solstice, the end of the year. He is much concerned with endings. Any bringing of the threads to a conclusion is a Saturnian move. Closing is a part of his patterning: closing down sales, legal submissions before judgment, gates and doors, site hoardings. It is worth noting that the Latin word *claudere* (= to close) is the root of seclusion, reclusive, cloister, as well as clause. Novation simultaneously ends one contract and brings another into being, like the snake imagined as Chronos.

The legal method with its categorising and distinguishing is based on the metaphor of cutting. A lawyer is said to possess a sharp mind; a judge cuts through the mass of evidence, sorting the reliable from the unreliable. A judgment doesn't waste words; it's incisive. Definitions are supposed to foster precision. Insolvency law is based on the rateable division of property among the creditors—dismembering the body, cutting the cake. The god's sickle is also reminiscent of the forfeiture of property on insolvency. But Saturn is also cut off from relationship with life. Everything is seen in terms of ownership of property. *Is there is a saturnine psychopathy in the way the law treats a contract or a demand bond as disposable property*?

The legal draftsman aims to close down the inherent generativity of words, to strip them of imaginal potential, of their power to move us and to stir memory. In the industry, the most extreme examples are contracts drafted on PFI projects, which are dominated by lengthy definitions clauses. Words are corralled into singleness of meaning. The same applies to the treatment of numbers by accountants. The aim is not so much clarity (Apollo) as control (Saturn). William Fulbecke's words quoted earlier now seem an understatement: these contracts are certainly "not pleasant to read". Law textbooks tend to follow a similar model; they are written as if the author is addressing the court and thus leave out anything not strictly relevant to the judicial function. From the point of view of the imagination, the end result is like a beggar slumped on a pallet, unseen in the shadows.

3. Athene the Worker

When Zeus was planning how to force Kronos to release his children, he consulted Metis. She was called "the most knowing" and "of many counsels". **22–009**
He found her near the river Okeanos, the living waters that coursed around the cosmos—her father. She knew the properties of herbs and provided Zeus with what he needed. When she later became pregnant by him, Zeus was told by Ouranos and Gaia that after Metis had had a daughter, she would give birth to a son who would usurp the place of Zeus as father of gods and men.

And so, as Kronos had done before him, he swallowed her whole. When her time came, the smith god Hephaistos split open Zeus's head with an axe, and out sprang their daughter Athene, fully armed.

This time the assimilation is different: Zeus becomes wise through Metis, and generates Athene to work the wisdom of Metis in the world. By incorporating her way of knowing, Zeus was able to remain in power; she ensured that his rule would not be of Saturn's fearful kind. As child of Metis and Zeus she mingles a deep intuitive knowing with a very public face. Although we now associate the head with the conscious mind, the Greeks understood it as the seat of the life-soul (Onians 1951, 154). Being born from Zeus's head, Athene is rational but not rationalistic; she is attuned to depth. If Saturn is heavy and difficult to work like earth, Athene brings an airy sense of swiftness and ease to legal practice.

Spear and spindle

22–010 A famous image of Athene shows her standing with a spear in her right hand and a spindle in her left: war and peace together. She is often shown fully armed, wearing a warrior's helmet and the aegis of Zeus with the head of Medusa. From Metis she inherited what is called "cunning intelligence", an awareness of the right moment to act. Her style of warfare was tactical and planned out. In this, she differs from the brute strength of Saturn and the titans. Perhaps we can return to her the rules of procedure governing civil litigation: elaborate and technical, yet capable of stopping a claim in its tracks. Her spear suggests an injunction, a well-timed pre-emptive measure. Rules of set-off whereby a cross-claim is accorded the status of a defence also feel part of her pattern. In the case of equitable set-off, the claim and cross-claim are interdependent. The court often uses the metaphor of weaving to describe them:

> "The two claims under consideration have their origin in the same portion of the same contract, where the obligations which give rise to them are intertwined in the closest manner" (*Governor of Newfoundland v Newfoundland Railway Co* (1888) 13 App. Cas. 199 at 212, *per* Lord Hobhouse).

It is worth pausing here to notice what has happened. The question of set-off arose in connection with defending (shield) but the image has changed to that of weaving (spindle). We have moved from one hand to the other: the defence is the weave. Things are not as they seem. The feeling of these images is different from those of Saturn. Now it is the walls of the city not the walls of Tartarus or Saturn's mouth that act as a defence. Athene promotes security in the sense of public safety not imprisonment. Perhaps Saturn fixes experience in the sense of separating elements, segregating me from you; whereas Athene joins phenomena together. Ann Shearer says of Athene:

> "This essential quality, this relatedness of hers, is what the Greeks used to call *sophia*. It is a word which means 'wisdom', but of a very particular sort; Homer would speak, for instance, of the *sophia* of the shipbuilder, of his supreme craft and skill. It is the wisdom that sees the relationship between

> idea and understanding, understanding and hand, hand and material in a sequential chain which leads to action fitting to time and place" (Shearer 1998, 123).

In the Old Testament, Wisdom declares: "when he [God] marked out the foundations of the earth,/ then I was beside him, like a master workman" (Proverbs, viii, 29–30). The word in Hebrew for master workman, *'amon*, might also be translated as architect, master craftsman, builder, bringer into harmony, or one who binds together. As Athene Ergane, "the worker", the goddess shows the divinity in crafting, even in making her own clothes. Potters, carpenters, shipbuilders, architects, goldsmiths, were all "children of Athene", or Minerva, as she was called by the Romans. She is credited with technological progress, in the forms of the plough, the horse's bridle, the potter's wheel. This way of knowing is important in the law. When Jackson J. says, "Let me now draw the threads together," he calls on Athene. The "threads" are the issues, the evidence, the law, the parties' submissions, and his own responses to them. Athene sat as judge in the trial of Orestes. She was also closely associated with Hephaistos who built golden palaces for the gods and Daedalus, the master-craftsman who built the labyrinth to hold the Minotaur. *Construction and law seem to live in the same community of images*. We construe a contract, construct a building, and reconstruct what happened from the evidence. One contract is often woven (incorporated) into another. Or it might combine legal and equitable principles, as with a construction trust (chapter 9). Perhaps Athene stands behind construction law.

Athene's sense of order is different from that of Saturn; it does not depend on static, rigid structures and hierarchies. Weaving was women's work and done at home. As a guiding metaphor for legal process, "weaving" is elevated to the highest level of public life. At the same time, the judge who "hands down" his judgments, assumes the humble role of the weaver. Judges as weavers, weavers as makers of a just society. Athene's "art of fitting" is subtle and profound.

In the Archaeological Museum in Athens, there is a stone relief showing Athene leaning against her spear, her head on her shoulder, looking away from the viewer. It is known as "mourning Athene". We do not know the context of the scene. It may relate to a myth in which she unintentionally killed her friend Pallas. But it may also reflect a deeper connection between law and weaving, that they both mediate grief. While the hands work, the soul meditates: finding a place for this here, saving that for another time, if ever. Things belong to particular places. Little groupings form, at first provisionally, then formally. Pattern-making with cases or threads imitates nature: fixed positions break up and start to flow again. An intuition comes that there is something greater and more mysterious than at first appears. For the Greeks, grief melted or dissolved the body (Onians 1951, 33 and 48).

In the *Odyssey*, Penelope tells the suitors she is making a shroud for **22–011**
Laertes, Odysseus's father. By night she unwinds what she has woven by day, over and over again, until Odysseus returns. Archetypal psychologist Thomas Moore says of the myth of Penelope: "This is the great mystery of the soul: wherever something is being accomplished, it is also in some way being undone" (1992, 34). A poem by Adam Horovitz written to celebrate the bicentenary of Brunel's birth, described him as "Odysseus of industry/ a flawed hero." In the *Iliad*, Achilles tells Priam that "the gods, who have no cares themselves, have woven sorrow into the pattern of our lives" (quoted in

Shearer 1998, 9). Athene's melancholy is worked through; for Saturn it is permanent.

Athene may be behind this chapter interweaving law and myth, seeing through law to its mythic foundations. Myths that themselves are woven from the encounters of gods and humans. "Seeing through" Athene offers a chance to look at bonds and guarantees from a different perspective. Again, a correspondence appears between spear and spindle. References in the following discussion are to Onions (1951). The Greeks envisaged battle as a living creature. If one of its sinews were cut one side would lose. The same word is used for cutting corn and "mowing down" an army (p.188). War was imagined as a bond (*peirar*) spread over both armies, as if the ends of a rope were crossed or tied loosely and the battle field was in the space enclosed (p.319). *Peirar* meant thread or wool as well as rope: "the same fortunes which the gods spin for men, they also fasten upon them in the form of a cord or bond" (p.335). Binding and weaving follow spinning; the loom as fate, as battle. The poet Simonides sang of death as hanging over us and we recall the sword of Damocles which began this book. "On the field of battle the presence of the bond may be felt as a kind of physical paralysis" like a fetter or shackle (p.327). We say that something is bound to happen. "To bind" in this context meant "to spread a bond over" (p.331). The bond was sometimes shown in Greek art as a wreath carried by a winged figure hovering above a person. Onians understands both bond and figure as indicating the person's *daimon* or guiding spirit (p.402); it could portend love.

22–012 "If two things had to be joined together or fixed relatively to each other, binding was the obvious means" (p.371). Onians argues that binding was understood to include riveting and nailing. Atropos, one of three Fates, was depicted with a nail in her hand or piercing a man's head with a nail (p.374); but despite this, humans could affect their fate by taking the proper attitude to the gods (p.391). Heads were pierced with spikes above the central arch of Temple Bar (Ch.1). We speak of paying on the nail, after the posts erected in Bristol. But the posts as nails echoed classical sources associated with binding (p.375). Distraint for debt was effected by tying a withy on the debtor's property (p.358). Gods bound humans with sickness or ill luck. A bond might also be imagined as putting on a garment (p.361).

What are we to make of these glimpses into the world of the Greeks? I suggest that they can help us to take the step of psychological faith in imagination I referred to at the beginning of this chapter. A construction contract and a debt are both forms of bond or fate hanging over the parties: failure to complete the works and failure to pay sums due are cognates, both implying death. A surety or demand bond is therefore an attempt to overcome death; but only the gods are deathless. Are creditors who take security taking a risk? There are many myths in which a mortal is killed or transformed for claiming what belongs to the gods. Athene, for example, changed Arachne into an owl for claiming that her weaving was superior to the goddess's. It is not surprising that the chapters on bonds and termination are the longest in this book or that employers and contractors are so concerned with security (other forms of binding that are intended to work like spells protecting the creditor). Activities such as litigation (battle) and construction share the same root metaphor. In the mythic perspective of the Greeks, litigation has an animal nature, or *is* an animal. "Myths do not tell us how. They simply give the invisible background which starts us imagining, questioning, going deeper" (Hillman 1976, 158). Compare the demanding and conditional bonds of Saturn with the social, interdependent bonds of Athene. The goddess also helped the women of Sparta in the *Lysistrata* of Aristophanes. The name Lysistrata means "army-disbander" but could equally mean "bond-loosener".

The gods are powers that bind. Jung famously said that the gods have become diseases. We no longer recognize Zeus in his Greek form. But are there gods in the "binding powers" considered in this book: contracts, companies, debts, bonds, charges and mortgages, set-off, and the panoply of security devices discussed in Ch.2? If so, law still has a religious dimension. One myth leads to another, is already implicated inside another. The urge to master this form of knowing has to be abandoned and each image valued in its own right. Law mimics myth in its case reports, where one refers to another, moving back in time. One way of bringing images into mainstream legal education would be to introduce insolvency not by reference to legal definitions but by looking at images of the goddess Fortune and her wheel or by reading a scene from Shakespeare's play *Timon of Athens*. Lawyers often invoke Shylock in *The Merchant of Venice* as a cultural reference to the conditional bond as used in the construction industry but it would be equally interesting to study the relationship between Prospero and Ariel in *The Tempest*. Ariel appears on demand but has been promised his freedom if his bond is performed.

Juris Prudentia

There is a manuscript in the Fitzwilliam Museum, Cambridge (MS McClean **22–013** 139) dated about 1300 showing a Tree of Actions, a presentation of forms of action (lawsuit), as 180 circles set out in two grids of ten rows and nine columns each, with text surround. Beside one of the tables is painted an image of a woman. It has been suggested that she is Juris Prudentia, mother of actions (L'Engle and Gibbs 2001, 158). She has golden hair and wears a crown. She is dressed in scarlet with a cape of purple. Her right hand grasps the frame (the trunk) of the "tree"; in her left, she holds a lily. A male figure dressed in similar colours stands next to her holding the other grid.

In medieval jurisprudence it was vital to choose the correct form of action otherwise your claim would founder. I wonder whether the images of Juris Prudentia and her consort are not purely decorative but are vehicles to attract her *sophia* to the text and to mediate between the lawyer's desire to serve his client well and the principle of justice which she embodies. Could the lawyer have asked her in his imagination to guide his interpretation of the text? Could she help him fit the remedy to the claim? Perhaps the choice was hers and a successful lawyer understood how to allow intuition and logic to co-exist.

The figure of Prudentia has a long history in which Athene is strongly implicated. She is concerned with the art of memory which, as Frances Yates (1992) shows, was developed by Cicero as a means of delivering his speeches in court but became in the Renaissance a system for educating and containing the imagination. If, as I suggested in the previous section on Saturn, we need an archetypal jurisprudence, we could return to Juris Prudentia and be guided on the forms it should take. We could for example do for her what Curtis and Resnik (1987) did for the figure of Iustitia: make a collage out of myth, images, legal cases, and in the process let the right questions come.

If jurisprudence were re-visioned in this way, it may find new forms. In an ancient hymn, Apollo speaks of how he will build his temple as a place of "infallible counsel" to men. "When he had said this, Phoebus Apollo/ laid out the foundations/ which were broad and very long from end to end./ And upon them the sons of Erginos/ . . . built the threshold of well-based stones/ to be a theme of song forever" (Cashford 2003, 285). It is noteworthy that Apollo designed the temple but did not build it. To him belong abstract principles that others bring into materiality. Jurisprudence as currently envisioned has many forms, but leans towards Apollo, separating itself from its material. If it were returned to Athene, jurisprudence would be joined in a practical way to law. A textbook would then consider cases against the patterns of images and ideas to which they belong. Law would be closer to art and industry; we could "write as if law were art" (Young 2005, 8–13). There could be a renaissance of "the poetic art of law" (Goodrich 1995, 247). Hillman speaks of the poetic basis of mind; for him, all statements are psychological.

> "Psychology is taught not only in the department that bears its name. It is going on everywhere. Indeed it may be going on best where it is noticed least. . . . [It] refers less to a body of knowledge than to a perspective parallel to other bodies of knowledge, a running commentary to their direct and literal discourse" (1976 at 133, 159).

Perhaps law has always had such a perspective in Juris Prudentia but needs to reconnect with her. In one version of the myth of Pandora, when the first woman had been created Athene breathed the life soul into her. Athene–Prudentia might be seen as the soul of the law, giving legal work its interiority (see Sells 1994).

Each god understands security in a different way. In the pattern of Athene, there is a correlation between security and making things. While grieving for the loss of Pallas, the goddess made an image of her friend, a little statue, which was called a *palladium*. The term came to refer to the cult image of Athene herself which was kept in her temple. "The possession of a palladium was a pledge of security" (Larousse 1968, 109). As long as it remained safe and sound, so would the city. This has a very different feeling from the myth of Saturn and his children. With Athene, the image is valued and a public place is built to hold it; Saturn doesn't want any image-making and locks the gods privately away. In the perspective of Athene, "building" can apply to a shattered ego, a lost soul, "ruined love" (Shakespeare's Sonnet 119), as well as a community, or a livelihood; Saturn builds to rule.

4. Dionysos breaks down

22–014 In this chapter it is not my intention to explain myths in terms of law or vice versa, although it is easy to fall into this trap. The idea is to return the literal to the mythic, to see through legal devices to their imaginal background. In so doing, we might become more aware of the legal method, the perspective through which much of the lawyer's art is practised. We could be open to its positive and its negative aspects, and how it relates to other ways of seeing. It is better to tell the myths than to deal in metaphors. Literary criticism tends to lose the poetic impulse by objectifying. But mythical thinking is more humble and keeps the stories going round until it is possible to say that we are lived by them, that Saturn and Athene are working *their* patterns in our lives.

Art historian Edgar Wind says of myth: "By calling one god, we call his affiliates; and by calling a few, we call them all. Polytheism leads to the Pantheon" (1967, 198). By invoking Saturn, we encounter Zeus in action and see a pattern of law that is not held back by rigid structures and can ask for help outside itself. Through Metis, we meet Athene weaving war and peace, and explore the bonds connecting gods and humans, through weavers like Penelope and Arachne. And now Dionysos—god of wine, body and emotions. He is known as a mask, as god of tragic theatre, and of community, especially the *thiasos* of maenads who accompany him on his wanderings.

Loosening

One of his titles is Dionysos Lysios, "the loosener". In his sculpture (Plate 5), **22–015**
Michelangelo shows the god as a youth, with body unbalanced, his eyes gazing on the wine cup. Rafael Lopez-Pedraza has pointed out the androgynous quality of this work, somewhere between dullness and brilliance, a particular kind of consciousness. Perhaps what I termed the "insolvency perspective" in Ch.1 could be returned to Dionysos. Something familiar is being broken down, something new is on its way. The myths of the god's birth are especially violent:

> In a deep cave, weaving a robe on which is shown a picture of the cosmos, sits Persephone. In the guise of a snake, Zeus enters and mates with her. The child of their union, Dionysos, has two horns growing from his forehead. The infant is enthroned and called a "second Zeus". Two warriors with swords and shields perform a war dance around him and a woman holds up a mirror to enchant him. He is given toys to play with: a top, dice, a ball, golden apples, bull-roarer and wool. Suddenly Titans with faces whitened with chalk appear and attack and kill the child, tearing him apart into seven pieces. His flesh is thrown into a cauldron of boiling water and then roasted and eaten. Athene saw everything and preserved the only part of the body left untouched by the Titans. Some say it was the child's heart, others that only his phallus survived. She hid it in a covered basket and entrusted it to Zeus who sewed it into his thigh. The child god was born a second time from Zeus's thigh.

I prefer not to interpret the myth. Some of its images reverberate with the themes of this book without the need for heavy-handed treatment. We notice though the vital role of Athene, and her presence not just as witness but in the weaving and the sewing. The myth shocks and then 'stains', to use a metaphor of James Hillman's to describe the effect of myth, like the aftertaste of a good wine. We cannot touch myth, he says, without it touching us. In that state can we recall some of the loosening previously explored through the legal perspective?

Devices such as assignment and trust both have the capacity to dismember a contract. The link binding the benefit and burden of a contract is severed, making it possible to dispose of the benefit as a piece of property. In Saturn's eyes, this is a gain because the personal element has been jettisoned and full control can be exercised. As was seen in Ch.4, however, things are not that simple in construction because of the role of the certifier. When a company is informally insolvent, the directors must take the interests of the creditors into account. We could say that the company's attitude has to be loosened; it has to see the situation through the creditors' eyes and ask what they would expect to happen. Perhaps this is the first of many Dionysian changes of role that the company may then go through before its final dismemberment and destruction. Payment procedures in construction contracts have Dionysian qualities. One judge put it this way:

> " . . . the relationship between the plaintiff [contractor] and the defendant [employer] was fluid in terms of who from time to time might be the creditor and who might be the debtor. . . . the roles of the defendant and the plaintiff could be reversed in terms of debtor and creditor": (*Main Roads Corporation v Samary Enterprises* [2006] VSC 144 at para.36, *per* Habersberger J.

The industry itself is often criticised for being fragmented and unable to speak with one voice. Law too can be said to dismember phenomena through its cutting methods (fact-finding, distinguishing, judging, categorising). Activities such as outsourcing and subcontracting cut the ties of direct employment. The liquidation process is like a Dionysian ritual with each stage laid down with precision and repeated countless times.

Mythic thinking in Jung's terms is only possible by loosening the grip of literalism. Any work on building, however apparently technical and ordinary, is involved with an image of the utmost value to the psyche.

> "For the house the psyche actually inhabits is a compound of connecting corridors, multi-leveled, with windows everywhere and with large ongoing extensions 'under construction,' and sudden dead ends and holes in the floorboards; and this house is filled already with occupants, other voices in other rooms, reflecting nature alive, echoing again the Great God Pan alive, a pantheism rekindled by the psyche's belief in its personified images" (Hillman 1976, 42).

The play of words reminds us that "building" is both thing and process. Construction insolvency may simply be saying that a building (a psychic structure) can never be completed because it is always also building (psychologising). In his poem "Milton" William Blake speaks of the golden builders of imagination who will never finish their work on:

> Golgonooza, the spiritual Four-fold London eternal,
> In immense labours & sorrows, ever building, ever falling. (Blake 1972, 485)

In his late poem "Jerusalem", he describes the work as "continually building & continually decaying desolate" (1972, 684). With these lines in mind, Kathleen Raine writes of "the archetype of the ever-present, never-realized pattern of the *sancta civitas*, the pattern of the 'golden builders' be they architects or poets, painters or musicians" (1991, 118).

Grief and horror

22–016 I mentioned earlier that Dionysos is god of emotions and the body. Writers on law are beginning to take seriously the presence of emotions in legal work. In her introduction to *The Passions of Law*, Susan A Bandes states that "the emotions that pervade law are often so ancient and deeply ingrained that they are largely invisible" (1999, 2). Among many others she mentions vengeance, disgust, fear, and shame. Interestingly, grief is not considered in the book. The significance of this emotion was noted above in connection with Saturn and Athene. In the *Bacchae*, a tragedy by Euripides, the principal character is Pentheus, from *penthos* which means grief.

The play begins with Dionysos revealing that he has returned to Thebes, the city of his birth, over which Pentheus rules as king. In response to reports that women from the city have been worshipping the god in the mountains, Pentheus issues a warrant for his arrest. When the god appears before him disguised as a priest, Pentheus cross-examines him and orders him to be tied up and thrown into prison; but fetters could not hold the god. Pentheus is warned not to deny Dionysos but persists in trying to repress him and his cult. Eventually his mind is turned by the god and he goes up to the mountains disguised as a woman only to be torn to pieces by the maenads, and decapitated by his own mother.

There is much play on Pentheus's name. It is implied that it embodies his fate, that he will "come to grief". But could it have been grief that led him to take refuge in the security systems of the state? Could his denial of Dionysos, god of joy and ecstasy, have been the tragic outcome of suicidal grief? Dionysos appears among the buildings of the city and shakes them to their foundations. In the madness and dismembering of Pentheus the god sees himself as in a mirror. Could an addiction to security reflect a secret identity with the god, as in the name that Dionysius of Syracuse chose for himself?

There is another aspect of the god which resonates with this book—his **22–017**
wandering. He was called "He who comes and goes" because of the suddenness of his epiphany and his vanishing. As a wanderer, especially across borders of cities and countries, he aroused suspicion. Historians of the Tudor period, when insolvency law first became formalised in England and Wales, have often commented on the severity of the vagrancy laws. As well as beggars, they were applied to tinkers, pedlars, unlicensed actors, and astrologers. There were two other groups who could easily be classed as vagrants: debtors and builders. The former might be evading creditors, the latter looking for daywork.

Vagrants were punished by public whipping or mutilation (loss of an ear), and later in the sixteenth century by slavery, branding, enforced service in the army, transportation, even death. As Foucault (1979) argues, power manifested itself through its treatment of the bodies of prisoners. William Carroll investigates possible correspondences in the minds of the authorities between beggars (or "masterless men" as some were called) and traitors. In our terms it is as if insolvency were being equated with communism at the height of the Cold War. Vagrants were the ultimate "other" who attracted all kinds of prejudice just by being who they were (the scapegoat). They embodied an inversion of the established order at the head of which was the Crown, hence the equation with treason, and therefore disorder in the cosmos. An excess of liabilities over assets as the balance sheet test has it. "The inescapable conclusion is that Tudor authorities feared vagrants far out of proportion to their actual menace" (Carroll 1996, 36). Perhaps people who were tied to where they were born showed a misplaced envy of the freedom attributed to vagrants. Possibly vagrants were feared because their lives imitated the wandering courses of the planets; or their evident helplessness and powerlessness were perceived as threats to the precarious security of everyone else. But these sound like rationalisations. Could the vagrant have presented a deeply pathologised face of soul which an increasingly iconoclastic age wanted to repress? Dionysos as the mask? The figure recalls Edgar as Poor Tom in King Lear: vagrancy, suffering in body and mind, reversals of fortune, all bring into question the supremacy of power in Shakespeare's play. As shadow figures for those in power, debtors and bankrupts attracted a stigma consistent with illegitimacy, idiocy, lunacy, and treason. The draconian laws do not appear to have had any effect other than to institutionalise and reinforce the stigma.

Various questions arise from this Dionysian digression. Could the myriad of security devices employed against the contractor and its property reviewed in Ch.2 be modern substitutes for actual bodily harm against or imprisonment of the debtor's body? Should the attitude which craves security in all situations that Wood (1998) calls "the banker's mind" be returned to the pattern of Pentheus–Dionysos?

Rebirth

22–018 In the myth of Dionysos told earlier the god was reborn from Zeus's thigh. The Greeks associated the marrow of the thigh bone with the substance of life and therefore with new birth (Onians 1951, 183). A similar movement takes place towards the end of the myth of Ariadne.

> After Theseus vanquished the Minotaur, he left the island of Crete with Ariadne, the king's daughter who out of love for him had supplied the string by which he found his way out of the labyrinth. At dusk their ship reached another island where they stayed the night in a cave. Shortly before dawn Theseus rose and departed, abandoning Ariadne to her fate. She woke just in time to see his ship pass over the horizon. In despair she contemplated suicide. Half out of her mind she heard gentle singing and laughing coming from the forest and a procession emerged of nymphs and satyrs leading Silenos tipsy astride a donkey. Following them was Dionysos who offered her wine. She consented to marry him and he crowned her with rubies he had obtained on his wanderings in India. They remained faithful to one another.

In Ch.1, I briefly discussed the novation procedure in the broader context of *renovatio* or spiritual rebirth. Perhaps it can be returned to the mythic pattern of Dionysos, and in particular to the story of Ariadne. Theseus the hero betrays her; he fails to honour his promise (as she understood it) to take her home with him. There is a repudiation and Ariadne suffers. Dionysos takes his place and fulfils his vow to marry her.

James Hillman says that: "A fantasy of decay and degeneracy belongs with the archetype of *renovatio*: rebirth appears together with rot" (1976, 203). The alchemical engraving (Plate 6) shows a grave and a corpse together with seeds being sown and corn ready to harvest. "No generation without corruption", as the alchemists say. In the myth, Ariadne enters a dark night of the soul after her abandonment to which we can revert the effect of the termination clauses in the standard forms. Where one of the parties to a contract becomes insolvent there is often a period of loss and uncertainty. How will it be completed and by whom? This may be archetypally necessary. Hillman continues: "For we have learned from Renaissance psychology that rebirth is coupled with defeat, failure is its precondition, Hades its deepest secret" (1976, 221).

Dionysos is the liberator. Walter F Otto describes how "the appearance of Dionysos brings with it nourishing intoxicating waters that bubble up from the earth. . . . Everything that has been locked up is released . . . Age-old laws have suddenly lost their power, and even the dimensions of time and space are no longer valid." Women doing Athene's work who tried to resist the god were overwhelmed. "The loom on which [the daughters of Minyas] are working is suddenly overgrown with ivy and grape vines, and wine and milk trickle down from the ceiling of their chamber" (1965, 95–7). They went mad and tore one of their children to pieces.

5. The Firebird

In the myth of Dionysos's birth, Kerényi says that the snake was Zeus **22–019**
Cthonios, "subterranean Zeus". In this respect he is in the place of his brother Hades. In Plate 7, Zeus stands on the island of Delos, releasing two eagles, one to the east, the other to the west. It is the beginning of the alchemical work. I have commented several times on the alchemical language of the law. As insolvency emerged as a body of law during the heyday of alchemy in the sixteenth and seventeenth centuries perhaps there is more than a fanciful connection. The alchemists had a motto: "*Solve et Coagula*", dissolve and coagulate, which could be reformulated as "liquidate and construct". Otto says that in the Dionysian pattern "life and death, mortality and eternity are mixed up with one another in a miraculous way in those who are near to the god" (1965, 185). As an image, construction insolvency implies the arrestment of development as a governing idea. Perhaps it also suggests life and death together, the loss of a fixed perspective being sustained by a vision of a deeper archetypal order in which all the gods are recognised.

This sense of being conscious at the same time of blossoming and withering is voiced most nobly by the poet Rainer Maria Rilke. In his *Duino Elegies*, as translated by Stephen Cohn, he says:

And we, we stay spectators; turned towards
all things and still transcending none.
All overwhelms us. We set all in order.
All falls apart. We order it once more
and fall, collapse, disintegrate ourselves.

How were we first persuaded to perform
our every act as though it were our last?
As one might halt upon the last high ground,
which shows him his own valley one last time,
and turn; and linger; and hang back . . .
. . . so we dwell here, forever taking leave.
(Rilke 1989, 69)

One of the questions left open in Ch.1 was: if construction is earth, insolvency is water, and law is air, where is fire? The question was intended to lead to mythical thinking rather than hard answers. Walter Burkert observes: "Zeus is the world as a whole, and especially the thinking fire which pervades everything, forms everything, and holds everything in limits" (1989, 131). Bird and fire combine in the myth of the phoenix. The following version is by the artist Thetis Blacker, who died a few months before this book was completed.

> "The great miraculous bird, Phoenix, lives alone in an earthly Paradise, feeding upon the light of the stars. At the end of a thousand years, knowing that death is approaching, he descends into the mortal world below. There in the tallest palm tree he builds a nest of spices, and at dawn, lifting his voice, he sings a hymn so ravishingly beautiful that the sun stops in his track to listen. In that instant the universe stands still, but sparks from the flaming halo of the sun set fire to the aromatic phoenix nest. Thus the phoenix, the only phoenix, is consumed in flames; yet, as he burns, an egg appears from the ashes of the bird, which, hatching, reveals a new phoenix, himself reborn. Rapidly growing strong, the young phoenix stretches his radiant wings, and bearing the burned nest that was the funeral pyre of his parent-self flies to the temple of the sun in Heliopolis, where he lays it upon the altar. Thousands of birds follow him. They fly together in friendship, the hawk with the sparrow, the eagle with the dove. Then soaring aloft the mighty bird wings his way towards Paradise. The multitude of birds follow him singing" (Blacker 2001, 75).

Is it not strange that the law should use the image of the phoenix as shorthand for a shady business practice? The "phoenix syndrome" is the name given to the mischief which s.216 of the Insolvency Act 1986 is designed to address, whereby a director of a company which goes into liquidation begins trading through a new company with the same or virtually the same name shortly afterwards (Chs 8 and 20). The law appropriates the cyclical aspect of the myth but places it in a quasi-criminal context. It is true that the court has distinguished between honest and dishonest phoenix companies: *Official Receiver v Zwirn* [2002] B.C.C. 760 at para.13. But even then, where are the colours, the aromatic scent, the entrancing song, the images of eternity? Could the fate of the phoenix be saying something about law's relationship with imagination? Or should we just marvel that the miraculous bird has appeared in such an unexpected and inhospitable place?

These are serious questions because of the fact that working for a long time with the legal method is bound to have an effect: toiling in Saturn's fields we slowly become like him. It's interesting in this context to note the way that "desire" is used in s.239 of the Insolvency Act 1986. As appropriated by the law, this Dionysian word is also tainted with wrongdoing, this time in preferring a creditor. There seems to be a paradox at work. In the image of the company, the law demonstrates its extraordinary imagination, even if multinationals now rule the world. In this sense insolvency undermines the *hubris* of the modern company, its titanic greed and overweening pride. Fuelled by human projections, the company needs insolvency to impose an inhuman solution on it. But in the treatment of the phoenix, the law shows that it also disparages, degrades and rubbishes images. Perhaps that is the role of a writer on the law—to search among the fragments and return what he finds to the gods.

Glossary

This glossary consists of simplified definitions to assist the general reader.

Abatement: Defence that value of work done or goods supplied should be reduced because of defects.
ACE: Association of Consulting Engineers, which publishes forms of engineers' conditions of engagement.
Adjudication: Interim dispute resolution procedure in construction contracts.
Administration: Formal insolvency procedure with the aim of rescuing a company.
Administrative Receiver: Insolvency practitioner appointed by the holder of a **floating charge.**
Administrator: Insolvency practitioner appointed to take control over a company in administration.
Arrestment: Form of **diligence**, similar to a **freezing order** obtained on issuing proceedings (Scotland).
Assignee: Person to whom an asset is assigned.
Assignment: Procedure for transferring assets.
Assignor: Person who assigns.
Attachment: Enforcing a judgment by ordering a person who owes a debt to a judgment debtor to pay it direct to the judgment creditor.

Back-to-back contracts: Where the terms of one contract are referred to or mirrored in another to promote easier enforcement of rights.
Balance sheet test: Test of **insolvency** where the value of a company's assets is compared with the amount of its liabilities, including contingent and prospective liabilities.
Bankruptcy: Formal insolvency procedure for individuals rather than companies or partnerships.
Bankruptcy set-off: Mandatory **set-off** of all mutual dealings where one party is bankrupt.
Benefit of contract: Rights which one party to a contract has against the other.
Bills of quantity: Schedules containing each item of work and materials required in the construction process individually priced by the contractor.
Bill of sale: Document transferring ownership of a chattel.
Bond: Undertaking under seal to pay money.
Bondsman: Person who gives a bond.
Book debt: Debt arising in the course of a business which would normally be entered in the accounting records of the type of business concerned.
Building out: Completing an unfinished structure after a contractor defaults.
Burden of contract: Obligations which one party under a contract owes to the other.

Cash flow test: See **going concern test**.
CEDR: Centre for Effective Dispute Resolution, which has issued a set of rules for adjudication.
Certified sum: Money certified for payment to a contractor or a subcontractor by an architect or an engineer normally on a monthly basis.
Charge: Form of security whereby an asset of a debtor is identified and appropriated towards payment should the debtor fail to pay.
Charge holder: Person to whom a charge is given.
Chattel: Any property except land and **choses in action**.
Chose in action: Property right enforceable by proceedings, e.g. a debt, a claim for damages, an insurance policy, copyright.
CIC: Construction Industry Council, industry body which has published an adjudication procedure, and standard forms of warranty, novation and consultants' appointment.
CIS: Construction Industry Scheme whereby the Revenue permits registered subcontractors to be paid gross of tax.
Collateral warranty: Separate contract often between an employer and subcontractor to overcome the absence of **privity of contract**.
Company voluntary arrangement: Formal insolvency procedure whereby creditors agree to accept a certain proportion of their debts in full settlement.
Completion contract: Contract entered into with a new contractor after the original contractor's failure to complete.
Compulsory liquidation: Formal court-based insolvency procedure started by **winding up petition.**
Construction (of a contract): Ascertaining the intention of the parties by interpreting the words used.
Construction management: Means of procurement whereby a contractor manages the work and the employer enters into contracts direct with subcontractors.
Contingent liability: Liability under an existing obligation subject to an event which may or may not happen.
Contract sum: The sum for which a contractor agrees to carry out construction work.
Contractor: Person or company that carries out or procures construction work for an employer.
Contractor's employment: The contractor's right and duty to carry out the works.
Conversion: Tort of interfering with another's goods.
Cost-plus contract: Contract where the contractor is paid his costs plus an agreed percentage for overheads and profit.
Counter-indemnity: Document between a bondsman and its client entitling the bondsman to call for cash security or payment as a result of a call on a bond issued on that client's behalf.
Court of Session: High Court (Scotland).
Credit agreement: Loan agreement between the funder and the employer for the construction cost.
Critical path: The order of work in a construction programme which cannot be changed without causing delay and disruption to the whole.
Crown debts: Debts owed to the government, e.g. VAT, National Insurance contributions, PAYE.
Crystallisation: Conversion of a **floating charge** into a **fixed charge**.
Debt: Right to payment of money enforceable by action.

Deceit: Tort of fraudulent misrepresentation.
Decree: The judgment of a court or arbiter (arbitrator) in civil proceedings (Scotland).
Defeasance: The process by which a right to payment can be lost if a condition to its enforceability (or even existence) is never satisfied.
Defects liability period: Period between **practical completion** and final completion on a building contract.
Defender: Defendant (Scotland).
Diligence: The methods of obtaining security and/or enforcing unpaid debts due under decrees of the Scottish courts.
Direct agreement: An agreement between a funder and a contractor or an employer and subcontractors similar to a **collateral warranty** and a **step-in agreement**.
Direct payment: Payment made by an employer to a subcontractor or a supplier by-passing the contractor.
Disqualification: Procedure resulting in a court order or an undertaking preventing a director from acting in the management of a company for a specific period.
Disruption: Interference to the regular progress of construction work, measured by the degree of alteration caused to the contractor's programme.
Dividend: Proportion of creditor's debt receivable from an insolvency procedure where the assets are insufficient to pay the debt in full.

Election: Choice between two inconsistent remedies.
Employer: Client who wishes to procure construction work.
End-user: The eventual customer of a facility, e.g. a school under a **PFI** contract or a purchaser under a gas supply agreement.
Entire contract: Contract where nothing becomes payable to the contractor until it is substantially completed.
Equity: 1. A defence of a debtor binding an assignee 2. (equity of redemption) The right of a debtor to recover property offered as security on performing the secured obligation. 3. A separate system of law which gave rise to trusts and guarantees etc., which was fused with the common law in the nineteenth century.
Equitable assignment: Transfer of personal property where formalities have not been complied with.
Equitable set-off: Set-off of a cross-claim so closely connected with the claim it would be unjust not to allow the set-off.
Escrow account: A bank account set up for a particular purpose from which payment can only be made by complying with the special terms under which it was set up.
Estimator: Person employed by contractor to prepare and cost tenders.
Executory contract: A contract which is incomplete and ongoing at the start of a formal insolvency procedure.
Execution: Enforcement of a judgment by the seizure and sale of the assets of the judgment debtor.

Factoring: Sale of debts for less than their face value in return for immediate payment.
FIDIC: Federation Internationale des Ingenieurs-Conseils, which publishes international forms of engineering and process contracts under its name.
Fixed charge: Charge over a specific asset preventing its owner from dealing with it in the ordinary course of business.

Flawed asset: Property subject to a contingency such as a blocked bank account.
Floating charge: Charge over an asset permitting its owner to deal with it in the ordinary course of business.
Fluctuations clause: Contractual term entitling a contractor to recover increases in the cost of labour and materials since the date of his tender.
Formal insolvency: Legal procedures under which an insolvency practitioner assumes control of a company or partnership or an individual's property for the benefit of creditors, e.g. receivership, liquidation, administration, bankruptcy.
Framework agreement: An agreement between an employer and a contractor governing their commercial relationship which is intended to apply to any contract they enter into with each other.
Fraudulent trading: Carrying on business with intent to defraud creditors.
Freezing order: Court order preventing a defendant dealing with its assets above a certain value (formerly a "Mareva" injunction).
Front-end loading: Common practice in tendering of placing higher values on early items of work so as to generate a positive cash flow for the contract.

Garnishee: Person ordered to pay another's judgment creditor rather than his own creditor (now pursuant to a third party debt order).
GC/Works: Standard form used on government contracts
General law: Common law.
Going concern test: The ability to pay debts as they fall due.
Guarantee: Contract whereby a person agrees to answer for the debt or default of another.
Guarantor: Person who gives a guarantee.

ICC: International Chamber of Commerce, which hosts an important system of arbitration and publishes internationally recognised commercial codes such as the Uniform Customs and Practice.
ICE: Institution of Civil Engineers, a professional body which publishes the standard form of engineering contract for use in the UK.
I Chem E: Institution of Chemical Engineers, which publishes its own standard form of the same name.
I Mech E: Institution of Mechanical Engineers, which publishes its own standard form of the same name.
Indemnity: Document giving right to compensation on the occurrence of an event.
Informal insolvency: Failure to pass the **going concern test** or **the balance sheet test**.
Injunction: Court order compelling a person to act or preventing a person from acting in a particular way.
Insolvency: Inability to pay debts.
Insolvency practitioner: Person licensed to act on behalf of a company placed in **formal insolvency.**
Intellectual property rights: Rights protecting inventions, designs, drawings, e.g. copyright.
Interim certificate: Certificate issued by an architect or an engineer showing the amount payable by the employer in respect of the work done by the contractor during the previous month.
Interpleader: Court procedure whereby a person in possession of property not his own which is claimed by two or more persons can apply to the court to decide who owns it.

JCT: Joint Contracts Tribunal, an industry body responsible for drafting the standard forms of building contract.
Judicial management: Formal insolvency procedure in overseas jurisdictions such as Singapore and South Africa which is analogous to administration.

Knock-on effect: Phenomenon where a company or an individual becomes insolvent as a consequence of the insolvency of another.

Latent defects: Work which does not conform to the contract specification but which is not apparent from reasonable inspection.
Legal assignment: Transfer of personal property which complies with the formalities of the Law of Property Act 1925.
Legal set-off: Set-off of independent mutual debts which are both liquidated (i.e. quantified) or ascertainable by the time the defence is due.
Letter of intent: Written instruction to a contractor to commence work against an undertaking to pay a reasonable sum for it if a contract is never concluded with the employer.
Licence to the site: Right to temporary possession of a construction site for the purpose of carrying out the works.
Lien: Security interest entitling holder to retain property until payment.
Liquidated and ascertained damages: A genuine pre-estimate of loss agreed by the parties when entering into the contract.
Liquidation: Formal insolvency procedure leading to the dissolution of the company.
Liquidation set-off: Mandatory set-off of all mutual dealings where one party is in liquidation.
Liquidator: Insolvency practitioner appointed to conduct a **liquidation**.
Loss and expense: Compensation payable to the contractor under the terms of a construction contract for delay or disruption to the work.

Main contract: Construction contract between the employer and the contractor.
Maintenance period: Period between substantial completion and final completion on an engineering contract.
Management contract: Means of **procurement** whereby the contractor does no site work but manages the works entering into subcontracts for that purpose.
Mechanics' lien: A form of **charge** on the employer's property to secure payment to a person who has provided work or materials for the project (US, Canada).
Mediation: Informal procedure for resolving disputes intended to avoid arbitration or litigation.
Misfeasance: A claim against a director for breach of duty owed to the company brought by a liquidator.
Mitigation of loss: Minimising loss caused by breach of contract by acting reasonably.
Moratorium: Suspension of creditors' rights for an agreed period.
Mortgage: Form of security where property is transferred to a creditor on terms that it be transferred back to the debtor after the debt is paid or the secured obligation is performed.
Mutuality: The position where two persons have claims against each other in the same capacity.

NHBC: National House-Builders' Council.
NEC3: Current (2005) edition of the Engineering and Construction Contract published by the **ICE**.
Negative pledge: Contractual term where a person agrees not to grant security over his assets.
Negligence: Tort of breach of a duty of care.
Negotiated contract: Contract where an employer agrees a construction contract with a contractor without inviting tenders.
Nemo dat quod non habet: Legal maxim meaning: "you cannot give what you do not have".
NSC: Nominated subcontractor, i.e. a subcontractor appointed on an architect's instruction expending a prime cost sum.
Non-assignment clause: A contractual term restricting the transfer of the benefit of the contract.
Notice of assignment: Notice given by an assignee to a debtor following an assignment removing the debtor's right to obtain a good discharge by paying the assignor.
Novation: Three-way agreement where one party to a contract is released by the other in consideration of a third person agreeing to be bound as if it had been named as a party originally.

Official Referee: Former title of a judge in the Queen's Bench Division of the High Court designated to hear construction disputes (now judges of the Technology and Construction Court).
OGC: Office of Government Commerce.

Pari passu rule: Rule that all unsecured creditors are paid the same proportion of their debts out of sums remaining after payment of secured and **preferential** creditors and the costs and expenses of the liquidation.
Pay when paid clause: Clause in a subcontract that the subcontractor will become entitled to payment only after the contractor has been paid (also known as a "contingent payment" clause).
Payee: Person to whom money is paid.
Penalty: Contractual term imposing financial consequences out of proportion to the breach which activates it.
Permanent works: Construction works forming the subject matter of an engineering contract where **FIDIC** or **ICE** is used.
Performance bond: Form of payment undertaking generally enforceable by serving a demand.
Pledge: Form of security where possession of property is given to a creditor as security for payment of a debt, entitling the creditor to sell the chattel if the debtor defaults.
Post-petition disposal: Disposal of property by a company after the issue of a **winding up petition** against it which is void unless validated by the court.
Practical completion: Completion of building work to a stage where the employer can go into occupation.
Preference: Payment made to a creditor (or surety of a creditor) within a defined period before the start of liquidation or bankruptcy which is influenced by the desire to improve the creditor's position in that event.
Preferential debt: Class of debt given priority by the Insolvency Act 1986 over amounts due to the holder of a floating charge or to unsecured creditors.
Prescribed part: Percentage of floating charge realisations payable to unsecured creditors in priority to the charge holder.

Prime cost sum: Amount included in a construction contract to be expended on work to be carried out by a **nominated subcontractor**.
PFI: Private finance initiative, a system of procuring infrastructure such as schools and hospitals by central and local government whereby a private consortium finances, builds, owns and operates the facility in return for charges payable over say 25 years.
Privity of contract: Rule of law that only a party to a contract can sue or be sued under it.
Project finance: Lending which relies primarily on repayment out of the cash flows generated by the project.
PPP: Public-private partnership, similar to PFI except that the facility remains in public ownership throughout.
Procurement: Contractual method chosen for the construction process (e.g. design and build).
Progress payment: Periodic payment made by an employer to the contractor on account of the contract sum.
Proof of debt: Creditor's claim to have a debt admitted by a liquidator.
Proprietary right: A right or interest in property.
Provisional liquidator: Liquidator appointed by the court in urgent situations before a **winding up petition** is heard.
Provisional sum: Sum inserted in a construction contract to cover work whose scope is uncertain at the time of tender.
Pursuer: Plaintiff (Scotland).

Qualifying floating charge: charge entitling the holder to appoint an **administrator**.
Quantity surveyor: Construction professional who prepares **bills of quantity** and measure and values work in progress.
Quantum meruit: Reasonable sum for work done and materials supplied at the request of another.
Quicquid plantatur solo, solo cedit: Legal maxim meaning: "anything fixed to the land becomes part of it."
Rateable distribution: Payment to ordinary unsecured creditors in proportion to the amounts they are owed.
Realisation: Sale of property and collection of debts.
Receivable: Sum payable or to become payable.
Receiver: Person appointed by a secured creditor to enforce security.
Receivership: Procedure for the enforcement of a security by the appointment of a receiver over the asset charged.
Remeasurement contract: Contract where the contract sum is not ascertained until after completion when the work done is valued by an engineer.
Repudiation: Conduct by one party to a contract showing an intention no longer to be bound by its terms entitling the other to claim damages.
Reputed ownership: Bankruptcy concept (now repealed) whereby goods apparently in the ownership of a bankrupt could be claimed by a **trustee in bankruptcy** in priority to the real owner.
Rescheduling: Postponement of payment of debt on agreed terms as to interest and costs.
Retention: Fixed percentage of the contract sum withheld from each progress payment until the end of a construction contract.
Retention of title: Term in a sale of goods contract where the seller withholds ownership until the goods have been paid for.

Retention trust: Term contained in some building contracts that the employer holds the retention on trust for the contractor.
RIBA: Royal Institute of British Architects, publishes forms of appointment for architects and project managers.
Right of re-entry: Right to enter on another's property for the purpose of re-possessing goods or land.
Ring-fencing: Protecting a company or an asset from the effects of insolvency.

Scheme of arrangement: Formal insolvency procedure similar to **company voluntary arrangement** requiring meetings of different classes of creditors.
Secured creditor: Creditor with a security interest in the debtor's property.
Security for costs: Court procedure where a plaintiff who is insolvent can be ordered to pay money into court in respect of the defendant's costs as a condition of continuing its claim.
Security interest: An interest in another's property enforceable in the event of default but which comes to an end if the secured obligation is performed.
Set-off: Procedure whereby a debtor pays a debt by using its own claim against its creditor.
Shadow director: A person in accordance with whose instructions and directions the directors are accustomed to act.
Sheriff: Judge (Scotland).
Sheriff court: County court (Scotland).
Snagging: Correction of defects following **practical completion**.
SPV: A company set up as a "special purpose vehicle" in a **project finance** setting to act as the employer.
Specific performance: Court action to compel the carrying out of a contract.
Standard forms: Agreed forms of contract published by industry bodies comprising the parties involved in construction work.
Standby letter of credit: A letter of credit which operates as a **performance bond**.
Statutory demand: Demand for payment of a debt which is due and payable and exceeds £750 non-compliance with which deems the debtor to be insolvent.
Statutory scheme: Order of priority of payment to creditors in a liquidation prescribed by the Insolvency Act 1986.
Step-in agreement: Contract between a funder and a contractor to protect the funder in the event of default by the employer by entitling it to substitute its own nominee as employer and thus prevent the contractor terminating its involvement.
Subcontractor: Individual, partnership or company to whom a contractor contracts out part of the work.
Subordination: Agreement whereby one creditor agrees to defer payment of its debt until after another creditor has been paid in full.
Subrogation: Equitable remedy allowing an insurer or a **guarantor** to enforce the rights of the beneficiary they have indemnified in order to recoup moneys outlaid.
Substantial completion: See **practical completion**.
Summary judgment: Court procedure for obtaining final judgment at an early stage in the action.
Surety: See **guarantor**.
Suspension: 1. Contractor's remedy for non-payment. 2. (Suspension of payment) Employer's right to withhold further payment to the contractor following a termination until the works have been completed.

Temporary works: Works of a temporary nature necessary to construct the **permanent works** on an engineering contract.
Tracing: Legal process of identifying a new trust asset as the substitute for an old one.
Trustee: A person who holds property on behalf of another.
Trustee in bankruptcy: Insolvency practitioner appointed by the court to conduct the bankruptcy of an individual.
Turnaround practitioner: Person employed by a company in financial difficulty with a view to facilitating an informal rescue.

Under-certification: Where an architect or engineer includes as the gross value of the contractor's work a sum less than the true value of the work properly done.
Undertaking: 1. Business and assets of a company. 2. Promise to pay money, especially in a **bond**. 3. (Undertaking in damages) Indemnity given to the court by the applicant for an injunction in respect of loss suffered by the defendant if it later appears that the **injunction** ought not to have been granted.
Unliquidated claim: Claim for damages which have not yet been assessed.
Valuation: Process of applying rates or prices to work in progress resulting in measured work ready for certification.

Vesting clause: Contractual term giving the employer a **security interest** or **proprietary right** in the contractor's plant or materials.
Voluntary liquidation: Form of liquidation initiated by the directors in which the creditors choose the liquidator.

Winding up petition: Document presented to the court seeking a compulsory liquidation.
Withholding notice: A pre-condition for **abatement** or **set-off** where the construction contract is governed by the Housing Grants, Construction and Regeneration Act 1996.
Work and materials contract: Contract for the supply and fixing of goods.
Wrongful trading: Civil claim brought by a liquidator against directors for compensation in respect of credit incurred by the company after the date when they knew or must have known there was no reasonable prospect of avoiding insolvent liquidation.

Bibliography

General works

Chitty on Contracts: (2004) 29th edn, Sweet & Maxwell, London.
Halsbury's Laws of England, 4th edn, Butterworths, London.
Ramsey, V., and Furst, S, (eds): (2006) *Keating on Building Contracts*, 8th edn, Sweet & Maxwell, London.
Ramsey, V., et al, (eds): (2007) *Construction Law Handbook*, Thomas Telford, London.
Sealy L., and Milman, D.: (2006) *Annotated Guide to the Insolvency Legislation*, 9th edn, 2 vols, Sweet & Maxwell, London.
Totty, P., and Moss, G.: (1986) *Insolvency*, Sweet & Maxwell (looseleaf).
Lightman, G., and Moss, G.: (2007) *The Law of Administrators and Receivers of Companies*, 4th edn, Sweet & Maxwell, London (in press).

Websites

www.bailii.org (British and Irish Legal Information Institute) gives free access to law reports world wide.
www.opsi.gov.uk/stat.htm (Office of Public Sector Information) gives the text of statutes and statutory instruments.
www.r3.org.uk (Association of Business Recovery Professionals) has a bibliography as well as annual reviews, statistical analysis, statements of insolvency practice, and general guides to insolvency procedures.
www.insolvency.gov.uk (The Insolvency Service) is a government resource with a searchable register of disqualified directors.
www.jctltd.co.uk gives details of all current JCT standard forms.
www.hm-treasury.gov.uk/documents/public_private_partnerships/ppp_standardised_contracts.cfm gives the text of Standardisation of PFI Contracts (SoPC) Version 4 (March 2007).
www.hmrc.gov.uk/contractors/index.shtml gives details of the Construction Industry Scheme (see Ch.21).
www.constructionhistory.co.uk (Construction History Society) provides industry cultural background.
www.woodchestermansion.org.uk tells the story of a country house abandoned during construction in the 1870s. The income from the estate would not cover its running costs.
www.building.co.uk has a useful archive for checking construction-related companies which have become insolvent since 1997.
www.etymonline.com is a good resource for researching the origins of words.

Chapter 1: Law in context

Attwater, D.: (1965) *The Penguin Dictionary of Saints*, Penguin, London.

Barber, R.: (trans): (1992) *Bestiary, Bodleian MS 764*, London, Folio Society.

Brindle, S.: (2005) *Brunel: The Man who Built the World*, London, Weidenfeld & Nicolson.

Brownlee, D.B.: (1984) *The Law Courts: Architecture of George Edmund Street*, London, The MIT Press.

Campbell, JWP: (2002) "Seventeenth-century bricklayers' contracts: Wren's City churches", *Construction History Society Newsletter No. 64*, October 2002, 7–12.

Cicero, trans. Grant, M.: (1971) "Discussions at Tusculum" in *On the Good Life*, Penguin, London.

Davis, R.: (1996) "Payment issues and legislation" in Davis, R., and Odams AM, (eds) (1996) *Security for Payment*, Construction Law Press, King's College, London.

Delmon, J.: (2005) *Project Finance, BOT Projects and Risk*, Kluwer Law International.

Dunkeld, M.: (2003) "Establishing a Postgraduate Programme in Construction History: The Experience of South Bank University, London", *Construction History Society Newsletter No. 65*, February 2003, 20–25.

Emden, A.: (1882) *The Law Relating to Building Leases and Building Contracts*, 1st edn, Sweet & Maxwell: London.

Finch, V.: (2002) *Corporate Insolvency Law: Perspectives and Principles*, Cambridge University Press.

Finley, M.I., Mack Smith, D: and Duggan, C.: (1986) *A History of Sicily*, Chatto & Windus, London.

Hillman, J.: (1979) *The Dream and the Underworld*, Harper & Row, New York.

Knowles, D.: (1948) *The Religious Orders in England*, Vol.1, Cambridge University Press, Cambridge.

Kostal, R.W.: (1997) *Law and English Railway Capitalism 1825–1875*, Clarendon Press, Oxford.

Lester, V.M.: (1995) *Victorian Insolvency*, Clarendon Press, Oxford.

Milman, D.: (2005) *Personal Insolvency Law, Regulation and Policy*, Ashgate Publishing, Aldershot.

Powell, C.G.: (1986) "He that runs against time: life expectancy of building firms in nineteenth century Bristol" (1986) 2 Construction History 64.

Selby, P.: (1997) *Grace and Mortgage: The Language of Faith and the Debt of the World*, Darton, Longman and Todd, London.

Summerson, J.: (1973) *The London Building World of the Eighteen-Sixties*, Thames and Hudson, London.

Summerson, J.: (1978) *Georgian London*, 3rd edn, Barrie & Jenkins, London.

Vaughan, A.: (1991) *Isambard Kingdom Brunel: Engineering Knight-Errant*, London: John Murray.

The following list was compiled by Peter Fenn for the 2nd edn of this book:

Acland, A.: (1990) *A Sudden Outbreak of Common Sense*, Hutchinson Business Books, London.

Baden Hellard, R.: (1988) *Managing Construction Conflict*, Longman, London.
Ball, M.: (1990) *Rebuilding Construction*, Routledge, London.
CIEC (Construction Industry Employers Council): (1994) *Final Report by the CIEC to Sir Michael Latham*.
DoE (Department of the Environment): (1990) *Housing and Construction Statistics 1979–1989: Great Britain*, HMSO.
Fleming M.C.: (1980) *Construction and the Related Professions*, Pergamon Press.
Harvey, J.: (1992) *Urban Land Economics*, Macmillan.
Higgins and Jessop: (1965) *Communications in the Construction Industry*, The Tavistock Institute, London.
Hillebrandt, P.: (1984) *Analysis of the British Construction Industry*, Macmillan.
Hillebrandt, P.: (1985) *Economic Theory and the Construction Industry*, 2nd edn, Macmillan.
Hillebrandt, P. and Cannon, J. (eds): (1989) *The Management of Construction Firms: Aspects of Theory*, Macmillan.
Hillebrandt, P. and Cannon, J.: (1990) *The Modern Construction Firm*, Macmillan.
Hillebrandt, P. and Cannon, J. and Lansley, P.: (1995) *The Construction Company in and out of Recession*, Macmillan.
Raftery, J.: (1991) *Principles of Building Economics*, B.S.P., London.
Smith and Wiede Nebbeling: (1986) *The Shadow Economy in Britain and Germany*, Anglo-German Foundation, London.
World Bank: (1984) *The Construction Industries: Issues and Strategies*, World Bank, Washington DC.

Chapter 2: Elements of Construction Security

Alhajeri, M.A.: (2000) "Use of guarantee bonds in public works contracts—the legal framework in Kuwait" [2000] I.C.L.R. 415.
Cahill, F.: (1988) "Security for performance clauses" (1988) B.C.L. 18 (Australian).
Cavill, N.: (1999) "Arts Council faces £3.5m of Bristol claims", *Building*, 16 April 1999.
Cole, M.: (2000) "Restructuring of project finance debt in emerging markets" (2000) 28(9) I.B.L. 415.
Cole, T.R.H.: (2003) *Final Report of the Royal Commission into the Building and Construction Industry (Australia)*, *www.royalcombci.gov.au*.
Coote, B.: (2001) "The performance interest, Panatown, and the problem of loss" (2001) 117 L.Q.R. 81.
Delmon, J.: (2005) *Project Finance, BOT Projects and Risk*, Kluwer Law International.
Goode, R.M.: (2003) *Legal Problems of Credit and Security*, 3rd edn, Sweet & Maxwell, London.
Gough, W.J.: (1996) *Company Charges*, 2nd edn, Butterworths, London.
Gu, W.: (2005) "Security for costs in international commercial arbitration", *Journal of International Arbitration*, 22(3), 167–206, 2005.
Hughes, W., Hillebrandt, P. and Murdoch, J.: (1998) *Financial Protection in the UK Building Industry*, E. & F.N. Spon, London.

Jones, D.F.: (1992) "How the construction contract can protect those in the construction industry from the effects of insolvency" (1992) 8 B.C.L. 246.

Jones, D.: (2007) "Proportionate liability—reform or regression?" [2007] I.C.L.R. 62–101

Latham, M.: (1993) "Trust and money", HMSO, London.

Latham, M.: (1994) *Constructing the Team*, HMSO, London.

McGaw, M.: (1994) "Insolvency, project integrity and the JCT standard forms" Const. L.J., 1994, 10, 266–300.

Mead, P.: (2007) "Current trends in risk allocation in construction projects and their implications for industry participants" Const. L.J., 2007, 23(1), 23–45.

Merity, P.: (2002) "Paradise postponed: a history of attempts to ensure payment in the building and construction industry of New South Wales" (2002) 18 B.C.L. 169–179.

Milman, D.: (1998) "Security for costs: principles and pragmatism in corporate litigation" in Rider, B., (ed) (1998) *The Realm of Company Law*, Kluwer, London.

Neate, F.W.: (ed): (1990) *Using Set-off as Security*, Graham & Trotman and International Bar Association.

Newman, P.: (1999) *Bonds, Guarantees and Performance Security in the Construction Industry*, Jordans, London.

Odams, A.M.: (1996) "Lien, charge and payment security" in Davis, R., and Odams A.M., (eds) (1996) *Security for Payment*, Construction Law Press, King's College, London.

Oditah, F.: (1992) "Assets and the treatment of claims in insolvency" (1992) 108 L.Q.R. 459.

Runeland, P., and Blanke, G: (2007) "On provisional measures in English arbitrations: a brief overview," (2007) 73 *Arbitration* 189–198.

Soo G.: (2001) "Invoking security in Hong Kong construction contracts" [2001] I.C.L.R. 130.

Vinter, G., and Price, G.: (2005) *Project Finance*, 3rd edn, Sweet & Maxwell, London.

Wallace, I.N.D.: (1995) *Hudson's Building and Engineering Contracts*, 11th edn, Sweet & Maxwell, London.

Wallace, I.N.D.: (1986) *Construction Contracts: Principles and Policies in Tort and Contract*, Sweet & Maxwell, London.

Wallace, I.N.D.: (2000) "People in glass houses—the need for unconditional warranties" [2000] I.C.L.R. 124–129.

Watts, P.: (1995) "Does a subcontractor have restitutionary rights against the employer?" [1995] L.M.C.L.Q. 398.

Whiteson, J.: (1992) "Insolvency and the NHBC" (1992) 8 (1) I.L. & P. 5.

Chapter 3: Payment

Banwell: (1964) *The Placing and Management of Contracts for Building and Civil Engineering Work*, HMSO.

Barber, J: (2007) "Late Payment of Commercial Debts (Interest) Act 1998—no laughing matter," Const. L.J., 2007, 331–343.

BSRIA (2002) *Project improvements through abolishing retentions*, *www.bsria.co.uk*.

Buisson, A.: (2004) "PFI subcontracts and equivalent project relief", MSc dissertation, Centre of Construction Law and Management, King's College, London.

Cork, K.: (1982) *Insolvency Law and Practice: Report of the Review Committee*, HMSO.

Davis, R.: (1996) "Insolvency and the bill", *Building*, 22 March 1996.

Davis, R.: (2000) "The insolvency perspective" in Paterson, F.A., and Britton, P. (eds) (2000) *The Construction Act: Time for Review*, Centre of Construction Law and Management, King's College, London.

Department of the Environment (DoE): (1995) *Fair Construction Contracts*.

Department of Trade and Industry (DTI): (2006) *Improving payment practices in the construction industry—Analysis of the consultation on proposals to amend Part II of the Housing Grants Construction and Regeneration Act 1996 and Scheme for Construction Contracts (England and Wales) Regulations 1998, www.dti.gov.uk/files/file20826.pdf*.

House of Commons: (2002) House of Commons Trade and Industry Committee, "*The use of retentions in the UK construction industry*", 2nd report of session 2002–2003, HMSO.

Goldsmith, I. and Heintzman, T.G.: (1988) *Goldsmith on Canadian Building Contracts*, 4th edn, Carswell (looseleaf).

Goode, R.M.: (1983) *Payment Obligations in Commercial and Financial Transactions*, Sweet & Maxwell, London.

Goode, R.M.: (2003) *Legal Problems of Credit and Security*, 3rd edn, Sweet & Maxwell, London.

Hayton, D.: (1994a) "The significance of equity in construction contracts" [1994] 2 Con. L. Yb. 19.

Hillebrandt, P. and Cannon, J. (eds): (1989) *The Management of Construction Firms: Aspects of Theory*, Macmillan.

Hosie, J.: (1997) "How will pay when paid clauses be affected by the Construction Act?" (1997) 8(7) *Construction Law* 236.

Hughes, W., Hillebrandt, P. and Murdoch, J.: (1998) *Financial Protection in the UK Building Industry*, E. & F.N. Spon, London.

Keating, D.: (1983) "Sub-contracts under English law" in *Selected Problems of Construction Law: International Approach*, Fribourg University Press and Sweet & Maxwell.

Loftus, G.: (2002) "Retention—is it time to let it go?", MSc dissertation, Centre of Construction Law and Management, King's College, London.

MacLaughlin, W.: (2006) "Courts v construction: accrual of a cause of action for payment in engineering contracts" Const. L.J., 2006, 22(7), 445–460.

McCosker, B.: (1995) "Back to back payment clauses: 'if and when'" [1995] C.I.L.L. 1029.

McGuinness, K.P.: (1983) *Construction Lien Remedies in Ontario*, Carswell Legal Publications.

Murphy, H.J.: (1989) "Pay when paid clauses in construction sub-contracts: conditions precedent or terms of payment?" (1989) 4 I.C.L.R. 207.

Oditah, F.: (1991) *Legal Aspects of Receivables Financing*, Sweet & Maxwell.

OGC (Office of Government Commerce): (2007) *Guide to Best 'Fair Payment' Practices*, http://www.ogc.gov.uk

Pilcher, R.: (1985) *Project Cost Control in Construction*, Collins.

Price, J.: (1994) *Sub-Contracting under the JCT Standard Forms of Building Contract*, MacMillan.

Salinger, F.R.: (2000) *Factoring Law and Practice*, 2nd edn, Sweet & Maxwell, London.
Sheridan, P.: (2006) "Construction Act Review" Const. L.J., 2006, 22(5), 324–335 [pay when paid].
Stebbings, S.: "Performance bonds" (1997/8) 8(10) *Construction Law* 336.
Sweet, J., and Schreier, M.M.: (2004) *Legal Aspects of Architecture, Engineering and the Construction Process*, 7th edn, Thomson (American).
Stockenberg, RA and Woodbury, JS: (1996) "Retainage revisited: a time to revise and reform" (1996) 16(1) *The Construction Lawyer* 41 (American).
Subramaniam, S: (2006) "Pay-when-paid clauses: a comparative study", MSc dissertation, Centre of Construction Law and Management, King's College, London and National University of Singapore.
Upson, A: (1987) *Financial Management for Contractors*, BSP Professional Books.
Wood, PR: (1989) *English and International Set-Off*, Sweet & Maxwell, London.
Wright, JD: (1997) "Credit insurance for the construction industry" (1997) 8(1) *Construction Law* 25.
Yendall, A: (1997) "The outlawing of 'pay-when-paid' clauses: can regulation be justified?" MSc dissertation, Centre of Construction Law and Management, King's College, London.

Chapter 4: Assignment

Allcock, R.: (1983) "Restrictions on the assignment of contractual rights" (1983) C.L.J. 328.
Cartwright, J.: (1990) "The assignment of collateral warranties" (1990) 6 Const. L.J. 14.
Cartwright, J.: (1993) "Remedies in respect of defective buildings after Linden Gardens" (1993) 9 Const. L.J. 281.
Davis, R.: (1996) "Payment issues and legislation" in Davis, R, and Odams, AM, (eds) (1996) *Security for Payment*, Construction Law Press, King's College, London.
Flannery, A.: (2002) "Security over Contractual Rights and Tripartite Agreements" (2002) 13 J.B.F.L.P. 179.
Goode, R.M.: (1979) "Inalienable rights?" (1979) 42 M.L.R. 553.
Goode, R.M.: (1976) "The right to trace and its impact in commercial transactions: Part I" (1976) 92 L.Q.R. 360, (Part II) (1976) 92 L.Q.R. 528.
Hayton, D.J.: (1994a) "The significance of equity in construction contracts" [1994] 2 Con. L. Yb. 19.
Hayton, D.J.: (2003) *Underhill and Hayton: Law Relating to Trusts and Trustees*, 16th edn, Butterworths, London.
Jones, G. and Goodhart, W.: (1996) *Specific Performance*, 2nd edn, Butterworths.
Latham, M.: (1994), *Constructing the Team*, H.M.S.O., London.
McCormack, G.: (1997) *Proprietary Claims and Insolvency*, Sweet & Maxwell, London.
McKnight A.: (2003) "Contractual Restrictions on a Creditor's Right to Alienate Debts": Part 1 (2003) 18(1) J.I.B.L. 1–8, Part 2 (2003a) 18(2) J.I.B.L. 43–51.

Megens, P., and Ang, B.: (1994) "Assignment, novation and sub-contracting: who cares what you call it?" [1994] B.C.L. 319.
Millett, P.J.: (1991) "Tracing the proceeds of fraud" (1991) 107 L.Q.R. 71.
Prentice, G.: (1983) "Remedies of building sub-contractors against employers" (1983) 46 M.L.R. 409.
Stebbings, S.: (1997/98) "Performance bonds" (1997/8) *Construction Law*, 8(10), 336.
Tettenborn, A.M.: (1987) "Fraud, cross-claims and the assignment of choses in action" (1987) Conv. 358.
Tolhurst, G.J.: (1999) "Assignment, equities, The Trident Beauty and restitution" (1999) 58 C.L.J. 546.
Tolhurst, G.J.: (2004) "The Efficacy of Contractual Provisions Prohibiting Assignment" [2004] Syd. L. Rev. 8.
Turner, P.G.: (2004) "Charges of Unassignable Rights" (2004) 20 *Journal of Contract Law*, 97–124.

Chapter 5: Set-off, abatement and deduction

Aeberli, P.: (1992) "Abatements, set-offs and counterclaims in arbitration proceedings" [1992] A.D.R.L.J. 130.
Barrett, K.J.: (1998) "Withholding payment under the Housing Grants, Construction and Regeneration Act 1996", (1998) 14 Const L.J. 180.
Berger, K.P.: (1999) "Set-off in international economic arbitration", (1999) 15 *Arbitration International* 53.

Chapter 6: Plant and equipment

Barber, P.: (1998) "Title to goods, materials and plant under construction contracts" in Palmer N., and McKendrick, E. (eds) (1998) *Interests in Goods*, 2nd edn, Lloyd's of London Press, London.
Emden, A.: (1882) *The law relating to building leases and building contracts*, 1st edn, Sweet & Maxwell, London.
Goode, R.M.: (2004) *Commercial Law*, 3rd edn, Lexis Nexis, London.
Goode, R.M.: (2005) *Principles of Corporate Insolvency Law*, 3rd edn, Sweet & Maxwell.
Hudson, A.: (1891) *The Law of Building and Engineering Contracts*, 1st edn, Sweet & Maxwell, London.
Lonergan, R.: (2005) "A principal's rights in relation to contractor's plant under NZS3910:2003: a plea for conceptual clarity" [2005] I.C.L.R. 151.
Newman, P.: (1998) "Plant vesting under civil engineering contracts" (1998) 9(6) *Construction Law* 195.
Palmer, N.: (1996) "ICE (5th) Conditions: title to plant and contractor's insolvency" (1996) 13 Build. L.M. 1.
Palmer, N.: (1997) "Employer's rights over plant: Cosslett in the Court of Appeal" (1997) 14 Build. L.M. 1.
Pickin, A.: (1998) "The registrability of liens as security interests" *Insolvency Intelligence, 1998, 11, 60–61.*
Summerson, J.: (1978) *Georgian London*, 3rd edn, Barrie & Jenkins, London.

Vaughan, A.: (1991) *Isambard Kingdom Brunel: Engineering Knight-Errant*, John Murray, London.

Wallace, I.N.D. (1995) *Hudson's Building and Engineering Contracts*, 11th edn, Sweet & Maxwell, London.

Chapter 7: Goods and materials

Ballard, D.: (1994) "Payment for materials or goods not yet incorporated into the works" (1994) 10 Const. L.J. 203.

Barber, P.: (1998) "Title to goods, materials and plant under construction contracts" in Palmer N., and McKendrick, E. (eds) (1998) *Interests in Goods*, 2nd edn, Lloyd's of London Press, London.

Buckland, W.W.: (1963) *A Textbook of Roman Law from Augustus to Justinian*, Cambridge University Press.

Cooper, D.: (1991) "Retaining title to fixtures" (1991) 4 Auckland Univ. L.R. 477.

Crowther: (1971) *Report on the Committee on Consumer Credit*, Cmnd 4596, HMSO.

RIBA: (1978) *Retention of Title (Ownership) by Suppliers of Building Materials and Goods*, Royal Institute of British Architects.

Feld: (1992) "Retention of title: Seller v Receiver", (1992) L.S.G. July 1, 1992.

Goode, R.M.: (1989) *Proprietary Rights in Insolvency and Sales Transactions*, Sweet & Maxwell, London.

Goode, R.M.: (2004) *Commercial Law*, 3rd edn, Lexis Nexis, London.

Goodhart, W., and Jones, G.: (1980) "The infiltration of equitable developments into English commercial law" (1980) 43 M.L.R. 489.

Guest, A.G. and Lever, J.: (1963) "Hire-purchase, equipment leases and fixtures" (1963) 27 Conv. 30.

Holdsworth, W.: (1956) *A History of English Law*, 7th edn, Methuen, London.

ICC (International Chamber of Commerce): (1993) *Retention of Title*, 2nd edn, Publication No. 501.

Latham, M.: (1994) *Constructing the Team*, HMSO, London.

McCormack, G.: (1995) *Reservation of Title*, 2nd edn, Sweet & Maxwell, London.

Parris, J.: (1986) *Effective Retention of Title Clauses*, Collins.

Tettenborn, A.M.: "Reservation of title: insolvency and priority problems" (1981) J.B.L. 173.

Wallace, I.N.D.: (1995) *Hudson's Building and Engineering Contracts*, 11th edn, Sweet & Maxwell, London.

Ward, N.: (2001) "The unwanted enigma: reservation of title in the construction industry" [2001] I.C.L.R. 147–177.

Weathered, J.: (1992) "Administrative receivers and leased assets" (1992) 8 I.L. & P.3.

Williams, G.A.: (1987) "Reservation of title in the construction industry: who wants it: some economic perspectives on risk allocation" (1987) 40 Current Legal Problems 233, (1987) 3 Const. L.J. 252–273.

Wylie, O.P.: (1978) "Reservation of ownership: a means of protection for unsecured creditors of bankrupt builders" (1978) 42 Conv. 37.

Chapter 8: Informal insolvency

Abidali, A.F.: (1990) "A methodology for predicting company failure in the construction industry", Ph. D. thesis, Loughborough, 41–6571 (referenced in Morris, 2005).

Adamson, S.: (1991) "Restructuring", unpublished paper.

Goode, R.M.: (2003) *Legal Problems of Credit and Security*, 3rd edn, Sweet & Maxwell, London.

Goode, R.M.: (2005) *Principles of Corporate Insolvency Law*, 3rd edn, Sweet & Maxwell, London.

Grant Thornton: (1999) *Industry Watch on Construction*.

Gyles, R.V.: (1992) *Royal Commission into Productivity: Report of the Hearings*, Sydney: State Government of New South Wales.

Haig, C.: (2000) "Preparing a blueprint for disaster", *Contract Journal*, October 11, 2000.

Harrison, M.: (2002) "PFI Casualty: How Amey went from buccaneer to basket case," *The Independent*, November 9, 2002, p.26.

Hillebrandt, P.M.: (1977) "Going bust: what are the facts?" (1977) 232 *Building*, 52–53.

Hillebrandt, P.M.: (1984) *Analysis of the British Construction Industry*, MacMillan.

Kenley, R.: (2003) *Financing Construction: cash flows and cash farming*, Spon Press, London.

Kent, P.: (1997) "Corporate workouts—a UK perspective" (1997) 6 Int. Insolv. Rev. 165.

Lee Beng Tat: (1993) "Claiming a pound of flesh as a contingent or prospective creditor under the Companies Act" [1993] *Singapore Journal of Legal Studies* 144.

Leftly, M.: (2003) "Going Ballistic", *Building*, Issue 48.

Leftly, M.: (2006) "The temptation of Coverite", *Building*, Issue 18.

Morrell, D.: (1987) *Indictment: Power and Politics in the Construction Industry*, Faber and Faber, London.

Morris, S.: (2005) "Insolvency in construction: the collapse of Laing Construction plc in 2001", dissertation submitted to the University of Manchester for the degree of MSc in the Faculty of Engineering and Physical Sciences.

Oditah, F.: (1995) "Winding-up recalcitrant debtors" [1995] L.M.C.L.Q. 107.

R3 (Association of Business Recovery Professionals) (2004) *Corporate Insolvency in the UK*, 12th survey.

Summerson, J.: (1978) *Georgian London*, 3rd edn, Barrie & Jenkins, London.

White, D.: (2000) "The great sack race", *Building*, February 4, 2000.

White, J.: (1998) "Rescue v insolvency: the lawyer's perspective", unpublished paper.

Chapter 9: Construction trusts

Anderson, H.: (1992) "The treatment of trust assets in English insolvency law" in McKendrick, E.: (ed) *Commercial Aspects of Trusts and Fiduciary Obligations*, Clarendon Press, Oxford.

Cole, T.R.H.: (2003) *Final Report of the Royal Commission into the Building and Construction Industry (Australia)*, *www.royalcombci.gov.au*.

Critchlow, J., and Mulla, Z.: (1996) "Nominated sub-contractors: the trouble with name-borrowing" (1996) 7(3) *Construction Law* 96.

Davis, R.: "Payment issues and legislation" in Davis, R. and Odams, A.M. (eds) (1996) *Security for Payment*, Construction Law Press, King's College London.

Ettinger, L.P.: (1989) "Trusts in the construction industry" (1989) 27 Alberta L.R. 390.

Glaholt, D.: (1999) *Construction Trusts*, Carswell Legal Publications, Toronto.

Hayton, D.J.: (1994a) "The significance of equity in construction contracts" [1994] 2 Con L Yb 19.

Hayton, D.J.: (1994b) "Uncertainty of subject-matter of trusts" (1994) 110 L.Q.R. 335.

Hayton, D.J.: (2003) *Underhill and Hayton: Law Relating to Trusts and Trustees*, 16th edn, Butterworths, London.

Klein, R.: (2006) "We're banking on the project" *Construction News*, June 8, 2006, 24.

McGuire, T.J.: (1989) "Construction contract proceeds as trust funds" (1989) Flo. Bar. J. 31.

Merity, P.: (2002) "Paradise postponed: a history of attempts to ensure payment in the building and construction industry of New South Wales" (2002) 18 B.C.L. 169–179.

OGC (Office of Government Commerce): (2007) *Guide to Best 'Fair Payment' Practices*, http://www.ogc.gov.uk

Quick, R., and Davis, R.: (2002) "The construction trust—an empty remedy?" [2002] I.C.L.R. 474–487.

Chapter 10: Retention trusts

Blackler, A.: (1998) "Retention monies in UK building contracts" in Palmer N., and McKendrick, E. (eds) (1998) *Interests in Goods*, 2nd edn, Lloyd's of London Press, London.

Clarke, A.: (1992) "De Mattos v Gibson again" L.M.C.L.Q. 1992, 4, 448–459.

Dean, C.: (1996) "The JCT retention trust: an effective means of protecting a contractor's right to his own money?" in Davis, R., and Odams, A.M., (eds) (1996) *Security for Payment*, Construction Law Press, King's College, London.

Fitzpatrick, F.: (1991) "Retention funds in building contracts" (1991) N.L.J. 1007.

Hopper, R.: (1996) "Construction sector retention survey" in Davis, R., and Odams, A.M., (eds) (1996) *Security for Payment*, Construction Law Press, King's College, London.

Moss, G.: (1992) "Retention trusts" (1992) 5 *Insolvency Intelligence* 25.

Chapter 11: Pre-emptive measures

Bamford, J.: (2006a) "Abuse of process—part 2", *Insolvency Intelligence*, 2006, 19(10), 150–155.

Bamford, J.: (2006b) "Abuse of process—part 3", *Insolvency Intelligence*, 2006, 19(10), 155–166.

Paterson, S., and Marks, D.: (2004) "Administration orders and disputed creditors: to resolve or not to resolve", *Insolvency Intelligence*, 2004, 17, 40–44.

Chapter 12: Adjudication

Davis, R.: (2000a) "Adjudication and insolvency", *Construction Law*, May 2000, 11(3), 22.

Davis, R.: (2000b) "Security and construction contracts", unpublished paper delivered to the Society of Construction Law, 7 March 2000 (see *www.scl.org.uk*, paper no.97).

Davis, R.: (2001) "Elements of Construction Security", unpublished paper delivered at an IBC conference, March 19, 2001.

Gould, N.: (2005) "Construction Act Review" (2005) 21 Const. L.J. 435–455 [enforcement of adjudicators' decisions].

Hayford, O.: (2005) "Challenging security of payment adjudications after Brodyn" (2005) 21 B.C.L. 328–352.

Helps, D., and Sheridan P.: (2006a) "Construction Act Review", Const. L.J. 2006, 22(6), 378–393 [Stay of execution].

Helps, D., and Sheridan P.: (2006b) "Construction Act Review", Const. L.J. 2006, 22(8), 530–573 [Case index].

Kennedy, P., and Milligan J.L.: (2005) "Adjudication Reporting Centre, Glasgow Caledonian University, Report No. 7", *www.adjudication.gcal.ac.uk*.

Ndekugri, I., and Russell, V.: (2005) "Insolvency and resolution of construction contract disputes by adjudication in the UK construction industry" (2005) *Construction Management and Economics*, 23, 399–408.

Sheridan, P., and Helps, D.: (2002) "Construction Act Review" (2002) 18 Const. L.J. 39 [Adjudication and insolvency].

Sheridan, P., and Helps, D.: (2004) "Construction Act Review" (2004) 20 Const. L.J. 444.

The Technology and Construction Court Guide (2005), 2nd edn, (see *www.hmcourts-service.gov.uk*).

Chapter 13: Formal Insolvency

Blanchard, P.: (1989) "The contracts of a company in receivership" (1989) NZ Univ. L.R. 237.

Brown, D.: (1996) *Corporate Rescue: Insolvency Law in Practice*, John Wiley & Sons.

Chan, P.: (2004) *Casebook on Insolvency and the Construction Industry*, Sweet & Maxwell, Singapore.

Cork, K.: (1982) *Insolvency Law and Practice: Report of the Review Committee*, HMSO.

Fritz, D.F.: (2004) "Philipp Holzmann AG—insolvency of a construction giant", I.L. & P., 20(4), 2004, 166–170.

Grogan, F.: (1992) "A review of the administration order procedure in the context of the construction industry incorporating case studies", MSc dissertation. Centre of Construction Law and Management, King's College, London.

Hay, G., and McCulloch, C.: (2004) "UK directors' buyout rescues HLM from receivers" *Building* 2004, Issue 12.

Hillebrandt, P., and Cannon, J. (eds): (1989) *The Management of Construction Firms: Aspects of Theory*, Macmillan.

Homan, M.: (1989) *A Survey of Administration under the Insolvency Act 1986: The Result of Administration Orders Made in 1987*, Institute of Chartered Accountants in England and Wales.

Klein, R.: (2005) "The power of licensing bodies", *Construction News*, June 23, 2005, 16.

Klein, R.: (2007) "Restitution needs a test case", *Construction News*, March 22, 2007, 32.

Oditah, F.: (1991) *Legal Aspects of Receivables Financing*, Sweet & Maxwell, London.

Plant, S.: (2002) "The administration of Railtrack plc—law in the making", I.L. & P. 18(1), 2002, 18–20.

Simmons, M.: (1996) "The statutory declaration of solvency: voluntary winding up of companies: members or creditors?" (1996) 9 *Insolvency Intelligence* 33.

SPI (Society of Practitioners of Insolvency): (1993) Bulletin 17.

Stokes, D.: (2000) "How effective have company voluntary arrangements and administration orders been in rescuing insolvent companies with particular reference to the construction industry?" MSc dissertation, Centre of Construction Law and Management, King's College, London.

Totty, P. and Crystal, M.: (1982) *Corporate Insolvency*, McGraw-Hill.

Upson, A.: (1987) *Financial Management for Contractors*, BSP Professional Books.

White, J.: (1998) "Rescue v Insolvency: The Lawyer's Perspective", unpublished paper.

Chapter 14: Termination

Beale, H.: (1988) "Penalties in termination provisions" (1988) 104 L.Q.R. 355.

Bridge, S., Candi, E., and Wyburn, M.: (1987) "Copyright and architecture" (1987) B.C.L. 94.

Burke, T.M.: (1986) "The liability of the contractor for late completion" in LLoyd, H. (ed) *The Liability of Contractors*, Centre for Commercial Law Studies, Queen Mary College, University of London.

Carter, J.W.: (1989) "The effect of discharge of a contract on the assessment of damages for breach or repudiation" (1989) J.C.L. 113 and 249.

Carter, J.W.: (1990) "Termination clauses" (1990) 3 J.C.L. 90.

Carter, J.W.: (1991) *Breach of Contract*, 2nd edn, Sweet & Maxwell, London.

Countryman, V.: (1973) "Executory contracts in bankruptcy: Part I" (1973) 57 Minn. L.R. 439, Part II (1974) 58 Minn LR 479.

Davis, R.: (2000a) "Adjudication and insolvency", *Construction Law*, May 2000, 22.

Davis, R.: (2000b) "Security and Construction Contracts" unpublished, paper given to the Society of Construction Law on March 7, 2000, *www.scl.org.uk*.

Delemore, C.L.: (1994) *Copyright Explained*, RIBA Publications, London.

Jones, G., and Goodhart, W.: (1996) *Specific Performance*, 2nd edn, Butterworths.

Homan, M.: (1989) A *Survey of Administration under the Insolvency Act 1986: The Result of Administration Orders Made in 1987*, Institute of Chartered Accountants in England and Wales.

Keating, D.: (1986) "Employer's remedy for delay: termination" in LLoyd, H. (ed) *The Liability of Contractors*, Longman.

Lloyd, H.: (1990) "Termination clauses, worth more than a moment's thought", *Building*, May 25, 1990.

Oditah, F.: (1992) "Assets and the treatment of claims in insolvency" (1992) 108 L.Q.R. 459.

Opeskin, R.: (1990) "Damages for breach of contract terminated under express terms" (1990) 106 L.Q.R. 293.

Rubino-Sammartano, M.: (1983) "International construction agreements: employer's breach and consequent right of the contractor to withhold delivery of the site" (1983) I.B.L. 143.

Sims, J., and Powell-Smith, V.: (1985) *Determination and Suspension of Construction Contracts*, Collins.

Thomas, D.F.C.: (2004) "Contractual prohibitions on the assignment of copyright" L.Q.R. 2004, 120, 218–222.

Van Deventer, R.: (1993) *The Law of Construction Contracts*, John Wiley & Sons.

Wee, M.S.: (2005) "Insolvency and the survival of contracts", JBL, 2005, July, 494–521.

Wheeler, P.: (1991) "Copyright in construction drawings and works of architecture" (1991) 7 Const. L.J. 75.

Wheeler, P.: (1994) "Copyright—the Cinderella of construction agreements—Part 2" (1994) 5(1) *Construction Law* 27.

Wheeler, P., and Boyson, K.: (1999) "Copyright—an accident waiting to happen?" (1999) 10(5) *Construction Law* 24.

Chapter 15: Novation of contracts

Capon, G.: (1990) *Construction Industry*, Institute of Chartered Accountants in England and Wales.

Cullen, C.: (2005) "Novation", unpublished, a paper given to the Society of Construction Law in London March 1, 2005.

McDevitt, K.: (1985) *Contract Bonds and Guarantees*, Chartered Institute of Building.

McNicholas, P.: (1993) "Novation of consultants to design build contractors" (1993) 9 Const. L.J. 263.

RICS: (1997) *Construction Insolvency Information Paper*, Royal Institution of Chartered Surveyors.

Megens, P., and Ang, B.: (1994) "Assignment, novation and subcontracting—who cares what you call it?" [1994] B.C.L. 319.

Newman, P.: (1992) *Insolvency Explained*, RIBA Publications, London.

von Laun, R.: (2004) "Novation and other ways to exchange a party to a contract in England and Germany" MSc dissertation, Centre of Construction Law and Management, King's College, London.

Chapter 16: Completion contracts

Brindle, S.: (2005) *Brunel: The Man who Built the World*, London, Weidenfeld & Nicolson.
Fox, J., and Tott, N.: (1999) The *PFI Handbook*, Jordan Publishing, Bristol.
JCT, Practice Note 24 (1992), The Society of Practitioners of Insolvency and The Joint Contracts Tribunal, RIBA Publications, London.
Leftly, M.: (2006) "Why they pulled the plug on Curzon", *Building* 2006, Issue 15.
McDevitt, K.: (1985) *Contract Bonds and Guarantees*, Chartered Institute of Building.
Newman, P.: (1992) *Insolvency Explained*, Royal Institute of British Architects, London.
SBCC (Scottish Building Contract Committee): *Insolvency Practice Guide* (1991).
Scott, K. and Reynolds, P.: (1994) *Scott & Reynolds on Surety Bonds*, Carswell Legal Publications, Toronto (looseleaf).
Scriven J., Pritchard N., and Delmon J.: (1999) A *Contractual Guide to Major Construction Projects*, Sweet & Maxwell, London.
Stebbings, S.: (2000) "Satisfaction guarantees", *Building*, October 13, 2000.
Tan, K.: (2004) "To step-in or not to step-in? Direct agreements and PFI projects", MSc dissertation, Centre of Construction Law and Management, King's College, London.

Chapter 17: Direct payment

Baker, E., and Lavers, A.: (2004) "Worst Case Scenario: Anticipating Contractor's Insolvency—Lessons from Recent Cases", Const. L.J., 2004, 20(2), 58–70.
Bateson, D., and Barton, K.: (2002) "Sub-contractor insolvency—issues for main contractors in Hong Kong" [2002] I.C.L.R. 540–545.
Bridge, M.G.: (1991) "Company administrators and secured creditors" (1991) 107 L.Q.R. 394.
Bridge, M.G.: (2003) "Collectivity, management of estates and the *pari passu* rule in winding up" in Armour, J., and Bennett, H. (eds) (2003) *Vulnerable Transactions in Corporate Insolvency*, Hart Publishing, Oxford and Portland, Oregon, 1–36.
Capper, D.: (1998) "Direct payment clauses and the *pari passu* principle" CFILR, 2, 1998, 54–67.
Cole, T.R.H.: (2003) *Final Report of the Royal Commission into the Building and Construction Industry (Australia)*, *www.royalcombci.gov.au*.
Cushman, R.F., and Blick, G.L.: (1988) *Construction Industry Forms*, Wiley Law Publications.
DoE (Department of the Environment): (1995) "Fair construction contracts", Consultation Paper.
DTI (Department of Trade and Industry) (2006) *Improving payment practices in the construction industry—Analysis of the consultation on proposals to amend Part II of the Housing Grants Construction and Regeneration Act 1996 and Scheme for Construction*
European Commission: (1997) "The competitiveness of the construction sector".

Giocanti, X.: (1986) "Security for performance: conditional and on-demand bonds: the position of French law" in LLoyd, H. (ed) (1986) *The Liability of Contractors*, Longman.

Goode, R.M.: (2003) *Legal Problems of Credit and Security*, 3rd edn, Sweet & Maxwell, London.

HMSO: (1974): *Commentary on GC/Works/1*.

Latham, M.: (1994) *Constructing the Team*, HMSO, London.

Leftly, M: (2003) "Going Ballistic", *Building*, 2003, Issue 48.

Malinvaud, C.: (2006) "Protection of subcontractors under French law: an overview", unpublished, paper given to a meeting of the Society of Construction Law on September 5, 2006.

McCormack, G.: (1997) *Proprietary Claims and Insolvency*, Sweet & Maxwell, London.

McGaw, M.: (1994) "Insolvency, project integrity and the JCT Standard Forms" (1994) 10 Const. L.J. 266.

Merity, P.: (2002) "Paradise postponed: a history of attempts to ensure payment in the building and construction industry of New South Wales" (2002) 18 B.C.L. 169–179.

Ng, V.: (2006) "Statutory rights of lien, suspension and direct payment under The Building and Construction Industry Security of Payment Act Singapore: mere palliatives to claimants?" MSc dissertation, Centre of Construction Law and Management, King's College, London and National University of Singapore.

Oditah, F.: (1992) "Assets and the treatment of claims in insolvency" (1992) 108 LQR 459.

OGC (Office of Government Commerce): (2007) *Guide to Best 'Fair Payment' Practices*, http://www.ogc.gov.uk

Powell-Smith, V.: (1991) "Payment of sub-contractors when main contractor is insolvent" [1991] 2 I.C.L.R. 241.

Prentice, G.: (1983) "Remedies of building sub-contractors against employers" (1983) 46 M.L.R. 409.

Pulkowski, JF: (2004) "The sub-contractor's direct claim in international business law" [2004] ICLR 31–56.

Stephenson, A., and Harrison, B.: (2003) "Building and Construction Industry Security of Payment Act 2002 (Vic.)" (2003) 19 B.C.L. 7–24.

UN: (1988) *UNCITRAL Legal Guide on Drawing up International Contracts for the Construction of Industrial Works*, United Nations.

Wallace, I.N.D.: (1986) *Construction Contracts: Principles and Policies in Tort and Contract*, Sweet & Maxwell, London.

Wood, P.R.: (1989) *English and International Set-Off*, Sweet & Maxwell, London.

Chapter 18: Set-off in Insolvency

Berg, A.: (2002) "Cosslett—section 395 and set-off in the House of Lords—Part 2" *Insolvency Intelligence*, 2002, 15, 21–23.

Derham, R.: (2003) *The Law of Set-Off*, 3rd edn, Oxford University Press, Oxford.

Goode, R.M.: (1984) "The effect of a fixed charge on debts" [1984] J.B.L. 172.

Goode, R.M.: (2005) *Principles of Corporate Insolvency Law*, 3rd edn, Sweet & Maxwell, London.

Grantham, R.B.: (1989) "The impact of a security interest on set-off" [1989] J.B.L. 377.
Oditah, F.: (1991) *Legal Aspects of Receivables Financing*, Sweet & Maxwell, London.
Tettenborn, A.M.: (1987) "Fraud, cross-claims and the assignment of choses in action" (1987) Conv. 358.
Turing, D.: (2005) "The new insolvency set-off rules", I.L. & P., 21, 5, 2005, 165–167.
Wood, P.R.: (1989) *English and International Set-Off*, Sweet & Maxwell, London.

Chapter 19: Bonds and Guarantees

ABI (Association of British Insurers): (2002) *ABI Model Form of Guarantee Bond: An Explanatory Guide*.
Alhajeri, M.A.: (2000) "Use of guarantee bonds in public works contracts—the legal framework in Kuwait" [2000] I.C.L.R. 415.
Andrews, G., and Millett, R.: (2005) *Law of Guarantees*, 4th edn, FT Law & Tax.
Bailey, J.: (2003) "Unconditional bank guarantees" [2003] I.C.L.R. 240–288.
Bertrams, R.: (2004) *Bank Guarantees in International Trade*, 3rd edn, Kluwer Law International.
Bertrams, R.: (2000) "The new forms of security in FIDIC's 1999 Conditions of Contract" [2000] I.C.L.R. 369–383.
Bingham, A: (1993) "Whether to pay a bust subcontractor," *Building*, 16 April 1993, 28.
Byrne, D.: (2001) "Rights of the grantor under a performance bond" (2001) 17 B.C.L. 4.
Cahill, F.: (1988) "Security for performance clauses" (1988) B.C.L. 18.
Capper, P.: (1990) "Bonds and guarantees: their various types and problems" in *International and ICC Arbitration*, Centre of Construction Law & Management, King's College, London.
Chan, R.: (2006) "Recent legal developments in China in the use of bonds" [2006] I.C.L.R. 271–273.
Central Unit on Procurement (CUP): (1994) No. 48, *Bonds and Guarantees*, HM Treasury. *http://www.ogc.gov.uk/procurement_briefings—central_unit_on_procurement_cup_guidance.asp*.
Dixon, G., Gösswein, G., and Button, R.: (2005) "On-demand performance bonds in the international market and adjudication as a means of reducing the risks" [2005] I.C.L.R. 284.
DoE (Department of the Environment): (1996) *The Use of Performance Bonds in Government Construction Contracts*, Inter-Departmental Work Group for the Construction Sponsorship Directorate of the Department of the Environment.
Emden, A.: (1882) *The law relating to building leases and building contracts*, 1st edn, Sweet & Maxwell, London.
Goode, R.M.: (1986) "Unconditional bonds: the common law" in Lloyd, H (ed), *The Liability of Contractors*, Longman, London.
Goode, R.M.: (1992) *Guide to the ICC Uniform Rules for Demand Guarantees*, No.510, ICC Publishing SA, Paris.

Goode, R.M.: (2004) *Commercial Law*, 3rd edn, LexisNexis, London.
Herzfeld, E.: "Security for payments under major overseas projects" [1986] J.B.L. 446.
Horn, N.: (ed): (1989) *The Law of International Trade Finance*, Kluwer.
IBA (International Bar Association): (1992) *International Business Lawyer*, May 1992.
ICC (International Chamber of Commerce): (1986) *ICC Model Forms for Issuing Contract Guarantees*, No.406, ICC Publishing, Paris.
ICC: (1992) *ICC Uniform Rules for Demand Guarantees*, No.458, ICC Publishing, Paris.
ICC: (2006) *ICC Uniform Customs and Practice: UCP 600*, No.600, ICC Publishing, Paris.
ICC: (1993) *ICC Uniform Rules for Contract Bonds*, No.524, ICC Publishing, Paris.
ICC: (1994) *ICC Model Forms for Issuing Demand Guarantees*, No.503E, ICC Publishing, Paris.
ISP (1998) *International Standby Practices*, No.590, ICC Publishing, Paris.
Jack, R.: (1993) *Documentary Credits*, 2nd edn, Butterworths.
Jones, D.: (1990) *"Bid Bonds" in Formation of Contracts and Pre-Contractual Liability*, ICC Publication No.440/9.
Kennedy-Grant, T.: (1999) *Construction Law in New Zealand*, Butterworths, Auckland.
Kronfol, Z.A.: (1983–84) "Legal theory and practice of guarantee bonds in the Arabian Gulf" [1983–84] 1 I.C.L.R. 218.
Latham, M.: (1994), *Constructing the Team*, HMSO, London.
McDevitt, K.: (1985) *Contract Bonds and Guarantees*, Chartered Institute of Building
Marston, D.L.: (2002) "Pre-arbitral ADR techniques and conditional letter of credit performance guarantees" [2002] I.C.L.R. 526–530.
Moss G., and Marks, D.: (1999) *Rowlatt on Principal and Surety*, 5th edn, Sweet & Maxwell, London.
Muscat, A.: (1996) *The Liability of the Holding Company for the Debts of its Insolvent Subsidiaries*, Dartmouth, Aldershot.
NJCC (National Joint Consultative Committee for Building) (1995): *Guidance Note 2: Performance Bonds*.
Ndekugi, I.: (1999) "Performance bonds and guarantees in construction contracts: a review of some recurring problems" [1999] I.C.L.R. 294.
Petkovic, D.: (1995) "The proper law of letters of credit" [1995] 4 J.I.B.L. 141.
Phillips, J., and O'Donovan, J.: (1996) *The Modern Contract of Guarantee*, 3rd edn, LBC Information Services, Sydney.
Phillips, J.C. (1998) "Performance Bonds—some common issues" in "Construction Law: Looking to the Future", 11th Annual Conference, Centre of Construction Law & Management, Kings College London, September 18, 1998.
Pierce, A.: (1993) *Demand Guarantees in International Trade*, Sweet & Maxwell, London.
Pike, A.: (2004) "Review of the Association of British Insurers' Model Form of Guarantee Bond, July 2002" (2004) Const. L.J., 20(4), 197–205.
Robinson, N.M., Lavers, A.P. and Tan, G.K.H.: (1996) *Construction Law in Singapore and Malaysia*, 2nd edn, Butterworths.
Rowe, M.: (1987) *Guarantees, Standby Letters of Credit and Other Securities*, Euromoney Publications.

Rubino-Sammartano, M.: "Performance bonds: primary or secondary obligations?" (1985) I.B.L. 125.
Rubino-Sammartano, M.: "Performance bonds: injunctions" (1981) L.S.G., February 4, 1981.
Salzman, A.: (1952) *Building in England Down to 1540*, Oxford University Press, Oxford.
Scott, K. and Reynolds, P.: (1994) *Scott & Reynolds on Surety Bonds*, Carswell Legal Publications, Toronto (looseleaf).
Simpson, A.W.B: (1966) "The penal bond with conditional defeasance" (1966) 82 L.Q.R. 392–422.
Soo, G.: (2001) "Invoking security in Hong Kong construction contracts" [2001] I.C.L.R. 130.
Suen, H., and Cheung, S.O.: (2007) "Mareva injunctions: evolving principles and practices revisited", Const. L.J., 2007, 23(2), 117–136.
Wallace I.N.D.: (1986) *Construction Contracts: Principles and Policies in Tort and Contract*, Sweet & Maxwell, London.
Ward, A., and McCormack, G.: (2000) "Subrogation and bankers' autonomous undertakings" (2000) 116 L.Q.R. 121.
White, R.: (2001) "Appropriate use of bonds and guarantees in practice", unpublished, paper presented at IBC conference "Security and Construction Contracts" on March 19, 2001.
Wood, P.R.: (1995) *Comparative Law of Security and Guarantees*, Sweet & Maxwell, London.
Wunnicke, D.B. and Turner, B.S.: (1996) *Standby and Commercial Letters of Credit*, John Wiley & Sons.

Chapter 20: Insolvency claims

Anderson, H.: (1992) "The treatment of trust assets in English insolvency law" in McKendrick, E. (ed) *Commercial Aspects of Trusts and Fiduciary Obligations*, Clarendon Press, Oxford.
Armour, J., and Bennett, H.: (2003) *Vulnerable Transactions in Corporate Insolvency*, Hart Publishing, Oxford and Portland, Oregon.
Cole, T.R.H.: (2003) *Final Report of the Royal Commission into the Building and Construction Industry (Australia)*, *www.royalcombci.gov.au*.
Cork, K.: (1982) *Insolvency Law and Practice: Report of the Review Committee*, HMSO.
Davis, R.: (1988) "Wrongful trading and the construction industry" (1988) 4 Const. L.J. 185.
Goode, R.M.: (2005) *Principles of Corporate Insolvency Law*, 3rd edn, Sweet & Maxwell, London.
Lingard, J.: (1988) *Bank Security Documents*, 2nd edn, Butterworths, London.
Lingard, J.: (1989) *Corporate Rescues and Insolvencies*, 2nd edn, Butterworths, London.
Milman, D., and Parry, R.: (1997) *A Study of the Operation of Transactional Avoidance Mechanisms in Corporate Insolvency Practice*, Insolvency Lawyers Association Research Report, GTI Specialist Publishers.
Oditah, F.: (1992) "Misfeasance proceedings against company directors" [1992] L.M.C.L.Q. 207.

Chapter 21: Directors and employees

Benneyworth, R.: (2007) *The New Construction Industry Scheme: A Practical Guide to Compliance*, Lexis Nexis, Tolley.
Clark, G. de N.: (1967) "Industrial law and the labour-only sub-contract" (1967) 30 M.L.R. 6.
Drake, C.D.: (1968) "Wage slave or entrepreneur?" (1968) 31 M.L.R. 408.
Inland Revenue Consultative Document: (1991) "Taxation of sub-contractors in the construction industry".
Hillebrandt, P.M.: (1971) *Small Firms in the Construction Industry*, HMSO.
Mordsley, B.I.: (1975) "Some problems of the lump" (1975) 38 M.L.R. 504.
Phelps Brown, E.H.: (1968) *Report of the Committee of Inquiry into Certain Matters Concerning Labour in Building and Civil Engineering*, Cmnd 3714, HMSO.
Pollard, D.: (1994) *Tolley's Employment and Pension Rights in Corporate Insolvency*, Tolley.
Rear, J.: (1972) "Self employment in the building industry" (1972) 2 H.K.L.J. 150.
Ryley, M. and Goodwyn, E.: (2000) *Employment Law for the Construction Industry*, Thomas Telford, London.
Sadler, L.: (1999) "The CIS—what will the changes mean?" (1999) 10(5) *Construction Law* 16.
Sealy, L.S.: (2000) *Disqualification and Personal Liability of Directors*, 5th edn, CCH Editions, Bicester.
Tuite, T.: (1983) *The Construction Industry Tax Deduction Scheme*, Tolley.
Wallace, I.N.D.: (1988) "The lump and the landlord as exits from Anns: the D & F case" (1988) 4 Const. L.J. 100.
Walters, A., and Davis-White, M.: (2005) *Directors' Disqualification and Bankruptcy Restrictions*, 2nd edn, Sweet & Maxwell, London.
Wheeler, S., and Wilson, G.: (1998) *Directors' Liabilities in the Context of Corporate Groups*, GTI Specialist Publishers.

Chapter 22: Law into Myth

Bandes, S.A. (ed.): (1999) *The Passions of Law*, New York University Press, New York.
Blacker, T.: (1998) "Phoenix Reflections", Temenos Academy Review, 1, Spring 1998, 75–80.
Blake, W.: (1972) *Complete Writings*, edited by Keynes, G., Oxford University Press, London.
Burkert, W.: (1985) *Greek Religion: Archaic and Classical* (trans. John Ruffan), Blackwell Publishing.
Carroll, W.: (1996) *Fat King, Lean Beggar: Representations of Poverty in the Age of Shakespeare*, Cornell University Press, London.
Cashford, J. (trans): (2003) *The Homeric Hymns*, Penguin Books, London.
Curtis, D.E., and Resnik, J.: (1987) "Images of Justice", Yale Law Journal, 1987, 96, 1727–1772.
L'Engle, S., and Gibbs, R.: (2001) *Illuminating the Law: Medieval Legal Manuscripts in Cambridge Collections*, Harvey Miller Publishers, London.
Foucault, M.: (1979) *Discipline and Punish: The Birth of the Prison*, Penguin Books.

Goodrich, P.: (1995) *Oedipus Lex: Psychoanalysis, History, Law*, University of California Press, Berkeley.
Graves, R.: (1960) *The Greek Myths*, 2 vols, Penguin Books.
Greene, L.: (1976) *Saturn: A New Look at an Old Devil*, Samuel Weiser, York Beach, Maine.
Hillman J.: (1976) *Re-Visioning Psychology*, Harper & Row.
Hillman, J.: (1995) *Kinds of Power: A Guide to its Intelligent Uses*, Currency Doubleday, New York.
Hillman, J.: (2005) *Senex & Puer*, Spring Publications, Putnam, Connecticut.
Jung, C.G.: (1998) *Jung on Mythology*, edited by R.A. Segal, Routledge, London.
Kerényi, C.: (1951) *The Gods of the Greeks*, Thames and Hudson.
Klibansky, R., Panofsky, E., and Saxl, F.: (1964) *Saturn and Melancholy: Studies in the History of Natural Philosophy, Religion and Art*, Methuen, London.
Larousse: (1968) *New Larousse Encyclopedia of Mythology*, Paul Hamlyn, London.
Lopez-Pedraza, R.: (2000) *Dionysus in Exile*, Chiron Publications.
Moore, T.: (1989) *The Planets Within*, (revised ed), Lindisfarne Press.
Moore, T.: (1992) *Care of the Soul*, Piatkus, London.
Onians, R.B:. (1951) *The Origins of European Thought*, Cambridge University Press.
Otto, W.F.: (1965) *Dionysus: Myth and Cult*, Indiana University Press.
Raffield, P.: (2004) *Images and Cultures of Law in Early Modern England: Justice and Political Power 1558–1660*, Cambridge University Press, Cambridge.
Raine, K.: (1991) *Golgonooza City of Imagination: Last Studies in William Blake*, Golgonooza Press, Ipswich.
Rilke, R.M.: (1989) *Duino Elegies*, (trans. S. Cohn), Carcanet Press, Manchester (original published 1923).
Ripa website: *http://www.alchemywebsite.com/iconol02.html*
Sells, B.: (1994) *The Soul of the Law*, Element Books, Shaftsbury.
Selby, P.: (1997) *Grace and Mortgage: The Language of Faith and the Debt of the World*, Darton, Longman and Todd, London.
Shearer, A.: (1998) *Athene: Image and Energy*, Penguin Books.
Vaughan, A.: (1991) *Isambard Kingdom Brunel: Engineering Knight-Errant*, John Murray, London.
Wind, E.: (1967) *Pagan Mysteries in the Renaissance*, Penguin Books.
Yates, F.A.: (1992) *The Art of Memory*, Pimlico.
Young, A.: (2005) *Judging the Image: Art, value, law*, Routledge, London.
Wood, P.: (1997) *Maps of World Financial Law*, 3rd edn, Allen & Overy.
Wood, P.: (1998) "Maps of world financial law—background note" (1998) 14 I.L. & P. 173.

For a further bibliography of international aspects, see the second edition of this book.

Index